Directoire Revival Fashions
1888-1889

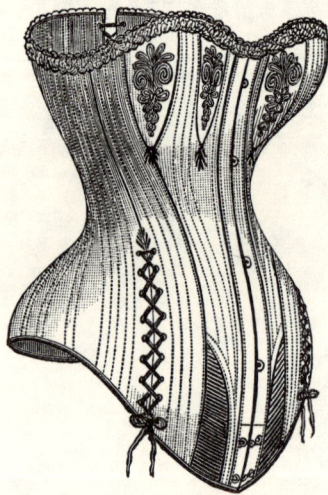

Scientific Garment Cutting

Directoire Revival Fashions 1888–1889

**57 Patterns
With Fashion Plates
And Suggestions for Adaptation**

Edited and with Additional Material by
Frances Grimble

Lavolta Press
20 Meadowbrook Drive
San Francisco, CA 94132
www.lavoltapress.com

Directoire Revival Fashions 1888–1889: 57 Patterns with Fashion Plates and Suggestions for Adaptation is a new work first published by Lavolta Press in 2010. All new text and illustrations; the selection and arrangement of period text, illustrations, and patterns; and revised versions of the period materials are protected by copyright. They may not be reproduced or transmitted in any form without prior written permission from Lavolta Press.

First edition

ISBN: 978-0-9636517-9-2

Published by:
Lavolta Press
20 Meadowbrook Drive
San Francisco, CA 94132
www.lavoltapress.com

Book design, cover design, scanning, scan editing, page layout, and production management by Frances Grimble and Allan Terry

Printed and bound in the United States of America

Cataloging-in-Publication Data

Directoire revival fashions 1888–1889: 57 patterns with fashion plates and suggestions for adaptation / edited and with additional material by Frances Grimble.
   p. cm.
   Includes bibliographical references and index.
   ISBN 978-0-9636517-9-2

1. Dressmaking --United States --Patterns. 2. Dressmaking --United States --History --19th century. 3. Costume --United States --History --19th century. 4. Fashion --United States --History --19th century.5. Millinery --United States --History --19th century.
I. Grimble, Frances. II. Directoire revival fashions 1888–1889: fifty-seven patterns with fashion plates and suggestions for adaptation. III. Title.

TT504.4 .D57 2010
646.4/78–dc22   2010925550

Acknowledgments

My husband, Allan Terry, helped to design the cover and interior. He edited the cover scans and draw the apportioning scales. He also did prepress work, kept my computer running, and performed countless other tasks. Our printer, McNaughton & Gunn, did their usual high-quality job.

To my mother-in-law, Aileen Terry

Contents

4. Skirts and Over-Skirts

5. Ensembles with Bodices, Skirts, And Draperies

Contents

Contents

Contents

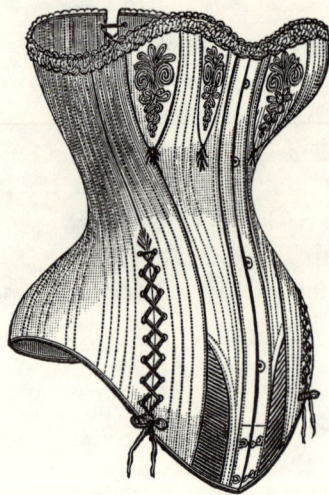

1. Introduction

This book contains 57 women's garment patterns from 1888 through 1889, the end of what is sometimes called the "second bustle period." The silhouette of early 1888 was much like that of 1887, with a close-fitting bodice worn with a full skirt, most of the skirt fullness being thrown to the back. The foundation garments consisted of a corset and a bustle; a pad and steels in the skirt back sometimes supplemented or substituted for the bustle. By the end of 1889, although back fullness and skirt draperies had not been entirely discarded, they had significantly deflated. The bustle, if worn, was long and slender, and there were fewer steels in the skirt. The over-skirt hung straight at the back, and had little fullness at the sides and front. It often consisted partly of "scarves," straight, unseamed panels that hung open to expose the skirt (see Chapter 4).

Most ensembles worn outside the home consisted either of two main garments, a long polonaise worn over a skirt (see Chapter 6), or of three, a bodice and over-skirt (or drapery) worn over a skirt (see Chapter 5). In addition, there were what might be more narrowly called dresses, consisting of only a bodice and a straight skirt, or with a foundation skirt that was mostly or entirely concealed. (See Chapter 7.) Specialized costumes were required for riding and even lawn tennis (see Chapter 8).

At home, women wore simpler dresses, wrappers, and tea gowns. (See Chapter 3.) The two latter were distinguished not by their cut, but by their materials and trimmings. Illustrations showing them with flowing fronts and sashes loosely tied below the abdomen hint at maternity use.

Many garments and garment sections exhibited historical inspiration. Smocking, and sleeves with shoulder puffs, were "Old English." Very long, pointed sleeves seemed borrowed from the Middle Ages, and there was a kind of organ-plaited cloak that resembled a houppelande. Leg-of-mutton sleeves echoed the 1820s and 1830s. Empire dresses featured visually higher waists (aided by wide sashes) and simple skirts. The most popular inspiration was late 18th century. Elbow-length evening sleeves, with lace frills at the bottom, and puffy fichus were "Marie Antoinette." Single or double-breasted polonaises with large lapels, with the skirt cut far back to reveal a large portion of the under-skirt in front, were "Directoire."

Under-garments consisted of a chemise, a corset cover, drawers, and at least a short and a long petticoat. (See Chapter 2.) The bulk was often reduced by wearing "combinations" of chemise and drawers, or corset cover and drawers, or corset cover and short petticoat.

Outer wear included jackets (which sometimes doubled as street bodices), long coats, long and short dolman wraps, and short capes. (See Chapter 9.)

Although some street suits and coats were plainly tailored, garments could be highly decorated. This task was facilitated not only by widespread ownership of sewing machines, but by the availability of commercially made braids and braid appliqués; tucked, plaited, and ruched trimmings; beaded laces, appliqués, and passementeries; and machine-embroidered trimmings, including large ones shaped for specific garment sections. (See Chapter 10.)

Toilettes were often varied (even from day to evening wear) by the use of accessories. These included home-made jabots, chemisettes, gilets, collars, hats, bonnets, and muffs, as well as purchased fans, parasols, belts, and other articles. (See Chapter 11.)

Using This Book

The patterns in *Directoire Revival Fashions 1888–1889* are designed to be enlarged by drafting with the National Garment Cutter, one of a number of popular Victorian and Edwardian apportioning scale systems. Apportioning scales are special rulers that make it easy to accurately

1

draft the patterns designed for that system to fit an individual's body measures. Each scale has units of a different size. The scales for smaller sizes have smaller units, and the ones for larger sizes have larger units. Therefore, the units printed on the pattern can be used to draft any size. No arithmetic or drafting experience is required; you "draft by the numbers."

Most pattern measures are projected in proportion to one crucial body measure—the bust measure for bodices, and the waist for skirts. That is, these patterns have built-in sizing. However, the system recognizes that height is not necessarily in direct proportion to the bust or waist. The instructions explain how to draft patterns for the taller or shorter person after checking a few important measures with an inch ruler.

The National Garment Cutter System. The National Garment Cutter scales were reconstructed for this book by comparing two sets of wooden originals. The units were mathematically corrected to account for variations in manufacture (including duplications of the same units on supposedly different scales), and shrinkage in the wood. The scales were also visually redesigned for ease of use. (See Appendix A.)

The set of National Garment Cutter tools included a large combination curve or "scroll." The scroll provides a variety of curves on the different sides and ends, enabling you to turn it to draw the exact shapes of the armholes, bodice center backs, skirt bottoms, etc., used in the National Garment Cutter system patterns. It is provided in Appendix A.

Figure 1 shows the remainder of the tools in the National Garment Cutter set. These are a patent folding L-square to hold the scales during drafting, an inch tape measure, and a tracing wheel. You will need an ordinary modern L-square; an inch ruler (preferably transparent); pattern paper; and, of course, a pencil, eraser, and scissors. If you do not wish to use the scroll, you will need a modern hip/armhole curve. In addition, you may find it handy to have a set of French curves, a flexible or "spline" curve, a yardstick, and a double tracing wheel.

The Patterns and Instructions. These patterns are drawn from *The National Garment Cutter Book of Diagrams* and *The Voice of Fashion*. The *National Garment Cutter Book of Diagrams* was packaged with the drafting tools and contained patterns drawn from *The Voice of Fashion*. It changed comparatively little from year to year; and except for such basics as under-garments and wrappers, it tended to be rather outdated. *The Voice of Fashion* was a quarterly magazine that provided more up-to-date patterns.

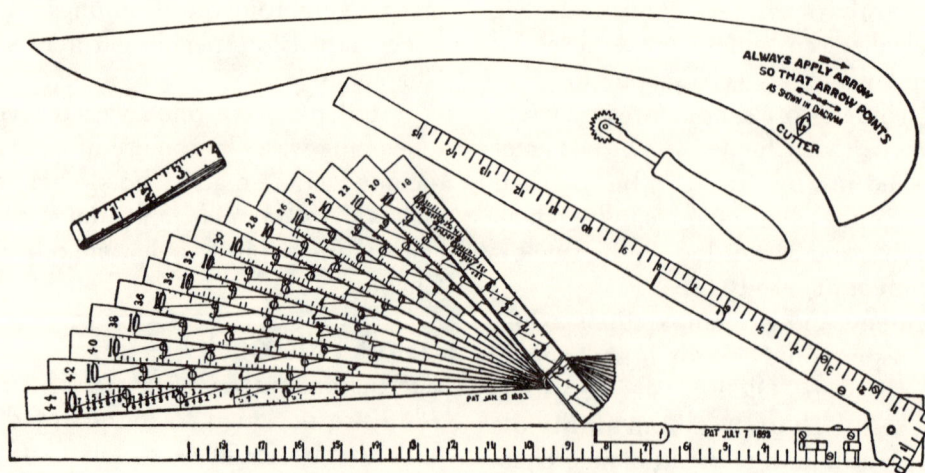

Figure 1. The National Garment Cutter tools

The firm that sold the tools and publications was Goldsberry, Doran & Nelson. (It may be of interest to know that the man in Figures 2–5 resembles published photographs of William H. Goldsberry.)

All of the patterns that were chosen have been redrawn for greater ease of use. Those too small or crowded with labels to see clearly were enlarged, and those too large to fit on a page were divided. The straight lines and right angles have been trued. More legible labels have been applied, and missing ones have been added. The originals contained some errors in measures and text labels, which have been corrected. All of the edited patterns have been proofread several times.

Some new diagrams have been drawn for pattern pieces that were described but not provided. More commonly, the publication omitted some section (typically a sleeve) or an essential entire garment (typically a skirt), and directed readers to use one from another pattern, or to choose from "any other pattern in this issue." The patterns were reorganized for this book, and numerous cross-referenced parts would have inconvenienced readers. Therefore, suitable ones have been chosen and included with the relevant pattern. The patterns for the main parts of all ensembles are listed separately in the index. You can freely select from and combine the sections that compose a garment, and the garments that compose an ensemble. As the original instructions say, "Often a pleasant result is obtained by using parts of different patterns. That is to say, the back of one and the front of another, etc. Take care to put the different parts together so that the seam lines, waistlines, etc., come out properly." The pattern pieces are arranged the way they are sewed together, as well as the page size allows.

The patterns in *The National Garment Cutter Book of Diagrams* and *The Voice of Fashion* are so similar to those published some months earlier by Butterick, that it seems likely Goldsberry, Doran & Nelson copied Butterick patterns. Some of their illustrations strongly resemble ones in Butterick's *Delineator* magazine, and the pattern pieces correspond to the *Delineator's* descriptions. Many others are patchworks of *Delineator* illustrations—a bodice drawn from one illustration and an over-skirt from

another, or the trimmings for one garment transferred to another. Again, the descriptions of the elements correspond.

However, the fashion descriptions and assembly instructions in *The Delineator* are significantly more detailed. Wherever possible, the relevant information from *The Delineator* has been included after each *National Garment Cutter* or *Voice of Fashion* pattern. The text has been edited for clarity and consistency, and the illustrations have been edited to correct deterioration. Also included after each pattern, are illustrations and descriptions sufficiently similar that readers already familiar with modern flat pattern techniques can use the *National Garment Cutter* or *Voice of Fashion* pattern as a base for developing more Butterick styles. Other readers may simply enjoy browsing the extra illustrations, or try their hand at flat patterning with the aid of the books recommended in Appendix D.

Victorian dressmakers consulted sewing manuals for basic, conservative techniques, and fashion magazines for details on how to make up the latest styles. In that spirit, each chapter of this book has been prefaced with a series of edited quotes from other publications. (See Appendix D.) In addition to *The Delineator,* one main source is *Home Dressmaking,* a manual published in 1892 but largely describing construction techniques that were appropriate a few years earlier. Another is *Harper's Bazar,* a magazine that published home-dressmaking patterns, but which was more stylish than *The Delineator.* Also useful are the patterns and supplementary material in this book's companion volume *Bustle Fashions 1885–1887,* which complements this book rather than overlapping it.

Using Apportioning Scales

Using the National Garment Cutter scales to draft the patterns in *Directoire Revival Fashions 1888–1889* is quite easy. It is a matter of enlarging them to your size, rather than designing styles from scratch. First take your measures over the foundation garments and under-garments you will wear. Choose the correct scales for your measures and the garment section. The scales have size labels that correspond to inch measures. Suppose you wish to draft a

three-piece ensemble with a 34-inch bust and a 27-inch waist. You would choose the size 34 scale to draw the bodice, and the size 27 scale to draw the skirt and over-skirt.

Drafting the Pattern. After choosing your scales, lay out a large piece of pattern paper printed with marks at 1-inch intervals. Pencil a vertical baseline, and use your scale to mark off the measures shown on the pattern piece. From these, draw horizontal cross-lines to the measures shown. You then draw the curves. Choose a curve tool that fits to the ends of the lines you drew and looks like the pattern shape. You may need parts of two tools.

The fitted bodice patterns, such as tight linings, were designed with very little ease. It is best to use a scale one to two sizes larger than your bust and leave large seam allowances. The proportionally determined waist size is small for many modern women, but can be enlarged. Check all back waist, sleeve, and skirt lengths until you become familiar with the system's fitting standards. Remember that skirt length measures must include the hem and the belt (waistband) seam. "Drafting a Ladies' Basque" recommends making most corrections for individual measures during the drafting process. However, the patterns can be drafted as given, then altered by standard modern techniques and/or during fitting.

Finishing the Pattern. Measure edges that will be seamed together. If they are different lengths, check the original measures and redraw as necessary. Add pattern markings such as notches and stars. Sometimes you must true seam lines where material will be folded into darts, plaits, or facings. Fold the pattern like the material and redraw lines that do not match.

The instructions and pattern labels claim that seam allowances are provided, but some are overly narrow by modern standards. It is safest to use 1 to 2 inches on side seams, 1 inch on seams of sections that fit tightly, and 1/2 inch on seams of loose-fitting sections. To add a seam allowance, measure out from the pattern edge with a clear plastic ruler. For straight edges, measure each end and connect the lines. For curved edges, draw short lines at such frequent intervals that they connect. Or use a double tracing wheel to indent the paper, then pencil over the indents.

To finish the pattern piece, draw a grain line following a vertical row of pattern paper dots. Label the piece with the pattern source, garment type, and style date. Indicate how many times each piece will be cut from the outer material, the lining, the underlining, and/or the interfacing. Add any markings or notes you find helpful.

Although the National Garment Cutter system produces a good fit, Victorian patterns assume the dressmaker adjusts a lining or a muslin before cutting garment material. This is strongly recommended.

Chapter 10 gives many suggestions for trimmings. Draft and mark them with an inch ruler after completing the rest of the pattern. You can test size and placement on the muslin.

The step-by-step instructions that appeared in the 1885 *National Garment Cutter* and other publications are given below. They have been rewritten and reorganized to eliminate the confusion and repetition that resulted from Goldsberry, Doran & Nelson having layered new text onto old without integrating it. However, one continually stressed point does bear repetition here. If you are unaccustomed to drafting, you need to not only read the instructions for the Ladies' Basque before drafting the pattern you plan to sew, but use those instructions to practice drafting before moving on to other patterns. Most people cannot fully absorb technical instructions without carrying them out.

Frances Grimble

Drafting a Ladies' Basque

These instructions should be very carefully studied by the beginner before trying to draft this or any other garment. This will save much valuable time and be far more efficient. All garments are drafted on the same general plan of work. The instructions for different garments apply only to their special features.

Taking the Measures. The first step is to carefully take the measures, as no one can get a well-fitting garment with improper measures. Take the bust measure with the tape measure straight around

Figure 2. Measuring the bust

Figure 3. Measuring the waist

the largest part of the bust, high up under the arms (see Figure 2). Take a snug, close measure, neither too tight nor too loose. Take the measure around the waist as tight as the dress is to be worn (see Figure 3). Take the length of the waist from the large joint, where the neck and body join, down to the waist (see Figure 4). The sleeve measure is taken from the center of the back to the wrist joint, with the arm raised and the elbow bent (see Figure 5).

This basque is in six pieces: Front, back, side back, collar, and two sleeve pieces. In cutting out, place the narrow end of the collar on a crosswise fold of the material to avoid a center seam. Cut all of the other parts lengthwise. The quantity of material required is 4 yards if 22 inches wide, and 2 1/2 yards if 48 inches wide.

Drafting the Bodice. Supposing the bust measure to be 32 inches, use the scale marked 32. Or if the bust measure is 36 inches, take the scale marked 36, etc. Fasten this scale on the square by passing the screw through the scale and both parts of the square.

Draft the back piece first. Square the draft by drawing the first cross-line and the base-line, as shown by Figure 6. The upper-right corner of a draft is the starting point.

Measure all of the numbers on the base-line as given on the diagram. Always keep the angle of the square to your right. Measure down from the upper-right corner to 1 1/4 spaces, and make a dot; 2 1/2 and 6 1/4 the same. At 10 make an X to show it to be the place to commence measuring again. Move the square down and measure 5 more spaces from the X, or 15 from the starting point. At the end of the scale make an X again and move the square, measuring 2 1/4 more, or 22 1/4, then 28 and 28 1/4.

Now turn the scale without taking it off the square, from the long blade to the short blade of the square. Beginning at the base-line, measure out 2 1/4 on the first cross-line and mark. This is to get the width of the garment. Do not measure from 1 1/4 as it is to cut to. Place the square on the base-line point exactly on the measure. At 2 1/2 measure out 6 1/2 spaces, and draw a cross-line following the diagram. From the third point, 6 1/4

on the base-line, measure 6, drawing a line as before. Draw a line from 10 as before.

Correcting the Waist Length. Before measuring the width from the point at 15, take the tape measure and measure down from 1 1/4 along the base-line, the waist length of the person you are cutting for. If this distance is the same as that of the scale measure, which if scale 32 is used will be 16 inches, you make no change. But supposing the person's measure is more or less than the scale measure, change the point and measure from the point given by the tape measure. Say the person's waist length is 15 inches; measure 15 from 1 1/4. Measure from this point 1/2 and 2 3/4 spaces, drawing a

Figure 4. Measuring the back waist length

Figure 5. Measuring the sleeve length

First cross-line

Square when moved down to locate points on base-line beyond end of scale

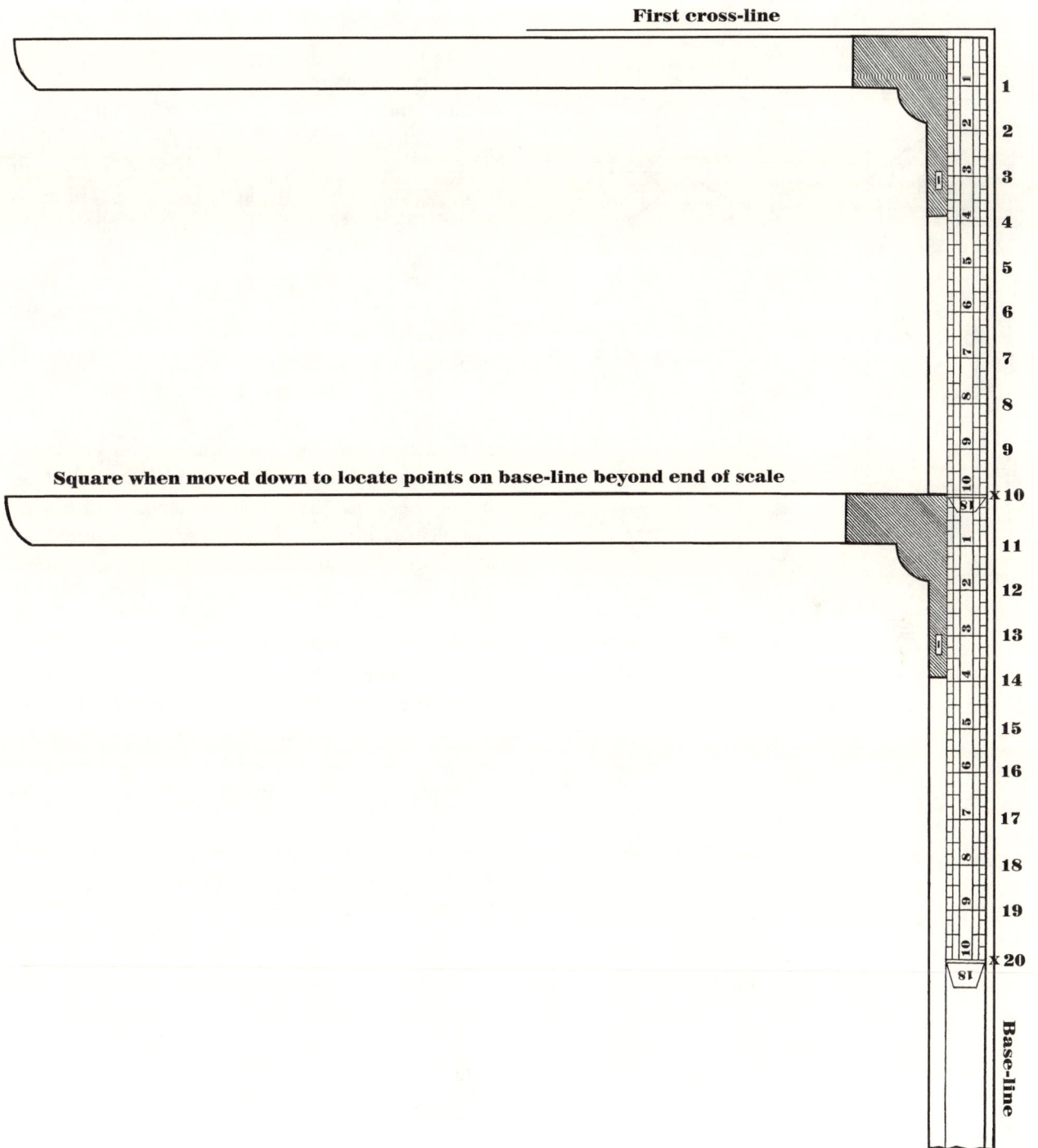

Figure 6. Drawing the first cross-line and the base-line

(See Figure 7.) Draw a curve from the armhole to the next line, then down to the waist-line. Draw curves on all of the other points as shown by the diagram.

The arrows on the diagrams show which way to turn the scroll, which is always with the largest part in the direction in which the arrow points. The arrows are not given on all diagrams, as one diagram mastered is the key to all others. In many cases a slight variation of the exact location of the scroll does not impair the results of the work.

Next draft the side back on the same general plan. If the waist-line on the back has been raised or lowered, raise or lower the waist-line on the side back to correspond.

Draft the front next. If the waist-line has been raised or lowered on the back, raise or lower it the same distance on the front. Raise or lower the top dart line, at 11 3/4, half of the distance. All lines below the waist-line should be changed the same distance as the waist-line. Never change any lines above the dart line. Draw all straight and curved lines except for the under-arm dart lines. Figure 8 shows how to draw the curves.

Correcting the Waist Size. Before drawing the under-arm darts, measure off 1 1/2 spaces on the front for the hem, and 1 1/4 spaces on the side back for the same purpose. For seams, measure off 1/2 space on each side of the back, the side back next to the back, and on each side of the under-arm darts.

Then measure the pattern across at the waist-line, omitting seams already marked off and darts. If the pattern measures the exact size of the waist measure of the person to be fitted, between the seams and hems, the size is correct. If it is not, change the under-arm dart to the correct size, changing a quarter of the amount on each side of the under-arm dart. If the change to be made is greater than 3 inches, change part of it equally at 15 1/2 on the front and on the side back. Because the material is cut double, this will give the correct size. Now draw the dart and seam lines.

Drafting the Sleeve. For the upper sleeve piece, measure from the upper-right corner down to 2, and make a dot. Measure 4 spaces with the

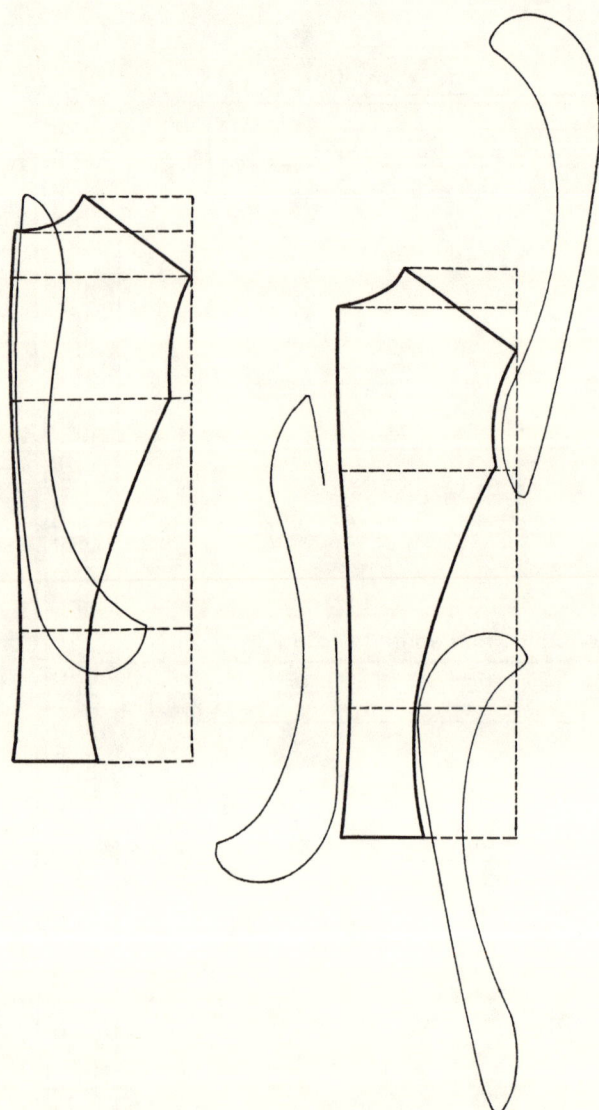

Figure 7. Positions of the scroll for backs

cross-line to the base-line. If this line has been raised or lowered, raise or lower the lines at 22 1/4, 28, and 28 1/4 the same distance; measure and draw a line as before. These are all of the measures.

For the shoulder, draw a diagonal line to connect 2 1/4 on the first cross-line to 6 1/2 on the second cross-line. For the neck, take the scroll and connect the first point on the first cross-line and the first point on the base-line, following the diagram. Draw the curve for the back part of the armhole.

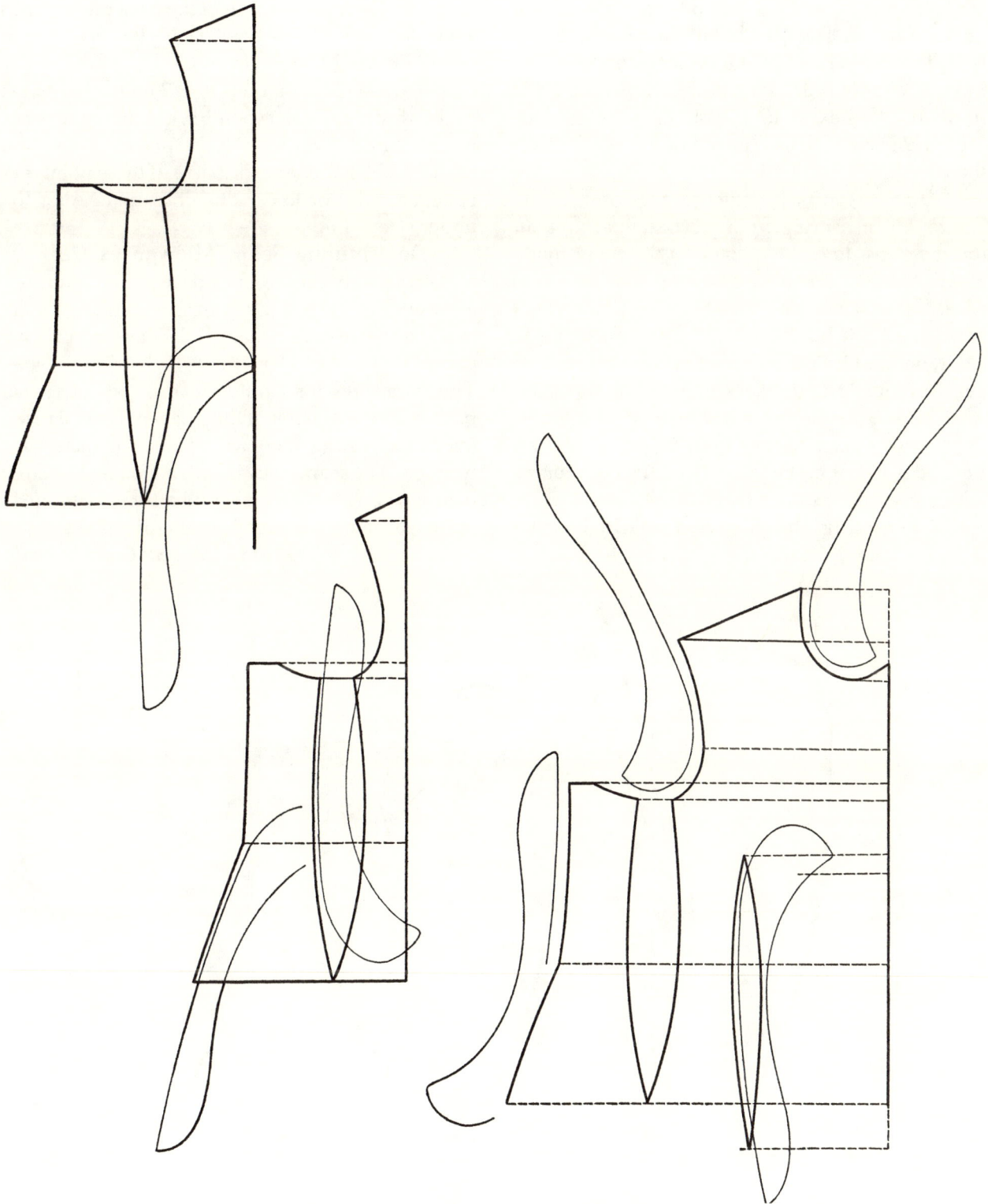

Figure 8. Positions of the scroll for fronts

scale, then at 10 make an X and move the square down to the X. The next number on the base-line is 11. This is obtained by measuring 1 from 10. The next number is 17 1/2; get this by measuring 7 1/2 from 10. The next is 19 1/2, obtained by measuring 9 1/2 from 10. These are all of the numbers on the base-line.

Draw the cross-lines, to get the width of the sleeve, by measuring from the base-line to 4 on the first cross-line. Next come to the point made at 2; place the square exactly on the base-line. Measure 1 1/4 and dot, then 8 and dot, drawing a cross-line to the base-line, connecting the points 8, 1 1/4, and 2. Omit drawing a line at 4 as that is to cut to. From 11 and 19 1/2 draw a line the same as at 2 using the numbers as shown on those lines; then draw a diagonal line from 17 1/2 to 4. Draft the under sleeve in the same way. Draw the curves with the scroll as shown by Figure 9.

Correcting the Sleeve Length. Use the person's measure from the center of the back to the wrist. Deduct the width of the back piece minus 1 inch for seams; then you will have the exact length of the sleeve. Measure from the top of the upper sleeve to the point marked 19 1/2 on the base-line. Make this point correspond to the tape measure, by raising or lowering it. Raise or lower the point marked 17 1/2 the same distance. If these points are changed, raise or lower the elbow line. Alter the under sleeve in the same way.

Determining Seam Allowances. Cut your pattern exactly on the lines drawn. All seams are allowed. They are of different sizes and are usually marked. Seams are usually 1/2 space on dresses, except for the shoulder seam, which is 1 1/4 spaces. The extra width for shoulder seams and under-arm parts is allowed so that if the garment is to be made over after wearing, there will be plenty of material to work on. The seams may be made smaller if desired before cutting, which makes no difference to the fit of the garment. Use small seams for sleeves.

1885 *National Garment Cutter*

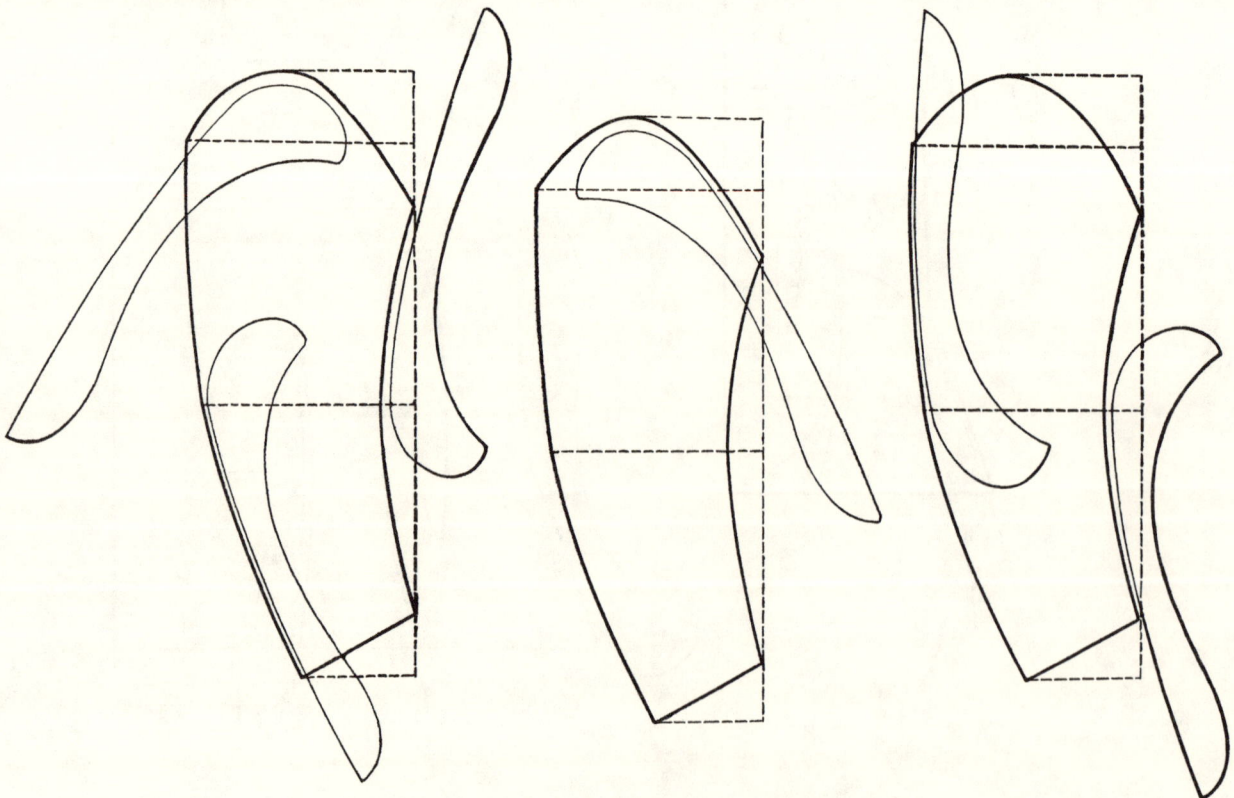

Figure 9. Positions of the scroll for sleeves

Ladies' Basque Pattern

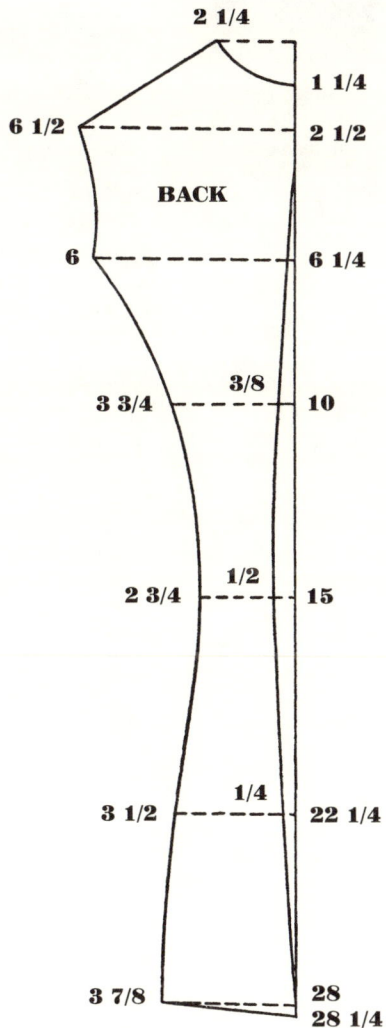

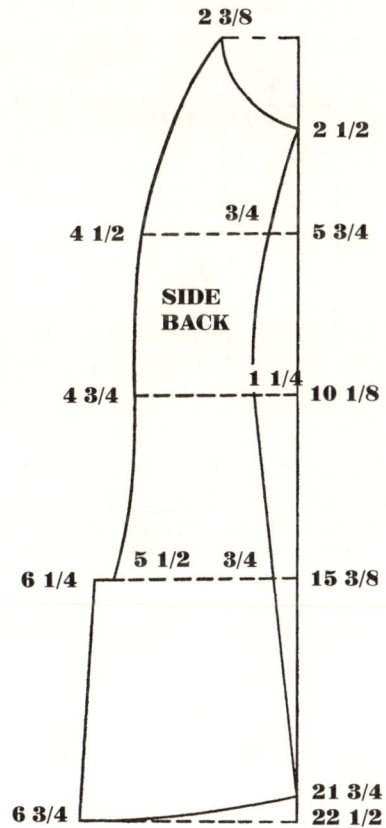

BACK

2 1/4

1 1/4

6 1/2 — 2 1/2

6 — 6 1/4

3 3/4 — 3/8 — 10

2 3/4 — 1/2 — 15

3 1/2 — 1/4 — 22 1/4

3 7/8 — 28
28 1/4

SIDE BACK

2 3/8

2 1/2

4 1/2 — 3/4 — 5 3/4

4 3/4 — 1 1/4 — 10 1/8

6 1/4 — 5 1/2 — 3/4 — 15 3/8

6 3/4 — 21 3/4
22 1/2

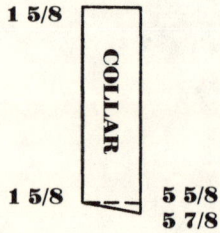

COLLAR

1 5/8

1 5/8

5 5/8
5 7/8

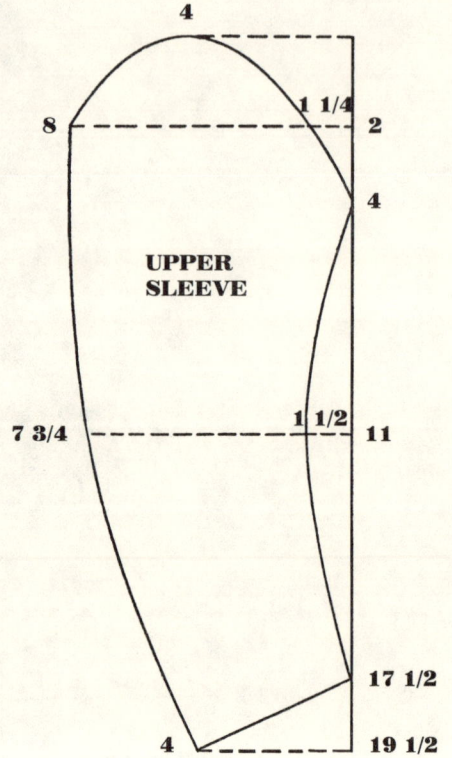

4

8   1 1/4   2

4

UPPER
SLEEVE

7 3/4   1 1/2   11

17 1/2

4   19 1/2

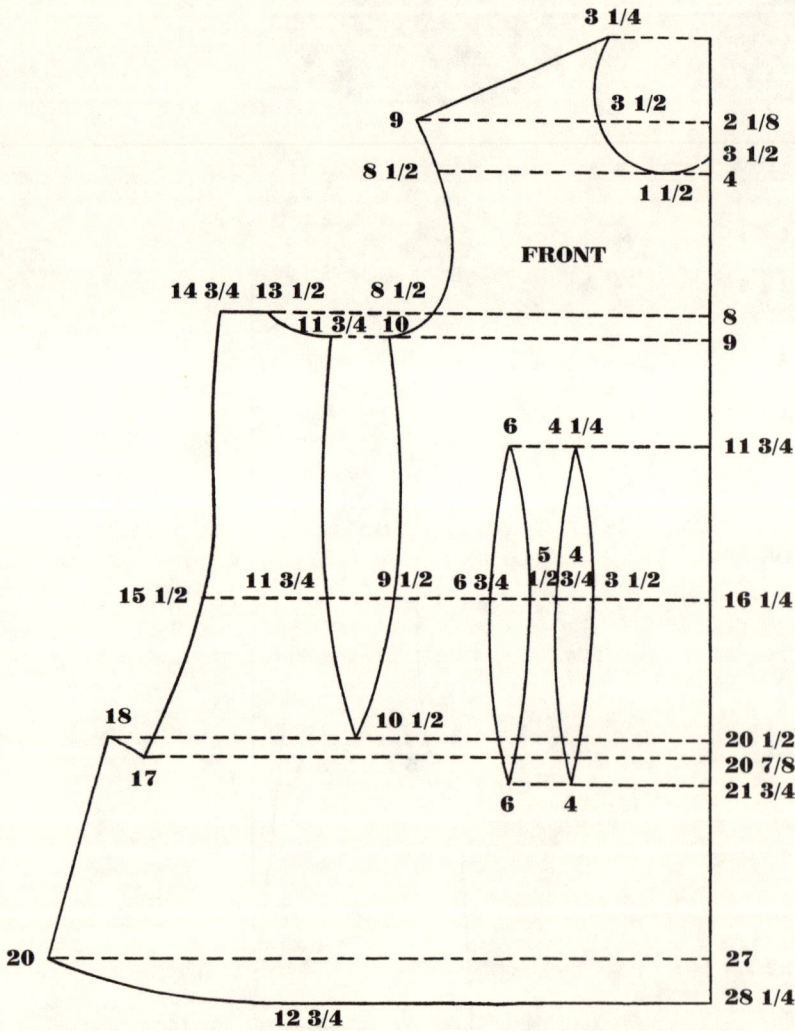

3 1/4

3 1/2

9   2 1/8
3 1/2
8 1/2   4
1 1/2

FRONT

14 3/4 13 1/2   8 1/2   8
9
11 3/4 10

6   4 1/4   11 3/4

5   4
11 3/4   9 1/2   6 3/4 1/2 3/4 3 1/2
15 1/2   16 1/4

10 1/2   20 1/2
18   20 7/8
17   6   4   21 3/4

20   27
28 1/4
12 3/4

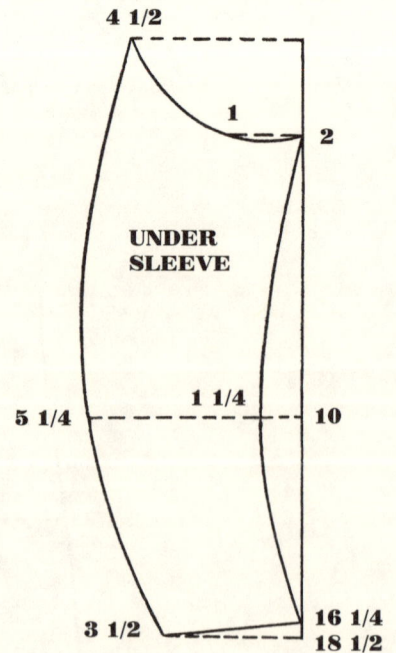

4 1/2

1
2

UNDER
SLEEVE

5 1/4   1 1/4   10

3 1/2   16 1/4
18 1/2

2. Under-Garments, Négligé Wear, and Night-Gowns

For under-garments, silk, linen, lawn, batiste, percale, cambric, muslin, mull, flannel, and similar materials are used, according to the season, climate, and taste of the wearer. China silk is usually used for colored under-garments. The cut and fit of a given garment is the same no matter what material is used.

If any difference is shown, drawers should be made of heavier linen, cambric, or muslin than any other under-garment, as there is more strain on them. Closed drawers should be made with a deep yoke over the hips, thus bringing the closing at the back below the corset. The best patterns for open drawers overlap at the back, and the seat is longer in proportion. If this is not done, the drawers are likely to draw apart and not give the needed protection.

The lower part of drawers permits of considerable trimming. Clusters of tucks separated by feather-stitching, insertions of lace or embroidery, and lace or embroidered ruffles may all be seen on one pair. First do all this trimming on each leg, then stitch together and fell each leg. If the drawers are closed, seam and fell the legs together, and then put on the yoke or belt. If the drawers are open, after the legs are closed face each side with a straight piece of the material and then join the legs to the belt. Use medium-sized flat pearl buttons for the closings.

Chemises are either made with the fullness gathered into a band over the shoulders, or in the sack shape. The sack shape is cut to fit without fullness over the back and front. Four darts are made below the bust to shape it to the waist. The armholes are not supplied with sleeves, but finished with embroidery or lace. Some chemises have shoulder straps that button on and may be removed when worn under a low bodice; the chemise being so closely fitted by darts that it does not need to be suspended from the shoulders.

Embroidery done on the material itself is the most durable trimming, but Hamburg and Russian embroideries, and Valenciennes and torchon laces, are exquisite. The bottom of the chemise may be finished by a hem 2 to 4 inches deep, or by ruffles 2 to 6 inches wide, which may be edged with lace, tucks, or embroidery. Ribbons are used in narrow widths run through casings of the material, or through woven beadings that may be used with both lace and embroidery. They are drawn through and tied in loops. Bows and rosettes of wider ribbons are set about on the shoulders or in front.

After the chemise has been cut out, baste up the seams and any darts, and try on the chemise. Then sew the side seams and fell them down. Hem or trim the bottom, then finish the neck and armholes.

A corset cover should fit as perfectly as a basque, and no better pattern can be found than a tried and true basque pattern. Corset covers are cut with a high or a low neck; a great number are high at the back with open V-shaped or square-necked fronts. Sometimes very small sleeves are added; or else the armhole is faced, or scalloped, or finished with a narrow embroidery or lace edging. The corset cover should be basted together and fitted before its seams are stitched. If the neck is to be low, it is cut into the desired shape during this fitting.

After a good fit is obtained, stitch the seams and fell them. Either the ordinary flat fell or the French fell may be used. The front closing edges should be curved as for a well-fitted basque and require to be faced. The facing should be wide enough to take button-holes, which should be placed about 2 inches apart. The corset cover should be closed with small pearl buttons. The bottom of the corset cover should be finished by a 1/2-inch hem. The neck should have a 1/2-inch facing unless the trimming gives the necessary stay. When Hamburg embroidery is used, the top of the corset cover can be turned over 1/2 inch and then stitched down on the embroidered edge. When lace is used, a facing of the material must be supplied.

The petticoat for wear under the ordinary walking skirt is cut 3 inches shorter than the skirt. For a medium-sized woman, the petticoat should measure 2 1/2 yards around the bottom. It is made with a front gore, side gores, and a straight back breadth. The top is finished with a yoke when the hips are large enough to require it. The seams are stitched and overcast, and the bottom is finished with a 2-inch hem. The trimming should be done on deep flounces of scanty fullness, tucks, lace, and embroidery being used together and alone. The same trimmings are applied to silk, cambric, and cloth petticoats.

The styles of night-gowns vary, but the gown with long breadths gathered into a square, round, or pointed yoke is always in favor. The yoke should be made double with shoulder seams and a front closing. The shoulder seam of four thicknesses should be stitched together so that the seam is within. The seams of the skirt of the gown should be felled. The sleeves should be made and completely trimmed before they are inserted into the armholes. The front of the gown may be closed with small pearl buttons and button-holes placed 4 inches apart. More luxurious gowns are closed with tied ribbons instead.

A dressing sack is best made with a close-fitting back and a loose front. Cut the sack out of the material. Baste the seams and lay the hem down each side of the front closing. Try on the garment and make any necessary alterations before stitching the seams. If the material is cotton, linen, or China silk, fell the seams. If some material that will not fray is used, the edges of the seams may be cut in fine notches and the seams pressed open flat. Heavy silks, cloths, cashmeres, flannels, and most wools are finished in this way. The sleeves may be full and held in by wristbands, or be simply flowing.

Dainty dressing sacks are made of white nainsook, trimmed with insertions of both lace and nainsook embroidery, and a gathered lace edging. Torchon and Valenciennes are prettiest and wear best. Ribbons in white, or some bright becoming shade, are knotted and basted on according to the taste of the wearer.

1892 Home Dressmaking

Petticoats to be worn with summer dresses are made of French percale, cambric, or light-weight domestic muslins. Two lengths are used—the walking-length petticoat, 1 or 2 inches shorter than the dress skirt, and the short under-petticoat. Trained petticoats are not now used, as each trained skirt is supplied with inside flounces of muslin and lace, shaped to fit in the facing and move with the train, as a separate garment will not.

The walking petticoat is 2 1/2 yards wide at the bottom. The front and sides are gored to meet a yoke that is fitted to the figure there, but is drawn into shape across the back by a string at the top. The back breadth is straight and full. When the bottom is hemmed the trimming is sewed to the edge, making it full like a balayeuse, and outside trimmings of flounces or of embroidered bands fall to the bottom of this foot trimming.

Tucked nainsook flounces with the tucks lengthwise, with insertions of lace or embroidery between the clusters of tucks, and lace on the edge of the flounce, trim handsome hand-made petticoats. Some of these have a deep Spanish flounce from the knees down, while others have two or three narrower ruffles. Valenciennes and Medici laces are used on such petticoats, and also the point de Paris lace with large strong meshes as a foundation for closely wrought vines and flowers.

Machine-made petticoats are made with a yoke all around gathered with a tape, instead of a belt. The fullness at the back is cut off halfway below the top and gathered to narrower top breadths. These petticoats are trimmed with flounces of Hamburg embroidery, done in open patterns of bars, stripes, leaves, stars, etc., with scalloped or pointed edges. Some have a cambric flounce with two or three insertions of Medici, torchon, or point de Paris lace. Underneath is a narrower flounce to hold the outer one in place and give fullness at the bottom.

Petticoats of silk taffeta with many pinked flounces are made in cream, pink, and pale blue shades, and also in the darker changeable silks. They have one or two ruffles all around, and are covered from the belt to the bottom across the back with five or six narrow flounces, or with three or four wider ones.

Short under-petticoats fall just below the knees. They are closed all around, without a placket opening, the yoke being very large and drawn in to fit the figure by tapes at the back. Some are covered from the yoke down with a fall of tucked nainsook, the lengthwise tucks stopping a few inches below the bottom, and falling open below as a flounce, which is tucked around and edged with lace. Plainer cambric petticoats have a scant flounce of Hamburg embroidery, which is set in the edge of the hem to fall below it.

Chemises are made in sack shapes that are partly fitted to the figure by two or four darts. They are without sleeves, the armholes being merely trimmed with embroidered or lace edging, or with needle-work done on the garment. Banded and yoke chemises are again coming into favor. Fine batiste, sheer French percale, and very light-weight linen are used for imported chemises. Some have four darts, fitting the front as smoothly as a corset cover, and doing away with all fullness just below the waist. The dart seams are neatly joined by beading, which is a tiny narrow insertion of ladder-like bars.

Wider beading than that used for joining seams is placed around the neck and armholes of chemises, and also of corset covers, night-gowns, etc. Very narrow ribbons—white, blue, rose, or lavender—are drawn through and tied in bows of many loops. Some chemises have the top entirely of lace, Valenciennes yokes being especially liked. These yokes pass over the arms or under them, the chemise being so closely fitted by darts that it does not need to be suspended from the shoulders.

Drawers are made very wide at the knees, measuring 5/8 yard around, or even more. The top is deeply faced in yoke shape, the fronts fit easily, and a tape draw-string is added across the back. Belts are no longer seen. Some drawers open on the sides and are buttoned there, while others open at the back and are widely lapped. Drawers are made of percales, durable muslins, and linens of heavier weight than that used for other under-garments.

Drawers may be trimmed with bands of nainsook with lengthwise tucks and rows of feather-stitching between them. The lower part of the nainsook is left free for a ruffle, and lace or embroidery is added. Some drawers have two or three lengthwise clusters of tucks and feather-stitching up the outside of the legs to the top. Others have the trimming at the knees curved upward on the outside, or else are simply caught up there in plaits, and decorated with a ribbon bow. Still others have fine needle-work done in squares on the edge, falling over a plaited frill of Valenciennes or torchon lace.

Cambric or linen corset covers may have high or low necks. A great number are high at the back, with open V-necked or square-necked fronts made of embroidery or lace, with tucks, feather-stitching, and insertion. Sometimes very slight sleeves are added, or the armhole is scalloped, or it is finished with a bit of lace or embroidery. When a chemise is not worn, this trimming is important. Drapery of lace or embroidery trims handsome corset covers, lapping to the left side. Others have a vest of embroidery set in V shape.

Combination garments are made in cambric or linen. They come in two shapes, one with the corset cover and drawers combined, and the other with the corset cover and short petticoat combined.

Dressing sacks have the back partly fitted to the figure, and the fronts loose, with tucks holding the fullness at the top in a pointed yoke. Other dressing sacks have tucks down the center of the front and back. Hair-striped batistes and speckled mulls are liked for these garments, with blue or red scallops wrought in their edges, or finished with a ruffle that has Valenciennes on both edges. They are trimmed with many loops of ribbon, a collar band of ribbon, and a ribbon belt sewed in the under-arm seams to confine the full fronts. Full sleeves, or else flowing sleeves, complete these garments.

Night-gowns are made fuller than formerly, and serve for room gowns in the morning and for invalids' day wrappers. The yoke gown with full breadths gathered to it remains a general favorite. However, the newer gowns carry the fullness up to the shoulders in continuous breadths, gathering

it just below the neck, tucking the shoulders, and putting box-plaits across the back. A favorite style has the front lapped to the left side, after being fully gathered at the neck. The fullness is then shirred at the waist-line, and trimming is placed down the left side at the opening. Full straight sleeves are liked for night-gowns. They are gathered at the armholes, and again to wristbands large enough for the arm to pass through. Two standing ruffles of embroidery or lace trim the neck of many gowns. Others have a rolling collar of tucked nainsook, or of embroidery edged with lace.

One design has the full front of the night-gown tucked lengthwise in a point like a yoke, then tucked again at the waist-line in points like those of a Swiss girdle. Diagonal rows of insertion and tucks, with beading and feather-stitching, trim other gowns from shoulder to bust. Fine torchon lace is used as insertion in ruffles, and in entire yokes wrought in shape. Cambric, percale, batiste, linen, lawn, brilliantine, and dotted mull are the materials most used for summer night-gowns.

August 18, 1888 *Harper's Bazar*

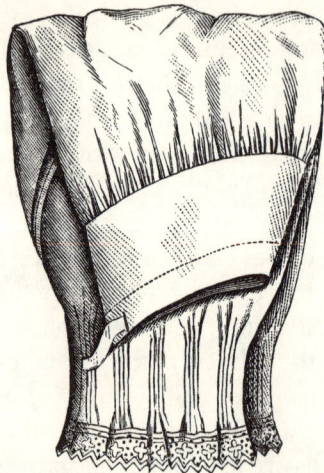

Drawers with Yoke

This garment is drafted with the scale corresponding to the waist measure. The length is regulated with the tape measure. Add all allowances for tucks. There are two pieces: Half of the body and half of the yoke. The drawers may be closed or left open. Gather the extra fullness at the top and sew it to the yoke.

Fall 1888 *Voice of Fashion*

Drawers with Yoke

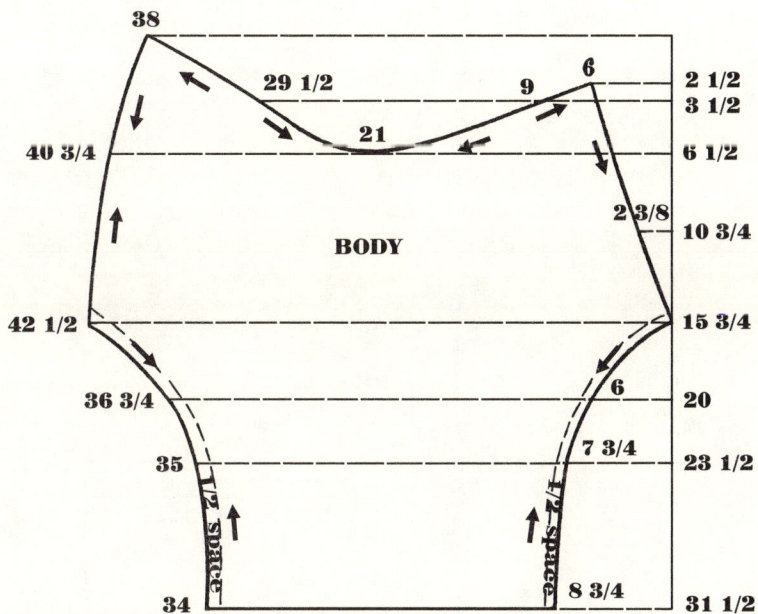

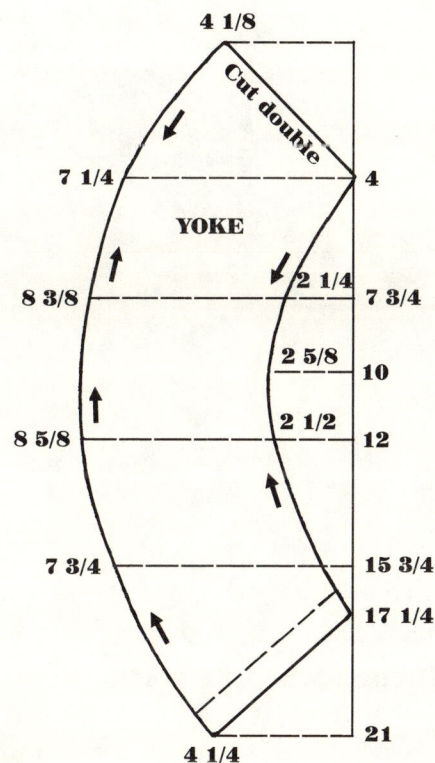

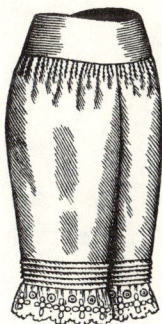

38 **29 1/2** **9** **6** **2 1/2**
21 **3 1/2**
40 3/4 **6 1/2**
BODY **2 3/8** **10 3/4**
42 1/2 **15 3/4**
36 3/4 **6** **20**
35 **7 3/4** **23 1/2**
1/2 space 1/4 space
34 **8 3/4** **31 1/2**

4 1/8
Cut double
7 1/4 **4**
YOKE **2 1/4**
8 3/8 **7 3/4**
2 5/8 **10**
2 1/2 **12**
8 5/8
7 3/4 **15 3/4**
17 1/4
21
4 1/4

Drawers with Yoke. Bleached muslin was used for this example, Hamburg edging and tucks providing the trimming. Each leg is formed of a single section, which is folded lengthwise and has its inner edges seamed together. The corresponding front and back edges of each section are finished with an underfacing. The upper edges are scantily gathered and sewed to a fitted yoke, which is lined with the material and closed at the back with button-holes and buttons. Each leg is trimmed with a frill of edging surmounted by a cluster of five small tucks, which are made before cutting out the garment.

For the construction of these drawers cambric, linen, flannel, or silk may be used. For the lighter materials, lace or embroidery is liked for trimming. Insertion may separate clusters of as many tucks as desired, and edging may be sewed below. The tucks may be omitted and insertion used only above the edging, and the material cut away beneath. Cotton or crocheted laces are serviceable and neat for trimming cotton materials. Knitted worsted laces are liked for flannel drawers. To make the garment for a lady of medium size, requires 2 yards of material 36 inches wide.

February 1888 *Delineator*

Pompadour Chemise

This garment is drafted with the scale corresponding to the bust measure. The length is regulated with the tape measure. There are two pieces: A quarter of the chemise and the yoke.

Spring 1889 *Voice of Fashion*

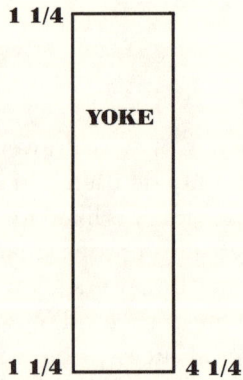

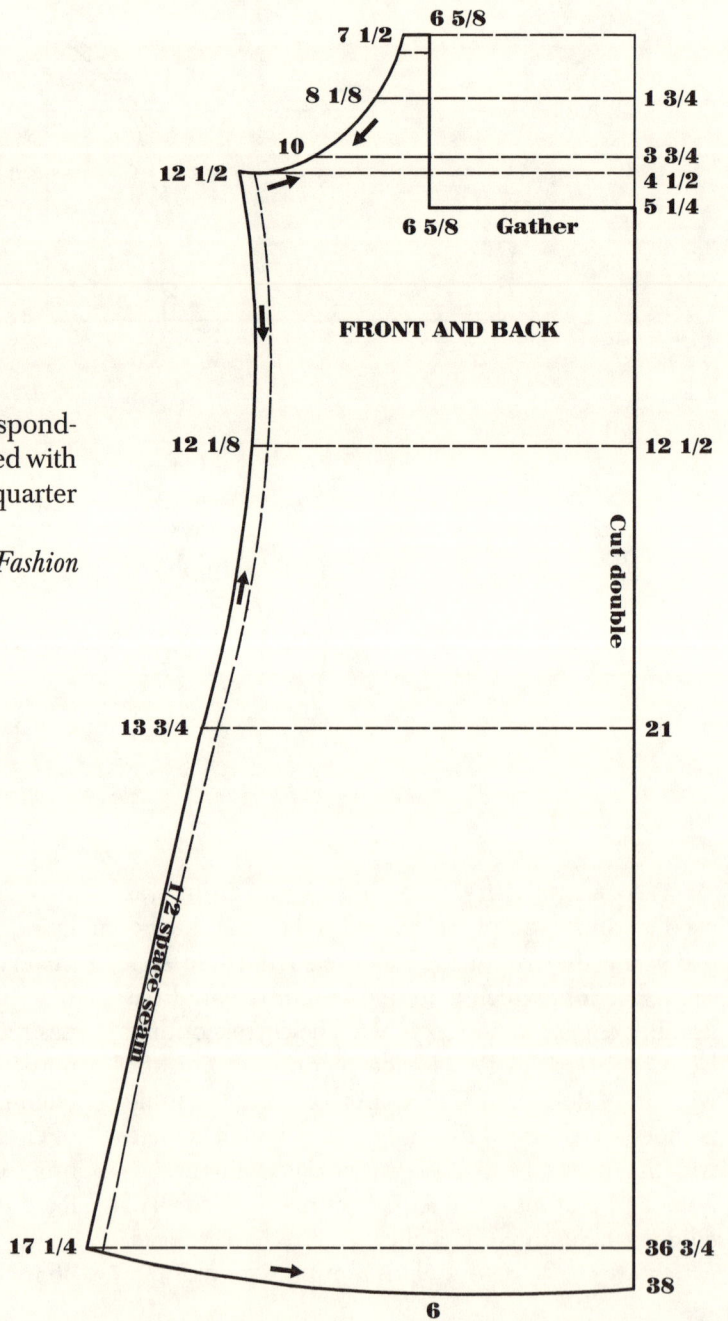

YOKE

1 1/4

1 1/4   4 1/4

7 1/2   6 5/8

8 1/8   1 3/4

10   3 3/4
4 1/2

12 1/2   5 1/4

6 5/8   Gather

FRONT AND BACK

Cut double

12 1/8   12 1/2

13 3/4   21

1/2 space seam

17 1/4   36 3/4

38

6

Ladies' Chemise. This example is made of cambric, and trimmed with Italian lace, insertion, and fine tucks. When the garment is cut out, the material is folded crosswise. Consequently no seams are made at the shoulders, where the width is sloped off to allow the neck to be cut out in a square outline and drawn into the proper space by a line of gathers at the front and back. The gathered edges are sewed to bands of lace insertion surmounted by lace edging, the latter decoration being carried all about the neck edges. The armholes are also bordered with lace and insertion. A comfortable width for the lower part of the garment is obtained by springing the side seams out toward the bottom. A petticoat effect is given by ornamenting the lower edge with edging and a cluster of three fine tucks. This decoration is not shown by the engraving, which does not illustrate the full length of the garment. The lower edge may, of course, be plainly finished.

Hamburg embroidery, rick-rack, torchon, and all kinds of washable decorations are suitable trimmings. To make the chemise for a lady of medium size, requires 2 3/8 yards of material 36 inches wide.

August 1884 *Delineator*

UPPER SLEEVE

4 1/4   3 1/4

1 1/8   2

7 5/8

4 1/2

8   6 1/2

8 1/4   1 3/4   12

1/2 space

1/2 space

5 1/4   21

19 1/4

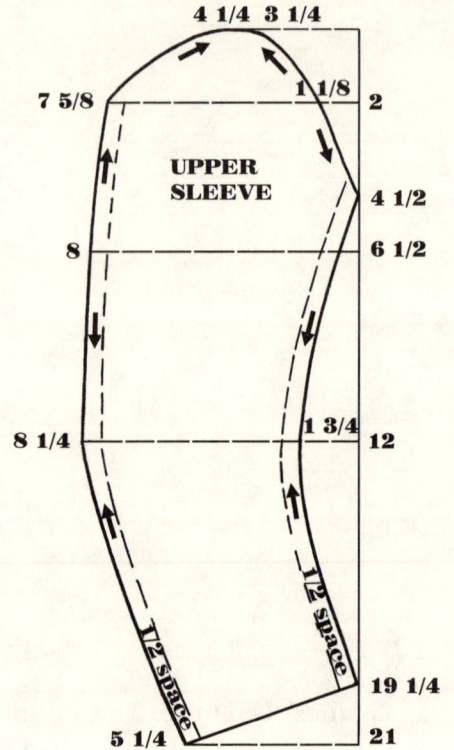

Night-Gown with Yoke Front

This night-gown has a Mother Hubbard front and a plain back. The entire garment is drafted with the scale corresponding to the bust measure. The length is regulated with the tape measure. There are six pieces: Front yoke, front shirring, back, collar, and two sleeve pieces.

Spring 1889 *Voice of Fashion*

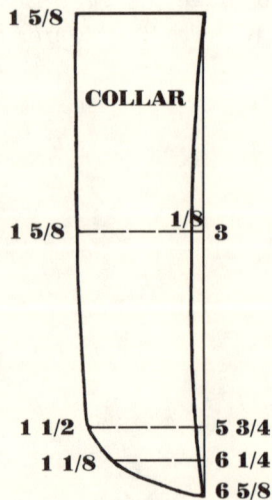

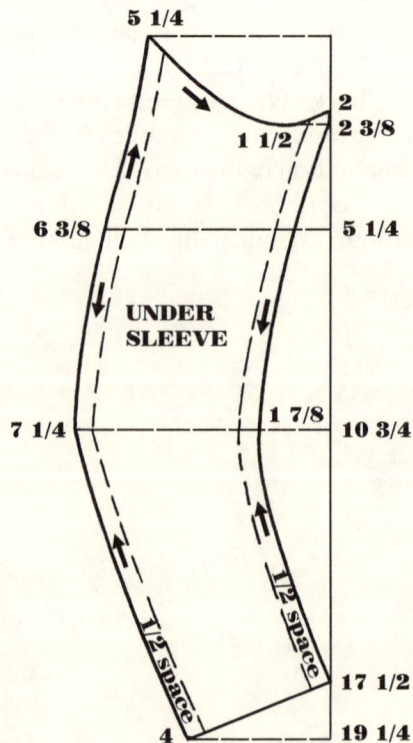

COLLAR

1 5/8

1 5/8   1/8   3

1 1/2   5 3/4
1 1/8   6 1/4
6 5/8

UNDER SLEEVE

5 1/4

2
1 1/2   2 3/8

6 3/8   5 1/4

7 1/4   1 7/8   10 3/4

1/2 space

1/2 space

4   19 1/4

17 1/2

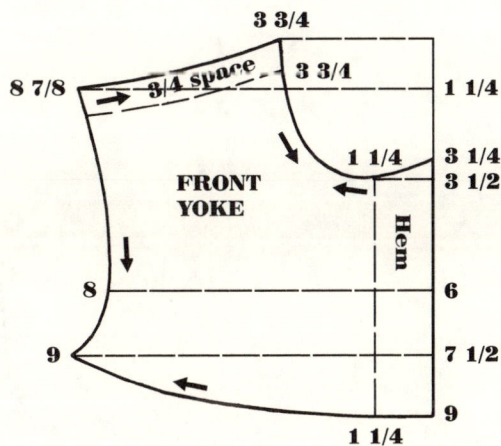

3 3/4

8 7/8   3/4 space   3 3/1   1 1/4

1 1/4   3 1/4
3 1/2

**FRONT
YOKE**   Hem

8   6

9   7 1/2

9

1 1/4

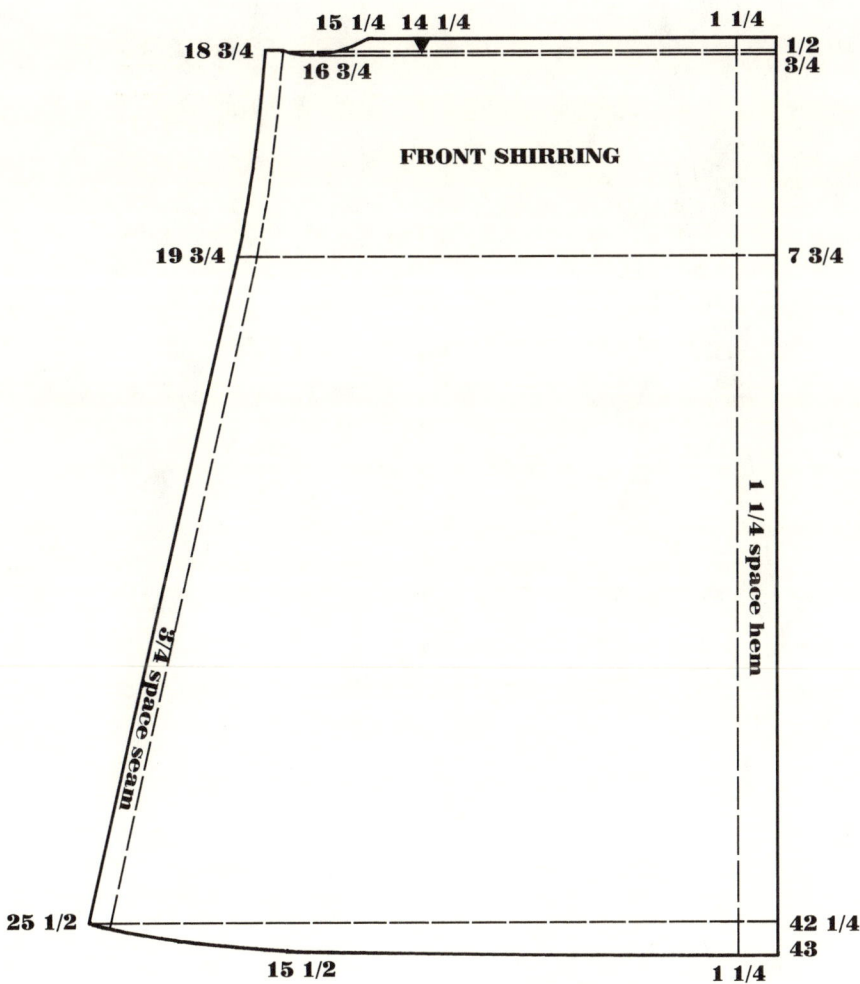

15 1/4   14 1/4   1 1/4
18 3/4   1/2
16 3/4   3/4

FRONT SHIRRING

19 3/4   7 3/4

1 1/4 space hem

3/4 space seam

25 1/2   42 1/4
43

15 1/2   1 1/4

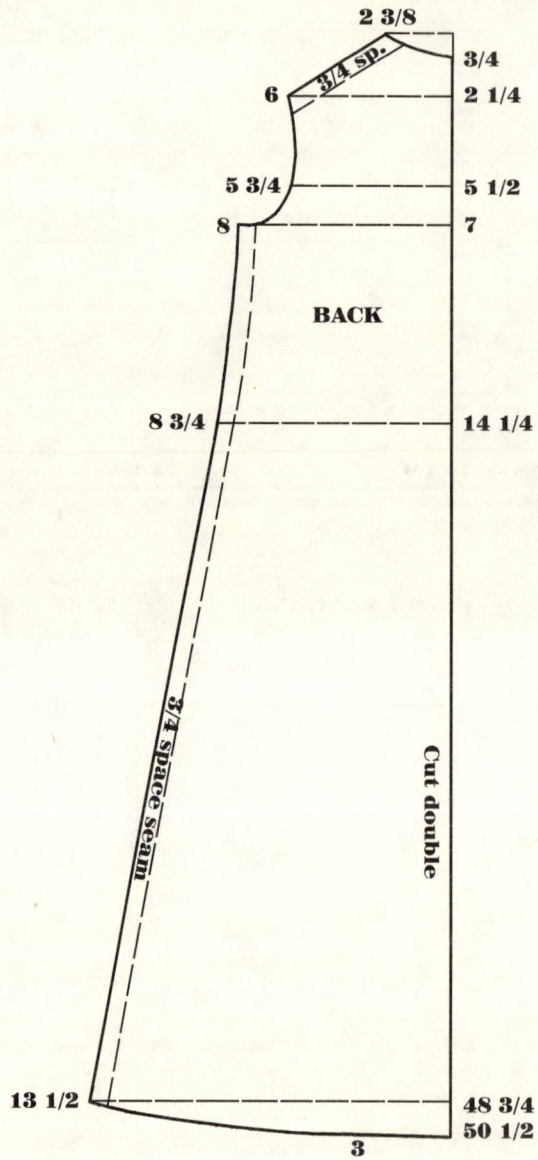

2 3/8

3/4 sp.

3/4

6   2 1/4

5 3/4   5 1/2

8   7

BACK

8 3/4   14 1/4

3/4 space seam

Cut double

13 1/2   48 3/4

                    50 1/2

3

Night-Gown with Yoke Front. Muslin was selected for making this night-gown, and Hamburg edging forms the trimming. The back is in one length from the neck to the lower edge. The fronts are in yoke shape at the top, the lower parts being gathered before being sewed to the yoke. The upper parts are smoothly fitted by the shoulder seams. The side seams spring out toward the lower edge to supply the requisite width at the hem. The front edges are hemmed, and closed with button-holes and pearl buttons. A standing collar is sewed to the neck. Its edges, as well as the lower and overlapping front edges of the yoke and the wrists of the coat sleeves, are finished with Hamburg edging.

Cambric is cooler than muslin for summer wear, and is selected in both plain and printed varieties. The yoke is sometimes cut from all-over embroidery or from plain or lace tucking, and the back faced to correspond. The lower hem of the night-gown may be trimmed. Colored embroideries, as well as white, are used for trimming white night-gowns. To make the garment for a lady of medium size, requires 4 3/8 yards of material 36 inches wide.

June 1887 *Delineator*

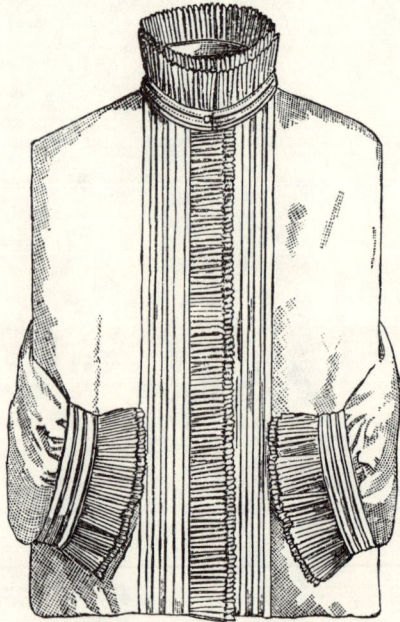

Sack Night-Gown

This garment is drafted with the scale corresponding to the bust measure. The length is regulated with the tape measure. There are four pieces: Front, back, sleeve, and cuff. Gather the sleeve at the bottom and sew it to the cuff. Gather it between the notches at the top and sew it into the armhole.

Fall 1889 *Voice of Fashion*

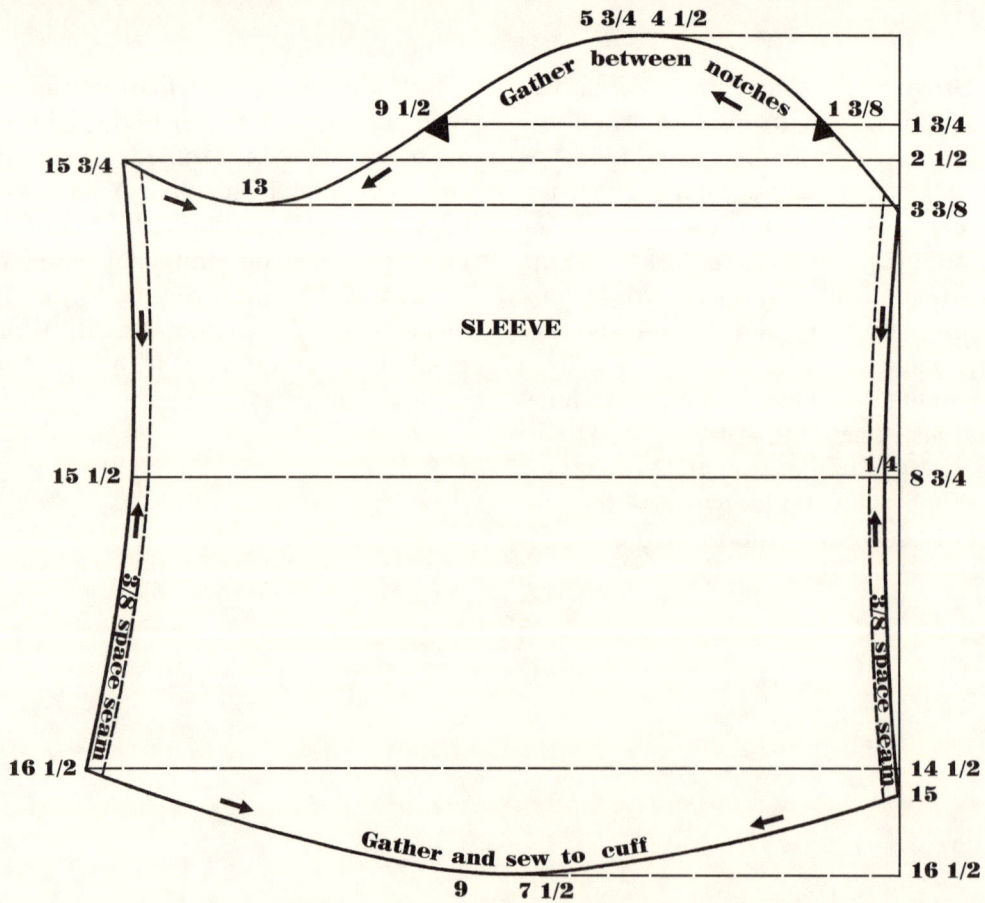

SLEEVE

5 3/4 4 1/2

Gather between notches

9 1/2   1 3/8

1 3/4

15 3/4   2 1/2

13   3 3/8

1/4   8 3/4

15 1/2

3/8 space seam   3/8 space seam

16 1/2   14 1/2

15

Gather and sew to cuff

9   7 1/2   16 1/2

Sack Night-Gown

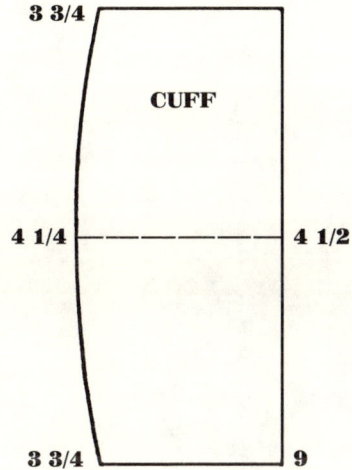

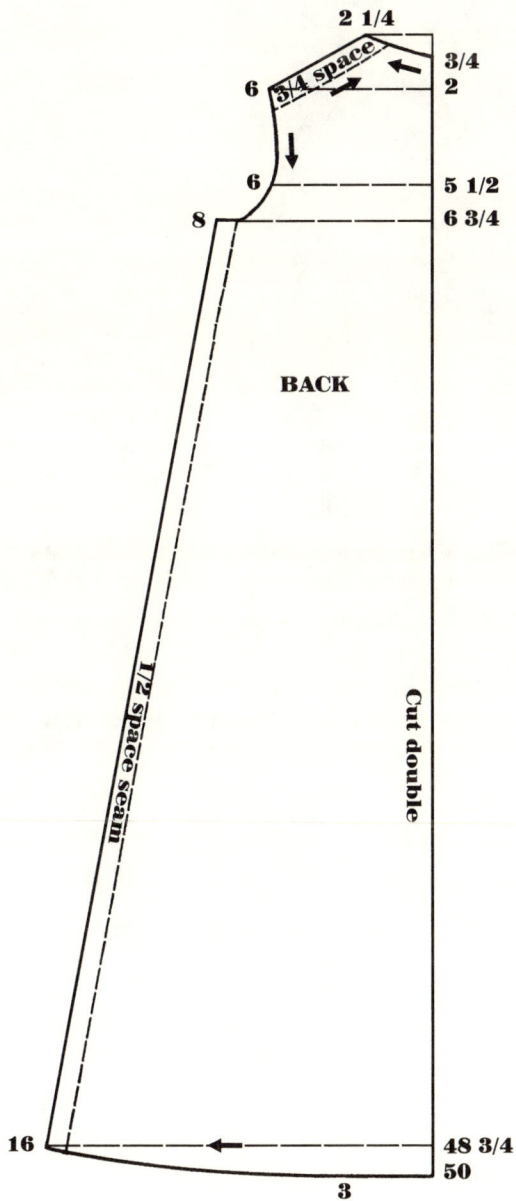

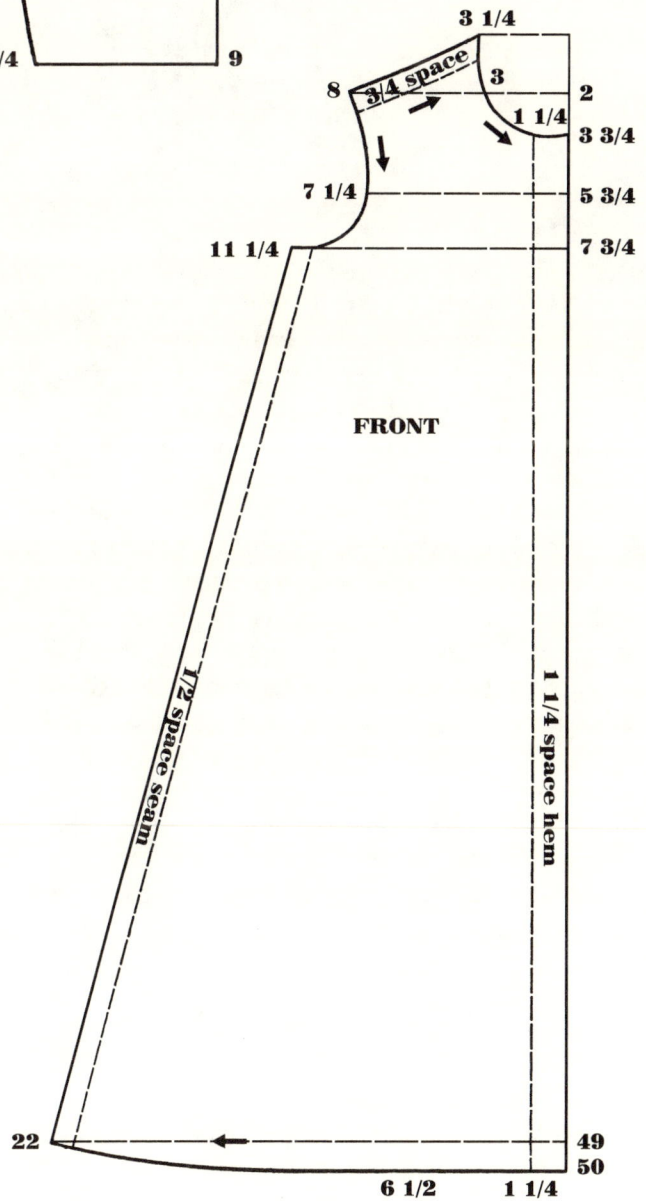

CUFF

3 3/4

4 1/4 — 4 1/2

3 3/4 — 9

BACK

2 1/4
3/4
6 3/4 space 2
6 — 5 1/2
8 — 6 3/4

1/2 space seam

Cut double

16 — 48 3/4
50
3

FRONT

3 1/4
8 3/4 space 3 — 2
1 1/4 — 3 3/4
7 1/4 — 5 3/4
11 1/4 — 7 3/4

1/2 space seam

1 1/4 space hem

22 — 49
50
6 1/2 1 1/4

25

Sack Night-Gown. Fine white muslin was used for this example, and the trimming is Hamburg edging. The gown is seamless at the back, being cut on a fold of the material at the center. The upper part of the back is overlaid with a yoke that is pointed at its lower edge. The upper part of each front is overlaid with a yoke that is pointed at the lower front corners. These applied yokes strengthen the upper part of the back and fronts. They are included in the shoulder seams; the lower edges are stitched flatly in place and outlined with a frill of embroidered edging. The garment is shaped by side seams, which are sprung out to give the desired width at the lower edge. The closing is made with buttons and button-holes, the closing edges being turned under for hems. A collar of comfortable height encircles the neck and is trimmed with a row of embroidered edging. The coat sleeves fit easily, and are trimmed at the wrists with a frill of embroidered edging.

This style of night-gown may be developed in cambric, linen, flannel, silk, etc., and trimmed with lace, embroidery, or narrow cambric ruffles. If desired, the trimming may be carried along the edge of the front overlap, and feather-stitching may be worked along the edging. The yokes may be made of all-over embroidery or lace tucking, the fronts and back being cut away underneath. Flannel is desirable for heavier gowns; and fancy stitching wrought in silk floss at the edges, or narrow worsted lace applied with only a trifle of fullness, provide dainty trimmings. For a lady of medium size, this night-gown requires 4 3/4 yards of material 36 inches wide.

August 1887 *Delineator*

Short Sack Night-Wrapper. The wrapper is here made of muslin, with lace tucking and lace edging for trimming. The construction is in sack style, the only seams being those on the shoulders and at the sides. The fronts are turned under for hems and closed invisibly. Each side is faced for some distance back of the front edge with lace tucking, the material underneath being cut away or not, as preferred. The upper part of the back is faced in a deep pointed outline with lace tucking, which is even at the shoulders with the facings on the front. A band of the decorative material is carried about the bottom of the garment, and the lower edge is bordered with embroidery. The coat sleeves are loose enough to be entirely comfortable. They are completed with cuff-facings of lace tucking bordered at the lower edge with lace edging. The narrow bias collar or band about the neck is also bordered with edging.

Night-wrappers of this kind may be made of any material admired. Invalids often have them made of flannel or cashmere and trimmed with cotton or wool lace. Pongee and raw silks are also liked, and permit of any pretty trimmings. Lace tucking and embroidered webbing, with edgings of lace or embroidery, are always in good taste. For a lady of medium size, this garment requires 2 3/8 yards of material 36 inches wide, together with 1 5/8 yards of lace tucking 20 inches wide for trimming.

January 1885 *Delineator*

Morning Dress

The dressing sack is drafted with the scale corresponding to the bust measure. There are seven pieces: Front, side back, back, two sleeve pieces, cuff, and collar. The kilt skirt is drafted with the scale corresponding to the waist measure. The length is regulated with the tape measure. The skirt is drafted in one piece; parts A and B are to be put together before drafting; but it is also cut double. Lay the plaits according to the notches.

Winter 1888–1889 *Voice of Fashion*

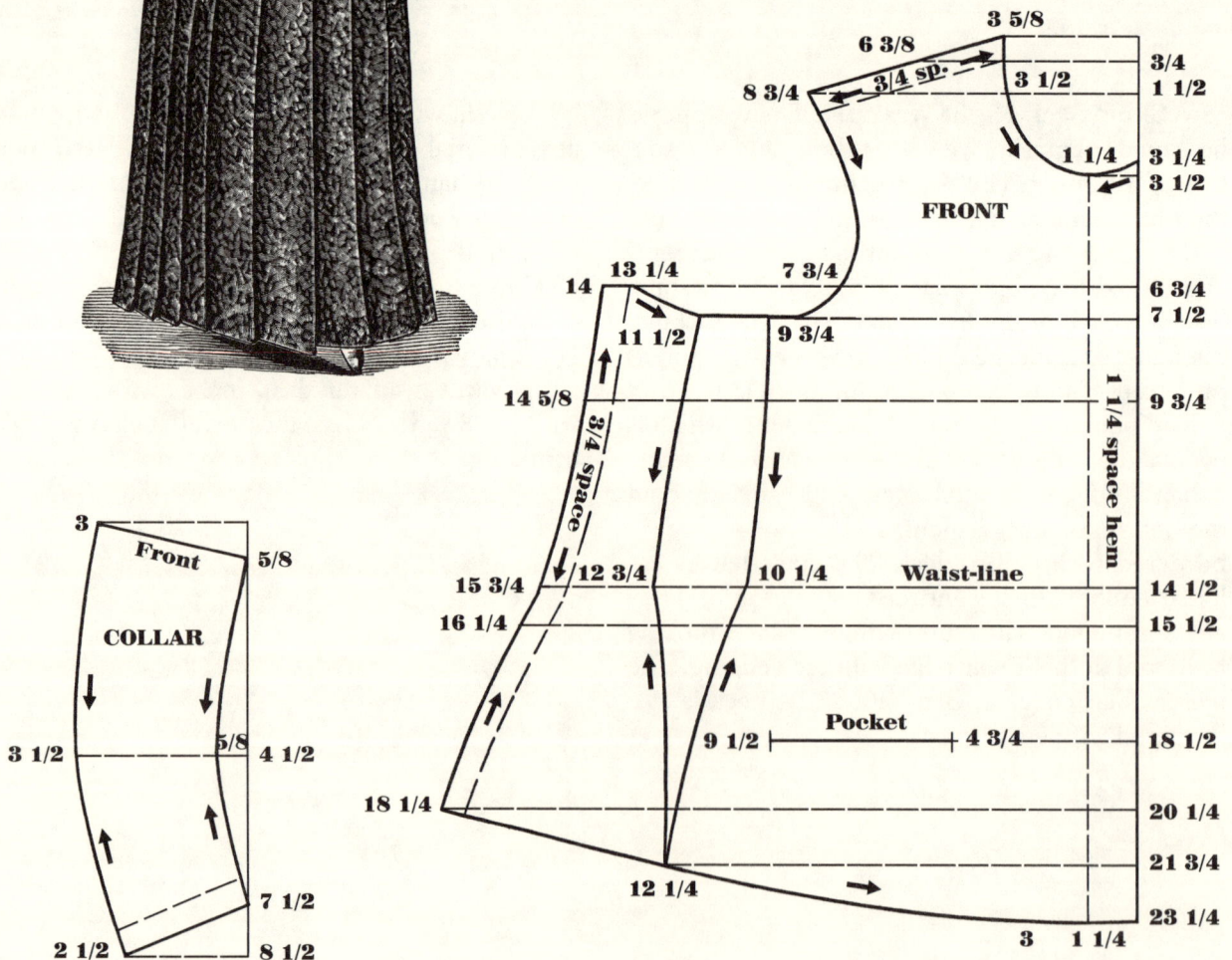

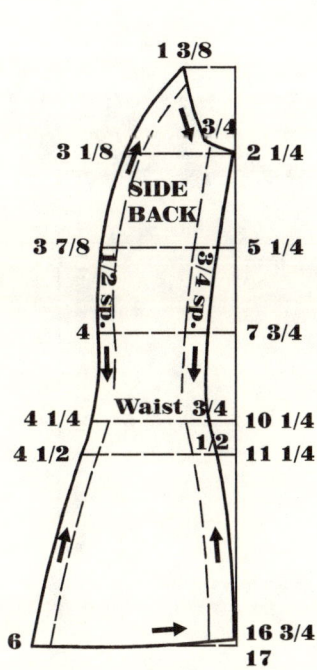

SIDE BACK

1 3/8

3/4

3 1/8   2 1/4

3 7/8   5 1/4

1/2 sp.   3/4 sp.

4   7 3/4

4 1/4   Waist 3/4   10 1/4

4 1/2   1/2   11 1/4

6   16 3/4

17

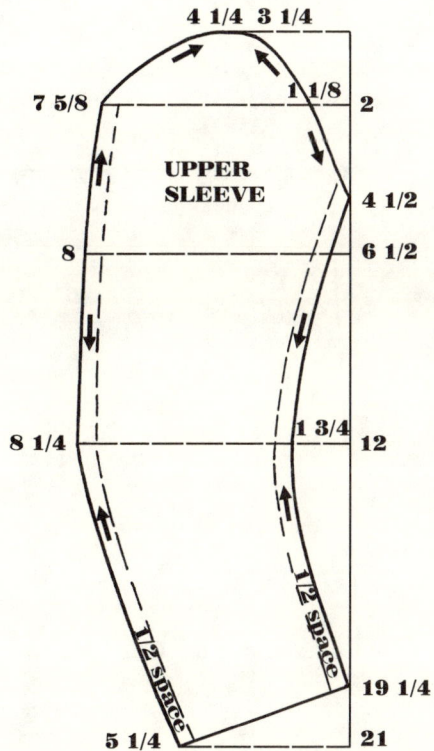

UPPER SLEEVE

4 1/4   3 1/4

7 5/8   1 1/8   2

4 1/2

8   6 1/2

8 1/4   1 3/4   12

1/2 space

1/2 space

19 1/4

5 1/4   21

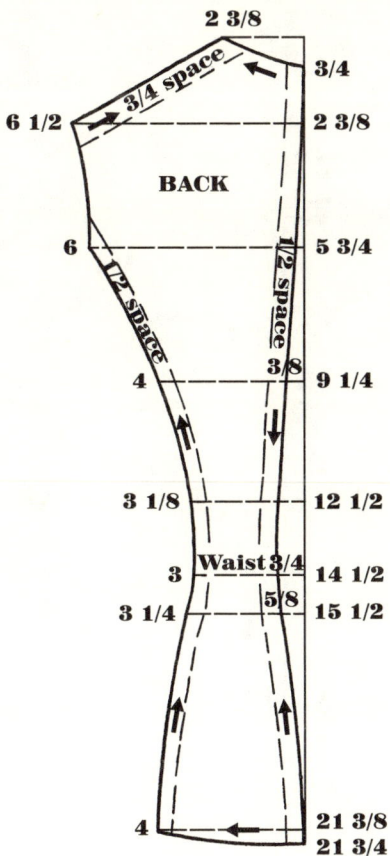

BACK

2 3/8

3/4 space   3/4

6 1/2   2 3/8

6   5 3/4

1/2 space   1/2 space

4   3/8   9 1/4

3 1/8   12 1/2

3   Waist 3/4   14 1/2

3 1/4   5/8   15 1/2

4   21 3/8

21 3/4

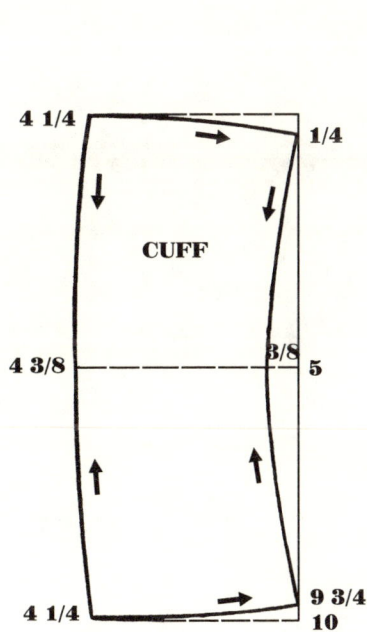

CUFF

4 1/4   1/4

4 3/8   3/8

5

4 1/4   9 3/4

10

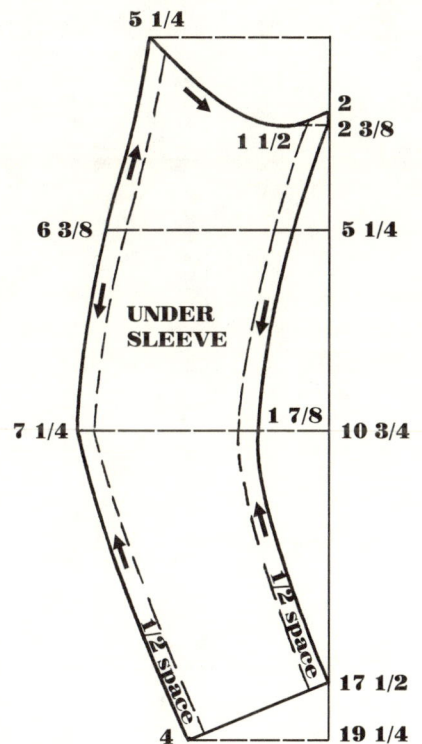

UNDER SLEEVE

5 1/4

2

1 1/2   2 3/8

6 3/8   5 1/4

7 1/4   1 7/8   10 3/4

1/2 space   1/2 space

17 1/2

4   19 1/4

29

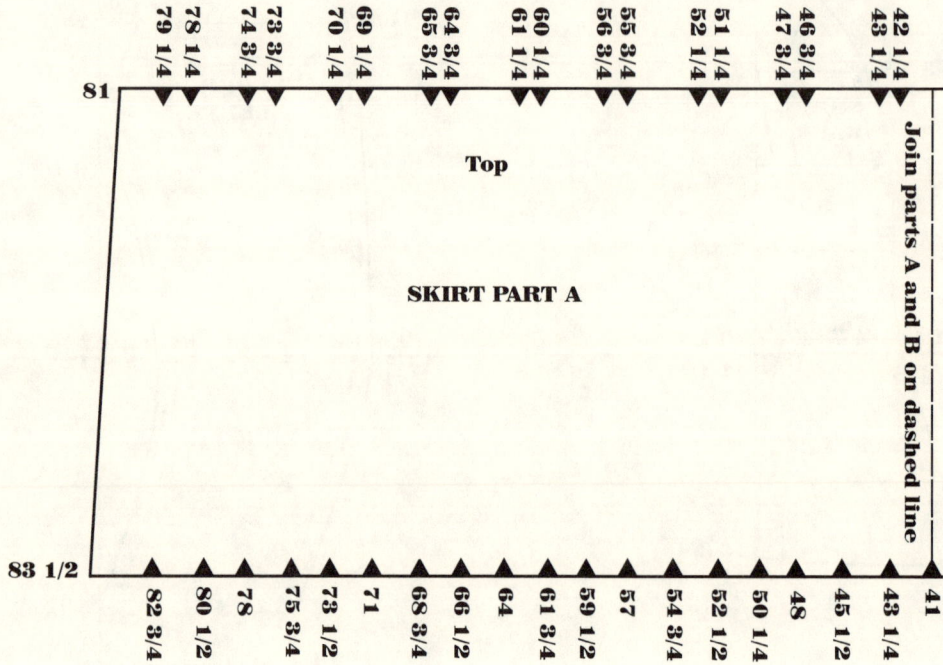

Top

SKIRT PART A

Join parts A and B on dashed line

81

83 1/2

42 1/4 · 43 1/4 · 46 3/4 · 47 3/4 · 51 1/4 · 52 1/4 · 55 3/4 · 56 3/4 · 60 1/4 · 61 1/4 · 64 3/4 · 65 3/4 · 69 1/4 · 70 1/4 · 73 3/4 · 74 3/4 · 78 1/4 · 79 1/4

41 · 43 1/4 · 45 1/2 · 48 · 50 1/4 · 52 1/2 · 54 3/4 · 57 · 59 1/2 · 61 3/4 · 64 · 66 1/2 · 68 3/4 · 71 · 73 1/2 · 75 3/4 · 78 · 80 1/2 · 82 3/4

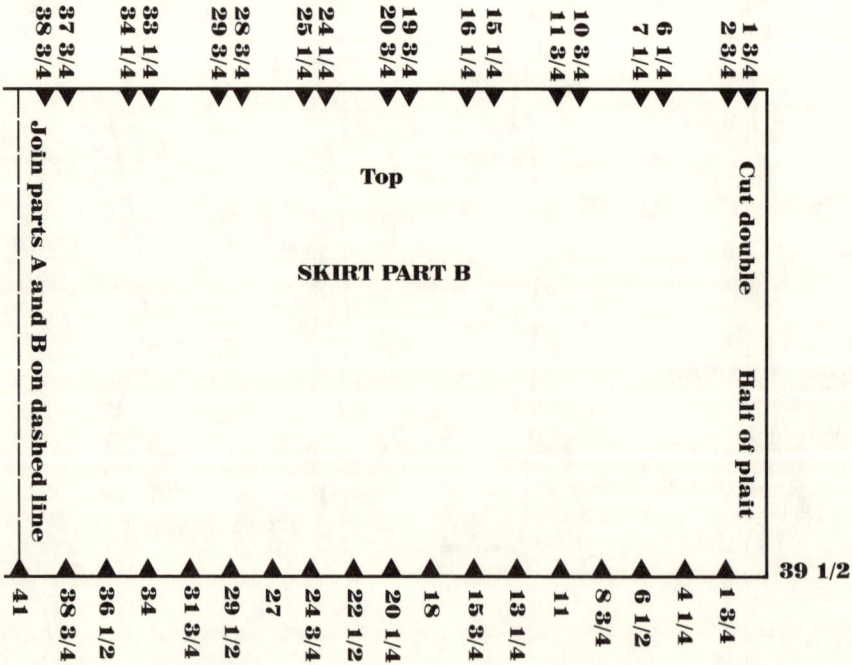

Top

SKIRT PART B

Join parts A and B on dashed line

Cut double

Half of plait

39 1/2

38 3/4 · 37 3/4 · 34 1/4 · 33 1/4 · 29 3/4 · 28 3/4 · 25 1/4 · 24 1/4 · 20 3/4 · 19 3/4 · 16 1/4 · 15 1/4 · 11 3/4 · 10 3/4 · 7 1/4 · 6 1/4 · 2 3/4 · 1 3/4

41 · 38 3/4 · 36 1/2 · 34 · 31 3/4 · 29 1/2 · 27 · 24 3/4 · 22 1/2 · 20 1/4 · 18 · 15 3/4 · 13 1/4 · 11 · 8 3/4 · 6 1/2 · 4 1/4 · 1 3/4

Négligé Toilette. A skirt and a dressing sack are combined in this négligé, which may with propriety be worn as a breakfast toilette at home. The four-gored skirt is made from a walking skirt pattern. It is here made of fine nainsook, the gores being dart fitted and the back breadth gathered. A knife-plaiting of the material provides the foot trimming, above which the skirt is covered nearly to the belt with two flounces of nainsook embroidery.

Here the dressing sack is made of white flannel. The fronts are in loose sack style, close all the way down with button-holes and buttons, and are held in to the figure by ribbon ties inserted in the side seams and bowed over the closing. A long under-arm dart in each front produces a smooth effect at the sides, and together with the side and shoulder seams, completes the adjustment. The back is cut on a fold of the material. At the center of the back are six backward-turning tucks, which extend from the neck to a little below the waist-line and have their fullness pressed in plaits below.

A frill of embroidery, headed by a band of insertion, trims the lower edge of the sack. Down the left side of the closing is a full jabot of lace. The rolling collar is trimmed with a lace frill, and a ribbon bow is fastened at the neck. The sleeves are shortened slightly and trimmed with a lace frill, headed by a band of insertion; and a ribbon bow is basted on the outside seam at the wrist.

This dressing sack may be made of basket flannel, eider-down flannel, cotton cloths and plushes, Turkish cloth, gingham, nainsook, lawn, piqué, delaine, nun's veiling, pongee, or China silks. Its decoration may be as simple or as elaborate as desired. Lace, embroidery, braid, ruffles, insertion, ribbons, contrasting bands, hand embroidery, appliqué ornaments, etc., are all suitable. To make the dressing sack for a lady of medium size, requires 3 1/2 yards of material 22 inches wide, 2 1/2 yards of material 36 inches wide, or 1 3/4 yards of material 48 inches wide.

June 1885 *Delineator*

Ladies' Négligé. This toilette consists of a morning sack and a four-gored skirt made from a walking skirt pattern. The gores are smoothly fitted to the belt, and the back breadth is gathered. The skirt is shown made of pink étamine suiting. A narrow knife-plaiting of silk trims the bottom. Above this a gathered flounce of the material trims the bottom of the gores. Falling over the top of this flounce is a plaited flounce that extends to the belt. It is trimmed at the bottom, like the gathered flounce, with three bands of crimson ribbon. The back breadth is covered with four deep, gathered flounces of the material similarly trimmed at the bottom. The skirt may be used for street as well as for house wear. It may be finished without any trimming, or it may be elaborately trimmed with lace, embroidery, applied bands, braid, ruffles, or plaitings of the material.

Ladies' Négligé

The morning sack is made of figured cashmere. It has loose-fitting fronts. At the back and sides it is conformed to the figure by side pieces, side backs, and a center back seam, all of the seams being continued in their curves to the lower edge. It is shortest at the back and gradually deepens toward the closing, which is made with button-holes and buttons. A white lace frill trims the lower edge, and is arranged in a cascade up each side of the closing and outside the standing collar. The coat sleeves fit comfortably and are shortened somewhat. They are trimmed with a lace frill, headed by a band of narrow pink ribbon that is arranged in a full-looped bow near the back of the wrist. Long ties of wide pink ribbon are inserted in the under-arm seams at the waist-line, and bowed at the back. The ties may be bowed in front if desired, or omitted altogether.

All kinds of pretty wools, cottons, and silks are used for morning sacks. Foulard, cambric, sateen, linen lawn, crinkled and plain zephyr ginghams, soft serge, plain and embroidered cashmeres, nun's veiling, lawn, nainsook, chambray, pongee, etc., are much liked for summer wear. All kinds of becoming colors may be selected, and embroidery or inexpensive lace may be used for trimming. To make the morning sack for a lady of medium size, requires 3 1/4 yards of material 22 inches wide, 2 yards of material 36 inches wide, or 1 1/2 yards of material 48 inches wide.

May 1886 *Delineator*

3. Wrappers and Tea Gowns

The term "wrapper" conveys widely different meanings. There are two faults into which wrappers may fall. They may be made entirely too négligé to be worn except in the bedroom, and they may be made as elaborate as an evening or dinner dress and so lose all comfort. The comfortably fitted princess dress is the best kind of wrapper. On this various changes of loose fronts, Watteau backs, long wrappers, and walking-length wrappers are rung.

Cotton wrappers are seldom lined. The seams are long and often bias; consequently they must be securely stitched and stayed. When the wrapper is of silk or wool material, French cambric makes the best lining. The bottom of the skirt may be faced with the same; nothing heavier is required. The sleeves and neck are finished just like those of a basque. If the front of the wrapper is made to fit snugly, its closing edges should be curved as for a basque, and must be faced. When the front falls loose, the straight hemmed edges are easily finished.

1892 *Home Dressmaking*

Muslin wrappers are so elaborate that they resemble tea gowns, and are sometimes worn over a slip of colored surah, or a China silk corset cover and petticoat. India lawn, Victoria lawn, and French nainsook wrappers are more useful. They are made with wide straight fronts, which have only an under-arm dart, meeting the side backs, which are of continuous length. The center backs are cut off in a point below the waist-line, and a full breadth is shirred to this point to give fullness to the back of the skirt. These wrappers are very pretty when the fronts have three or four tucks their whole length, with a box-plait beyond the tucks, and two ruffles of open-work Hamburg edging scantily gathered between. The full sleeves have tucks and a box-plait at the top, with turn-over bands of the Hamburg edging forming a cuff. The neck may have frills to match those down the front, or a rolling collar similar to the cuffs. The bottom of the wrapper has one or two tucked ruffles of the material gathered scantily around it.

August 18, 1888 *Harper's Bazar*

Tea gowns are made in cashmere or camel's hair of light colors and trimmed with numerous rows and bows of black moiré ribbon. Tea gowns are in many cases simply Empire dresses, with a round full or plain bodice and a very full skirt of plain breadths. The skirt may be with or without long, broad sashes or panels. These are sometimes arranged with one on each side and two at the back, all slightly gathered at the top, falling quite to the foot of the skirt, and sometimes finished with a handsome fringe. Faced cloths and camel's hair serges in light shades are used for this purpose, and bordered silks seem especially appropriate for tea gowns in the Empire style.

Tea jackets made of soft silk or wool and lavishly trimmed with lace and ribbons, to be worn with various skirts, are preferred by many ladies to the more elaborate tea gowns.

December 1888 *Demorest's Monthly Magazine*

Tea Gown

Tea Gown

This tea gown is drafted with the scale corresponding to the bust measure. Regulate the length with the tape measure. There are six pieces: Bodice front, full front, back (drafted together with the side back), collar, and two sleeve pieces.

Turn down the top of the full front, gather it twice, and sew it onto the curved line on the bodice front, which forms a yoke. Lay two double box-plaits in the back; press them carefully but do not baste them down. Any style of trimming may be used on the bottom of the skirt, cuffs, yoke, and collar.

Summer 1888 *Voice of Fashion*

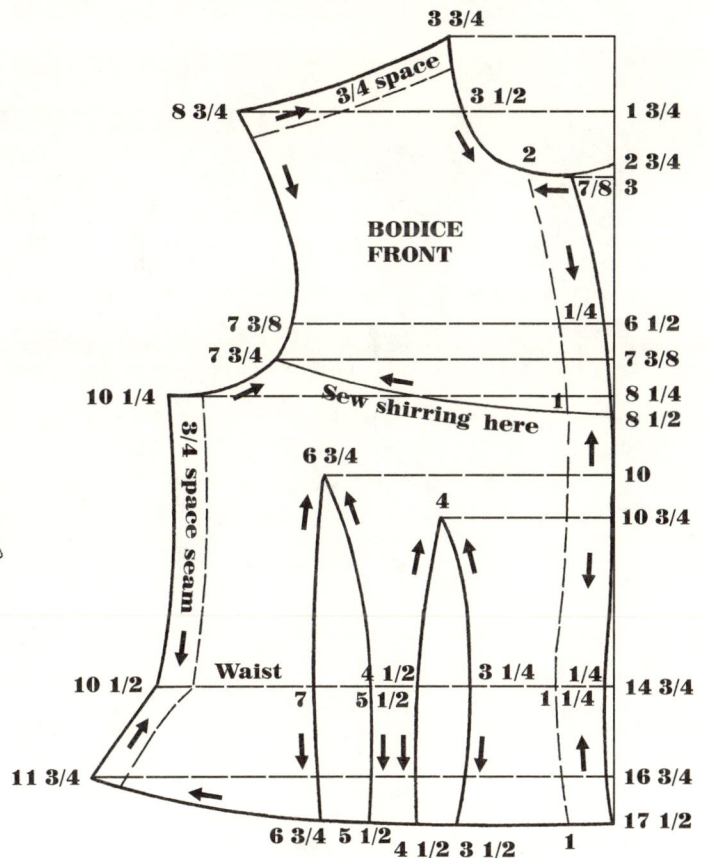

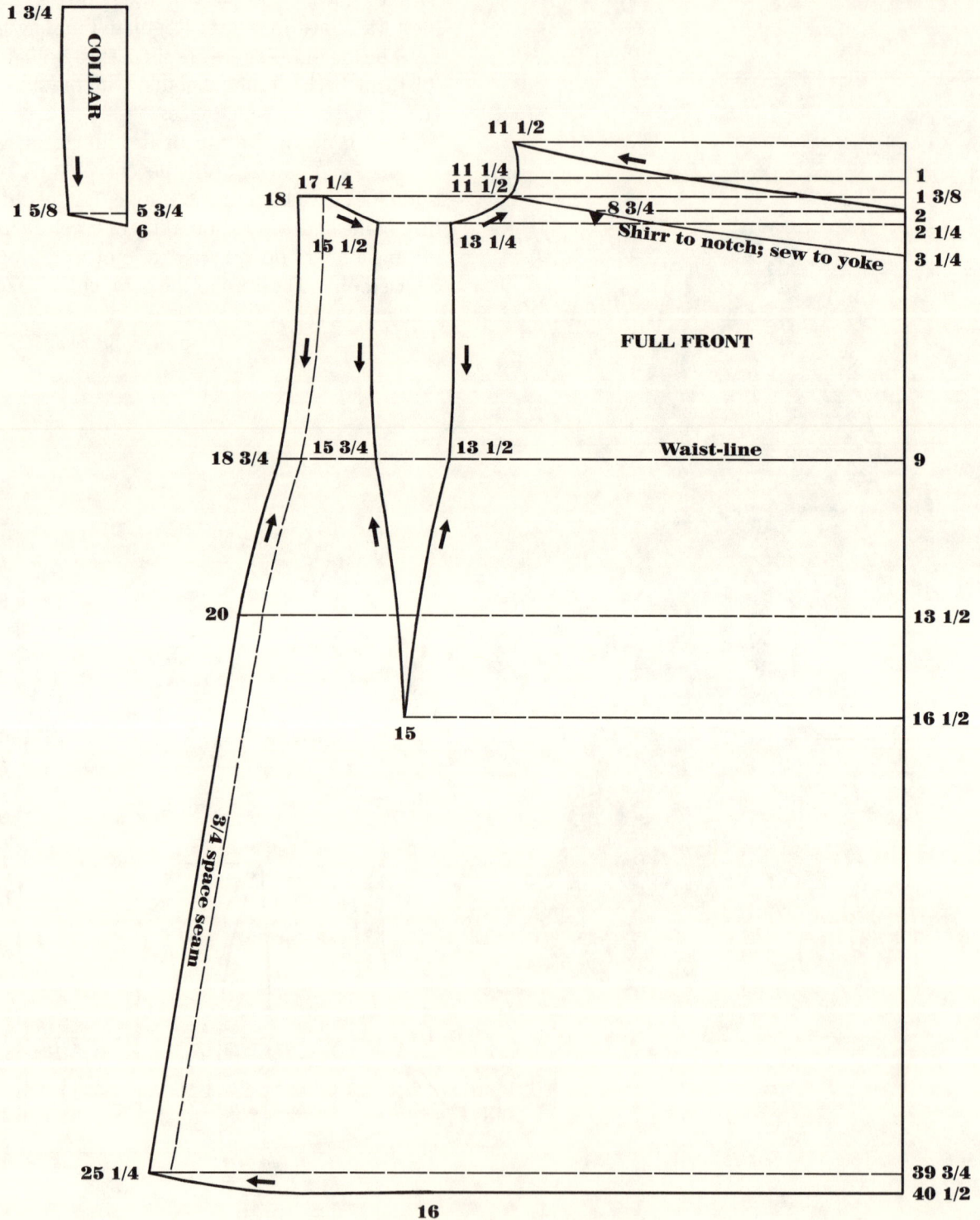

COLLAR

1 3/4

1 5/8   5 3/4
         6

11 1/2

17 1/4
18   11 1/4
          11 1/2   1
15 1/2   1 3/8
                    13 1/4   8 3/4   2
                                                       2 1/4
                         Shirr to notch; sew to yoke   3 1/4

FULL FRONT

18 3/4   15 3/4   13 1/2   Waist-line   9

20   13 1/2

                                                      16 1/2
         15

3/4 space seam

25 1/4   39 3/4
                                                      40 1/2
         16

UPPER SLEEVE

3 3/4

3/4 2 1/2

7 1/4

4 3/8

7 1/8 1/2 6

6 3/4 1 11

3/8 space

16

4 1/4 17 1/2

UNDER SLEEVE

5

1 3/4
2
1

5 1/8 3 3/4

5 3/8 1 1/8 9

3/8 space

14

3 15 3/4

BACK

5

2 1/2 3/4

9 3/4 space 2

1/2 space 4 1/2

14 8 7/8 5 3/4

12 1/8 6 3/4

15 1/4 3/4 space 11 1/4 7 1/8 3 1/2 8 3/4

10 5/8 6 1/8 11 1/4

1/2 sp. 10 1/2 5 3/4 4 Waist 14

13 3/4 10 3/8 6 4 15

8 3/4 3 1 5/8

15 3/8 18

17 24

3/4 space seam

21 1/2 44 1/2

46 1/2

10 47 1/4

Cut double

Wrapper or Tea Gown. This example is made of suit material and trimmed with material of a darker shade. The back is suggestive of a princess, with center back and side-back seams ending a little below the waist-line at the top of extra widths. These are folded to form a double box-plait underneath at the end of the center back seam, and a plait turning backward at the end of each side-back seam.

The bodice is in basque style in front, with double bust darts fitting it snugly to the figure. On its fronts, at about yoke depth below the neck, are adjusted the full fronts, which are shirred and finished with a self-heading at the top as far back as the armholes. Beneath the armholes, the fronts extend to meet the side backs and are fitted by long under-arm darts. The full fronts extend only to the under-arm darts, into which they are sewed. They can be closed beneath the skirt parts with buttons and button-holes, hooks and eyes, or cords laced through eyes or eyelets, as desired. Above the skirt they are closed with buttons and button-holes, which may be in a fly. This mode of construction adjusts the fronts and back closely to the figure, and leaves the front skirts to fall loosely in Mother Hubbard fashion. Ribbon ties are inserted in the lower part of the under-arm darts and are tied in a bow in front, appearing to hold the fullness in place. The wrapper is of uniform length at the bottom.

Wrapper or Tea Gown

The coat sleeves are finished at the wrists with medium-wide cuff-facings of the darker material. A standing collar, also of the darker material, finishes the neck. A broad band of the darker material borders the bottom of the wrapper.

This style also does good service as a tea gown. It may be made of eider-down flannels and cloths, striped and plain flannels, Turkish cloth, serge, cashmere, wool sateen, plain and brocaded silks, satin merveilleux, and all kinds of soft, pretty dress materials. Lace, feather or down trimming, or embroidery are suitable decorations; and braid, contrasting bands, or pipings are also much admired. For a lady of medium size, this garment requires 8 1/4 yards of material 22 inches wide, 5 3/4 yards of material 36 inches wide, or 3 7/8 yards of material 48 inches wide.

January 1886 *Delineator*

Tea Gown

This garment is drafted with the scale corresponding to the bust measure. It is in ten pieces: Upper front, under front, front shirring, front plaiting, corselet, side back, back, under sleeve, upper sleeve, and full sleeve. Regulate the length of the sleeve pieces by the tape measure.

Lay plaits according to the notches in the back and side back. The under front is merely the lining, which is joined in the seams under the arm and on the shoulder, and closed with hooks and eyes.

Shirr the part given for that purpose with the lines 3/4 inch apart. Baste each line to a plain piece of material to stay the gathers. Place the center on the center of the front of the lining. Fasten securely on the right side, gather the bottom, and baste to the waist-line on the lining. Lay the plaits according to the notches. There are three forward-turning plaits on each side of the center. Press them carefully and stay them underneath. Baste them firmly to the lining, omitting the basting at the bottom. The corselet is made of velvet. Insert whalebone down the center of the front to keep it in place. Turn away the upper front and blind-stitch it onto the lining. Close the left side with hooks and eyes.

Gather the full sleeve at the top and bottom. Cut a lining or tight sleeve from the upper and under sleeve patterns, to the length required. A deep cuff may be used instead of the lace at the wrist.

Fall 1888 *Voice of Fashion*

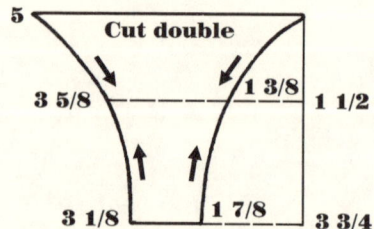

Corselet

5   **Cut double**

3 5/8   1 3/8   1 1/2

3 1/8   1 7/8   3 3/4

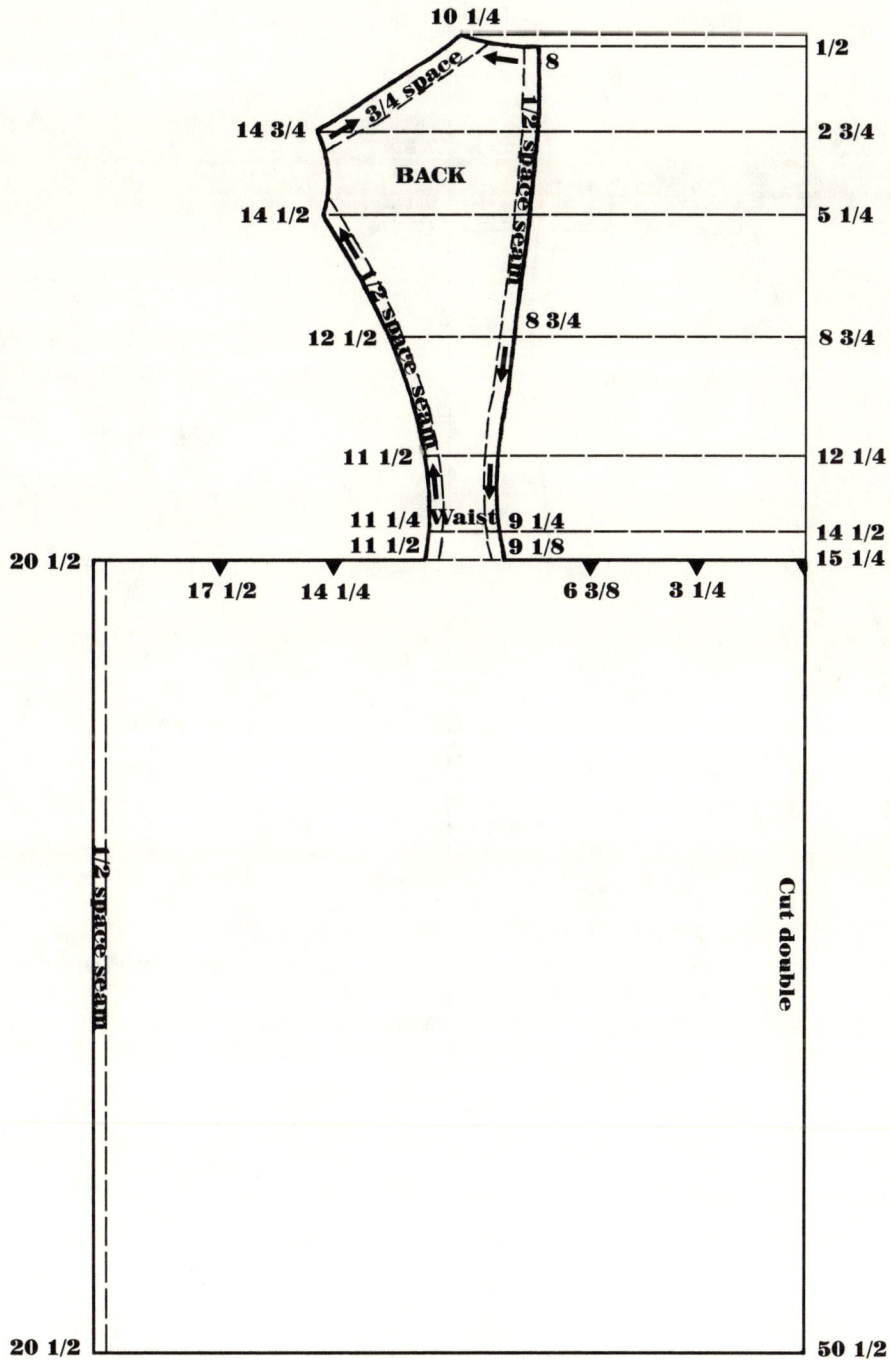

10 1/4

1/2

8

3/4 space

1/2 space seam

14 3/4

2 3/4

BACK

14 1/2

5 1/4

1/2 space seam

8 3/4

8 3/4

12 1/2

11 1/2

12 1/4

11 1/4 Waist 9 1/4

14 1/2

20 1/2

11 1/2

9 1/8

15 1/4

17 1/2

14 1/4

6 3/8

3 1/4

1/2 space seam

Cut double

20 1/2

50 1/2

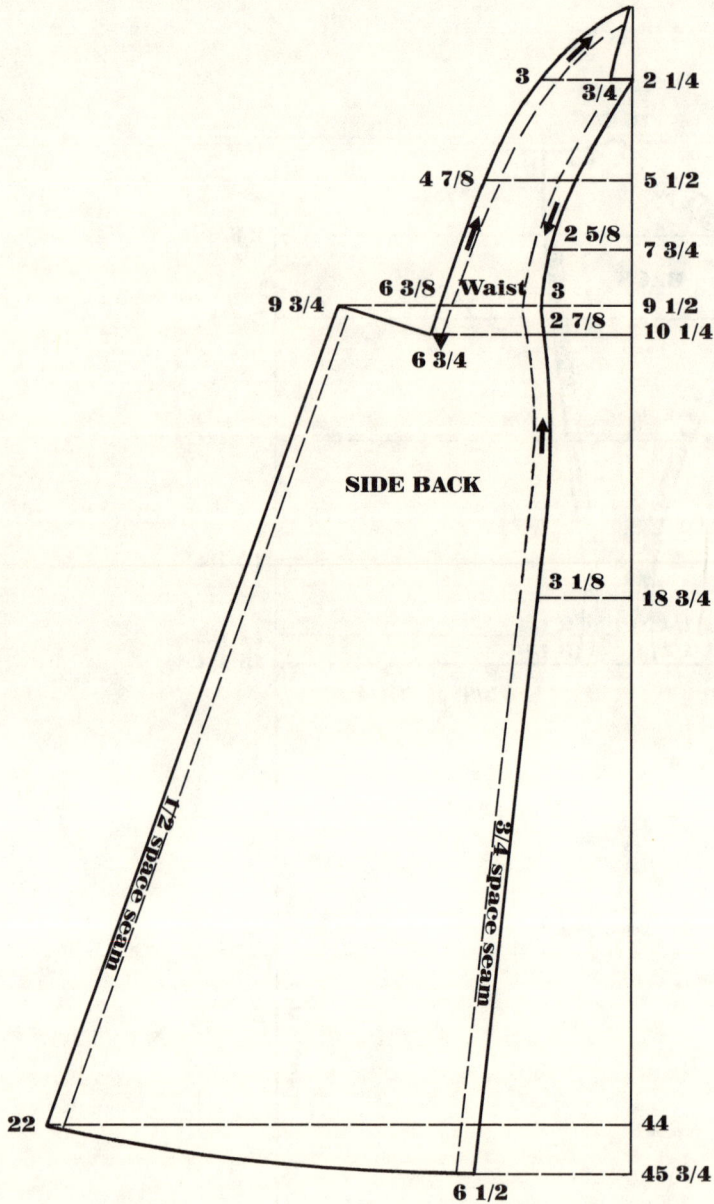

3   **2 1/4**
3/4

4 7/8   **5 1/2**

2 5/8
7 3/4

6 3/8   **Waist**   **3**   **9 1/2**
9 3/4   **2 7/8**   **10 1/4**
6 3/4

SIDE BACK

3 1/8   **18 3/4**

1/2 space seam

3/4 space seam

22

44

45 3/4

6 1/2

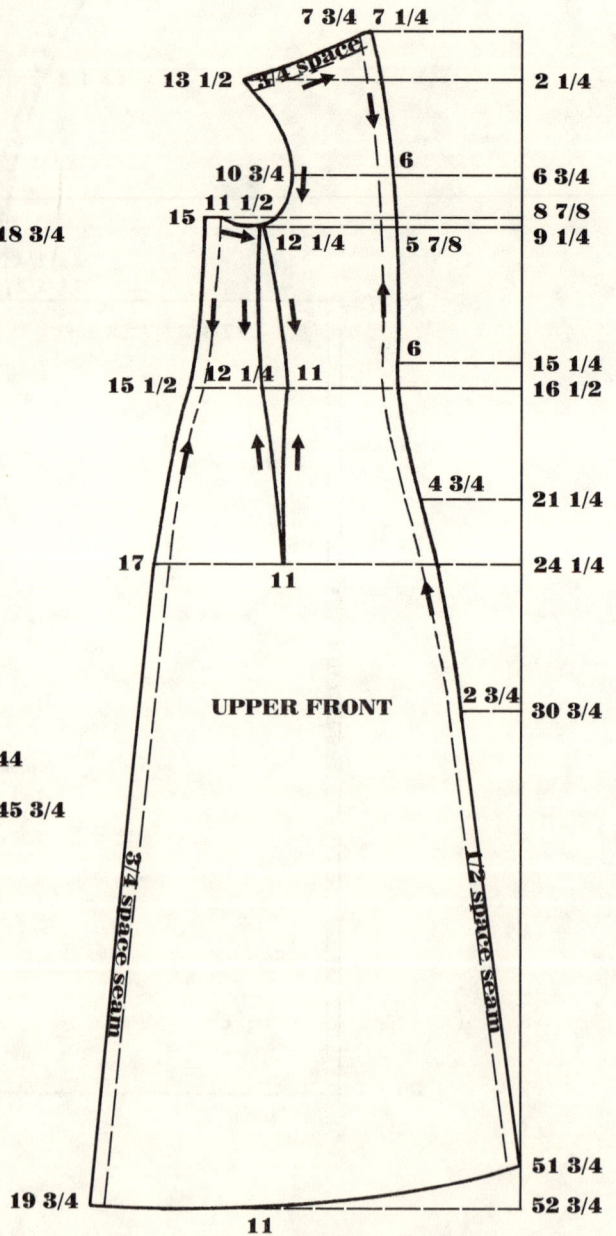

7 3/4   **7 1/4**

13 1/2   *3/4 space*

2 1/4

10 3/4   **6**
6 3/4

11 1/2   **8 7/8**
15   **12 1/4**   **5 7/8**   **9 1/4**

6

15 1/4

15 1/2   **12 1/4**   **11**   **16 1/2**

4 3/4   **21 1/4**

17   **11**   **24 1/4**

UPPER FRONT   **2 3/4**   **30 3/4**

3/4 space seam

1/2 space seam

51 3/4

19 3/4   **52 3/4**

11

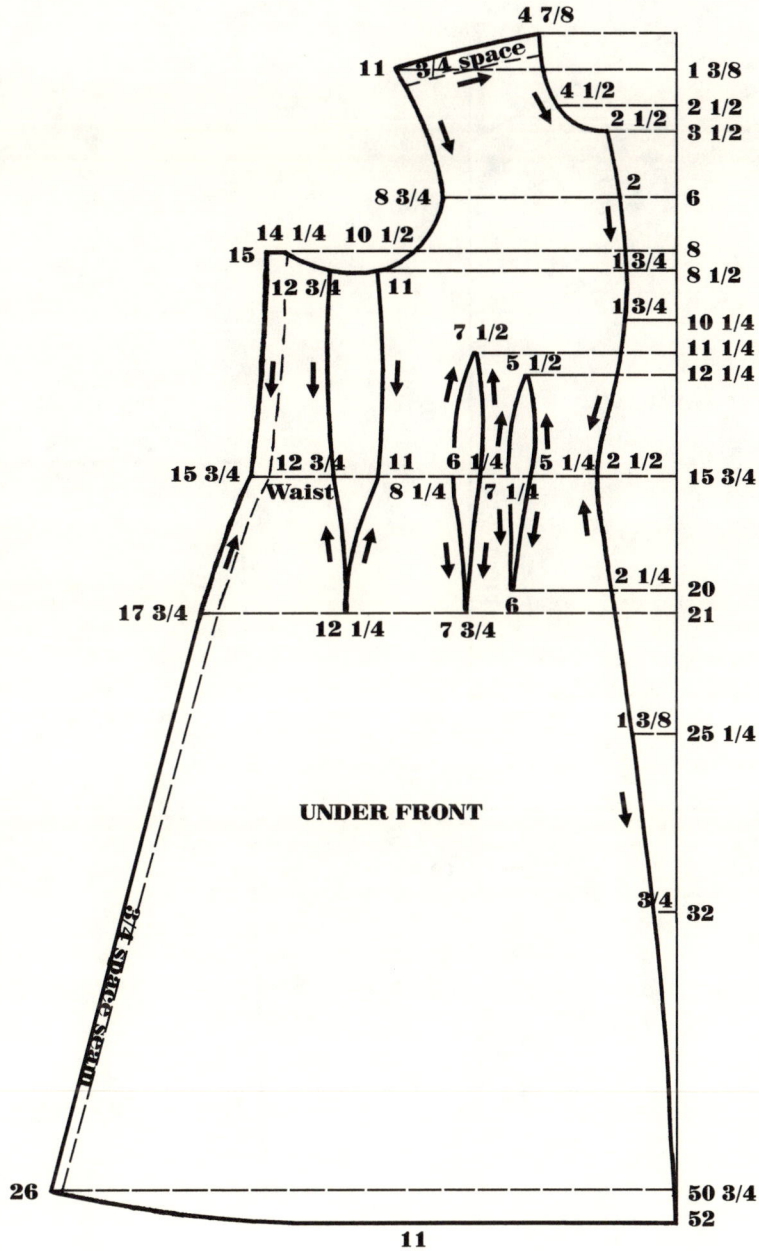

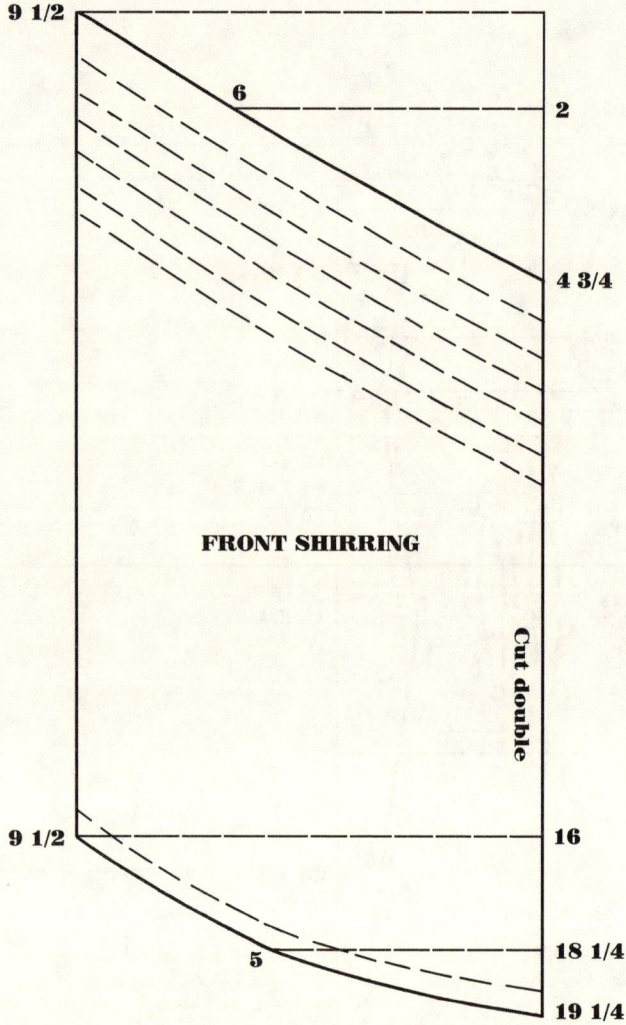

9 1/2

6 2

4 3/4

FRONT SHIRRING

Cut double

9 1/2 16

18 1/4

5

19 1/4

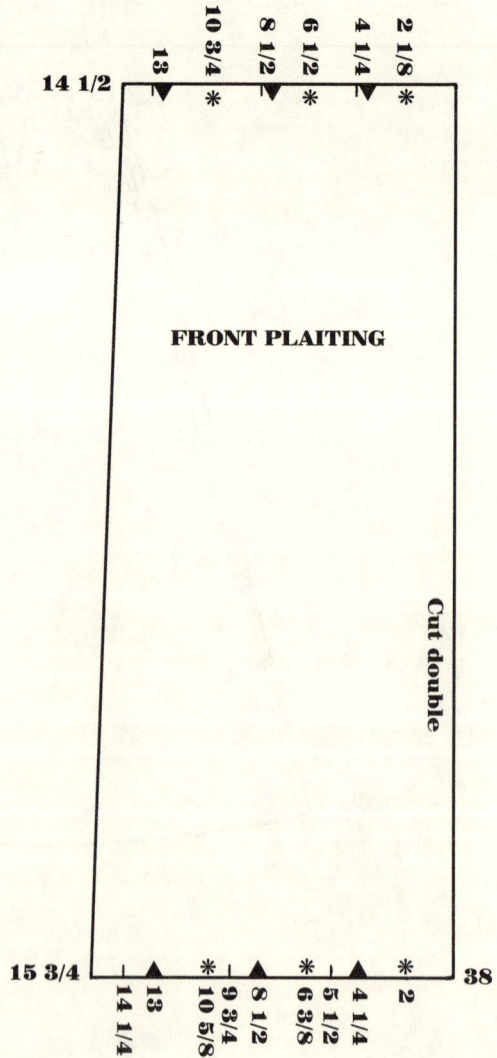

2 1/8
4 1/4
6 1/2
8 1/2
10 3/4
13

14 1/2

FRONT PLAITING

Cut double

15 3/4 38

14 1/4
13
10 5/8
9 3/4
8 1/2
6 3/8
5 1/2
4 1/4
2

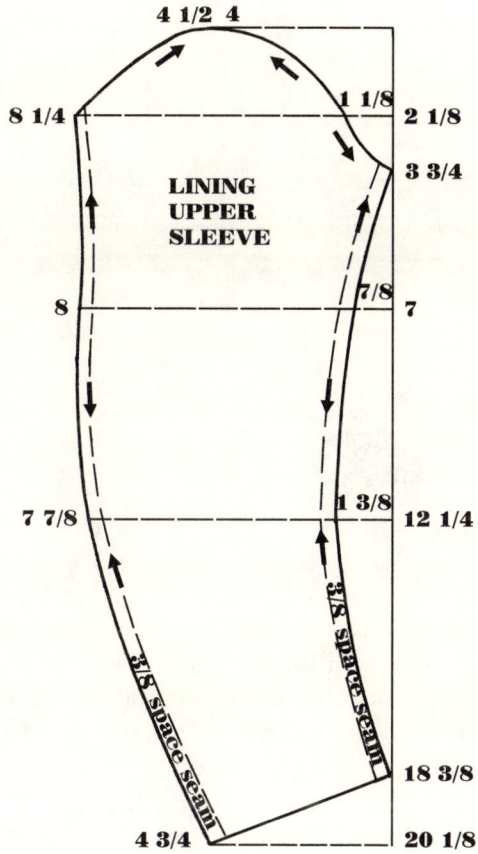

LINING UPPER SLEEVE

4 1/2 4

8 1/4

1 1/8 2 1/8

3 3/4

8

7/8 7

7 7/8

1 3/8 12 1/4

18 3/8

4 3/4 20 1/8

3/8 space seam

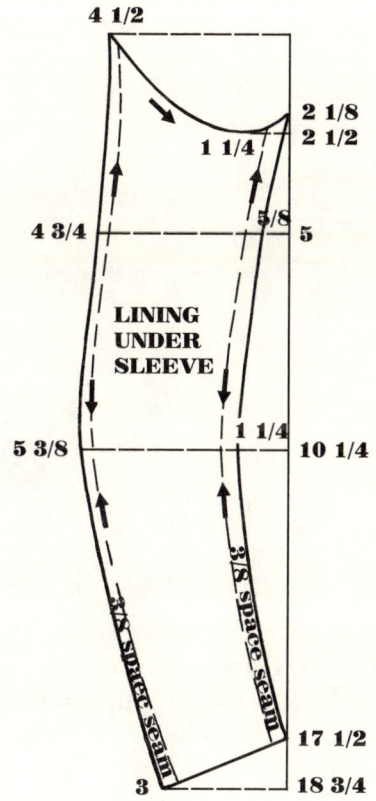

LINING UNDER SLEEVE

4 1/2

2 1/8
2 1/2

1 1/4

4 3/4

5/8 5

5 3/8

1 1/4 10 1/4

17 1/2

3 18 3/4

3/8 space seam

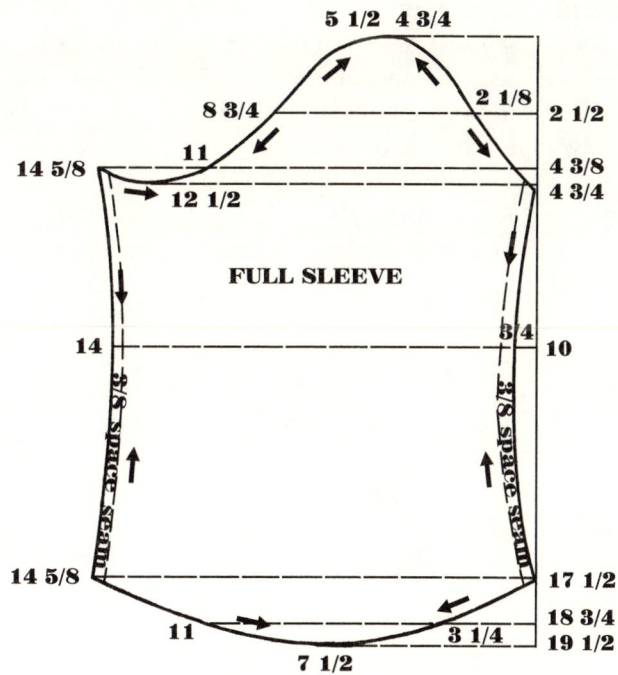

FULL SLEEVE

5 1/2 4 3/4

8 3/4

2 1/8 2 1/2

11

4 3/8

14 5/8

12 1/2 4 3/4

14

3/4 10

14 5/8

17 1/2

11

3 1/4 18 3/4
19 1/2

7 1/2

3/8 space seam

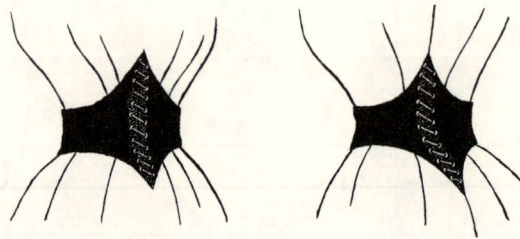

Spanish Girdle. One of the most popular accessories of a dressy or simple toilette is a Spanish girdle. Velvet was chosen for this example, and two sections are united in the formation. Each section is curved out narrowly over the hips and deepened toward the ends, so that when the corresponding edges meet they form points at the center of the front and back. Each section is lined and whaleboned. The ends are laced together at the front and back with silk cord run through eyelets, narrow underlaps being arranged to pass beneath the eyelets.

Such girdles are more frequently made of velvet than of any other material. However, girdles to match the costume are made up of the dress material, or of any contrasting material used in the construction. The finish may be entirely plain; or the girdle may be trimmed with tinsel cord or braid, jet sequins, embroidery, etc. For a lady of medium size, this girdle requires 5/8 yard of material 22 inches wide, or 1/2 yard of material 48 inches wide, with 3/4 yard of silk 20 inches wide for the lining.

September 1885 *Delineator*

Trained Wrapper

Trained Wrapper

The garment is drafted with the scale corresponding to the bust measure. The length is regulated with the tape measure. There are six pieces: Center front, front, back, two sleeve pieces, and collar. The train may be omitted if desired. The bell sleeve may be used instead of the two-piece coat sleeve shown by the engraving.

Any style of trimming may be used. Instead of the embroidered center front, a smocked or plaited front may be inserted, and the narrow center front used as a lining. Turn away the upper front and finish with a silk cord, velvet, plush, or lace.

Winter 1888–1889 *Voice of Fashion*

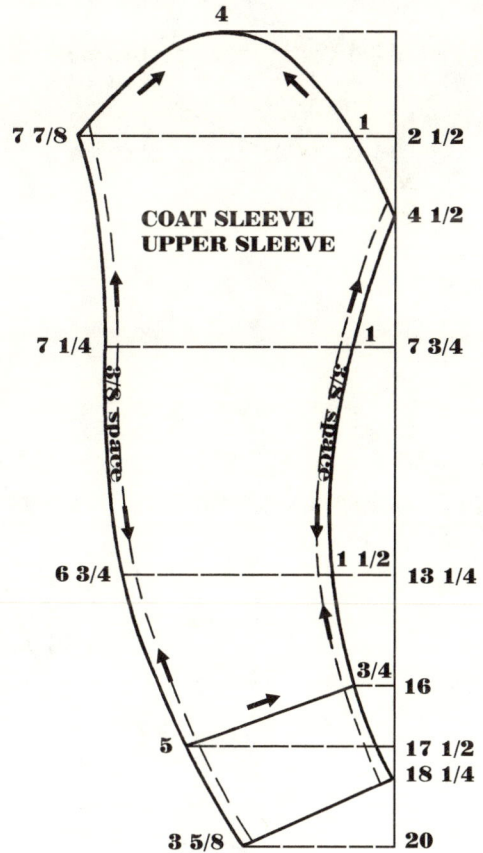

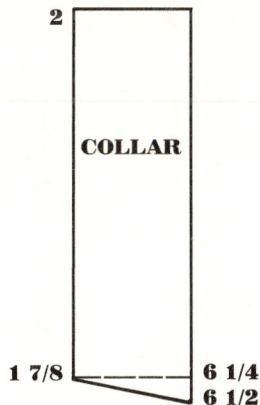

COLLAR

2

1 7/8   6 1/4
          6 1/2

4

7 7/8   1   2 1/2

COAT SLEEVE
UPPER SLEEVE   4 1/2

7 1/4   1   7 3/4

3/8 space   3/8 space

6 3/4   1 1/2   13 1/4

3/4   16

5   17 1/2
     18 1/4

3 5/8   20

Coat Sleeve Under Sleeve

5 1/2

2

2 1/4

**COAT
SLEEVE
UNDER
SLEEVE**

5 3/4

3/8 space

7/8

6 1/4

6

1 1/4

11 3/4

3/4

14 1/4

4 3/4

15 3/4
16 3/4

3 1/2

18 1/8

Front

1 7/8

6 7/8

3/4 space

1 3/4

1 3/4
2 3/4

1

6 3/8

7/8

7 3/4

13 1/4

10

7 1/2

8 1/2

13 1/2

3 1/4

1/2

11

13 3/4

9 3/4 Waist 7

17

14 1/2

3 3/4

1 1/2

18 1/4

16

8 1/4

21 1/4

FRONT

2 1/4

24 1/2

18 1/4

28 1/4

3/4 space seam

23 1/4

41 3/4

25 1/2

45 1/2

30

49 3/4

1 1/2

52

38
38

53

28

53 3/4

Trained Wrapper

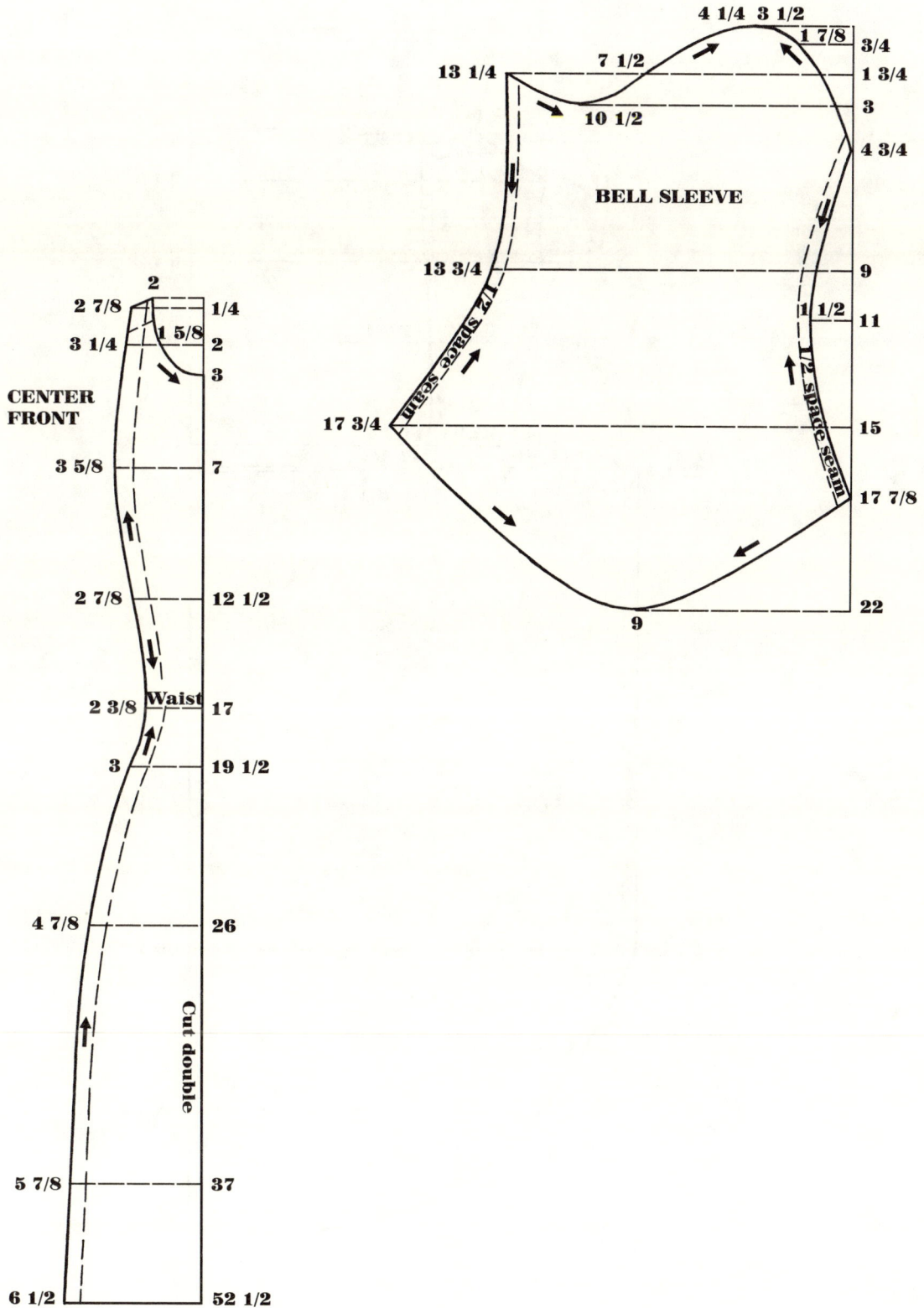

BELL SLEEVE

4 1/4 3 1/2

1 7/8   3/4

13 1/4   7 1/2   1 3/4

10 1/2   3

4 3/4

13 3/4   9

1/2 space seam   1 1/2   11

17 3/4   15

1/2 space seam   17 7/8

9   22

2

2 7/8   1/4

3 1/4   1 5/8   2

3

CENTER
FRONT

3 5/8   7

2 7/8   12 1/2

2 3/8   Waist   17

3   19 1/2

4 7/8   26

Cut double

5 7/8   37

6 1/2   52 1/2

49

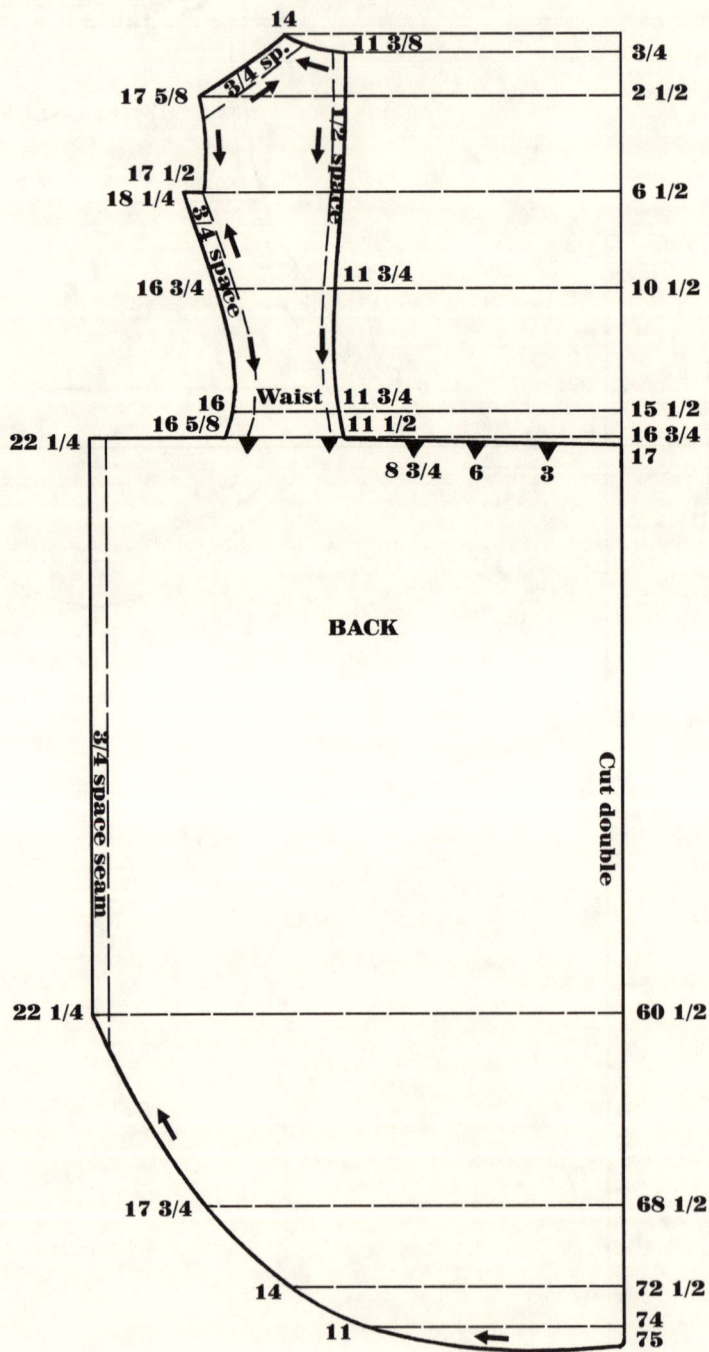

14   11 3/8   3/4
3/4 sp.
17 5/8   2 1/2
1/2 Space
17 1/2   6 1/2
18 1/4
3/4 Space
16 3/4   11 3/4   10 1/2

16   Waist   11 3/4   15 1/2
16 5/8   11 1/2   16 3/4
22 1/4   8 3/4   6   3   17

BACK

3/4 space seam

Cut double

22 1/4   60 1/2

17 3/4   68 1/2

14   72 1/2
74
11   75

Tea Gown

This garment is drafted with the scale corresponding to the bust measure. The length is regulated with the tape measure. It has eight pieces: Under front or lining, upper front, front plaiting, side back, back, collar, and two sleeve pieces.

The front plaiting is laid in five forward-turning plaits. Press them and baste them to the under front. Do not baste the plaits at the bottom of the skirt. Turn away the upper front to form lapels; face them with any suitable material. Make the cuffs and collar of the same material as the facing. Lay the plaits in the back and side back according to the notches. They can be either box-plaits or side-plaits.

Spring 1889 *Voice of Fashion*

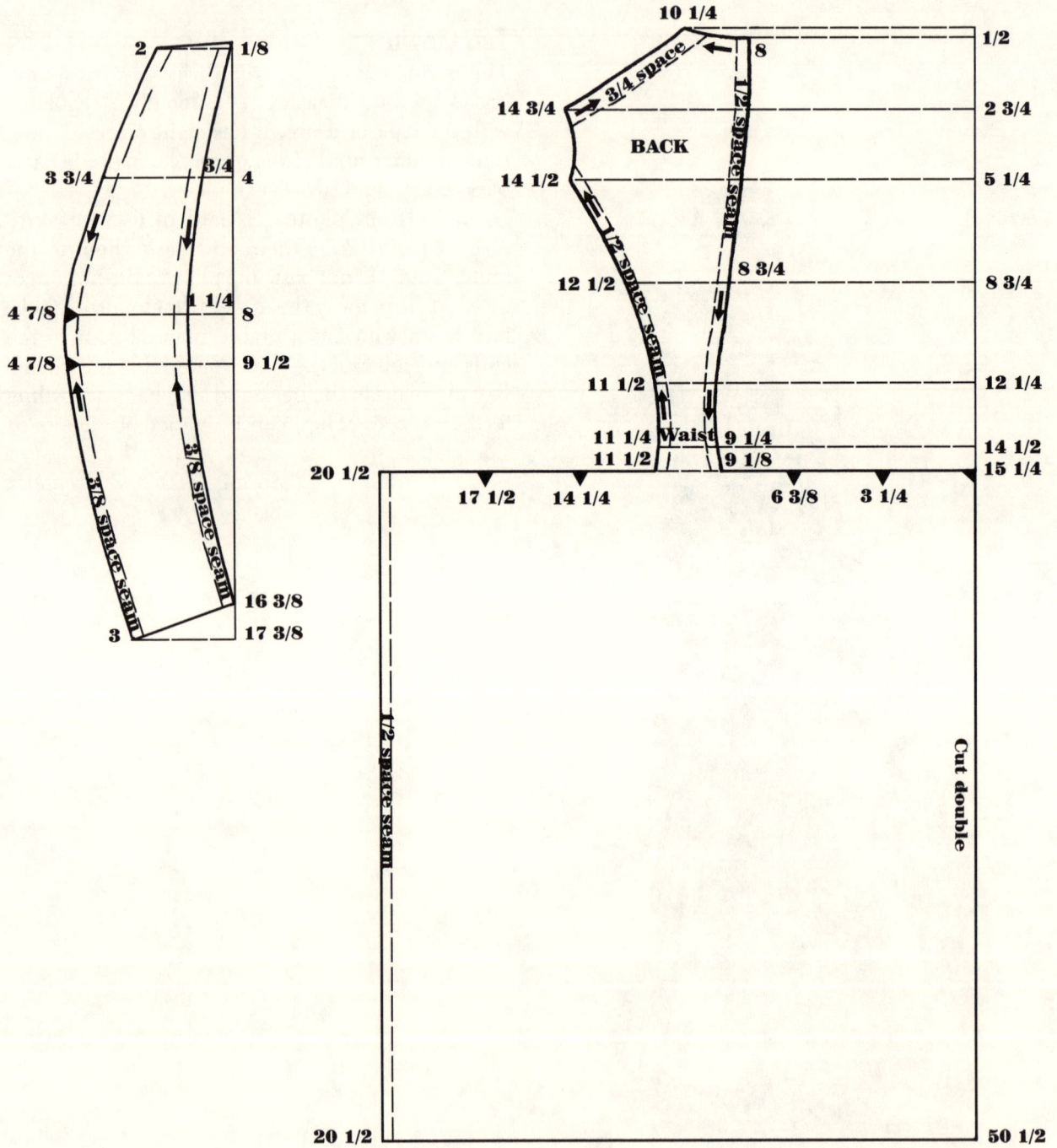

UNDER
SLEEVE

2   1/8

3 3/4   3/4   4

3/8 space seam

4 7/8   1 1/4   8

4 7/8   9 1/2

3/8 space seam

3/8 space seam

3   16 3/8
                17 3/8

10 1/4   1/2

8

3/4 space

14 3/4   2 3/4

1/2 space seam

BACK

14 1/2   5 1/4

1/2 space seam

12 1/2   8 3/4   8 3/4

11 1/2   12 1/4

11 1/4 Waist 9 1/4   14 1/2
11 1/2   9 1/8   15 1/4

20 1/2

17 1/2   14 1/4   6 3/8   3 1/4

1/2 space seam

Cut double

20 1/2   50 1/2

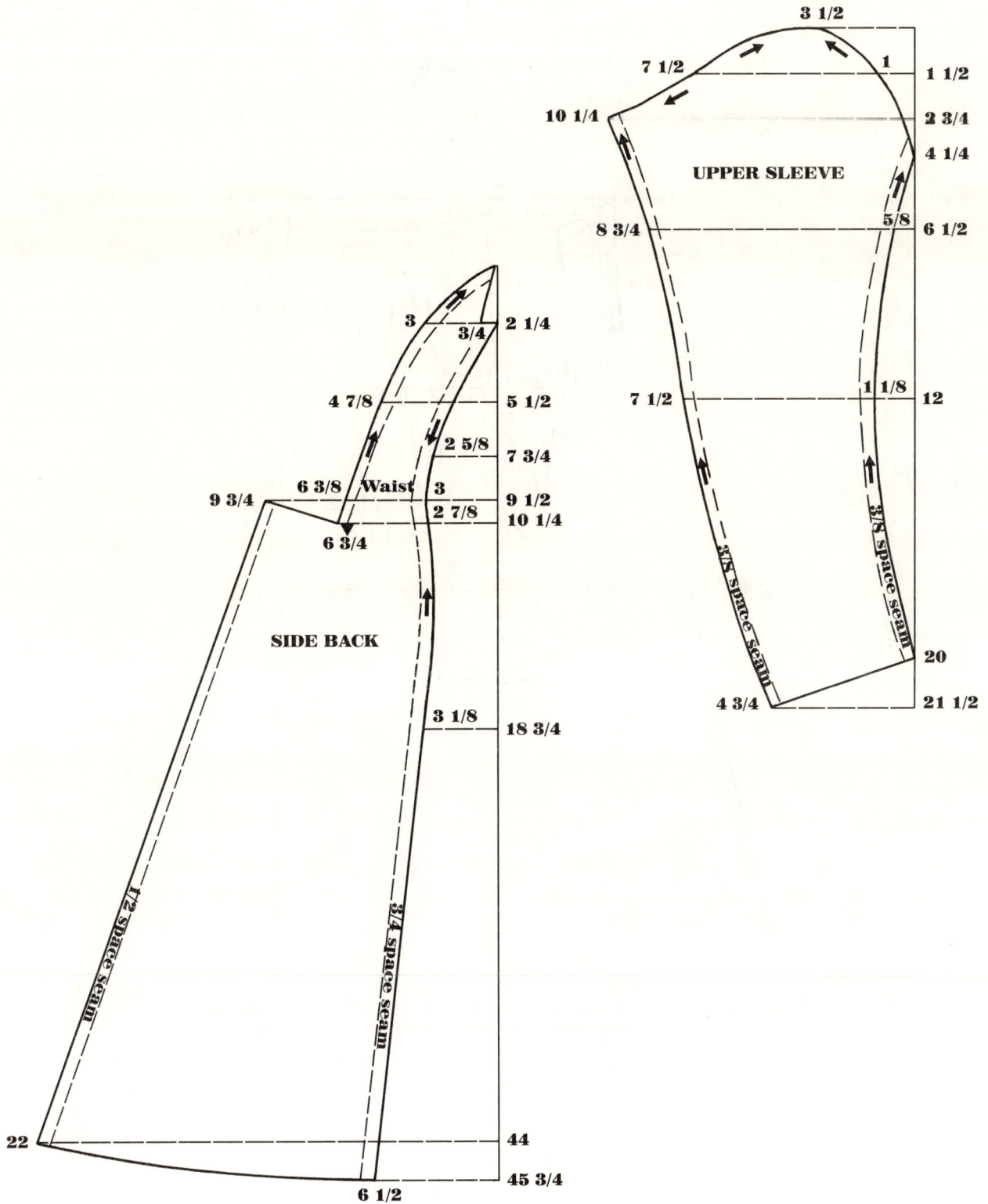

UPPER SLEEVE

3 1/2

7 1/2   1   1 1/2

10 1/4   2 3/4

                        4 1/4

8 3/4   5/8   6 1/2

7 1/2   1 1/8   12

3/8 space seam
3/8 space seam

                        20

4 3/4   21 1/2

SIDE BACK

3   3/4   2 1/4

4 7/8   5 1/2

              2 5/8   7 3/4

9 3/4   6 3/8   Waist   3   9 1/2
              2 7/8   10 1/4
        6 3/4

3 1/8   18 3/4

1/2 space seam

3/4 space seam

22

              44

              45 3/4

6 1/2

Wrappers and Tea Gowns

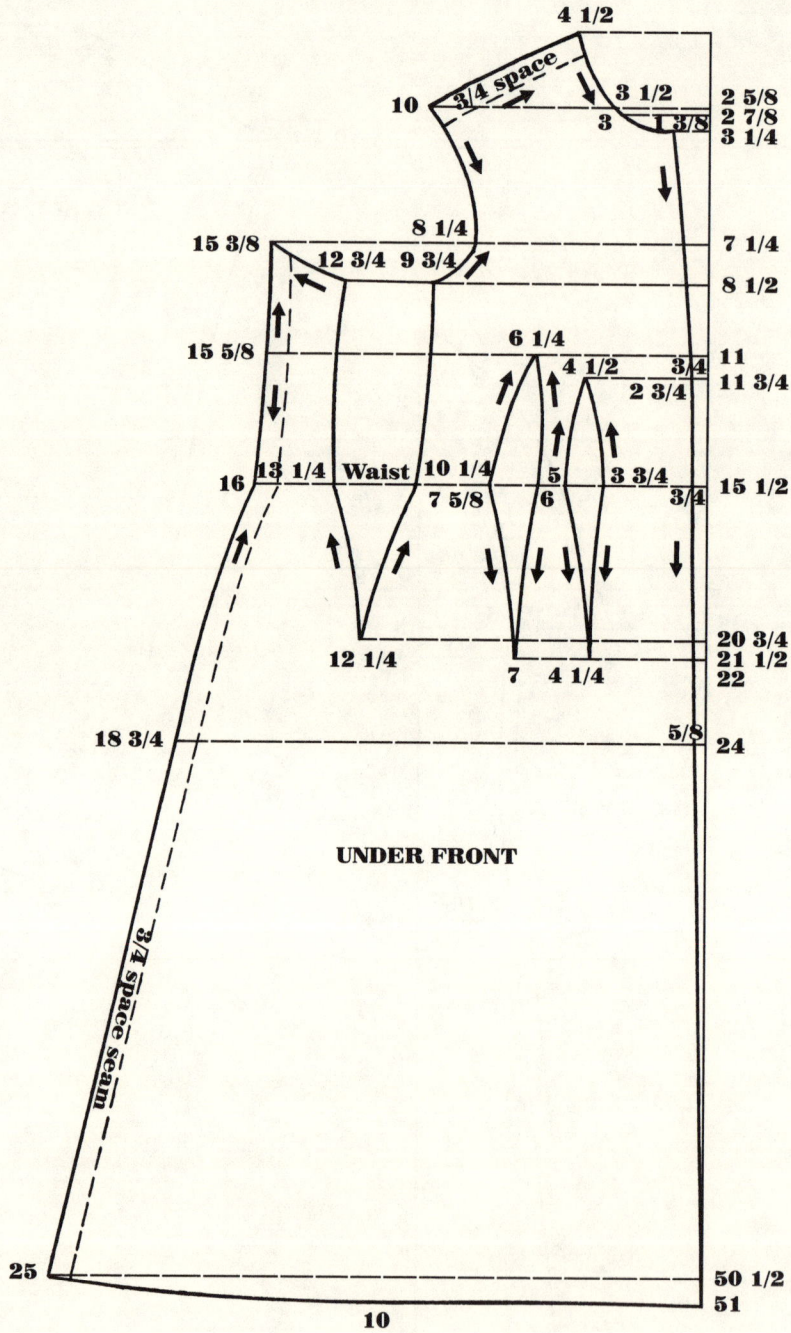

4 1/2

3/4 space

10

3 1/2

3

2 5/8
2 7/8
3 1/4

1 3/8

8 1/4

15 3/8

12 3/4   9 3/4

7 1/4

8 1/2

15 5/8

6 1/4

4 1/2

3/4

11

2 3/4

11 3/4

16   13 1/4   Waist   10 1/4

7 5/8

5

6

3 3/4

3/4

15 1/2

12 1/4

7   4 1/4

20 3/4
21 1/2
22

18 3/4

5/8

24

UNDER FRONT

3/4 space seam

25

10

50 1/2
51

54

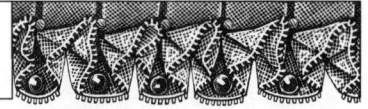

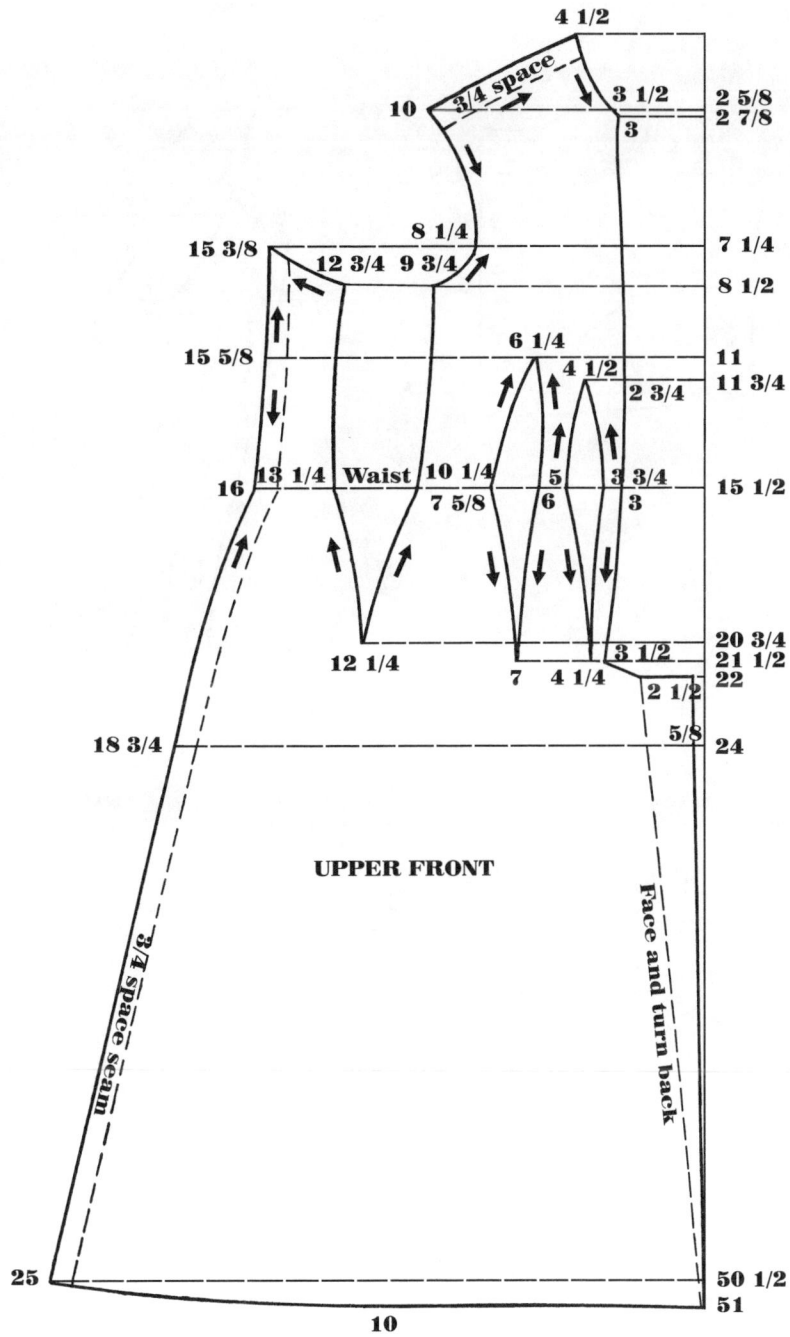

UPPER FRONT

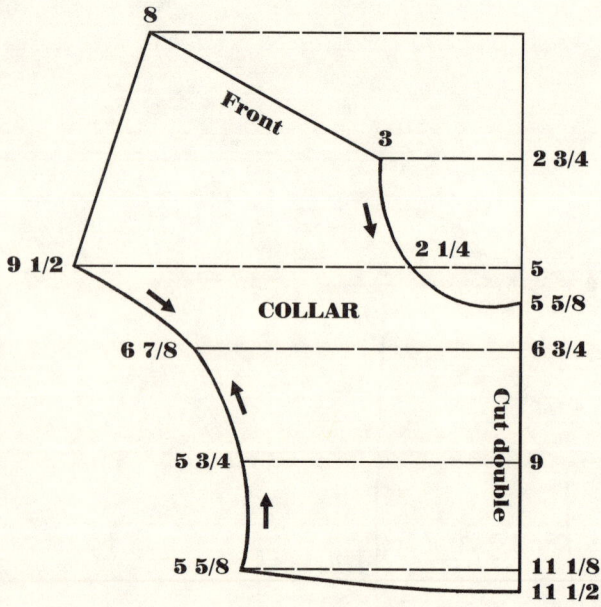

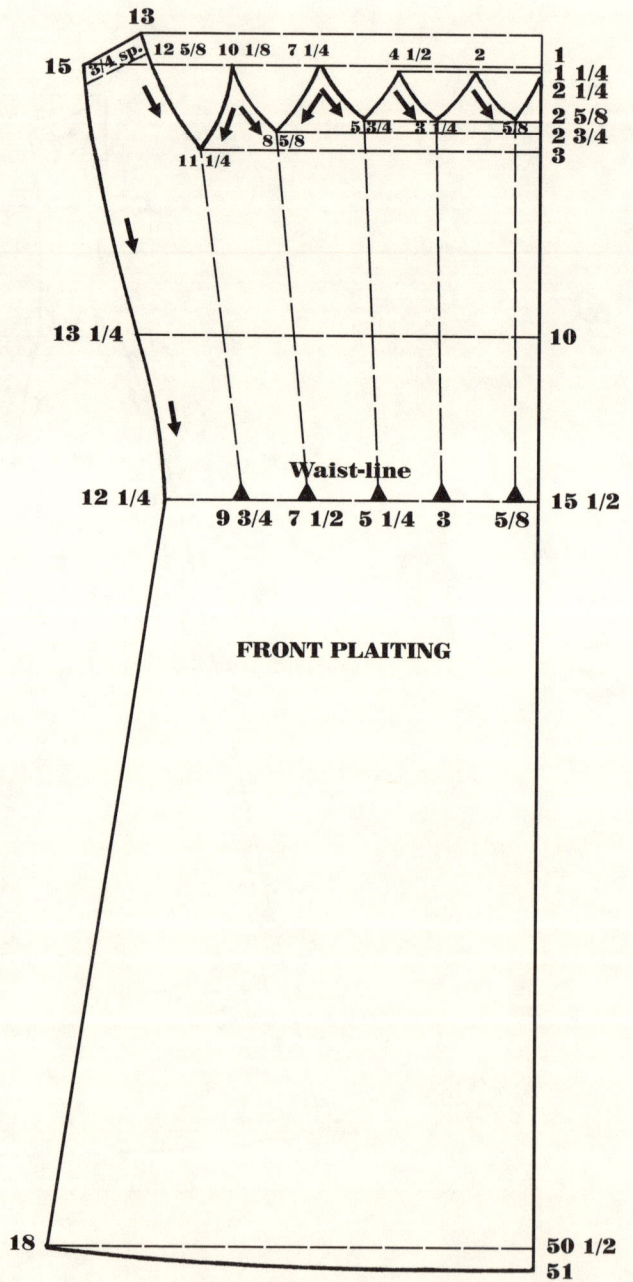

Tea Gown

This garment is drafted with the scale corresponding to the bust measure. The length is regulated with the tape measure. There are nine pieces: Under front or lining, upper front, front shirring, vest, side back, back, collar, and two sleeve pieces. The demi-train may be omitted if preferred.

Connect the stars under the arm. Cut open the under-arm dart on the upper front–but do not cut on the lines, cut down the center of the dart. Join on the vest next, with the curved seam from 8 3/4 to 7 sewed into the under-arm dart. Then join the front shirring, and last the under front, both with the side seam sewed into the under-arm dart.

Turn back the vest on the dashed line that runs diagonally from 3 3/4 to 15 1/8, and face for lapels. Gather the shirred front at the top to fit the neck, and also on the two dashed lines at the waist. The lower part may be laid in side-plaits as illustrated, or it may hang in full folds to the bottom.

Lay the plaits in the back according to the notches, forming two triple box-plaits.

Summer 1889 *Voice of Fashion*

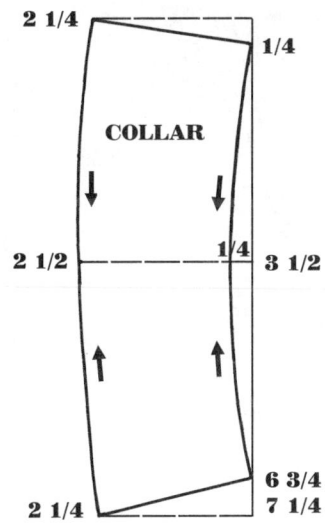

1 3/8

3 5/8 · 3/4 · 3 1/2

4 3/8 · 6 3/4

1/2 space · 3/4 space

5 1/2 · Waist · 2 · 10 1/2
7 1/2 · 2 · 11 1/2
6 1/4

1 7/8 · 17

SIDE BACK

2 1/4 · 24

1/2 space seam · 3/4 space seam

4 · 48
48 3/4
18 1/2 · 11 7/8 · 49 1/2

9 3/8 · 6 5/8 · 1/2
13 · 3/4 sp. · 1 3/4
12 7/8 · 5 1/4
1/2 space · 1/2 space
10 3/4 · 6 3/4 · 8 3/4
9 3/8 · 11
Waist · 6 3/4 · 14
9 · 6 1/2 · 15
15 1/4 · 9 1/8 · 15 1/4
13 3/4 · 11 1/4 · 4 5/8 · 2 3/8

BACK

1/2 space seam

Cut double

15 1/4 · 54 1/2

58
8 1/2 · 60

UNDER FRONT pattern diagram with measurements:

- 5 1/2
- 10 1/4 — 3/4 sp. — 5 3/8 — 1 1/2
- 1 1/2 — 2 3/4 — 3
- 3 1/2
- 8 5/8 — 6
- 11 — 7 3/4
- ✱
- 5 1/2 — 5/8 — 11
- Waist — 3/4 — 15
- 10 1/4 — 6 1/2 — 4 3/4 — 16
- 10 1/2
- 1/2 — 19 1/2
- 11 3/4 — 1/4 — 23
- 5 1/2
- 12 1/2 — 28 3/4
- **UNDER FRONT**
- 3/4 space seam
- 14 3/4 — 51
- 6 — 51 3/4

UPPER FRONT pattern diagram with measurements:

- 4 1/4
- 9 1/4 — 3/4 sp. — 2 3/8
- 7 1/4 — 6 1/4
- 3 5/8 — 8 1/2
- 12 1/2 — 8 3/4
- 10 1/4 — 8 1/2
- Cut open before basting
- 3 5/8 — 11 3/4
- Waist — 3 3/8 — 15 3/4
- 12 1/2 — 9 1/4 — 6 3/4 — 16 3/4
- 12 3/4
- 13 1/8 — 2 5/8 — 21 3/4
- 7 1/4
- **UPPER FRONT**
- Join under front and shirring to this line
- 3/4 space seam
- 52 1/2
- 53
- 13 3/4 — 53 1/4
- 7 1/4

59

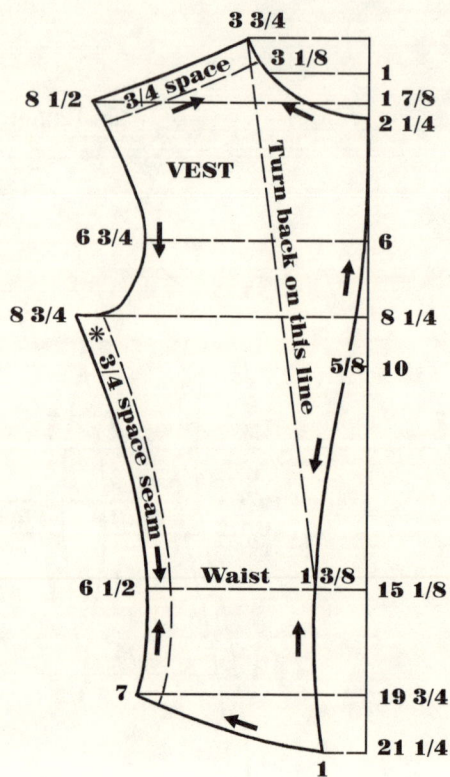

VEST

3 3/4

8 1/2   3/4 space   3 1/8   1
1 7/8
2 1/4

Turn back on this line

6 3/4   6

8 3/4   8 1/4
*   5/8   10
3/4 space seam

6 1/2   Waist   1 3/8   15 1/8

7   19 3/4
21 1/4
1

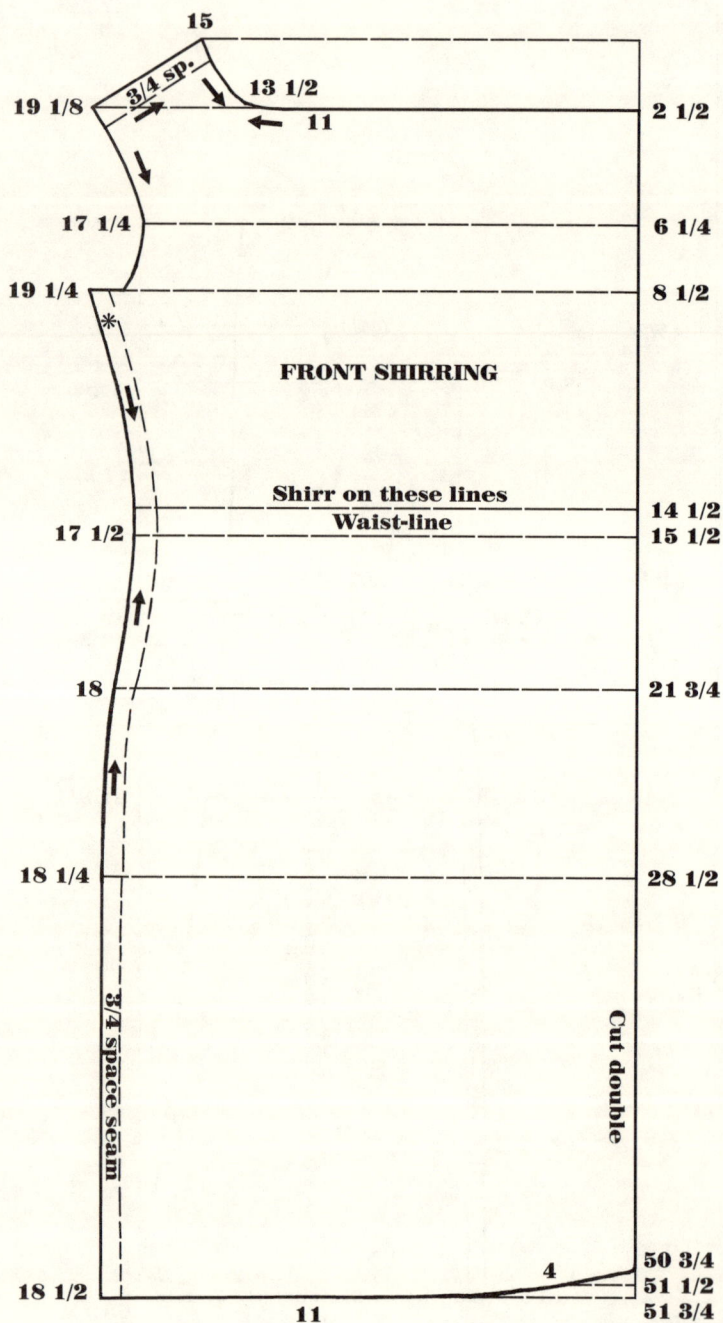

15

19 1/8   3/4 sp.   13 1/2
11   2 1/2

17 1/4   6 1/4

19 1/4   8 1/2
*

FRONT SHIRRING

Shirr on these lines
Waist-line   14 1/2
17 1/2   15 1/2

18   21 3/4

18 1/4   28 1/2

3/4 space seam

Cut double

50 3/4
4   51 1/2
18 1/2   11   51 3/4

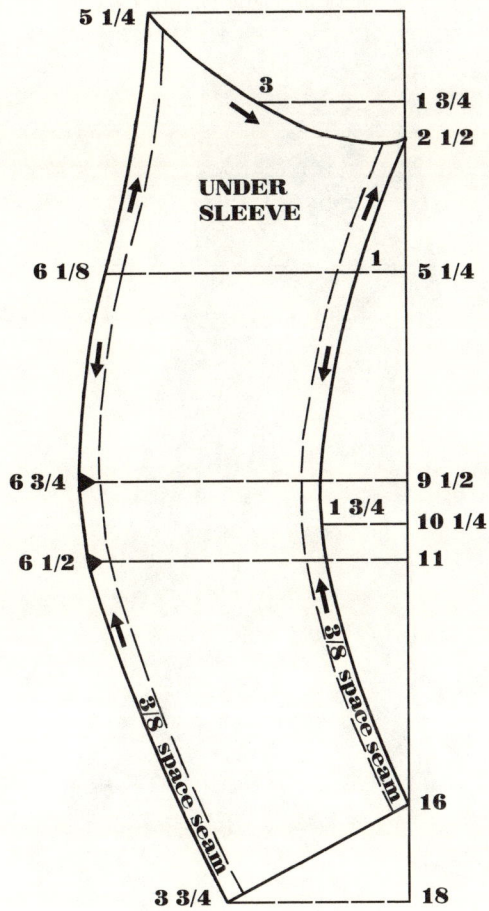

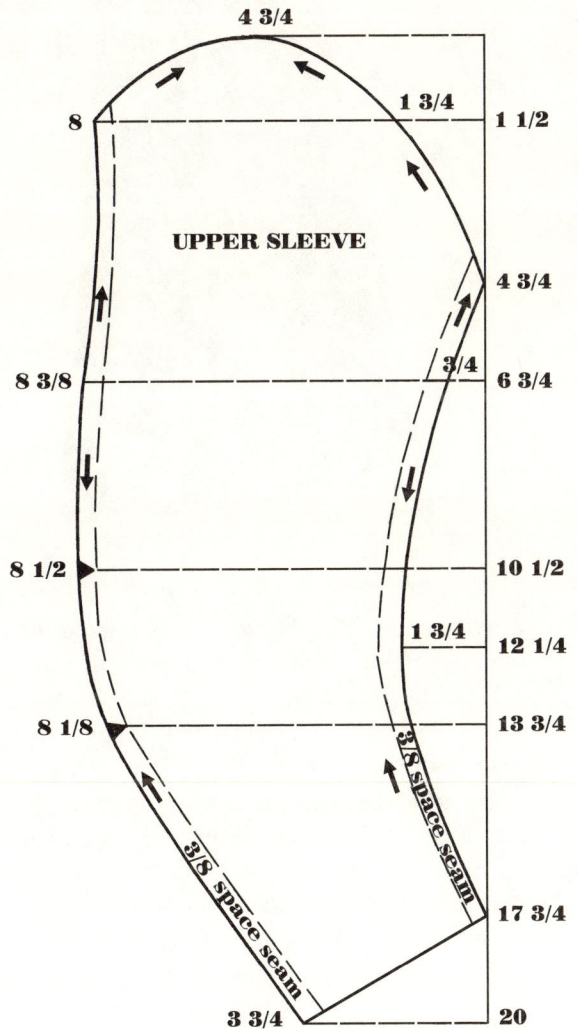

Wrapper or Tea Gown. This garment is pictured made of plain and striped flannel, trimmed with white feather-stitching. Single bust and under-arm darts, side backs, and a curved center back seam perform the adjustment. The center back seam is discontinued at the top of an underfolded double box-plait. Extra fullness is allowed on the front edges of the backs, and the back edges of the side backs are underfolded in two backward-turning plaits on each side, giving the effect of a double box-plait on each side of the center.

The fronts are turned back in lapels. These taper to points at the waist-line and extend about the neck to simulate a lapel collar, the parts being joined by a seam at the center of the back, below which is a notch. Between the fronts is disclosed a vest, which is laid in six forward-turning tucks at the top on each side of the invisible closing, the tucks flaring below the bust to the edge of the garment. Underlying the front and vest are dart-fitted linings, the back edges of which are sewed along the bust darts of the fronts and flatly above. The linings reach to the waist-line and are closed their depth with buttons and button-holes.

Wrapper or Tea Gown

The standing collar is decorated with feather-stitching, which also follows the edges of the lapels and is continued along the front edges of the fronts. The shirt sleeves are each finished at the wrist with a pointed cuff. The cuff is joined at the back by a short seam and turned over the sleeve, the edge being trimmed with feather-stitching.

This wrapper may be developed in flannelette, cashmere, foulé, silk-and-wool striped flannel, tamise, serge, etc. Combinations may be developed with the same material in different colors or with India silks, China silks, surah, or any soft silk. Ribbon, velvet ribbon, braid, lace, Arab trimmings, and Persian bands form pretty trimmings. To make the garment for a lady of medium size, requires 12 1/2 yards of material 22 inches wide, or 6 3/8 yards of material 44 inches wide. As represented, it needs 5 3/8 yards of plain flannel 44 inches wide, and 1 5/8 yards of striped flannel 44 inches wide.

October 1889 *Delineator*

Tea Gown

Use the scale corresponding to the bust measure to draft the entire garment. Regulate the length with the tape measure. There are eight pieces: Lining or under front, upper front, front shirring, side back, back, plain sleeve consisting of upper sleeve and under sleeve, and ornamental sleeve. This tea gown may be made of any soft material.

Lay the plaits in the back according to the notches. Shirr the full front at the top to fit the neck, also shirr on the two lines at the waist, and stay underneath. The part from the waist down to the bottom can either be laid in plaits or fall in loose folds. Join the sides in the under-arm dart and shoulder seams. Join the under front in the under-arm dart also. Face the upper front, and trim with passementerie or embroidery. Face the ornamental sleeve with silk or satin. Gather it at the top, and sew it into the armhole with the plain sleeve.

Winter 1889–1890 *Voice of Fashion*

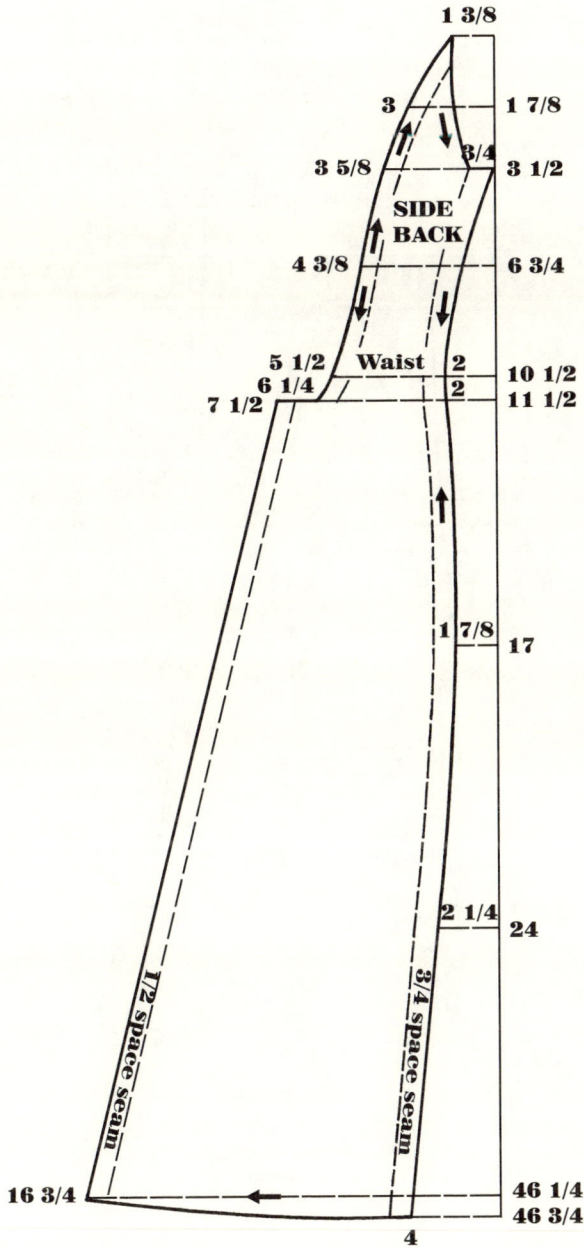

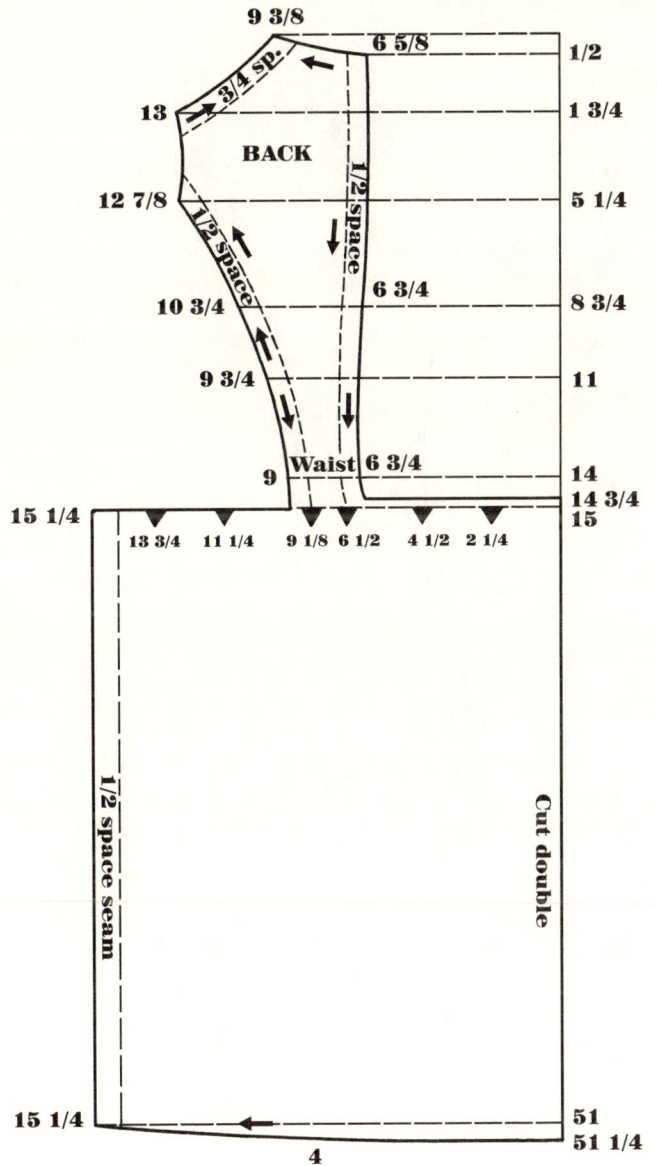

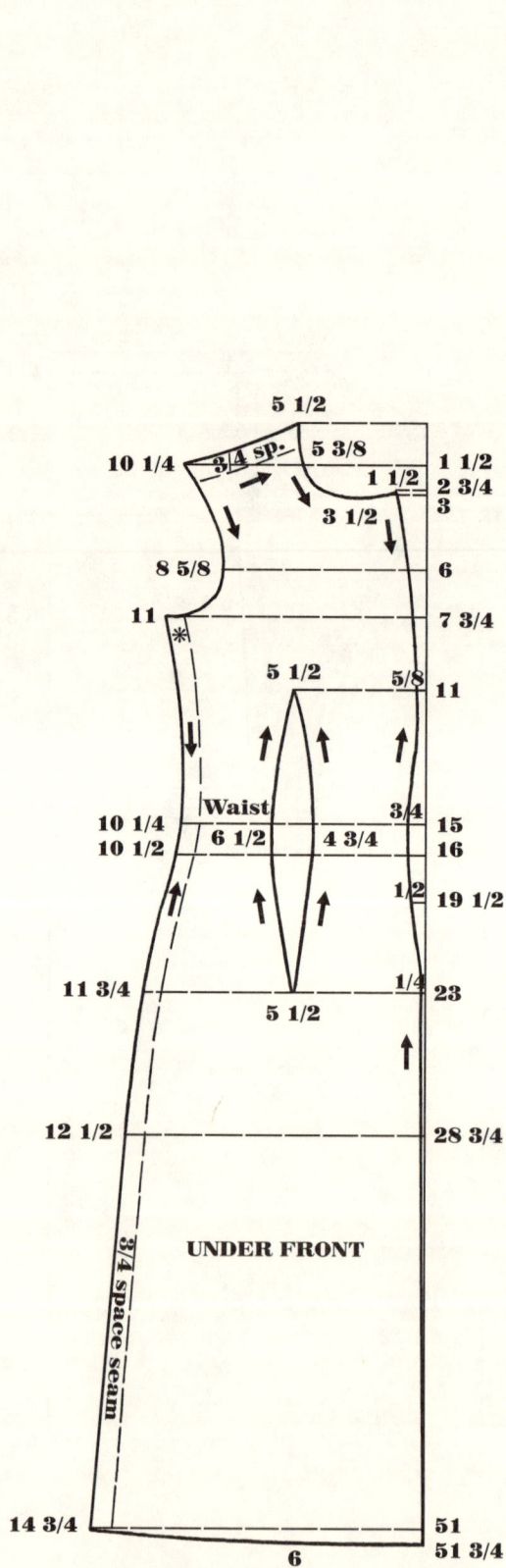

5 1/2

10 1/4   3/4 sp.   5 3/8   1 1/2

1 1/2   2 3/4
3 1/2   3

8 5/8   6

11   7 3/4
✳

5 1/2   5/8   11

Waist   3/4   15
10 1/4
10 1/2   6 1/2   4 3/4   16

1/2   19 1/2

11 3/4   1/4   23
5 1/2

12 1/2   28 3/4

3/4 space seam

UNDER FRONT

14 3/4   51
6   51 3/4

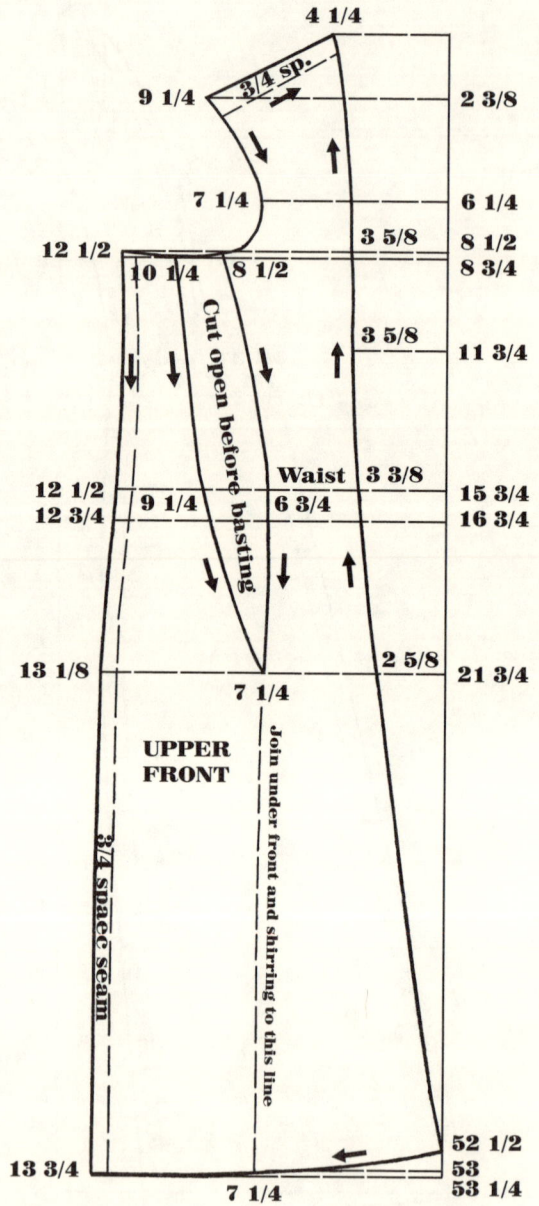

4 1/4

9 1/4   3/4 sp.   2 3/8

7 1/4   6 1/4

12 1/2   3 5/8   8 1/2
10 1/4   8 1/2   8 3/4

3 5/8   11 3/4

Cut open before basting

12 1/2   Waist   3 3/8   15 3/4
12 3/4   9 1/4   6 3/4   16 3/4

13 1/8   2 5/8   21 3/4
7 1/4

UPPER FRONT

Join under front and shirring to this line

3/4 space seam

52 1/2
53
13 3/4   7 1/4   53 1/4

 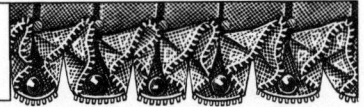

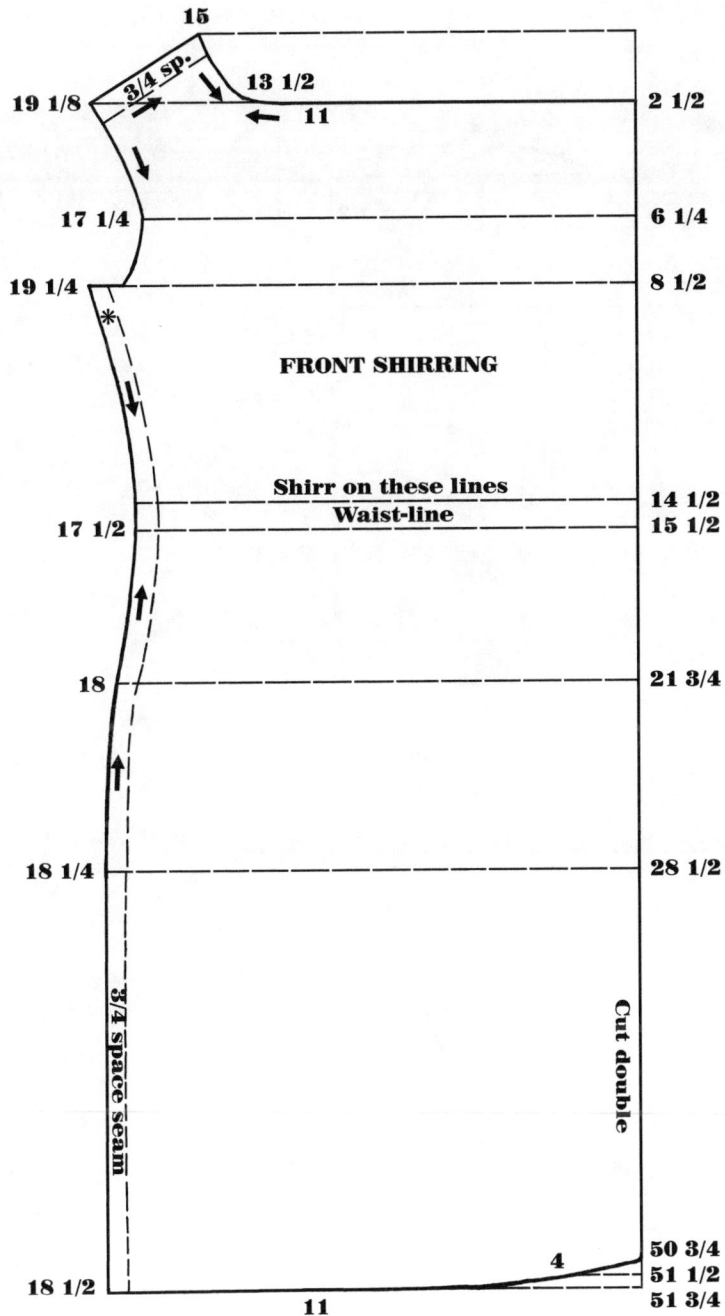

15

19 1/8   3/4 sp.   13 1/2   2 1/2
11

17 1/4   6 1/4

19 1/4   8 1/2

*

FRONT SHIRRING

Shirr on these lines   14 1/2
Waist-line   15 1/2
17 1/2

18   21 3/4

18 1/4   28 1/2

3/4 space seam   Cut double

4   50 3/4
51 1/2
18 1/2   51 3/4
11

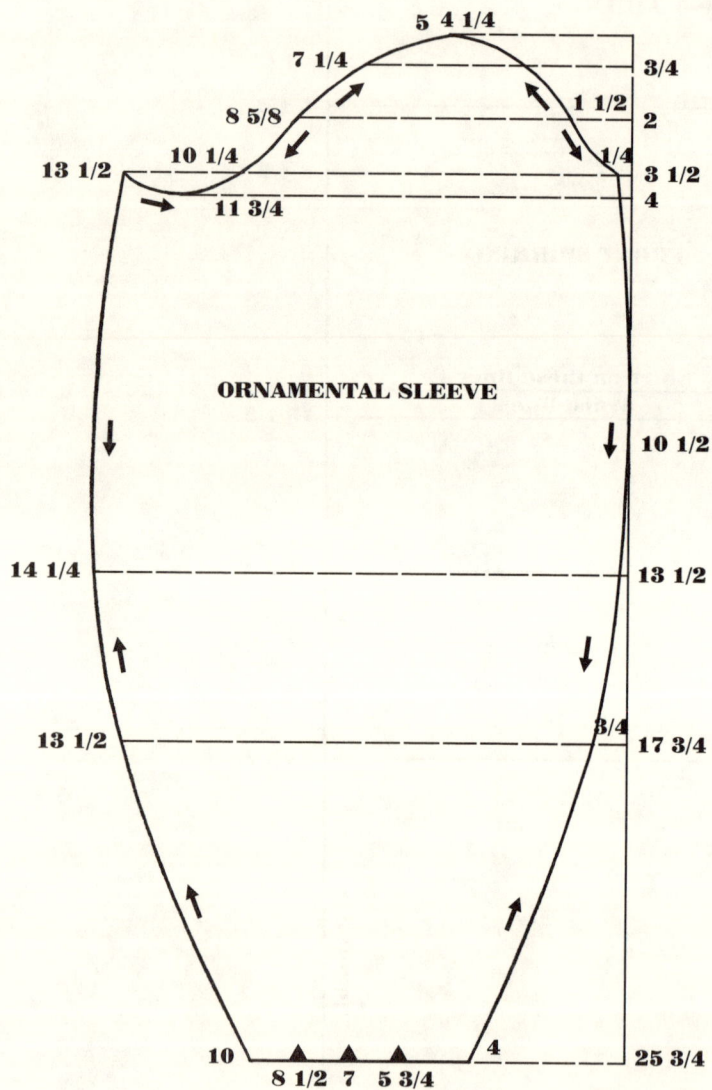

4 3/4

5   4 1/4

7 1/4   3/4

8 5/8   1 1/2

                 2

10 1/4   1/4

13 1/2   3 1/2

11 3/4   4

ORNAMENTAL SLEEVE

             10 1/2

14 1/4   13 1/2

13 1/2   3/4

             17 3/4

10   4

8 1/2   7   5 3/4   25 3/4

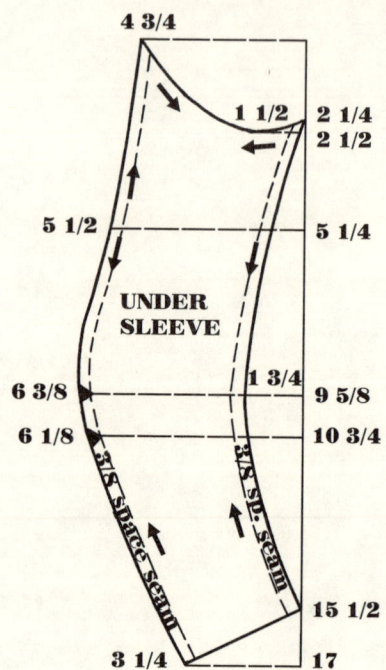

4 3/4

        1 1/2   2 1/4

               2 1/2

5 1/2   5 1/4

UNDER SLEEVE

6 3/8   1 3/4   9 5/8

6 1/8   10 3/4

3/8 space seam   3/8 sp. seam

3 1/4   15 1/2

             17

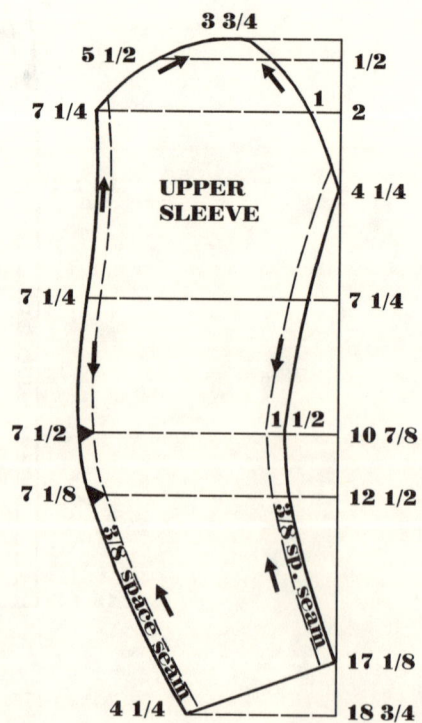

3 3/4

5 1/2   1/2

7 1/4   1   2

UPPER SLEEVE   4 1/4

7 1/4   7 1/4

7 1/2   1 1/2   10 7/8

7 1/8   12 1/2

3/8 space seam   3/8 sp. seam

             17 1/8

4 1/4   18 3/4

Directoire Tea Gown

Tea Gown in the Directoire Style. Olive green plush and apple green silk are combined in this tea gown. It is closely fitted by single bust darts, side pieces, side backs, and a curved center back seam. The fronts are of lining material. They serve as a foundation for side fronts that flare decidedly from the neck, and for a full vest that is shirred deeply at the neck and waist-line. The shirrings at the neck produce a yoke effect, and those at the waist-line that of a wide girdle. The fronts are closed down the center with buttons and button-holes to below the waist-line, and are basted together below that. At the center of the vest, an opening the length of the front closing is made, and fastened invisibly. The shirrings are basted to the fronts, and between and below them the vest falls in soft folds. The side fronts are folded back in Directoire lapels above the lower shirrings in the vest, and the lapels are faced with silk.

The back is short between the side-back seams, and to its lower edge is gathered the top of a full skirt that rolls over a pad and hangs in a demi-train. The standing collar is covered with silk laid in upward-turning folds.

The sleeves are gathered into the armholes. The fullness is collected into six lines of shirring at the wrists, the shirrings being stayed to an under cuff of lining, and giving the effect of shirred cuffs.

The wrists are trimmed with lace frills. The sleeves are overhung by long, ornamental sleeves that open from the armholes with the effect of Greek or angel sleeves, showing their silk lining. The ornamental sleeves may be omitted, as shown by the back view of the tea gown.

This gown may be made of fancy and plain wools combined, of cashmere, or of any pretty wool material, with silk, surah, or plush for the vest, lapel facings, and ornamental sleeve linings. The full sleeves and vest generally correspond when the ornamental sleeves are used, but the vest is like the rest of the garment when the ornamental sleeves are omitted. To make the tea gown for a lady of medium size, requires 10 7/8 yards of material 22 inches wide, or 5 yards of material 44 inches wide. Each requires 10 1/4 yards of silk 20 inches wide for the vest, etc., and 1 5/8 yards of lining 36 inches wide for the front linings, etc.

January 1889 *Delineator*

at the neck to fall in full, loose folds. The vest and fronts are arranged on a lining having curved front edges. These edges are closed to below the waist-line with button-holes and buttons, the right side being hemmed. Below the closing, the width of the hem and underlap is cut off and the edges are seamed. Single bust and under-arm darts taken in the fronts and lining together make a close adjustment that emphasizes the négligé look of the vest. Under the vest the lining is covered with silk, which is seen through the lace. The fronts are widely underfaced at the front edges, which are loose all the way down. The vest is sewed to the lining all the way down on the left side. It is sewed from the bottom to a little above the end of the closing on the right side, hooks and eyes fastening it the rest of the way to the neck. Below the end of the darts, the fronts are basted invisibly over the sides of the vest.

At the back, the effect of a princess dress with an oval train is achieved. In the adjustment only three curved seams are used—the side seams that join the back to the fronts and their lining, and the center back seam. The latter ends at the top of a broad double box-plait, which is folded underneath. On each front edge of the back skirt there is a wide extension that is arranged underneath in a single backward-turning plait, all of the plaits contributing to the ampleness of the train. The train lies flat on the floor, is broad enough to retain its pose, and is of exquisite length. The train should be lined to match the flowing sleeves, and a thick cord may edge it if desired.

The standing collar is high and close and is in two parts. The part on the vest is of silk covered with lace net put on full. The other part is of cashmere, with its ends overlapping the ends of the vest collar.

The sleeves are in flowing style, falling in long points suggestive of angel sleeves. Below the elbow they disclose full under-sleeves made of lace net. The flowing sleeves fit closely at the top and have a seam only at the inside of the arm, where they reach but a little above the elbow. They are lined with silk. The under-sleeve has a smooth-fitting upper part that reaches nearly to the elbow. To the

Tea Gown with Angel Sleeves. Being picturesque and elegant whether made up in rich or inexpensive materials, this tea gown is popular for four-o'clock teas, informal receptions, luncheons, etc. It is shown developed in cream cashmere, lace net, and apple green silk, the silk being used as lining and facings.

The vest is visible all the way down between the fronts, which flare from the neck, and is shirred

edge is joined the top of the lower part, which like the upper part has a seam only at the inside of the arm. The lower part is gathered at the top nearly to the seam, and is shortened slightly at the seam by a downward-turning plait laid near the top. At the bottom it is shirred once around far enough from the edge to form a frill.

Figured and plain wools of all kinds may be used for tea gowns. The vest may be of crêpe, plain silk, surah, bengaline, faille Française, lace net, Brussels net, China or India silk, plush, velvet, or contrasting wool material. Fancy-edged ribbons may be tied across the vest in bows. To make the tea gown for a lady of medium size, requires 15 yards of material 22 inches wide, or 7 3/4 yards of material 44 inches wide. As represented, it requires 7 1/4 yards of cashmere 40 inches wide, 2 1/2 yards of lace net 27 inches wide, and 3 3/4 yards of silk 20 inches wide for the flowing sleeve linings, etc. In any instance, 3 3/8 yards of silesia are required for the front linings.

November 1887 *Delineator*

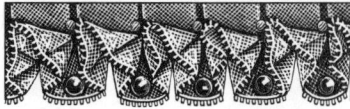

Watteau Wrapper

This garment is drafted with the scale corresponding to the bust measure. The length is regulated with the tape measure. There are nine pieces: Front, front shirring, side back, back, Watteau plait, collar, plain upper sleeve, plain under sleeve, and sleeve puff.

The front shirring is turned down on the cross-line from 1 5/8 to 21 1/4 for a facing. This is shirred twice and sewed to the front on the lines marked for the shirring. The part above the shirring forms a yoke. The Watteau plait is sewed to the center of the back from 1/2 to 23 on the base-line. The balance is joined together to form the fullness in the skirt.

After assembling the plain sleeve, gather the puff at the bottom and join it to the curved line on the plain sleeve marked for the puff. The part of the sleeve below the puff forms the cuff, and may be made of the same material as the front yoke and the collar. Turn the puff up to the top of the plain sleeve (the join at the bottom will be concealed). Connect the notches on the puff with the notches on the plain sleeve. Sew them into the armhole together.

1889 *National Garment Cutter Book of Diagrams*

73

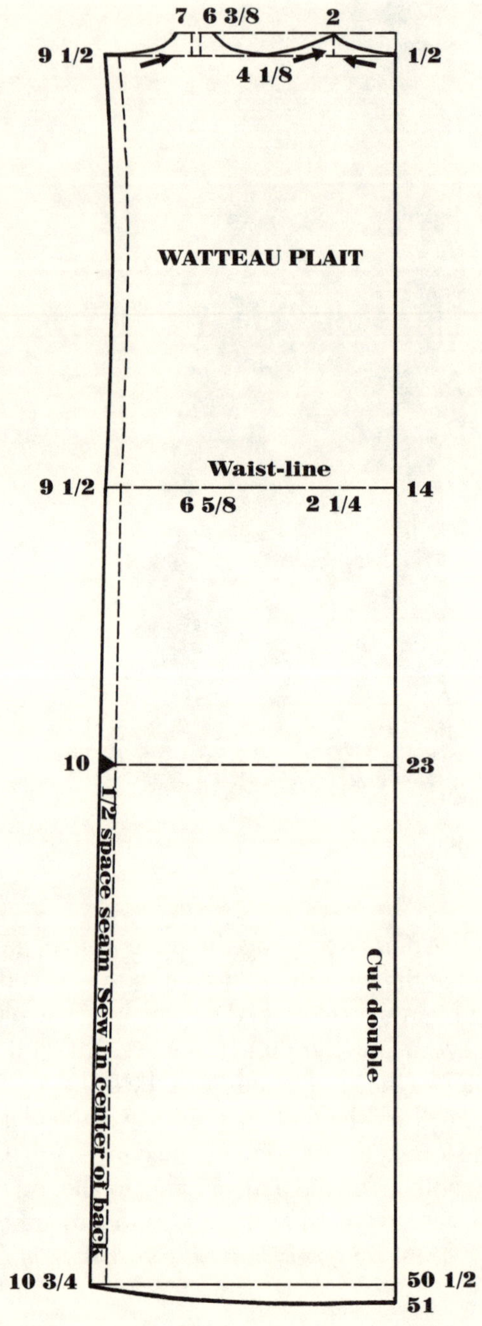

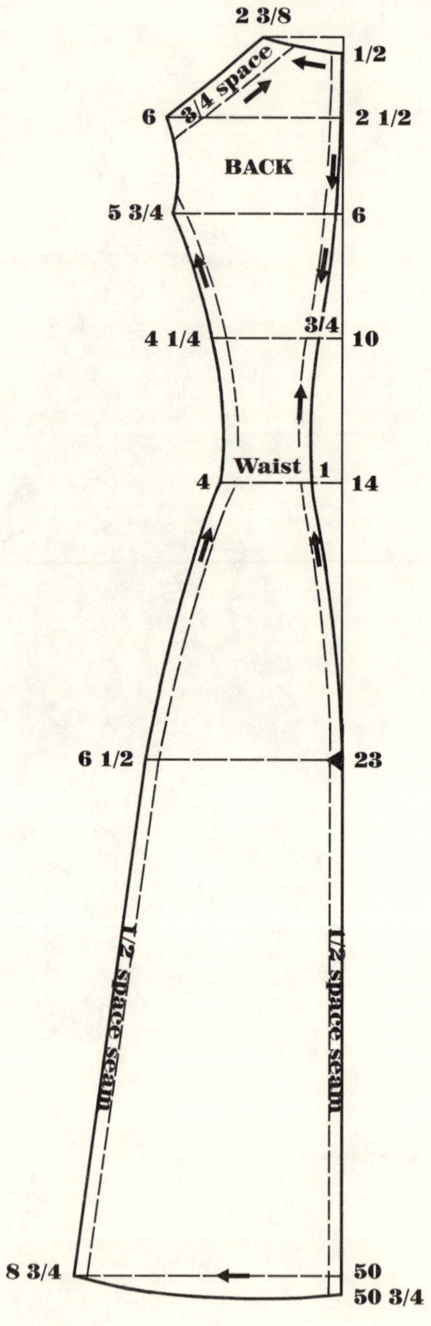

2 3/8

1/2

3/4 space

6

2 1/2

BACK

5 3/4

6

4 1/4

3/4

10

Waist

1

4

14

7   **6 3/8**   **2**

9 1/2   **1/2**

4 1/8

WATTEAU PLAIT

Waist-line

9 1/2

6 5/8   **2 1/4**   **14**

6 1/2

23

10   **23**

1/2 space seam Sew in center of back

Cut double

1/2 space seam

1/2 space seam

8 3/4

50

50 3/4

10 3/4   **50 1/2**

51

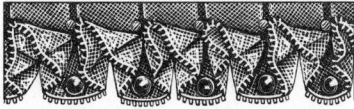

Watteau Wrapper

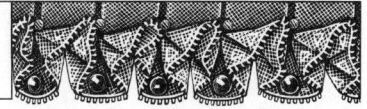

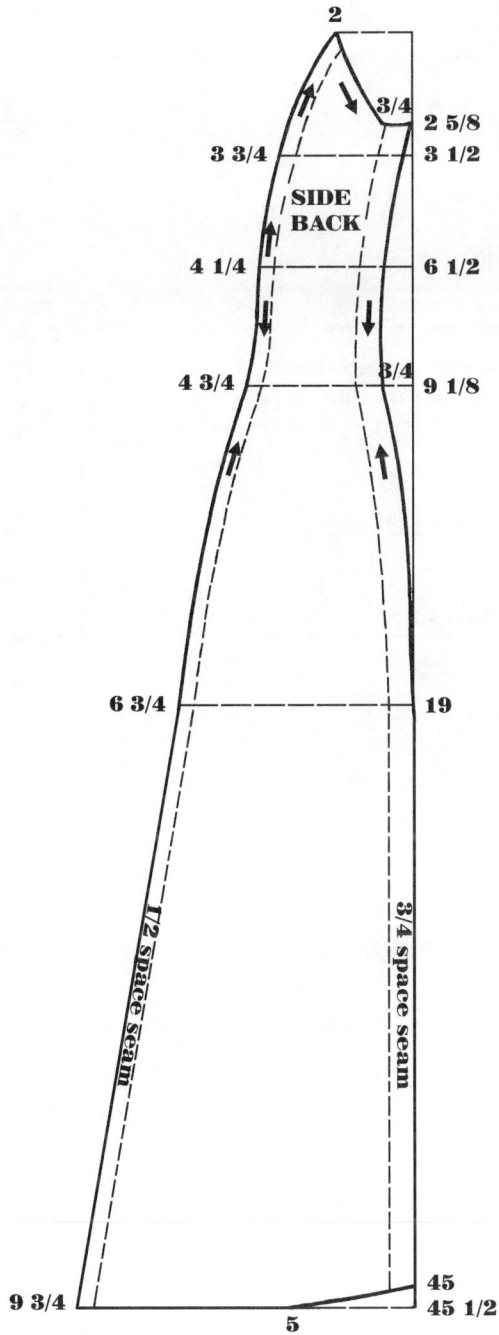

SIDE BACK

2

3/4
2 5/8

3 3/4 — 3 1/2

4 1/4 — 6 1/2

4 3/4 — 3/4 — 9 1/8

6 3/4 — 19

1/2 space seam

3/4 space seam

9 3/4 — 45 / 45 1/2

5

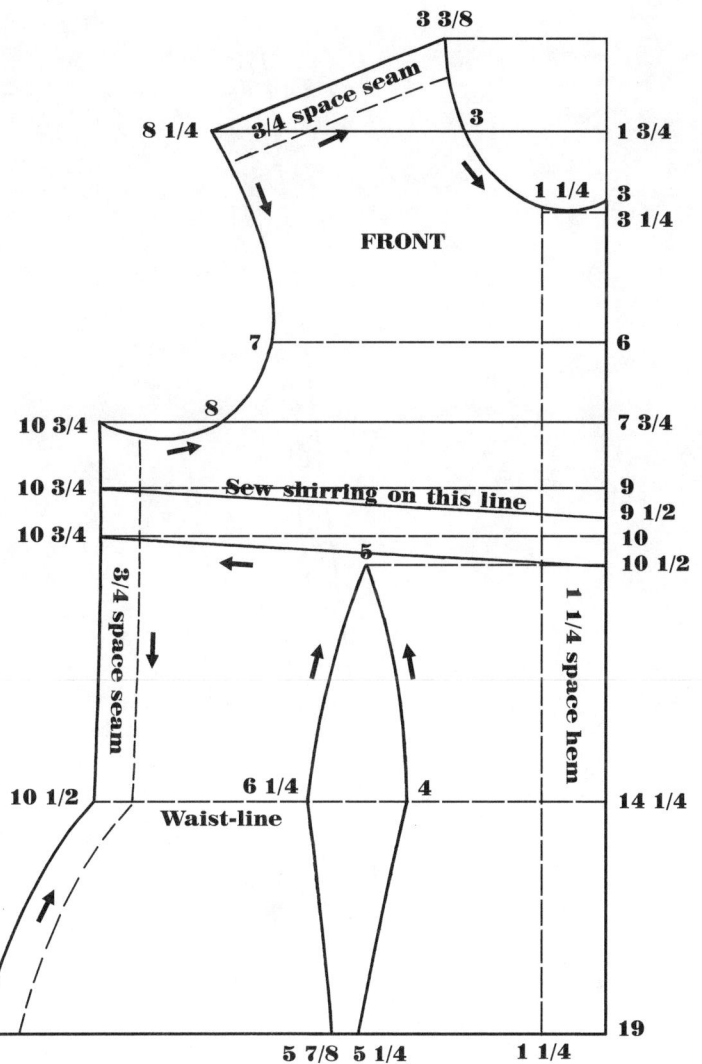

FRONT

3 3/8

8 1/4 — 3/4 space seam — 3 — 1 3/4

1 1/4 — 3 / 3 1/4

7 — 6

8 — 7 3/4

10 3/4 —

10 3/4 — Sew shirring on this line — 9 / 9 1/2

10 3/4 — 10

5 — 10 1/2

3/4 space seam

1 1/4 space hem

10 1/2 — Waist-line — 6 1/4 — 4 — 14 1/4

12 3/4 — 5 7/8 — 5 1/4 — 1 1/4 — 19

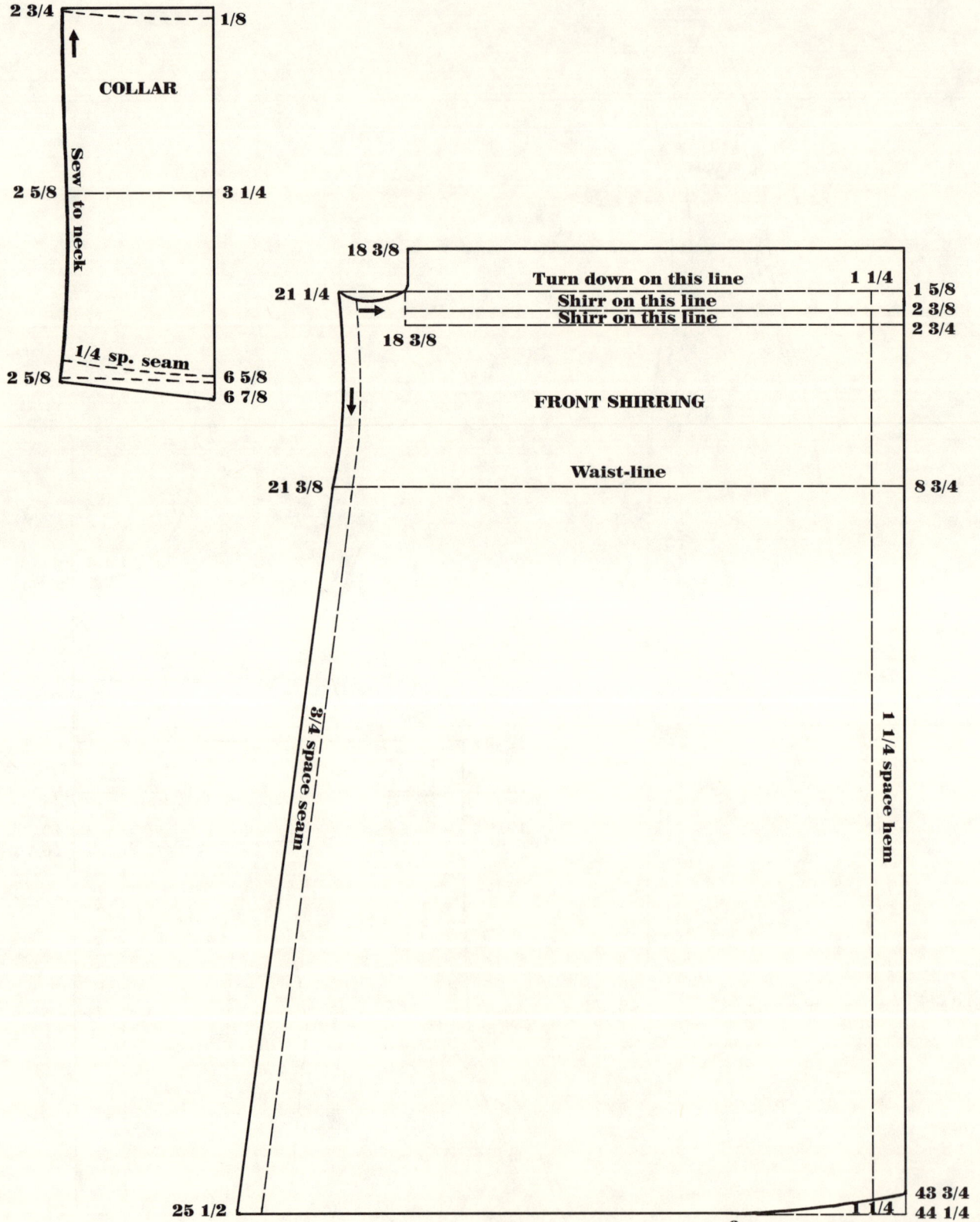

COLLAR

2 3/4 ... 1/8

Sew to neck

2 5/8 ... 3 1/4

1/4 sp. seam

2 5/8 ... 6 5/8
6 7/8

18 3/8

21 1/4

Turn down on this line ... 1 1/4 ... 1 5/8
Shirr on this line ... 2 3/8
Shirr on this line ... 2 3/4

18 3/8

FRONT SHIRRING

Waist-line ... 8 3/4

21 3/8

3/4 space seam

1 1/4 space hem

25 1/2

43 3/4
1 1/4 ... 44 1/4
6

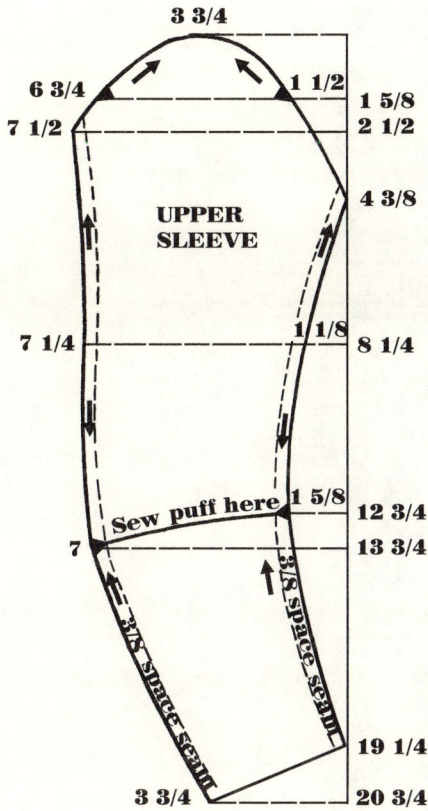

UPPER SLEEVE

3 3/4

6 3/4 | 1 1/2 — 1 5/8
7 1/2 — 2 1/2
4 3/8

7 1/4 — 1 1/8 · 8 1/4

Sew puff here · 1 5/8 — 12 3/4
7 — 13 3/4

3/8 space seam

3 3/4 — 19 1/4
20 3/4

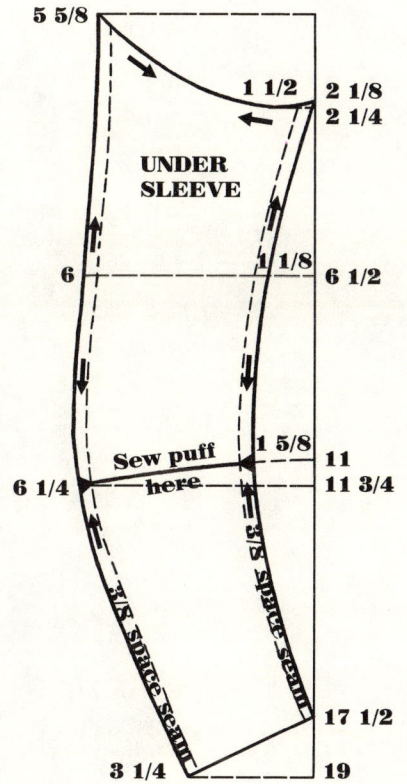

5 5/8

UNDER SLEEVE

1 1/2 — 2 1/8
2 1/4

6 — 1 1/8 · 6 1/2

Sew puff here · 1 5/8 — 11
6 1/4 — 11 3/4

3/8 space seam

17 1/2
3 1/4 — 19

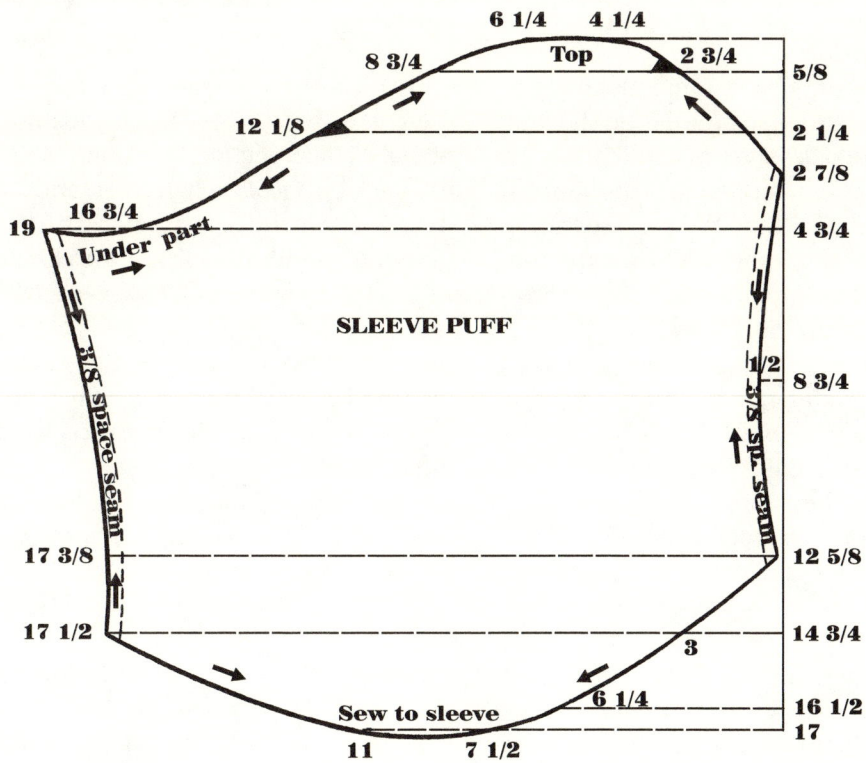

SLEEVE PUFF

6 1/4 · 4 1/4
8 3/4 · Top · 2 3/4 — 5/8
12 1/8 — 2 1/4
2 7/8
19 · 16 3/4 · Under part — 4 3/4
1/2 · 8 3/4

3/8 space seam

17 3/8 — 12 5/8
17 1/2 — 14 3/4
3
Sew to sleeve · 6 1/4 — 16 1/2
17
11 · 7 1/2

Ladies' Wrapper. This example is made of all-over embroidered cashmere, the design showing miniature acorns and oak leaves in cardinal silk on a dark green ground. The upper part of the front is in yoke shape. On each side the corresponding lower part is adjusted in Mother Hubbard fashion, the top being turned in for a finish and three lines of shirring made about 1/4 inch apart. These shirrings end a little in front of the armholes. The front edges of the corresponding yoke and lower parts are turned under for a hem on the right side and underfaced on the left, the closing being made with button-holes and buttons.

The back is fitted with side-back seams and a curved center back seam that ends below the waist-line. Over the center back is adjusted a Watteau section. After being appropriately narrowed off toward the top, its edges are joined in a seam on the inside, from the top to some distance below the waist-line. It is then laid in a double box-plait

and adjusted to overlie the wrapper to the end of the center back seam. Below this point, the edges of the Watteau section are joined to the corresponding back edges of the wrapper, and its fullness falls in with that of the back proper. The Watteau section is sewed in with the tops of the shoulder seams.

The wrapper is of walking length. Its lower edge is finished with two fine knife-plaitings of silk, the upper one being set on to form its own heading. Each of the coat sleeves is trimmed with two similar plaitings. The high standing collar is concealed by two standing knife-plaitings, the lower one being stitched far enough from its lower edge to form its own finish. Any other style of decoration may be applied instead. The lower edge may be left untrimmed.

To make the wrapper for a lady of medium size, requires 9 5/8 yards of material 22 inches wide, 7 yards of material 36 inches wide, or 4 1/2 yards of material 48 inches wide.

January 1885 *Delineator*

Ladies' Wrapper

Ladies' Wrapper. Cream challis with pale blue figures was used for this wrapper, with pale blue ribbon for trimming. The upper part of the wrapper is a square yoke shaped by shoulder seams. To its lower edge are seamed the full parts, which in front are turned in quite deeply at the upper edge for a finish. Three lines of shirring are made far enough from the top to leave a ruffled heading. The closing is made with buttons and button-holes, from the neck to the lower edge. The loose Mother Hubbard fronts form a contrast to the smoothly fitting side backs and back, a curved center back seam assisting the adjustment.

The center back seam terminates a short distance below the waist-line. Over it is arranged, in Watteau fashion, a double box-plait. The upper edge of the plait is included in the seam to the yoke. Its side edges are joined the same distance as the center back seam, below which the fullness falls into the skirt, the loose side edges being joined to the corresponding edges of the skirt.

The high collar fits closely about the neck, and the coat sleeves are finished plainly. The back end of a ribbon tie is included in each under-arm seam at the waist-line and is carried across to the center of the front, where the ties are bowed in loops and ends of different lengths.

The yoke and the Watteau plait may be made of surah of some contrasting color, or of velvet or novelty material in silk or wool. Striking contrasts are allowable. Soft lace may be cascaded over the closing, and loops of fancy-edged narrow ribbon may be placed among the folds of lace. Sometimes the yoke is all-over braided with one or two colors, or with metallic braid or cord. For a lady of medium size, this wrapper requires 10 yards of material 22 inches wide, or 5 yards of material 44 inches wide.

October 1888 *Delineator*

Watteau Wrapper. Plain cashmere was chosen for this example, with white lace and ribbon for trimming. The fronts close their entire length with buttons and button-holes. Single bust and under-arm darts, together with side-back seams and a center back seam, complete the adjustment.

The Watteau drapery is formed of a separate section. This section is seamed together at its corresponding edges for some distance from the top, and laid in a double box-plait. The top of this plait comes even with the neck, and its edges are included in the upper parts of the shoulder seams.

The center back seam of the wrapper terminates at a point in line with the end of the seam of the Watteau section. Below this the edges of the Watteau section are seamed to the corresponding edges of the backs, and the back is lengthened to form an oval train.

Lace is jaboted down each side of the front just back of the closing. A high standing collar, over which falls a lace frill, finishes the neck, and a ribbon bow is basted at the neck. The sleeves are in coat shape. The lower edge of each is turned under and trimmed with a frill of lace edging, a ribbon bow being placed on the upper side. The plaited ends of long ribbon ties are inserted in the side seams

at the waist-line, and the ribbons are arranged in a long loop and two ends a little to the left of the closing.

When this wrapper is intended for dressy wear, India and China silks, foulard, etc., are usually selected. However, it makes up well in challis, cashmere, serge, and numerous other wool materials, for which moiré ribbon provides an effective trimming. To make the wrapper for a lady of medium size, requires 11 3/4 yards of material 22 inches wide, 8 yards of material 36 inches wide, or 6 yards of material 44 inches wide.

August 1889 *Delineator*

Ladies' Wrapper. Striped flannel was used for this example, and the colors blended in it shade from a clear bright red to a very dark tone, and from dark gray to a gray that is almost white. Under-arm darts curve the fronts, but do not fit them closely. The fronts are closed with button-holes and buttons their entire depth, the right side being hemmed. Adjoining the fronts are side-back pieces.

At the back, a Watteau effect is formed by a seam that extends from the neck to about the waist-line. The upper portion of the part taken up by the seam is shirred across at intervals of 1/4 inch for some distance from the neck, and through each shirring it is sewed flatly to the body of the wrapper. The back and side backs are deepened to form a short oval train, and the fullness of the Watteau section sweeps out and merges into the fullness of the train.

The plaited ends of ribbon ties are fastened at the waist-line of the side-back seams, and knotted in a bow over the front closing. On the sides are placed pointed pockets with pointed, turn-over laps. The laps are bordered with bias bands of the material. A button is also placed on the point, and a ribbon bow is basted underneath. The collar is in the standing shape. The coat sleeves are ornamented at their wrists with wide bias bands.

Striped flannels are available in smooth, jersey, and eider-down weavings, and so are plain flannels. Cashmere, camel's hair, delaine, surah, and all materials in vogue for wrappers are just as well adapted to the mode. For a lady of medium size, this wrapper requires 8 7/8 yards of material 22 inches wide, 6 1/2 yards of material 36 inches wide, or 4 7/8 yards of material 44 inches wide.

December 1886 *Delineator*

Tea Gown

This tea gown is drafted with the scale corresponding to the bust measure. The length is regulated with the tape measure. There are ten pieces: Upper front, under front, front yoke, front shirring, side back, back, skirt back, upper sleeve, under sleeve, and sleeve puff.

Cut the back double. Sew the side back on as usual. This will form a deep point down the center. Sew the skirt back to the side back, and lay the plaits according to the notches, turning all of the plaits toward the center. Do not press or baste the plaits; allow them to fall gracefully to the floor.

Join the upper front and the side back in the under-arm seam. Join the under front in the under-arm dart. On the upper front take up the dart, and sew the front shirring on the dashed line on the under front. Gather the shirring at the top and sew it to the yoke. Any style of trimming may be used down the front.

Spring 1890 *Voice of Fashion*

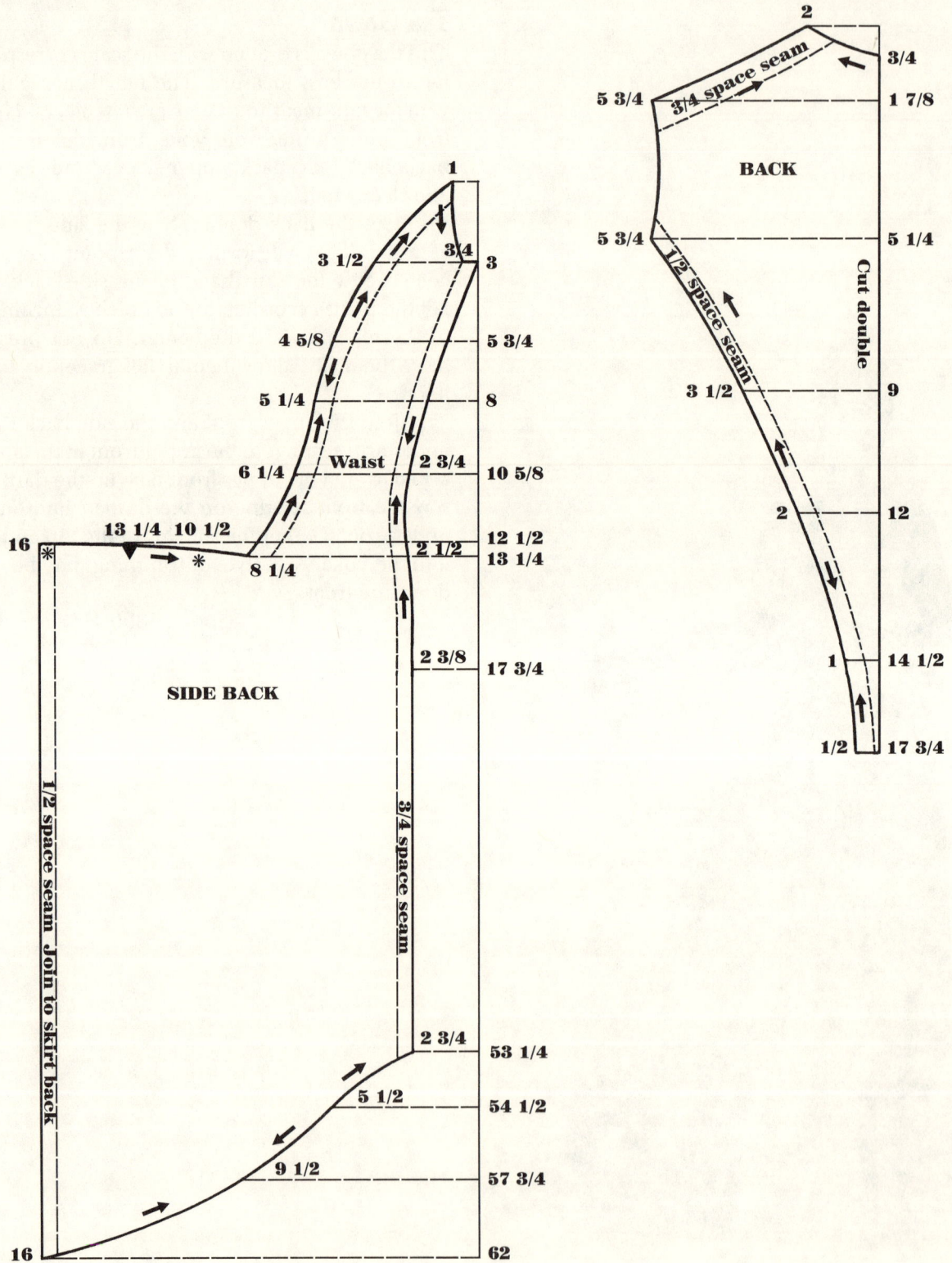

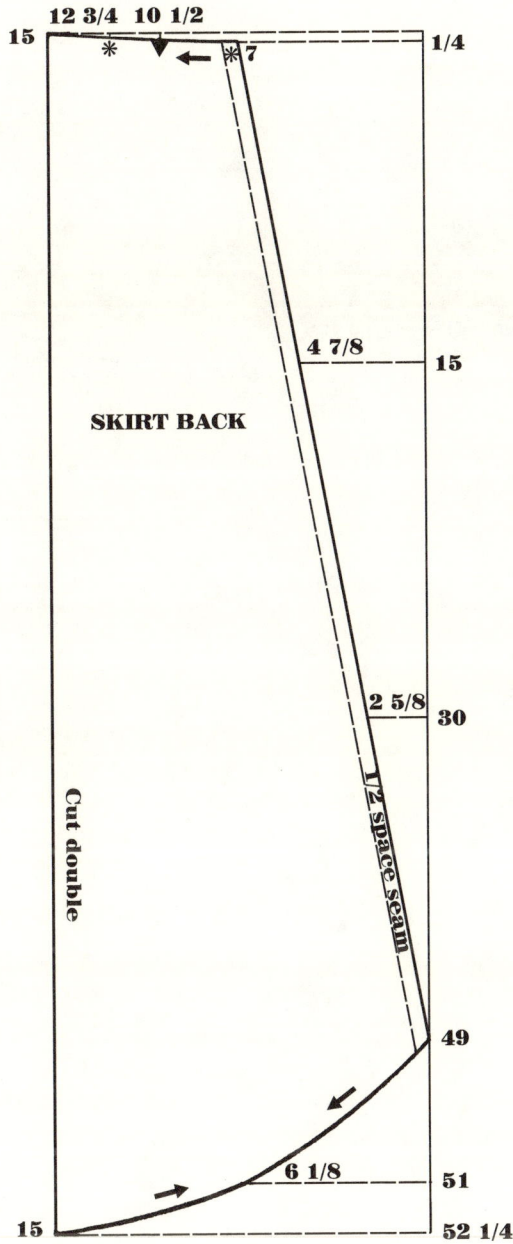

12 3/4   10 1/2

15   ✳   ▼   ←   ✳ **7**   **1/4**

SKIRT BACK

4 7/8   **15**

2 5/8   **30**

Cut double

1/2 space seam

49

6 1/8   **51**

15   **52 1/4**

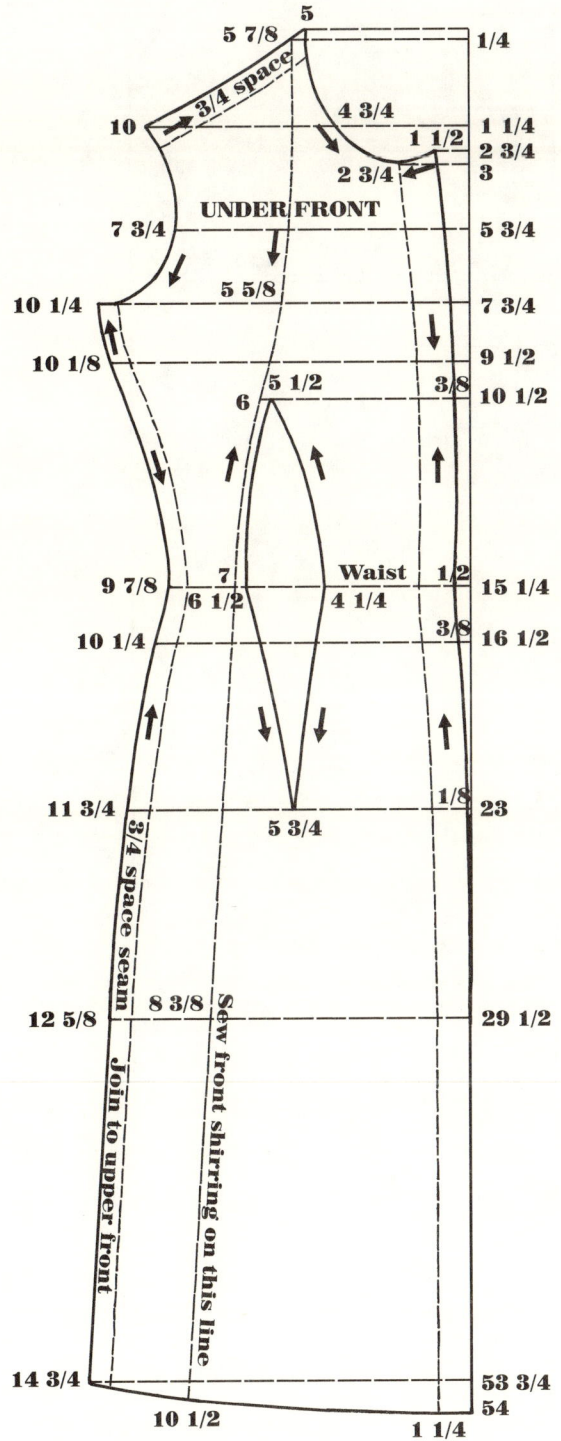

5 7/8   **5**   **1/4**

3/4 space

10   **4 3/4**   **1 1/2**   **1 1/4**
2 3/4   **2 3/4**   **3**

UNDER FRONT

7 3/4   **5 3/4**

10 1/4   **5 5/8**   **7 3/4**

10 1/8   **9 1/2**

6   **5 1/2**   **3/8**   **10 1/2**

9 7/8   **7**   **Waist**   **1/2**   **15 1/4**
6 1/2   **4 1/4**

10 1/4   **3/8**   **16 1/2**

11 3/4   **1/8**   **23**
5 3/4

3/4 space seam
Join to upper front

Sew front shirring on this line

12 5/8   **8 3/8**   **29 1/2**

14 3/4   **53 3/4**
54
10 1/2   **1 1/4**

85

 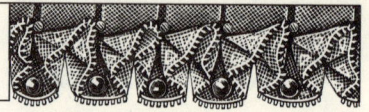
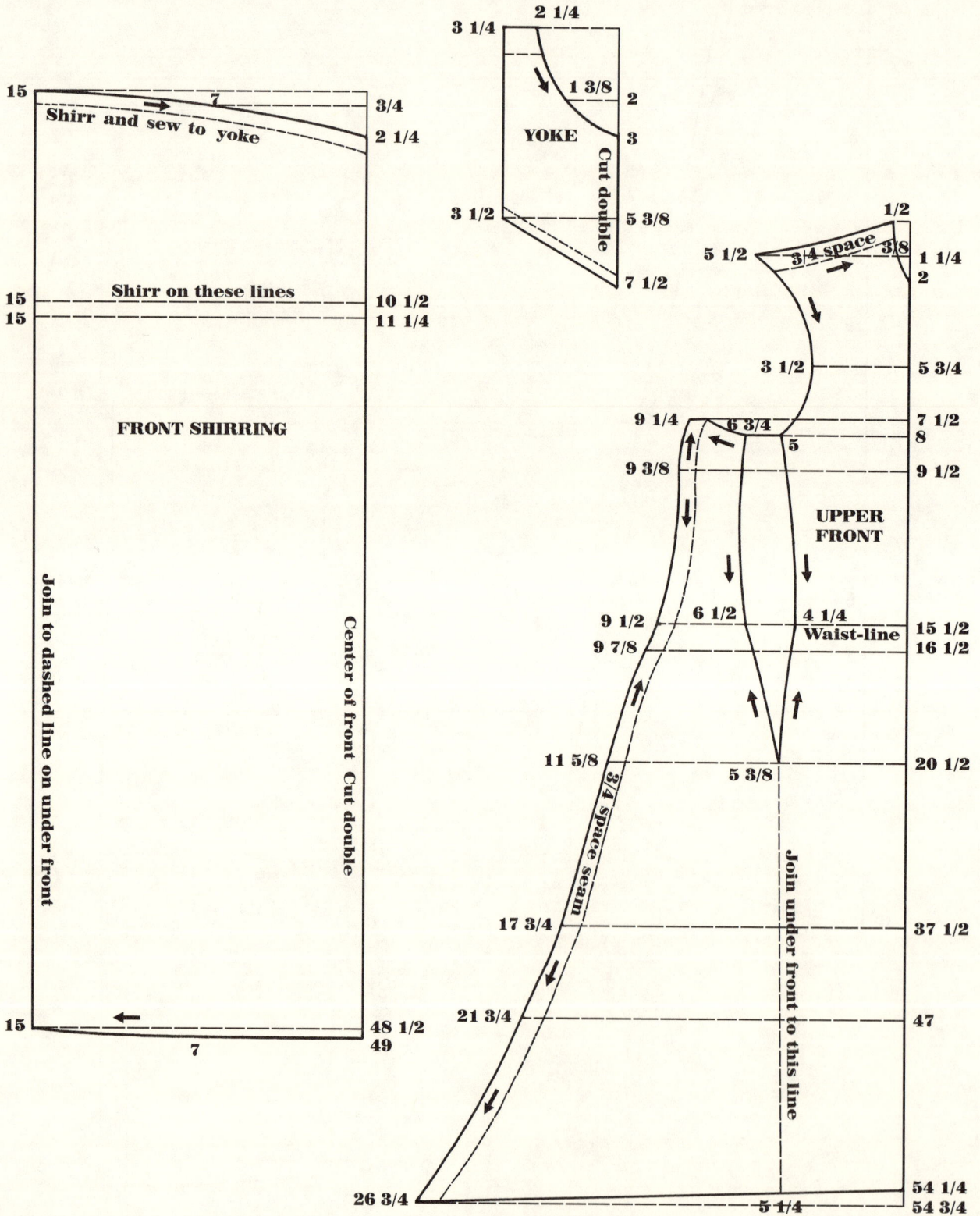

15
7
3/4
Shirr and sew to yoke
2 1/4

3 1/4
2 1/4
3 1/4
1 3/8
2
YOKE
3
Cut double
3 1/2
5 3/8
7 1/2

1/2
5 1/2
3/4 space
3/8
1 1/4
2

Shirr on these lines
15
10 1/2
15
11 1/4

3 1/2
5 3/4

FRONT SHIRRING

9 1/4
6 3/4
7 1/2
5
8
9 3/8
9 1/2

UPPER FRONT

Join to dashed line on under front

Center of front Cut double

9 1/2
6 1/2
4 1/4
15 1/2
9 7/8
Waist-line
16 1/2

11 5/8
5 3/8
20 1/2

3/4 space seam

Join under front to this line

17 3/4
37 1/2

21 3/4
47

15
48 1/2
7
49

26 3/4
5 1/4
54 1/4
54 3/4

86

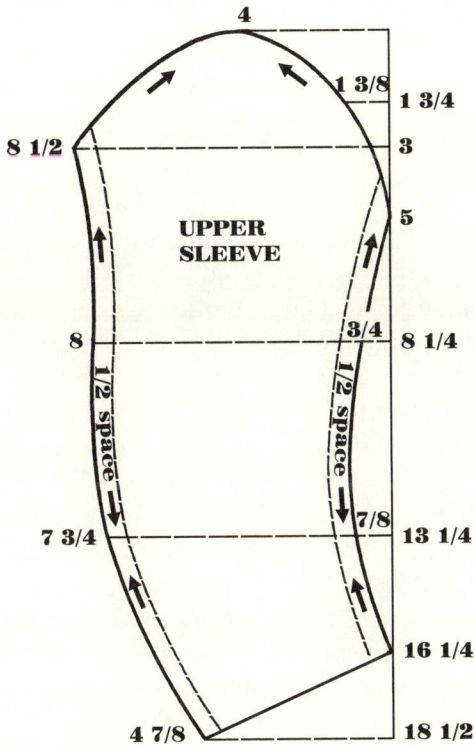

4

1 3/8   1 3/4

8 1/2   3

UPPER SLEEVE   5

1/2 space   1/2 space

8   3/4   8 1/4

7 3/4   7/8   13 1/4

16 1/4

4 7/8   18 1/2

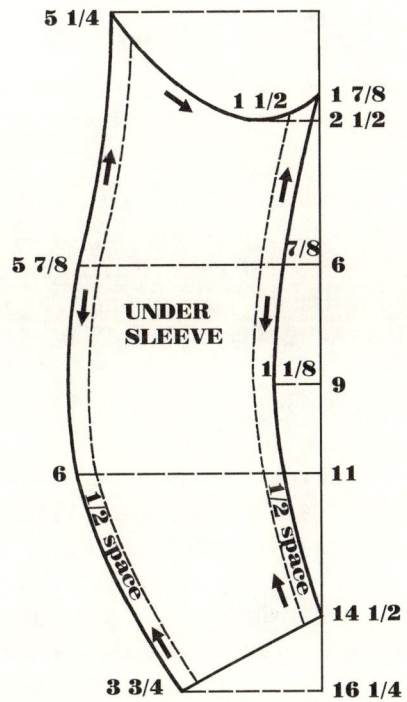

5 1/4

1 1/2   1 7/8

2 1/2

5 7/8   7/8   6

UNDER SLEEVE

1 1/8   9

6   11

1/2 space   1/2 space

14 1/2

3 3/4   16 1/4

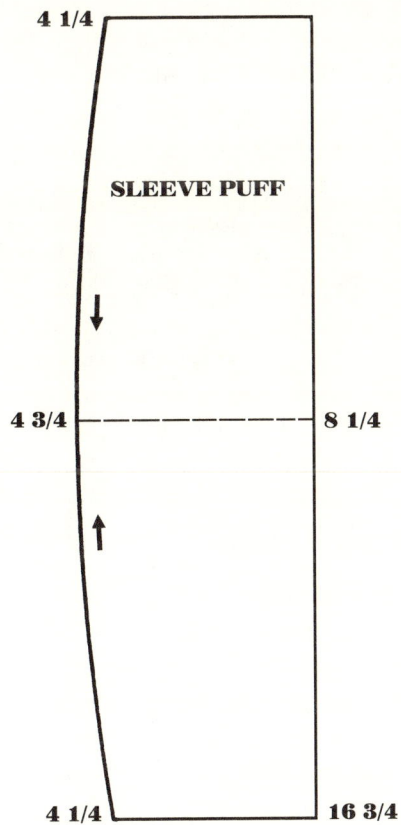

4 1/4

SLEEVE PUFF

4 3/4   8 1/4

4 1/4   16 3/4

4. Skirts and Over-Skirts

Every skirt should be made with a perfectly fitted foundation. It should be of easy walking length. It is usually cut with one front gore, two side gores, and a straight back breadth. The materials used include lining silk, sateen, silesia, and French cambric.

Cut the front gore and back breadths on a lengthwise fold of the material. Cut the side gores with their front edges on the straight edges of the material. The seams of the foundation skirt are sewed up separately from the outside or draped parts. Begin to sew each seam (there are four in all) at the top, allowing all unevenness to fall at the bottom. Be careful not to stretch any bias edges. If you are a novice, it is best to both pin and baste the seams before stitching them. After stitching the seams, press each one down flat, turning them always toward the back, which is better than laying the seams open. In either case the edges should be overcast or top-sewed, and thoroughly pressed with a warm iron. Then, on a table, lay the skirt folded down the center at the front and back so that the corresponding seams are together. Let them be even at the top, and pare off any unevenness at the bottom. For heavy skirts, it is better to slash the front gore for at least 4 inches on its lower edge to give greater freedom in walking.

Most foundation skirts are faced with the drapery material for 4 inches on the upper side, under the draperies. This facing is laid on each part of the skirt with its upper edge turned under and stitched down on the lining, before the skirt seams are sewed. The skirt seams can be sewed so that the smooth surfaces are on the under side of the skirt, and the rough edges next to the draperies. In that case, the facings should all be cut to fit the skirt after its seams are closed.

A supportive facing is required to neatly finish the bottom of the skirt and to obviate any clinging about the limbs when walking. Some dressmakers prefer a 5-inch piece of crinoline or canvas, and then a piece of alpaca. Some demand a hem lined for 12 inches with horsehair cloth, canvas, or buckram. However, skirt padding used alone is the best thing. This material is called by other names, but it is a medium-weight material glazed on one side and like Canton flannel on the other. It is sufficiently stiff, but also pliable. It sheds the dust, and when required it may be wiped with a damp cloth. Its durability is also a great recommendation.

After the lower edge of the skirt has been pared, cut the facing 8 inches deep and to fit it exactly. Then seam the lower edges of the skirt and the facing on the inside, and turn. Cut the upper edge of the facing in fine notches, and just below them stitch it down on the skirt lining. Then finish the smooth edge with braid wrapped around the edge. Some dainty dresses for house wear are not bound with braid, but are simply faced with silk. Attached to this facing inside the skirt is a pinked frill of silk, which can be cut on the straight or on the cross.

The best foundation skirts are given a foot plaiting 5 or 6 inches wide. This should be stitched fast to the upper side of the foundation skirt.

The top of the foundation skirt must be finished before the draperies are adjusted. A placket opening must be provided either at the back or on one side. This is done by making an opening in a seam, or by cutting the material the depth of 10 inches from the top. Face the upper or overlapping side with a strip of the drapery material 2 inches wide. Then sew in a seam, to the opposite side, a double lap of the same material. Let it extend under the faced side, basting it fast at its lower end to the opposite facing.

A pocket should then be put in along the second right-side seam. It may be made of silk or silesia, and must be faced with the dress material on each side of its opening. Then the skirt must be thoroughly pressed on the long skirt board with a hot iron.

The darts in the front and the side gores are stitched, then the back is gathered. The belt may be added in one of two ways. First, the edge may be

basted on the wrong side of the skirt. Baste the center of the belt to the center of the front, and the tops of the seams on each side at corresponding distances on the belt. Then try on the skirt, and make sure that it hangs perfectly even, or make any changes necessary. When you are satisfied, stitch the belt and the upper edge of the skirt together. Turn over the belt with the seam inside, and stitch it down on the skirt.

The second method of attaching the belt, is to first make it the required size (a piece of belting may be used). Then turn under the edge of the skirt 1/4 inch, securing it with a running stitch. Baste the center of the front and the seams to the belt, in their respective positions. Lay the fullness of the back in plaits or gathers, after which fell the belt to the skirt edge by hand with a strong thread. The parts at the back that are sewed to the belt are the stitches of the gathering themselves. The intervals between them supply the deep plaits, which are secured in place by strong stitches made about 1/2 inch below the line of gathering. When there is a great deal of material to gather into a small compass, the gathering stitches are discarded, the intervals between them being too wide to sew across. The material is evenly plaited up and sewed as plaited to the belt. The difference between these gathered plaits and real plaits is that the gathered plaits are upright, and the material below hangs freely.

For a stout woman, a belt mars the fit of the bodice worn over it. Instead, face the entire top of the skirt, gathering the back fullness on tapes.

To finish the skirt, along the belt, sew two braid loops by which to hang it up. Use two hooks and eyes to close the belt. Add two large hooks to correspond to two large eyes placed at the waist-line of the bodice.

After the draperies are cut out, stitch all of the sections together and press the seams. Turn up the lower edge in a medium-sized hem. For bordered materials, silks, and cottons, it is best to secure this hem with a fine blind-stitch, but cloths and suitings are often enhanced by machine-stitching the hem. Unless the material is heavy and firm, it is best to stiffen the hem with crinoline before stitching.

The edges of draperies are often best finished by a false hem of the foundation material about 6 inches wide, after a muslin interlining has been overcast to the lower edge of the drapery. After finishing the false hem, place braid at the lower edge, not doubled over the edge, but sewed inside the skirt and left quite flat.

For cloths and heavy wools, the tailor's hem makes the neatest finish. The stitches are invisible from the right side. Thin paste is employed to make the halves of the hem adhere together, and to facilitate flattening with the iron. Three inches from the edge, baste a straight line that is to be the edge of the skirt. Have the paste and a hot iron at hand. Apply the paste inside with a brush, not too thickly, where the hem is to fold over, on the 3 inches below the basting. As you paste, turn the hem over at the basting, and iron it flat and smooth.

Baste down the hem for greater safety. Then hem it invisibly, passing the needle only half through the cloth, so that no vestige of the stitch appears on the right side. Use silk of the cloth color, not cotton. The silk must be strong and of excellent quality. Cheap silk is not strong enough, and the constant dampening necessary in tailoring injures its color. Remove the basting, and iron a second time. In spite of the thickness of the cloth, your hem should be flat, smooth, and even.

When draperies or a tunic are edged with one or more rows of machine-stitching, the tailor's hem is not necessary. However, it is advisable to paste and iron the hem before it is stitched.

When the hem has been carefully ironed, turn under 1/2 inch at the top of the draperies and fell them into place on the foundation skirt, at the waist. Cover this edge with a flat galloon or braid.

A trained skirt should be lined with silk of a shade that contrasts or harmonizes with the material. The under side should be finished as neatly as possible, since it is liable to become visible. Trains made of heavy silks or wools require no extra stiffening. Soft silks may be interlined with soft crinoline. However, it should be used with the greatest discrimination, as the goal is only to avoid stringiness. Tapes must be adjusted on the under side to draw the front and sides back into their proper places, as well as to hold the fullness of the back together.

1892 Home Dressmaking

Plain Skirt with Drapery

Use the scale corresponding to the waist measure. Regulate the length with the tape measure. The skirt is in three pieces: Front, side gore, and back. The drapery is in two pieces: Front and back.

Summer 1888 *Voice of Fashion*

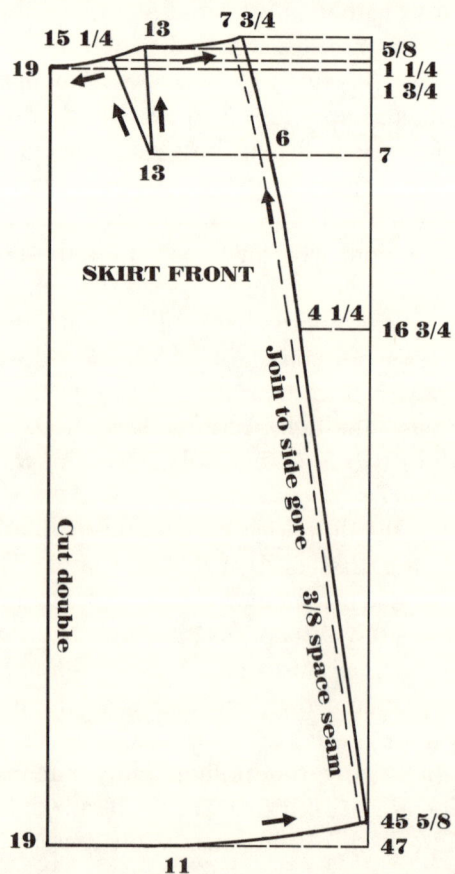

SKIRT FRONT

Cut double

15 1/4   13   7 3/4

19

5/8
1 1/4
1 3/4

6   7

13

4 1/4   16 3/4

Join to side gore   3/8 space seam

19

11

45 5/8
47

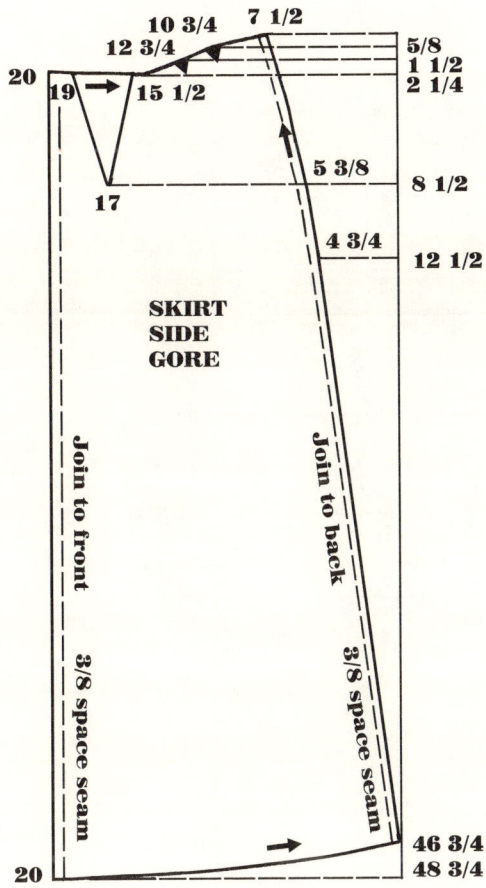

10 3/4   7 1/2
12 3/4   5/8
                         1 1/2
20   2 1/4
19 →   15 1/2

                  5 3/8   8 1/2

17

                  4 3/4   12 1/2

**SKIRT
SIDE
GORE**

Join to front   Join to back

3/8 space seam   3/8 space seam

20   46 3/4
                  48 3/4

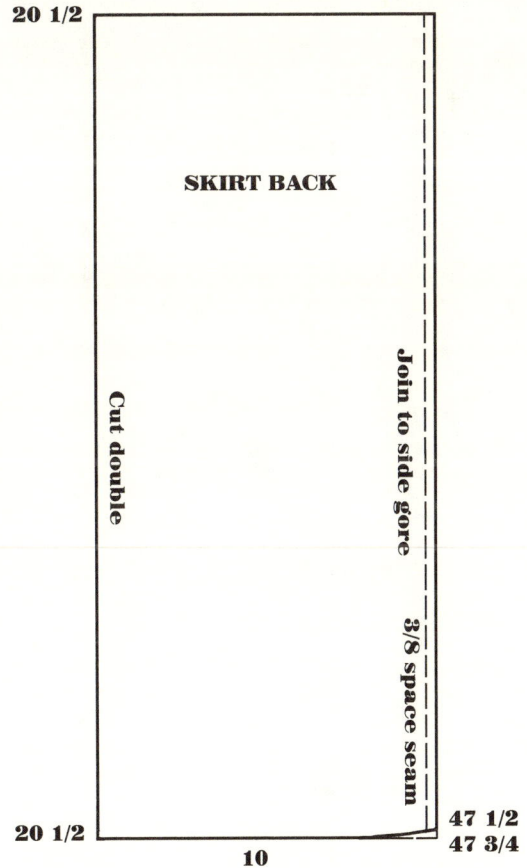

20 1/2

SKIRT BACK

Cut double   Join to side gore   3/8 space seam

20 1/2   47 1/2
          10   47 3/4

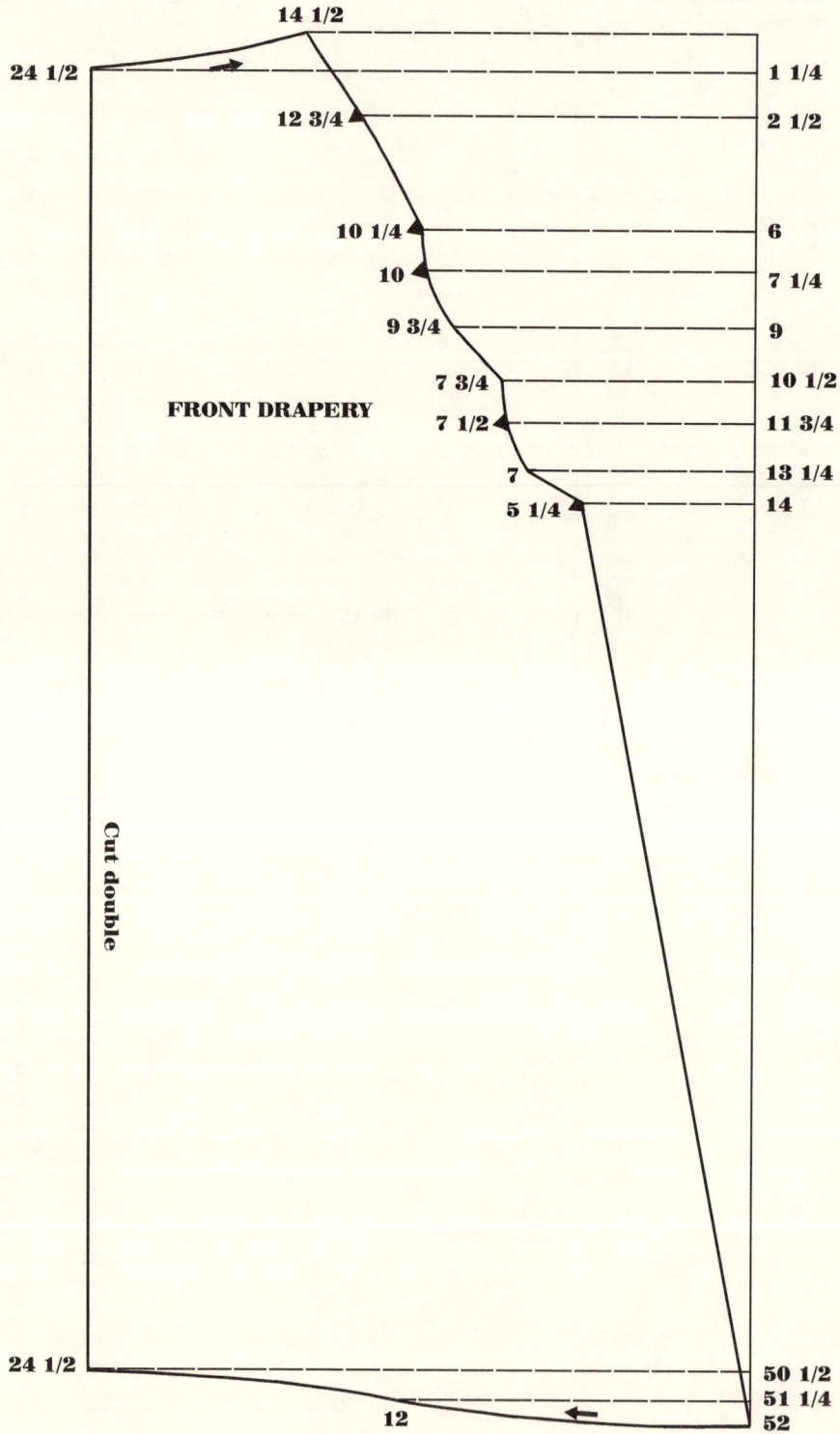

14 1/2

24 1/2

1 1/4

12 3/4

2 1/2

10 1/4

6

10

7 1/4

9 3/4

9

7 3/4

10 1/2

FRONT DRAPERY

7 1/2

11 3/4

7

13 1/4

5 1/4

14

Cut double

24 1/2

50 1/2

51 1/4

12

52

Plain Skirt with Drapery

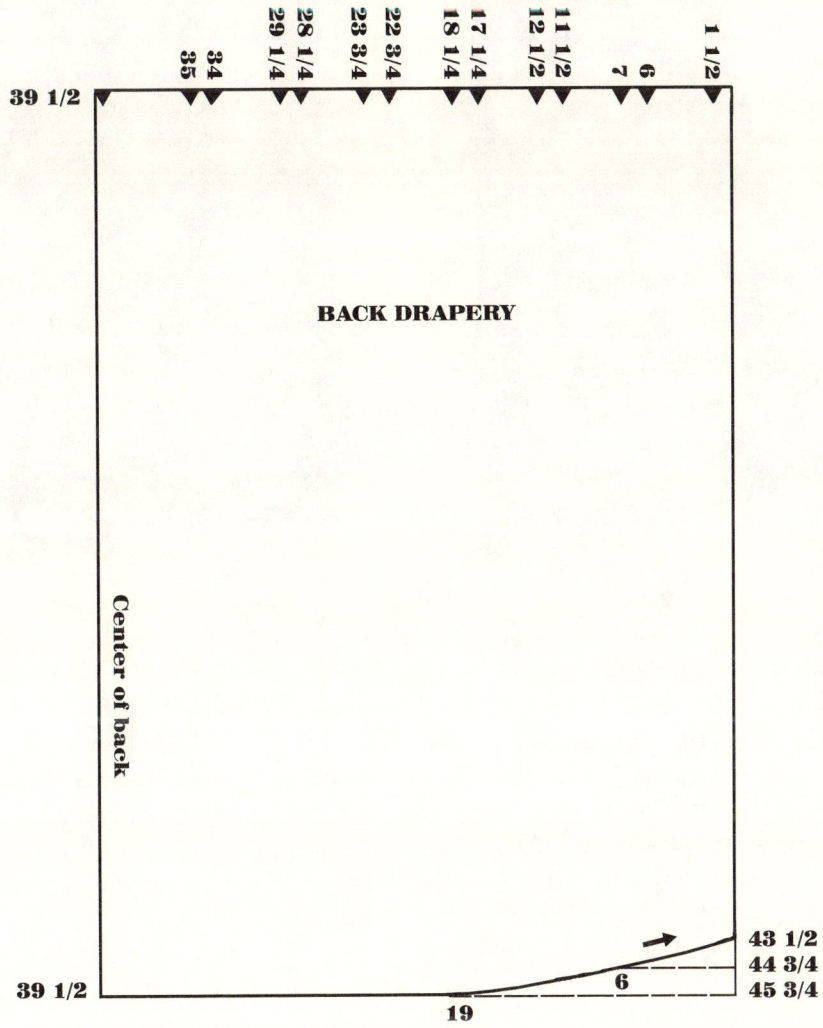

BACK DRAPERY

Center of back

39 1/2

35 3-4 29 1/4 28 1/4 23 3/4 22 3/4 18 1/4 17 1/4 12 1/2 11 1/2 7 6 1 1/2

39 1/2

43 1/2
44 3/4
45 3/4

6

19

Walking Skirt. The foundation or skirt proper is composed of three gores and a full breadth for the back. The gores are fitted smoothly by darts, and the breadth is gathered across the top. The placket is finished at the center of the back. Provision for a bustle is made by curving the back breadth across the top, and to further increase the bouffant effect steels are run through casings. Tapes, sewed at the ends of the casings and tied together, draw the steels into curves. The foundation skirt can always be made of lining material.

On the front is a deep tablier, which is conformed to the shape of the gores by darts, and has three upward-turning plaits folded diagonally to each side not far from the top. These plaits produce soft, wavy folds, and bastings made through the drapery to the skirt preserve a smooth adjustment about the top.

The back drapery consists of a wide breadth. This breadth has its top gathered, then folded through its center and seamed along the gathers for some distance from the center. The seamed edges are finished by a binding. The rest of the top is sewed with the skirt, as is also the front drapery,

to the belt. This arrangement produces ample fullness at the top of the back without bringing it all close to the belt.

The placket opening for the drapery is finished on the left side, an underlap being sewed to the front drapery and a facing to the back drapery. Both draperies fall nearly even with the bottom of the skirt, and below them a narrow foot plaiting is visible.

Plain suit material was here chosen for the skirt, but very often the front drapery contrasts with the back. Striped and plaid materials are fashionable for the back when the front is plain. A handsome skirt has its front drapery of soft serge and its back of plush-striped serge. Another has the widths forming the back drapery joined so as to bring a breadth of velvet between two of silk, the entire front drapery being of silk. To make the skirt for a lady of medium size, requires 11 5/8 yards of material 22 inches wide, or 5 5/8 yards of material 44 inches wide.

March 1887 *Delineator*

Walking Skirt

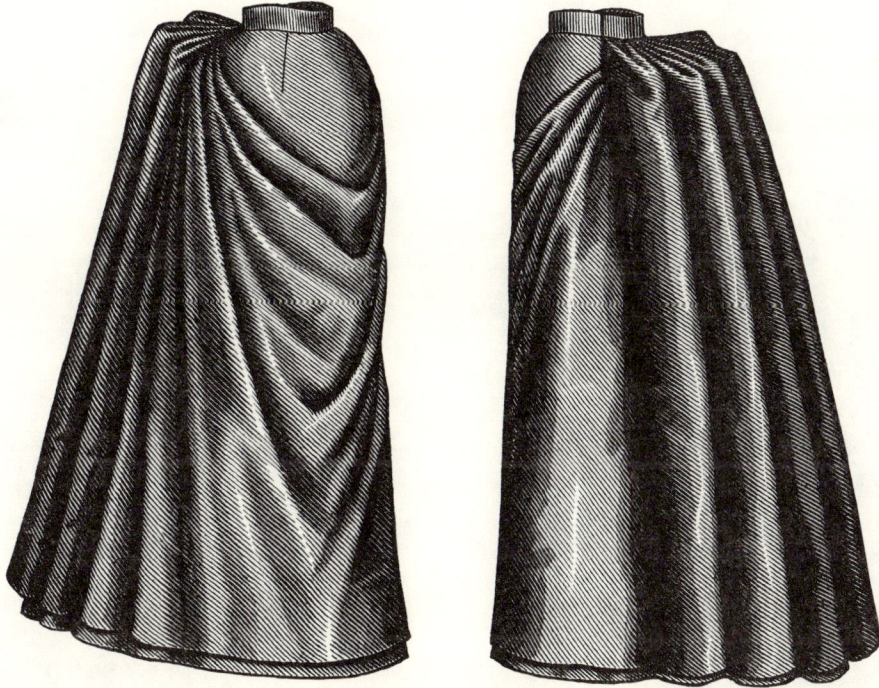

Walking Skirt. This skirt is pictured made of cedar green cloth and finished plainly. The four-gored foundation skirt is of lining, and is faced several inches up from the bottom with the material. The back breadth is also faced as far down from the top as necessary with the material, and the long draperies extend nearly to its lower edge. Two steels across the back breadth add to the bouffant effect of the back drapery. A pad may also be worn if desired.

In the side edges of the front drapery, a little below the waist-line, are laid three shallow, upward-turning plaits that pass into the drapery diagonally from each side. A dart on each side makes a close adjustment at the top. The upper edge of the back drapery is hemmed and caught to the belt to form five burnous loops of uneven length, from which the drapery falls in full, straight folds nearly to the bottom of the skirt. Bastings made through the drapery to a strap placed underneath preserve their lines of direction.

This skirt is suitable for house wear, or as part of a walking costume. Henrietta, serge, lady's cloth, tricot, and cashmere are adaptable to this style. It may be decorated with braid, bands of embroidery, or Persian trimming. To make the skirt for a lady of medium size, requires 8 yards of material 22 inches wide, or 3 7/8 yards of material 44 inches wide. Each requires 3 1/8 yards of lining 36 inches wide for the foundation skirt and the strap.

April 1889 *Delineator*

Skirt with Scarf Drapery. The skirt and drapery are drafted with the scale corresponding to the waist measure. The length is regulated with the tape measure. The skirt consists of three pieces: Front, side gore, and back. The drapery consists of two pieces: Side panel and back. It should be just the same length as the skirt. Gather the back drapery, interline the panel, and make one plait over the hip.

Fall 1889 *Voice of Fashion*

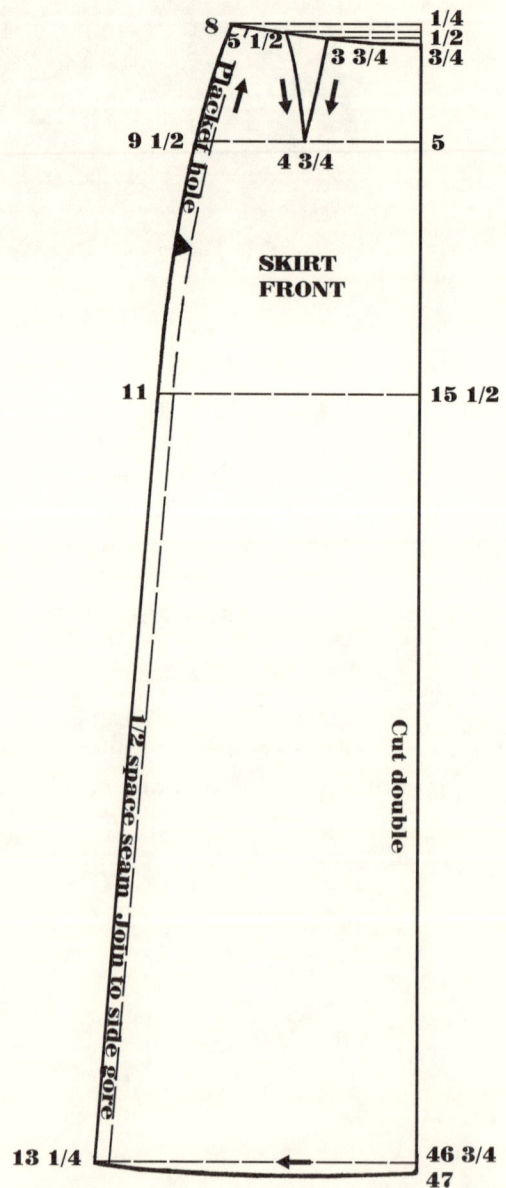

8   5 1/2   3 3/4   1/4   1/2   3/4

Placket hole

9 1/2   4 3/4   5

SKIRT FRONT

11   15 1/2

1/2 space seam join to side gore

Cut double

13 1/4   46 3/4   47

Skirt with Scarf Drapery

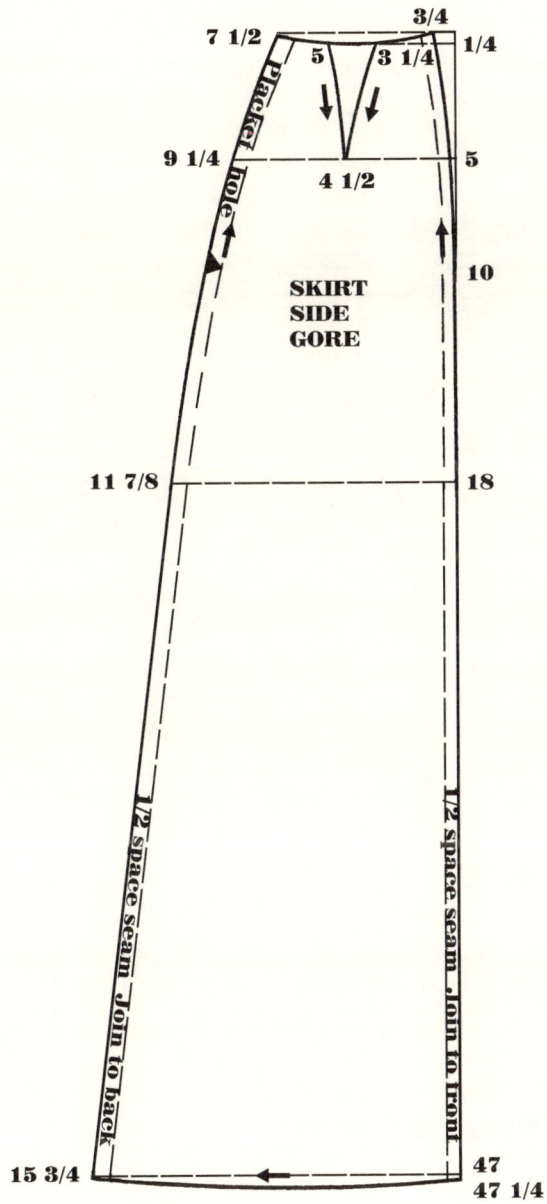

SKIRT SIDE GORE

7 1/2

3/4

5   3   1/4

1/4

9 1/4

4 1/2

5

Placket hole

10

11 7/8

18

1/2 space seam Join to back

1/2 space seam Join to front

15 3/4

47
47 1/4

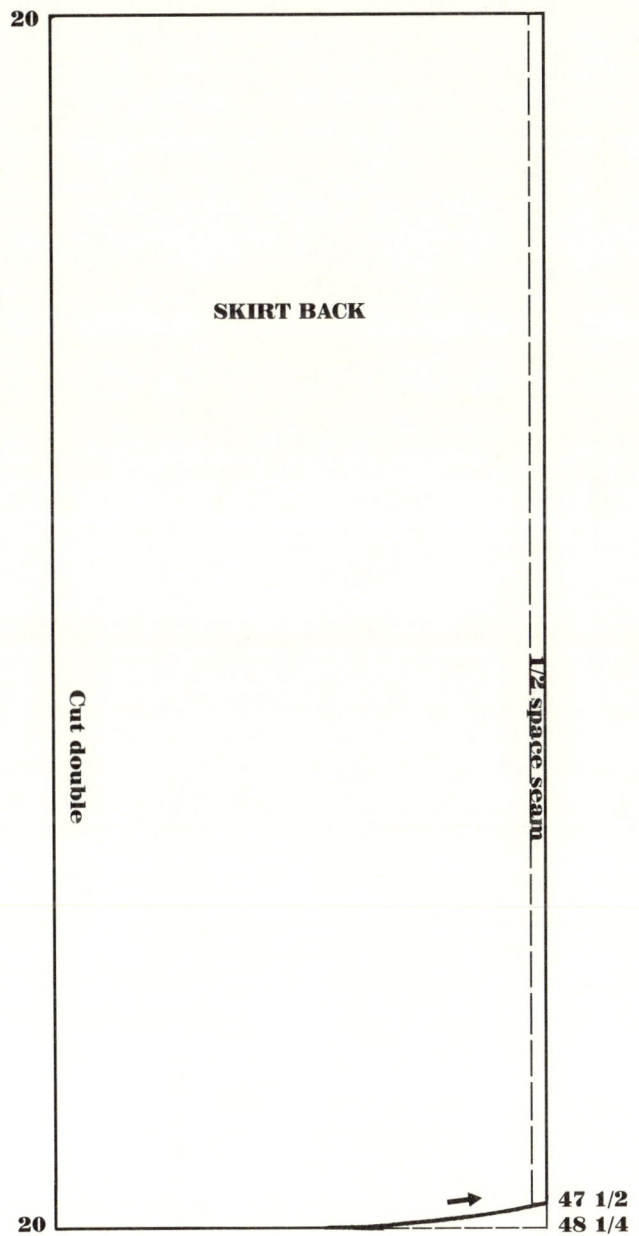

SKIRT BACK

20

20

Cut double

1/2 space seam

47 1/2
48 1/4

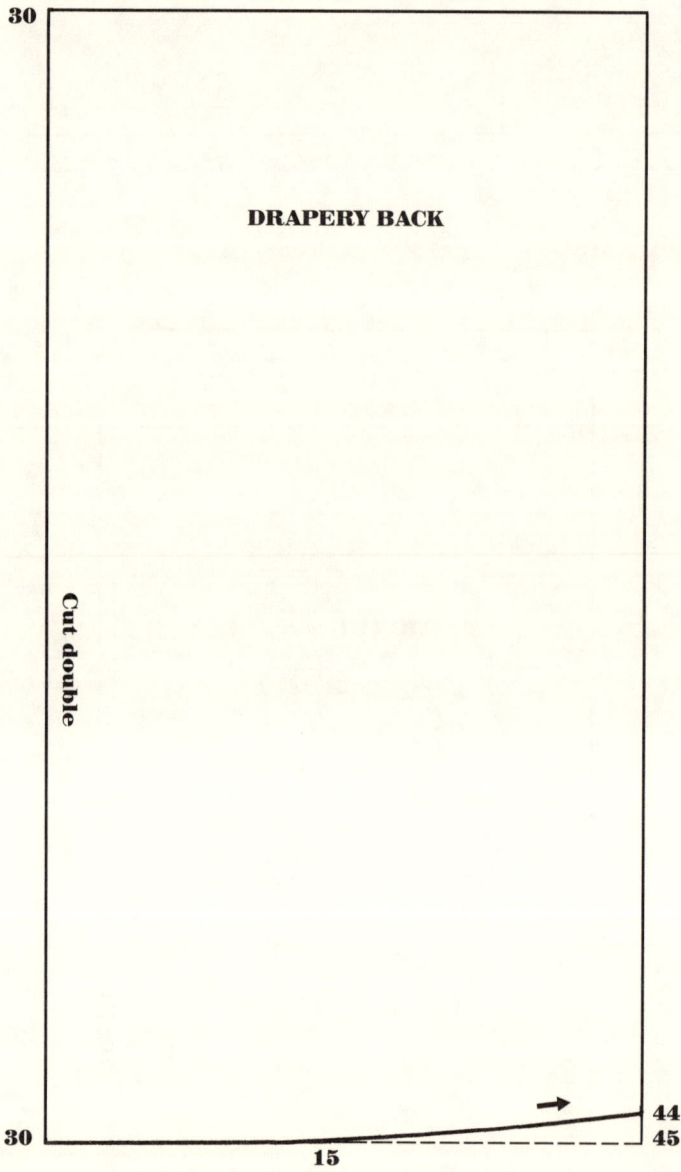

30

DRAPERY BACK

Cut double

30 44
    45
15

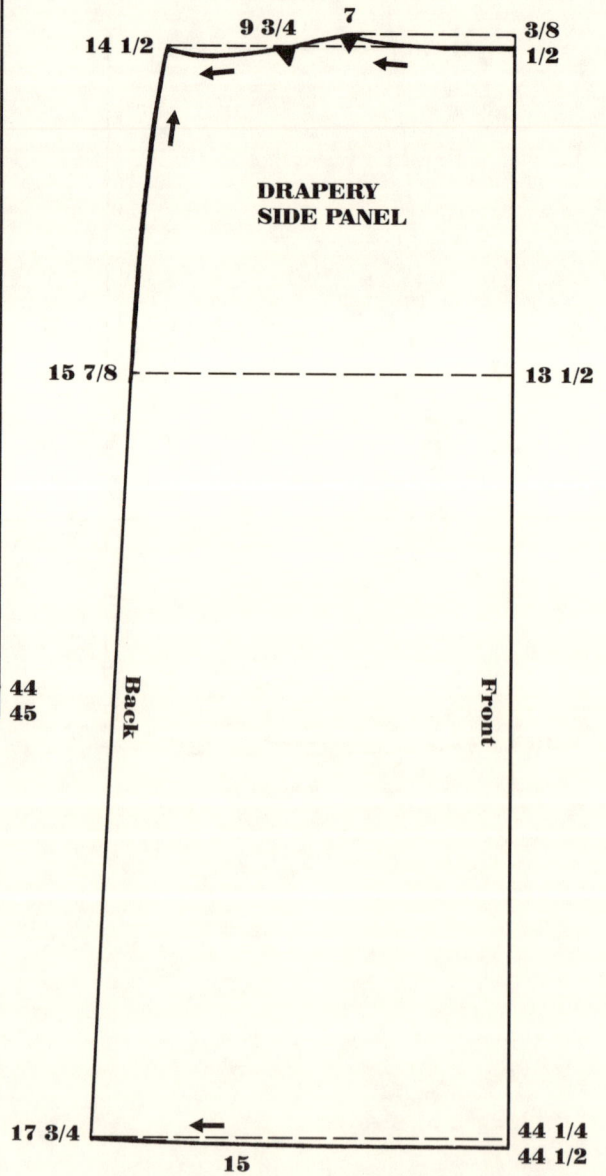

9 3/4   7   3/8
14 1/2   1/2

**DRAPERY
SIDE PANEL**

15 7/8   13 1/2

Back   Front

17 3/4   44 1/4
                          44 1/2
        15

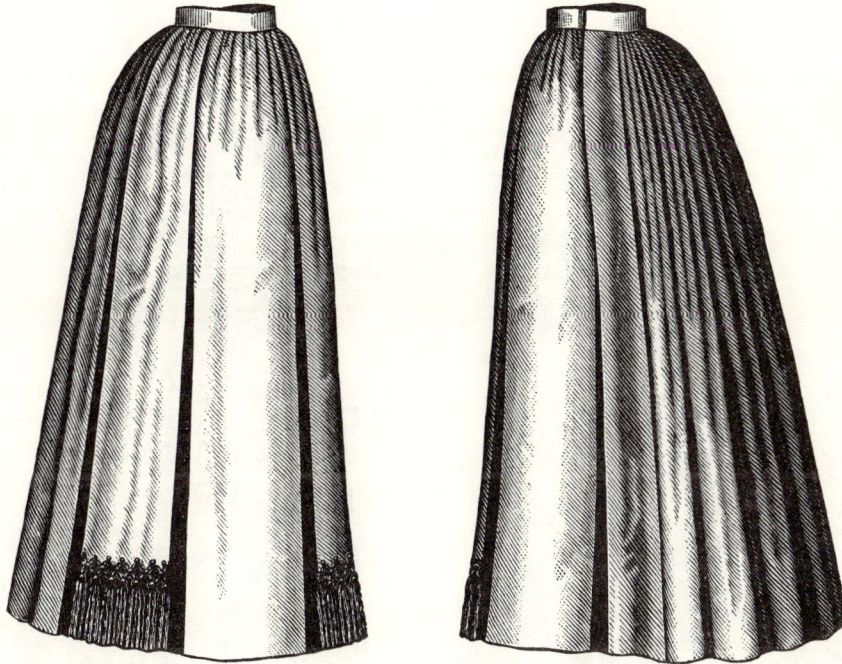

Walking Skirt. The skirt is shown developed in suit material. It is trimmed with bengaline of a contrasting color, and with fringe. The skirt is in the regulation style, with two steels and a pad. The front and side gores are covered with bengaline. The back breadth, which is of lining, is faced up several inches from the bottom with bengaline.

On the front of the skirt are five panels that almost cover the gores, the bengaline showing between the long edges. The center panel is the widest and comes at the center of the front gore. Two panels are arranged on each side of it. The panels are gathered at the top and lined with bengaline, the one next to the center on each side being trimmed with deep, rich fringe. The panels are usually interlined with crinoline to make them hang well.

The back drapery is laid in seven deep, backward-turning plaits on each side of the center, and hangs to the edge of the skirt. The upper edge is finished with a belt. The front edges are turned under for hems, and basted here and there to the side-back seams along the sewing of the hems.

Bordered materials develop nicely in this way, as the border may substitute for the fringe, and trim the other panels and the edge of the skirt as well. The panels may be the same color as the rest of the costume, with lining of a different shade. To make the skirt for a lady of medium size, requires 7 1/2 yards of material 22 inches wide, 4 3/4 yards of material 36 inches wide, or 3 3/4 yards of material 44 inches wide. Each requires 3 3/4 yards of bengaline 22 inches wide, and 3 1/8 yards of lining 36 inches wide for the foundation skirt.

May 1889 *Delineator*

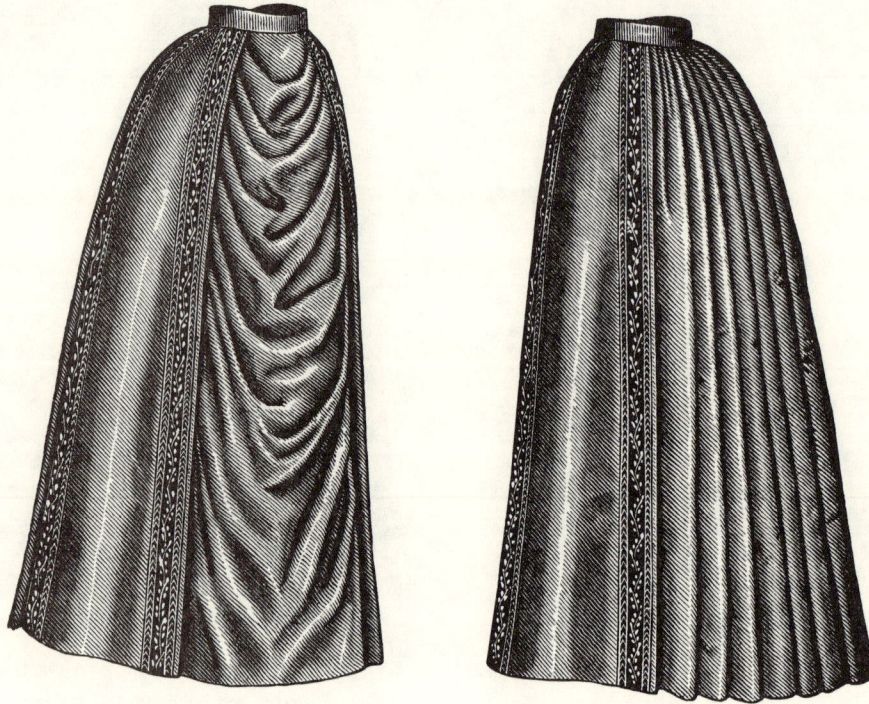

Walking Skirt. Plain suit material was selected for this skirt, with Persian bands for trimming. The foundation skirt is of lining material and is in the four-gored style. The effect is good when a long, slender bustle is worn, although steels in the foundation skirt may be used. Tapes are sewed underneath the side-back seams to draw the fullness back.

Over the foundation skirt is arranged a drapery that hangs to the bottom of the skirt. Six forward-turning plaits are laid on each side of the front drapery and flare out, producing pretty folds and wrinkles. A broad panel shaped at the top by a dart depends from the belt on each side, its long edges being trimmed with Persian bands. The top of the back drapery is laid in four backward-turning plaits on each side of the center, the plaits being pressed in their folds to the bottom of the drapery.

This mode develops well in bordered materials. The panels invite trimmings of appliqué embroidery, passementerie, etc. When a striking effect is desired, they may differ from the rest of the costume. To make this skirt for a lady of medium size, requires 11 yards of material 22 inches wide, 6 7/8 yards of material 36 inches wide, or 5 1/2 yards of material 44 inches wide. Also required are 3 1/8 yards of lining 36 inches wide for the foundation skirt.

July 1889 *Delineator*

5. Ensembles with Bodices, Skirts, and Draperies

Round bodices and shirred basques are the styles used for handsome embroidered dresses. The round bodice is made without fullness on the shoulders, but is gathered into a belt in front and back. It may be made on a lining, but it is better to make it without one, making very small seams and covering the edges neatly. The pointed neck, or the surplice front lapped to the left side at the waist-line, is used for dressy toilettes. When the neck is high, a rolling Byron collar takes the place of a standing band. Yoke bodices are also worn, with the yoke made of the embroidery, and also the collar, pointed epaulettes, and cuffs. Sometimes a V of embroidery in back and front is used instead of a yoke that covers the entire shoulders. Plain muslin is then shirred next to this V on the shoulders and the waist-line. When the embroidery is striped, the basque may be plain, the fronts and the center backs having the stripes coming diagonally toward the center, forming a series of Vs.

The full round skirt gathered to a belt and without drapery is made both in embroidered and in plain muslins. The latter are hemmed and tucked, or trimmed around with bands of insertion. A favorite design has vines of embroidery passing around the skirt and alternating with clusters of drawn-work. When the embroidery is used for an over-skirt above a plain muslin skirt, it is arranged in very simple apron shape, either pointed to the bottom in front, or drawn slightly to one side. Or else the over-skirt droops to the bottom of the dress all around, and is very slightly caught up alike on both hips. Belts and drooping sashes of ribbon complete such dresses. Flounces of embroidered muslin are chosen wide enough for three or four to cover the back of the skirt. Or else they are narrower, and are put around the skirt with a short pannier over-skirt of plain muslin edged with embroidery.

February 11, 1888 *Harper's Bazar*

Bodices with full fronts are in great favor for dresses of various materials, from heavy silks to the thinnest gauzes. This fullness is easily added, and it will improve the simplest bodice. For plain muslins, ginghams, and other cotton materials, and also for dinner silks, it is only necessary to add 2 or 3 inches of breadth to the front edges, gathering this fullness at the neck and waist-line. In wash dresses, the darts are not taken in the outside, but merely in the lining. In silks, however, the darts are sewed in both.

To make a V-shaped opening in a dress high on the shoulders, the straight edges of the fronts of the dress material are carried back to the shoulder seams, and the fullness is gathered along these seams. Lapped bodices have the fullness carried still farther back on the shoulder seams. A material of contrasting color (such as surah, tulle, or Brussels net) partly fills in the pointed neck-line. It passes around the neck, and is carried in folds down the front, lapping to the left side at the waist-line. It is finished there with a ribbon rosette or a flowing bow.

Irregular arrangements are preferred for double-breasted bodices, such as lapping the right side nearly to the left armhole, then turning over the top to form a triangular lapel, and sloping the space below back to the center at the waist-line. Another fancy has the doubled part only below the darts, while the upper part has a gathered plastron of silk or lace. This is edged by a velvet or moiré collar, which also crosses with the lower parts to the left side, where it is buttoned.

February 25, 1888 *Harper's Bazar*

Full skirts and long draperies give ample effects without exaggerated tournures. The lines of most draperies are straight and flowing, instead of being bunched up and wrinkled across. In many dresses there is but a single skirt, which is draped slightly at the top and hangs in very full plaits on

the foundation skirt. The back of the foundation skirt has crosswise steels, but they are shortened, and are not tied closely enough to give an extended bustle. When pads are added, they are small and very nearly flat.

For simple wool dresses, a single skirt is made 4 yards wide, with its only sloping at the top of the side seams. The front and sides are lengthened a trifle, and are draped at the top. The back is laid in close plaits that fall in natural folds to the bottom. Sometimes a fold of contrasting material is added around the bottom, showing 1 inch below it.

Bordered wool dresses have a full lower skirt made of 4 yards of the bordered material, with the border and the selvage showing at the bottom all around. Such skirts are made over a foundation skirt, with which they are joined only at the belt. They are gathered in front, and loosely plaited at the back. A large, well-defined plait extends up each side to the belt. This is slit at the top to allow a sash drapery of striped material to pass under, forming an apron in front, and dropping in two points at the back.

March 10, 1888 *Harper's Bazar*

Blouse bodices are most comfortable for summer dresses. They may be made of the dress material, or of some other material that may be worn with various skirts of harmonizing colors. Surah, pongee, India silks, Irish linen, lawn, and striped flannel are the materials most used for separate blouses. There are also many of plain flannel for the country, for wearing with mountain, tennis, or yachting dresses. Moreover, they are made for dressy occasions of bengaline, with gilt or silver galloon, or of black or white lace, or of insertion, with ribbon or jet stripes. Striped silk blouses are made of undressed silks in 1/4-inch stripes of pale rose with green and cream, and finished with a green or rose surah collar, cuffs, and belt. Stripes 1 inch or more wide are chosen in contrasting colors—blue with red, écru with brown, fawn with blue or red, and black with white—and these have dots of the light color woven in the dark stripe.

These blouses are gathered basques made without a lining and worn with a belt. Bodices of surah and other opaque materials may have a yoke-like piece of silk lining serge set across inside the top, from the armholes to the collar, to keep the garment in shape. However, this is not added in lace or thin white Victoria lawn blouses. These blouses extend below the belt a depth of 6 inches in front, 4 inches on the hips, and 5 inches at the back, and are simply hemmed around. They may be gathered all around the top next to the standing collar in three lines of shirring. Or else they are gathered only in the center of the front and back with one line of shirring just below the collar. The backs have a narrow side back, but the fronts are full and straight. Both fronts and back are gathered or plaited in the center at the waist-line, this shirring or plaiting being set on an inside belt ribbon.

The fronts have a broad box-plait for holding three stud-like buttons. Blouses of flannel or surah have a fly front fastening. The sleeves have but one seam, and are full shirt sleeves attached to a wristband, and gathered into the armhole. The collar is a high standing band fastened by three hooks, or else it is a rolling Byron collar. The belt is of the material, 2 inches wide, cut lengthwise; that is, parallel to the selvage. It is hooked in front, but laps with a pointed end passing toward the left side, which may also have a strap over it.

June 2, 1888 *Harper's Bazar*

In mounting a skirt of straight breadths to the belt there is opportunity for variety. Some are simply gathered all around; some are gauged; some are shirred to a greater or lesser depth, either all around, on one or both hips, or across the front only. Others have lengthwise tucks in front, from the top to any desired depth, gradually lengthening toward the middle, and forming a kind of pointed cuirass.

August 1889 *Demorest's Monthly Magazine*

Street Costume with Wrap

The French basque is drafted with the scale corresponding to the bust measure. It consists of eight pieces: Front, first side piece, second side piece, side back, back, collar, and two sleeve pieces. If preferred, the front may be turned away on the diagonal dashed line to form a V shape, and a vest inserted. Also, allowance may be made for plaits in the back. The sleeves may be finished with a cuff if desired.

The drapery is drafted with the scale corresponding to the waist measure. The length is regulated with the tape measure. It is in two pieces: Front and back. Lay the plaits according to the notches and the engravings.

The skirt is drafted with the scale corresponding to the waist measure. The length is regulated with the tape measure. It is in three pieces: Front, side gore, and back.

The wrap is drafted with the scale corresponding to the bust measure. It consists of four pieces: Front, back, loose sleeve, and collar. Almost any material and almost any style of trimming may be used. Join the parts according to the notches.

1889 *National Garment Cutter Book of Diagrams*

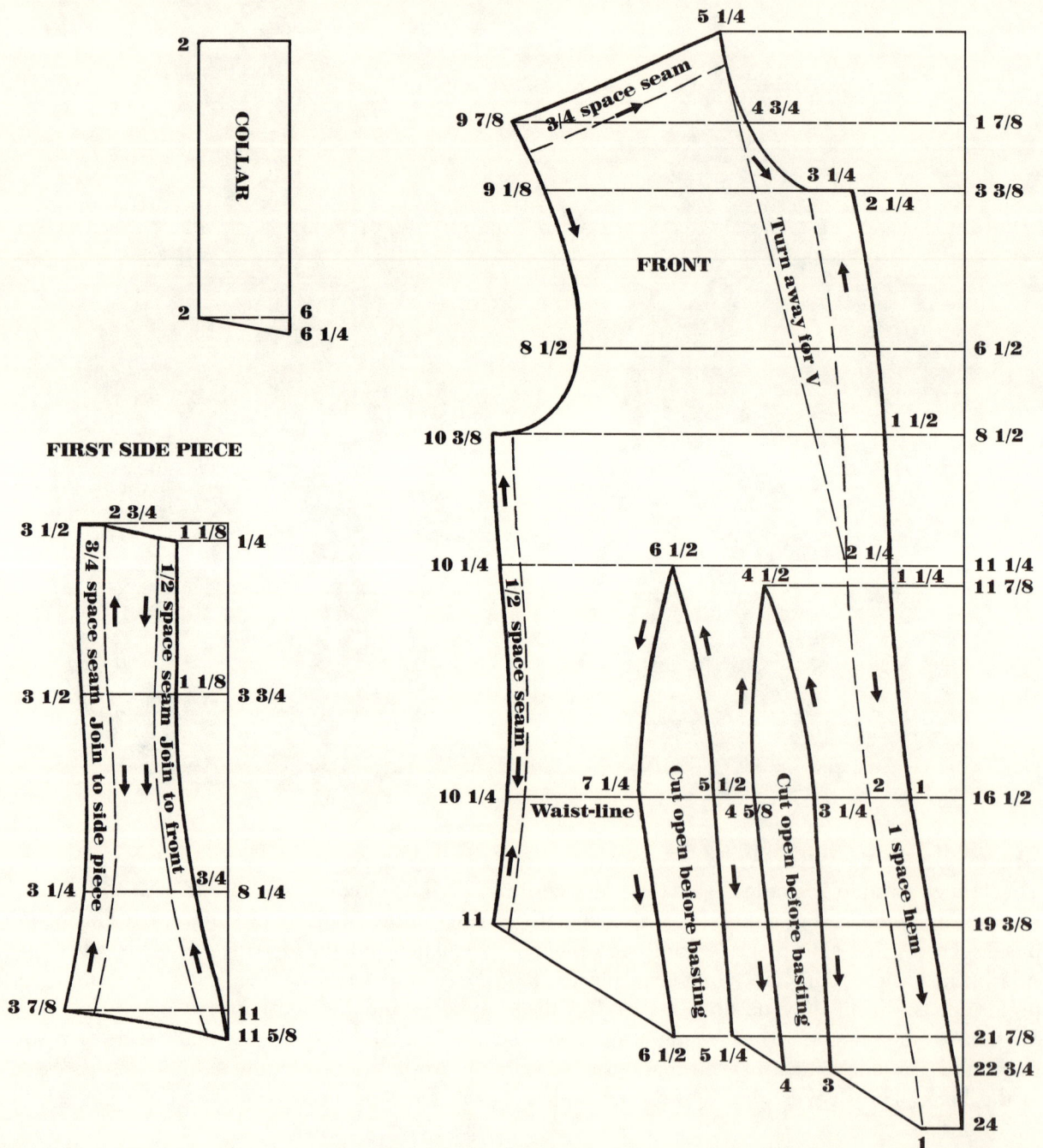

COLLAR

2

2

6

6 1/4

FIRST SIDE PIECE

3 1/2 2 3/4 1 1/8 1/4

3/4 space seam Join to side piece

1/2 space seam Join to front

3 1/2 1 1/8 3 3/4

3 1/4 3/4 8 1/4

3 7/8 11

11 5/8

5 1/4

9 7/8 3/4 space seam 4 3/4 1 7/8

9 1/8 3 1/4 2 1/4 3 3/8

FRONT

Turn away for V

8 1/2 6 1/2

10 3/8 1 1/2 8 1/2

10 1/4 6 1/2 4 1/2 2 1/4 11 1/4

1/2 space seam 1 1/4 11 7/8

7 1/4 5 1/2 2 1 16 1/2

10 1/4 Waist-line 4 5/8 3 1/4 1 space hem

Cut open before basting

Cut open before basting

11 19 3/8

6 1/2 5 1/4 21 7/8

4 3 22 3/4

24

1

104

SECOND SIDE PIECE

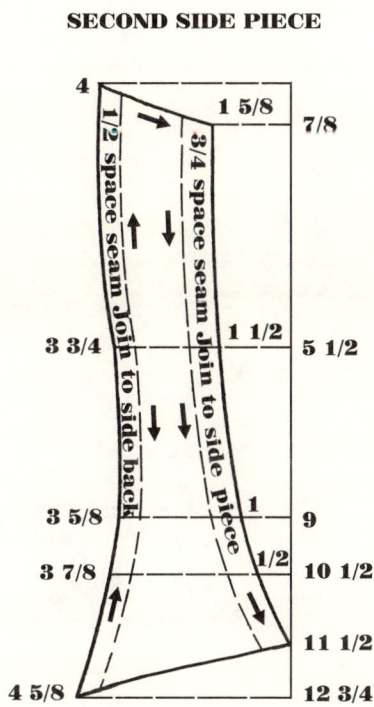

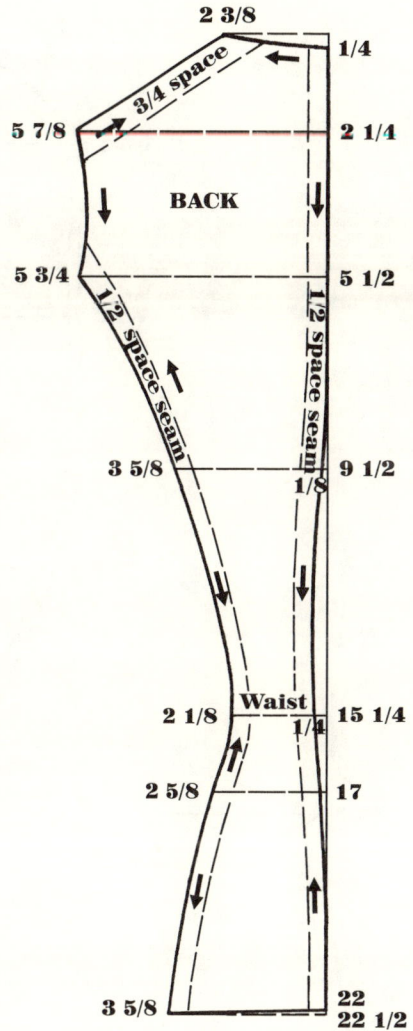

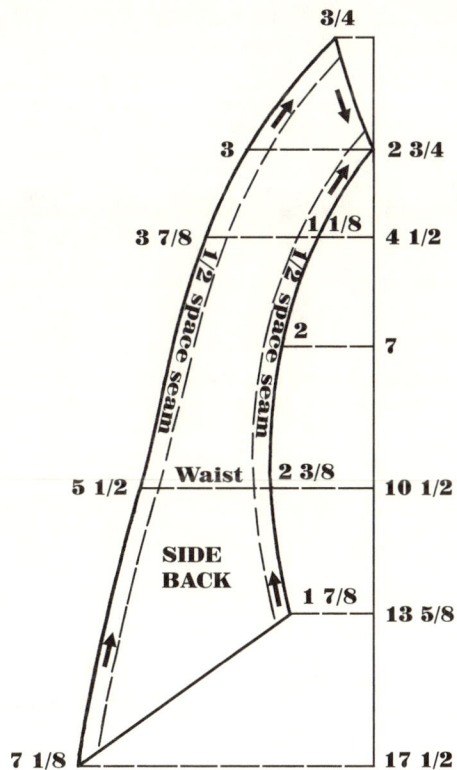

4   1 5/8   7/8

1/2 space seam Join to side back

3/4 space seam Join to side piece

3 3/4   1 1/2   5 1/2

3 5/8   1   9

3 7/8   1/2   10 1/2

11 1/2

4 5/8   12 3/4

2 3/8   1/4

3/4 space

5 7/8   2 1/4

BACK

5 3/4   5 1/2

1/2 space seam

1/2 space seam

3 5/8   1/8   9 1/2

2 1/8   **Waist**   15 1/4
1/4

2 5/8   17

3 5/8   22
     22 1/2

3/4

3   2 3/4

3 7/8   1 1/8   4 1/2

1/2 space seam

1/2 space seam

2   7

5 1/2   **Waist**   2 3/8   10 1/2

SIDE BACK

1 7/8   13 5/8

7 1/8   17 1/2

105

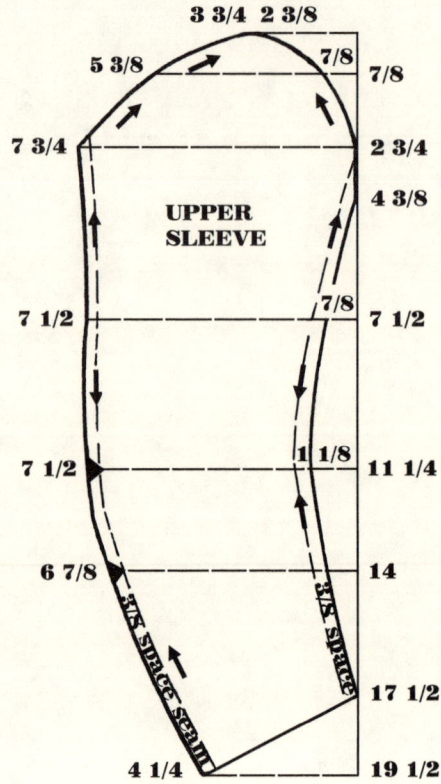

UPPER SLEEVE

3 3/4   2 3/8
5 3/8   7/8   7/8
7 3/4   2 3/4
4 3/8
7 1/2   7/8   7 1/2
7 1/2   1 1/8   11 1/4
6 7/8   14
3/8 space seam
17 1/2
4 1/4   19 1/2

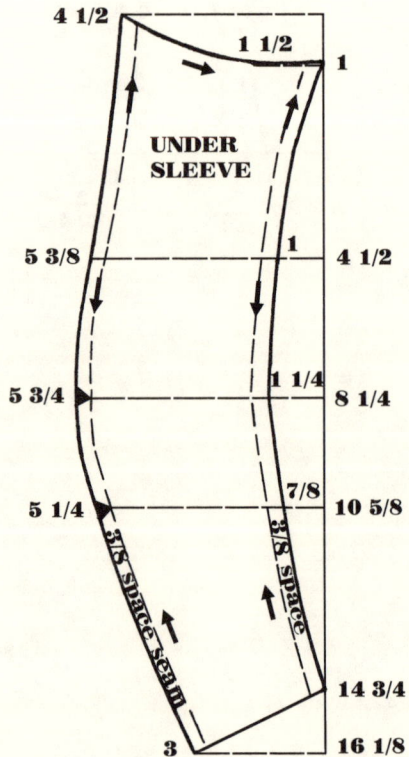

UNDER SLEEVE

4 1/2
1 1/2   1
5 3/8   1   4 1/2
5 3/4   1 1/4   8 1/4
5 1/4   7/8   10 5/8
3/8 space seam   3/8 space
14 3/4
3   16 1/8

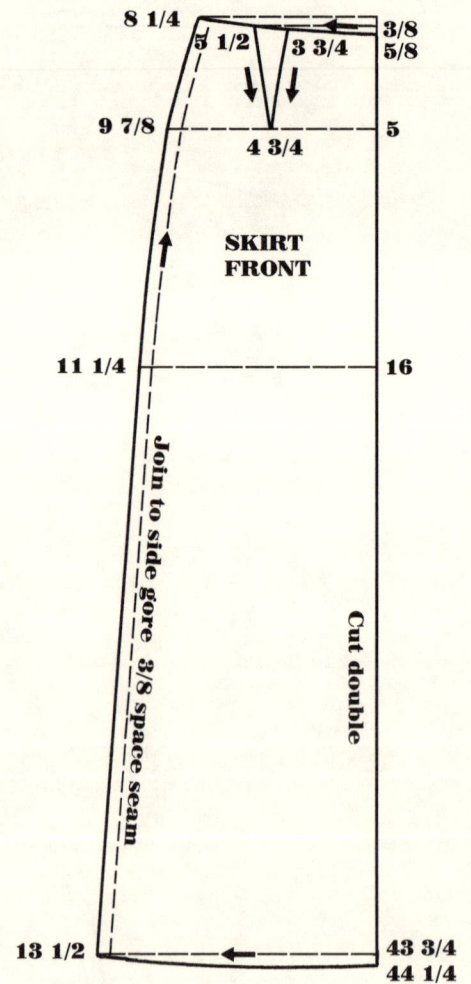

SKIRT FRONT

8 1/4   5 1/2   3 3/4   3/8
5/8
9 7/8   4 3/4   5
11 1/4   16
Join to side gore 3/8 space seam
Cut double
13 1/2   43 3/4
44 1/4

106

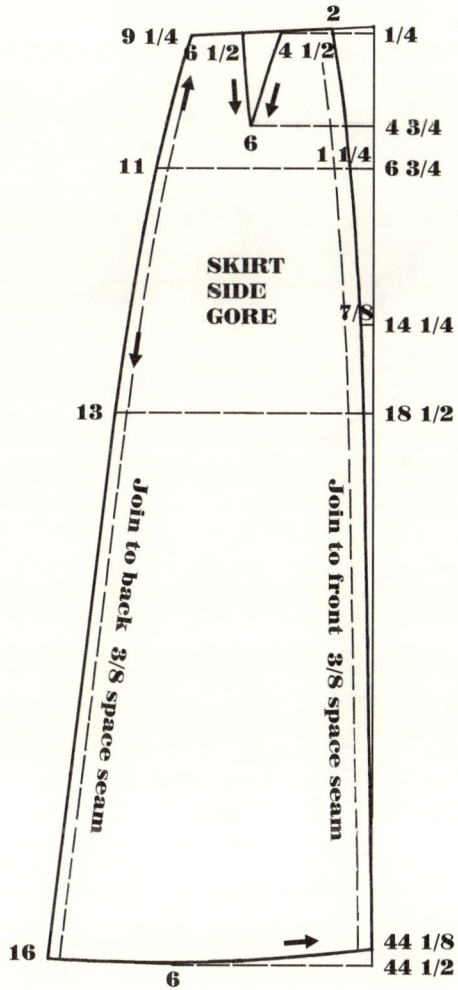

SKIRT
SIDE
GORE

Join to back 3/8 space seam

Join to front 3/8 space seam

9 1/4
2
1/4
6 1/2
4 1/2
4 3/4
6
11
1 1/4
6 3/4
7/8
14 1/4
13
18 1/2
16
44 1/8
6
44 1/2

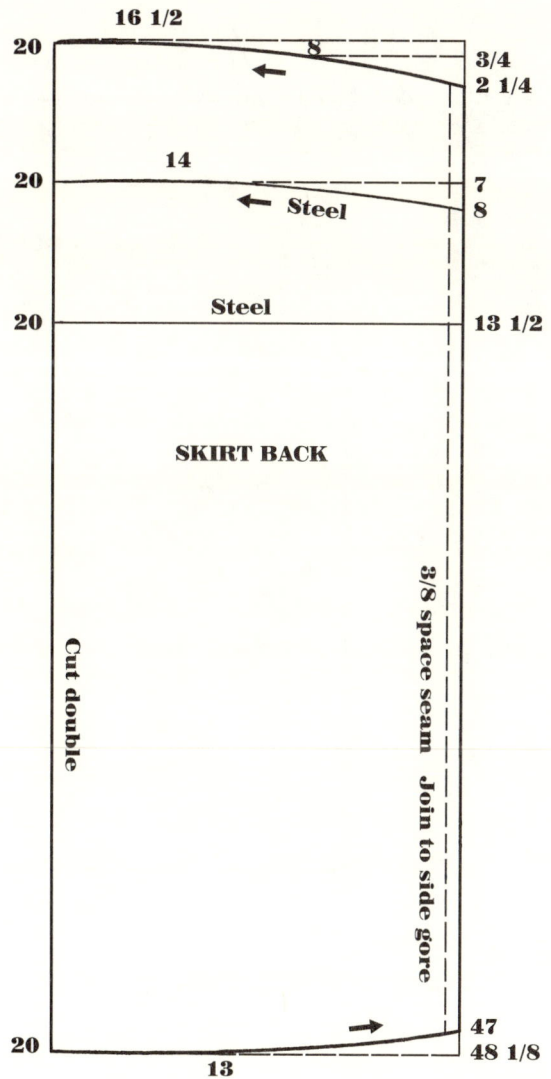

SKIRT BACK

Cut double

3/8 space seam   Join to side gore

Steel
Steel

16 1/2
20
8
3/4
2 1/4
20
14
7
Steel
8
20
Steel
13 1/2
20
47
13
48 1/8

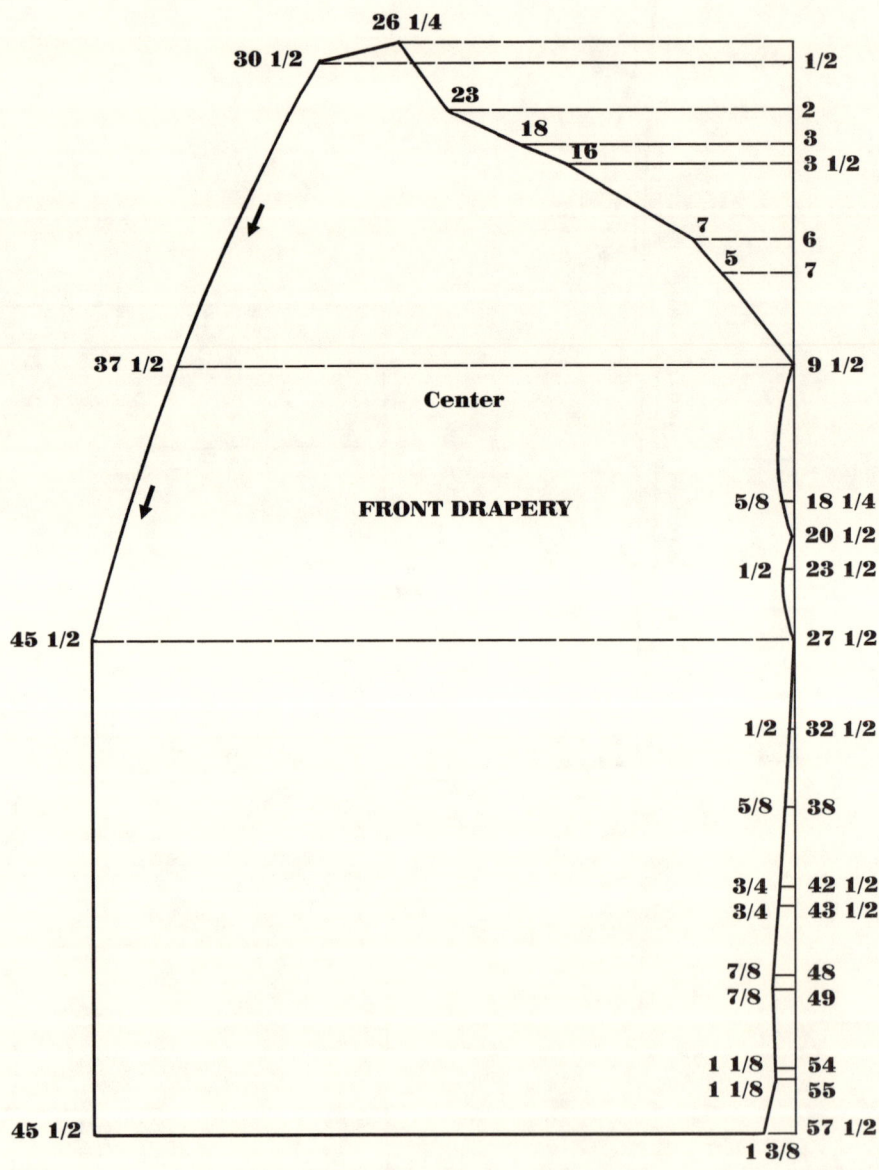

26 1/4

30 1/2

1/2

23

2

18

3

16

3 1/2

7

6

5

7

37 1/2

9 1/2

Center

FRONT DRAPERY

5/8

18 1/4

20 1/2

1/2

23 1/2

45 1/2

27 1/2

1/2

32 1/2

5/8

38

3/4

42 1/2

3/4

43 1/2

7/8

48

7/8

49

1 1/8

54

1 1/8

55

45 1/2

57 1/2

1 3/8

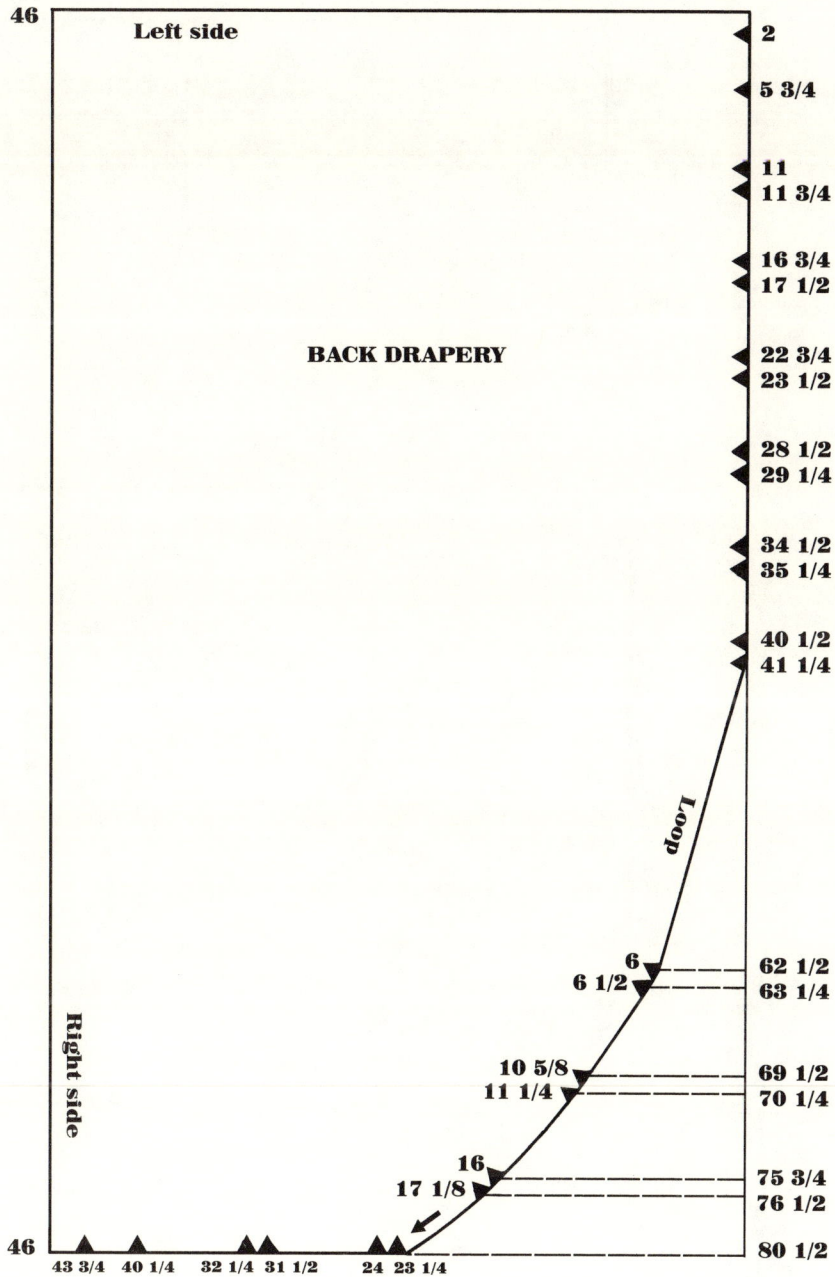

Left side

46

2

5 3/4

11
11 3/4

16 3/4
17 1/2

BACK DRAPERY

22 3/4
23 1/2

28 1/2
29 1/4

34 1/2
35 1/4

40 1/2
41 1/4

Loop

Right side

6
6 1/2

62 1/2
63 1/4

10 5/8
11 1/4

69 1/2
70 1/4

16
17 1/8

75 3/4
76 1/2

46

80 1/2

43 3/4 40 1/4   32 1/4 31 1/2   24 23 1/4

WRAP COLLAR

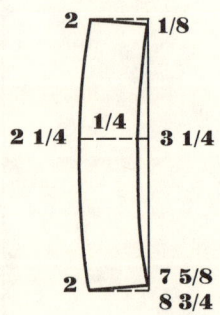

2   1/8

2 1/4   1/4   3 1/4

2   7 5/8
          8 3/4

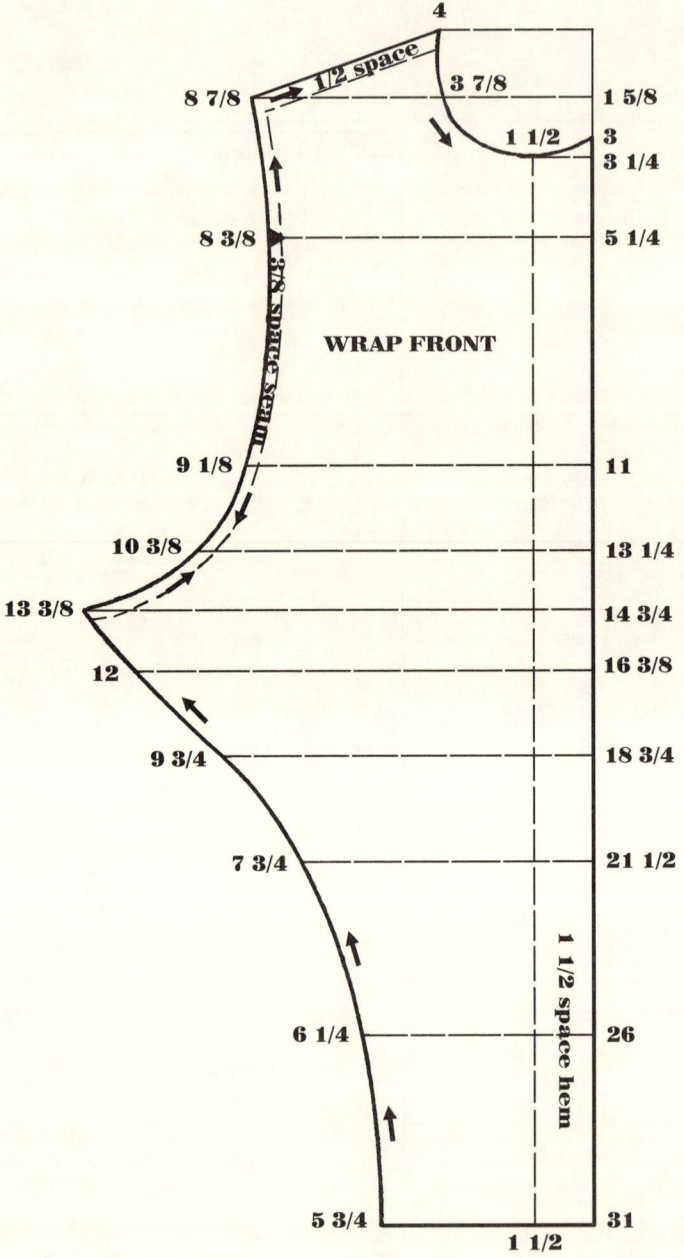

WRAP FRONT

4

8 7/8 1/2 space 3 7/8   1 5/8

1 1/2   3
              3 1/4

8 3/8   5 1/4

3/8 space seam

9 1/8   11

10 3/8   13 1/4

13 3/8   14 3/4

12   16 3/8

9 3/4   18 3/4

7 3/4   21 1/2

1 1/2 space hem

6 1/4   26

5 3/4   31
   1 1/2

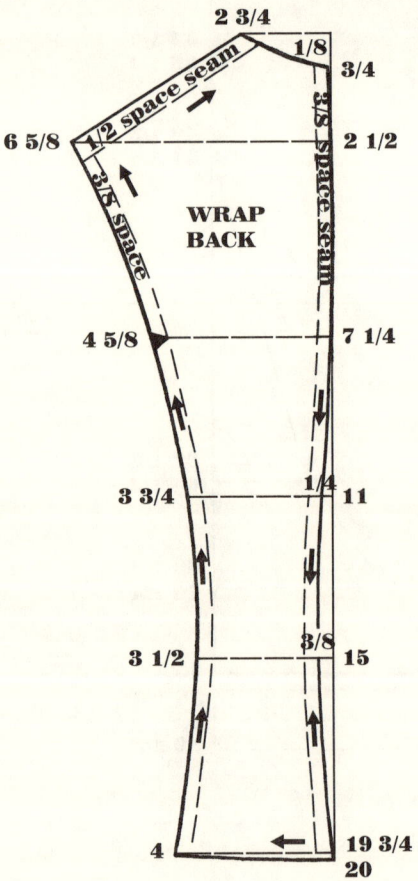

WRAP BACK

2 3/4
    1/8
    3/4

1/2 space seam

6 5/8   2 1/2

3/8 space seam

3/8 space

4 5/8   7 1/4

3 3/4 1/4 11

3 1/2 3/8 15

4   19 3/4
    20

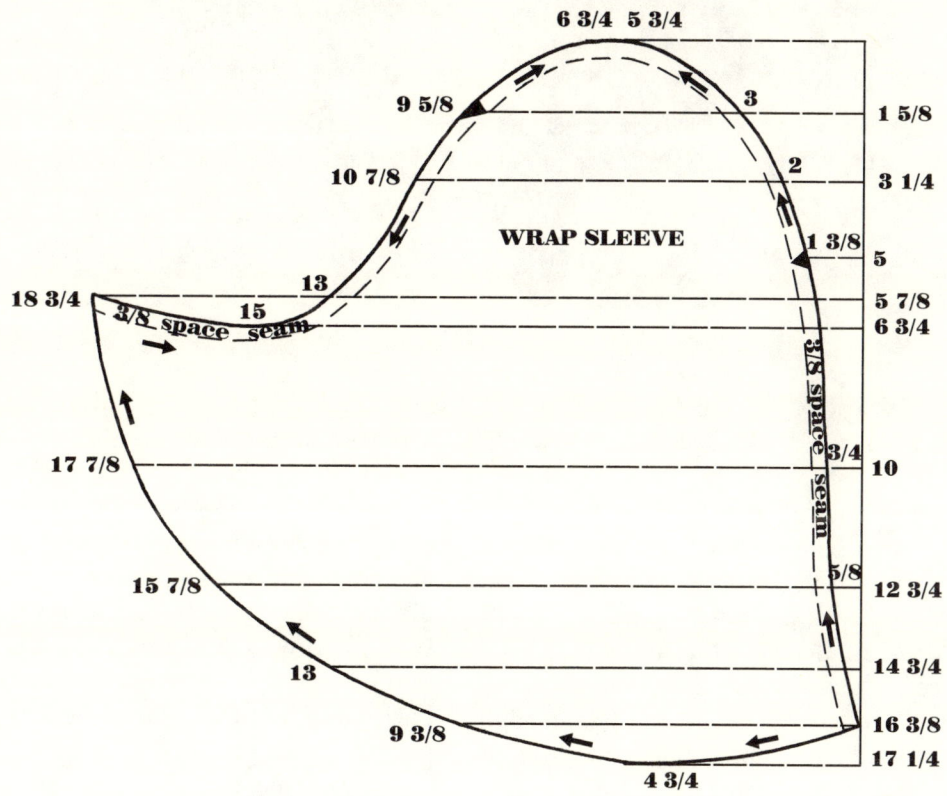

WRAP SLEEVE

6 3/4 5 3/4

9 5/8

10 7/8

13

18 3/4

15

3/8 space seam

17 7/8

15 7/8

13

9 3/8

4 3/4

3

1 5/8

2

3 1/4

1 3/8

5

5 7/8

6 3/4

3/8 space seam

3/4

10

5/8

12 3/4

14 3/4

16 3/8

17 1/4

Ladies' Wrap. This wrap has the effect of a dolman but is closer in fit. It is pictured made of corded silk and striped beaded net. The loose, narrow fronts fall in tabs considerably below the waist-line, to which point they are closed with hooks and eyes. The back falls short and plain on the tournure, and is closely fitted by side-back and center back seams. Between the fronts and back are side pieces, which extend some distance above the waist-line and are curved at the lower edge continuously with the front. The sleeves are of beaded net lined with silk and fall gracefully over the arms, presenting a rounded lower outline. Each is formed of a large upper part, and a small under part, joined by a curved seam along the inside of the arm. The high dolman curve is visible at their sewing to the armholes. Below these they pass into the side-back seams to the lower edge of the back, the under parts falling in points and being invisible when the garment is adjusted.

A frill of lace headed by a band of passementerie borders the lower edges of the back, side pieces, and sleeves, and is continued down the back edges of the fronts. At the lower edges of the tabs and along the front edges of the fronts, the lace is arranged in soft jabots. A V-shaped passementerie ornament overlies the center of the back nearly to the waist-line. A band of passementerie passes across the shoulder along the seaming of the sleeve, and down this seam to the bust in front and to below the waist-line at the back. The high standing collar is overlaid with passementerie, and its ends close in the front. A belt-tape basted to the seams at the back and closed in front is generally required to perfect the adjustment.

Sicilienne, faille Française and imperiale, bengaline, and merveilleux are favored for this wrap. Beaded nets are stylish over colored or black satins, and they are especially fancied in combination with velvet. Passementerie, jet, and jetted lace are the preferred trimmings, but braid or cord passementerie or feather bands may be used. The wrap may be made to match a special costume. For a lady of medium size, this wrap needs 3 3/8 yards of material 22 inches wide, 1 5/8 yards of material 44 inches wide, or 1 3/8 yards of material 54 inches wide. As represented, it calls for 2 1/8 yards of silk 20 inches wide, and 1 3/8 yards of beaded net 27 inches wide.

May 1888 *Delineator*

Street Costume with Wrap

Draft the basque with the scale corresponding to the bust measure. It is in seven pieces: Front, vest, side piece, side back, back, and two sleeve pieces. Lay four side-plaits on each side of the back. Turn away the front on the dashed line, and fasten it firmly to the vest. The vest may be of the same material or of a contrasting color.

The skirt is drafted with the scale corresponding to the waist measure. The length is regulated with the tape measure. The skirt is in three pieces: Front, side gore, and back. Any kind of trimming may be used; braid is very stylish.

The skirt drapery is drafted with the scale corresponding to the waist measure. It is in two pieces: Front and back. Lay plaits according to the notches in the front and back. The front drapery forms a point on each side of the skirt; therefore, cut two pieces just alike. The back, when plaited up, forms one point. The loop is in the center of the back. It is not necessary to cut the material on the curved diagonal line running from 28 on the first cross-line to 29 1/4 on the base-line. Simply turn it away, mark the plaits with a tracing wheel, and lay the plaits.

The wrap is drafted with the scale corresponding to the bust measure. It is in four pieces: Front, back, sleeve, and collar. This wrap may be made of silk, satin, velvet, or the same material as the dress–that is, the front and back. The sleeves are generally made of some kind of jetted material and finished with fringe, with an ornament down the back and front.

Summer 1888 *Voice of Fashion*

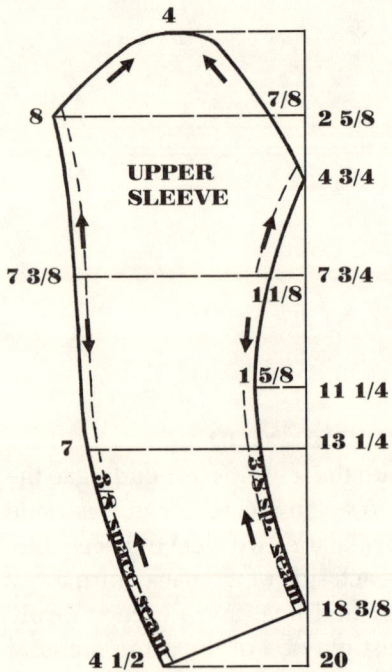

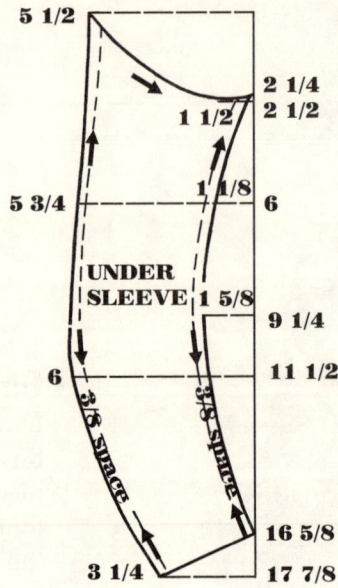

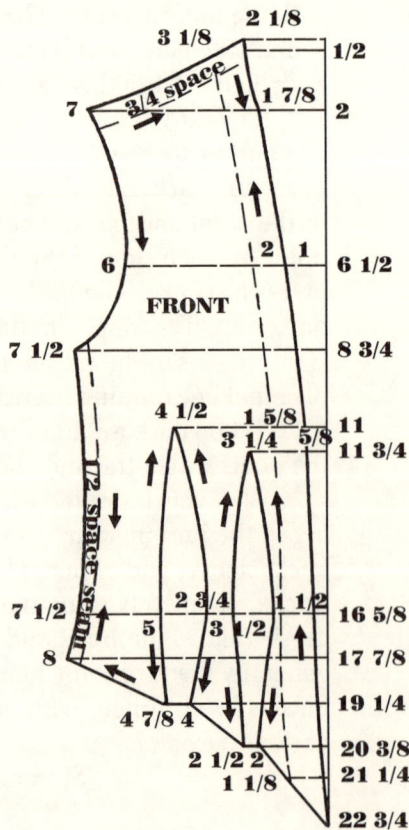

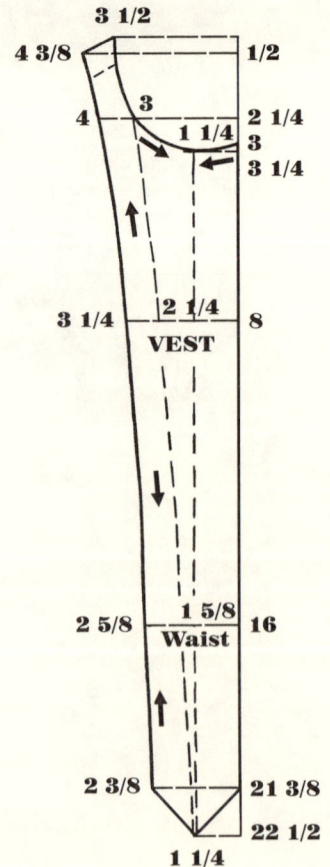

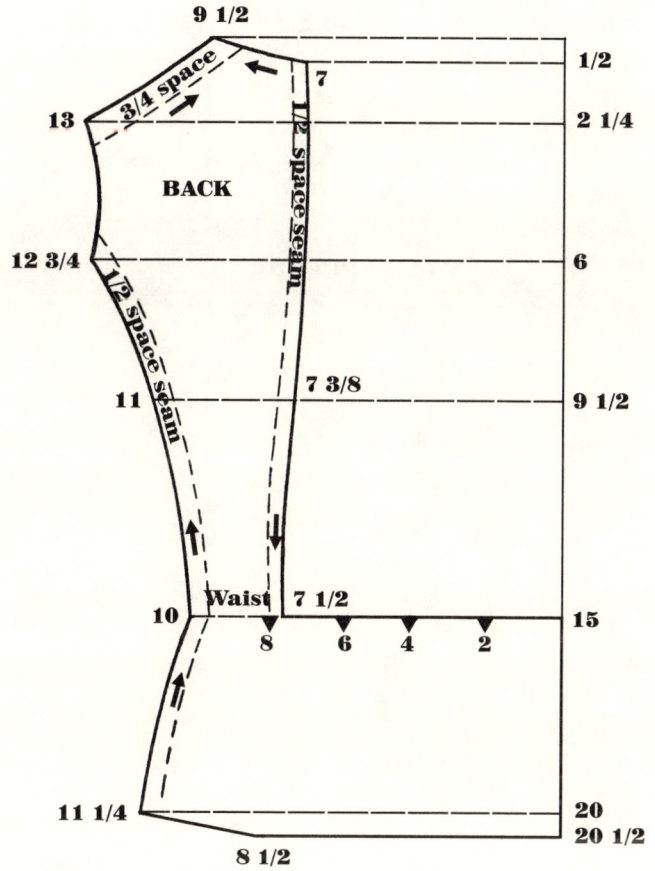

9 1/2

1/2

2 1/4

3/4 space

7

13

BACK

1/2 space seam

12 3/4

6

1/2 space seam

11

7 3/8

9 1/2

Waist

7 1/2

10

15

8 6 4 2

11 1/4

20

20 1/2

8 1/2

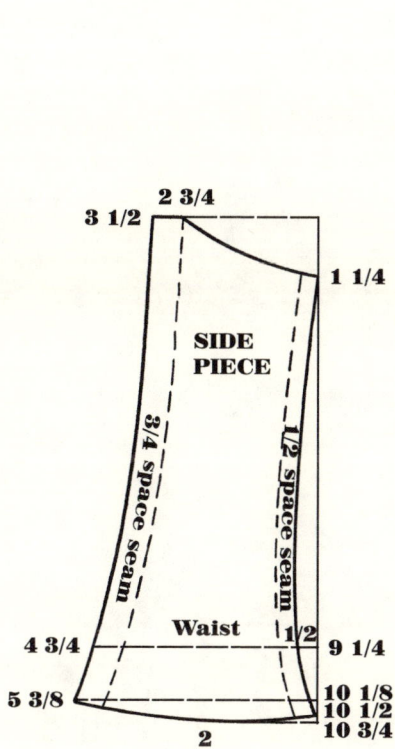

2 3/4

3 1/2

1 1/4

SIDE
PIECE

3/4 space seam

1/2 space seam

Waist

4 3/4

1/2

9 1/4

5 3/8

10 1/8
10 1/2

2

10 3/4

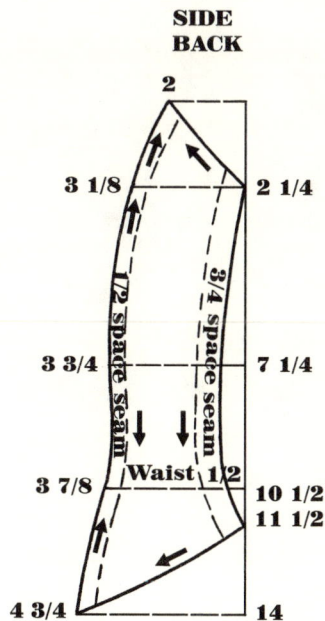

SIDE
BACK

2

3 1/8

2 1/4

1/2 space seam

3/4 space seam

3 3/4

7 1/4

Waist

3 7/8

1/2

3 7/8

10 1/2
11 1/2

4 3/4

14

115

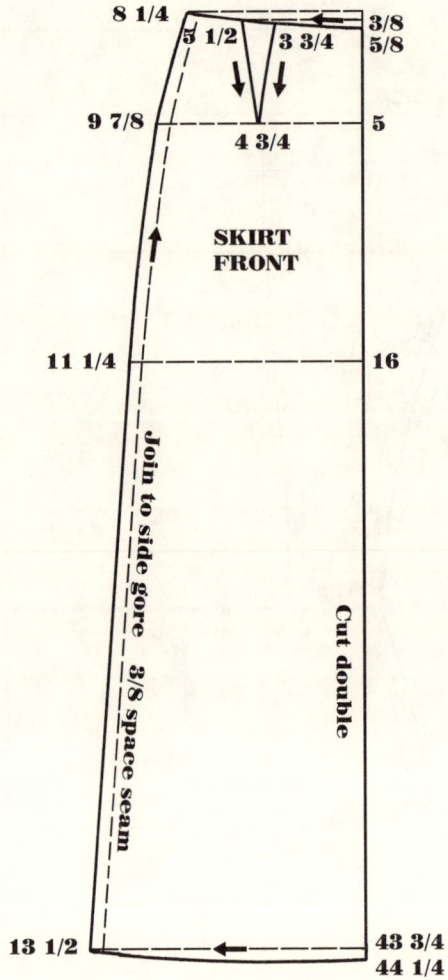

SKIRT FRONT

8 1/4

5 1/2   3 3/4   3/8 / 5/8

9 7/8   4 3/4   5

11 1/4   16

Join to side gore   3/8 space seam

Cut double

13 1/2   43 3/4 / 44 1/4

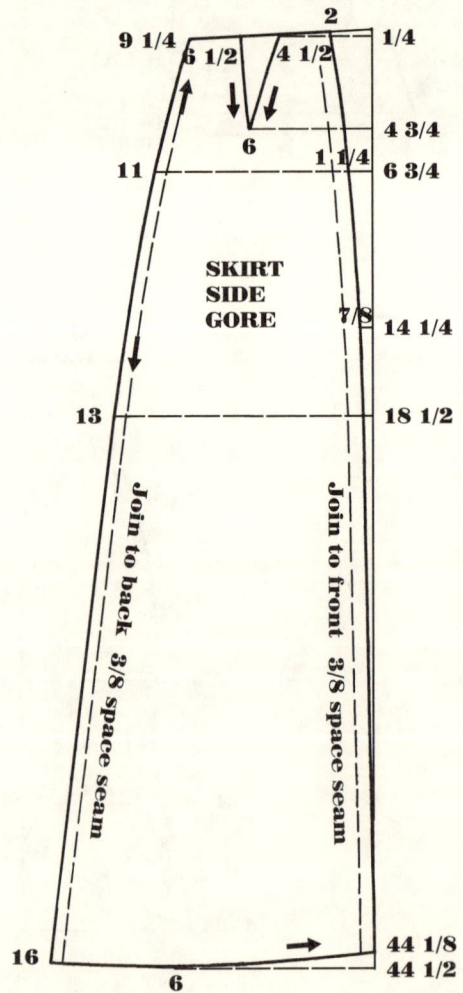

SKIRT SIDE GORE

2   1/4

9 1/4   6 1/2   4 1/2

4 3/4

11   6   1 1/4   6 3/4

7/8   14 1/4

13   18 1/2

Join to back   3/8 space seam

Join to front   3/8 space seam

16   44 1/8 / 44 1/2

6

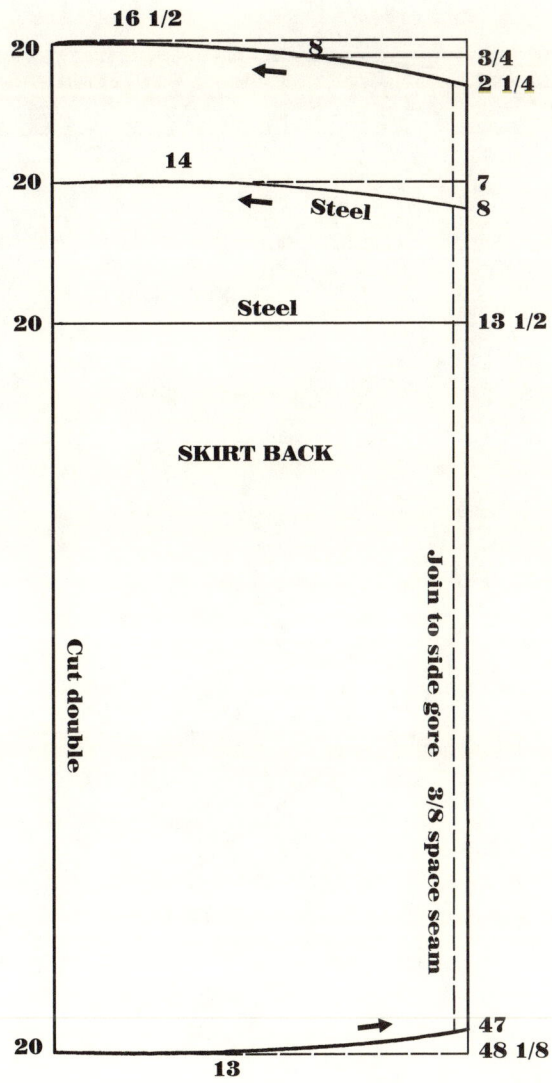

16 1/2

20

8

3/4
2 1/4

20

14

7
8

Steel

20

Steel

13 1/2

SKIRT BACK

Cut double

Join to side gore   3/8 space seam

47
48 1/8

20

13

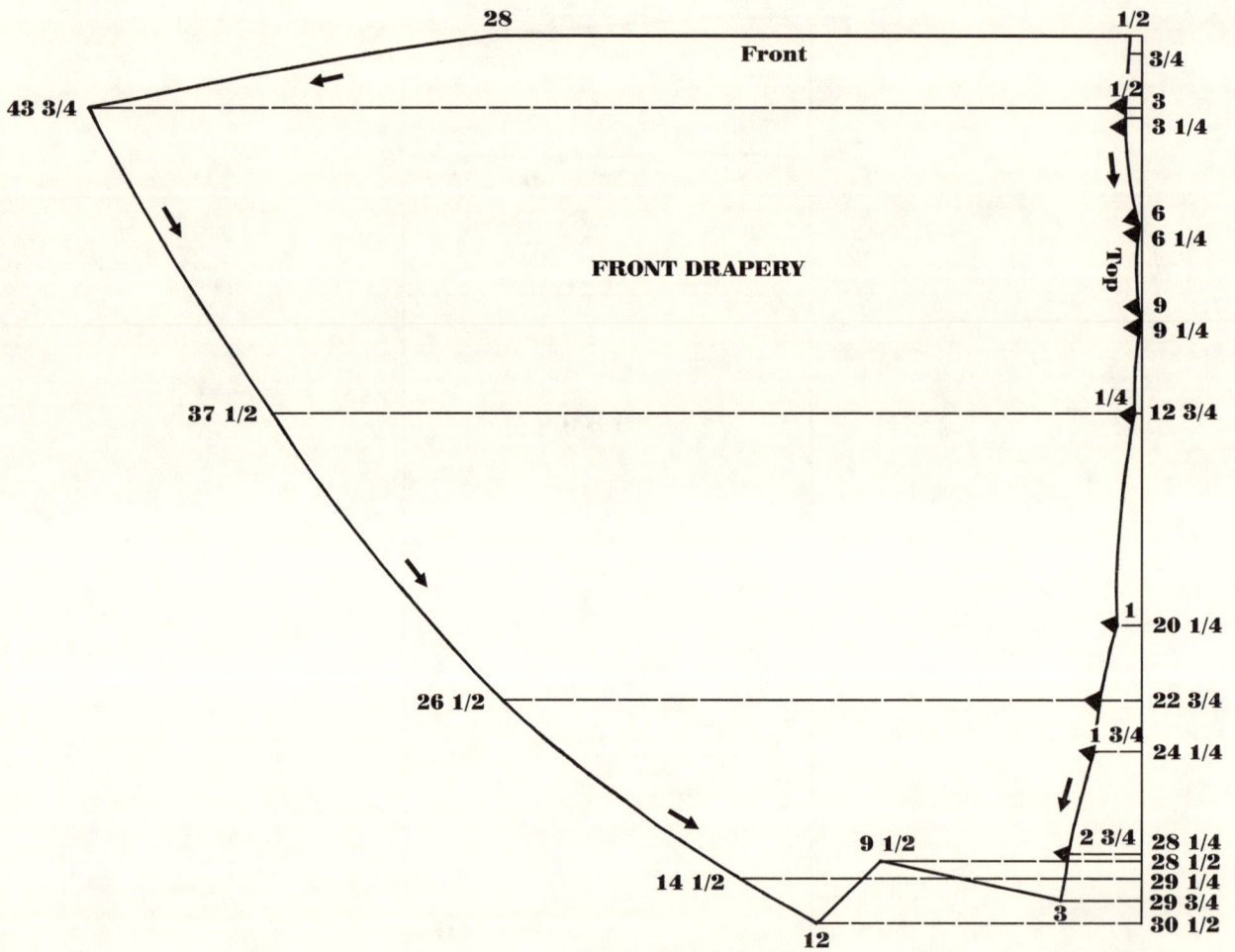

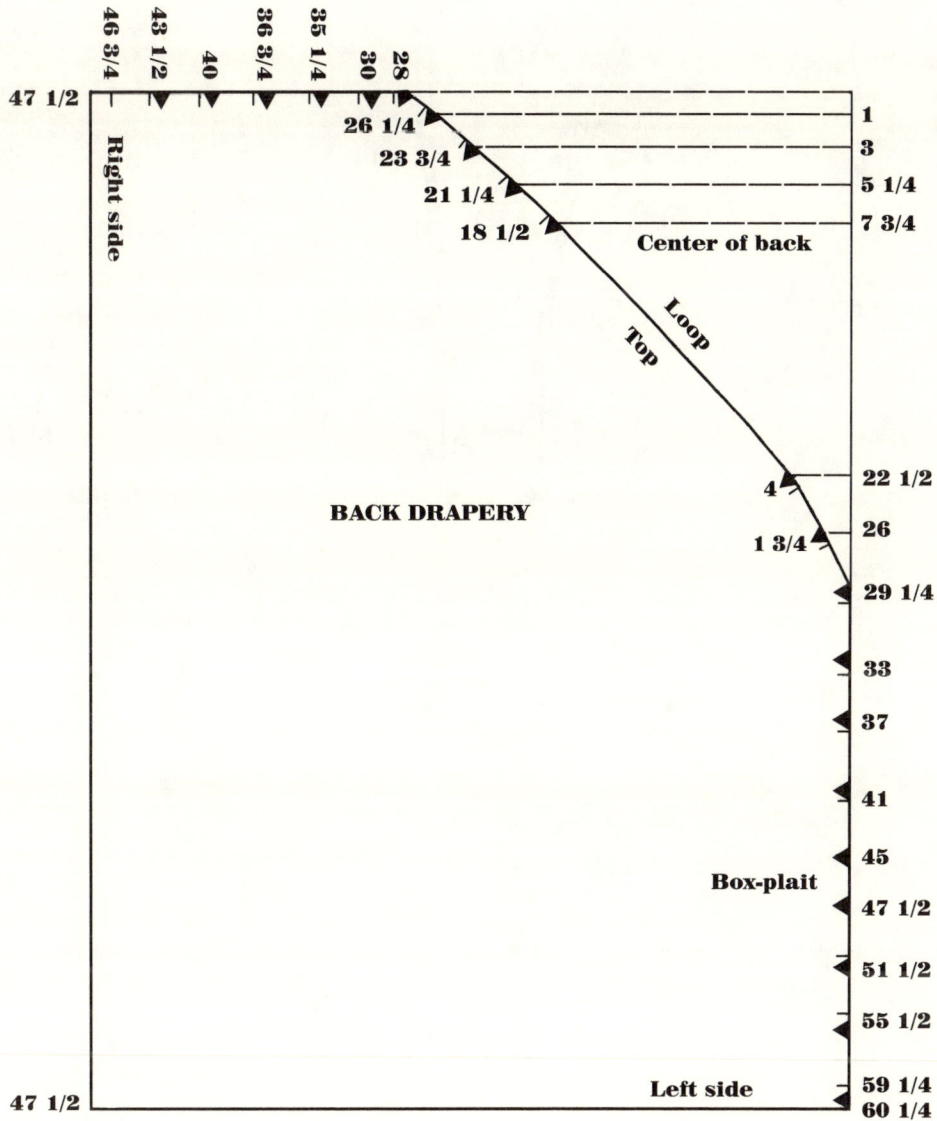

47 1/2

46 3/4   **43 1/2**   **40**   **36 3/4**   **35 1/4**   **30**   **28**

Right side

26 1/4

23 3/4

21 1/4

18 1/2

1

3

5 1/4

7 3/4

Center of back

Loop

Top

BACK DRAPERY

4   **22 1/2**

1 3/4   **26**

29 1/4

33

37

41

45

Box-plait   **47 1/2**

51 1/2

55 1/2

Left side   **59 1/4**

47 1/2   **60 1/4**

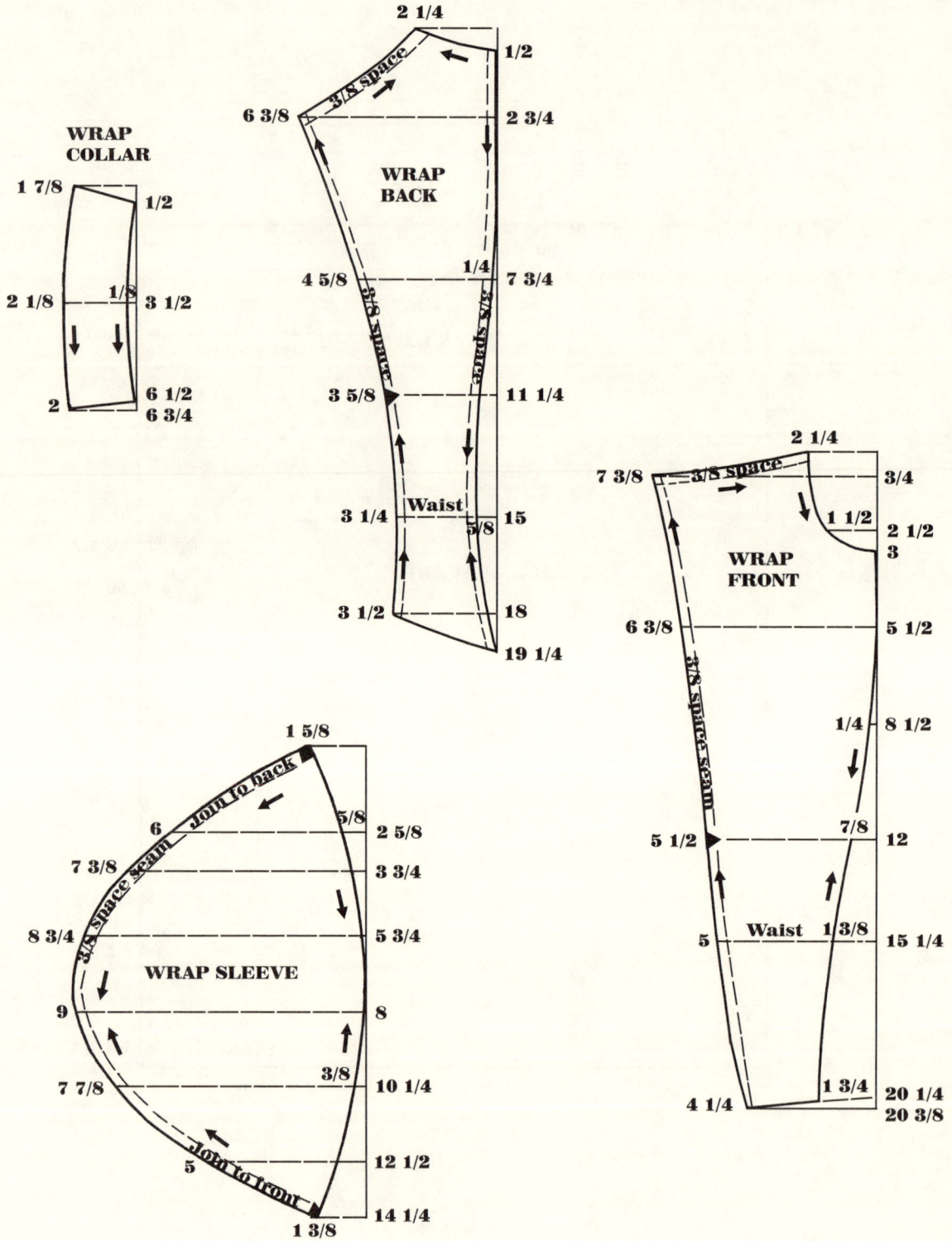

WRAP COLLAR

1 7/8   1/2

2 1/8   1/8   3 1/2

2   6 1/2   6 3/4

WRAP BACK

2 1/4   1/2

3/8 space

6 3/8   2 3/4

4 5/8   1/4   7 3/4

3/8 space

3 5/8   11 1/4

3 1/4   Waist   15

5/8

3 1/2   18

19 1/4

WRAP FRONT

2 1/4

7 3/8   3/8 space   3/4

1 1/2   2 1/2

3

6 3/8   5 1/2

3/8 space seam

1/4   8 1/2

5 1/2   7/8   12

5   Waist   1 3/8   15 1/4

4 1/4   1 3/4   20 1/4

20 3/8

WRAP SLEEVE

1 5/8

Join to back   5/8   2 5/8

6

3/8 space seam

7 3/8   3 3/4

8 3/4   5 3/4

9   8

7 7/8   3/8   10 1/4

Join to front

5   12 1/2

1 3/8   14 1/4

Ladies' Wrap

Ladies' Wrap. Beaded grenadine is united with velvet in the formation of this wrap. The fronts extend in slender tabs a little below the waist-line and are closed with hooks and eyes, each front being hemmed. The back is tapered off to a sharp point, which extends to about the same distance below the waist-line. The back has no center seam, the seams joining it and the front to the side parts being curved so as to render such a seam unnecessary. The side parts extend quite high on the shoulders. The shoulder seam is carried along the top of each until it meets a dart seam, which crosses the top of the arm and is indispensable to the high curved effect. When the dart seam is being closed the lower edge is held a little full, and by this means the curve is rendered prominent but not exaggerated. The side parts fall to a graceful length on the arms. The front and back are drawn in to the figure by elastic straps, which are fastened at the lower edges of the sides beneath the side-back and side-front seams.

A high standing collar finishes the neck, and outside it is a band of passementerie. A similar decoration passes along the side-back and side-front seams and below the side parts to the lower edges of the back and front. On the side parts are passementerie epaulettes, which are curved at their tops to follow the direction of the dart seams and have pendants hanging from their lower edges. A fringe of passementerie drop ornaments attached to a gimp borders the lower edges of the side parts and fronts, and a passementerie ornament heads the trimming on each side of the front.

In wraps of this style the side parts are often of lace net, and the decoration consists of lace edging. This mode may be made up in any kind of suit material or summer wrap material. To make the wrap for a lady of medium size, requires 2 yards of material 22 inches wide, 3/4 yard of material 48 inches wide, or 5/8 yard of material 54 inches wide. In the combination shown, it needs 7/8 yard of beaded grenadine and 1 1/8 yards of velvet, each 20 inches wide.

July 1886 Delineator

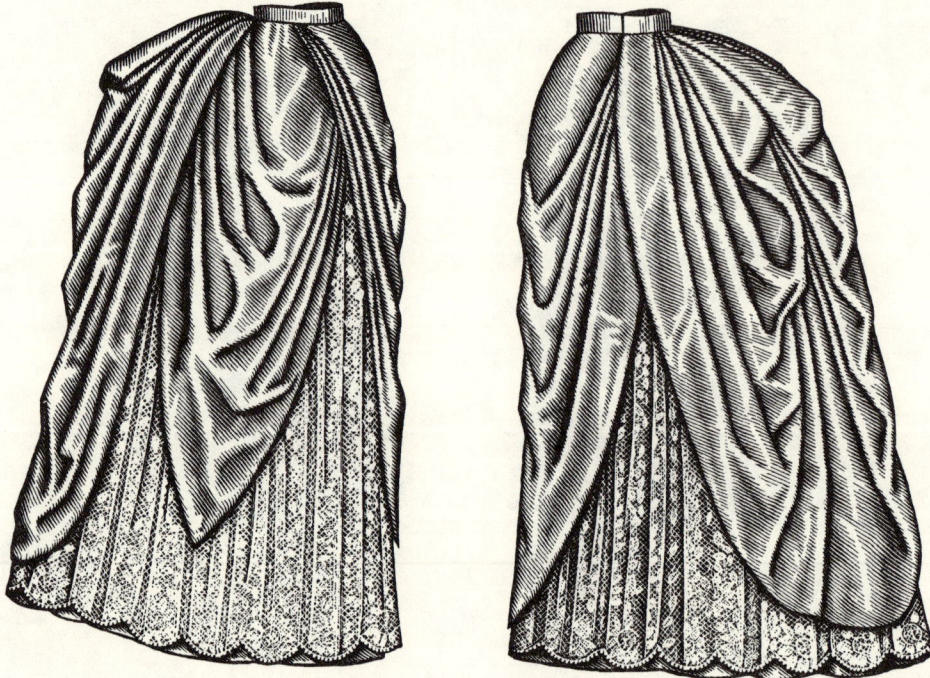

Walking-Length Skirt. This engraving depicts silk trimmed with lace flouncing. The foundation skirt is composed of three gores and a full back breadth. The gores are fitted smoothly by darts, while the breadth is gathered across the top. The extra length at the top may be cut off if a bustle is not worn. Steels run through casings are tied into bouffant curves by tapes sewed at their ends, but the steels may be omitted. The skirt should be as long as it can be worn without the edge dragging on the ground.

The drapery consists of three sections, two of which fall on the gores. The narrower of these two has four diagonal, upward-turning plaits folded in its back edge near the top, this edge being sewed into the right side-back seam of the skirt. Turning toward the front edge are three overlapping plaits, which are folded in at the top. Back of these plaits, enough fullness to produce an easy adjustment over the hip is held in place by a few gathers. This section is overlapped at the top by the wider front drapery, which has three forward-turning plaits and a short gathering at its top. It has four deep, overlapping, upward-turning plaits in its back edge. Below the point where they cease to lap, the front edges of these draperies flare

widely, and the back edge of the wider drapery is sewed along the front edge of the placket opening and is included in the seam below it. Both draperies fall with a pointed effect. The wider one is considerably deeper than the narrower and has a little fullness at its top.

The back drapery is a wide breadth. It is draped into an oval shape by means of plaits in the top and two deep burnous loops. Between the burnous loops are two plaits that turn toward the center, and turning toward each loop are six overlapping plaits.

Both skirt and drapery are sewed to the same belt. A basting is made through the front drapery to the skirt on each side, not far from the top, to prevent its being disarranged.

For a lady of medium size, the skirt requires 13 yards of material 22 inches wide, or 7 yards of material 44 inches wide. The lace flounce extends well up beneath the drapery and falls even with the bottom of the skirt. If the lace flounce is omitted, a box-plaiting or side-plaiting deep enough to extend well up under the drapery may take its place, or a narrow foot plaiting may be added.

February 1887 *Delineator*

Ladies' Costume

The basque is drafted with the scale corresponding to the bust measure. It is in seven pieces: Front, side piece, side back, back, two sleeve pieces, and collar. The basque is drafted in the same way as any other basque, but the effect when cut and made up is different. When cutting out the front, lay its front edge straight along the selvage. This gives the much sought-for bias appearance under the arm.

The skirt is drafted with the scale corresponding to the waist measure. The length is regulated with the tape measure. The skirt is in three pieces: Front, side gore, and back.

Draft the drapery with the scale corresponding to the waist measure. It is in three pieces: Front together with the right side, plaited panel for the left side, and half of the back. The back drapery is drafted differently, as you will see by examining the diagram. Instead of drawing cross-lines to the base-line, run down from the first cross-line. This is done to avoid extra lines and figures. Take care to keep the square even with the first cross-line.

Lay six upward-turning plaits on the right and front drapery according to the notches. The point is the upper part of the plait, and the star the under part. The left side panel consists of one double box-plait. Lay the plaits according to the notches, press them carefully, and stay them underneath with tape. On the first cross-line of the back drapery, the space between 8 3/4 and 29 1/2 is a loop turned wrong side out. Join the stars and sew them together on the wrong side. Lay the two remaining plaits, and baste them to the center of the skirt. Lay the plaits at the top of the drapery according to the notches.

Summer 1888 *Voice of Fashion*

SIDE PIECE

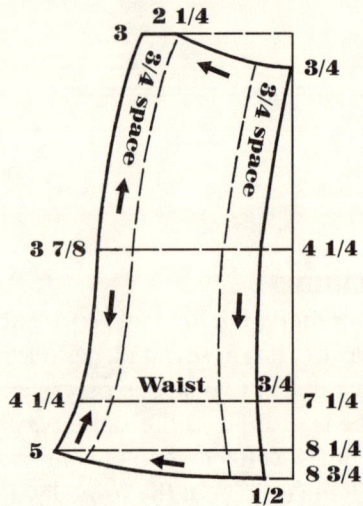

COLLAR

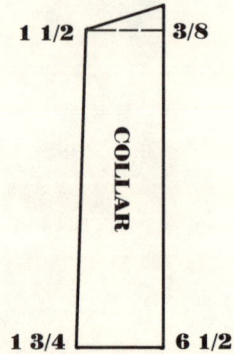

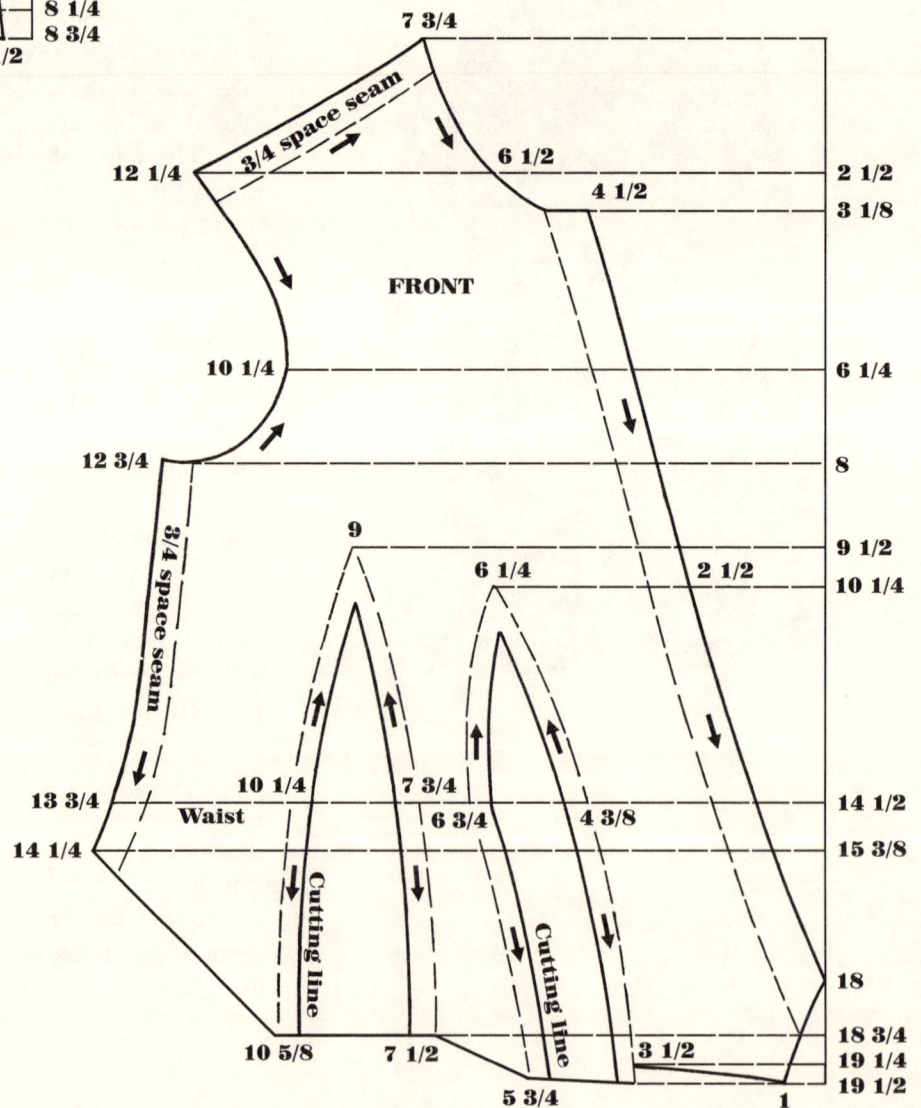

FRONT

Ladies' Costume

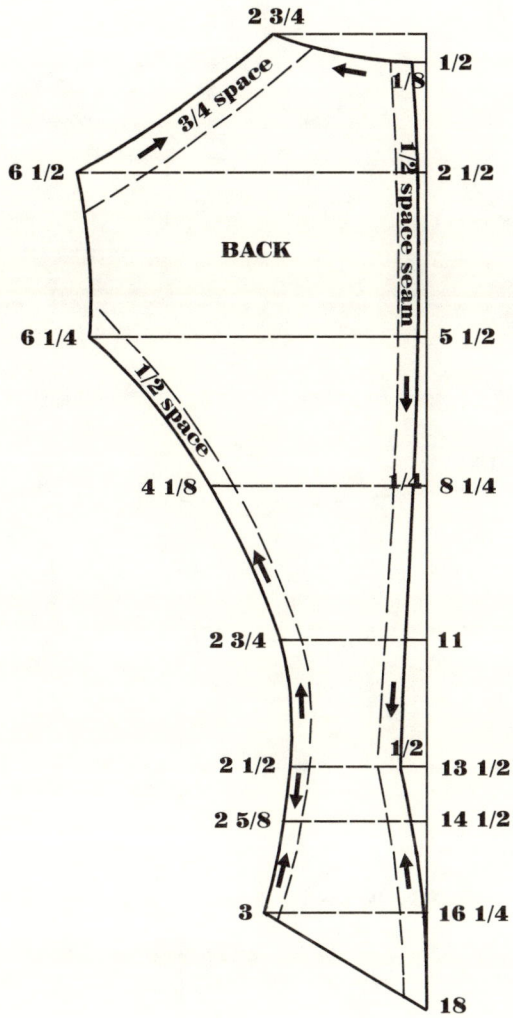

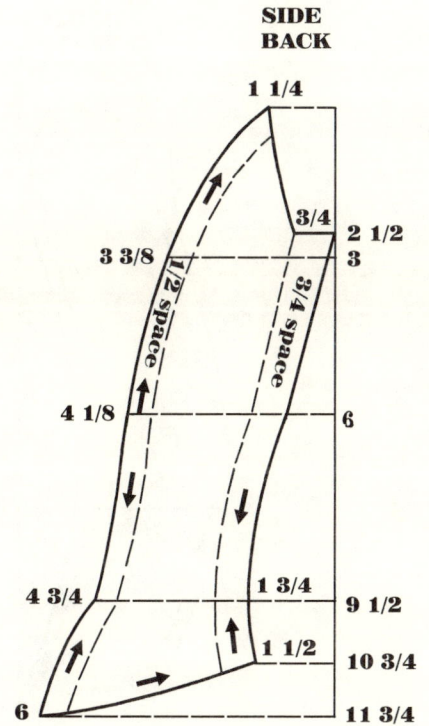

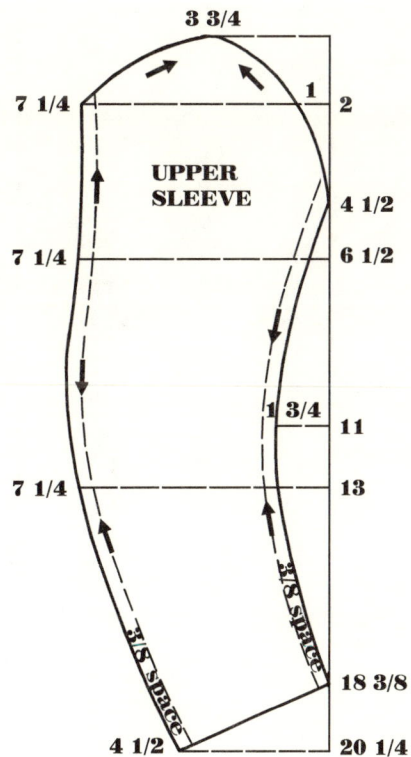

UNDER SLEEVE

4 3/8

2 1/4
1 1/4   2 1/2

5 1/4   5 1/4

1 3/4   9 3/4

6   11 1/4

3/8 space   3/8 space

16 3/4
3   18 3/8

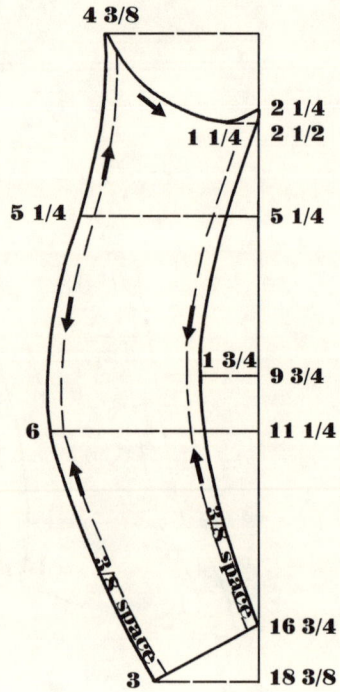

16 1/2

20   8   3/4
                       2 1/4

20   14   7
            Steel   8

20   Steel   13 1/2

SKIRT BACK

Cut double

Join to side gore 3/8 space seam

20   47
        13   48 1/8

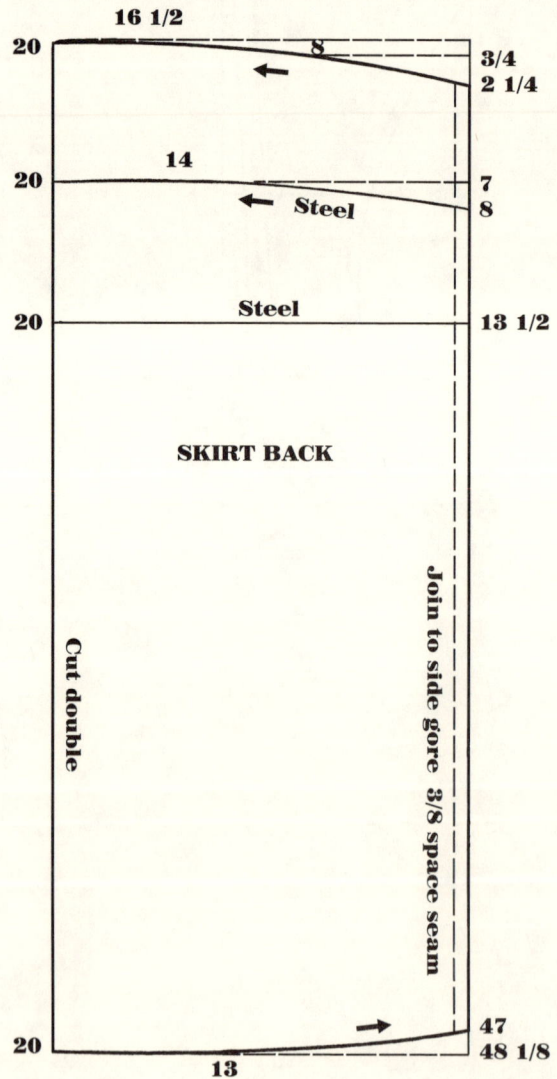

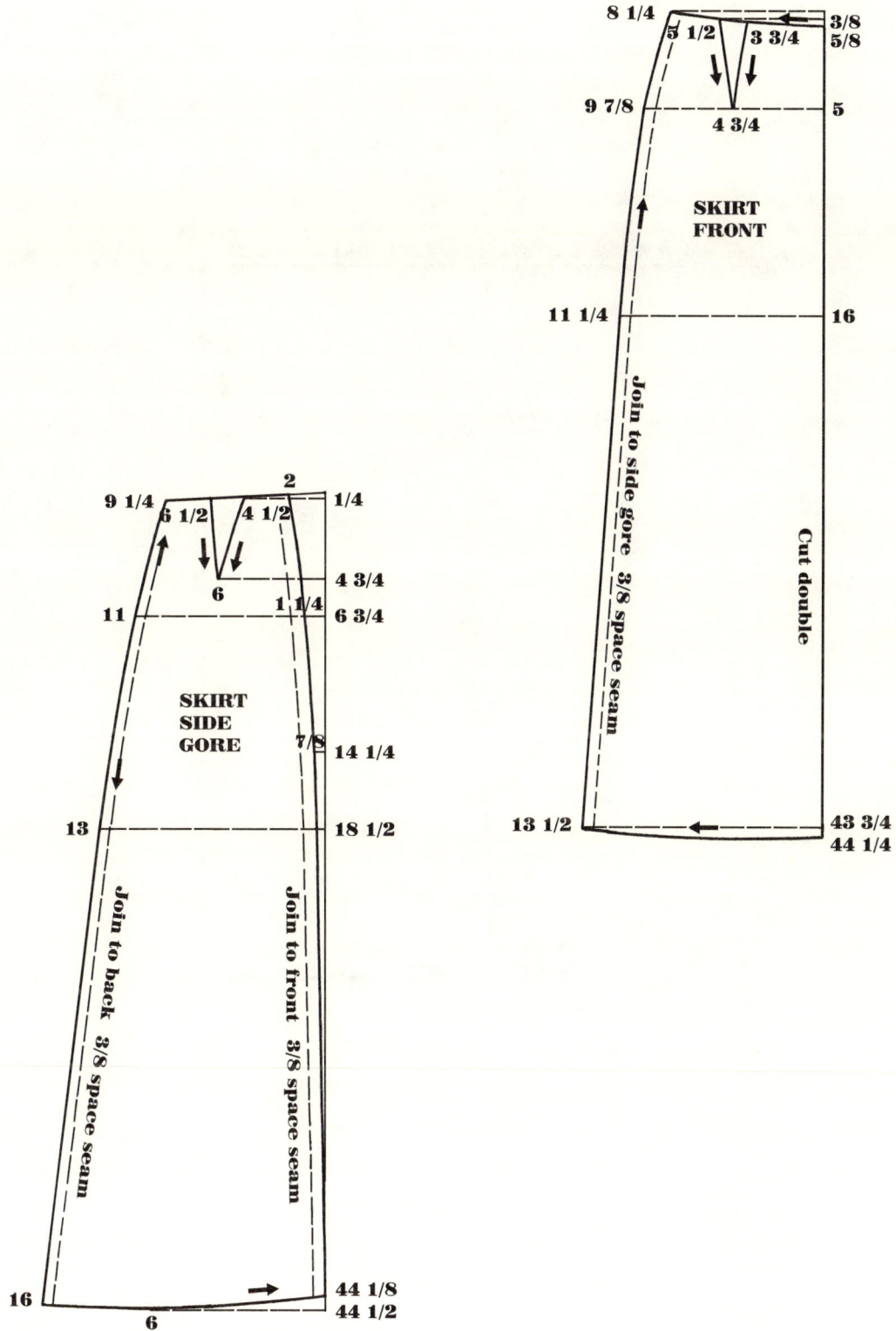

SKIRT FRONT

8 1/4   5 1/2   3 3/4   3/8
5/8

9 7/8   4 3/4   5

11 1/4   16

Join to side gore 3/8 space seam

Cut double

13 1/2   43 3/4
44 1/4

SKIRT SIDE GORE

2   1/4
9 1/4   6 1/2   4 1/2

6   4 3/4

11   1 1/4   6 3/4

7/8   14 1/4

13   18 1/2

Join to back 3/8 space seam

Join to front 3/8 space seam

16   44 1/8
6   44 1/2

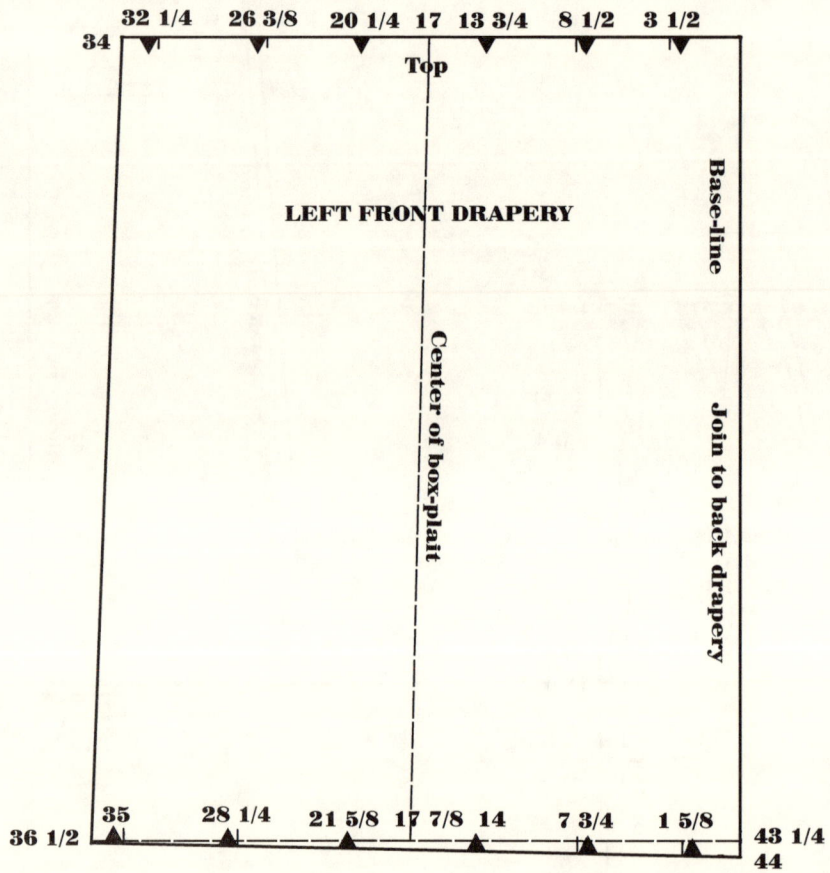

34   32 1/4   26 3/8   20 1/4   17   13 3/4   8 1/2   3 1/2

Top

LEFT FRONT DRAPERY

Base-line

Center of box-plait

Join to back drapery

36 1/2   35   28 1/4   21 5/8   17 7/8   14   7 3/4   1 5/8   43 1/4   44

33

26

1 5/8

3 3/4

30 3/4 *

19 1/4

5 1/2

38 3/4

25 *

7

18 1/4 *

9 1/2

13 3/4

10

12 1/2 *

14

8

15

7 *

18

39 3/4

4

20

2 3/4 *

23 1/4

RIGHT AND FRONT DRAPERY

26 3/4

1 3/4

33 1/4

42 1/4

1 7/8

35

1 1/4

40 1/2

43 1/2

46 1/4

3/4

54 3/4

1/2

63 3/4

66 1/2

44

67 1/2

129

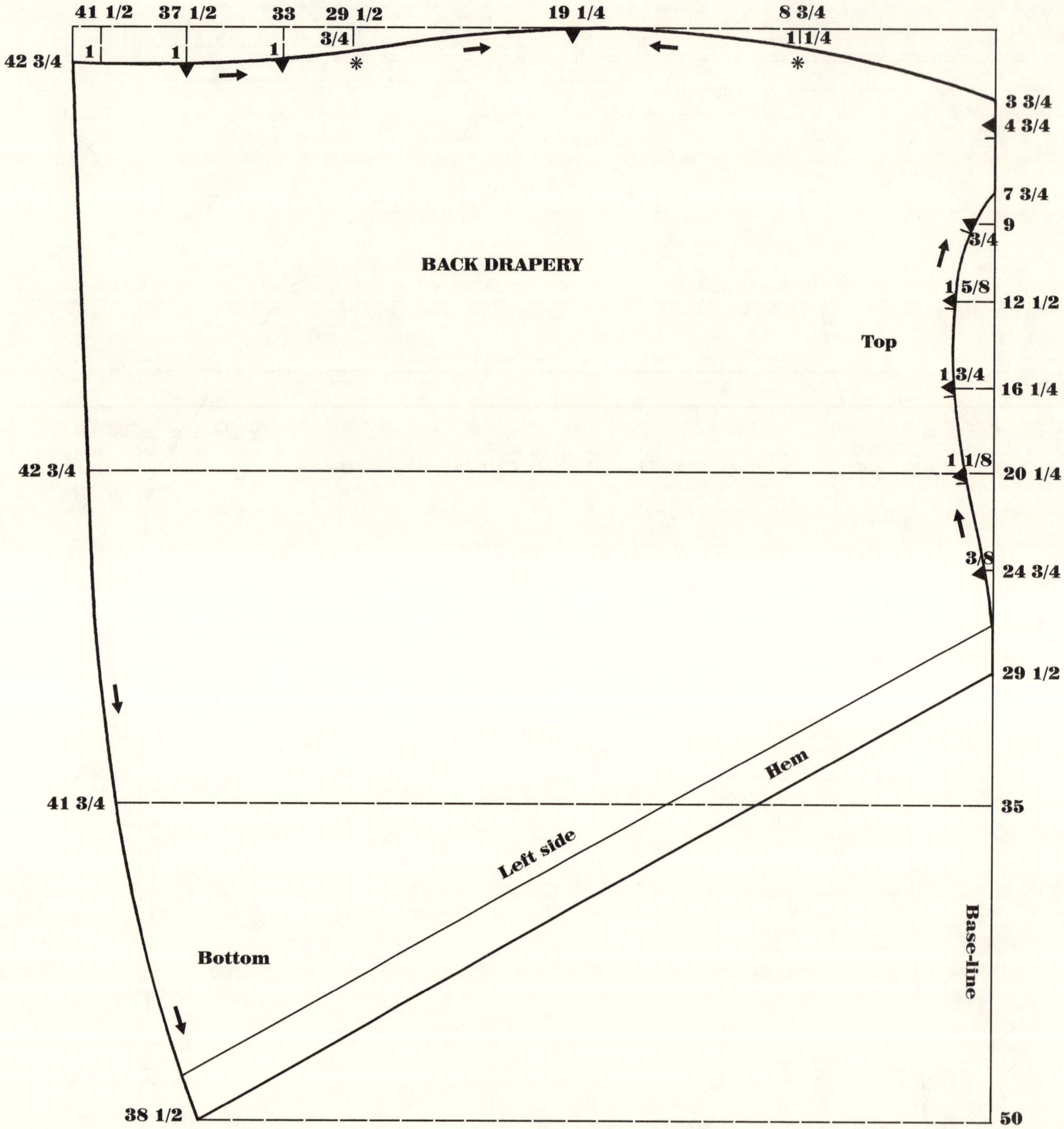

41 1/2   37 1/2   33   29 1/2   19 1/4   8 3/4

1   1   1   3/4   1 1/4

42 3/4

BACK DRAPERY

3 3/4
4 3/4

7 3/4
9
3/4

1 5/8   12 1/2

Top

1 3/4   16 1/4

42 3/4   1 1/8   20 1/4

3/8   24 3/4

29 1/2

Hem

41 3/4   35

Left side

Base-line

Bottom

38 1/2   50

130

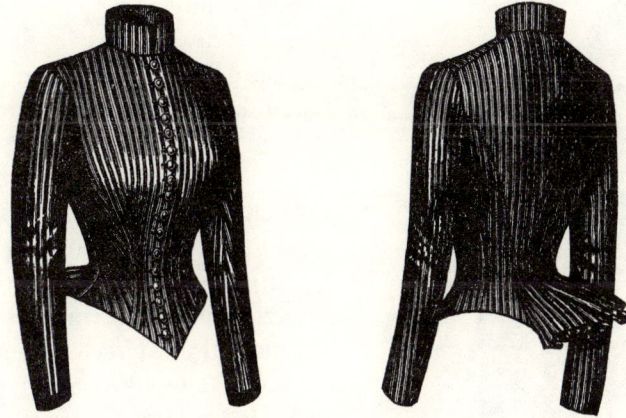

French Basque. This example was made up in suit material showing narrow stripes in alternation with hair-lines of a contrasting color. It is, of course, quite as well adapted to any other dress material. Any kind of decoration may be applied, from a braid binding to the most elaborate application of passementerie or galloon. For a lady of medium size, the basque requires 3 1/4 yards of material 22 inches wide, or 1 5/8 yards of material 44 inches wide.

The fronts are curved at their closing edges. The right side is underfaced, the closing being made with button-holes, and buttons to match the stripe. There are two bust darts in each side of the front. At the back are side backs and a curved center back seam, while there are side pieces between the back and front. On the front edges of the center back, below the waist-line, are allowed extensions. These, in conjunction with extra width allowed below the center back seam, are under-folded to form two double box-plaits. These spring out, and, being deeper than the rest of the basque, present something of a postilion effect. The lower edge curves upward over the hips and deepens to a point toward the center of the front. The sleeves are in coat shape and plainly finished. The standing collar is so skillfully curved and adjusted that its height is as comfortable as it is fashionable.

December 1886 *Delineator*

Ladies' Costume

The basque is drafted with the scale corresponding to the bust measure. It is in six pieces: Front, side back, back, two sleeve pieces, and collar. The front is cut double. Close the back with buttons and button-holes.

The drapery is drafted with the scale corresponding to the waist measure. The length is regulated with the tape measure. It is in two pieces: Front and back.

Lay the plaits according to the notches. However, at the back ten lines of shirring 3/4 inch apart will give a pretty and equally stylish effect. If you shirr the back drapery, use the skirt pattern given; each line of shirring should be basted to a plain foundation. The lower part of the back drapery should fall to the bottom of the dress skirt, and also the left side of the front drapery.

Fall 1888 *Voice of Fashion*

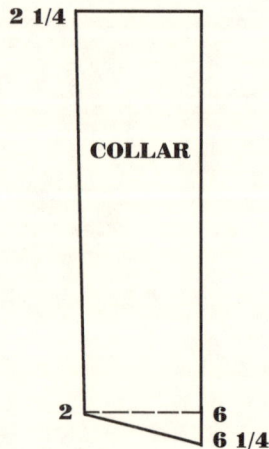

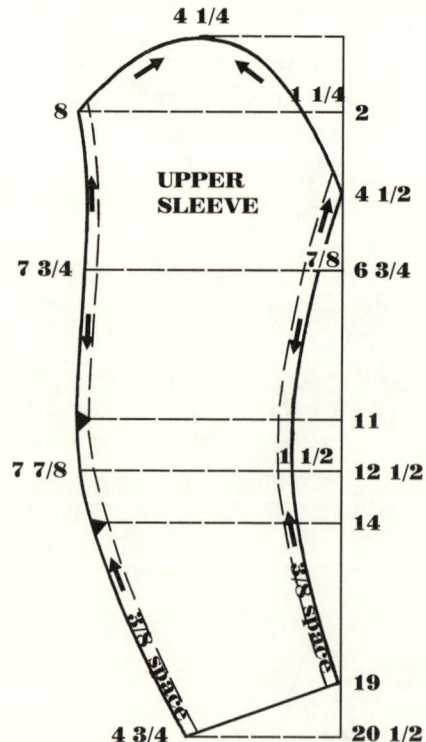

COLLAR

2 1/4

2   6
     6 1/4

UPPER SLEEVE

4 1/4
8   4 1/4   2
             4 1/2
7 3/4   7/8   6 3/4
                    11
7 7/8   1 1/2 12 1/2
                    14
3/8 space   3/8 space
                    19
4 3/4   20 1/2

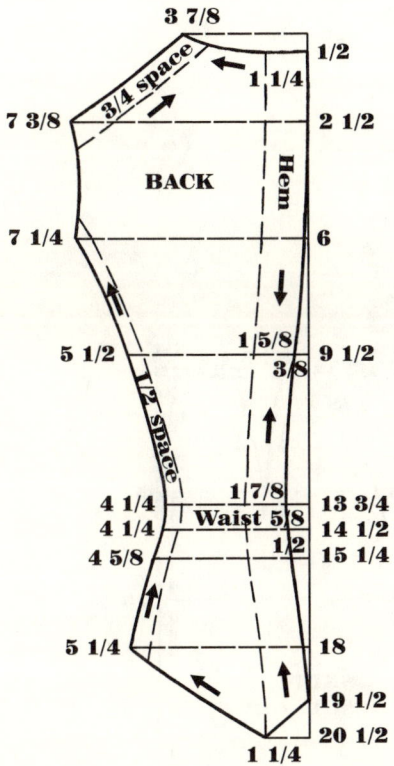

BACK

3 7/8
3/4 space
1 1/4
1/2
1 1/4
7 3/8
2 1/2
Hem
7 1/4
6
1/2 space
5 1/2
1 5/8
9 1/2
3/8
1 7/8
4 1/4   Waist 5/8   13 3/4
4 1/4   14 1/2
4 5/8   1/2   15 1/4
5 1/4   18
19 1/2
20 1/2
1 1/4

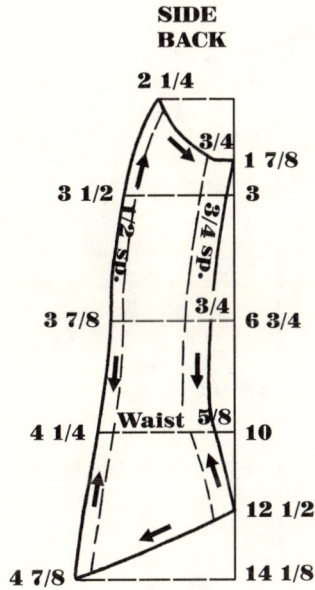

SIDE
BACK

2 1/4
3/4
1 7/8
3 1/2
3
1/2 sp.
3/4 sp.
3 7/8
3/4
6 3/4
Waist 5/8
4 1/4
10
12 1/2
4 7/8
14 1/8

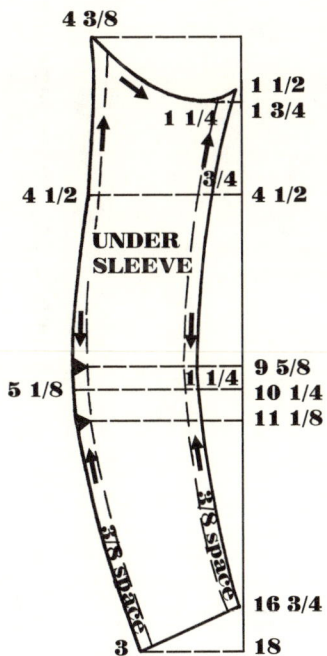

4 3/8
1 1/4
1 1/2
1 3/4
3/4
4 1/2   4 1/2
UNDER
SLEEVE
9 5/8
1 1/4
5 1/8
10 1/4
11 1/8
3/8 space
3/8 space
16 3/4
3   18

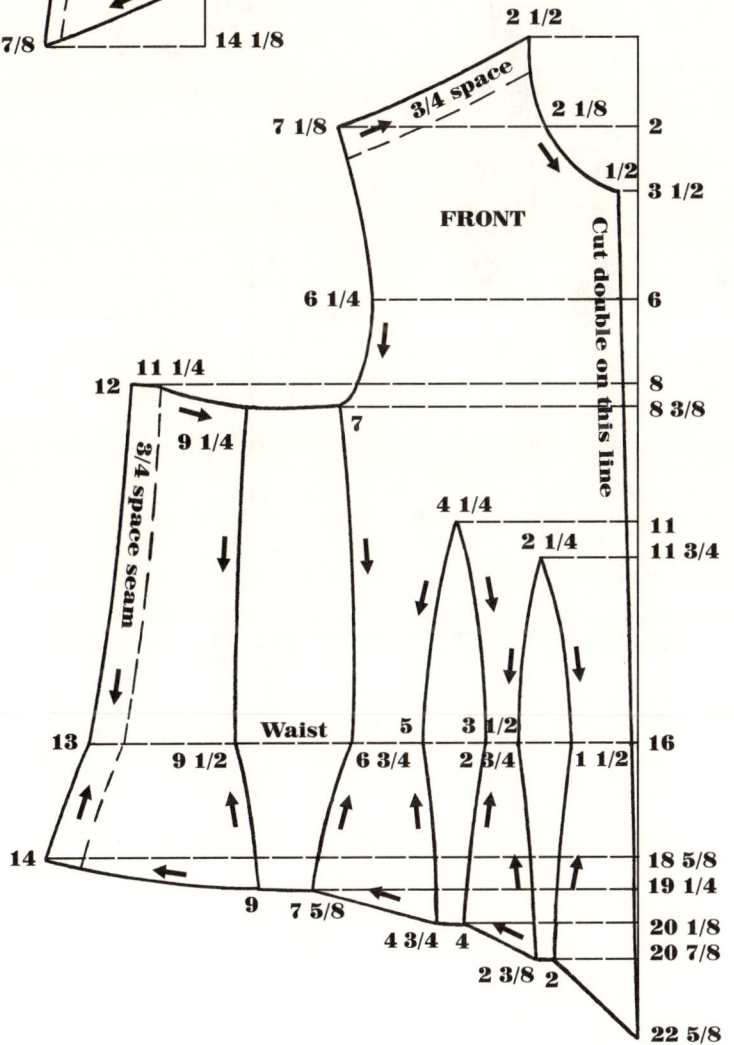

2 1/2
3/4 space
2 1/8
7 1/8
2
1/2
3 1/2
FRONT
Cut double on this line
6 1/4
6
8
8 3/8
11 1/4
12
7
9 1/4
3/4 space seam
4 1/4
11
2 1/4
11 3/4
Waist   5   3 1/2
13   9 1/2   6 3/4   2 3/4   1 1/2   16
18 5/8
14   19 1/4
9   7 5/8   20 1/8
4 3/4   4   20 7/8
2 3/8   2
22 5/8

133

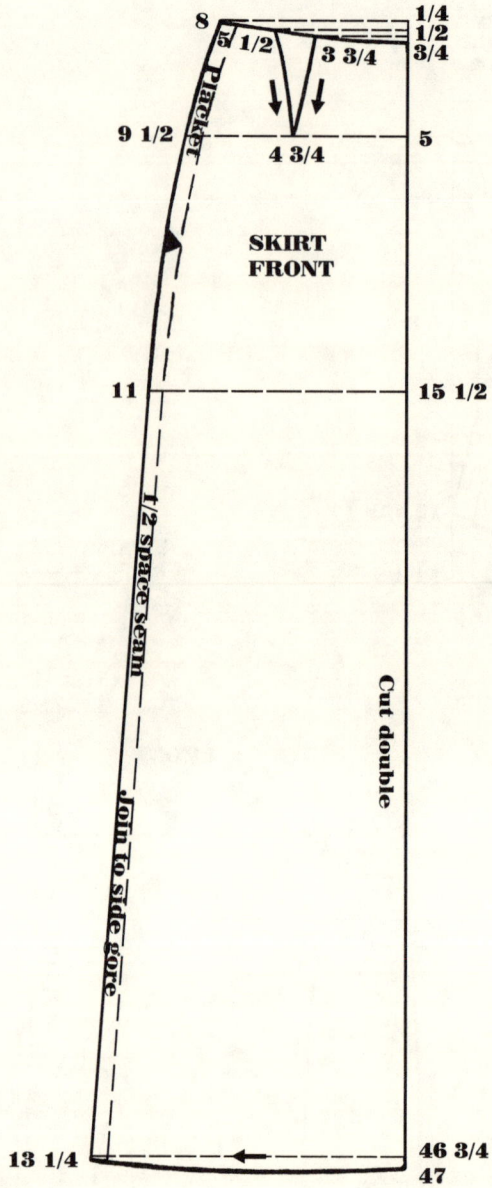

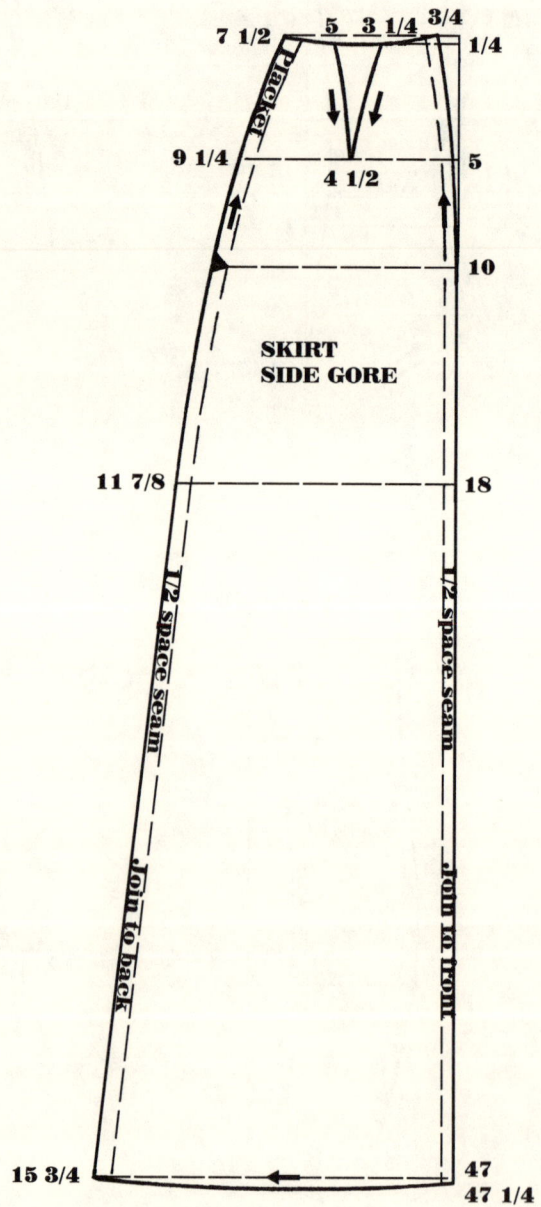

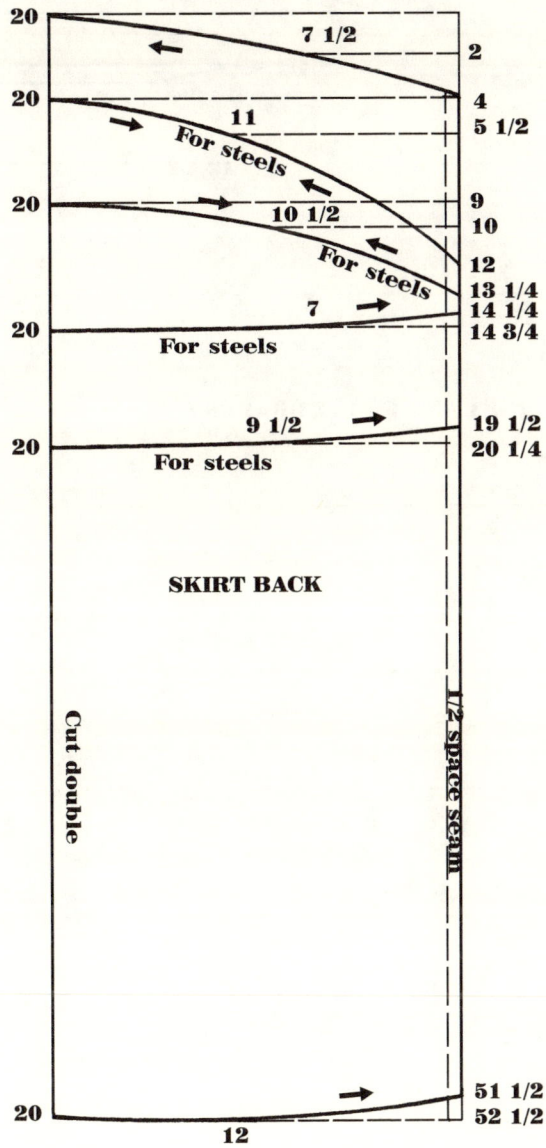

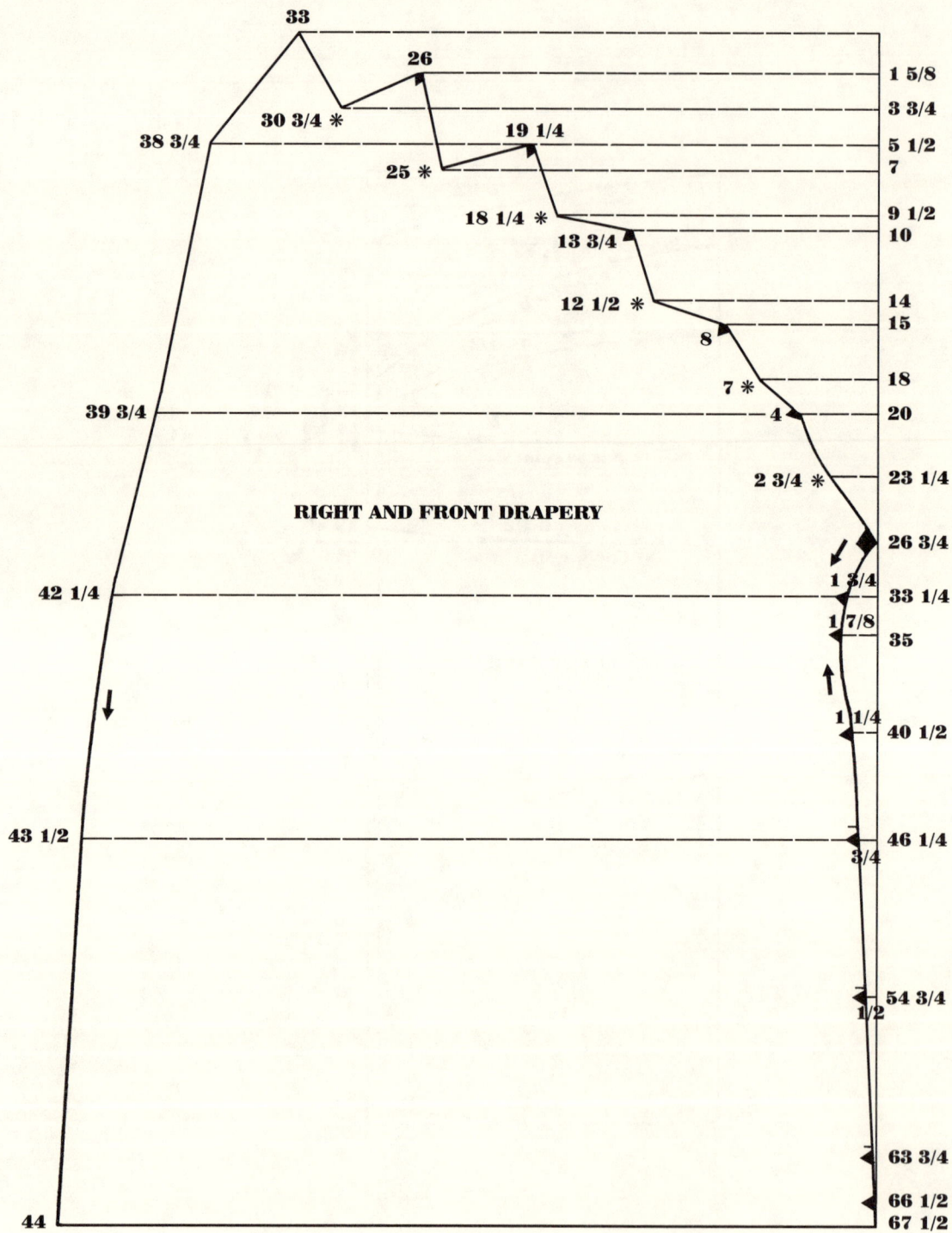

33

26   1 5/8

30 3/4 *   3 3/4

38 3/4   19 1/4   5 1/2
                              7

25 *

18 1/4 *   9 1/2
13 3/4   10

12 1/2 *   14
                 15
8

RIGHT AND FRONT DRAPERY   7 *   18

39 3/4   4   20

2 3/4 *   23 1/4

26 3/4

1 3/4   33 1/4

42 1/4   1 7/8   35

1 1/4   40 1/2

43 1/2   46 1/4
                3/4

54 3/4
1/2

63 3/4

66 1/2
44   67 1/2

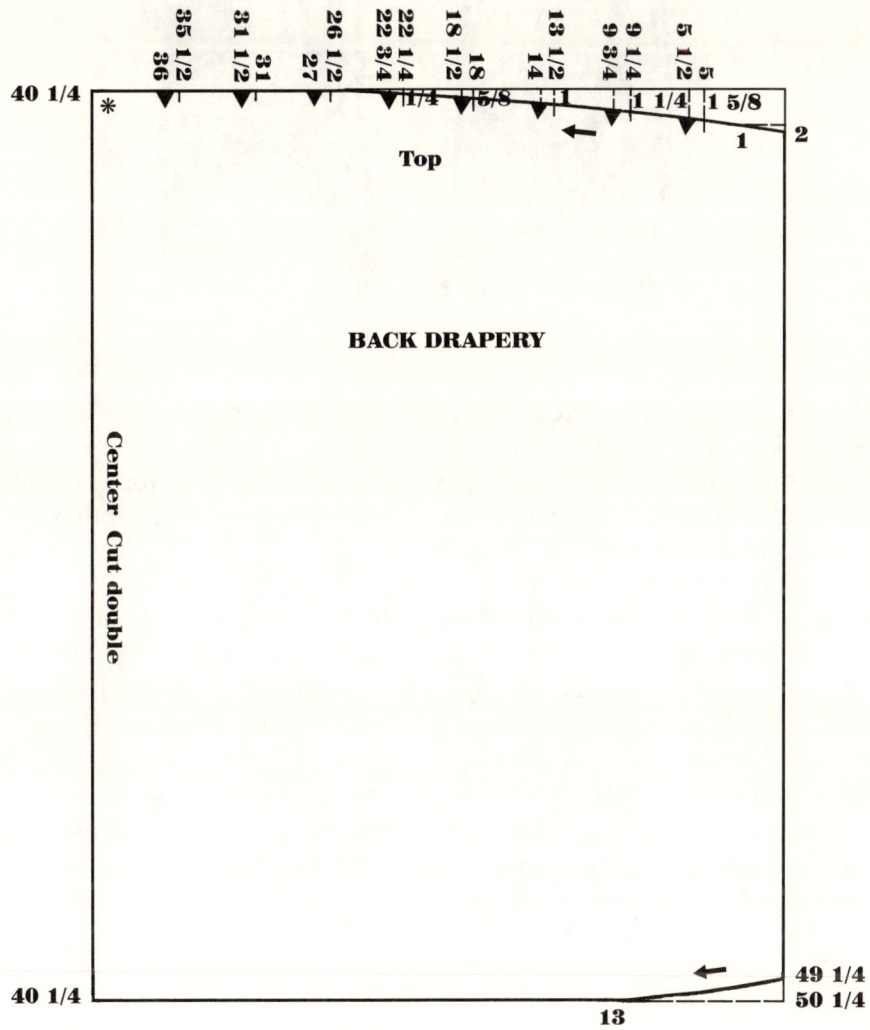

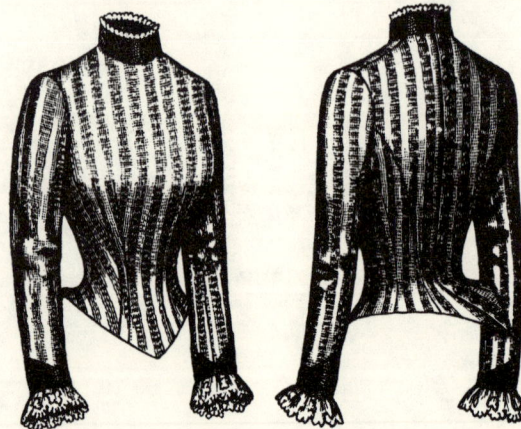

Basque That Buttons at the Back. The illustration shows this basque made of striped dress material, with velvet and lace for trimming. The front is cut on a fold of the material. It is adjusted to the figure by double bust darts in each side. A close fit is given to the back by side pieces and side-back seams. The closing is made down the center of the back by buttons and button-holes, the edges being curved to assist in the adjustment, and the right side being underfaced. The lower outline shows a point at the bottom of the back and front, and a high arch over the hips. A bias standing collar of velvet fits the neck closely, the closing being at the back. A fancy ruching shows above the collar. The coat sleeves are each trimmed at the wrist with a lace frill surmounted by a pointed cuff-facing of velvet.

This basque adapts itself to all kinds of fancy and plain dress materials. For evening wear the neck may be cut in a low, round outline. The basque may also be developed in cloth, with a tailor finish. All materials admit of trimmings, among them braid in worsted, silver, or gilt; ribbon; velvet; bands of the material; galloon; and jet passementerie. Braiding done in fancy patterns on the front and the wrists of the sleeves has a rich effect. Machine-stitching may finish the edges. To make the basque for a lady of medium size, requires 2 7/8 yards of material 22 inches wide, or 1 3/8 yards of material 44 inches wide. Each requires 3/8 yard of velvet 20 inches wide for the collar, etc.

December 1887 *Delineator*

Peasant Bodice

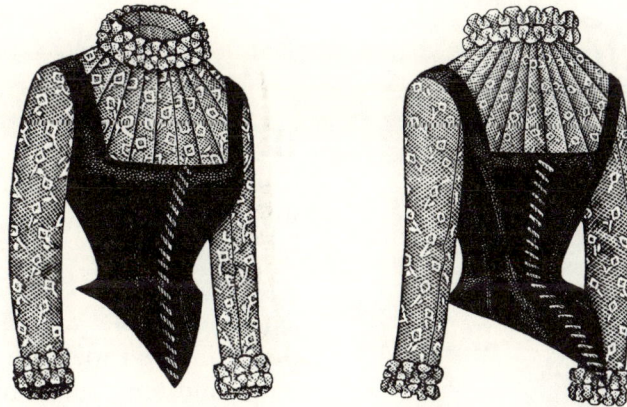

Peasant Bodice. This mode is especially popular for dressy wear, and is adapted to all kinds of lace and dress materials in vogue for such occasions. The under bodice or lining is of lining material. It has shoulder and side seams, and double bust darts in each side of the front. The front is cut in a fold at the center, while the back edges are underfolded for hems and closed with hooks and eyes. The yoke is of lace net and is all in one piece, being shaped to render shoulder seams unnecessary. Its back edges are bias. It is laid in plaits turning toward the center, which adjust it to the size of the neck. Shallower plaits conform its lower edges to the bodice, the length extending well under the lining. The lower edges are sewed flatly onto the lining, and the neck is seamed with the lining to the high standing collar. A lace ruching conceals the collar. The sleeves are of lace net and fit the arms closely, but not so tightly as to strain the material. They are finished at the wrists with full lace ruchings corresponding to that at the neck.

Velvet was selected for the peasant bodice proper. It is fitted by a curved center front seam, single bust darts, side pieces, side backs, and curved closing edges. The front and back are cut square at the top, leaving only narrow, strap-like extensions, which meet and are seamed at the shoulders. The closing edges are curved and underfaced, and the back closing is made with silk cord laced through eyelets. A closing is also simulated in front by the same means. The lower edges of the bodice are deeply pointed at the center of the front and back and curve high over the hips. Like the upper edges, they are plainly finished.

Spanish, Oriental, Escurial, or any kind of lace net, either black or white, may be used for the yoke and sleeves. The lining may be cut away from beneath the yoke if desired. The bodice may be like the skirt of the toilette or in decided contrast to it. The sleeves may be shortened to any length desired and finished to suit the fancy. Sometimes they are replaced by short, puffed sleeves.

For a lady of medium size, this garment requires 3 1/8 yards of material 22 inches wide for the lining, and 1 1/2 yards of material 22 inches wide for the bodice; or 1 5/8 yards of material 48 inches wide for the lining, and 3/4 yard of material 48 inches wide for the bodice. As represented, it needs 1 3/4 yards of velvet 20 inches wide for the bodice, and 1 7/8 yards of lace net 27 inches wide for the yoke and sleeves, together with 7/8 yard of lining 36 inches wide.

January 1885 *Delineator*

House Dress

The bodice is drafted with the scale corresponding to the bust measure. It is in eight pieces: Right front, left front, side back, back, collar, two sleeve pieces, and cuff. The right front is cut with a diagonal point. The button-holes are just inside the braid. A belt 3 or 4 inches wide, or a band of wide braid, with loops and long ends finished with fancy balls or tassels, extending from the left side nearly to the bottom of the skirt, would add greatly to the appearance of this costume.

The skirt has three pieces: Front, side gore, and back. The drapery also has three pieces: Side panel, side plaiting, and back drapery. Draft them with the scale corresponding to the waist measure. Regulate the length with the tape measure. Lay the plaits according to the notches. The back drapery is simply shirred or plaited at the waist. It falls straight to the bottom of the skirt; or to relieve the plainness it may be caught up in the center of the back or on one side.

Winter 1888–1889 *Voice of Fashion*

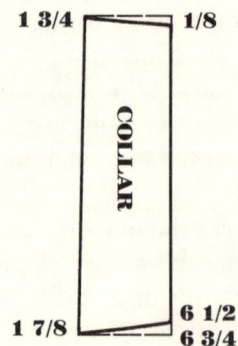

1 3/4   1/8

COLLAR

1 7/8   6 1/2   6 3/4

House Dress

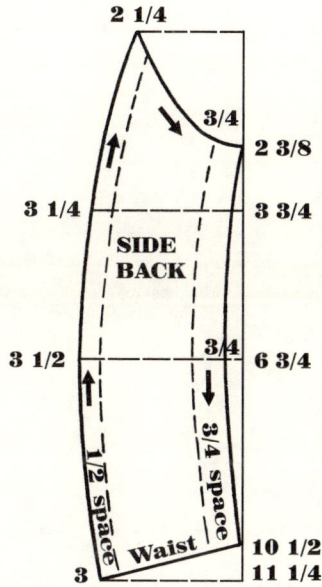

SIDE BACK

2 1/4

3/4

2 3/8

3 1/4   3 3/4

3 1/2   3/4   6 3/4

3/4 space

1/2 space

Waist   10 1/2

3   11 1/4

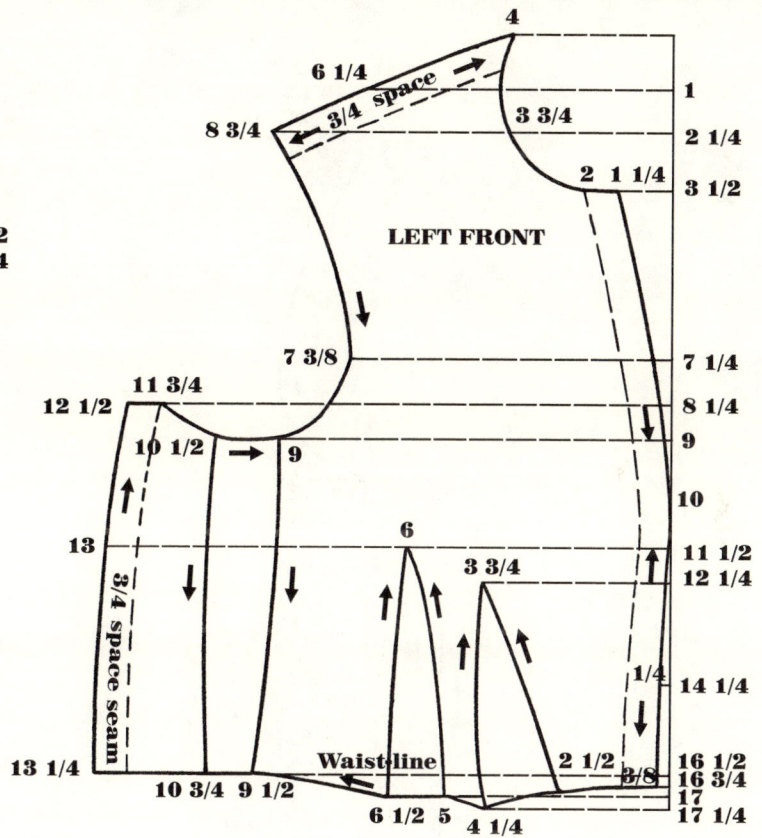

LEFT FRONT

4

6 1/4   3/4 space

8 3/4   3 3/4   1
          2 1/4
          2 1 1/4   3 1/2

7 3/8   7 1/4

12 1/2   11 3/4   8 1/4
          9

10 1/2   9   10

13   11 1/2
      12 1/4

3/4 space seam   6   3 3/4

13 1/4   1/4   14 1/4

Waistline   2 1/2   16 1/2
10 3/4 9 1/2   6 1/2 5   4 1/4   3/8   16 3/4
                                              17
                                              17 1/4

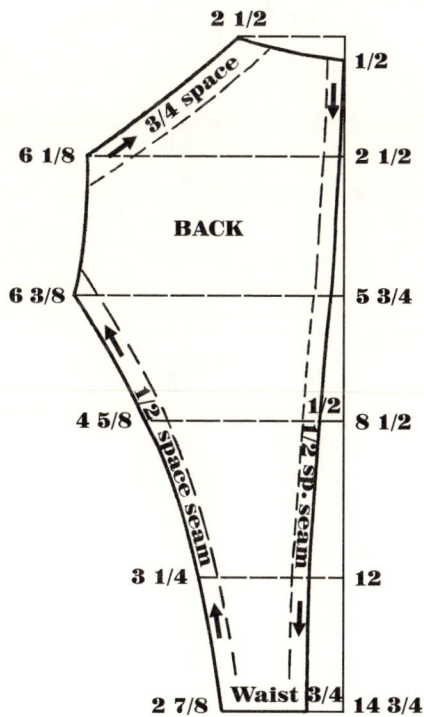

BACK

2 1/2   1/2

6 1/8   3/4 space   2 1/2

6 3/8   5 3/4

4 5/8   1/2 space seam   1/2   8 1/2

1/2 sp. seam

3 1/4   12

2 7/8   Waist 3/4   14 3/4

141

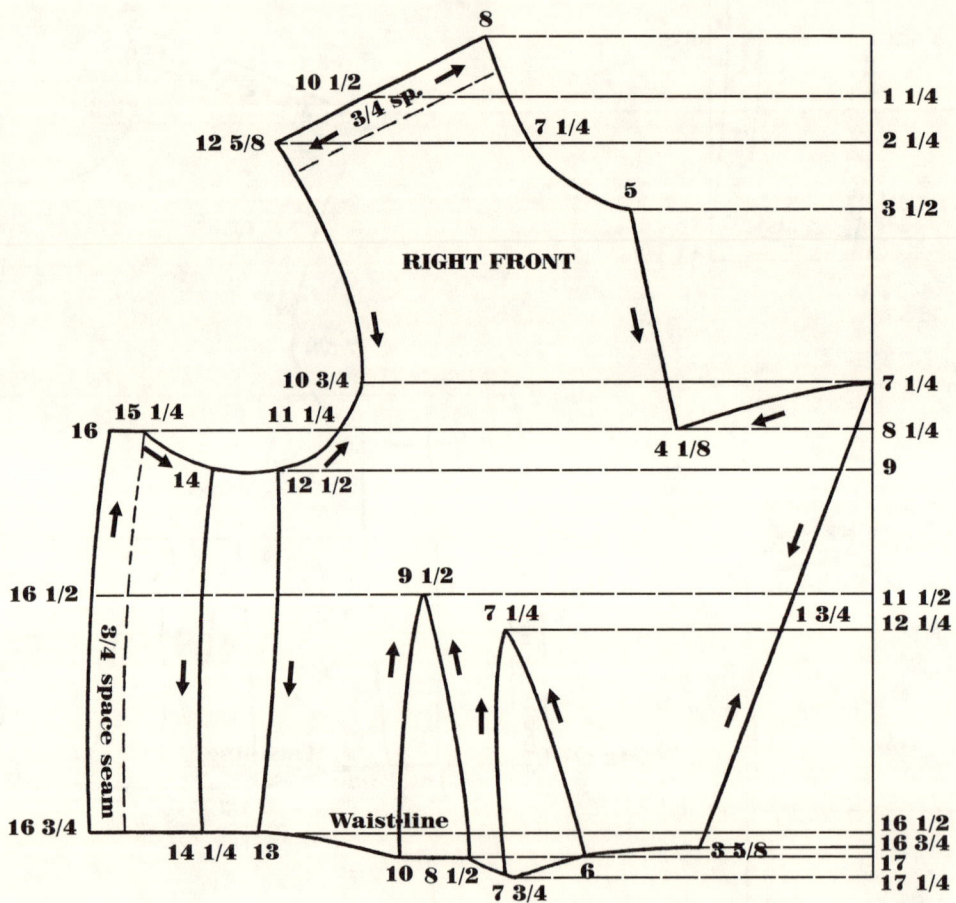

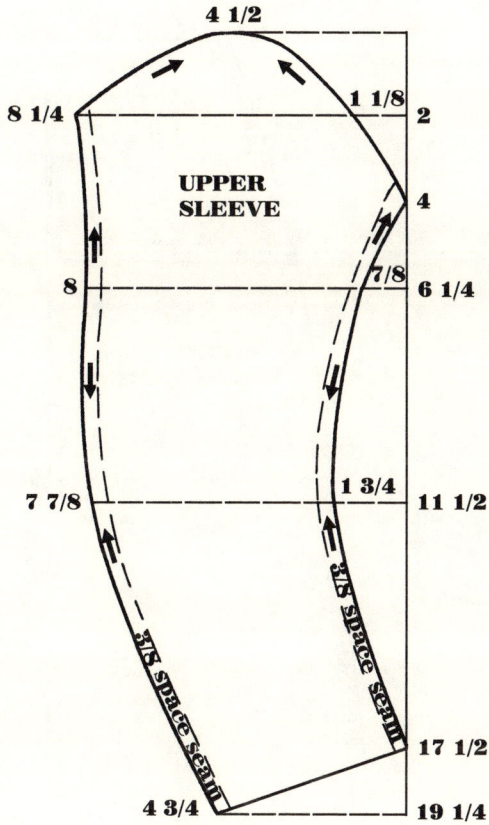

UPPER SLEEVE

4 1/2

8 1/4   1 1/8   2

4

8   7/8   6 1/4

7 7/8   1 3/4   11 1/2

3/8 space seam   3/8 space seam

4 3/4   17 1/2
             19 1/4

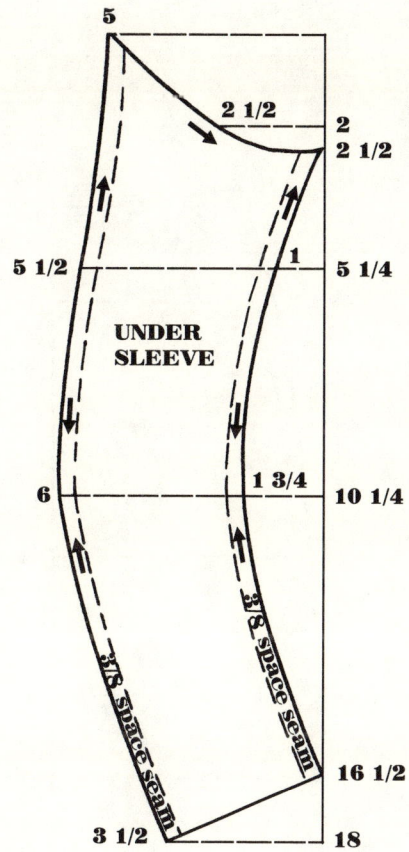

UNDER SLEEVE

5

2 1/2   2
             2 1/2

5 1/2   1   5 1/4

6   1 3/4   10 1/4

3/8 space seam   3/8 space seam

16 1/2

3 1/2   18

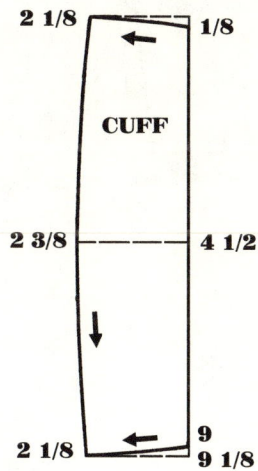

CUFF

2 1/8   1/8

2 3/8   4 1/2

2 1/8   9
             9 1/8

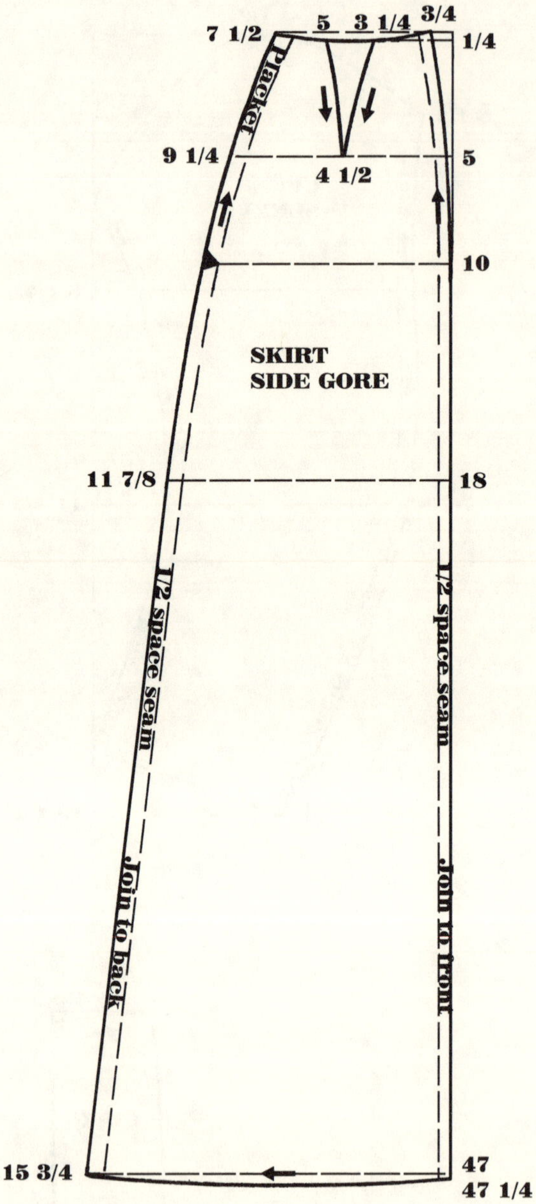

SKIRT SIDE GORE

7 1/2

5   3 1/4   3/4

1/4

Placket

9 1/4   4 1/2   5

10

11 7/8   18

1/2 space seam   Join to back

1/2 space seam   Join to front

15 3/4   47
47 1/4

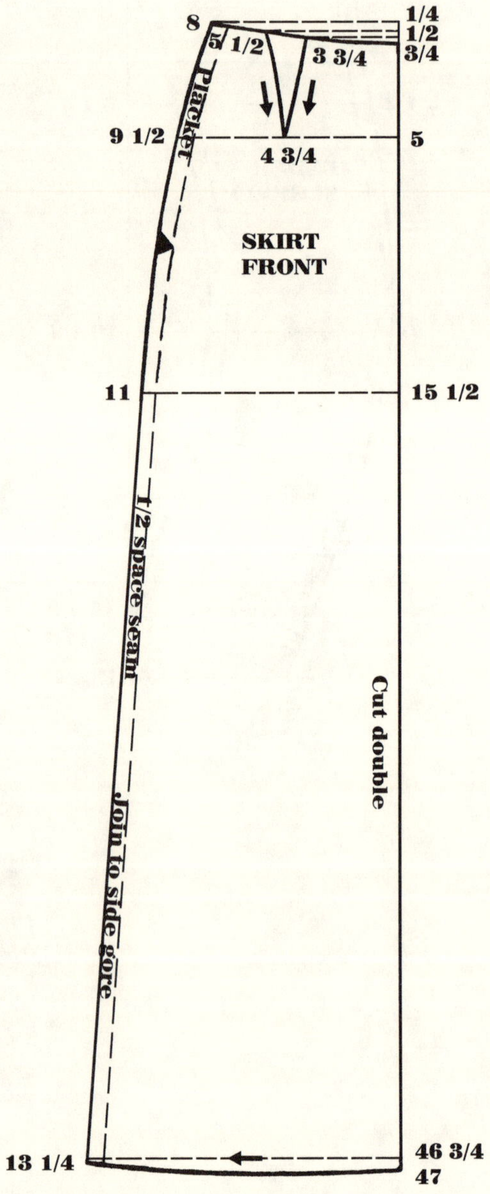

SKIRT FRONT

8

5 1/2   3 3/4

1/4
1/2
3/4

Placket

9 1/2   4 3/4   5

11   15 1/2

1/2 space seam   Join to side gore

Cut double

13 1/4   46 3/4
47

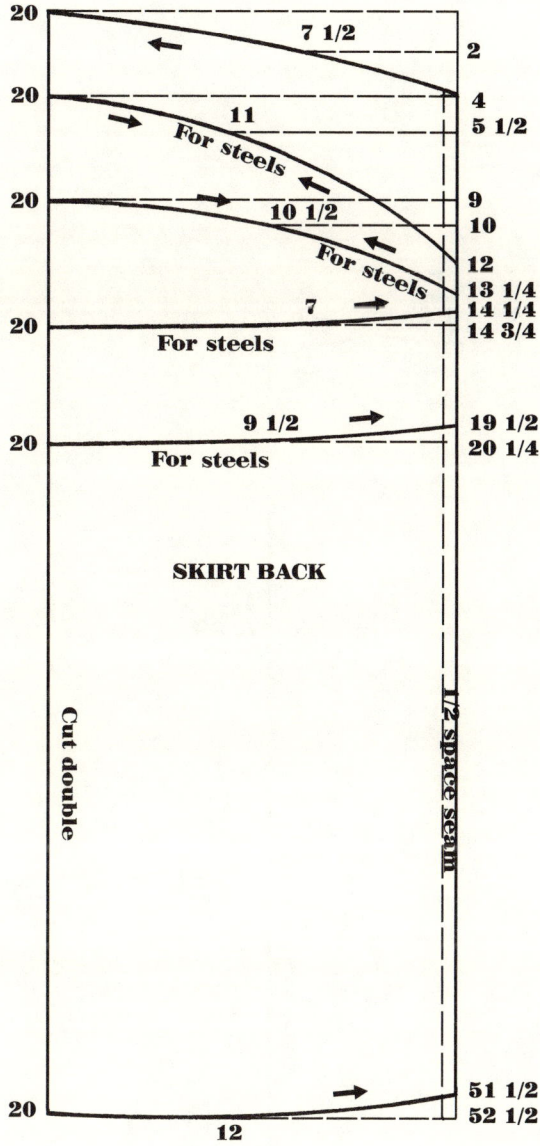

20   7 1/2   2
20   11   4
      For steels   5 1/2
20   9
      10 1/2   10
      For steels   12
20   7   13 1/4
      For steels   14 1/4
                              14 3/4
20   9 1/2   19 1/2
      For steels   20 1/4

SKIRT BACK

Cut double   1/2 space seam

20   12   51 1/2
                              52 1/2

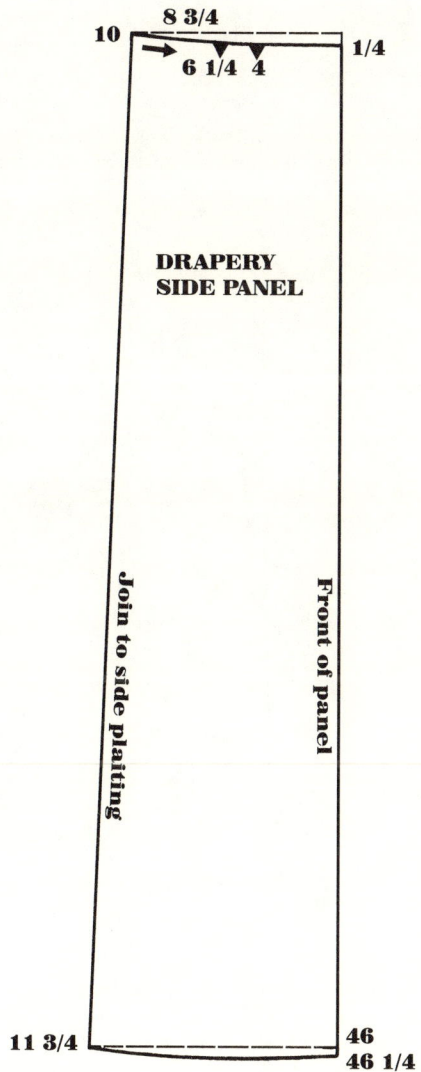

10   8 3/4   1/4
      6 1/4   4

**DRAPERY
SIDE PANEL**

Join to side plaiting   Front of panel

11 3/4   46
                              46 1/4

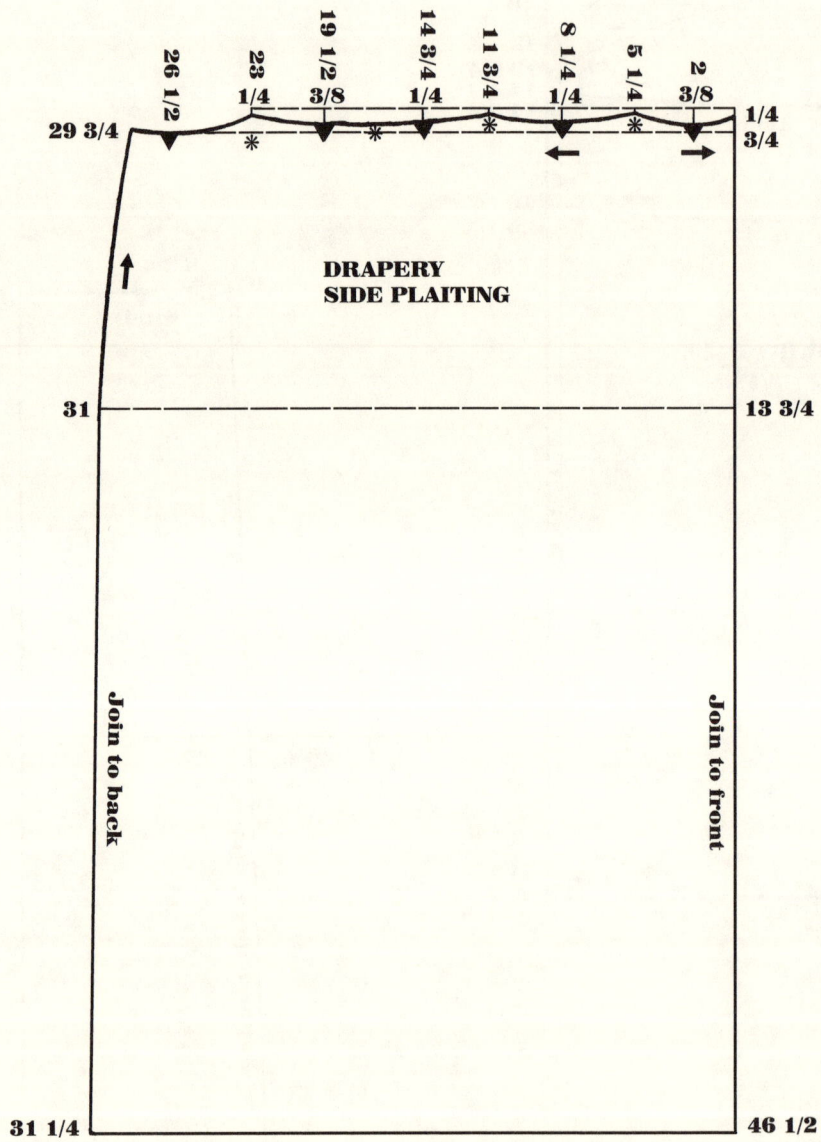

DRAPERY
SIDE PLAITING

29 3/4   26 1/2   23 1/4   19 1/2 3/8   14 3/4 1/4   11 3/4   8 1/4 1/4   5 1/4   2 3/8   1/4   3/4

31   13 3/4

Join to back   Join to front

31 1/4   46 1/2

146

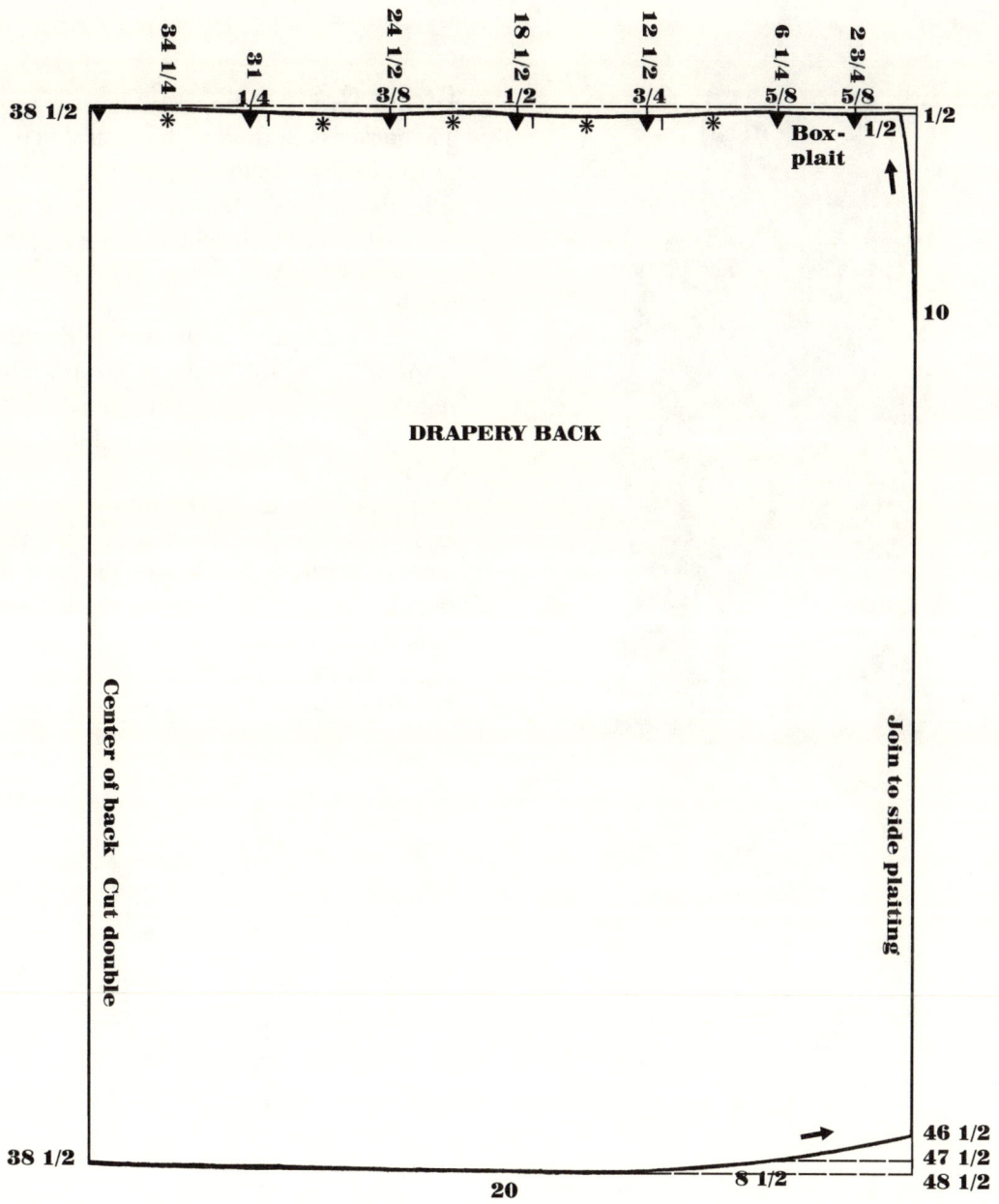

DRAPERY BACK

Box-plait

Center of back   Cut double

Join to side plating

Street Costume

The jacket is drafted with the scale corresponding to the bust measure. There are six pieces: Front, side piece, side back, back, bell sleeve, and collar. The two-piece coat sleeve also given may be used instead of the bell sleeve. The jacket is made of plush.

The drapery is drafted with the scale corresponding to the waist measure. The length is regulated with the tape measure. There are two pieces: Front and back. Lay the plaits according to the notches.

The skirt has three pieces: Front, side gore, and back. The width is drafted with the scale corresponding to the waist measure, and the length is regulated with the tape measure. A plain plush skirt to correspond to the jacket is as stylish as the one shown by the engraving.

Winter 1888–1889 *Voice of Fashion*

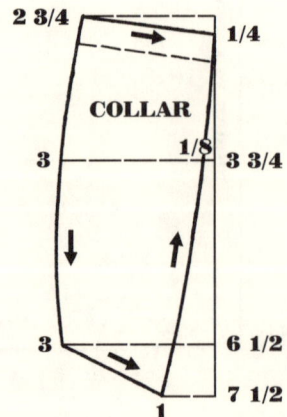

COLLAR

2 3/4   1/4
3   1/8   3 3/4
3   6 1/2
1   7 1/2

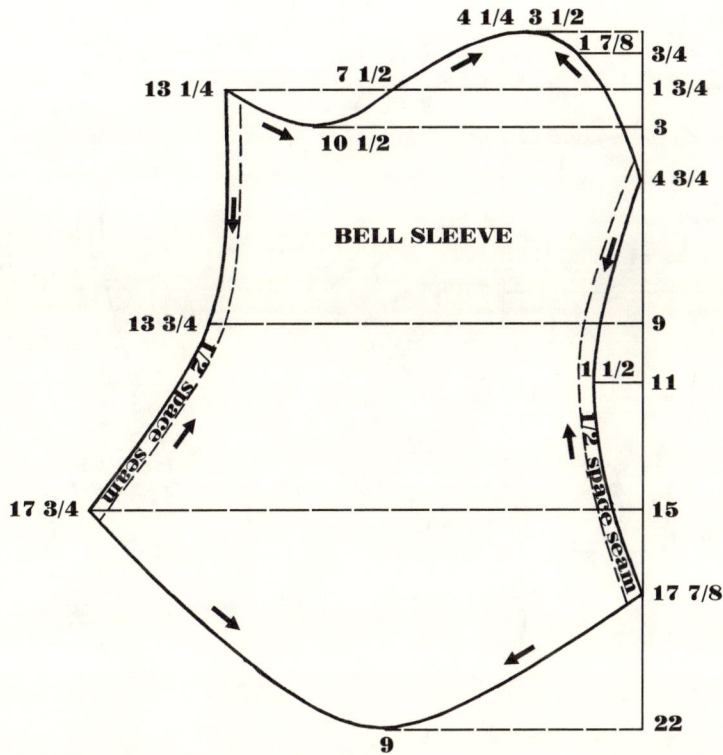

BELL SLEEVE

4 1/4 3 1/2
1 7/8 3/4
13 1/4 7 1/2 1 3/4
10 1/2 3
4 3/4
1/2 space seam
13 3/4 9
1 1/2 11
1/2 space seam
17 3/4 15
17 7/8
9 22

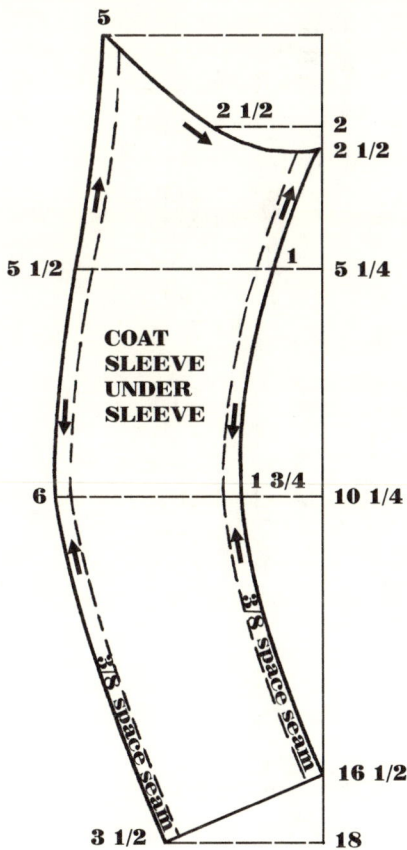

5
2 1/2 2
2 1/2
5 1/2 1 5 1/4
COAT
SLEEVE
UNDER
SLEEVE
6 1 3/4 10 1/4
3/8 space seam
3/8 space seam
3 1/2 18
16 1/2

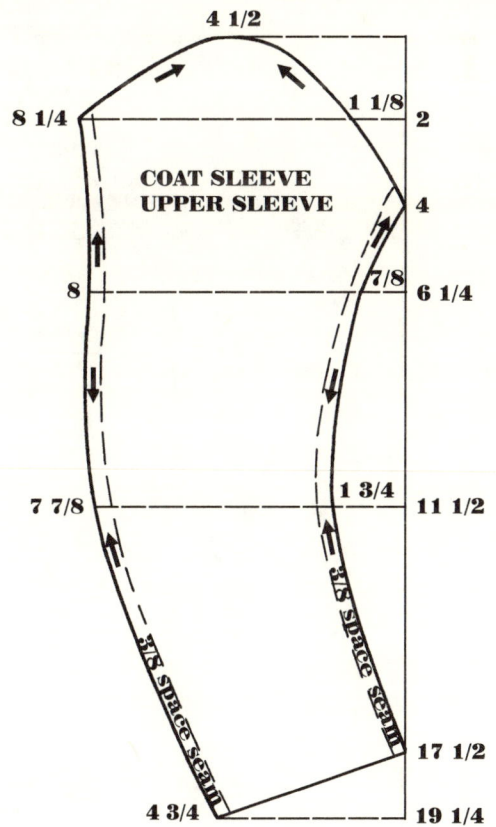

4 1/2
8 1/4 1 1/8 2
COAT SLEEVE
UPPER SLEEVE
4
8 7/8 6 1/4
7 7/8 1 3/4 11 1/2
3/8 space seam
3/8 space seam
4 3/4 17 1/2
19 1/4

149

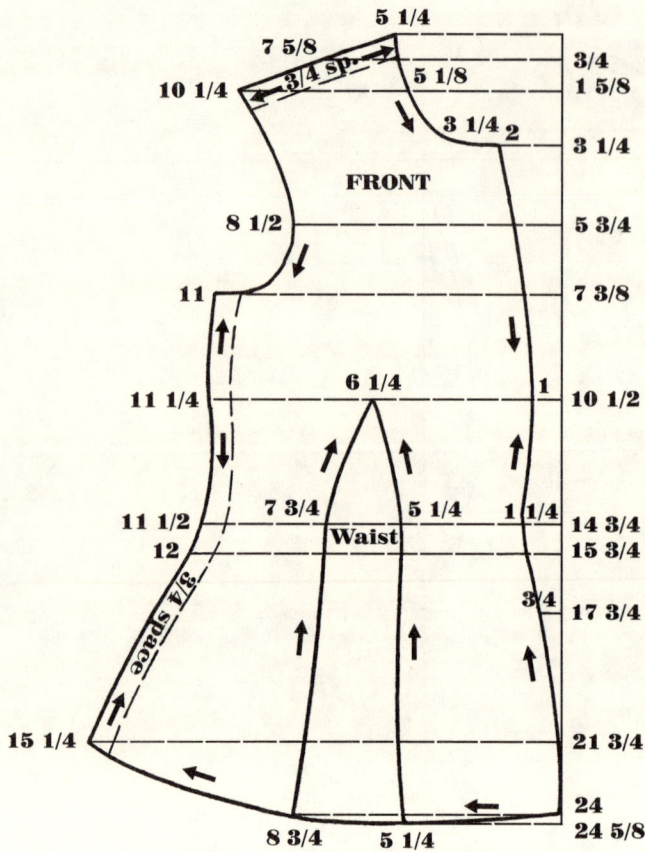

FRONT

5 1/4
7 5/8
3/4 sp.
10 1/4
5 1/8
3/4
1 5/8
3 1/4 2
3 1/4
8 1/2
5 3/4
11
7 3/8
11 1/4
6 1/4
1
10 1/2
11 1/2
7 3/4
5 1/4
1 1/4
14 3/4
Waist
12
15 3/4
3/4 space
3/4
17 3/4
15 1/4
21 3/4
24
8 3/4
5 1/4
24 5/8

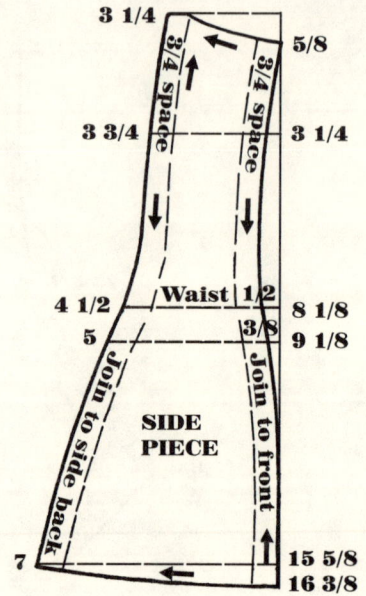

SIDE PIECE

3 1/4
5/8
3/4 space
3/4 space
3 3/4
3 1/4
4 1/2   Waist 1 2
8 1/8
5
3/8
9 1/8
Join to side back
Join to front
7
15 5/8
16 3/8

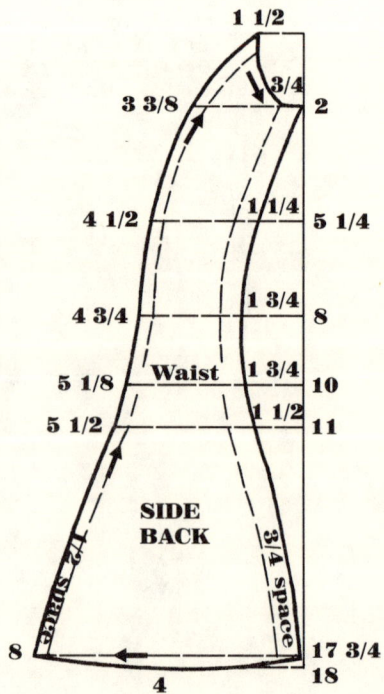

SIDE BACK

1 1/2
3 3/8
3/4
2
4 1/2
1 1/4
5 1/4
4 3/4
1 3/4
8
5 1/8   Waist 1 3/4
10
5 1/2
1 1/2
11
1/2 space
3/4 space
8
17 3/4
4
18

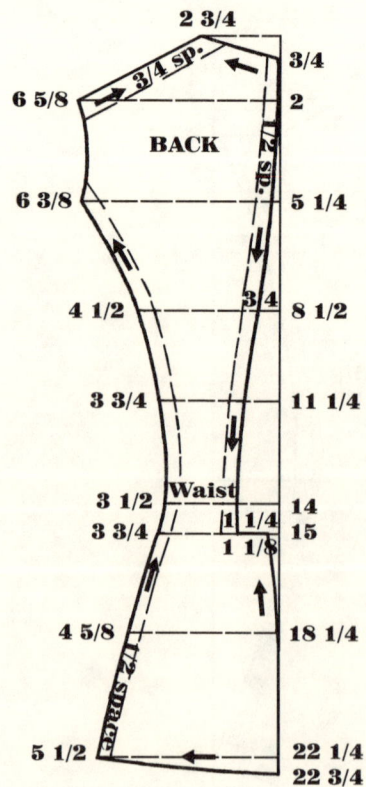

BACK

2 3/4
3/4 sp.
3/4
6 5/8
2
1/2 sp.
6 3/8
5 1/4
4 1/2
3/4
8 1/2
3 3/4
11 1/4
3 1/2   Waist 14
3 3/4
1 1/4
15
1 1/8
4 5/8
18 1/4
1/2 space
5 1/2
22 1/4
22 3/4

Street Costume

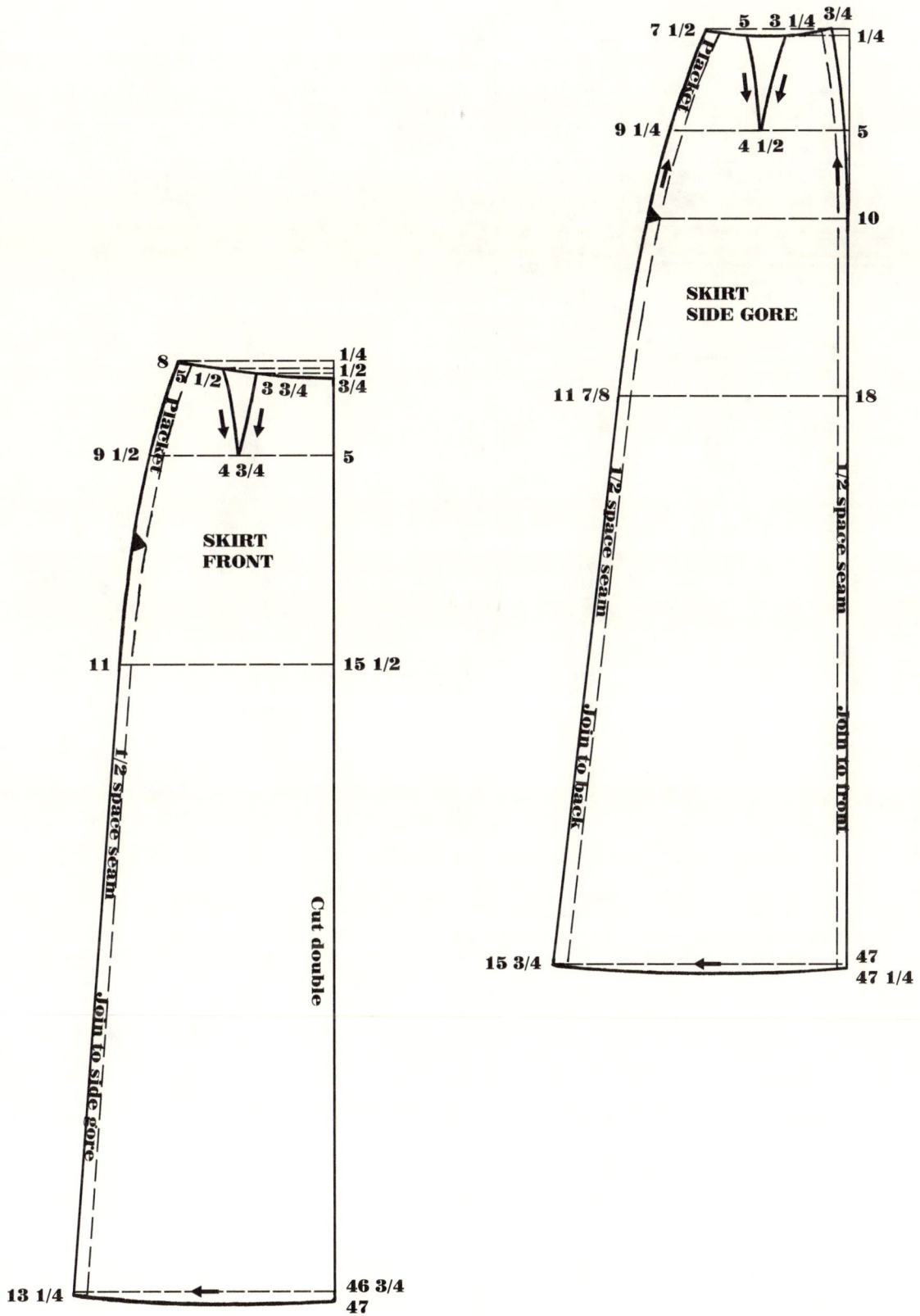

151

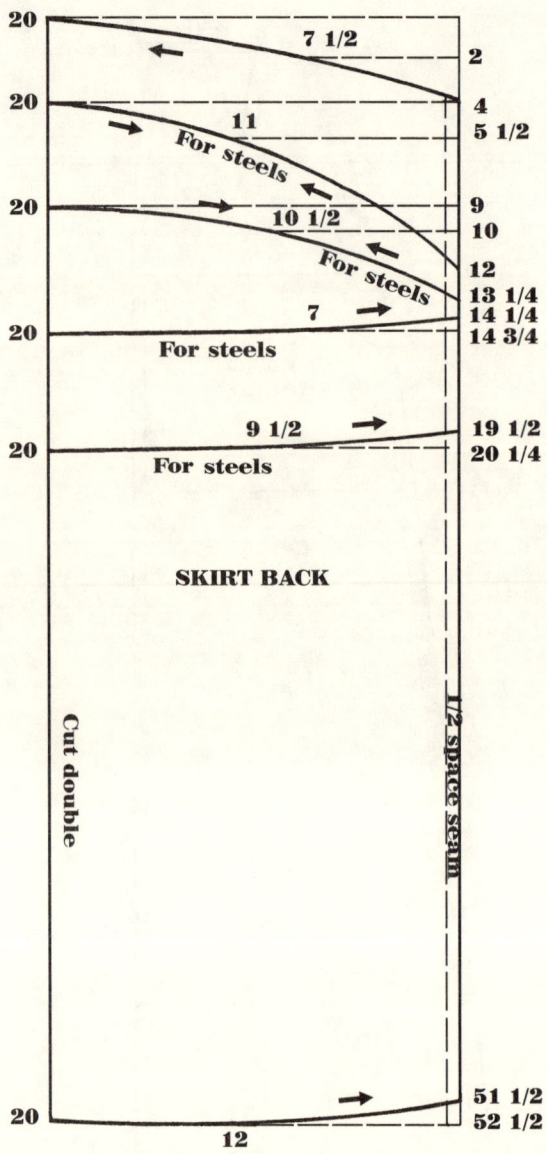

20

7 1/2 ← 2

20

11 → 4

For steels ← 5 1/2

20 10 1/2 → 9

For steels ← 10

12

13 1/4

7 → 14 1/4

20 For steels 14 3/4

9 1/2 → 19 1/2

20 For steels 20 1/4

SKIRT BACK

Cut double

1/2 space seam

20 51 1/2
12 → 52 1/2

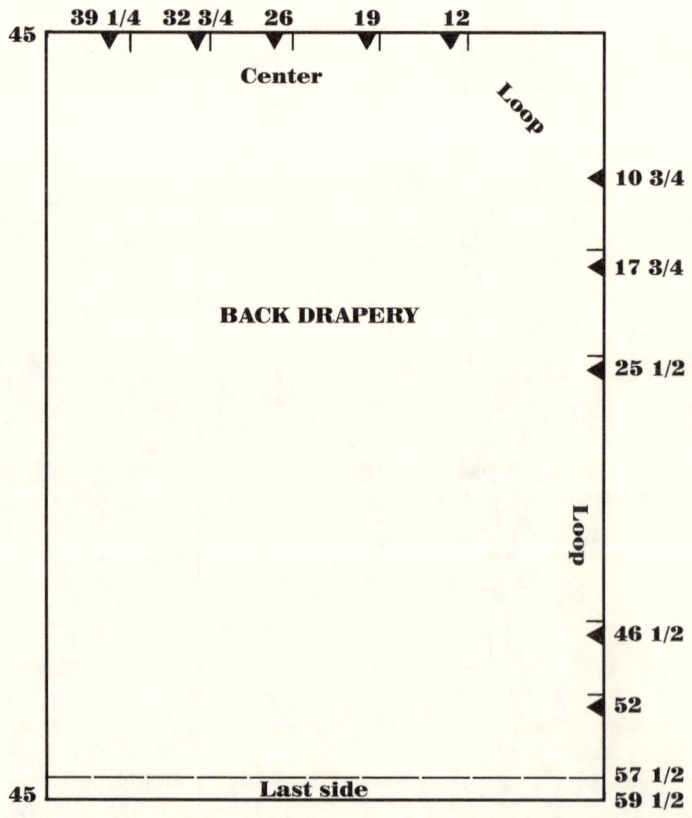

45

39 1/4 ▾ 32 3/4 ▾ 26 ▾ 19 ▾ 12 ▾

Center

Loop

▸ 10 3/4

▸ 17 3/4

▸ 25 1/2

BACK DRAPERY

Loop

▸ 46 1/2

▸ 52

57 1/2
45 **Last side** 59 1/2

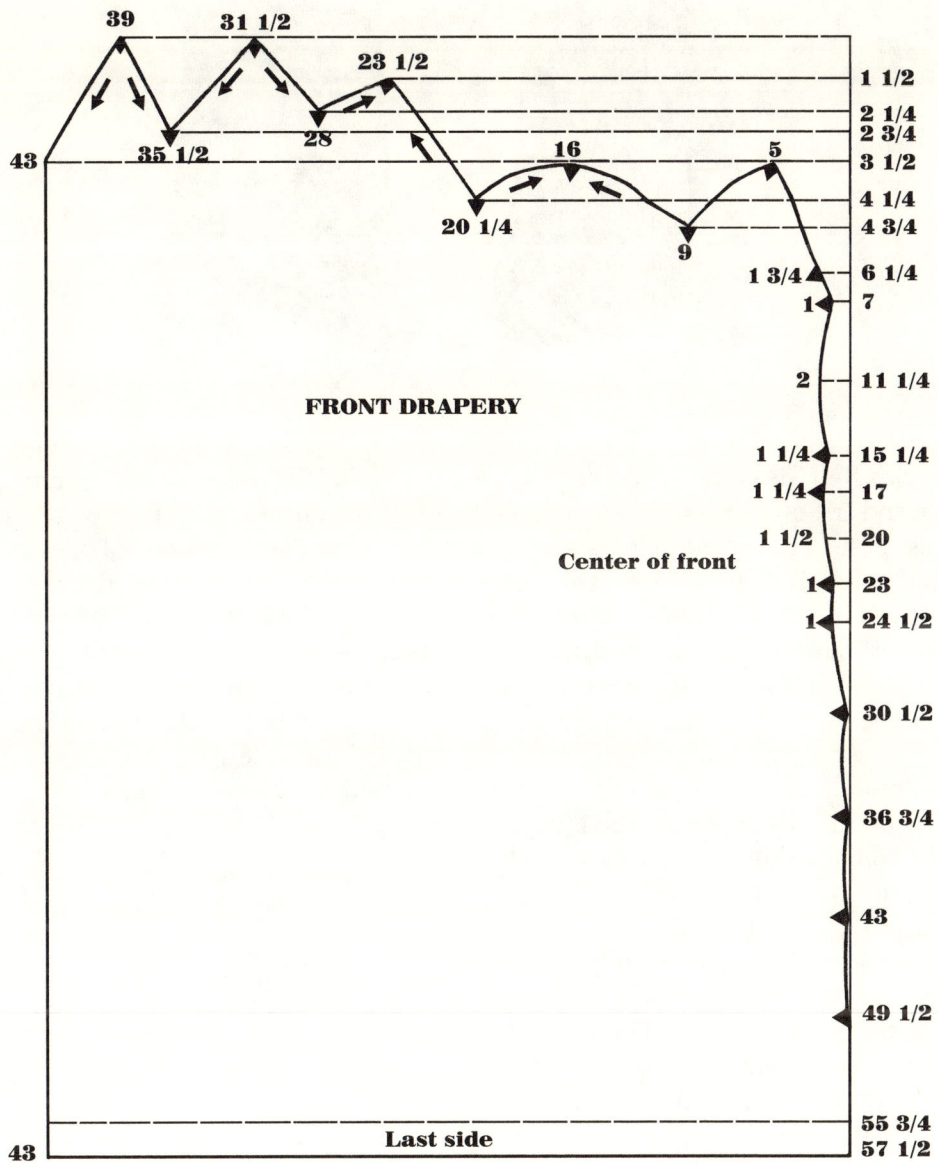

FRONT DRAPERY

39   31 1/2   23 1/2
43   35 1/2   28
20 1/4   16   5
9

1 1/2
2 1/4
2 3/4
3 1/2
4 1/4
4 3/4

1 3/4   6 1/4
1   7

2   11 1/4

1 1/4   15 1/4
1 1/4   17
1 1/2   20

Center of front

1   23
1   24 1/2

30 1/2

36 3/4

43

49 1/2

55 3/4
43   Last side   57 1/2

Jacket with Bell Sleeves. The jacket is shown made of cloth and elaborately braided. It is adjusted by single bust darts, curved side pieces and side backs, and a curved center back seam. The center back seam ends a little below the waist-line at the top of an underfolded box-plait, which fits well over the tournure. The other seams are continued to the lower edge, which is uniform in outline. The front edges are curved and underfaced, and are closed with buttons and button-holes.

Soutache braid in a floriated design is applied on each front from the shoulder to the lower edge, and also along the lower edge to the fold of the box-plait, on which it is continued to the center back seam. A similar design is carried out in V shape on the back from shoulder to shoulder. The high standing collar is covered with braiding. The sleeves are decorated at the wrists with braiding in cuff form, and on the outside at the top is a V-shaped application of braid, both patterns being in harmony with those on the rest of the garment.

Plain cloths in fawn or écru may be braided with an admixture of silver or gold and brown, and black braid may be applied on dark garnet, brown, blue, green, etc. If preferred, passementerie may be used in a similar manner. Trimming may be omitted if the severe tailor finish of binding or stitching is preferred. To make the jacket for a lady of medium size, requires 4 yards of material 22 inches wide, 2 yards of material 44 inches wide, or 1 5/8 yards of material 54 inches wide.

March 1888 *Delineator*

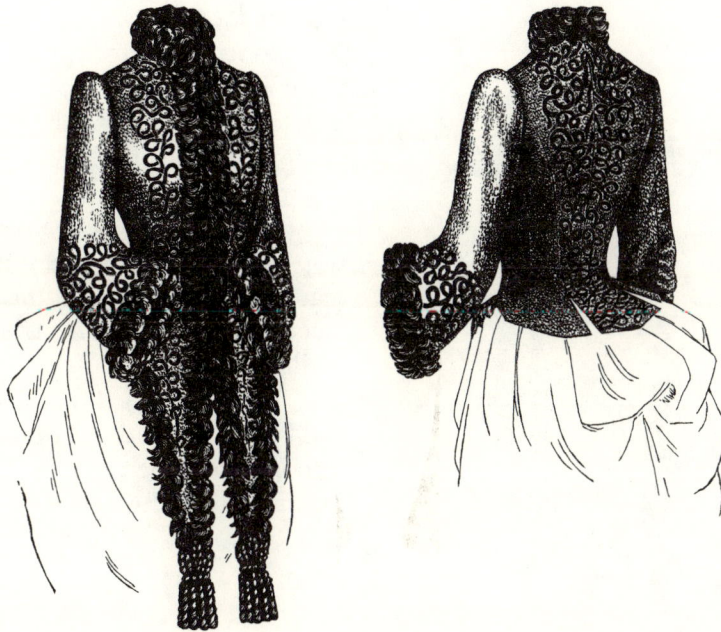

Wrap with Bell Sleeves. This wrap is a composite style, evolved from the trim, short jacket and the more dressy wrap. It is pictured made of gray plush, with black braid ornaments and feather trimming. The fronts are loose and fall in medium-long tabs, which are narrow at the ends. Side pieces, side backs, and a curved center back seam achieve a close adjustment at the sides and back, where the garment is quite short. The side-back seams are discontinued a trifle below the waist-line, the back falling in a square tab. The side backs are sloped to be shortest at their front edges. The lower part of the side pieces is also sloped to flare from the fronts. The fronts are hemmed and closed with hooks and eyes to below the waist-line.

Down each front hem is a band of black feather trimming, which is also carried up the back edges of the tabs to the under-arm seams. Back of the band, the front is braided in a simple scroll pattern with thick black braid, the width of the pattern being increased toward the shoulders. The back is similarly braided down each side of the center seam, the pattern being widest at the neck and narrowest at the waist-line. The high standing collar is hidden under a band of feather trimming, and the ends of the tabs are finished with a braid ornament.

The sleeves fit into the armholes in the coat style, which they closely resemble above the elbows; but below they are widened with a pronounced curve to give a bell shape at the wrist. They are each composed of an under and an upper part, the under part being much narrower. At the elbow, the back edge of the upper part is gathered with a slight fullness. A band of feather trimming follows the edge. Above the band the upper part is braided to accord with the front and back, the braiding being deepest at the back.

Sometimes two colors are laid side by side in the braiding, and often one kind with an admixture of gold, silver, copper, or other tinsel is used. On a black wrap copper and black braids, laid side by side, are very effective. All kinds of wrap materials are made up in this style, and a pretty lining is generally added. Fur, fringe, galloon, passementerie, pinked or raveled ruches, etc., may provide the trimming. Wraps of billiard cloth are pretty with pinked edges underlaid with another color, also pinked. To make the garment for a lady of medium size, requires 4 yards of material 22 inches wide, 2 yards of material 44 inches wide, or 1 5/8 yards of material 54 inches wide.

February 1888 *Delineator*

155

Street Costume

The basque is drafted with the scale corresponding to the bust measure. There are eight pieces: Front (drafted together with the side piece), vest lining, vest plaiting, side back, back, two sleeve pieces, and collar. The vest may be omitted if desired.

The drapery is drafted with the scale corresponding to the waist measure. The length is regulated with the tape measure. There are two pieces: Front and back. Lay the plaits according to the notches.

The skirt has three pieces: Front, side gore, and back. The width is drafted with the scale corresponding to the waist measure, and the length is regulated with the tape measure.

Winter 1888–1889 *Voice of Fashion*

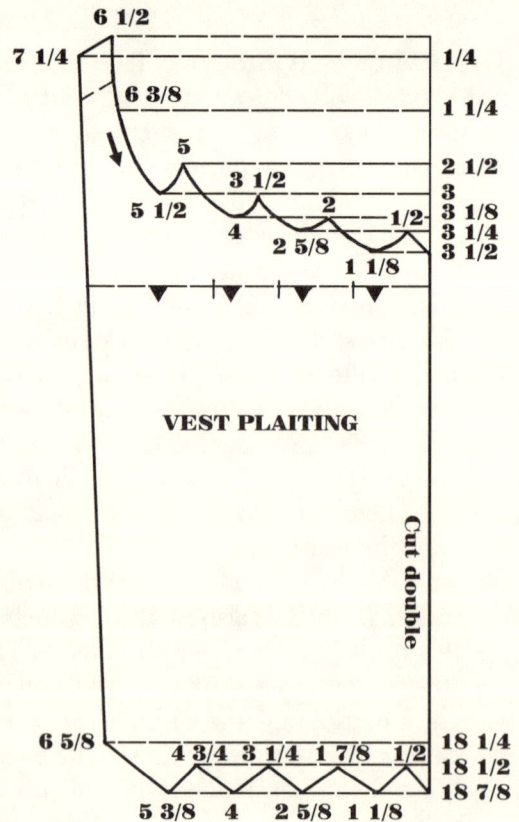

VEST PLAITING

Cut double

Street Costume

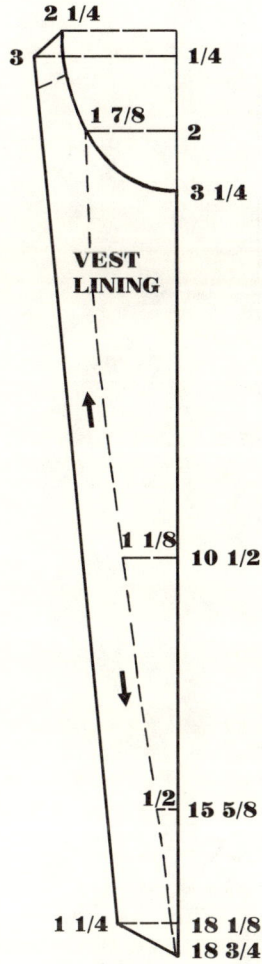

VEST LINING

2 1/4
3
1/4
1 7/8
2
3 1/4
1 1/8
10 1/2
1/2
15 5/8
1 1/4
18 1/8
18 3/4

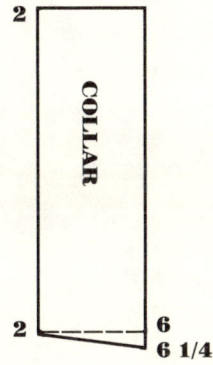

COLLAR

2
2
6
6 1/4

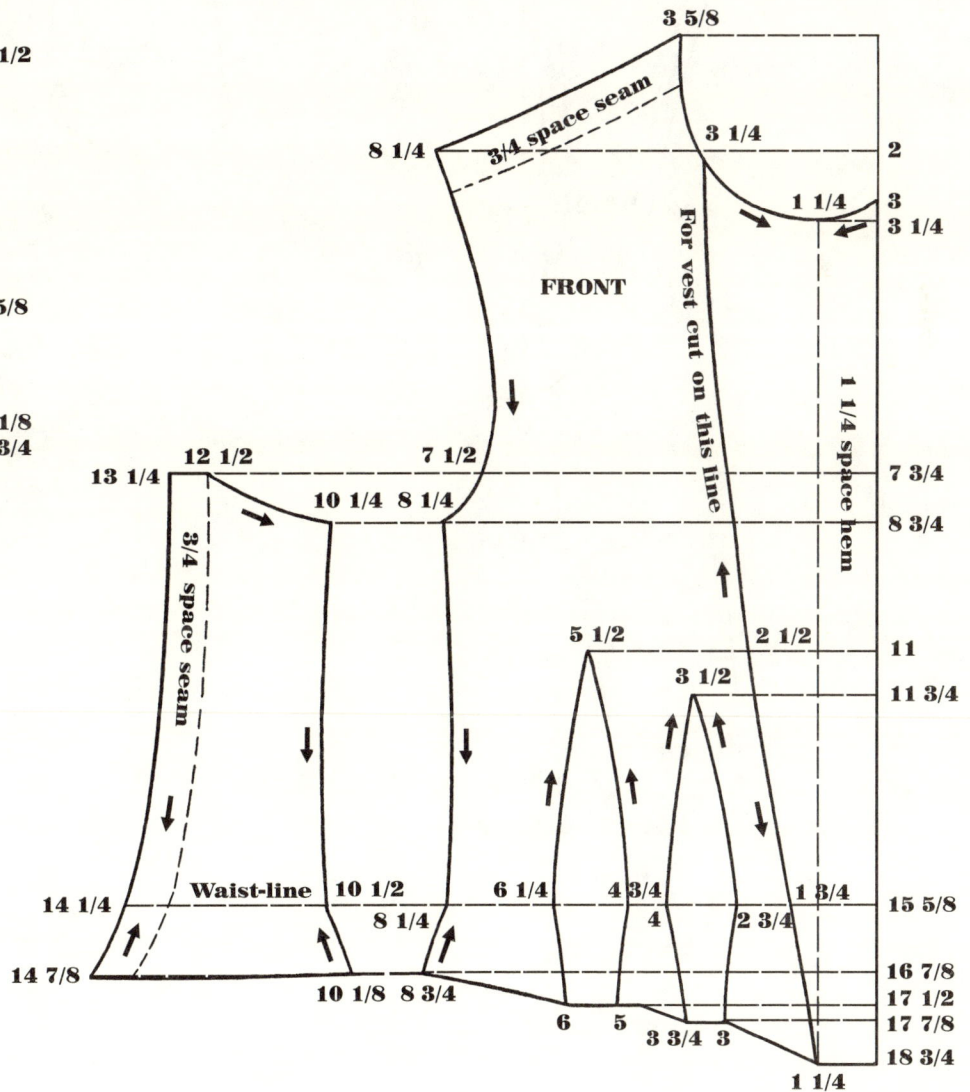

FRONT

3 5/8
3/4 space seam
8 1/4
3 1/4
2
1 1/4
3
3 1/4
For vest cut on this line
1 1/4 space hem
7 1/2
7 3/4
10 1/4 8 1/4
8 3/4
13 1/4 12 1/2
3/4 space seam
5 1/2
2 1/2
11
3 1/2
11 3/4
14 1/4 Waist-line 10 1/2
6 1/4 4 3/4 1 3/4
15 5/8
8 1/4
4
2 3/4
14 7/8
10 1/8 8 3/4
16 7/8
17 1/2
6 5
17 7/8
3 3/4 3
18 3/4
1 1/4

157

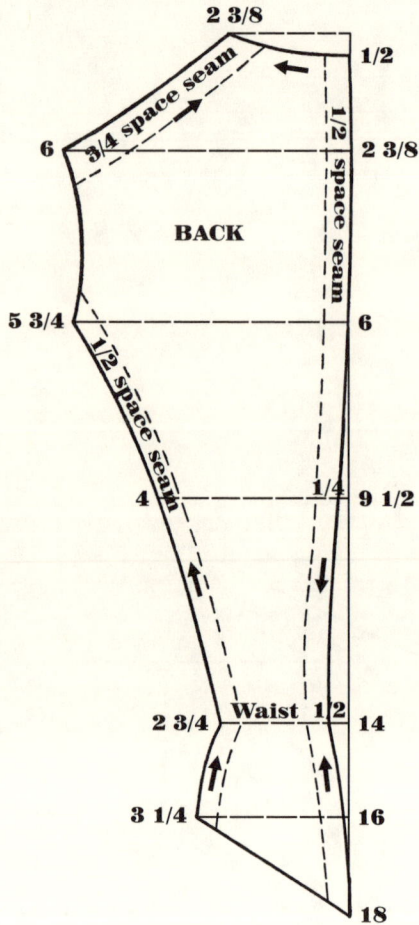

2 3/8

1/2

3/4 space seam

6   2 3/8

1/2 space seam

BACK

5 3/4   6

1/2 space seam

4   1/4   9 1/2

2 3/4   Waist   1/2   14

3 1/4   16

18

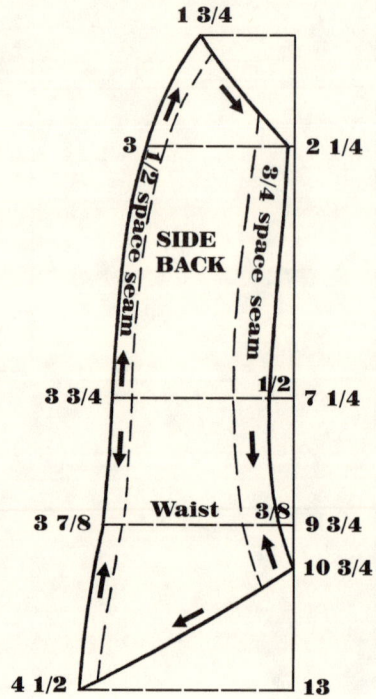

1 3/4

3   2 1/4

1/2 space seam   3/4 space seam

SIDE BACK

3 3/4   1/2   7 1/4

Waist

3 7/8   3/8   9 3/4

10 3/4

4 1/2   13

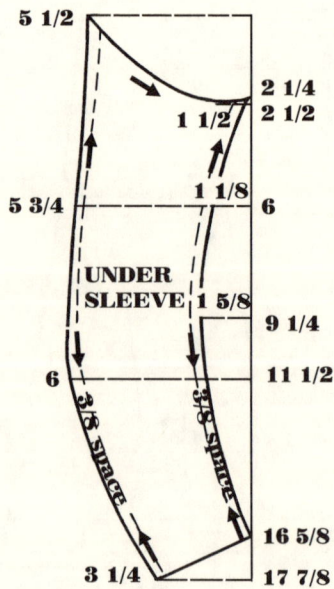

5 1/2

2 1/4
1 1/2   2 1/2

1 1/8
5 3/4   6

UNDER SLEEVE   1 5/8

9 1/4

6   11 1/2

3/8 space   3/8 space

16 5/8

3 1/4   17 7/8

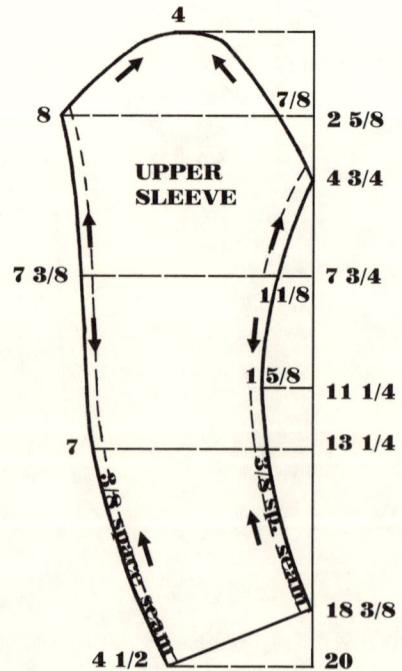

4

8   7/8   2 5/8

UPPER SLEEVE

4 3/4

7 3/8   7 3/4

1 1/8

1 5/8   11 1/4

7   13 1/4

3/8 space seam   3/8 space seam

18 3/8

4 1/2   20

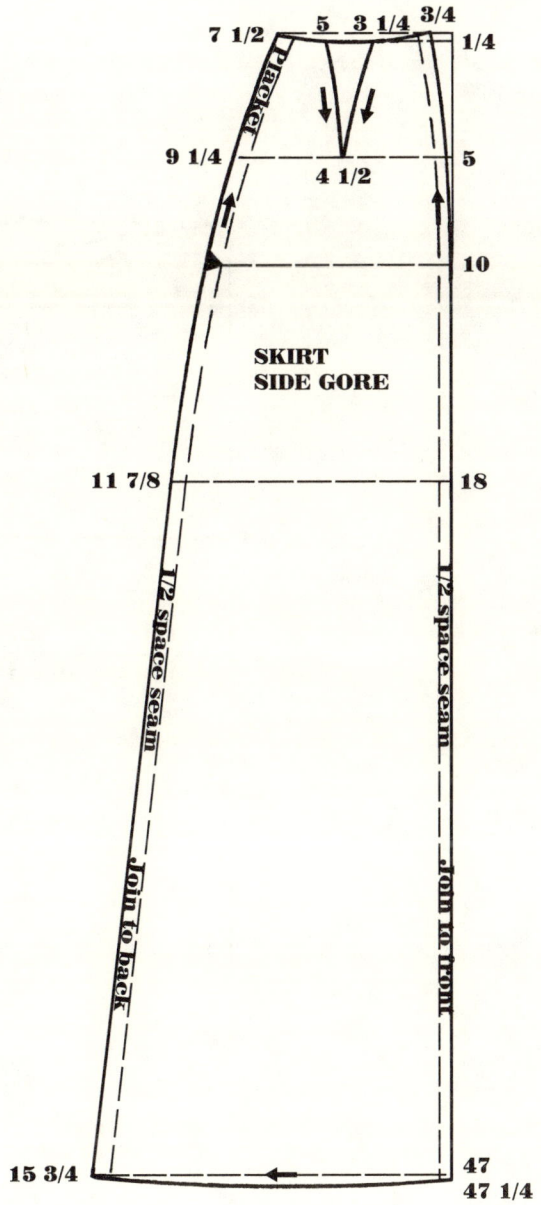

**SKIRT
SIDE GORE**

7 1/2   5   3 1/4   3/4   1/4
Placket   ↓   ↓
9 1/4   4 1/2   5
10
11 7/8   18
1/2 space seam   Join to back   1/2 space seam   Join to front
15 3/4   47   47 1/4

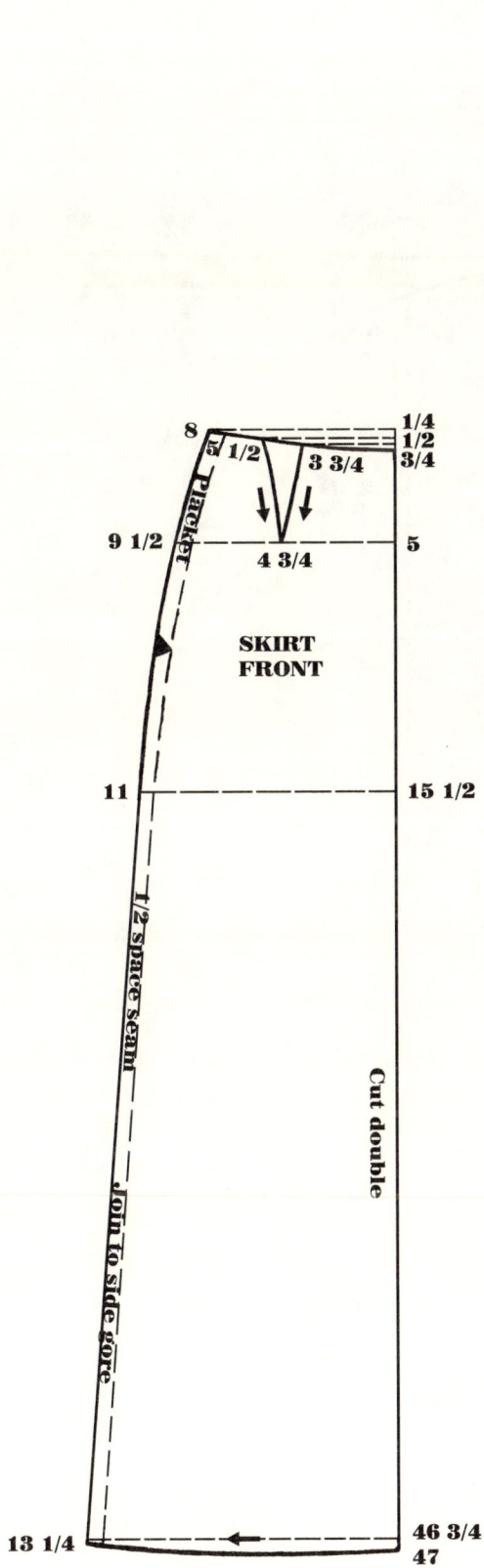

**SKIRT
FRONT**

8   1/4   1/2   3/4
5   1/2   3 3/4
Placket   ↓   ↓
9 1/2   4 3/4   5
11   15 1/2
Cut double
1/2 space seam   Join to side gore
13 1/4   46 3/4   47

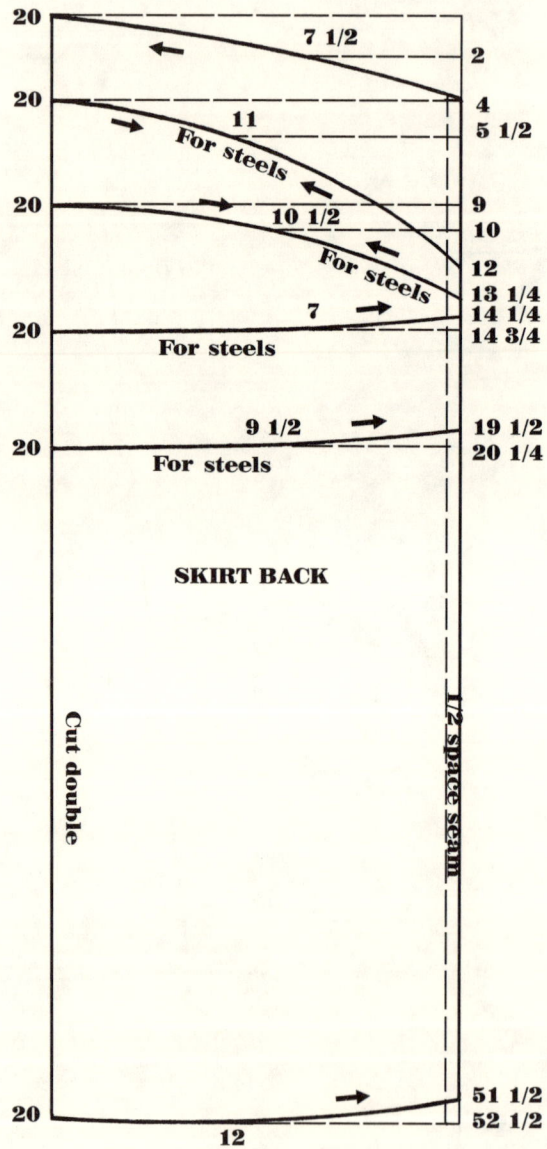

20   7 1/2   2

20   4

11   5 1/2

For steels

20   9

10 1/2   10

For steels   12

13 1/4

7   14 1/4

20   14 3/4

For steels

9 1/2   19 1/2

20   20 1/4

For steels

SKIRT BACK

Cut double

1/2 space seam

20   51 1/2

12   52 1/2

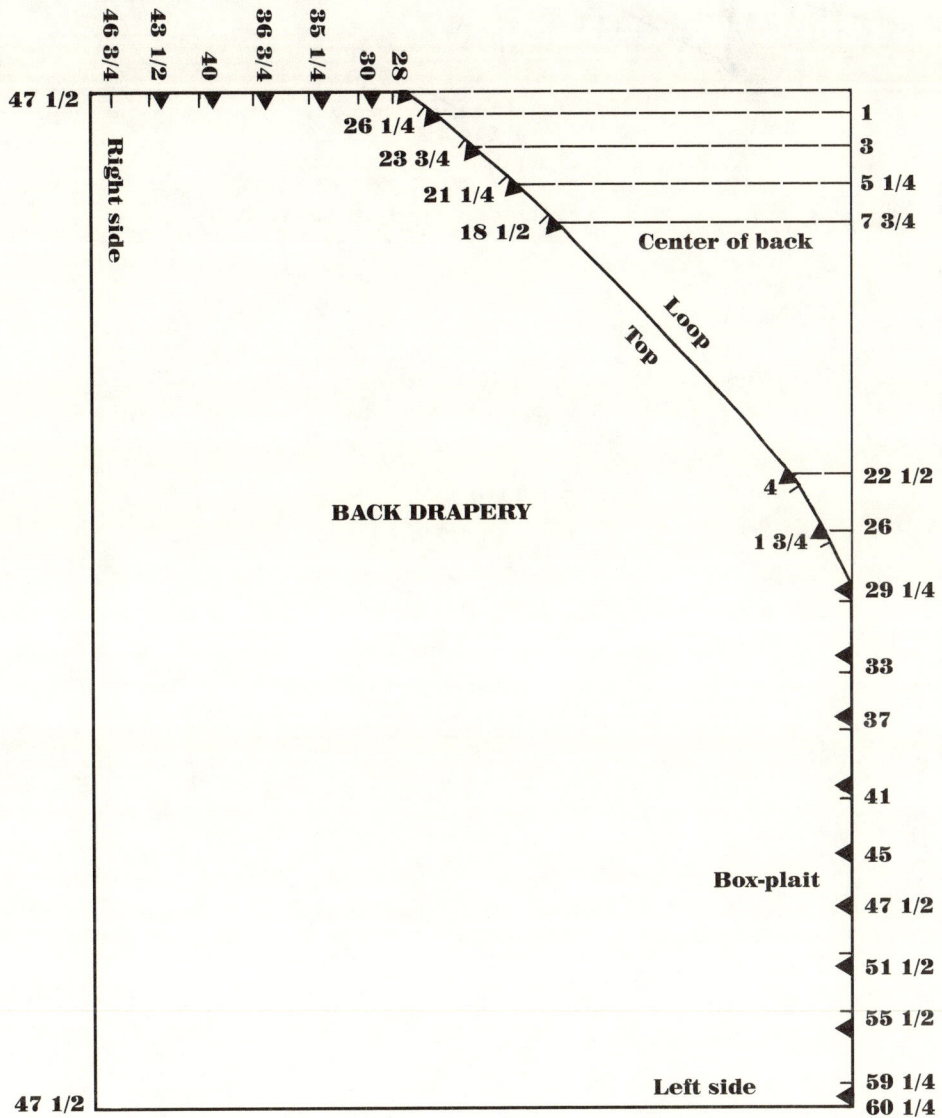

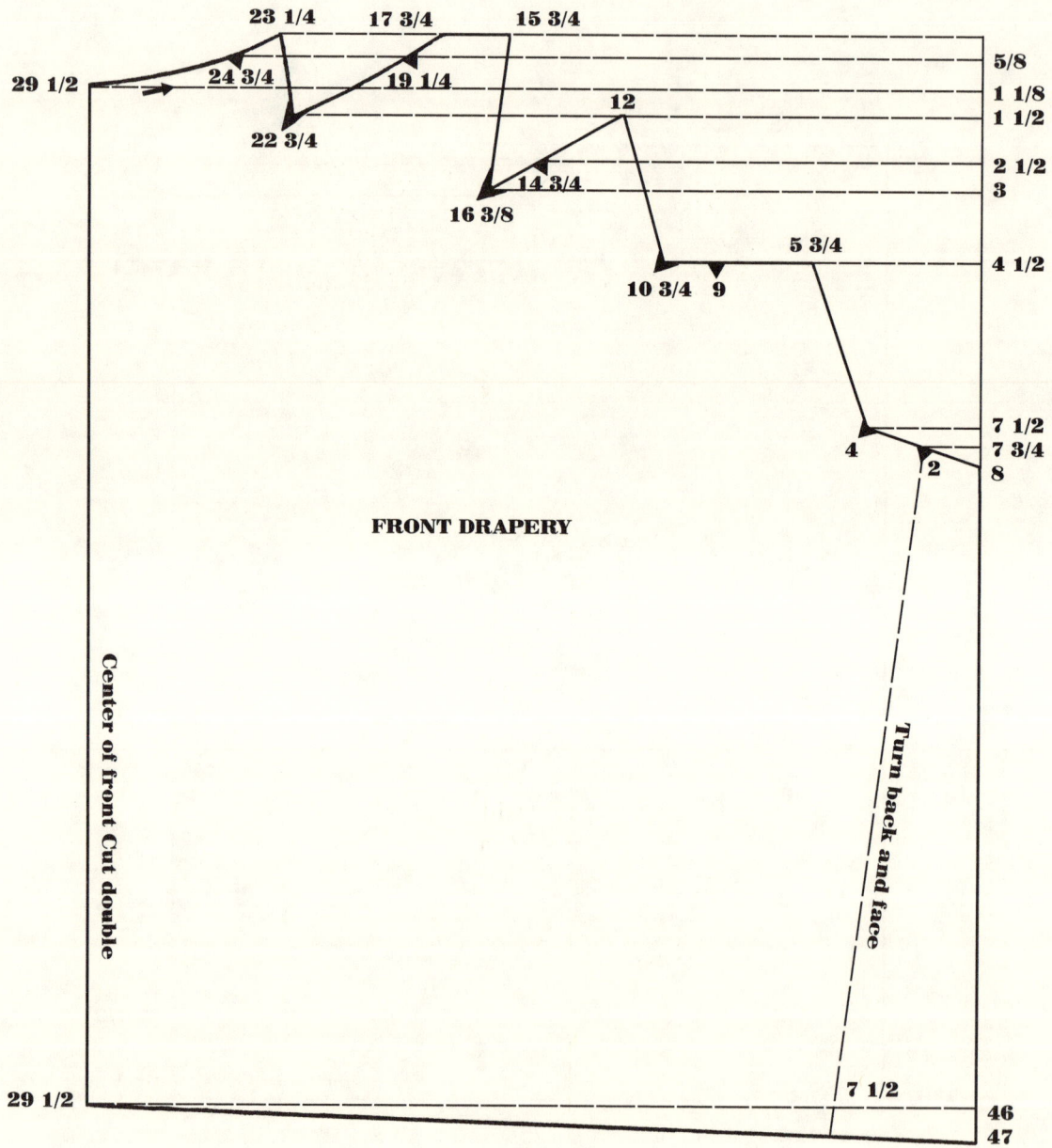

FRONT DRAPERY

Center of front Cut double

Turn back and face

Ladies' Basque

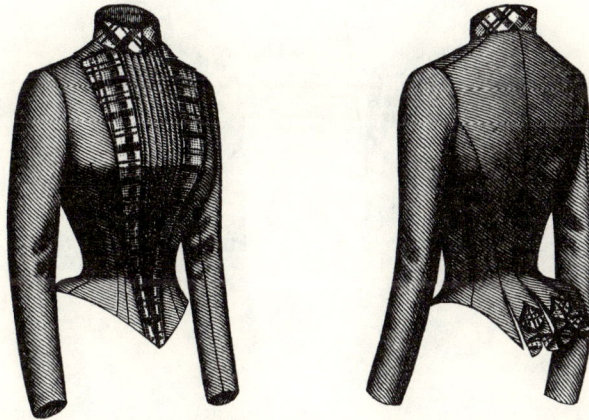

Ladies' Basque. Plain camel's hair and fancy plaid material are associated in this example. The basque proper is of plain material. It is adjusted by double bust darts, side pieces, side backs, and a curved center back seam. The center and side-back seams end a little below the waist-line. On the back edges below the terminations, extensions are allowed, which are underfolded to form two double box-plaits. These are curved out at their centers to show their underfolds, and present a sort of jaboted effect, which is rendered all the more ornamental by underfacing the plaited parts with plaid material. The basque curves high over the hips, and deepens to a point at the center front and the back edges of the side backs.

The front closes invisibly with hooks and eyes, the right side being underfaced. On each side, a little back of the closing, is a lapel ornament of plaid material, which tapers off narrowly toward the bottom of the basque and tends toward the closing at its lower extremity. These ornaments are basted at their tops to the basque. Between them and the closing, the fronts are covered with a section of the plain material laid in fine plaits. The sleeves are in coat shape. A high standing collar of plaid material finishes the neck.

Plaid materials having a serge-like surface crossed by bars of frisé or bouclé weaving are united with all kinds of plain wool materials and with velvet. Striped materials are also combined with all kinds of plain wool materials. Plain and figured sateens, and other plain and fancy cottons, are likewise associated. To make the basque for a lady of medium size, requires 3 1/4 yards of material 22 inches wide, or 1 5/8 yards of material 44 inches wide. In the combination represented, it needs 2 yards of camel's hair 40 inches wide, and 5/8 yard of plaid wool 22 inches wide.

March 1887 *Delineator*

163

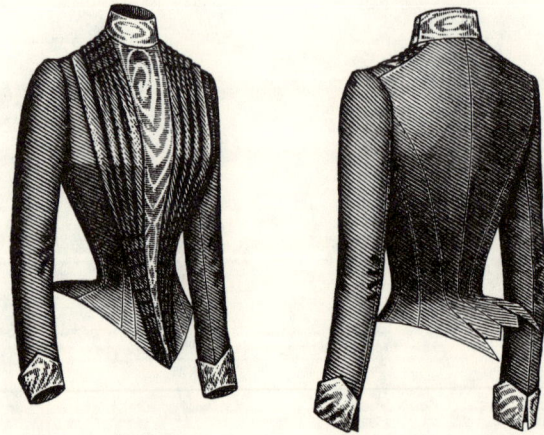

Ladies' Basque. The basque pictured is made up in suit material and moiré. The fronts close at the center with hooks and eyes. The closing is concealed by a pointed moiré vest, which is sewed in place on the right side and secured with hooks and eyes on the left. Framing the vest on each side is a surplice that is shirred across from the lower edge to a little above the waist-line, and also for some length at the top, where the shirrings end a short distance from the back edges. The tops of the surplices pass into the shoulder seams. The shirrings in the lower part are drawn up to give a pointed effect to the ends. The back edges of the surplices are sewed flatly in place, while the front edges are free and lap well on the vest.

The basque is adjusted by double bust darts, side pieces, side backs, and a curved center back seam. A contrast to the pointed front and the high curve of the sides is achieved by lengthening the side backs to points at their back edges and shaping the back in two short, pointed tabs on the tournure. The high standing collar is of moiré, and its ends lap above the left shoulder. The coat sleeves have a slight fullness gathered into the back edges

of their upper parts at the elbow. They are finished with pointed moiré cuffs, and are open the length of the cuff at the outside seam.

All kinds of materials make up well in this way. The vest may be made prominent by its color, material, or trimming. Braid in gold, silver, and copper, and beads of all colors, are appropriate. Crêpe, surah, fancy net, and beaded or embroidered gauze are sometimes draped over the vest and formed into puffs to give the effect of under-sleeves; of course, the sleeves must be shortened. Black lace bodices, made up over a moiré or silk lining and worn with a softly draped skirt to match, result in beautiful evening costumes. To make the basque for a lady of medium size, requires 3 5/8 yards of material 22 inches wide, or 1 7/8 yards of material 44 inches wide. Also required is 5/8 yard of moiré 20 inches wide for the vest, etc.

October 1888 *Delineator*

Street Costume

Street Costume

The under bodice and jacket are drafted with the scale corresponding to the bust measure. The under bodice has five pieces: Right front, left front, side piece, side back, and back. It may be made of the same material as the jacket if preferred.

The jacket has eight pieces: Front, lapel, side piece, side back, back, collar, and two sleeve pieces. Turn away the front of the jacket and face it with silk. Sew the skirt to the under bodice.

Both the drapery and the foundation skirt are drafted with the scale corresponding to the waist measure. The length is regulated with the tape measure. The drapery has three pieces: Side panel, side plaiting, and back. The skirt also has three pieces: Front, side gore, and back. Lay the plaits in the drapery according to the notches. The back and side gore of the foundation skirt may be made of silesia.

Spring 1889 *Voice of Fashion*

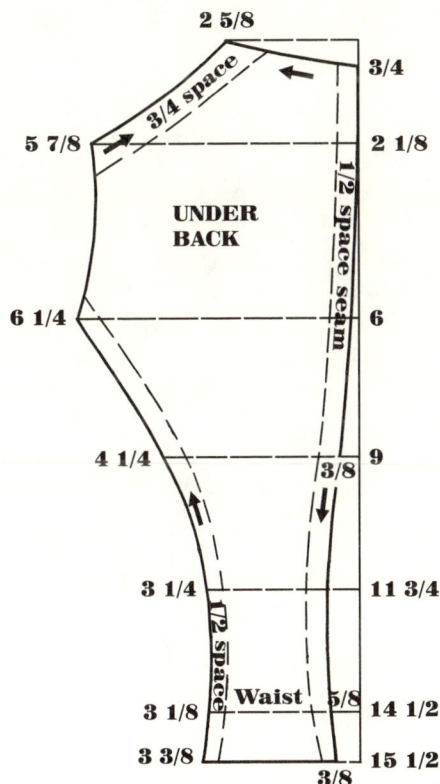

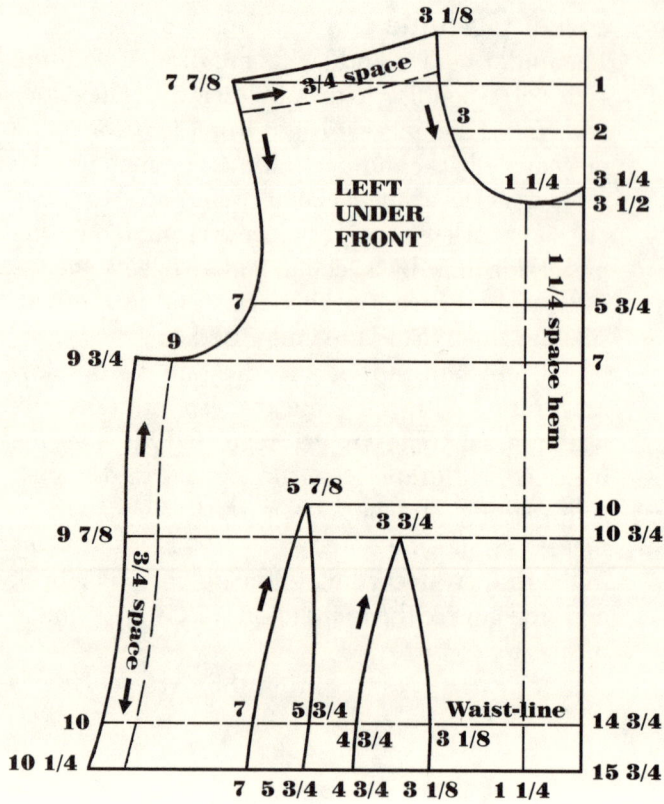

LEFT UNDER FRONT

3 1/8

7 7/8 3/4 space

1

3

1 1/4 3 1/4 3 1/2

1 1/4 space hem

5 3/4

7

7

9 3/4 9

3/4 space

5 7/8

3 3/4

9 7/8 10 10 3/4

3/4 space

10 Waist-line 14 3/4

10 1/4 7 5 3/4 4 3/4 3 1/8 15 3/4

7 5 3/4 4 3/4 3 1/8 1 1/4

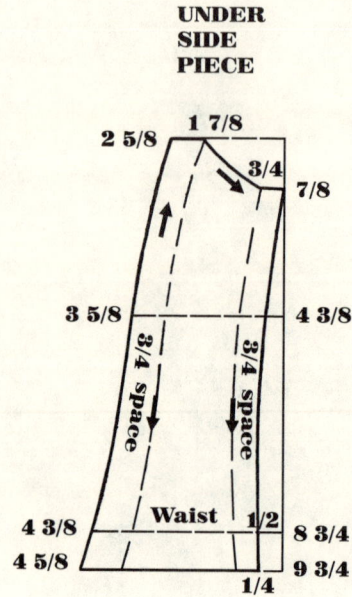

UNDER SIDE PIECE

2 5/8 1 7/8 3/4 7/8

3 5/8 4 3/8

3/4 space 3/4 space

4 3/8 Waist 1/2 8 3/4

4 5/8 1/4 9 3/4

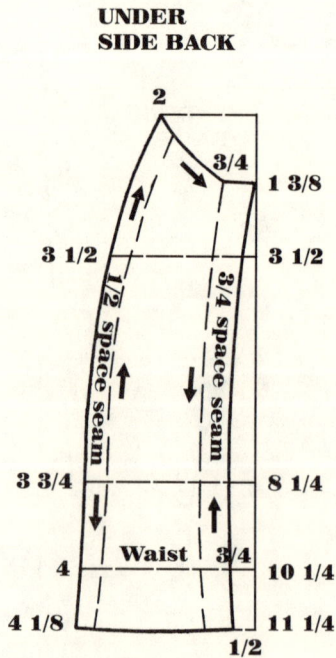

UNDER SIDE BACK

2

3/4 1 3/8

3 1/2 3 1/2

1/2 space seam 3/4 space seam

3 3/4 8 1/4

4 Waist 3/4 10 1/4

4 1/8 11 1/4

1/2

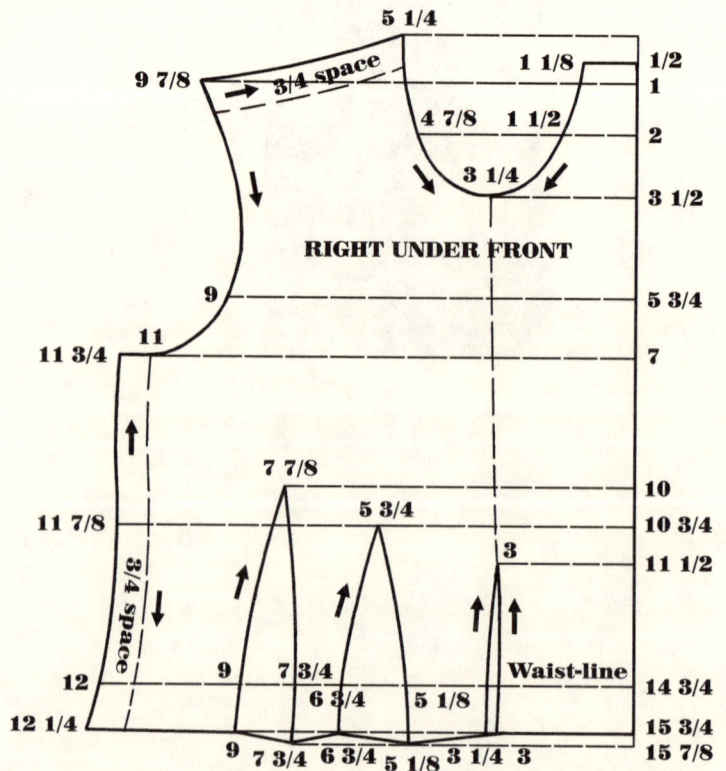

RIGHT UNDER FRONT

5 1/4 1 1/8 1/2

9 7/8 3/4 space 1

4 7/8 1 1/2 2

3 1/4 3 1/2

9 5 3/4

11 3/4 11 7

3/4 space

7 7/8 5 3/4 10

11 7/8 10 3/4

3 11 1/2

12 9 7 3/4 Waist-line 14 3/4

12 1/4 15 3/4

9 7 3/4 6 3/4 5 1/8 3 1/4 3 15 7/8

6 3/4 5 1/8

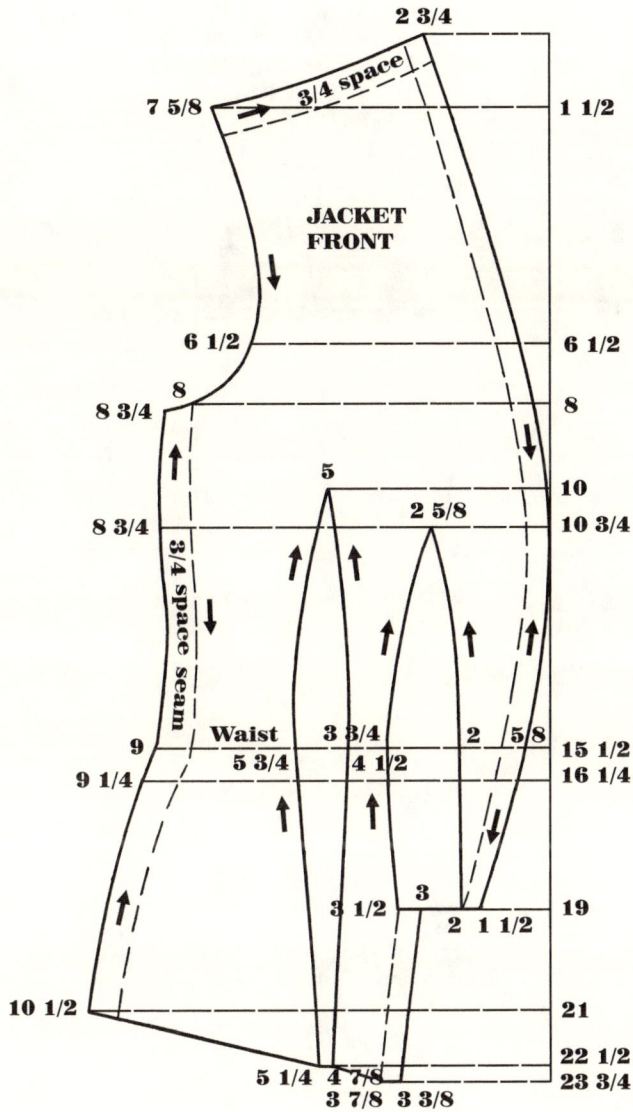

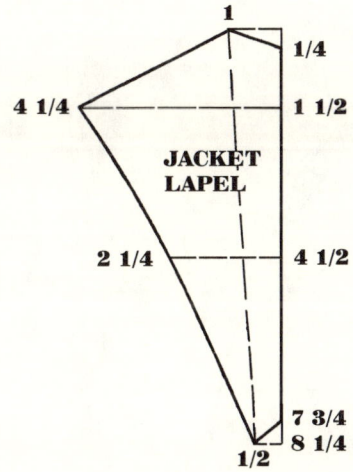

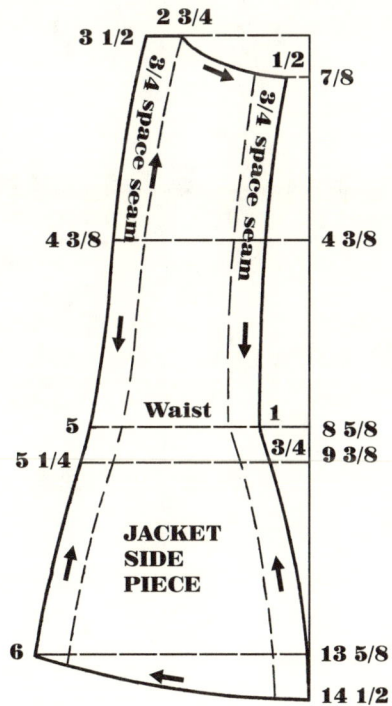

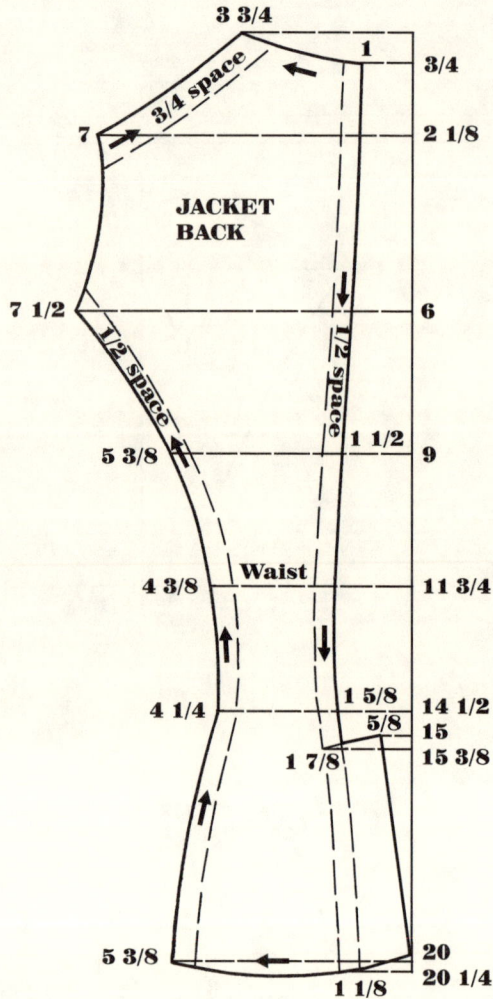

3 3/4

1

3/4

3/4 space

7

2 1/8

**JACKET
BACK**

7 1/2

1/2 space

1/2 space

6

5 3/8

1 1/2

9

4 3/8

Waist

11 3/4

4 1/4

1 5/8

14 1/2

5/8

15

1 7/8

15 3/8

5 3/8

20

20 1/4

1 1/8

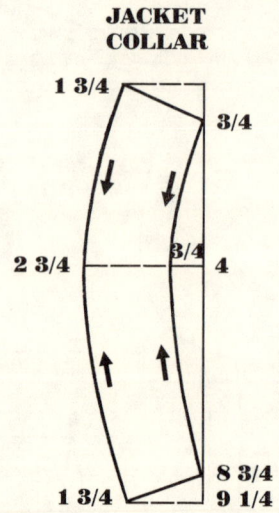

**JACKET
COLLAR**

1 3/4

3/4

2 3/4

3/4

4

1 3/4

8 3/4

9 1/4

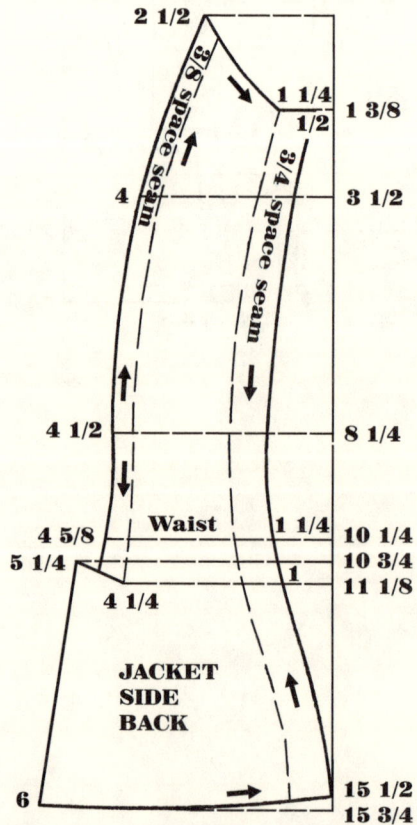

2 1/2

1 1/4

1 3/8

3/8 space seam

1/2

4

3/4 space seam

3 1/2

4 1/2

8 1/4

4 5/8

Waist

1 1/4

10 1/4

5 1/4

10 3/4

1

11 1/8

4 1/4

**JACKET
SIDE
BACK**

6

15 1/2

15 3/4

168

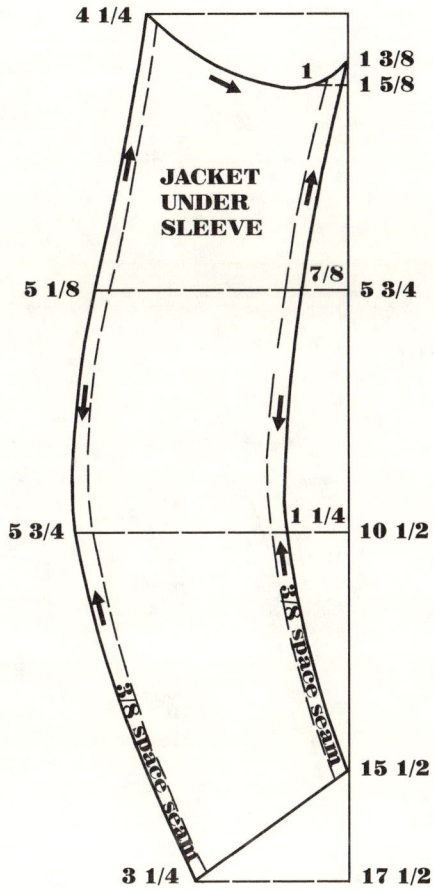

JACKET
UNDER
SLEEVE

4 1/4

1 3/8
1 5/8
1

5 1/8   7/8   5 3/4

5 3/4   1 1/4   10 1/2

3/8 space seam

15 1/2

3 1/4   17 1/2

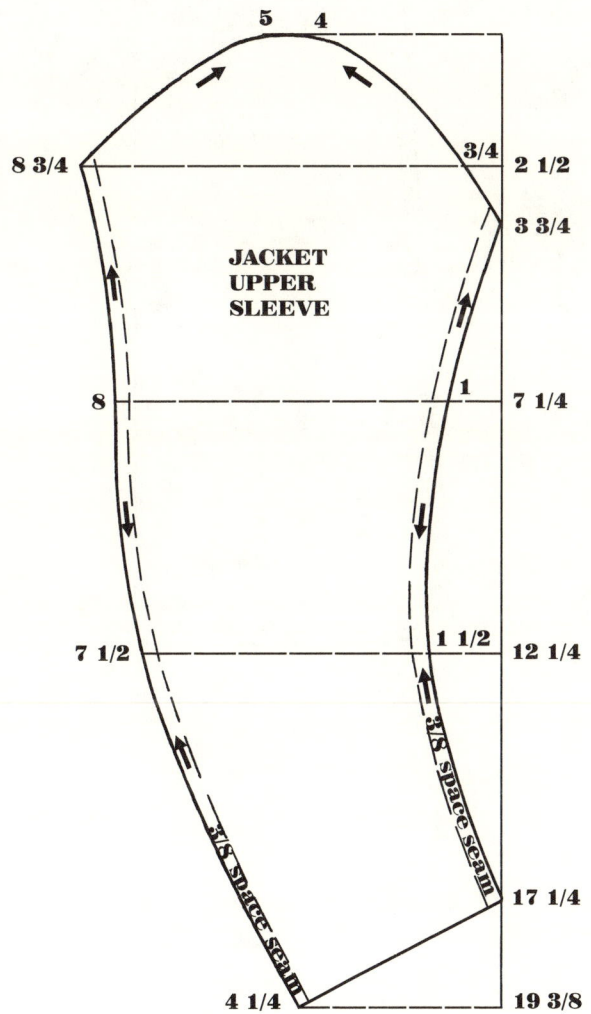

JACKET
UPPER
SLEEVE

5   4

8 3/4   3/4   2 1/2

3 3/4

8   1   7 1/4

7 1/2   1 1/2   12 1/4

3/8 space seam

17 1/4

4 1/4   19 3/8

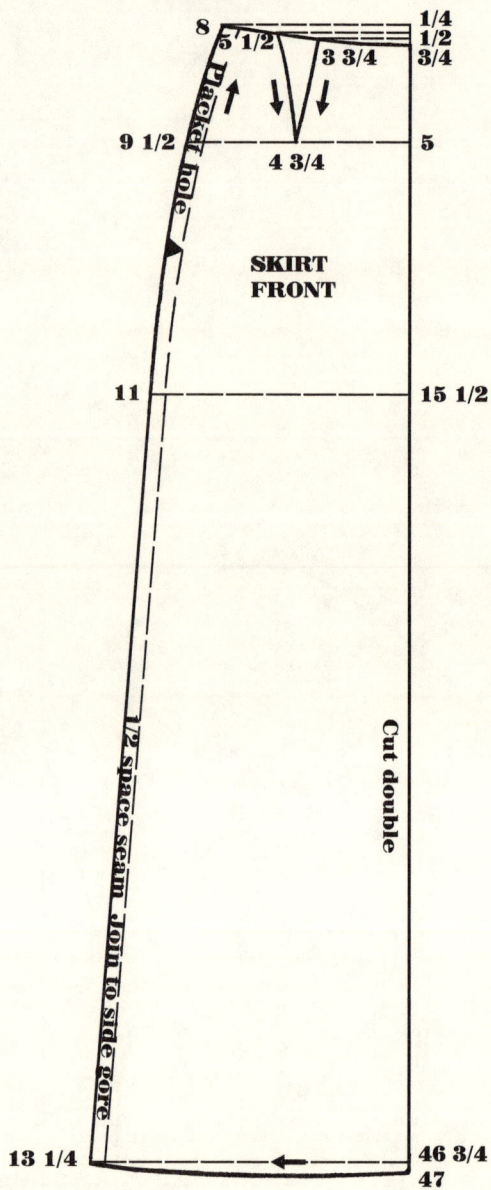

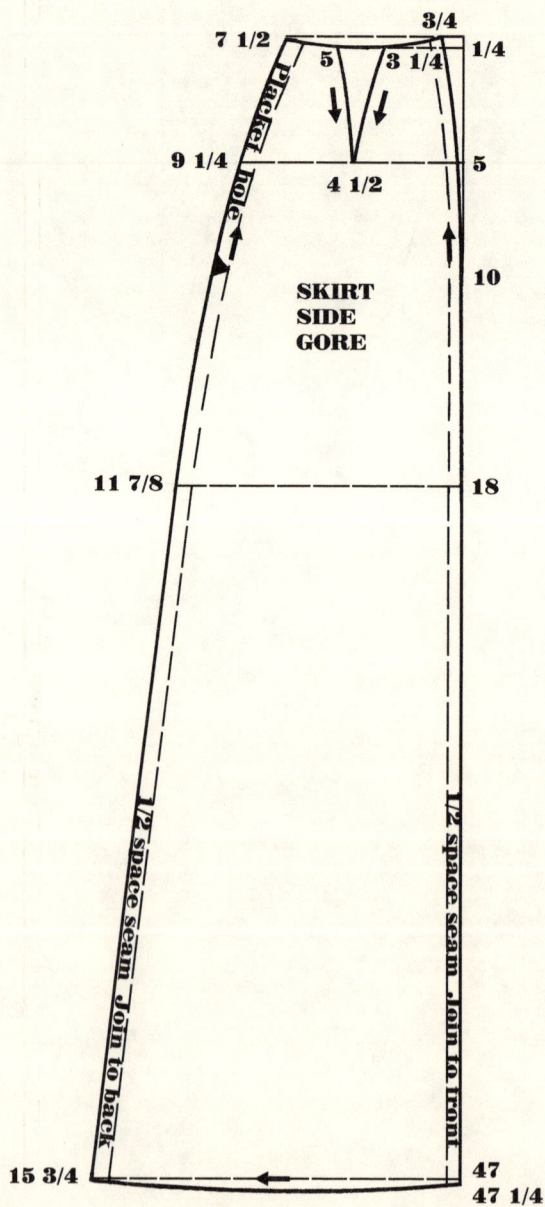

170

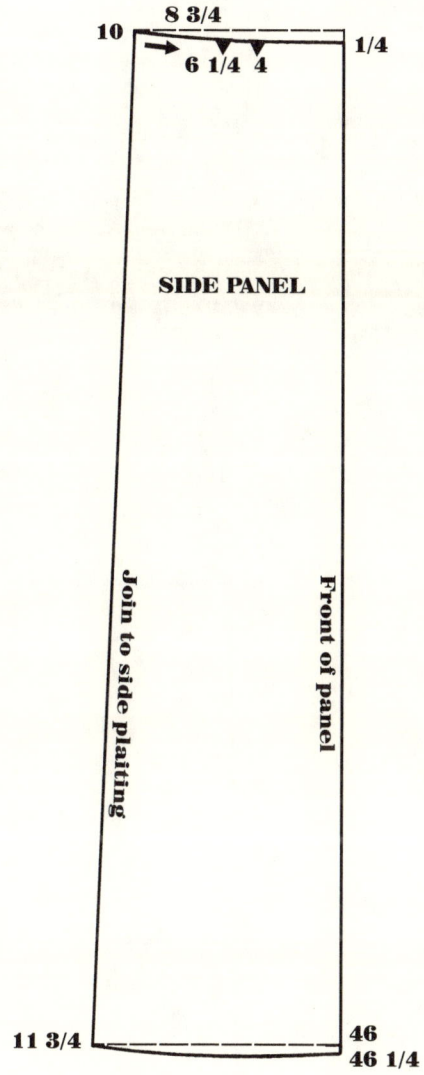

SIDE PANEL

8 3/4

10   1/4

6 1/4   4

Join to side plaiting

Front of panel

11 3/4   46
                46 1/4

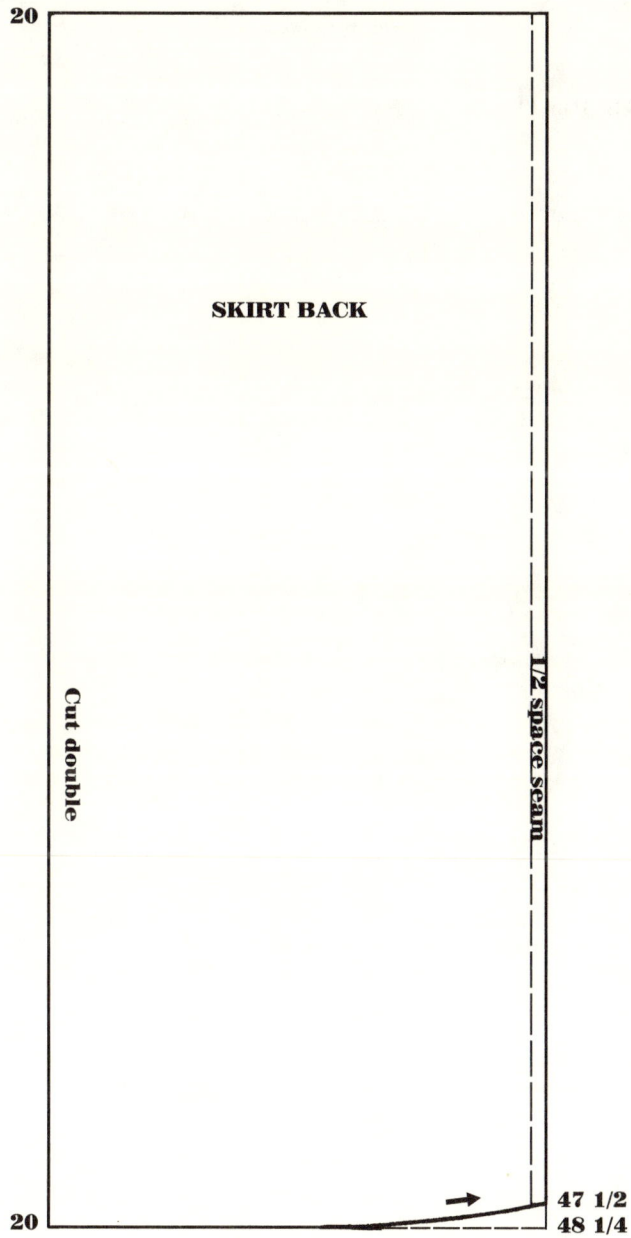

20

SKIRT BACK

Cut double

1/2 space seam

47 1/2
48 1/4

20

 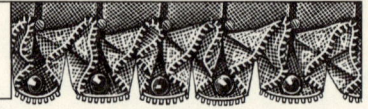
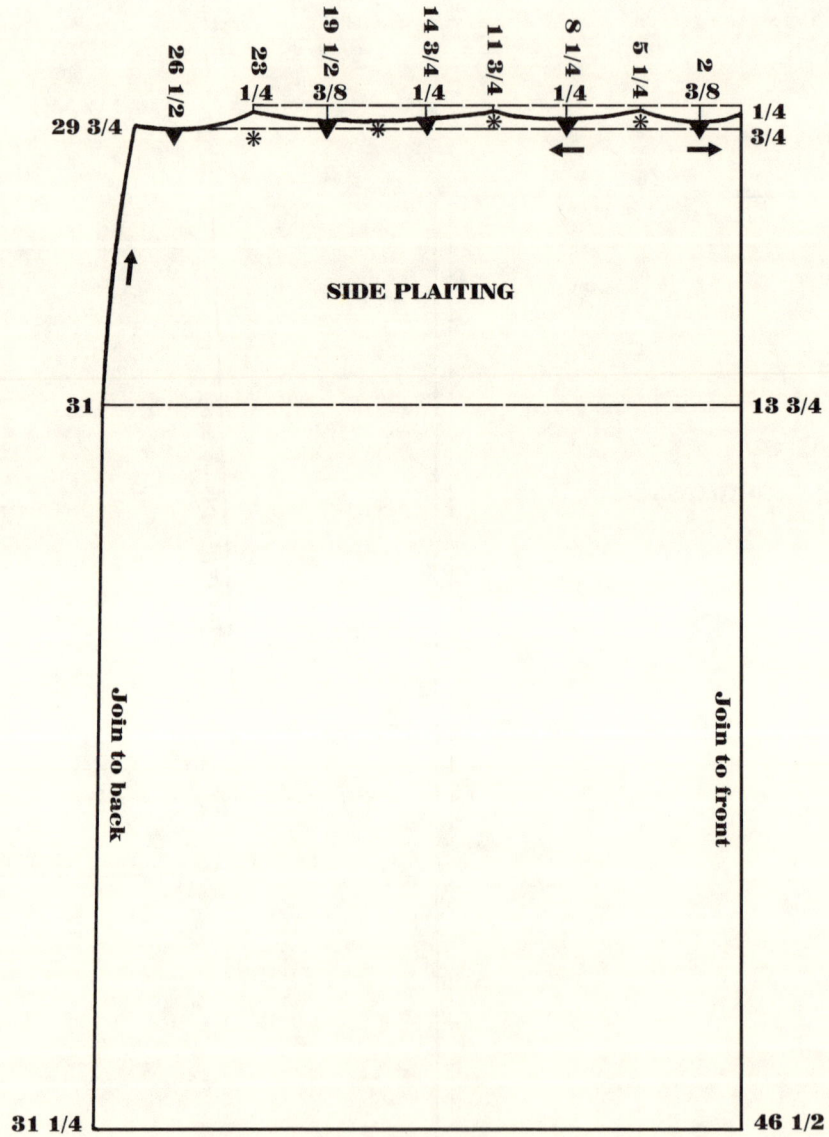

SIDE PLAITING

Join to back

Join to front

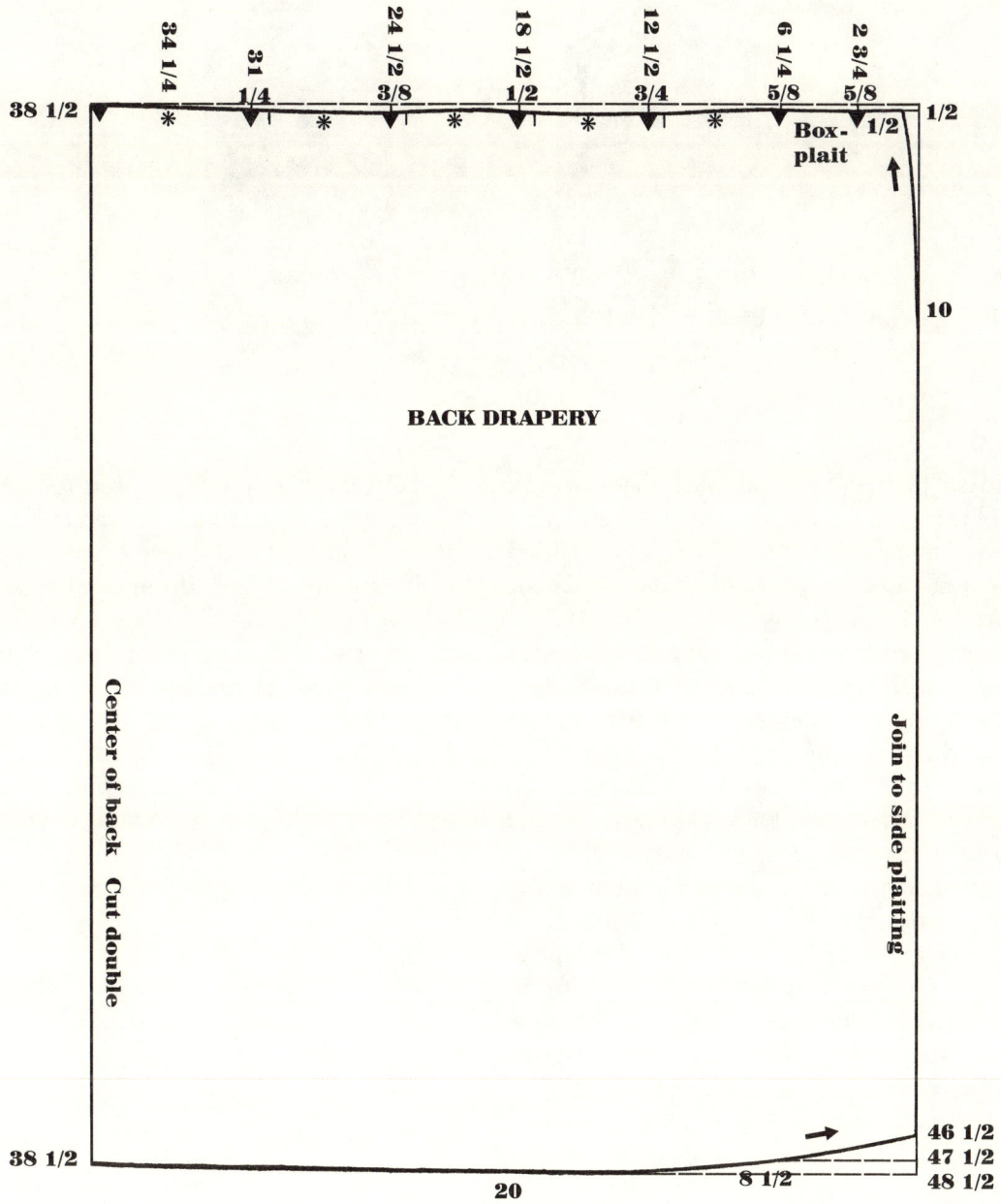

BACK DRAPERY

38 1/2

34 1/4

31 1/4

24 1/2 3/8

18 1/2 1/2

12 1/2 3/4

6 1/4 5/8

2 3/4 5/8

1/2

Box-plait

1/2

10

Center of back Cut double

Join to side plaiting

38 1/2

20

8 1/2

46 1/2

47 1/2

48 1/2

173

Ladies' Jacket. This example is made of dark cloth and trimmed with corded silk facings, appliqué bands, and fancy buttons. The fronts are fitted by single bust darts. They are turned back in lapels, which are faced with corded silk. The fronts flare over a narrow vest, which is considerably shorter and covered with appliqué bands. The back edges of the vest are sewed underneath to the fronts along the dart and flatly above. The curved front edges are closed with hooks and eyes. Side pieces, side backs, and a curved center back seam complete the adjustment. The center back seam ends at the top of coat laps, which are turned under and hemmed.

Three fancy buttons are placed decoratively along the edge of each front below the lapels. A curved pocket opening is made in each front, back of the dart. The edges of the opening are finished with machine-stitching, and the ends are stayed with triangular ornaments done with twist. The coat-shaped sleeves are each trimmed with an appliqué band, and so is the high standing collar.

All kinds of cloth are used for these jackets. Contrasts are very much in vogue, but one material may be used and the vest, collar, etc., braided in some pretty design. To make the garment for a lady of medium size, requires 4 yards of material 22 inches wide, 2 yards of material 44 inches wide, or 1 3/4 yards of material 54 inches wide. Each requires 3/4 yard of silk 20 inches wide for facing the lapels.

June 1889 *Delineator*

Street Costume

Use the scale corresponding to the bust measure to draft the bodice. It consists of ten pieces: Under front, upper front, jacket front, side back, back, collar, upper sleeve, under sleeve, sleeve puff, and sleeve band. It is closed at the back with buttons and button-holes. Cut the fronts double to avoid a seam down the center. Gather the upper front at the top to fit the neck. Gather the bottom between the notches from one to three times, as preferred. If the waist-line has been changed, change the lower line of the jacket; its edge should be at the waist-line when finished. Join it into the under-arm and shoulder seams. Fasten it in front with a hook and eye, or a clasp. Gather the sleeve puff on both sides. Sew the top to the sleeve, and the bottom to the band.

The sash (of which half is given), the panel, and the skirt (which is in one piece) are drafted with the waist measure. Regulate the length with the tape measure. Gather the panel slightly at the top to fit the hips. Line the under side with the same material, or a contrasting color. Trim it at the bottom with deep fringe the same shade as the costume. Trim the sash with long fringe that harmonizes with the sash color. Tie the sash in a large bow and sew it to the back. Tuck the front of the skirt as illustrated. Gather the back and sew the skirt to the bodice.

Fall 1889 *Voice of Fashion*

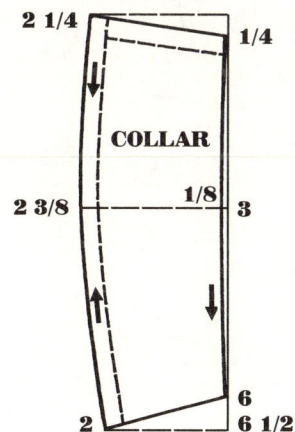

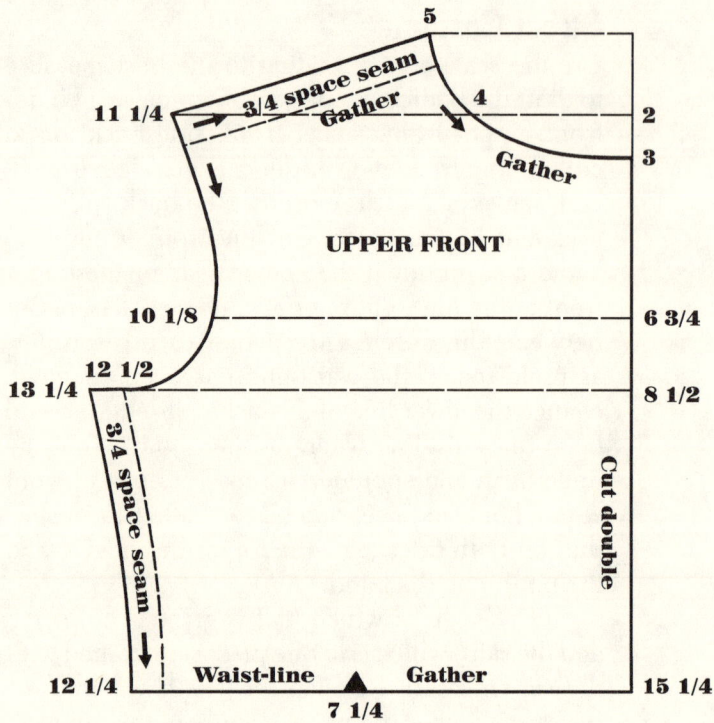

UPPER FRONT

5

11 1/4   3/4 space seam
Gather   4   2
Gather   3

10 1/8   6 3/4

12 1/2
13 1/4   8 1/2

3/4 space seam

Cut double

12 1/4   Waist-line   Gather   15 1/4
7 1/4

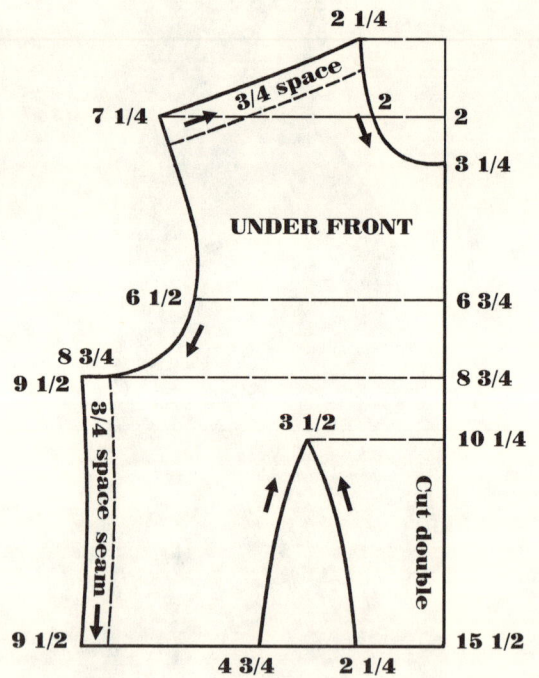

UNDER FRONT

2 1/4

7 1/4   3/4 space   2   2
3 1/4

6 1/2   6 3/4

8 3/4   8 3/4
9 1/2

3/4 space seam   3 1/2   10 1/4

Cut double

9 1/2   15 1/2
4 3/4   2 1/4

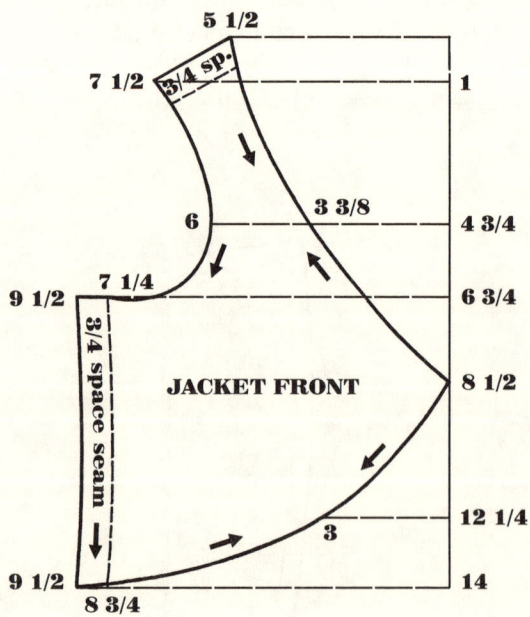

JACKET FRONT

5 1/2

7 1/2   3/4 sp.   1

6   3 3/8   4 3/4

9 1/2   7 1/4   6 3/4

3/4 space seam   8 1/2

9 1/2   3   12 1/4
8 3/4   14

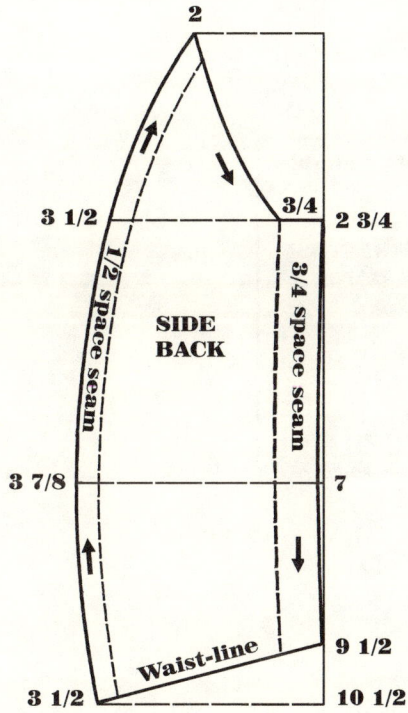

2

3 1/2   3/4   2 3/4

SIDE
BACK

1/2 space seam   3/4 space seam

3 7/8   7

Waist-line   9 1/2

3 1/2   10 1/2

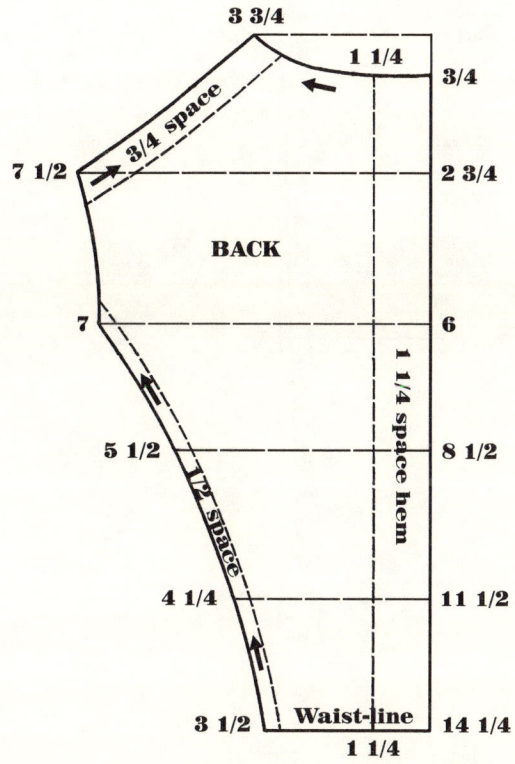

3 3/4   1 1/4   3/4

3/4 space

7 1/2   2 3/4

BACK

7   6

1 1/4 space hem

5 1/2   8 1/2

1/2 space

4 1/4   11 1/2

3 1/2   Waist-line   14 1/4

1 1/4

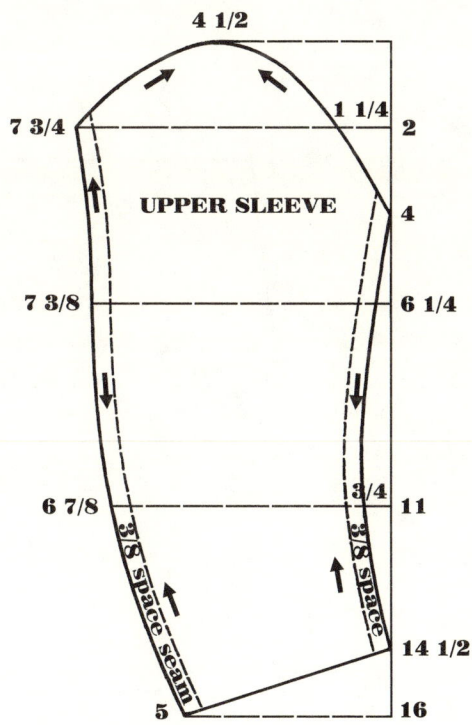

4 1/2

7 3/4   1 1/4   2

UPPER SLEEVE   4

7 3/8   6 1/4

6 7/8   3/4   11

3/8 space seam   3/8 space

5   16

14 1/2

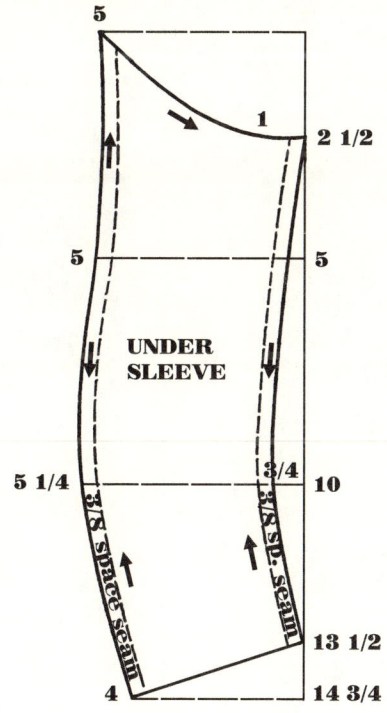

5

1   2 1/2

5   5

UNDER
SLEEVE

5 1/4   3/4   10

3/8 space seam   3/8 sp. seam

4   13 1/2

14 3/4

177

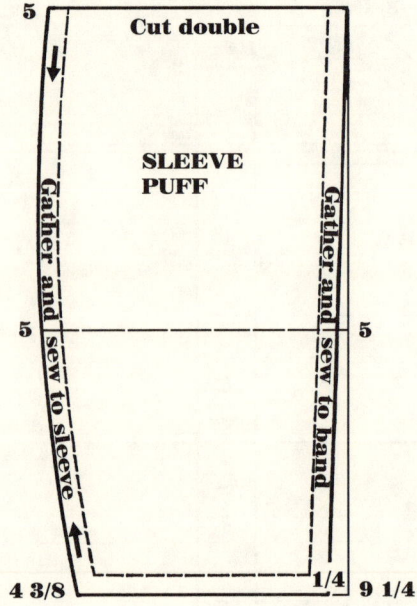

SLEEVE
PUFF

Cut double

5

Gather and sew to sleeve

Gather and sew to band

5 — 5

4 3/8   1/4 9 1/4

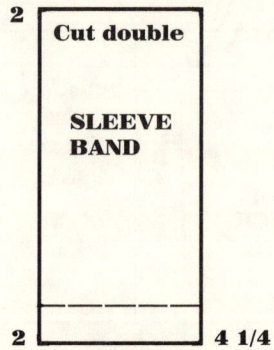

2   Cut double

SLEEVE
BAND

2   4 1/4

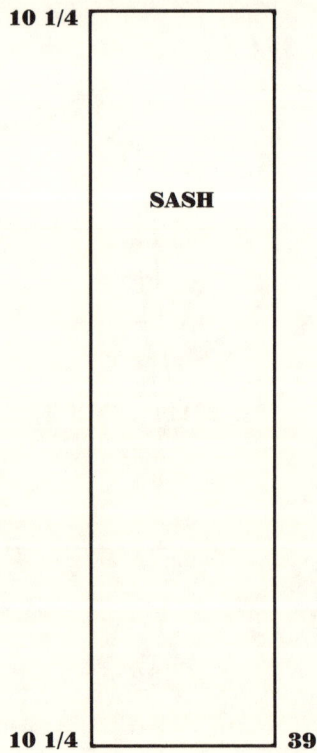

10 1/4

SASH

10 1/4   39

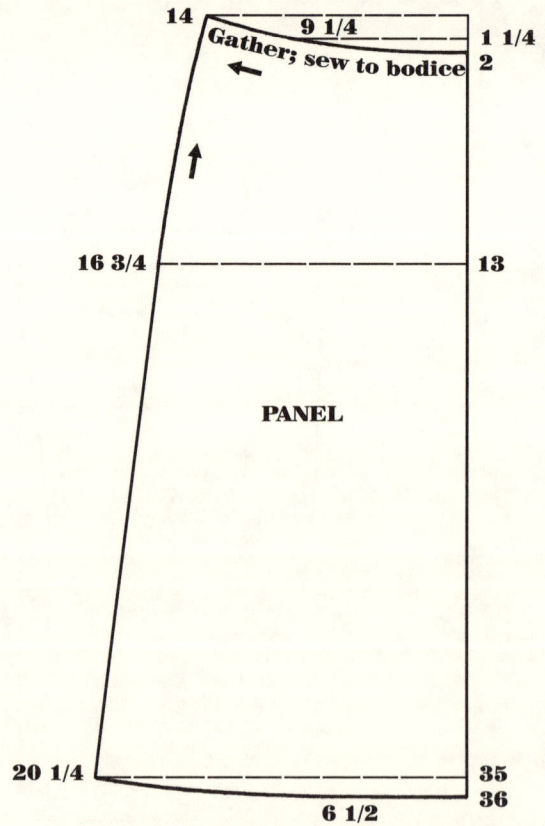

14   9 1/4   1 1/4
Gather; sew to bodice   2

16 3/4   13

PANEL

20 1/4   35
36
6 1/2

Street Costume

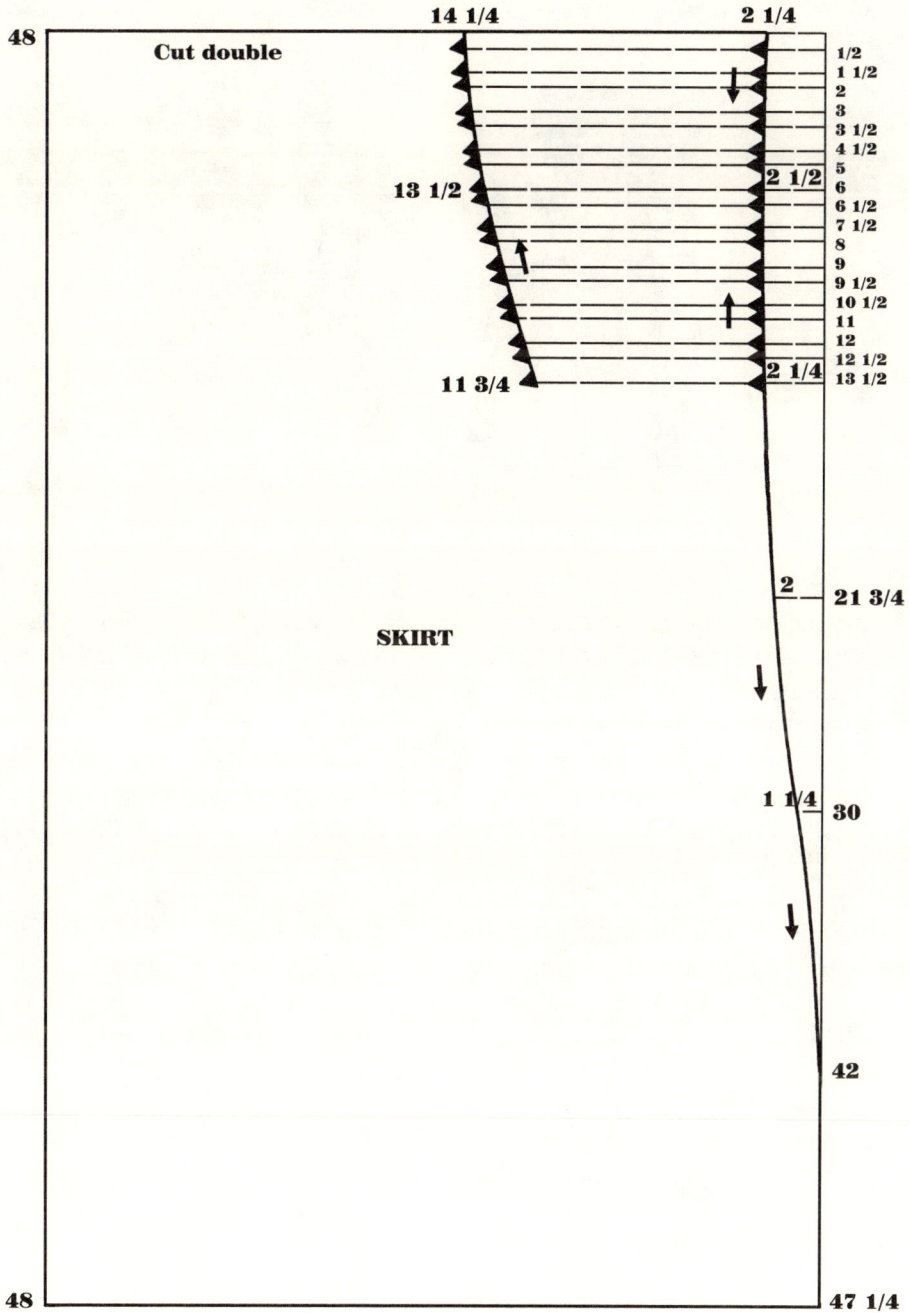

48   Cut double

14 1/4   2 1/4

1/2
1 1/2
2
3
3 1/2
4 1/2
5
2 1/2   6
6 1/2
7 1/2
8
9
9 1/2
10 1/2
11
12
12 1/2
2 1/4   13 1/2

13 1/2

11 3/4

SKIRT

2   21 3/4

1 1/4   30

42

48   47 1/4

Round Bodice. This bodice is shown made of figured dress material and velvet, the decorations consisting of velvet facings, velvet ribbon, and a belt of the material. The adjustment is effected by double bust darts, side pieces, side backs, and a center back seam. The front linings are closed with buttons and button-holes. The fronts are shirred halfway down the shoulder edges. At the waist-line the fullness is confined by three lines of shirring, which extend to the second dart and are basted to the linings. Bows of velvet ribbon are ornamentally placed on the front edge of the right front. The neck, which is rather low, is finished with a rolling collar, the front edges of which are slanted. The coat sleeves are trimmed at the wrists with velvet cuff-facings. The upper part of each sleeve is decorated with a puff, which is gathered at its long edges on the upper side. At the waist-line is a plaited belt, below which the bodice is worn under the top of the skirt, the arrangement holding it securely in place.

Nun's veiling, challis, cashmere, all-wool surah, serge, foulard, and other light-weight summer materials are suitable. Ribbon, velvet, braid, passementerie, galloon, etc., may be used for trimmings. A stylish bodice may be made of pistache Henrietta cloth, the collar, cuff-facings, bows, and belt being of white faille. Such bodices may be worn with different styles of skirts made of contrasting colors and materials. To make the bodice for a lady of medium size, requires 3 7/8 yards of material 22 inches wide, 2 5/8 yards of material 36 inches wide, or 2 yards of material 44 inches wide. Each requires 5/8 yard of lining 36 inches wide for the front linings, and 1/2 yard of velvet 20 inches wide for the collar, etc.

August 1889 *Delineator*

Walking Skirt

Walking Skirt. The four-gored skirt is shown made of suit material. A long, slender bustle is worn with it, tapes being sewed to the side-back seams to draw the fullness backward. Over the front gore is adjusted a drapery that is laid in tiny forward-turning tucks on each side of the center, the tucks being graduated in length to form a V-shaped outline. Overlapping the front drapery on each side is a drapery that is laid in four deep, forward-turning plaits and included in the side-back seams. The back drapery is widely hemmed at its side edges, turned down deeply at the top, and caught together underneath at the top and bottom of the reversed part to give the effect of coarse gauging. The top of the back drapery may be secured to the skirt belt when the basque skirt is to be worn outside, or to the outside of any style of basque if the round waist effect is desired at the back. The back view illustrates the location of the hook and eye for attachment to the belt.

This mode is adaptable to all kinds of wool and silk dress materials. Cashmere, poplin, foulé, silk-and-wool barège, etc., are especially appropriate. To make the skirt for a lady of medium size, requires 10 1/8 yards of material 22 inches wide, or 5 1/8 yards of material 44 inches wide.

November 1889 *Delineator*

Street Costume

Use the scale corresponding to the bust measure to draft the basque. It consists of seven pieces: Front, vest, side back, back, collar, and two sleeve pieces. Turn the front back on the dashed line for the lapels, and face with velvet or any suitable material.

The drapery is drafted with the scale corresponding to the waist measure. Regulate the length with the tape measure. It is in two pieces: Front and back. Lay the back drapery in two triple box-plaits. Lay the plaits in front according to the notches.

The skirt is drafted with the scale corresponding to the waist measure. Regulate the length with the tape measure. It is in three pieces: Front, side gore, and back.

Fall 1889 *Voice of Fashion*

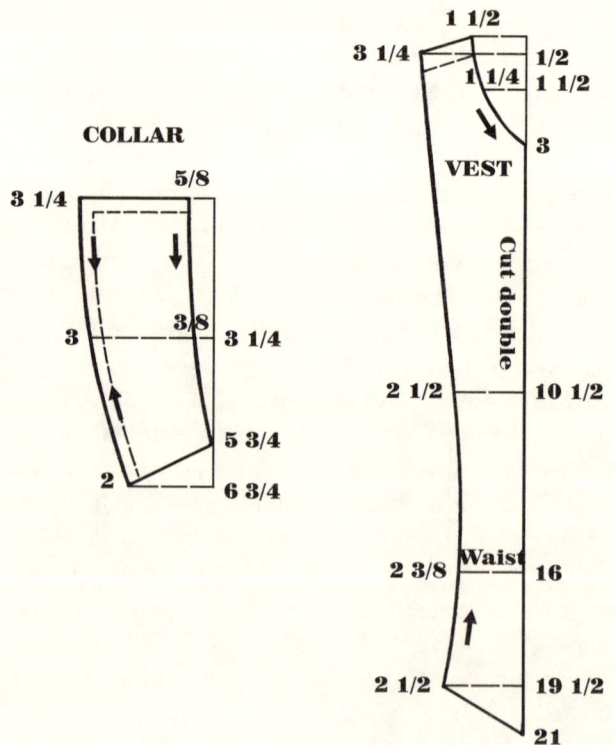

COLLAR

	5/8
3 1/4	
3	3/8 3 1/4
2	5 3/4
	6 3/4

VEST

1 1/2
3 1/4   1/2
1 1/4   1 1/2
3

Cut double

2 1/2   10 1/2

2 3/8 Waist 16

2 1/2   19 1/2
21

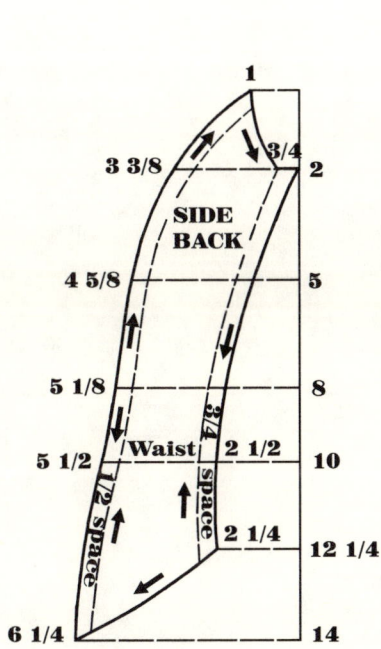

SIDE BACK

1
3 3/8
3/4
2
4 5/8 — 5
5 1/8 — 8
5 1/2 — Waist — 2 1/2 — 10
1/2 space — 3/4 space — 2 1/4 — 12 1/4
6 1/4 — 14

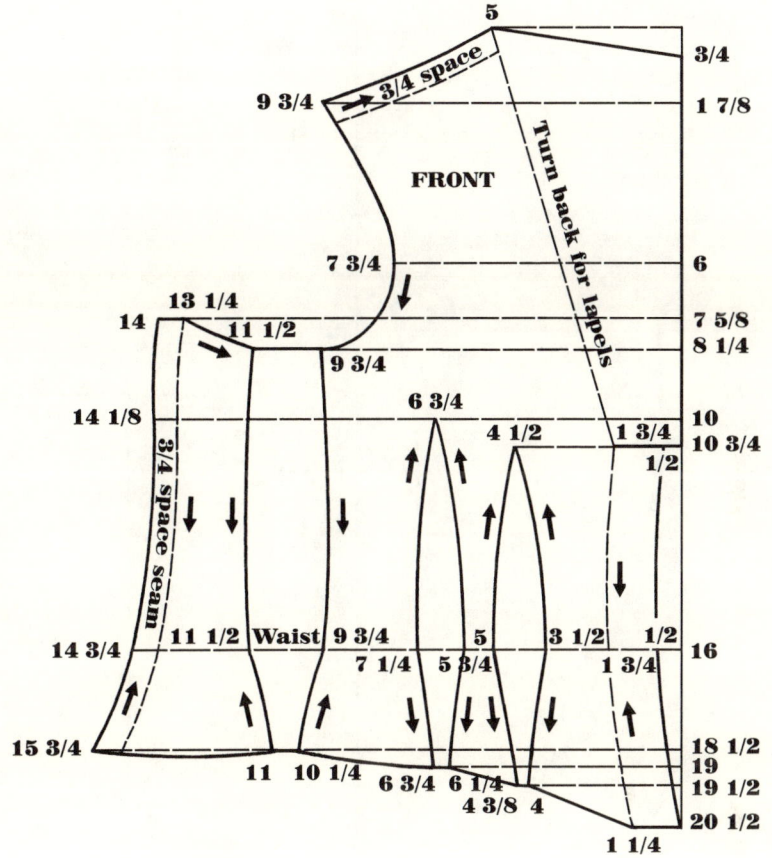

FRONT

5
3/4
9 3/4 — 3/4 space — 1 7/8
7 3/4 — 6
13 1/4 — 7 5/8
14 — 11 1/2 — 8 1/4
9 3/4
14 1/8 — 6 3/4 — 4 1/2 — 1 3/4 — 10
3/4 space seam — 10 3/4
1/2
14 3/4 — 11 1/2 — Waist — 9 3/4 — 5 — 3 1/2 — 1/2 — 16
7 1/4 — 5 3/4 — 1 3/4
15 3/4 — 18 1/2
19
11 — 10 1/4 — 6 3/4 — 6 1/4 — 19 1/2
4 3/8 — 4 — 20 1/2
1 1/4

Turn back for lapels

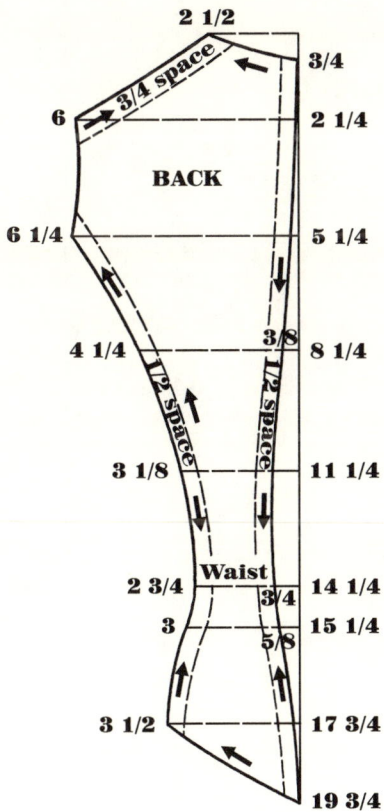

BACK

2 1/2
6 — 3/4 space — 3/4
2 1/4
6 1/4 — 5 1/4
4 1/4 — 3/8 — 8 1/4
1/2 space — 1/2 space
3 1/8 — 11 1/4
2 3/4 — Waist — 14 1/4
3/4
3 — 15 1/4
5/8
3 1/2 — 17 3/4
19 3/4

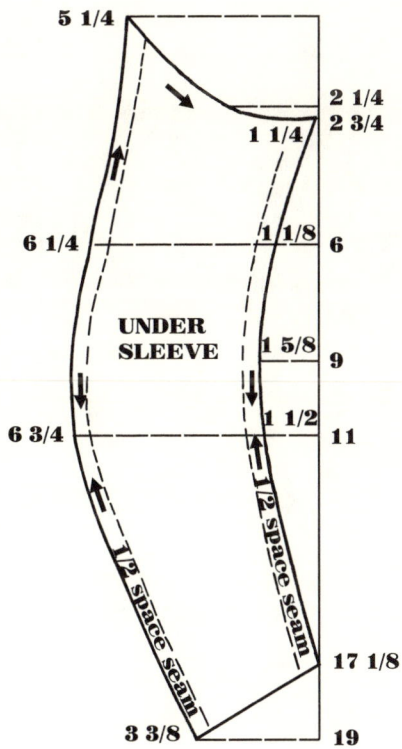

UNDER SLEEVE

5 1/4
2 1/4
2 3/4
1 1/4
6 1/4 — 1 1/8 — 6
1 5/8 — 9
1 1/2
6 3/4 — 11
1/2 space seam — 1/2 space seam
17 1/8
3 3/8 — 19

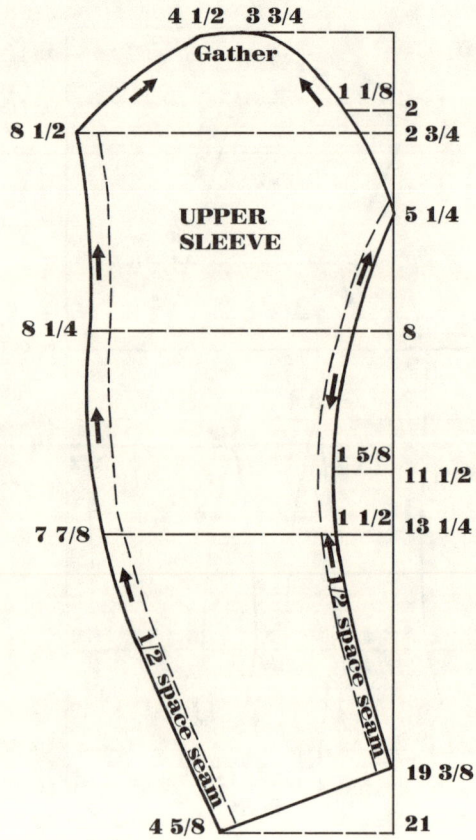

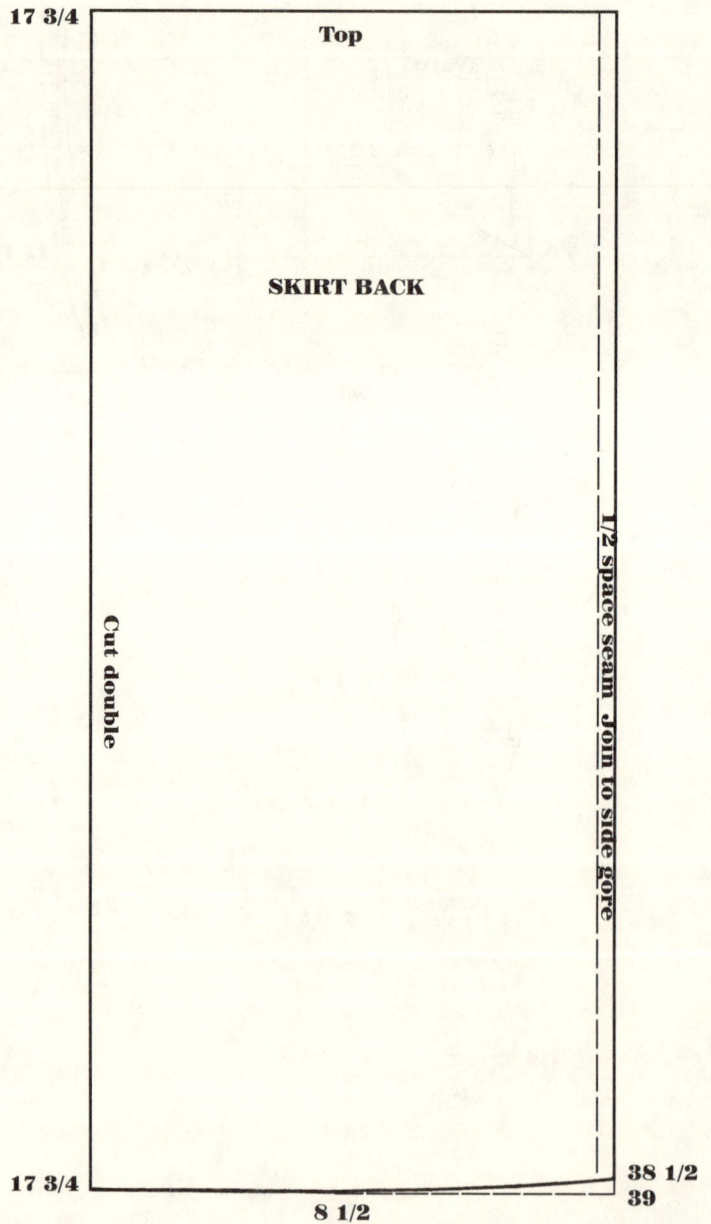

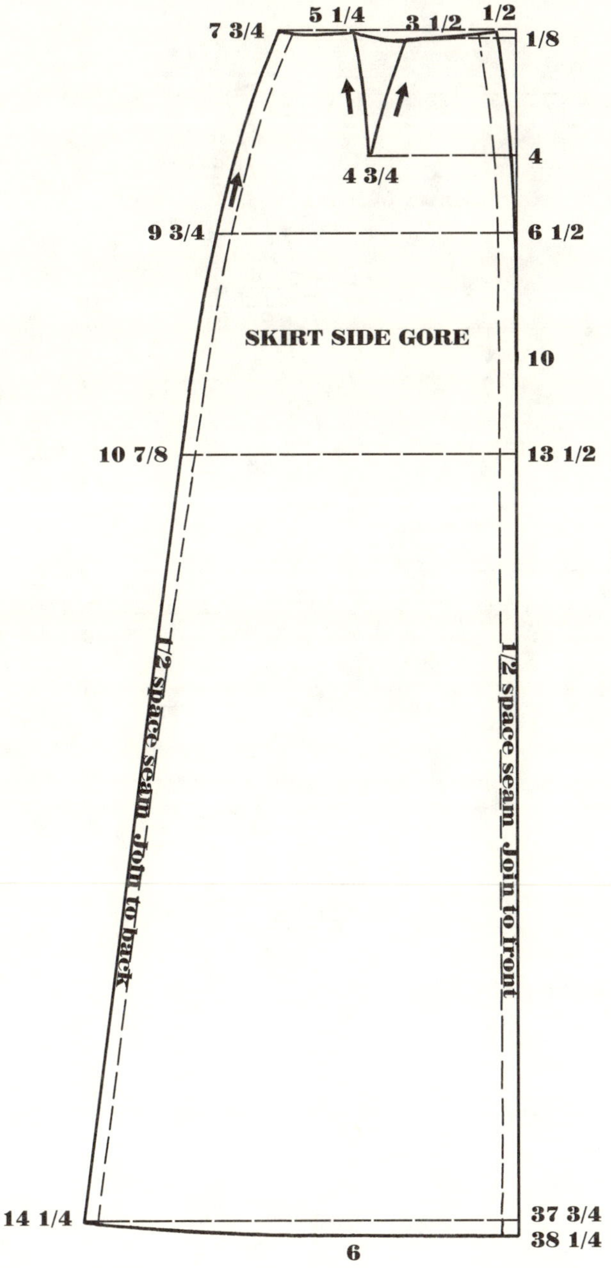

SKIRT SIDE GORE

7 3/4

5 1/4   3 1/2   1/2

1/8

4 3/4   4

9 3/4   6 1/2

10

10 7/8   13 1/2

1/2 space seam   Join to back

1/2 space seam   Join to front

14 1/4   37 3/4

38 1/4

6

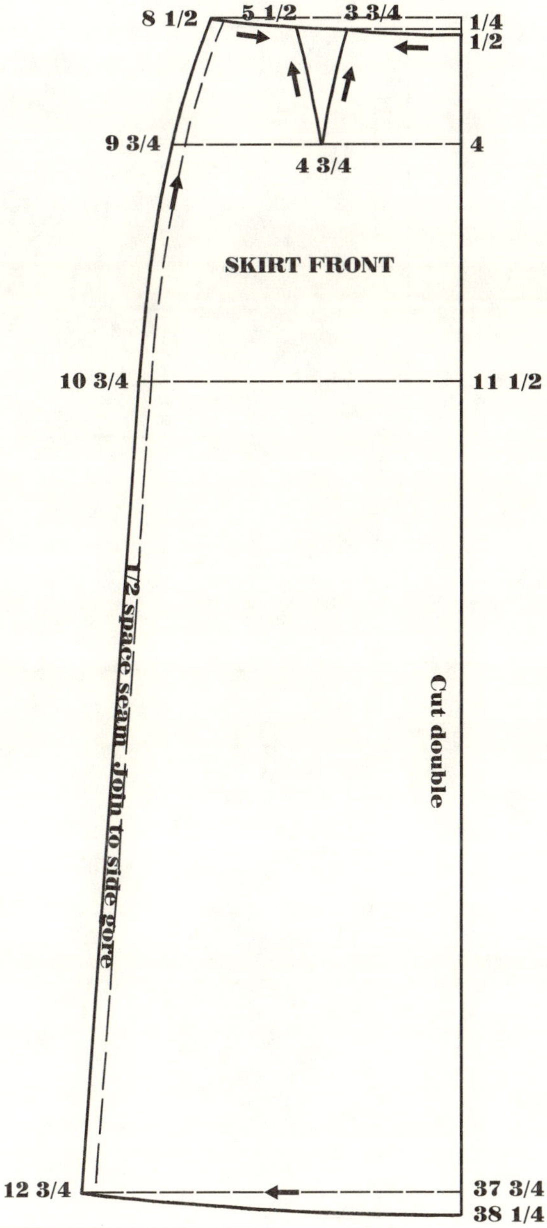

SKIRT FRONT

8 1/2   5 1/2   3 3/4   1/4

1/2

9 3/4   4

4 3/4

10 3/4   11 1/2

1/2 space seam   Join to side gore

Cut double

12 3/4   37 3/4

38 1/4

185

Ensembles with Bodices

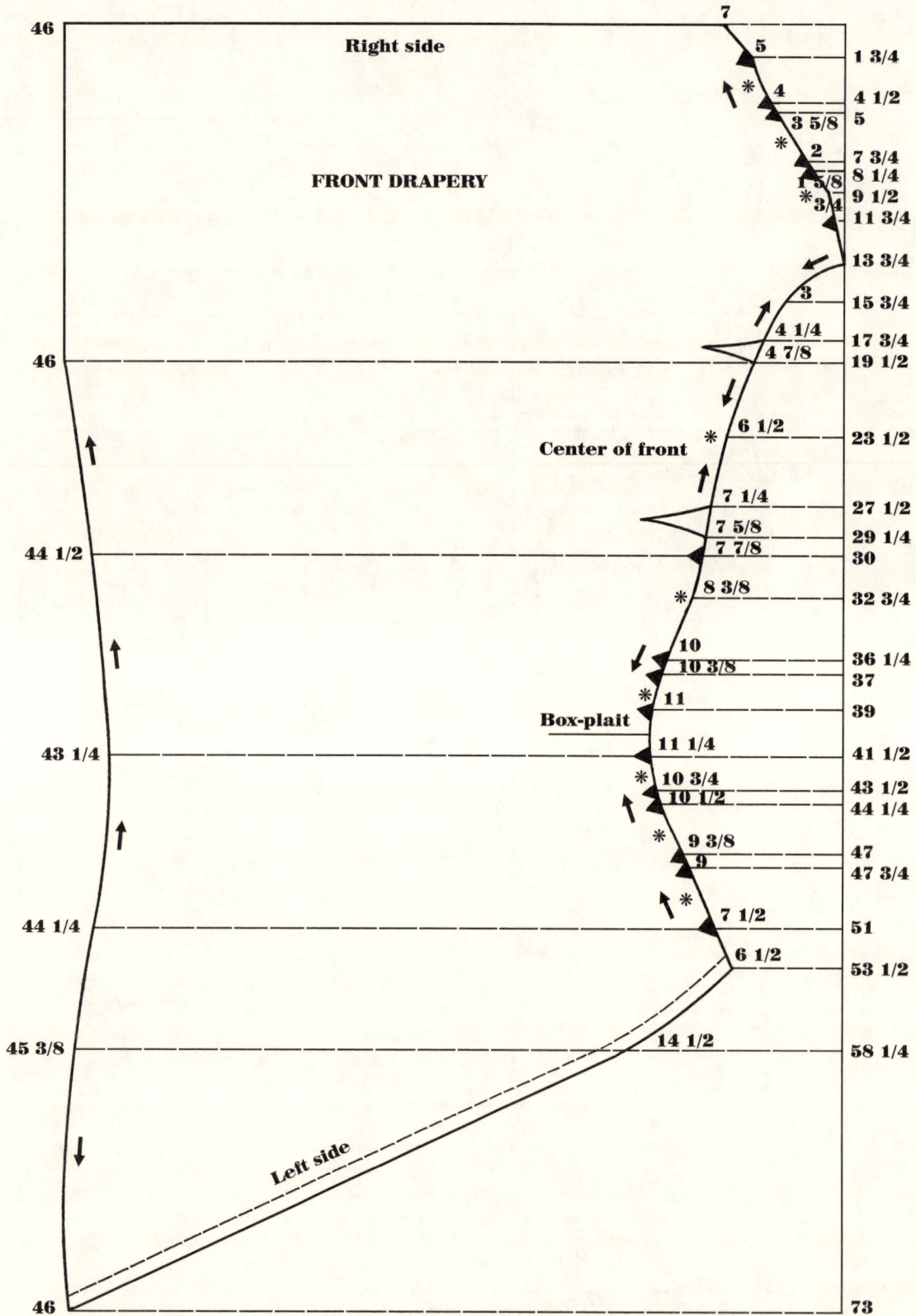

Right side

FRONT DRAPERY

Center of front

Box-plait

Left side

186

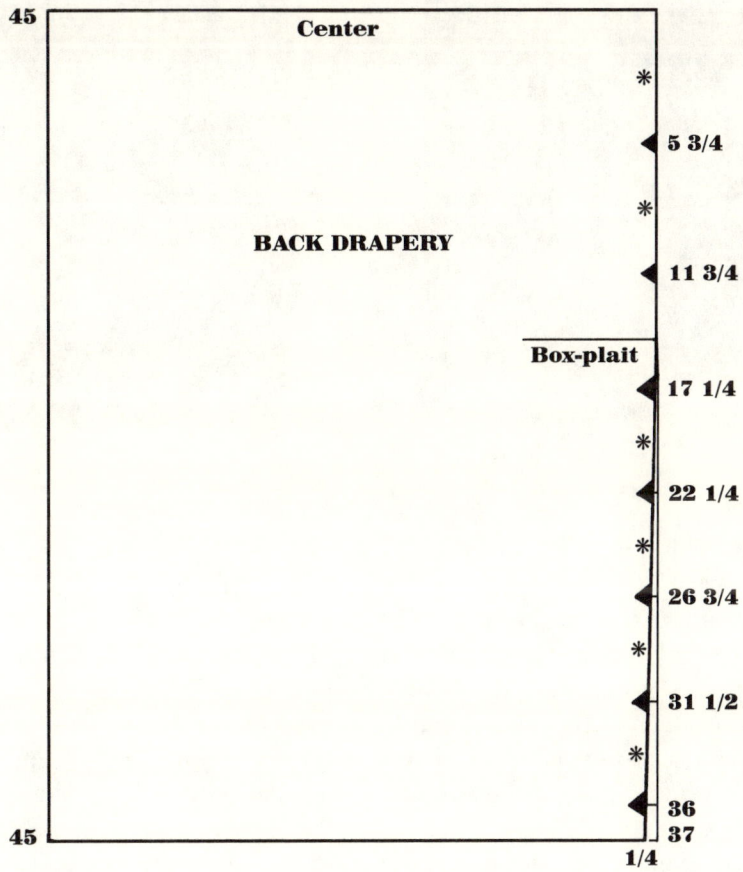

45 Center

❋

◀ 5 3/4

❋

BACK DRAPERY

◀ 11 3/4

Box-plait

◀ 17 1/4

❋

◀ 22 1/4

❋

◀ 26 3/4

❋

◀ 31 1/2

❋

◀ 36

45 37

1/4

Walking Skirt. The skirt is shown made of dress material, one edge of which has a striped border that is visible all around at the bottom of the drapery, forming its only finish. The foundation skirt is in the standard four-gored style. It has three steels inserted in casings across the back breadth, the steels almost meeting at the side-back seams and flaring toward the center. Tapes or elastic straps hold the steels in curves.

The drapery is all in one piece. It achieves the "natural effect," falling in free folds that are held only at the belt. It is draped to hang almost to the edge of the skirt at the back, to curve high and reveal the skirt well on the sides, and to droop quite near the edge at the center of the front. This varied effect is produced entirely by the unique mode of draping. The folds in the front and sides are produced by a group of six deep, forward-turning plaits in the top on each side of the center of the front, just back of a backward-turning plait, and a group of five backward-turning plaits a short distance back of these. At the back, the ends of the drapery are seamed save for the placket depth. On each side of the placket is a group of six deep, backward-turning plaits that lap so that their underfolds come even. Over these plaits, a forward-turning plait is formed in such a way that the drapery is thrown into jabot folds. The change of direction made in the plaits at the hip results very attractively, and the lower edge at the plaits is disposed in jabot folds. A basting made to each side gore, and another to each side of the back breadth, keeps them permanently in place.

Bordered materials and those with nice selvages look well when made up in this way, as the selvage should be left unfinished. Pinked edges are also stylish, and lace flouncing may be used for a lace dress. Embroidered flouncings often form the drapery on cotton materials. To make the skirt for a lady of medium size, requires 14 7/8 yards of material 22 inches wide, or 8 1/8 yards of material 44 inches wide.

August 1889 *Delineator*

Street Costume

Use the scale corresponding to the bust measure to draft the basque. It consists of eleven pieces: Under front, upper front, front shirring, yoke, girdle, side piece, side back, back, collar, and two sleeve pieces. The basque has a pannier back, and is finished at the back the same as a gentleman's coat. Turn the upper front back on the diagonal dashed line, and face it with suitable material. The plastron, composed of the shirring, yoke, and girdle, can be made separately. The material and color may correspond or contrast to the basque.

Draft the trimmed over-skirt with the scale corresponding to the waist measure. Regulate the length with the tape measure. There are three pieces: Front plaiting, side panel, and back drapery. Lay the back in two triple box-plaits, one on each side. Lay the plaits in the front according to the notches. Press them carefully, and stay them underneath with tape. Lay the plait in the side panel according to the notches, forming a single box-plait. Face with material that harmonizes in color. The bottom may be finished with fringe of the same shade.

Draft the foundation skirt with the scale corresponding to the waist measure. Regulate the length with the tape measure. There are three pieces: Front, side gore, and back.

Winter 1889–1890 *Voice of Fashion*

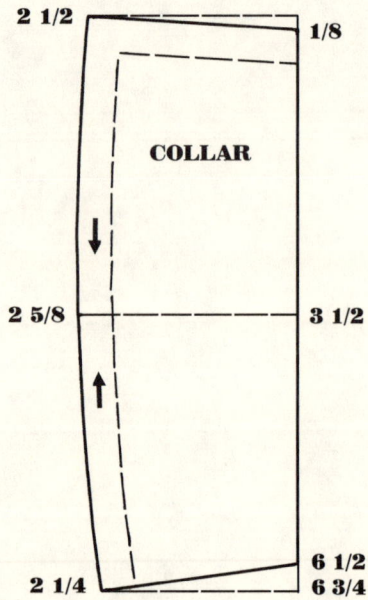

COLLAR

2 1/2 1/8

2 5/8 3 1/2

2 1/4 6 1/2
6 3/4

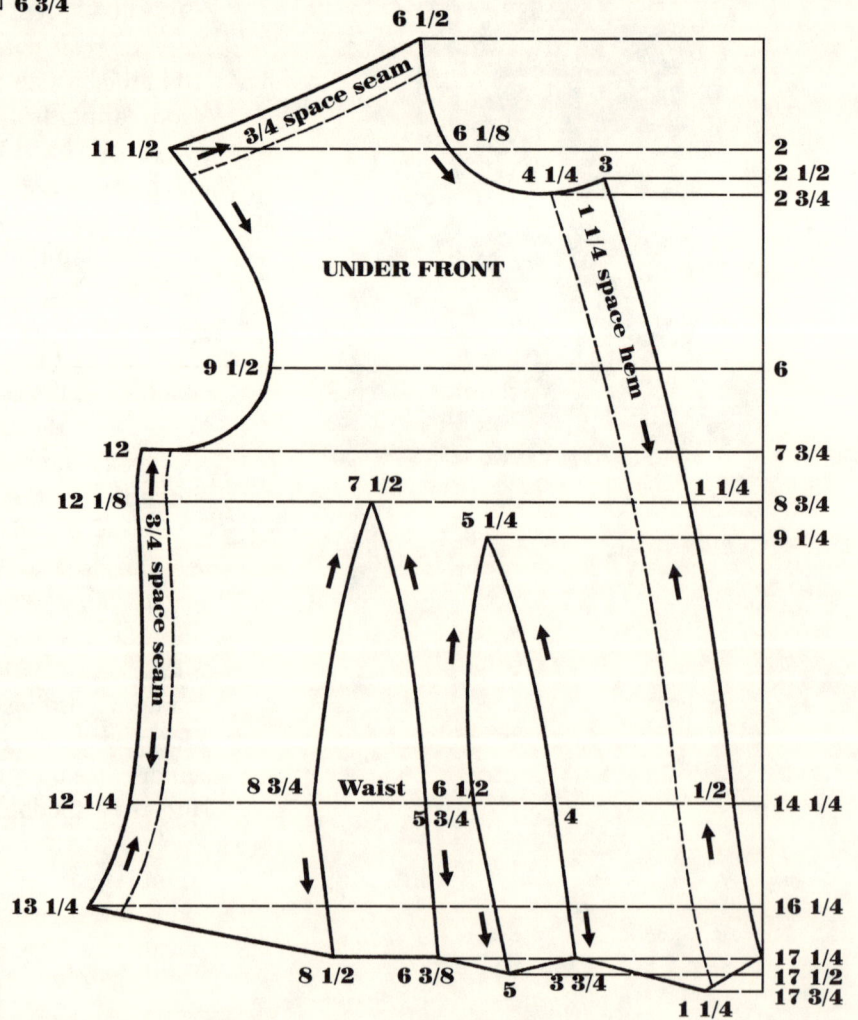

6 1/2

3/4 space seam

11 1/2   6 1/8   2
4 1/4 3   2 1/2
2 3/4

1 1/4 space hem

UNDER FRONT

9 1/2   6

12   7 3/4

12 1/8   7 1/2   5 1/4   1 1/4   8 3/4
9 1/4

3/4 space seam

12 1/4   8 3/4   Waist   6 1/2   1/2   14 1/4
5 3/4   4

13 1/4   16 1/4

8 1/2   6 3/8   5   3 3/4   17 1/4
17 1/2
1 1/4   17 3/4

Street Costume

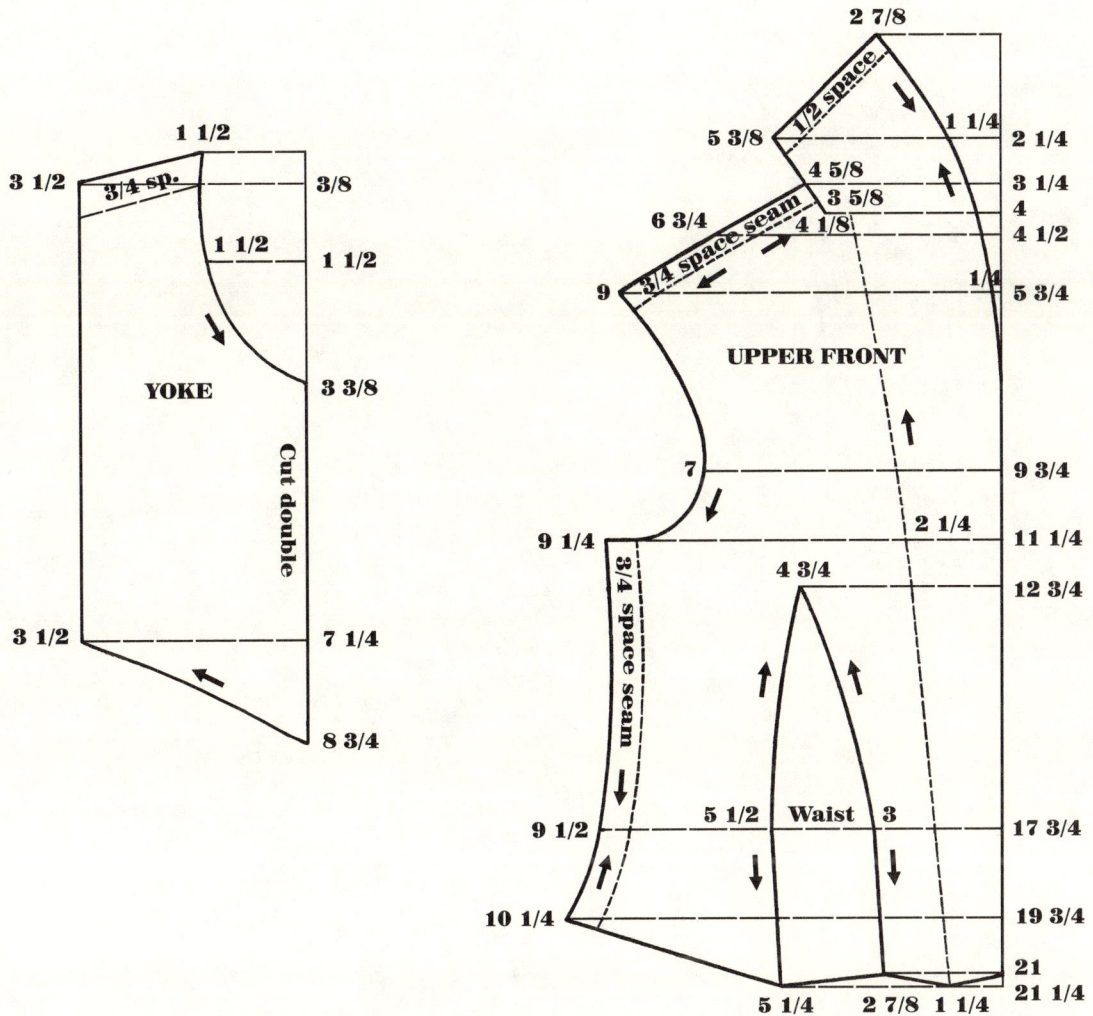

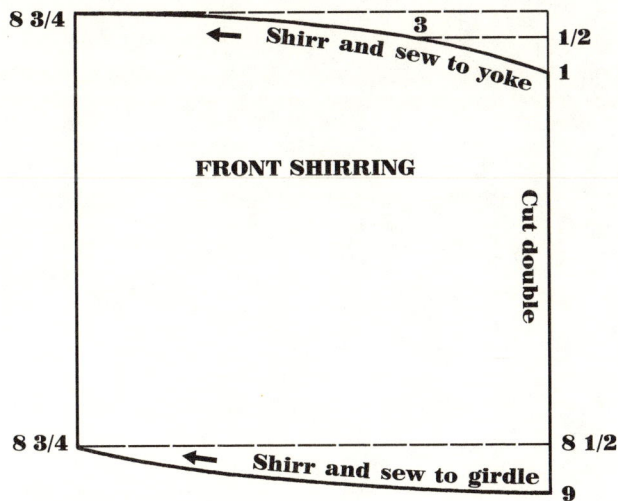

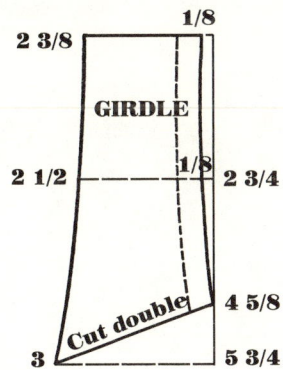

YOKE

1 1/2

3 1/2 · 3/4 sp. · 3/8

1 1/2 · 1 1/2

3 3/8

Cut double

3 1/2 · 7 1/4

8 3/4

UPPER FRONT

2 7/8

1/2 space

5 3/8 · 1 1/4 · 2 1/4

4 5/8 · 3 1/4

3 5/8 · 4

6 3/4 · 3/4 space seam · 4 1/8 · 4 1/2

9 · 3/4 space seam · 1/4 · 5 3/4

7 · 9 3/4

9 1/4 · 2 1/4 · 11 1/4

4 3/4 · 12 3/4

3/4 space seam

9 1/2 · 5 1/2 Waist 3 · 17 3/4

10 1/4 · 19 3/4

21

5 1/4 · 2 7/8 · 1 1/4 · 21 1/4

FRONT SHIRRING

8 3/4 · 3 · 1/2

← Shirr and sew to yoke · 1

Cut double

8 3/4 · 8 1/2

← Shirr and sew to girdle · 9

GIRDLE

2 3/8 · 1/8

2 1/2 · 1/8 · 2 3/4

Cut double

3 · 4 5/8

5 3/4

SIDE PIECE

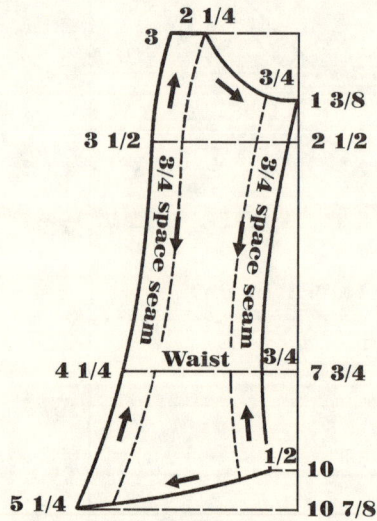

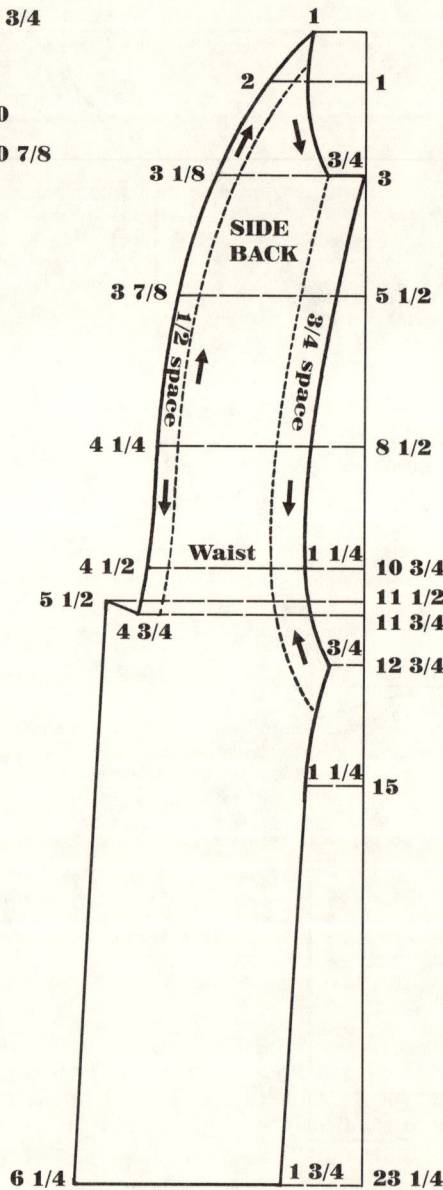

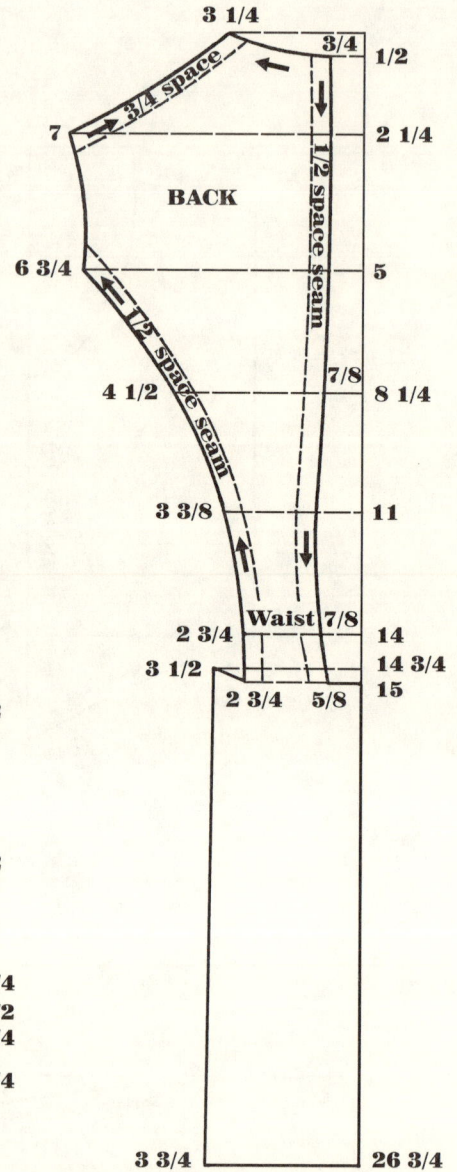

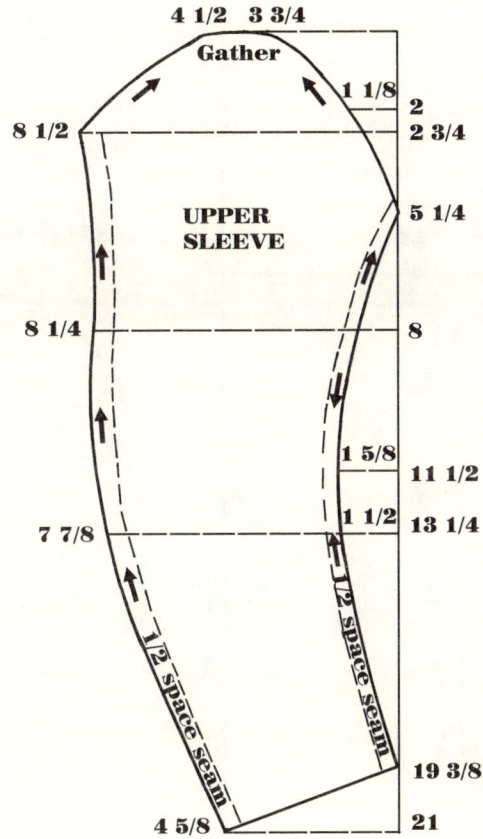

UPPER
SLEEVE

4 1/2   3 3/4
Gather
1 1/8
8 1/2
2
2 3/4
5 1/4
8 1/4
8
1 5/8
11 1/2
1 1/2
13 1/4
7 7/8
1/2 space seam
1/2 space seam
19 3/8
4 5/8
21

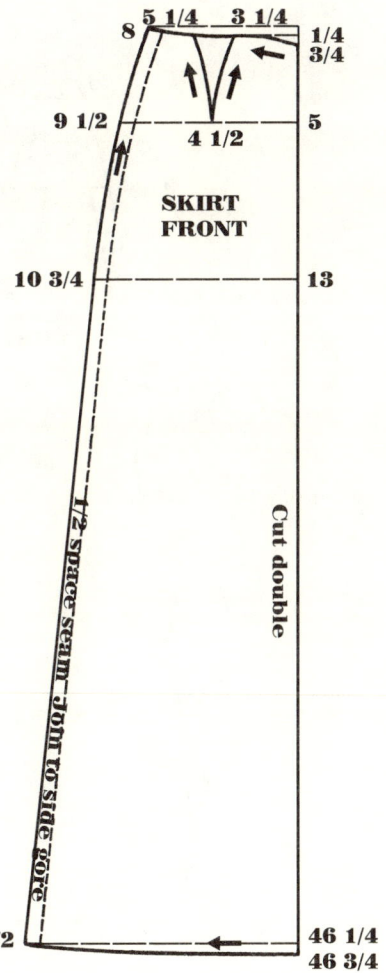

SKIRT
FRONT

5 1/4   3 1/4
8
1/4
3/4
9 1/2
4 1/2
5
10 3/4
13
1/2 space seam—joint to side gore
Cut double
14 1/2
46 1/4
46 3/4

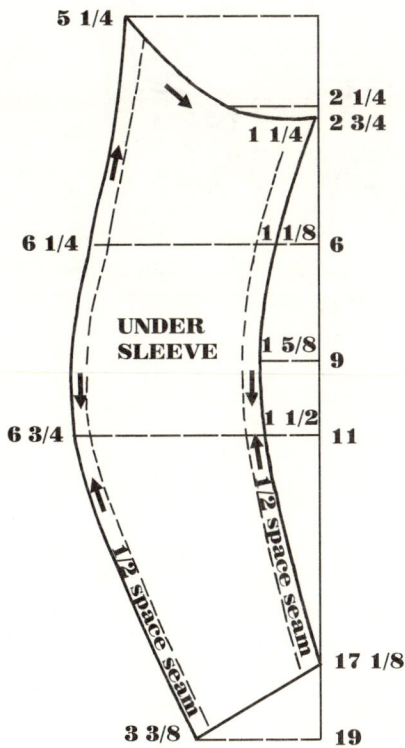

UNDER
SLEEVE

5 1/4
2 1/4
2 3/4
1 1/4
6 1/4
1 1/8
6
1 5/8
9
6 3/4
1 1/2
11
1/2 space seam
1/2 space seam
17 1/8
3 3/8
19

193

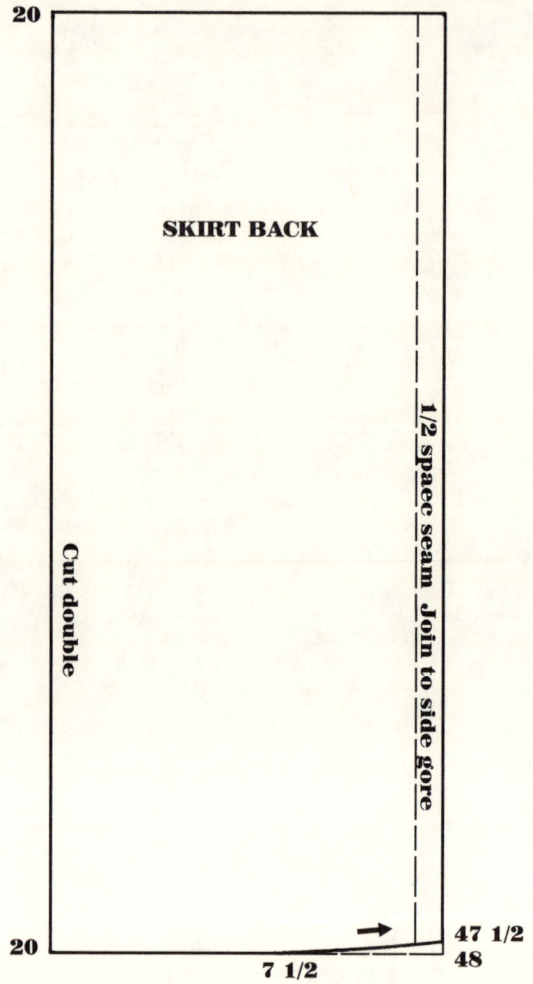

SKIRT BACK

20

Cut double

1/2 space seam Join to side gore

20

7 1/2   47 1/2
48

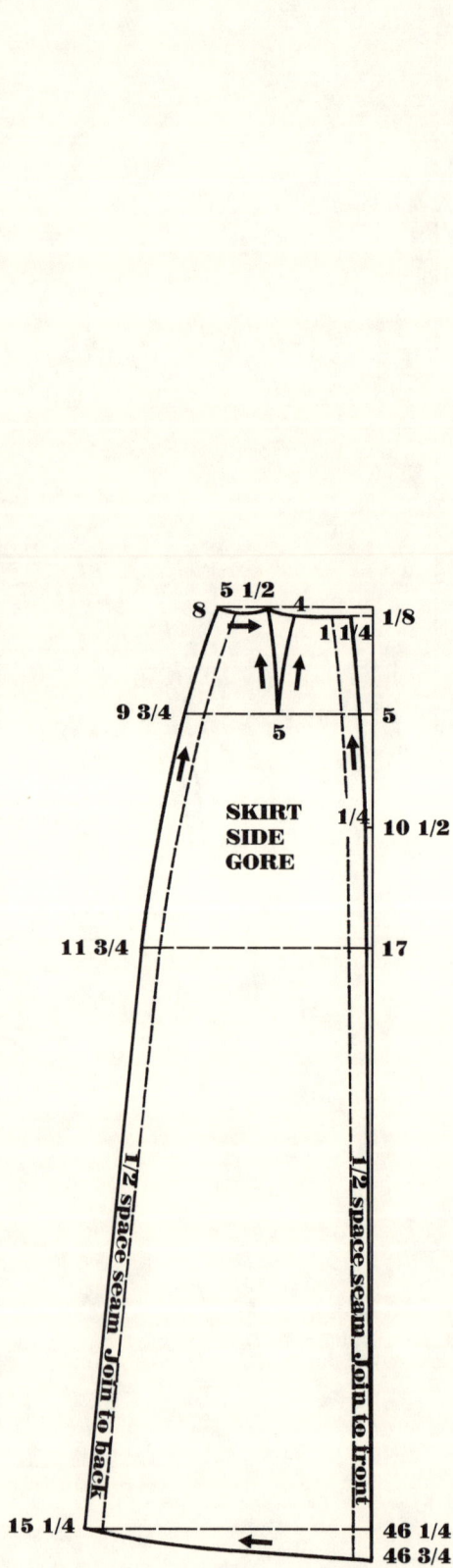

5 1/2   4
8   1/8
1 1/4

9 3/4   5

5

SKIRT SIDE GORE

1/4   10 1/2

11 3/4   17

1/2 space seam Join to back

1/2 space seam Join to front

15 1/4   46 1/4
46 3/4

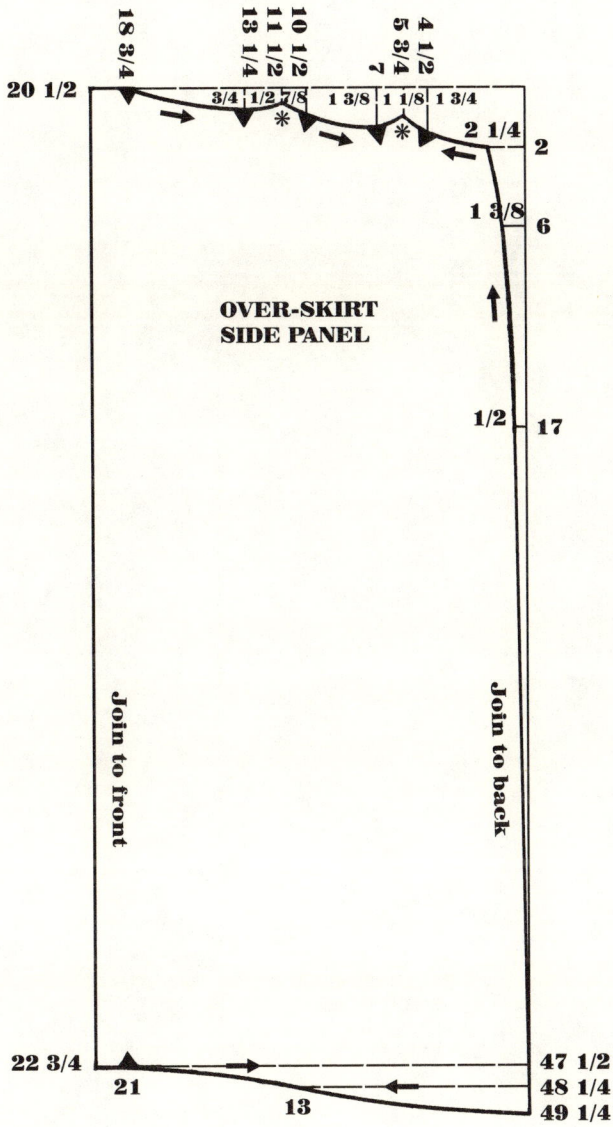

OVER-SKIRT
SIDE PANEL

Join to front

Join to back

18 3/4
20 1/2
13 1/4
11 1/2
10 1/2
7
5 3/4
4 1/2

3/4 1/2 7/8   1 3/8   1 1/8   1 3/4

2 1/4   2
1 3/8   6
1/2   17

22 3/4
21
13
47 1/2
48 1/4
49 1/4

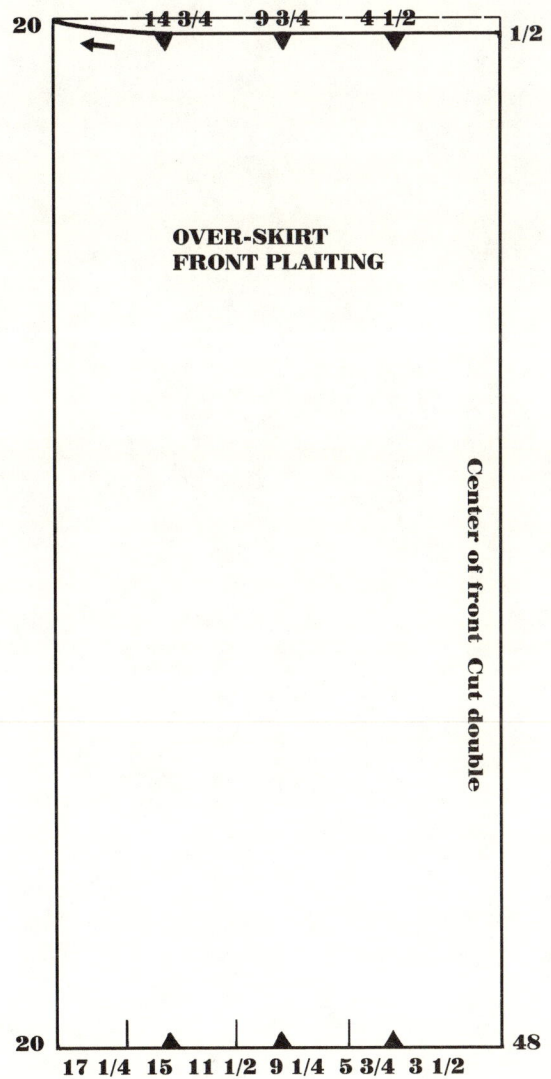

OVER-SKIRT
FRONT PLAITING

Center of front Cut double

20
14 3/4   9 3/4   4 1/2
1/2

20
17 1/4   15   11 1/2   9 1/4   5 3/4   3 1/2
48

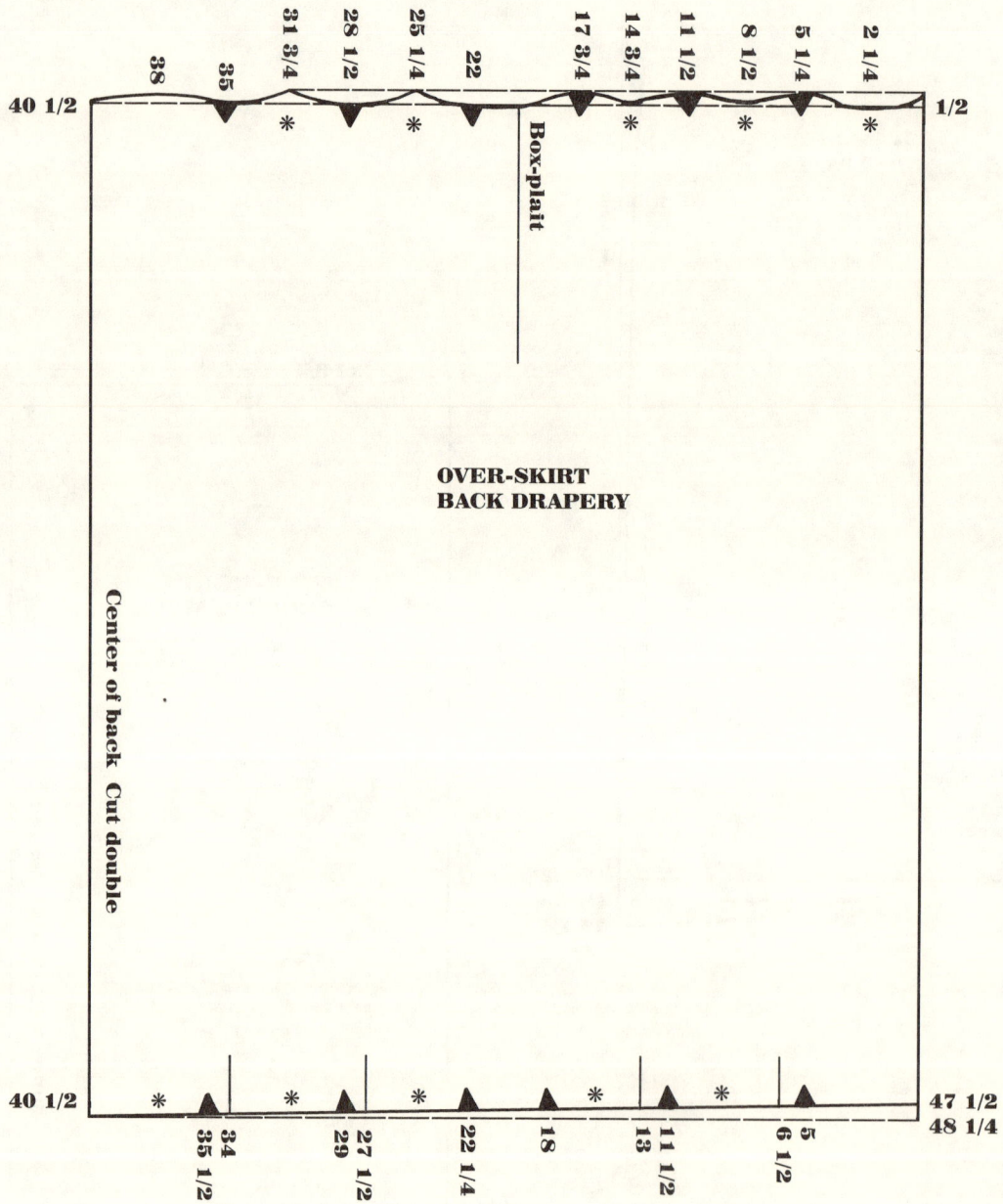

OVER-SKIRT
BACK DRAPERY

Box-plait

Center of back Cut double

40 1/2

38 35 31 3/4 28 1/2 25 1/4 22 17 3/4 14 3/4 11 1/2 8 1/2 5 1/4 2 1/4 1/2

40 1/2

47 1/2
48 1/4

35 1/2 34 29 27 1/2 22 1/4 18 13 11 1/2 6 1/2 5

Ladies' Basque. The basque is illustrated made of dress material, velvet, and silk. The back and sides are closely fitted by side pieces, side backs, and a center back seam. The latter ends above extra widths that are turned under for hems. Each side-back seam disappears below the waistline above fullness, which is underfolded to form a coat-plait that is marked at the top with a button. The close adjustment of the basque is completed by single bust darts in the fronts, and double bust darts in the under fronts. The under fronts are closed with buttons and button-holes. A full vest is sewed permanently along its back edge to the right under front, and buttoned invisibly on the left side. The vest is shirred twice at the upper part, the shirring being made far enough from the edge to leave a frill finish. The lower edge is gathered and concealed by a pointed girdle, which is sewed to the right under front, back of the vest, and fastened on the left side. The fronts open over the full vest, and are turned back in lapels, which are faced with velvet. The lapels are extended across the back to form a rolling collar, which has a seam at the center of the back. The neck is finished with a standing collar, which may be omitted as shown by the front view in the engraving. The sleeves are in the leg-of-mutton style.

Foulé, serge, cashmere, poplin, mohair, brilliantine, Thibet cloth, all-wool surah, etc., combined with velvet or silk in a contrasting color, will produce a handsome basque. Any style of walking skirt may be worn with it, and it may be of the same color and material or display a decided contrast. To make the basque for a lady of medium size, requires 4 7/8 yards of material 22 inches wide, or 2 3/8 yards of material 44 inches wide. As represented, it needs 1 1/2 yards of dress material 40 inches wide, 2 1/4 yards of velvet and 1 1/8 yards of silk each 20 inches wide, and 5/8 yard of lining 36 inches wide for the under fronts.

November 1889 *Delineator*

Walking Skirt. The skirt is pictured made of plain and fancy-striped materials. The foundation is a four-gored skirt, and a long, slender bustle is worn with it. The front drapery is arranged in three deep, overlapping plaits on each side of the center to produce a fan effect. Over each side is arranged a broad panel that is hemmed at the front edge, these panels meeting at the top and flaring below to disclose the fan. Two backward-turning plaits are laid in the upper edge to produce the adjustment over the hips. The back drapery is arranged in two triple box-plaits, which spread toward the edge.

Cashmere, serge, poplin, Henrietta cloth, all-wool surah, Thibet cloth, Pera material, all-wool royal armure, etc., are especially pretty made up in this way. Surah, armure, and faille Française will combine handsomely with any of the above materials, and so will striped, plaid, or fancy wool. For a lady of medium size, this skirt requires 8 7/8 yards of material 22 inches wide, or 5 yards of material 44 inches wide. As represented, it needs 3 7/8 yards of plain material 40 inches wide, and 1 1/4 yards of striped material 40 inches wide.

November 1889 *Delineator*

Ladies' Costume

Use the scale corresponding to the bust measure to draft the bodice. It is in eight pieces: Upper front, front shirring, girdle, under front, side piece, side back, back, and sleeve. Turn the upper front back on the diagonal dashed line, and face with velvet or silk. Gather the top with as many lines of shirring as desired, made 1 inch apart. Gather the bottom and sew it to the girdle. Sew it to the right side of the under front, and fasten it on the left side with hooks and eyes. Gather the sleeve at the top between the notches to fit the armhole. Finish it at the wrist with a cuff if desired.

Draft the over-skirt with the scale corresponding to the waist measure. Regulate the length with the tape measure. There are two pieces: Shirred front and draped back. Shirr the front, putting in as many lines as desired from 1 to 1 1/2 inches apart. Gather the back drapery and sew it to the waist.

The foundation skirt is drafted with the scale corresponding to the waist measure. Regulate the length with the tape measure. There are four pieces: Yoke, front, side gore, and back. Put all of the fullness at the back. This skirt pattern may also be used for a petticoat.

Winter 1889–1890 *Voice of Fashion*

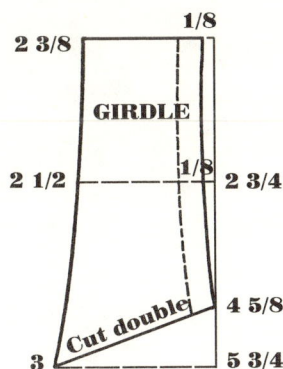

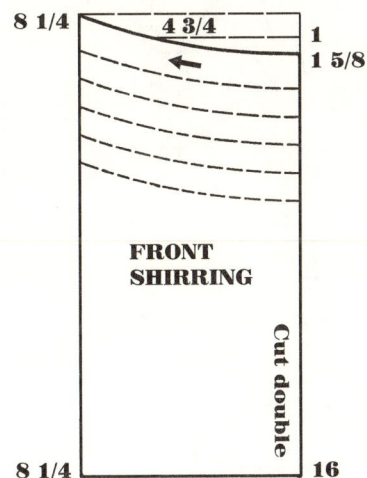

GIRDLE

2 3/8   1/8

2 1/2   1/8   2 3/4

Cut double

3   4 5/8   5 3/4

8 1/4   4 3/4   1
   1 5/8

FRONT SHIRRING

Cut double

8 1/4   16

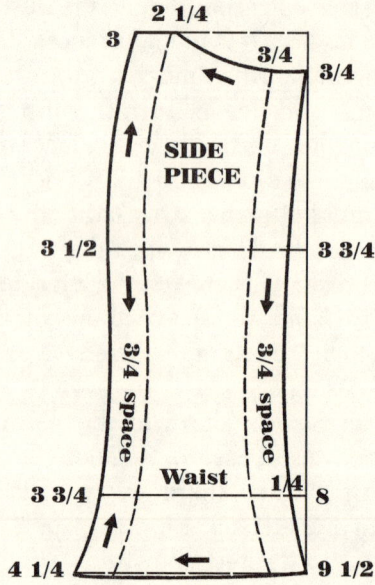

SIDE PIECE

2 1/4
3
3/4
3/4
3 1/2
3 3/4
3/4 space
3/4 space
Waist
3 3/4
1/4 8
4 1/4
9 1/2

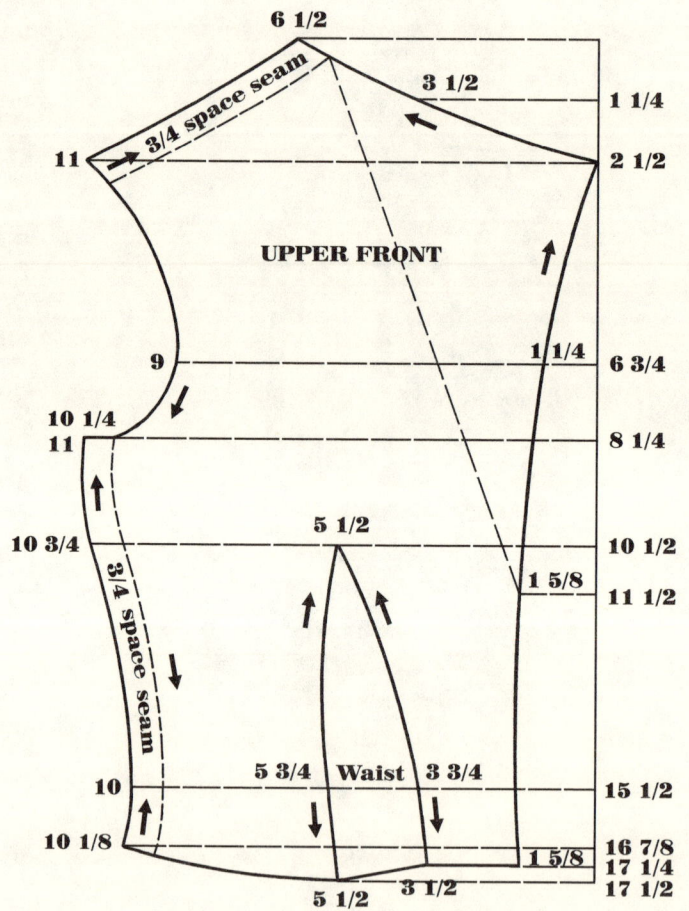

UPPER FRONT

6 1/2
3/4 space seam
3 1/2
1 1/4
11
2 1/2
1 1/4
6 3/4
9
10 1/4
11
8 1/4
10 3/4
5 1/2
10 1/2
1 5/8
11 1/2
3/4 space seam
5 3/4
Waist
3 3/4
15 1/2
10
10 1/8
16 7/8
1 5/8
17 1/4
5 1/2
3 1/2
17 1/2

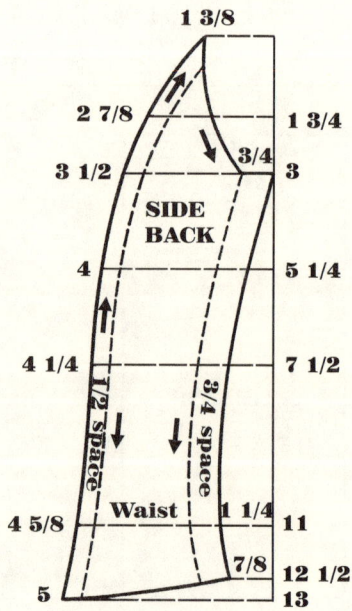

SIDE BACK

1 3/8
2 7/8
1 3/4
3 1/2
3/4
3
4
5 1/4
4 1/4
7 1/2
1/2 space
3/4 space
4 5/8
Waist
1 1/4
11
7/8
12 1/2
5
13

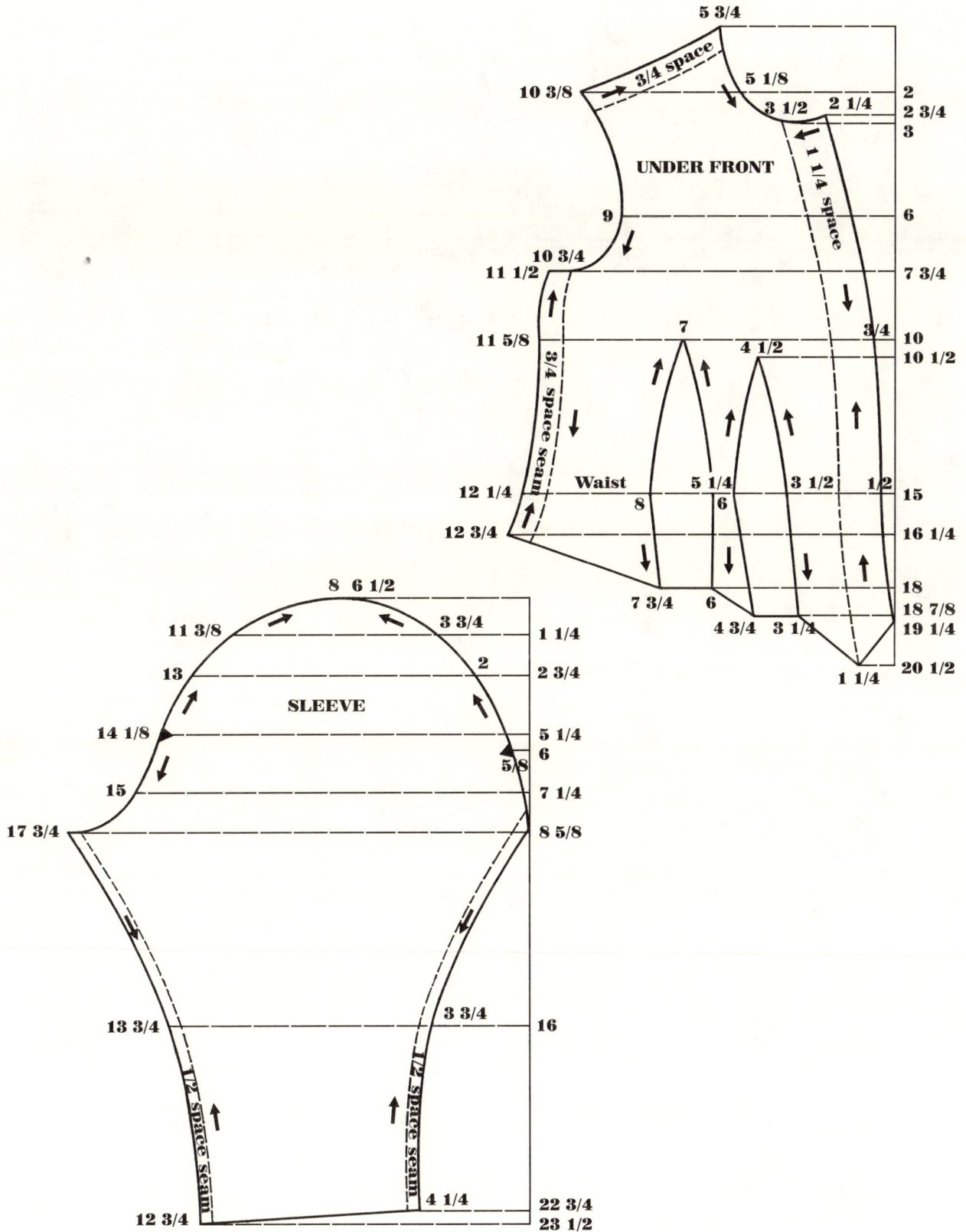

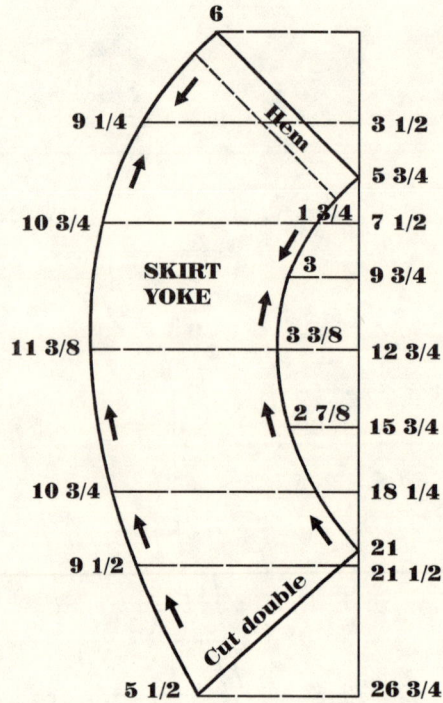

6

9 1/4   3 1/2

Hém

5 3/4

10 3/4   1 3/4   7 1/2

**SKIRT
YOKE**

3   9 3/4

11 3/8   3 3/8   12 3/4

2 7/8   15 3/4

10 3/4   18 1/4

9 1/2   21
          21 1/2

Cut double

5 1/2   26 3/4

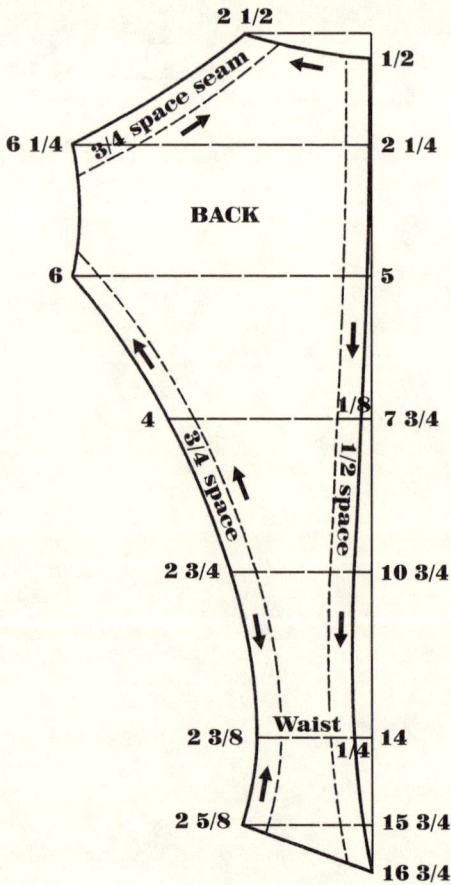

2 1/2

1/2

3/4 space seam

6 1/4   2 1/4

BACK

6   5

4   1/8   7 3/4

3/4 space   *1/2 space*

2 3/4   10 3/4

2 3/8   **Waist**   14
        1/4

2 5/8   15 3/4

16 3/4

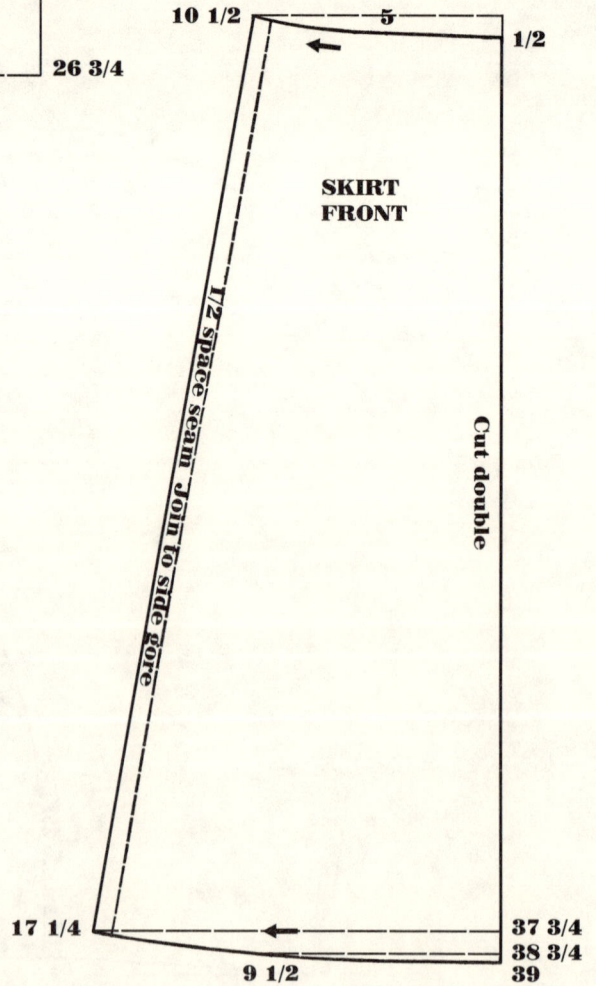

10 1/2   5   1/2

**SKIRT
FRONT**

1/2 space seam Join to side gore

Cut double

17 1/4   37 3/4
                 38 3/4
9 1/2   39

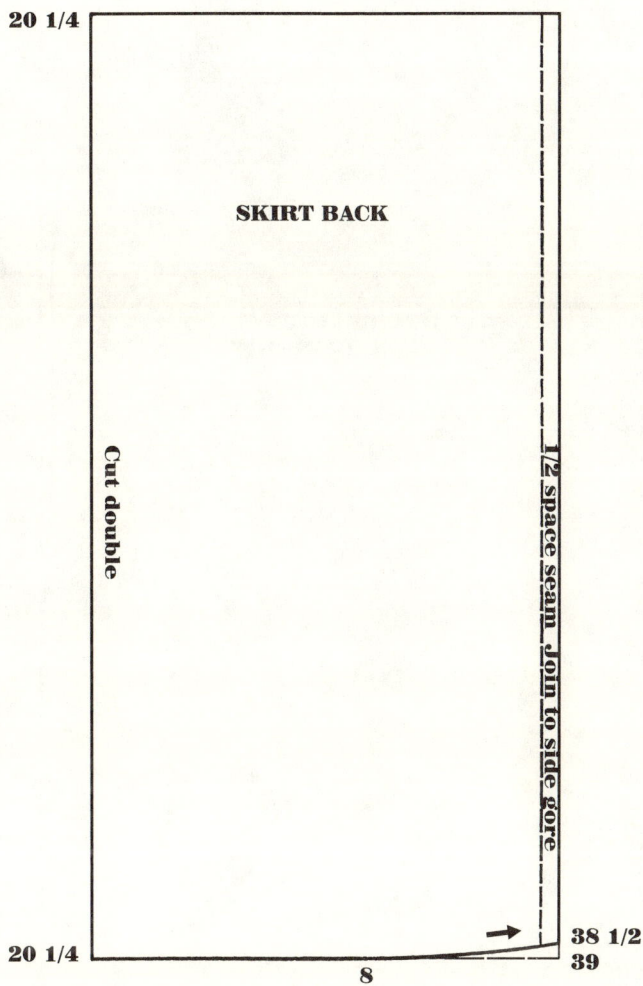

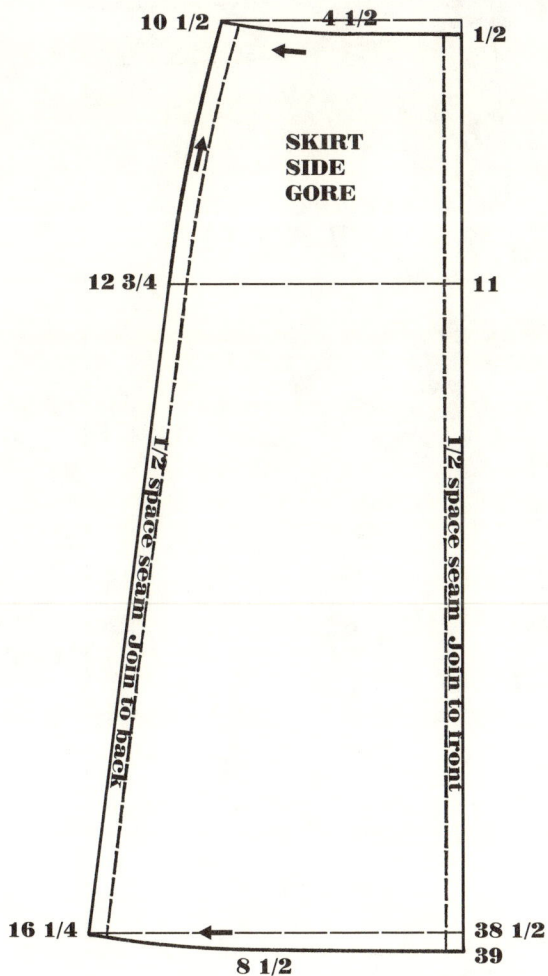

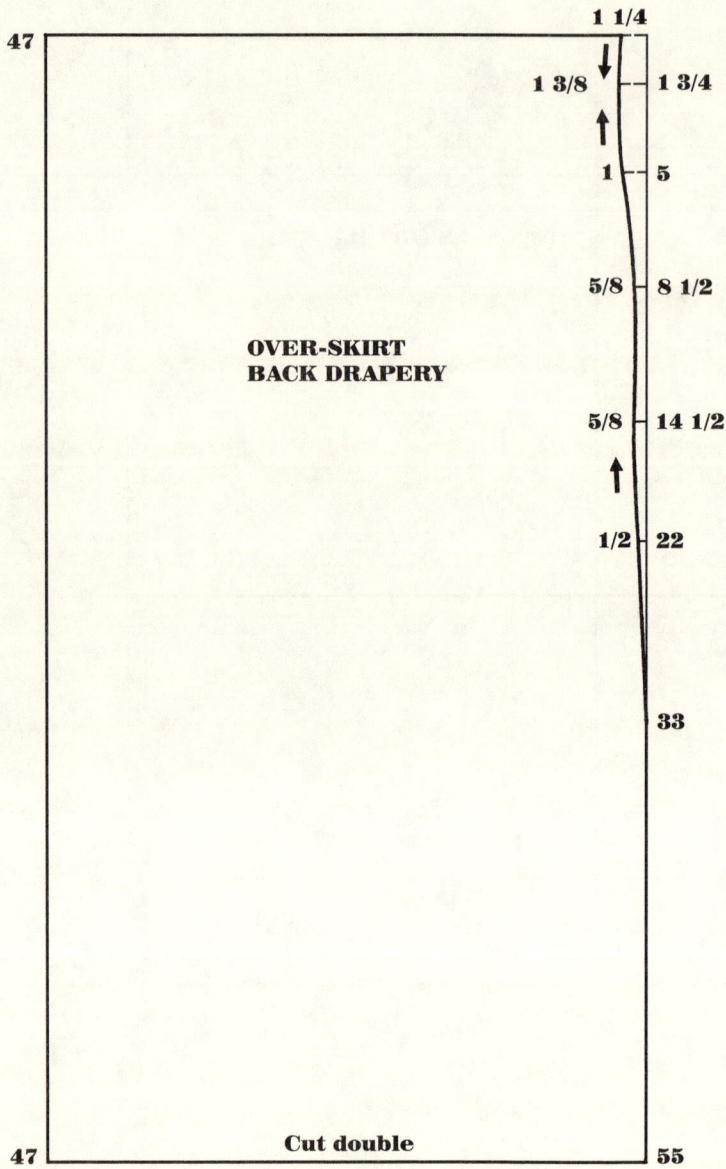

47

1 1/4

1 3/8 — 1 3/4

1 — 5

5/8 — 8 1/2

**OVER-SKIRT
BACK DRAPERY**

5/8 — 14 1/2

1/2 — 22

33

47   Cut double   55

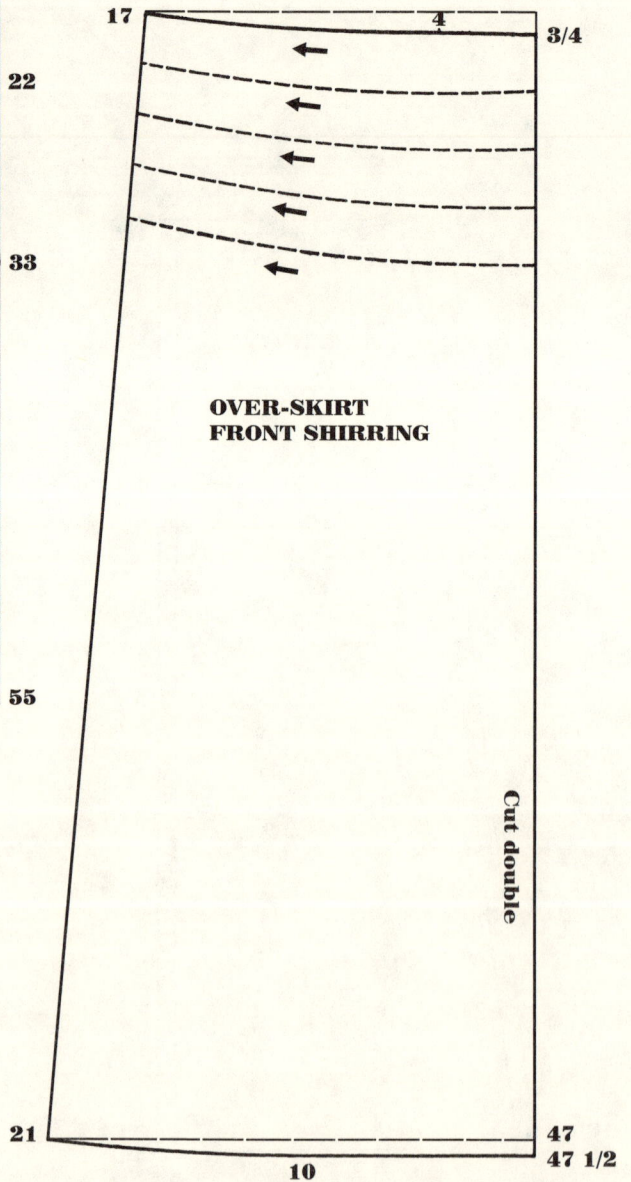

17   4   3/4

**OVER-SKIRT
FRONT SHIRRING**

Cut double

21   47

10   47 1/2

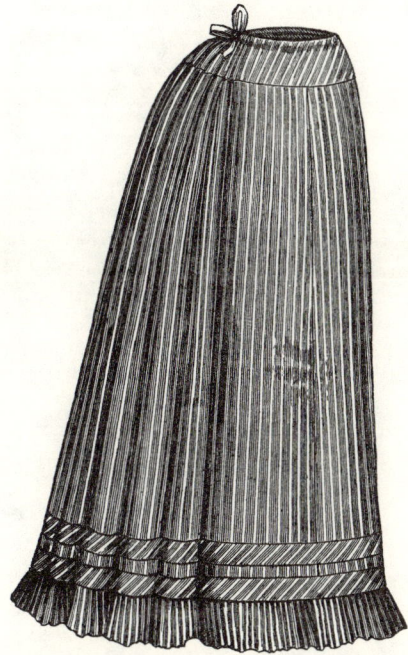

Walking Skirt. This skirt is adaptable to a great variety of suit materials, and when worn with a coat polonaise will complete a very stylish costume. It may be worn with any style of bodice or basque. A four-gored foundation skirt is used, and worn over a long, slender bustle. The gores of the foundation are completely covered by a drapery that is shirred nine times at the top, the fullness below falling to the edge. The back drapery is shirred twice at its upper edge and sewed to a short, narrow band, which is basted to the belt completing the top of the skirt.

Henrietta cloth, cashmere, serge, silk-and-wool barège, embroidered materials, camelette, etc., make up handsomely in this way. A broad band of silk passementerie or appliqué may be applied on the front drapery just above the lower edge. The polonaise may be of some contrasting color. To make the skirt for a lady of medium size, requires 10 5/8 yards of material 22 inches wide, or 5 1/4 yards of material 44 inches wide. Each requires 3 yards of lining 36 inches wide for the foundation skirt.

October 1889 *Delineator*

Petticoat with Yoke. Striped seersucker was used for this example. It is composed of a front gore, two side gores, and a back breadth, all joined to a shallow, round yoke. The back breadth is gathered at the top, and the gores are joined smoothly to the yoke. The placket opening is at the center of the back. The yoke is drawn in to the size of the waist by a tape inserted in a casing. The casing is formed by sewing the lining and the outside together near the top. The bottom of the skirt is trimmed with side-plaiting and two bias folds of seersucker, the lower fold serving as a heading to the plaiting.

Gingham; plain, striped, checked, and mixed flannels; all kinds of wool materials; mohair; alpaca; wash silks, etc., are suitable for this petticoat. All kinds of cotton, linen, and worsted laces; embroideries; scalloped edgings; bands of braid; tucking; etc., may be used for decoration. A deep hem-facing and large tucks feather-stitched in place constitute a desirable plain finish. To make the petticoat for a lady of medium size, requires 4 7/8 yards of material 27 inches wide, or 3 3/4 yards of material 36 inches wide.

February 1889 *Delineator*

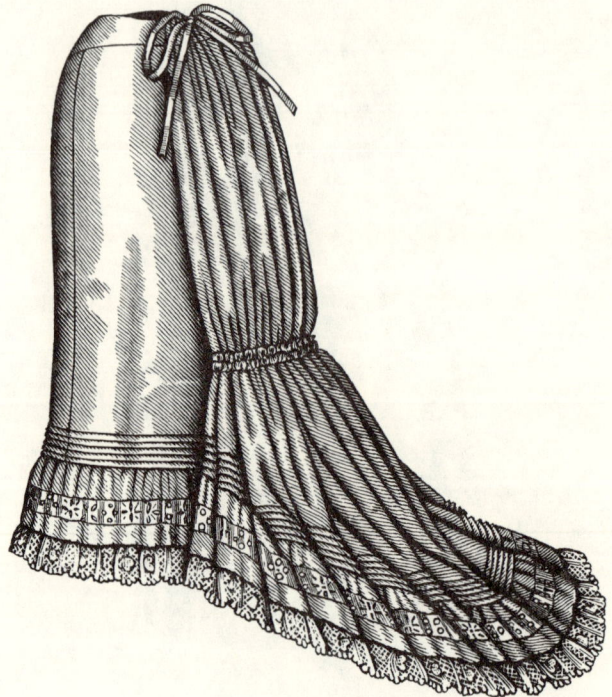

Petticoat at Full-Train, Demi-Train, or Walking Length. The view on the left of the en-graving shows the petticoat at walking length, and the one on the right shows it with a full-length train. It may be worn over a short or a long bustle. These examples are made of cambric. They are trimmed with a cambric flounce bordered with lace edging and having a band of insertion set in it, five narrow tucks being clustered just above the ruffles.

The petticoat has three gores for the front and sides, and a full breadth for the back. In addition there is a train part, consisting of a center breadth and two gores. These are gathered at the top and sewed to the lower edge of the back breadth, the latter being short enough to permit of this addition. Over the joining seam, and extending far enough above it to form a casing, is sewed a strip of the material. Through this casing are run tapes that are fastened at the side-back seams, their free ends being slipped through an opening at the center of the casing and tied together. The train part may be cut off to demi-train or walking length.

The gores and the back breadth are shortened and shaped at the top to permit of the addition of a yoke, which is composed of three sections. The center yoke section is pointed and extended across the top of the gores, its ends joining the back sec-tions at the side-back seams. The yoke is lined with the petticoat material. Near the top of each back section, a line of stitching is made to form a casing. Tapes are run into these casings, their front ends being sewed firmly in place and their free ends tied together above the placket opening.

The petticoat may be made of fine muslin, or for general wear of heavy, twilled skirting, pongee, gingham, seersucker, etc. Lace and embroidery are in vogue as trimmings, and both may be added to the same petticoat. For a lady of medium size, the petticoat with a full-length train requires 4 3/8 yards of material 36 inches wide. With a demi-train it requires 3 7/8 yards of material 36 inches wide, and for walking length 3 5/8 yards of material the same width.

September 1886 *Delineator*

Costume with Prince Albert Coat

Use the scale corresponding to the bust measure to draft the coat. It consists of nine pieces: Front, front lap, pocket lap, side back, skirt, back, collar, full sleeve, and cuff. Use the pattern given for the basque sleeve as the sleeve lining. This coat may be made of material to match the suit, or of any heavy material.

Take up the darts on the skirt parts. Baste the front and side back together, then sew them to the skirt, connecting the notches. Turn under the fullness on the back parts and lap it over the skirt. Also turn under the edge from 15 1/2 to 28 3/4, and let this remain open.

Use the scale corresponding to the bust measure to draft the French basque, which has a bias effect. It consists of seven pieces: Front, side piece, side back, back, collar, and two sleeve pieces. After drafting the front, cut out the pattern and lay it on the straight edge of the material. Cut the darts open down the center before basting.

Draft the drapery with the scale corresponding to the waist measure. Regulate the length with the tape measure. It has two pieces: Front and back. The back is laid in two double box-plaits. Press them carefully, but do not stay them underneath. Lay the plaits in front to correspond to the notches. The bottom may be slashed as represented, and faced with silk to correspond to the skirt, or made perfectly plain.

Draft the skirt with the scale corresponding to the waist measure. Regulate the length with the tape measure. There are three pieces: Front, side gore, and back.

Winter 1889–1890 *Voice of Fashion*

COAT COLLAR

4 3/8   2 1/4   1/4
1/2 space
4 3/8   2 3/4   1/8   3 3/4
5 1/4
3 1/8   6 1/4
7 1/4
2 3/8

COAT SIDE BACK

1 3/4
3 3/4   3/4   3 1/8
4 3/8   6
1/2 space seam   3/4 space seam
Waist-line
5 1/4   1 1/4   9 1/2
6   7/8   11 1/4
3 3/4

COAT FRONT

6 3/4
3/4 space seam   6   1 1/2
11 3/4   5 3/4   2 1/4
3 1/2   2 3/4
1/2 space
9   7
10 1/2   8 3/4
12
11 7/8   6 1/4   1 1/4   10
3/4 space   Cut open before basting
11 1/2   7   4 1/4   1/2   15 1/4
12   17
17 5/8
17 3/4
6 1/2   6 1/4   4 1/4

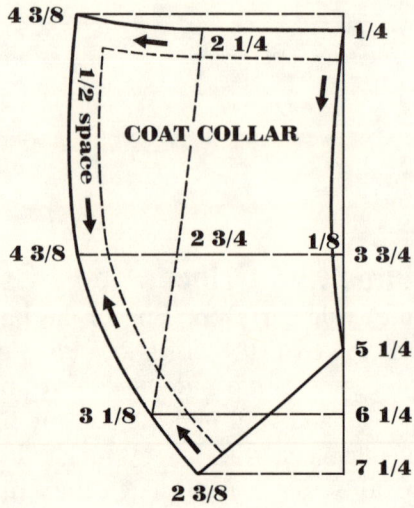

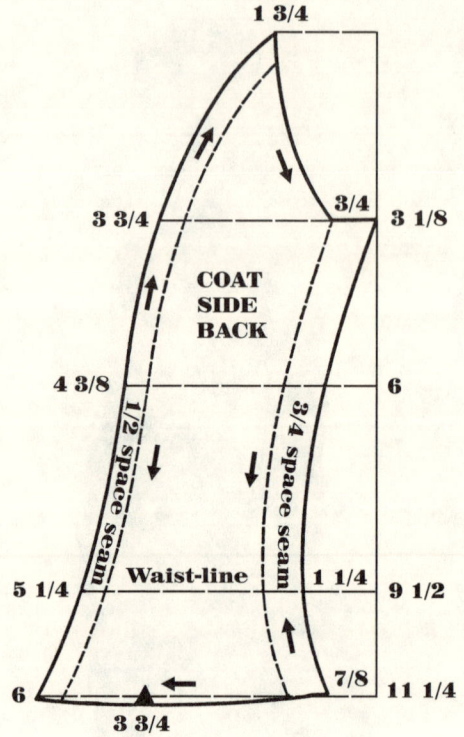

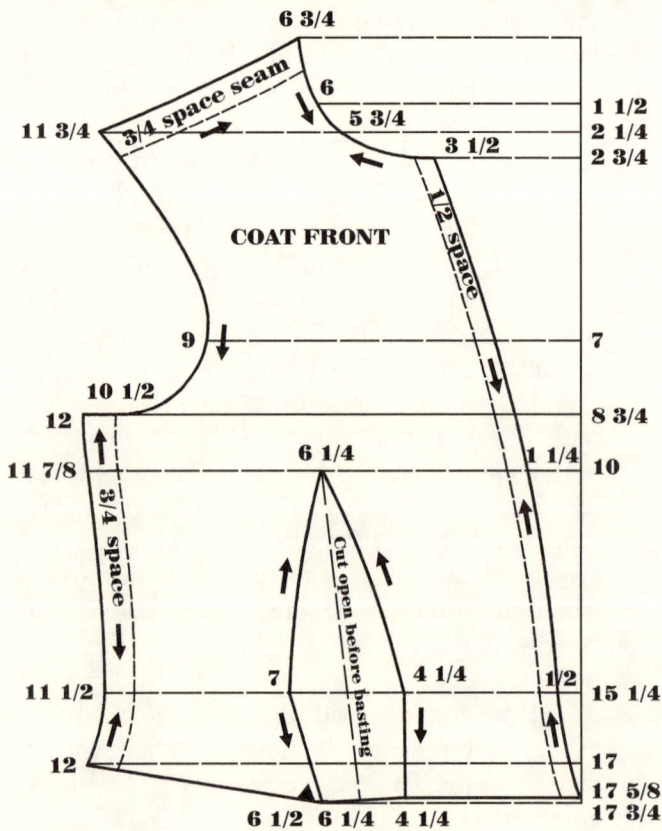

COAT FRONT LAP

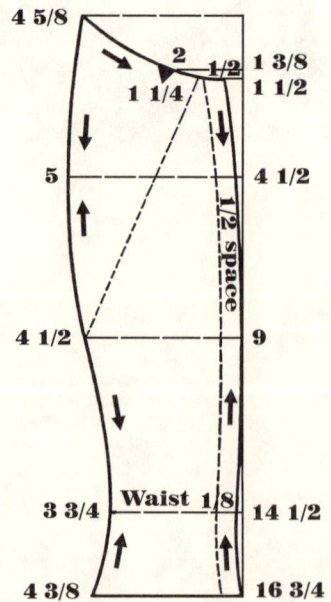

4 5/8   2   1 3/8
1 1/4   1/2   1 1/2
5   4 1/2
1/2 space
4 1/2   9
3 3/4   Waist 1/8   14 1/2
4 3/8   16 3/4

Prince Albert Coat

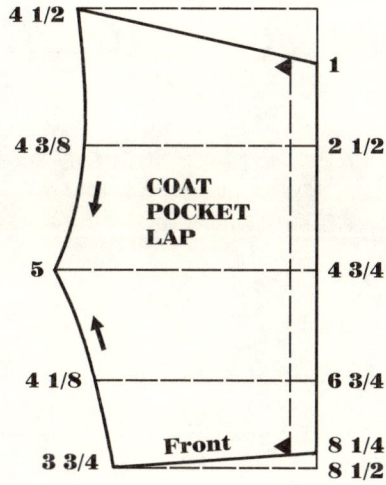

COAT POCKET LAP

4 1/2
1
4 3/8
2 1/2
5
4 3/4
4 1/8
6 3/4
Front
8 1/4
8 1/2
3 3/4

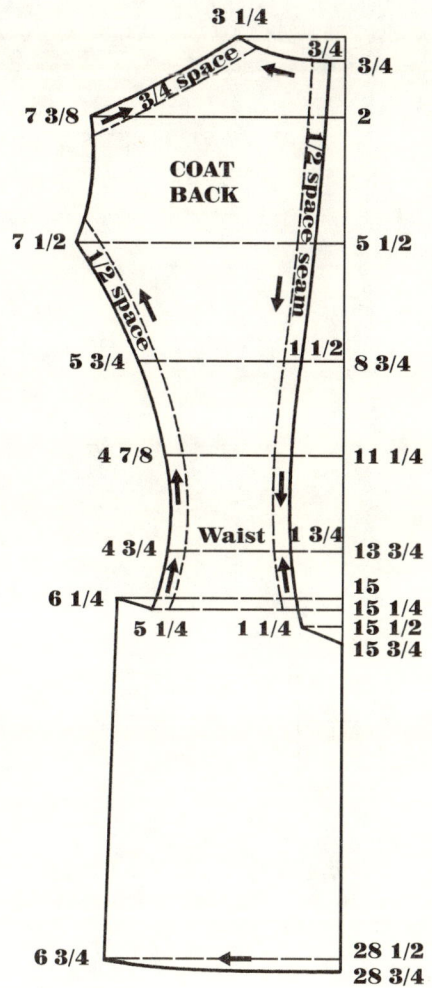

COAT BACK

3 1/4
3/4
3/4
7 3/8
3/4 space
2
7 1/2
1/2 space seam
5 1/2
1/2 space
5 3/4
8 3/4
1 1/2
4 7/8
11 1/4
4 3/4
Waist
1 3/4
13 3/4
6 1/4
15
15 1/4
5 1/4
1 1/4
15 1/2
15 3/4
6 3/4
28 1/2
28 3/4

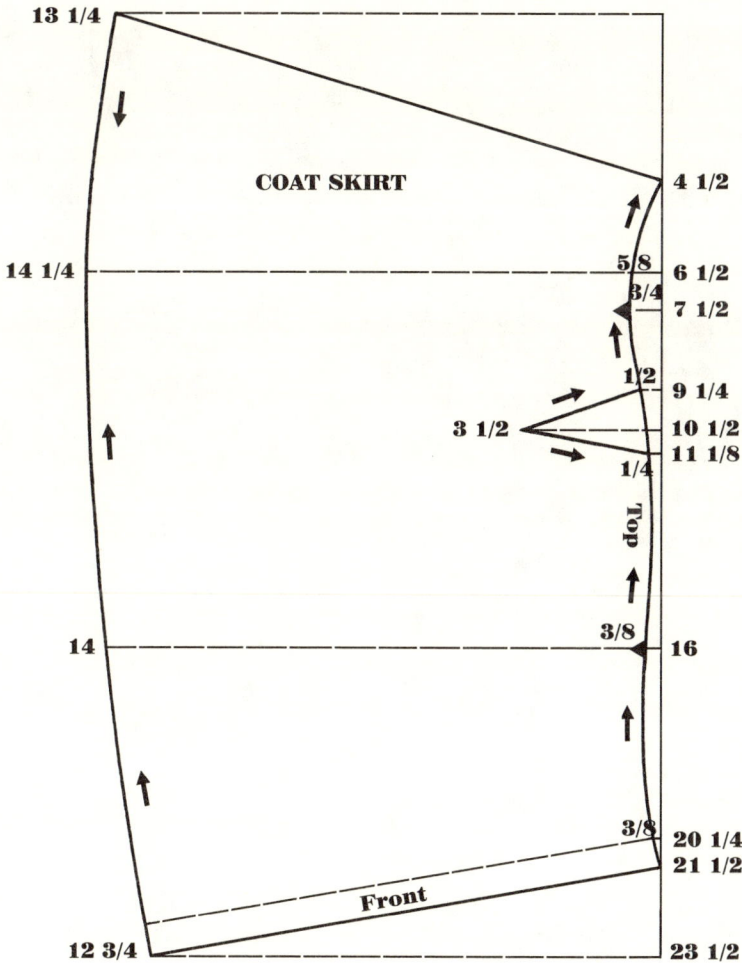

COAT SKIRT

13 1/4
14 1/4
5/8
4 1/2
6 1/2
3/4
7 1/2
1/2
9 1/4
3 1/2
10 1/2
11 1/8
1/4
Top
14
3/8
16
3/8
20 1/4
21 1/2
Front
12 3/4
23 1/2

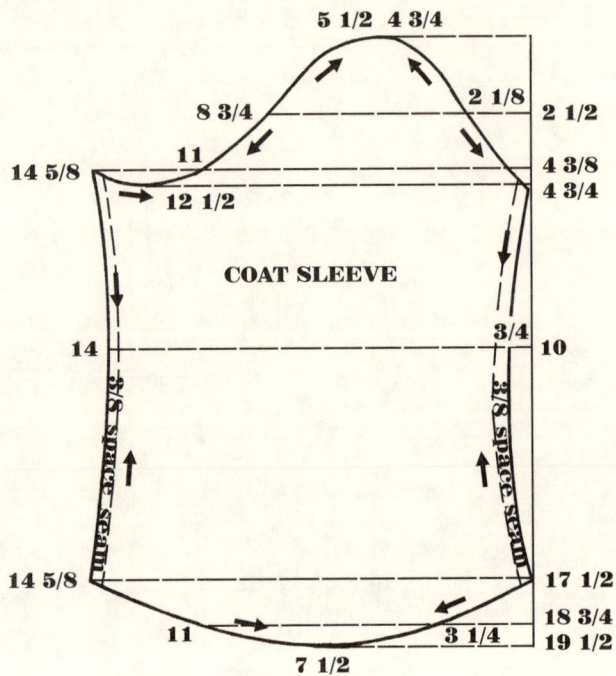

COAT SLEEVE

5 1/2 4 3/4

8 3/4 2 1/8 2 1/2

11 4 3/8

14 5/8 4 3/4

12 1/2

14 3/4 10

3/8 space seam 3/8 space seam

14 5/8 17 1/2

11 18 3/4

3 1/4 19 1/2

7 1/2

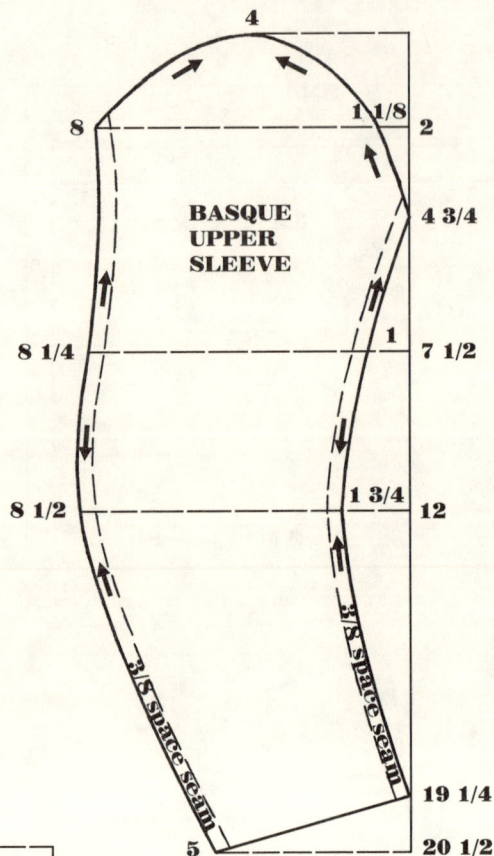

BASQUE
UPPER
SLEEVE

4

8 1 1/8 2

4 3/4

8 1/4 1 7 1/2

8 1/2 1 3/4 12

3/8 space seam

19 1/4

5 20 1/2

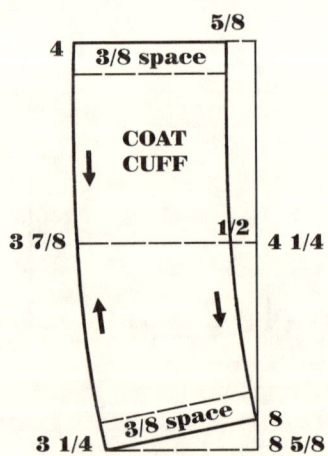

COAT
CUFF

5/8

4 3/8 space

3 7/8 1/2 4 1/4

3/8 space 8

3 1/4 8 5/8

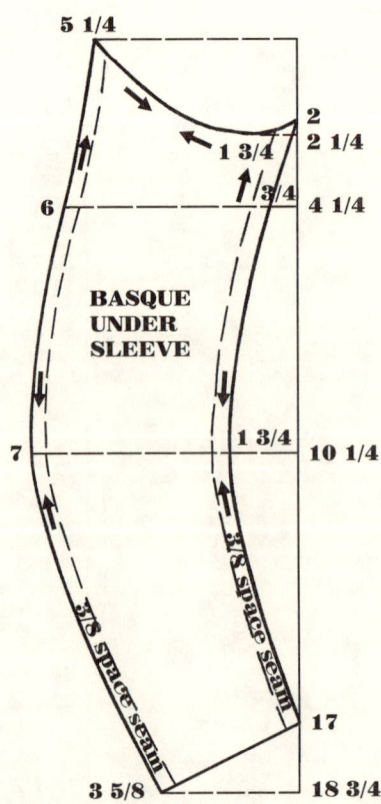

BASQUE
UNDER
SLEEVE

5 1/4

2
2 1/4
1 3/4

6 3/4 4 1/4

7 1 3/4 10 1/4

3/8 space seam 3/8 space seam

17

3 5/8 18 3/4

Prince Albert Coat

**BASQUE
SIDE PIECE**

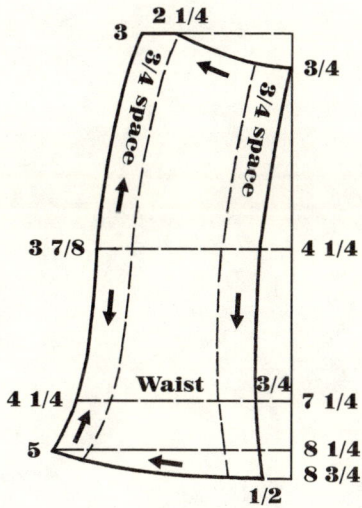

2 1/4

3

3/4

3/4 space

3/4 space

3 7/8   4 1/4

Waist

4 1/4   3/4   7 1/4

5   8 1/4
                       8 3/4
                       1/2

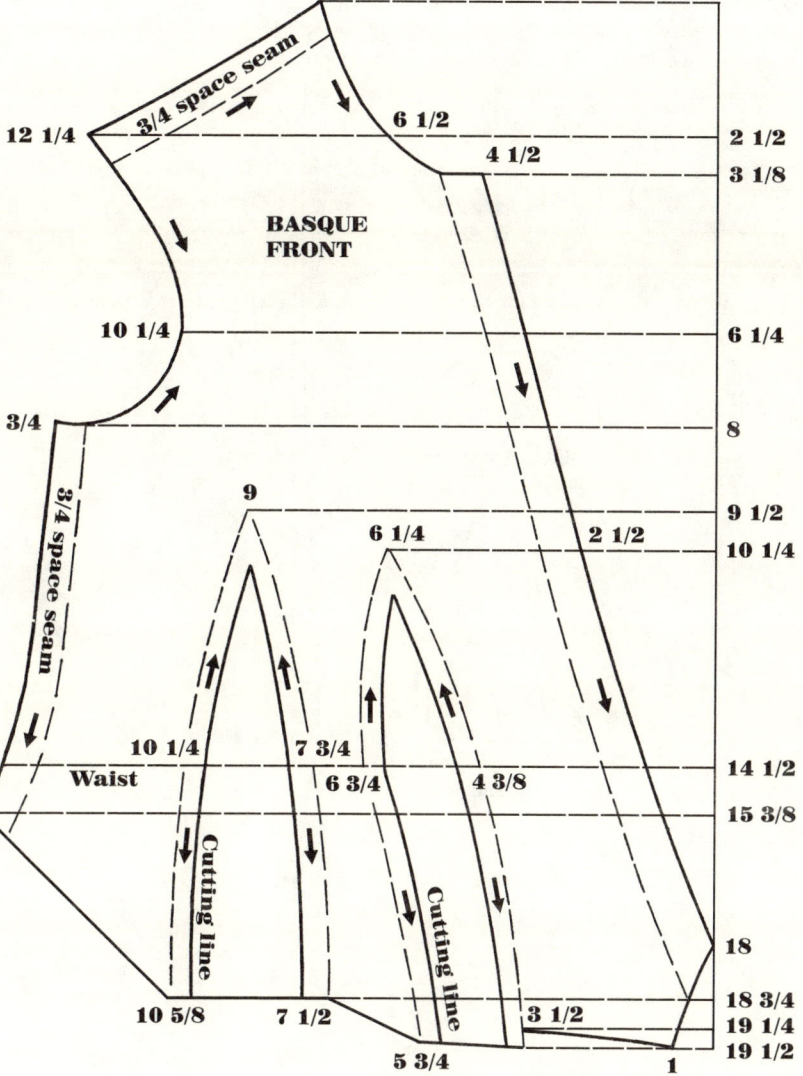

**BASQUE
SIDE BACK**

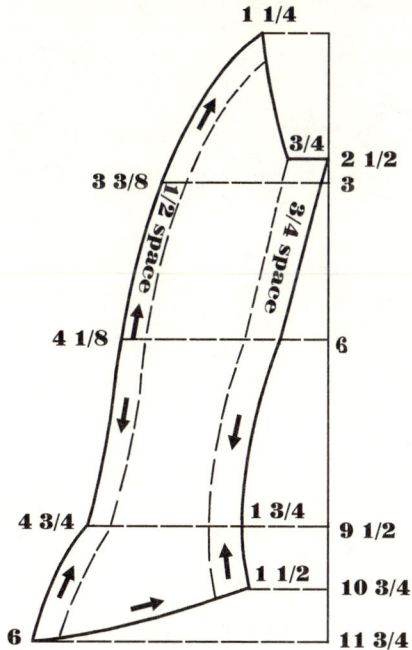

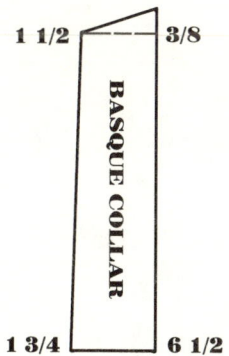

1 1/4

3/4

2 1/2
3

3 3/8

1/2 space

3/4 space

4 1/8   6

4 3/4   1 3/4   9 1/2

1 1/2   10 3/4

6   11 3/4

7 3/4

3/4 space seam

12 1/4   6 1/2   2 1/2
                     4 1/2   3 1/8

**BASQUE
FRONT**

10 1/4   6 1/4

12 3/4   8

3/4 space seam

9   9 1/2

6 1/4   2 1/2   10 1/4

Cutting line   Cutting line

13 3/4   10 1/4   7 3/4   14 1/2
Waist   6 3/4   4 3/8
14 1/4   15 3/8

18

10 5/8   7 1/2   3 1/2   18 3/4
                                     19 1/4
5 3/4   1   19 1/2

1 1/2   3/8

BASQUE COLLAR

1 3/4   6 1/2

211

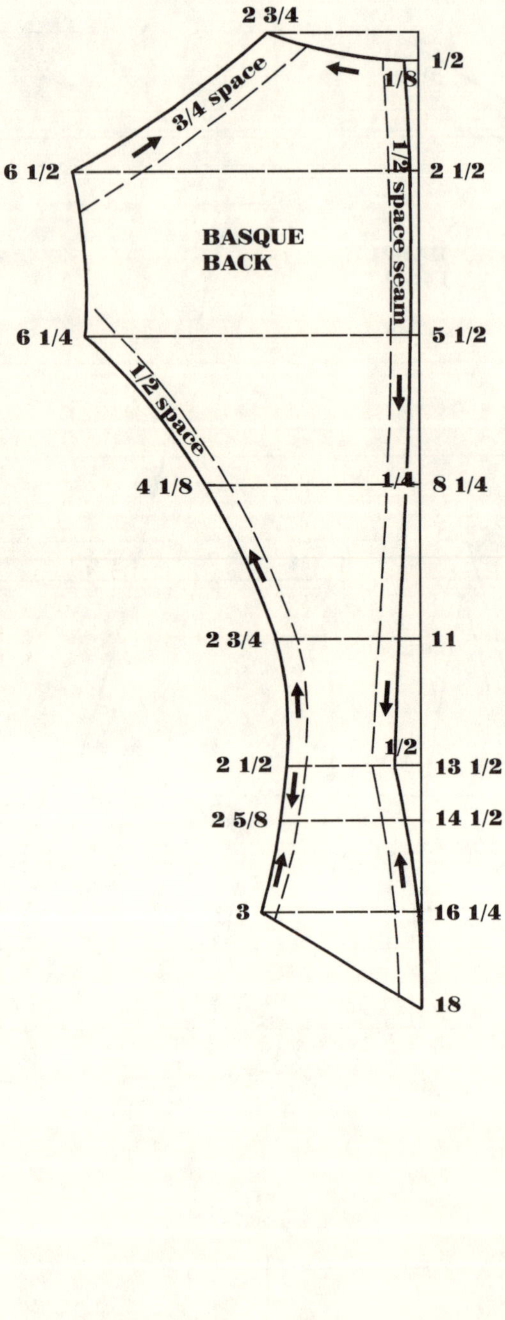

BASQUE
BACK

2 3/4

1/2

1/8

3/4 space

6 1/2 — 2 1/2

1/2 space seam

6 1/4 — 5 1/2

1/2 space

4 1/8 — 1/4 — 8 1/4

2 3/4 — 11

2 1/2 — 1/2 — 13 1/2

2 5/8 — 14 1/2

3 — 16 1/4

18

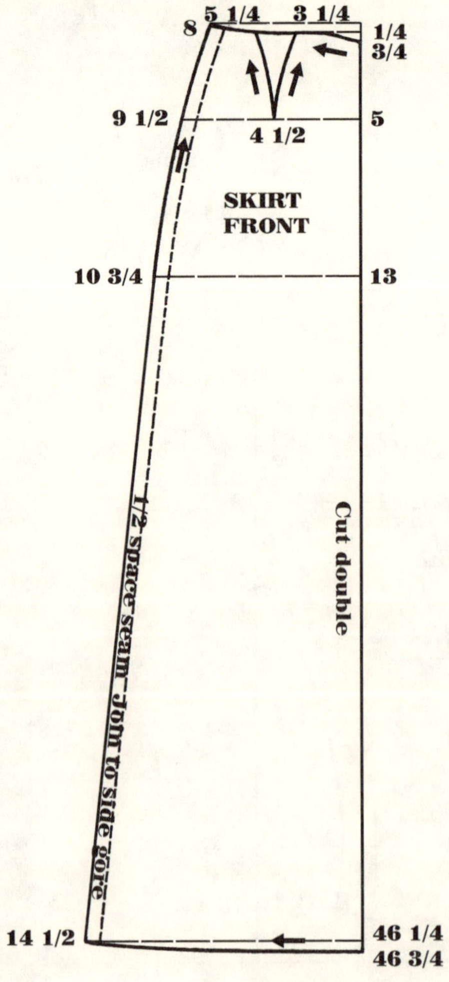

SKIRT
FRONT

8 — 5 1/4 — 3 1/4 — 1/4
3/4

9 1/2 — 5
4 1/2

10 3/4 — 13

1/2 space seam join to side gore

Cut double

14 1/2 — 46 1/4
46 3/4

SKIRT BACK

Cut double

1/2 spaec seam Join to side gore

20

20

47 1/2
48

7 1/2

SKIRT SIDE GORE

8   5 1/2   4   1/8
1 1/4

9 3/4   5   5

1/4   10 1/2

11 3/4   17

1/2 space seam Join to back

1/2 space seam Join to front

15 1/4   46 1/4
46 3/4

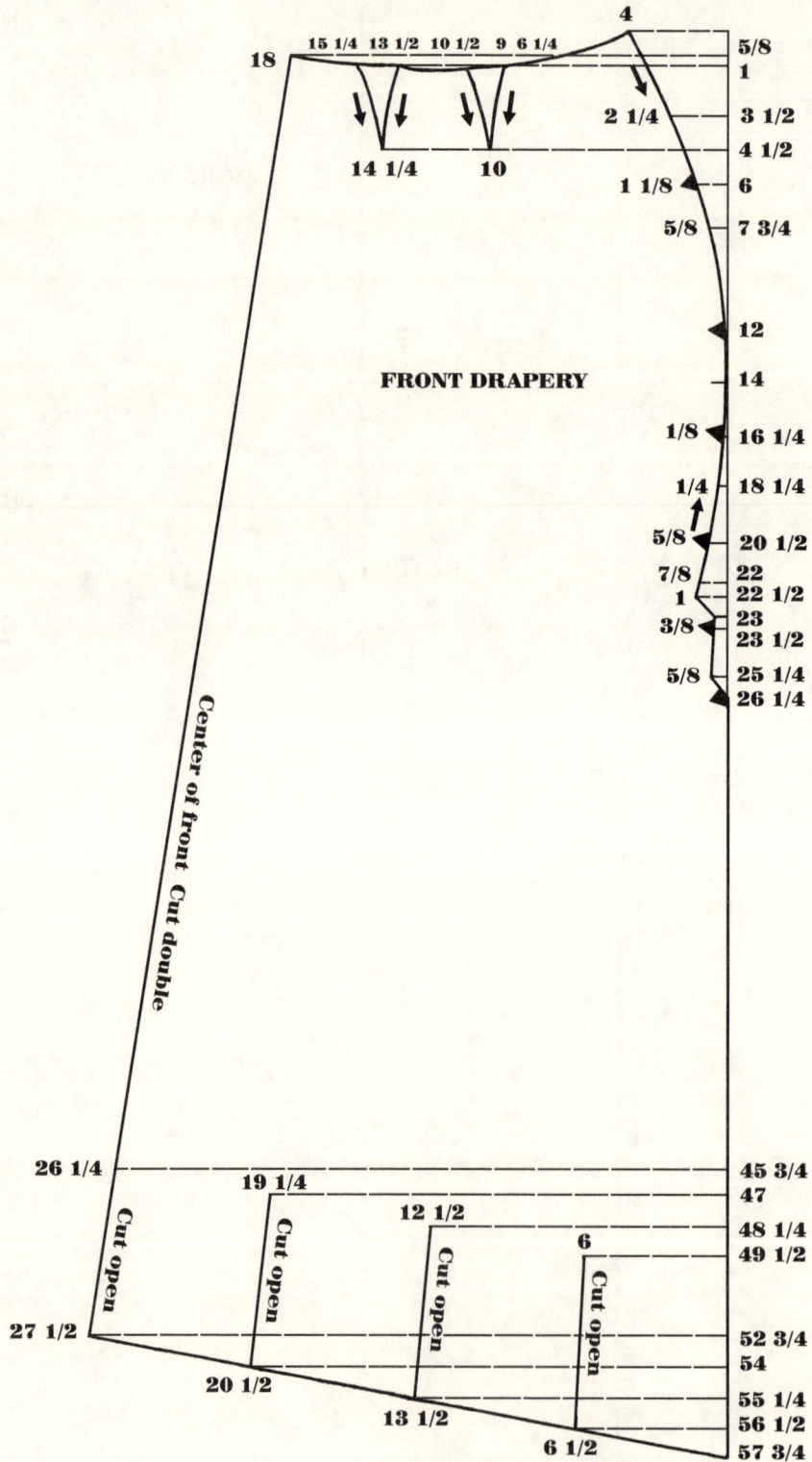

FRONT DRAPERY

4

18   15 1/4 13 1/2 10 1/2 9 6 1/4   5/8
                                              1
                              2 1/4   3 1/2
                                        4 1/2
        14 1/4   10   1 1/8   6
                                5/8   7 3/4

                                         12
                                         14
                                1/8   16 1/4
                                1/4   18 1/4
                                5/8   20 1/2
                                7/8   22
                                1   22 1/2
                                3/8   23
                                         23 1/2
                                5/8   25 1/4
                                         26 1/4

Center of front   Cut double

26 1/4   45 3/4
            19 1/4   47
                    12 1/2   48 1/4
                            6   49 1/2

Cut open Cut open Cut open Cut open

27 1/2   52 3/4
            20 1/2   54
                    13 1/2   55 1/4
                                          56 1/2
                            6 1/2   57 3/4

214

Prince Albert Coat

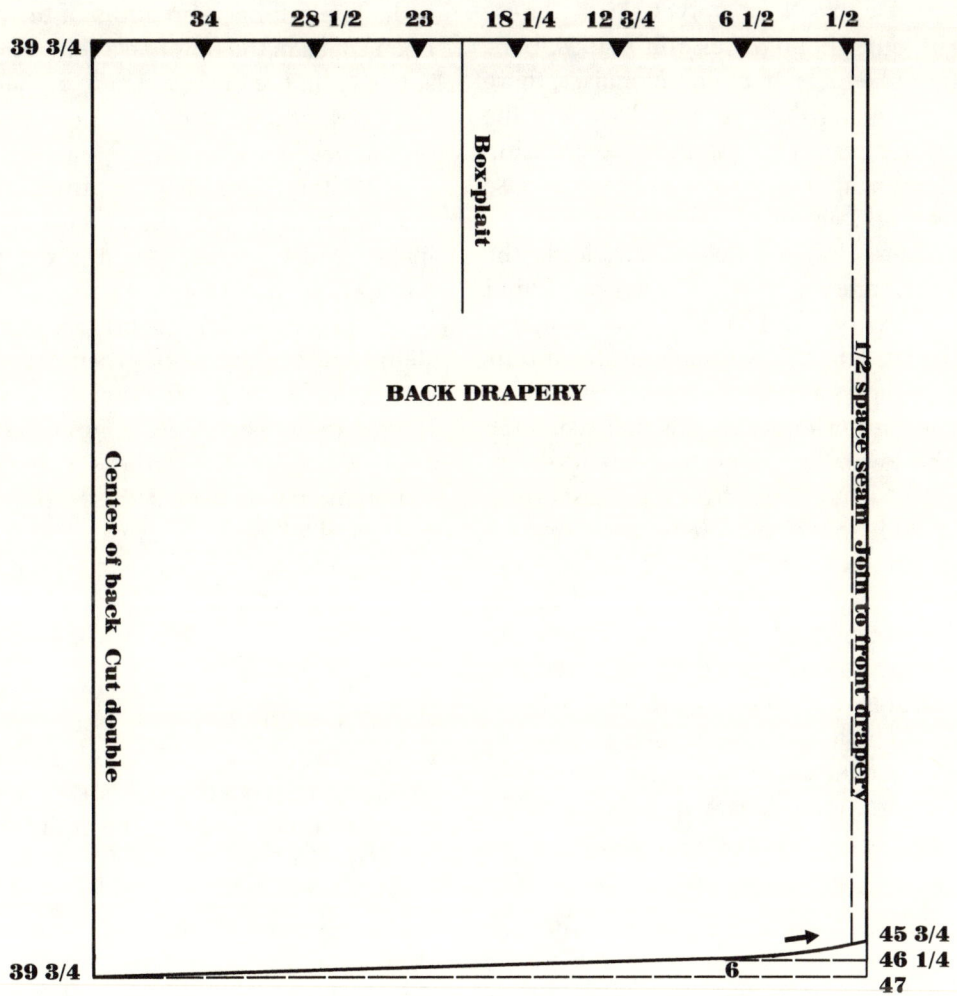

BACK DRAPERY

Box-plait

Center of back Cut double

1/2 space seam Join to front drapery

39 3/4

34   28 1/2   23   18 1/4   12 3/4   6 1/2   1/2

39 3/4

45 3/4
46 1/4
6
47

6. Ensembles with Polonaises

Wool materials of all kinds—cloth, cashmere, camel's hair, and chuddah—are preferred for polonaises, with silk or velvet skirts. These skirts may be quite plain, or else in stripes, bars, or great moon-like balls. In cloth polonaises, there is a fancy for making the vest and sleeves of the velvet used for the skirt. These may have a trimming of galloon, which may have jet beads, or else those of silver, gilt, or copper. Shirred polonaises, with their fullness drawn on cords parallel to the shoulder seams, are worn by slight figures. Other polonaises are very plain and severe in shape, without drapery. The fronts sometimes form only a square-cornered coat with a longer vest. Others are lengthened into slender panels that reach the bottom of the lower skirt. The back breadths are straight, with the center open from the waist down, and there are large square-cornered pockets on each side. Others open over a full gathered petticoat and vest of embroidered India cashmere, with lapels and panels of fur. Still others fall very low on the right side, but are curved quite short on the left hip in pannier fashion, displaying a skirt of moiré or of figured velvet. The latter design is liked for supple silks such as bengaline and peau de soie, with a skirt of velvet in stripes or cross-bars, or in Persian frisé figures outlined with a contrasting color.

January 21, 1888 *Harper's Bazar*

Many polonaise costumes give the effect of a princess dress, but consisting of two pieces—a long over-dress and a separate skirt. Two materials are usually employed, such as cashmere or other fine wool for the polonaise, and bengaline or any repped silk for the lower skirt. The most stylish polonaises are very long, and are fully draped, yet give a slender effect. The front of the bodice is lapped diagonally to the left side, and the skirt falls open in the center of the front and back alike. The fullness is drawn upward back on the tournure, making the back shorter than the front. In many designs, the center back pieces are cut off at the tournure, and finished with a passementerie ornament or a sash. The full back breadths of the skirt fill up the open space in the polonaise skirt. A vest of the skirt silk is set in the bodice. There are large pockets on the sides, or great buttons or ornaments like those on the back.

Other polonaise costumes are entirely of wool, trimmed with moiré sash ribbon 10 or 12 inches wide, arranged as a girdle and sash, and cut up to form a vest and revers. The front pieces of the polonaise are continuous. They are lapped slightly at the waist-line, then the skirt fronts are turned back, and wide revers of the moiré are arranged down each side. A moiré vest is V-shaped to the waist. A moiré girdle is set in plaits very wide in the under-arm seams, then tapered to a point in front, and falling thence in a long loop and ends on the plain wool skirt below. The center back pieces are completed by a sash of two loops and ends.

March 10, 1888 *Harper's Bazar*

The long Directoire coat worn over a plain skirt is a stylish design for wool street dresses. The coat is simply an undraped princess polonaise reaching nearly to the floor, of even length all around, and open down the entire front. The front of the bodice is turned back at the top in short broad lapels to show a vest underneath. The skirts hang open quite straight down the sides, disclosing the skirt front. There are large cuffs on the large coat sleeves, and broad square pockets are set on each hip. Cashmeres are used for the most elaborate Directoire costumes, and are richly embroidered with shaded silks down the front of the skirt and on the lapels of the long coat.

May 5, 1888 *Harper's Bazar*

The long Directoire redingote is used for rich velvet, silk, and cloth costumes. It hangs straight down the sides and back, and slopes away from the front to show the skirt beneath. The back breadths have additional fullness on the tournure, made by plaits folded in each seam. Or else the center backs are cut off in a point, and the skirt breadths are gathered to this point. The side backs and side pieces are continuous, but the fronts are cut off at the waist-line, and are turned back in wide lapels to show a vest beneath. This design is very elegant when made of an antique brocade with a skirt of plain royale, faille, or velvet. This arrangement is often reversed, the velvet serving for the long coat. Silk embroidery covering the vest is a feature of elegant redingotes. Large buttons of cut steel, old silver, or bronze, and some silk cord passementerie ornaments, are the trimmings. A wide folded silk sash crosses the vest.

October 6, 1888 *Harper's Bazar*

Embroideries on all kinds of materials are lavishly employed in bands to trim the plain falling breadths of Directoire redingotes. Rich Oriental gold and silver embroideries look quite in keeping. Even light veilings and crêpes have panels or insertions of embroidered silk. Often a handsome silk coat with an embroidered vest is worn with a skirt of plain veiling in the same or a contrasting color, plaited or with the fullness shirred to some little distance below the waist. Accordion-plaited skirts are worn with Directoire coats.

June 1889 *Demorest's Monthly Magazine*

Street Costume

The polonaise is drafted with the scale corresponding to the bust measure. It is in seven pieces: Front, side back, bodice back, skirt back, collar, and two sleeve pieces. The skirt back is gathered and sewed to the bodice back. Lay two upward-turning plaits in the front. Join it to the back, bringing the plaits up over the side back, and stay it underneath. The front is closed with buttons and button-holes.

The skirt is drafted with the scale corresponding to the waist measure. The length is regulated with the tape measure. The skirt is in three pieces: Front, side gore, and back.

Summer 1888 *Voice of Fashion*

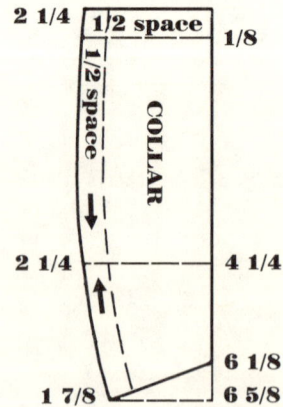

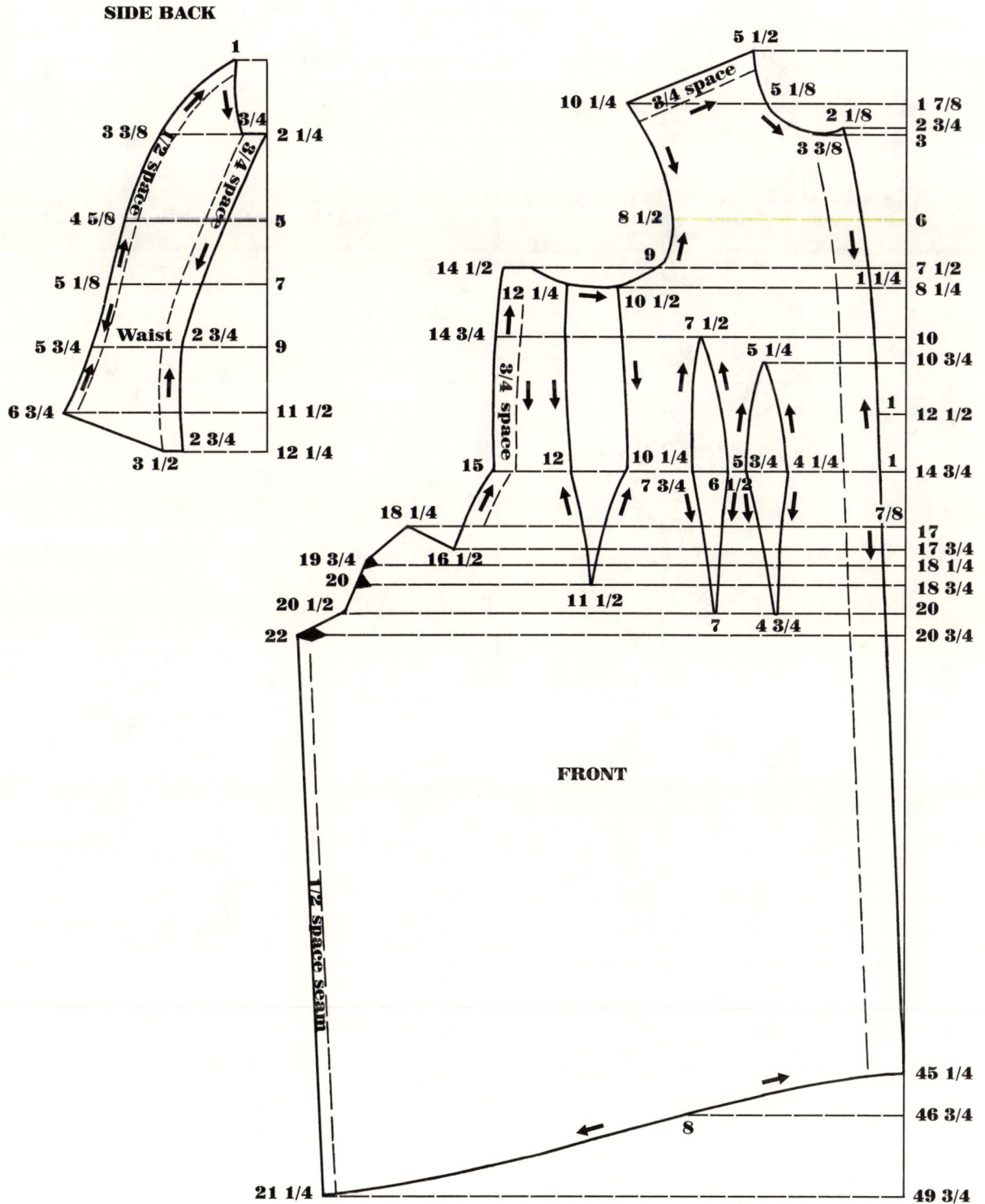

SIDE BACK

FRONT

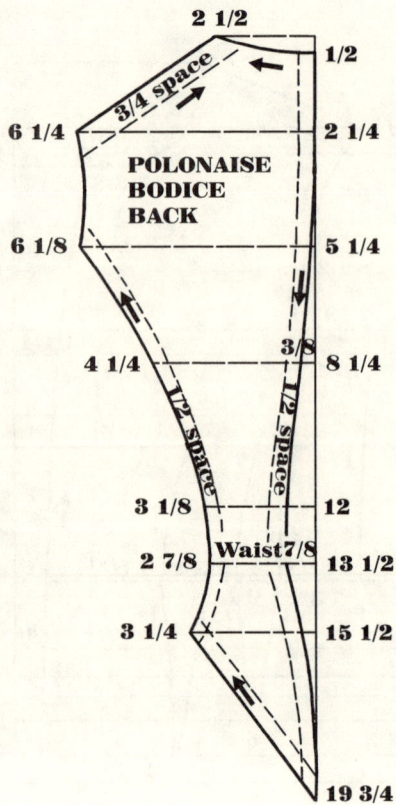

POLONAISE
BODICE
BACK

2 1/2
1/2
3/4 space
6 1/4
2 1/4
6 1/8
5 1/4
4 1/4
3/8
8 1/4
1/2 space
1/2 space
3 1/8
12
2 7/8   Waist 7/8
13 1/2
3 1/4
15 1/2
19 3/4

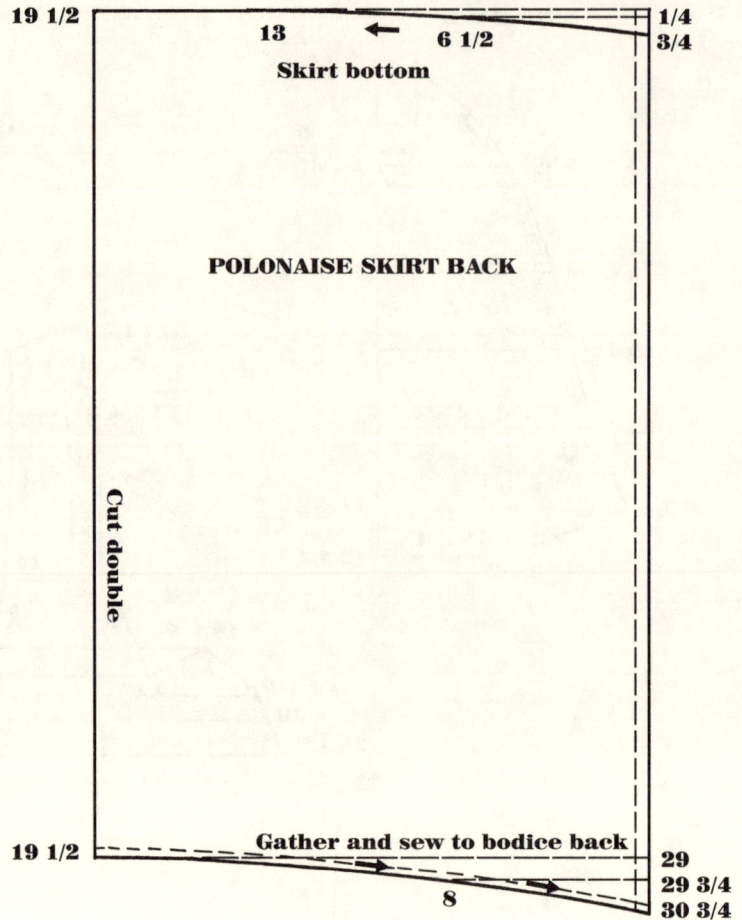

19 1/2
13
6 1/2
1/4
3/4
Skirt bottom

POLONAISE SKIRT BACK

Cut double

19 1/2
Gather and sew to bodice back
29
8
29 3/4
30 3/4

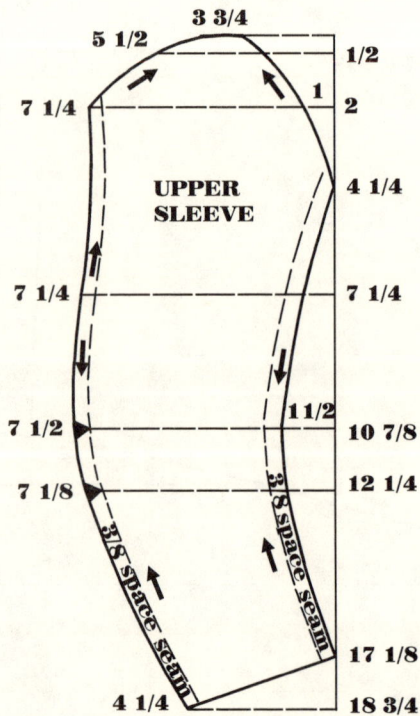

3 3/4
5 1/2
1/2
1
7 1/4
2

UPPER
SLEEVE

4 1/4
7 1/4
7 1/4
7 1/2
11 1/2
10 7/8
7 1/8
12 1/4
3/8 space seam
3/8 space seam
17 1/8
4 1/4
18 3/4

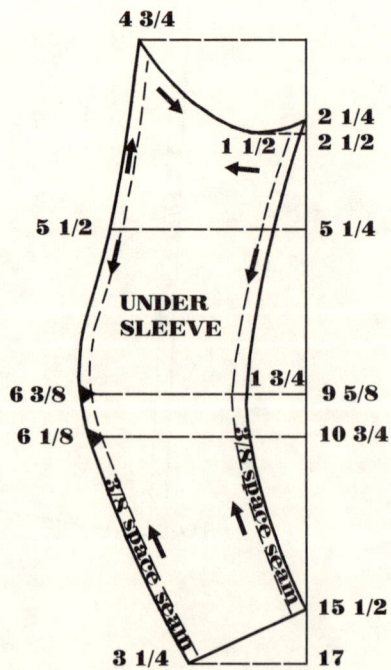

4 3/4
2 1/4
1 1/2
2 1/2
5 1/2
5 1/4

UNDER
SLEEVE

6 3/8
1 3/4
9 5/8
6 1/8
10 3/4
3/8 space seam
3/8 space seam
15 1/2
3 1/4
17

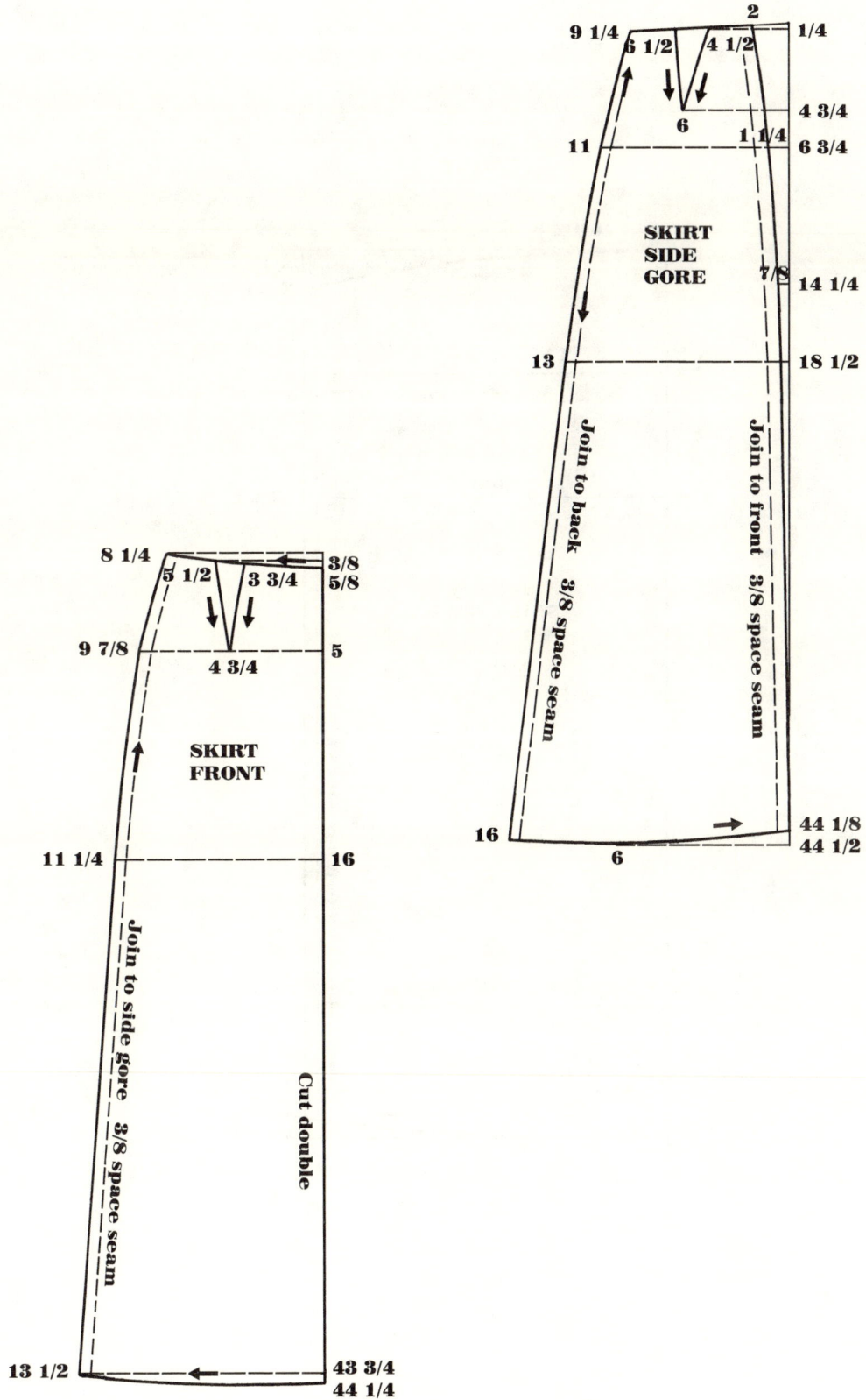

SKIRT SIDE GORE

9 1/4 5 1/2 4 1/2 2 1/4
6
4 3/4
11 1 1/4 6 3/4
7/8 14 1/4
13 18 1/2

Join to back 3/8 space seam
Join to front 3/8 space seam

16 44 1/8
6 44 1/2

SKIRT FRONT

8 1/4 5 1/2 3 3/4 3/8 5/8
4 3/4
9 7/8 5
11 1/4 16

Join to side gore 3/8 space seam
Cut double

13 1/2 43 3/4 44 1/4

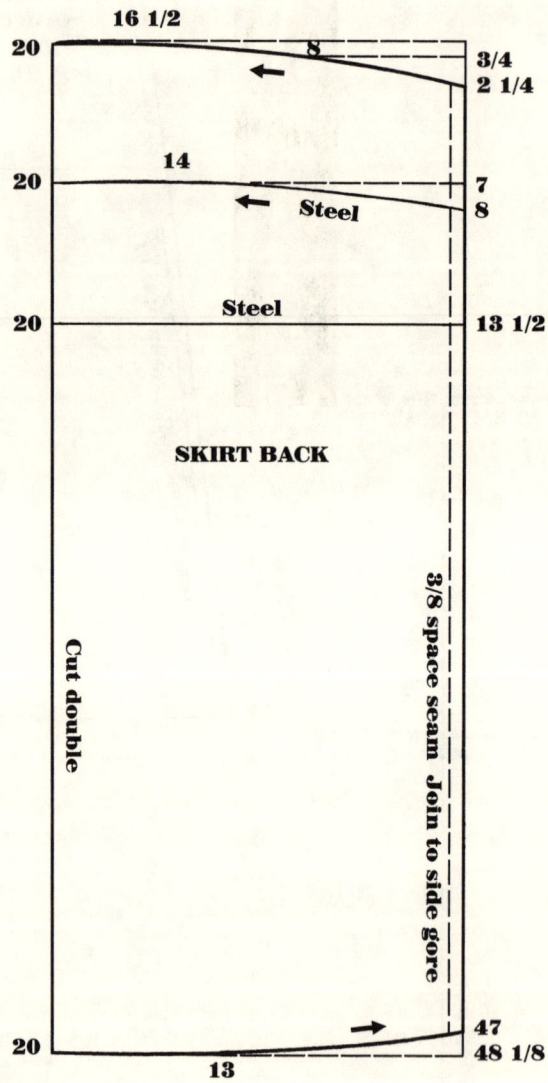

SKIRT BACK

Cut double

3/8 space seam Join to side gore

16 1/2
20
8
3/4
2 1/4
14
20
7
Steel
8
Steel
20
13 1/2
20
13
47
48 1/8

Four-Gored Skirt

Four-Gored Skirt. The engraving shows the skirt made up in plain suiting and plainly finished. Many fashionable walking skirts are untrimmed; however, trimming may be added. To make the garment for a lady of medium size, requires 4 7/8 yards of material 22 inches wide, 3 1/2 yards of material 36 inches wide, 3 yards of material 44 inches wide, or 2 3/8 yards of material 54 inches wide.

This skirt has three gores and a full back breadth. The gores are fitted smoothly by darts, while the breadth is gathered across the top. The skirt may be worn without a bustle, providing the extra length allowed for it at the top is cut off. The bouffant effect is further enhanced by steels run through casings, and tapes are sewed at their ends and tied together to regulate the final adjustment. The placket opening is finished at the center of the back breadth, and the top of the skirt is sewed to a belt.

The arrangement of the steels is most satisfactory when short pieces of elastic are sewed to the ends and the tying tapes attached to them. With either a long or a short bustle, the steels may be omitted. A lining is essential when the material is light or elastic. A crinoline facing is also in order, and in some instances it is carried so high that it might also be called a lining. However, this adds much to the weight of the skirt. A narrow facing of silesia or alpaca should always be applied over the crinoline. Many ladies complain that the edge of a skirt wears on the fronts of the boots. This can be avoided by slashing the skirt to a depth of about 2 inches at the center and on each side of the front; but this can only be done with a trimmed skirt, as the slashes should be covered by the trimming and finished like the bottom of the skirt.

January 1887 *Delineator*

Four-Gored Skirt. The skirt is portrayed made of dress material and plainly finished. Its three dart-shaped gores and full back breadth are shaped to hang evenly. Across the back breadth, two steels are adjusted in casings and tied into curves by tapes or elastics. A belt finishes the top of the skirt, and the placket opeing is made on the left side-back seam. A small pad is shaped in two parts, which are narrowest at the top and rounded at the bottom. They are filled with moss or curled hair, and caught together in upholstery fashion. The top of the pad is caught to the belt.

All kinds of seasonable dress materials, and also plain, corded, striped, and figured silks, velvets, etc., make up handsomely in this mode. Trimming may be added if desired, especially flat applications. To make the skirt for a lady of medium size, requires 5 3/8 yards of material 22 inches wide, 3 1/2 yards of material 36 inches wide, 3 yards of material 44 inches wide, or 2 1/2 yards of material 54 inches wide.

September 1888 *Delineator*

Ladies' Costume

The polonaise is drafted with the scale corresponding to the bust measure. It is in eleven pieces: Upper right front (in two parts to be put together before drafting), under right front, left front, side piece, side back, side panel, right back, left back, collar, and two sleeve pieces.

Draft the backs first. If the material to be used is sufficiently wide, omit the seams and cut double. The right side of the right back is straight, with the exception of the loop. Connect the notches to form the loop. Lay the plaits according to the notches on the left side of the left back.

The upper right front and the front drapery are drafted together. Close the darts. Sew the seams under the arm and on the shoulder. Face the front edge from 16 3/4 on the third cross-line down to 9 on the ninth cross-line. Lay plaits according to the notches from 9 to 20 1/4 on the base-line and baste them securely. Bring that part over to the left side and fasten with a hook and eye.

Turn away the left front on the dashed line and connect with the first dashed line on the under right front. This will form a V in front, which may be of shirring as represented, or of velvet.

Shirr the side panel and sew each shirring to the side back and side piece. Face the panel with the same material. Insert a lead weight at the bottom of the panel.

The over-skirt may be plaited as represented, or plain. The foundation skirt has three pieces: Front, side gore, and back. It is drafted with the scale corresponding to the waist measure, and the length is regulated with the tape measure. If steels are not desired, cut the back breadth straight on the line running from 4 on the base-line to 20. Leave the placket opening on the side instead of at the back, when the steels are used.

Fall 1888 *Voice of Fashion*

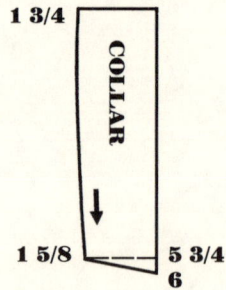

COLLAR

1 3/4

1 5/8   5 3/4
            6

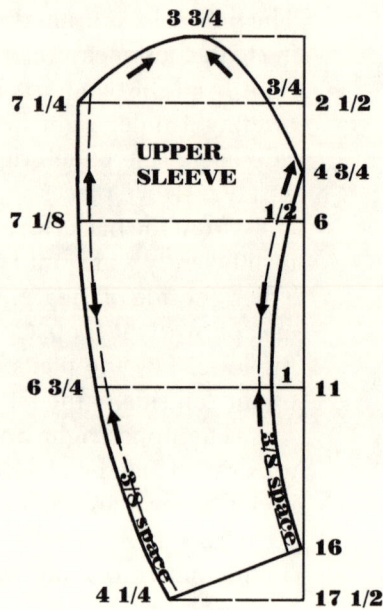

UPPER SLEEVE

3 3/4
3/4
7 1/4   2 1/2
               4 3/4
7 1/8   1/2 6
6 3/4   1   11
               16
4 1/4   17 1/2

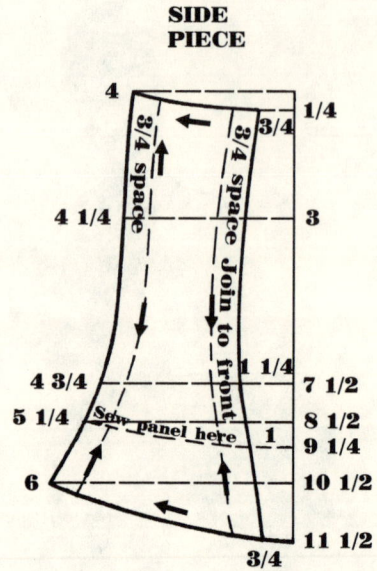

SIDE PIECE

4   1/4
        3/4
        3/4 space   Join to front
4 1/4
4 3/4   7 1/2
5 1/4   8 1/2
Sew panel here 1 9 1/4
               10 1/2
6
               11 1/2
        3/4

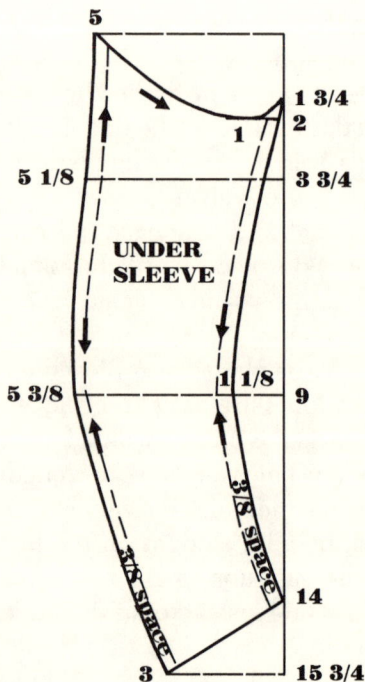

UNDER SLEEVE

5
           1 3/4
        1 2
5 1/8   3 3/4
5 3/8   1 1/8 9
           14
3   15 3/4
3/8 space

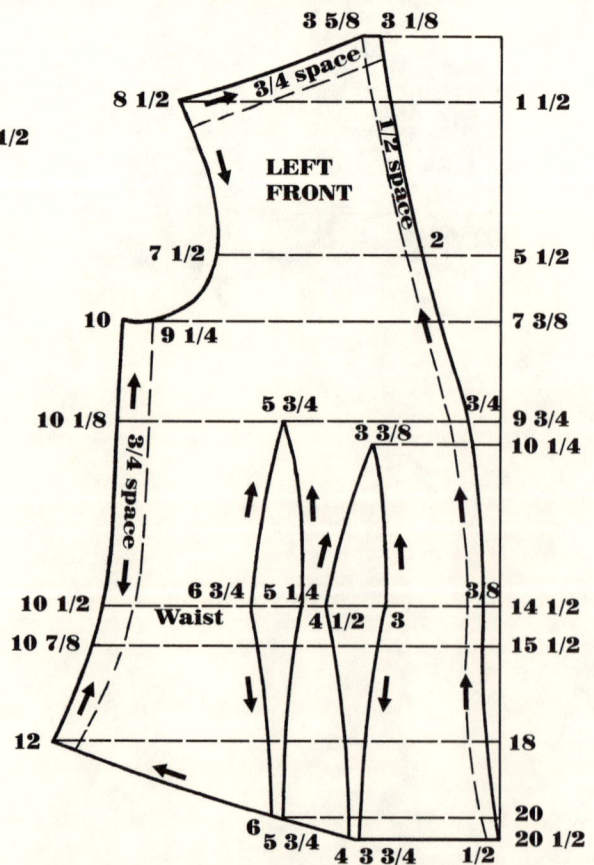

LEFT FRONT

3 5/8 3 1/8
8 1/2   3/4 space   1 1/2
                1/2 space
7 1/2   2   5 1/2
10   7 3/8
   9 1/4
10 1/8   5 3/4   3/4 9 3/4
          3 3/8   10 1/4
   3/4 space
10 1/2 6 3/4 5 1/4   3/8 14 1/2
Waist   4 1/2 3
10 7/8   15 1/2
           18
12
6   20
5 3/4   4 3 3/4 1/2 20 1/2

226

SIDE BACK

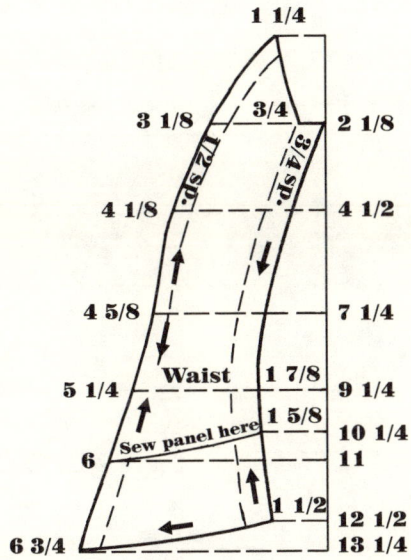

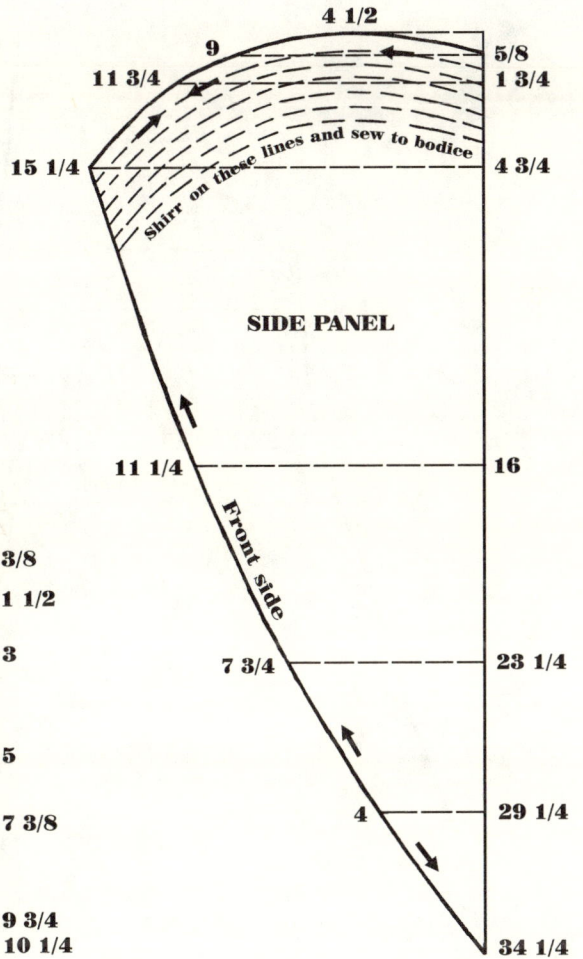

SIDE PANEL

Shirr on these lines and sew to bodice

Front side

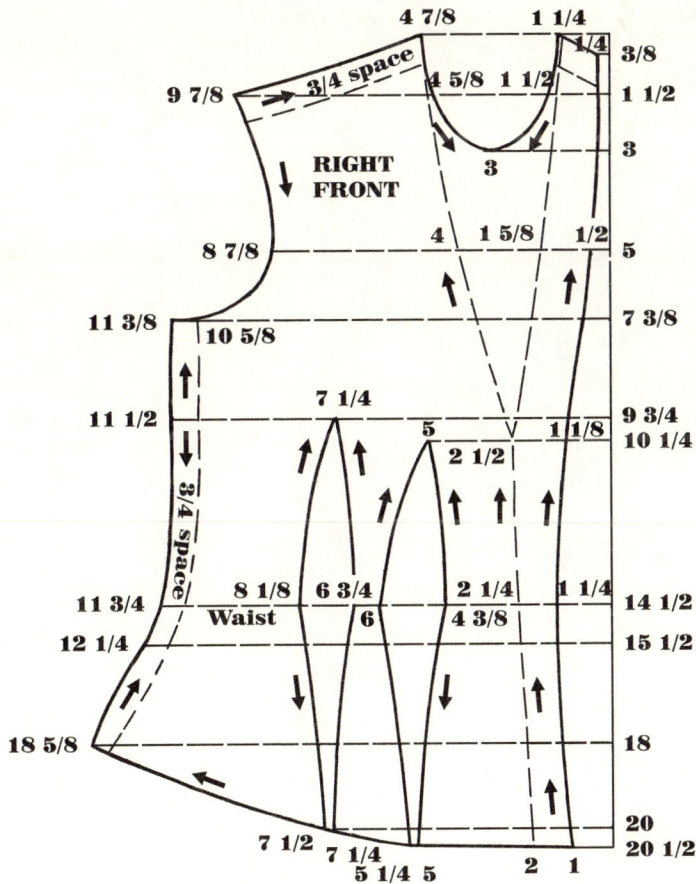

RIGHT FRONT

Waist

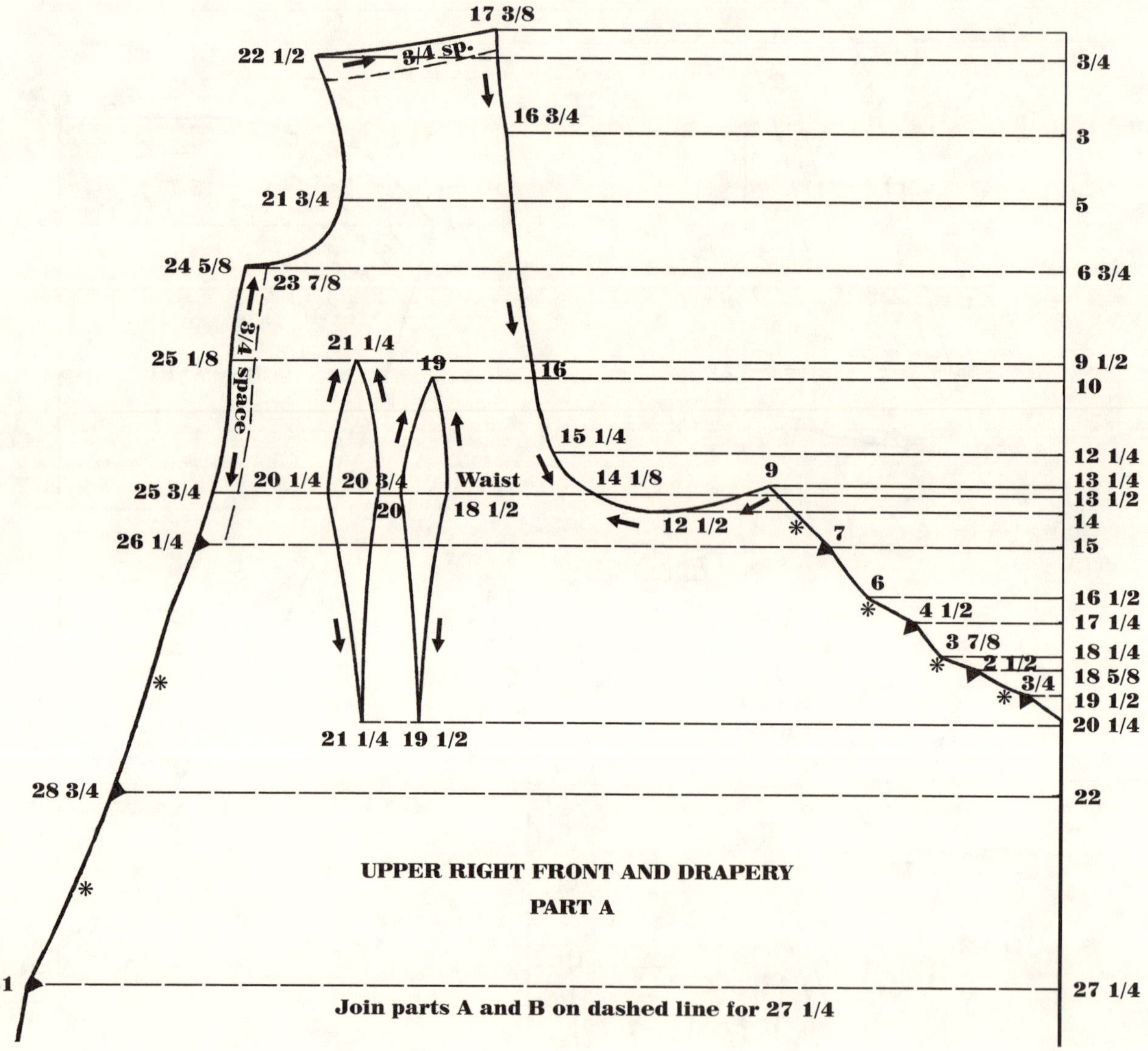

17 3/8

22 1/2   3/4 sp.

16 3/4   3/4

3

21 3/4   5

24 5/8   23 7/8   6 3/4

3/4 space

25 1/8   21 1/4   19   16   9 1/2

10

15 1/4   12 1/4

25 3/4   20 1/4   20 3/4   Waist   14 1/8   9   13 1/4

20   18 1/2   13 1/2

26 1/4   12 1/2   14

7   15

6   16 1/2

4 1/2   17 1/4

3 7/8   18 1/4

2 1/2   18 5/8

3/4   19 1/2

21 1/4   19 1/2   20 1/4

28 3/4   22

UPPER RIGHT FRONT AND DRAPERY

PART A

31   27 1/4

Join parts A and B on dashed line for 27 1/4

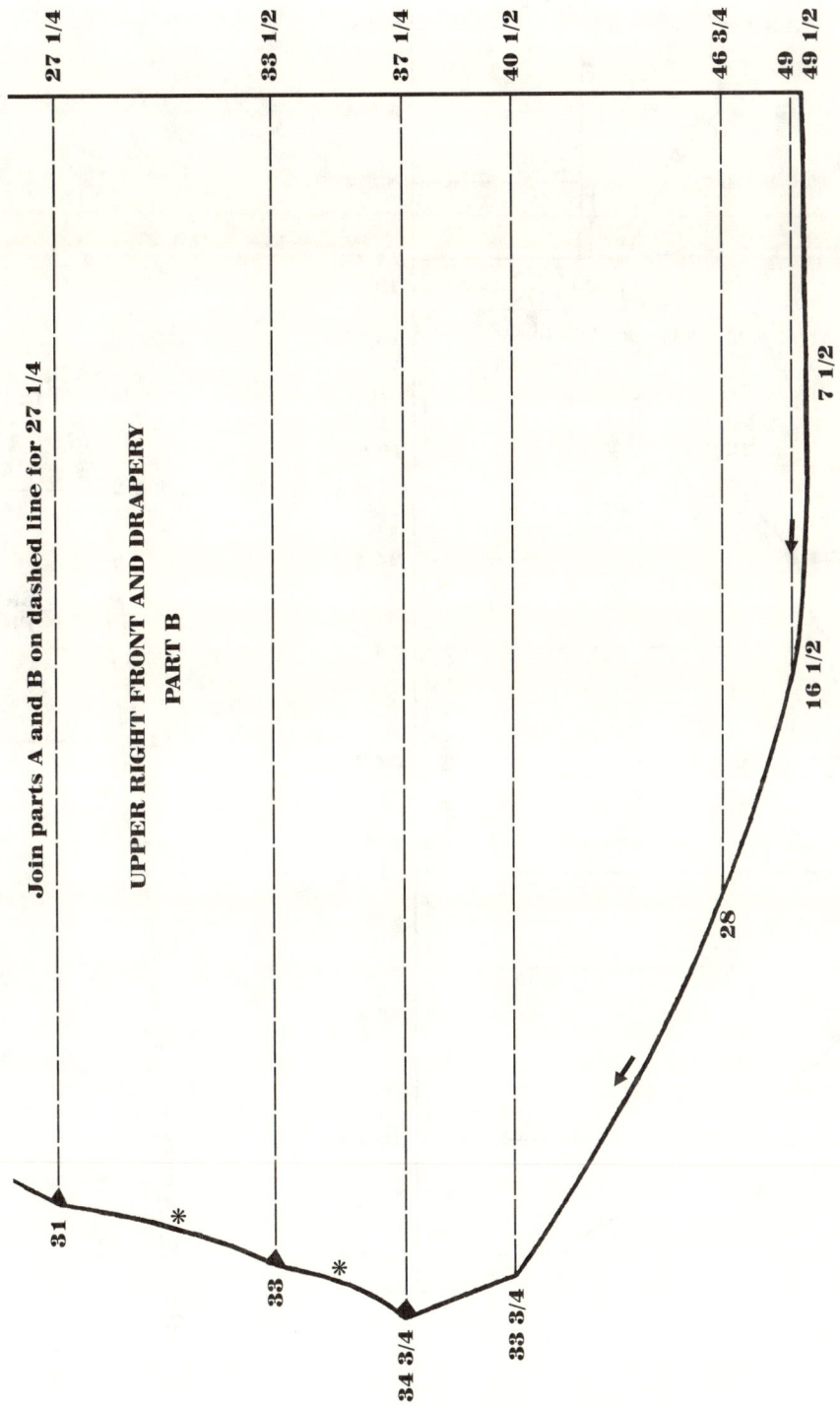

Join parts A and B on dashed line for 27 1/4

UPPER RIGHT FRONT AND DRAPERY

PART B

27 1/4

33 1/2

37 1/4

40 1/2

46 3/4

49

49 1/2

7 1/2

16 1/2

28

31

33

34 3/4

38 3/4

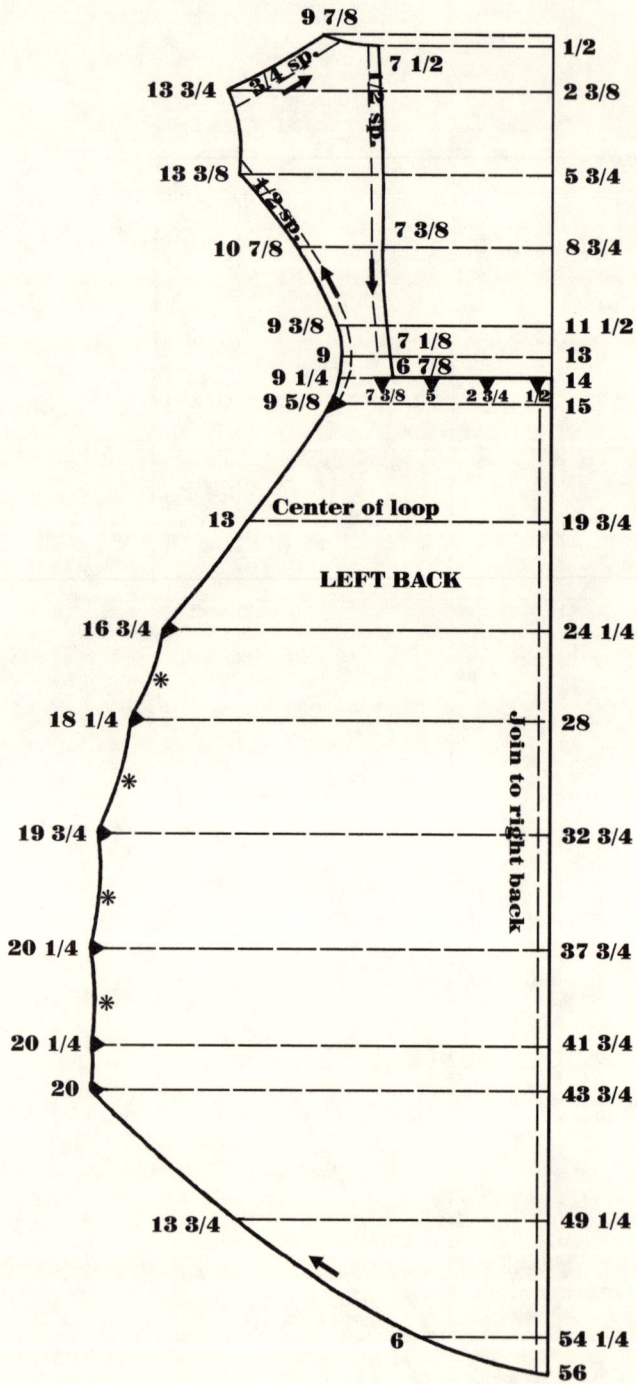

LEFT BACK

Center of loop

Join to right back

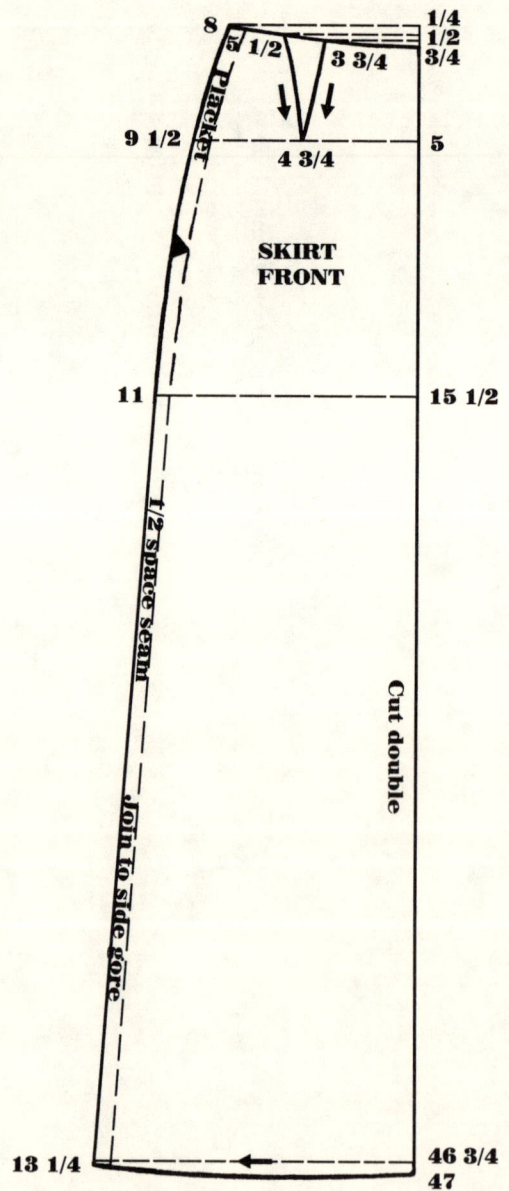

SKIRT FRONT

Placket

1/2 space seam

Join to side gore

Cut double

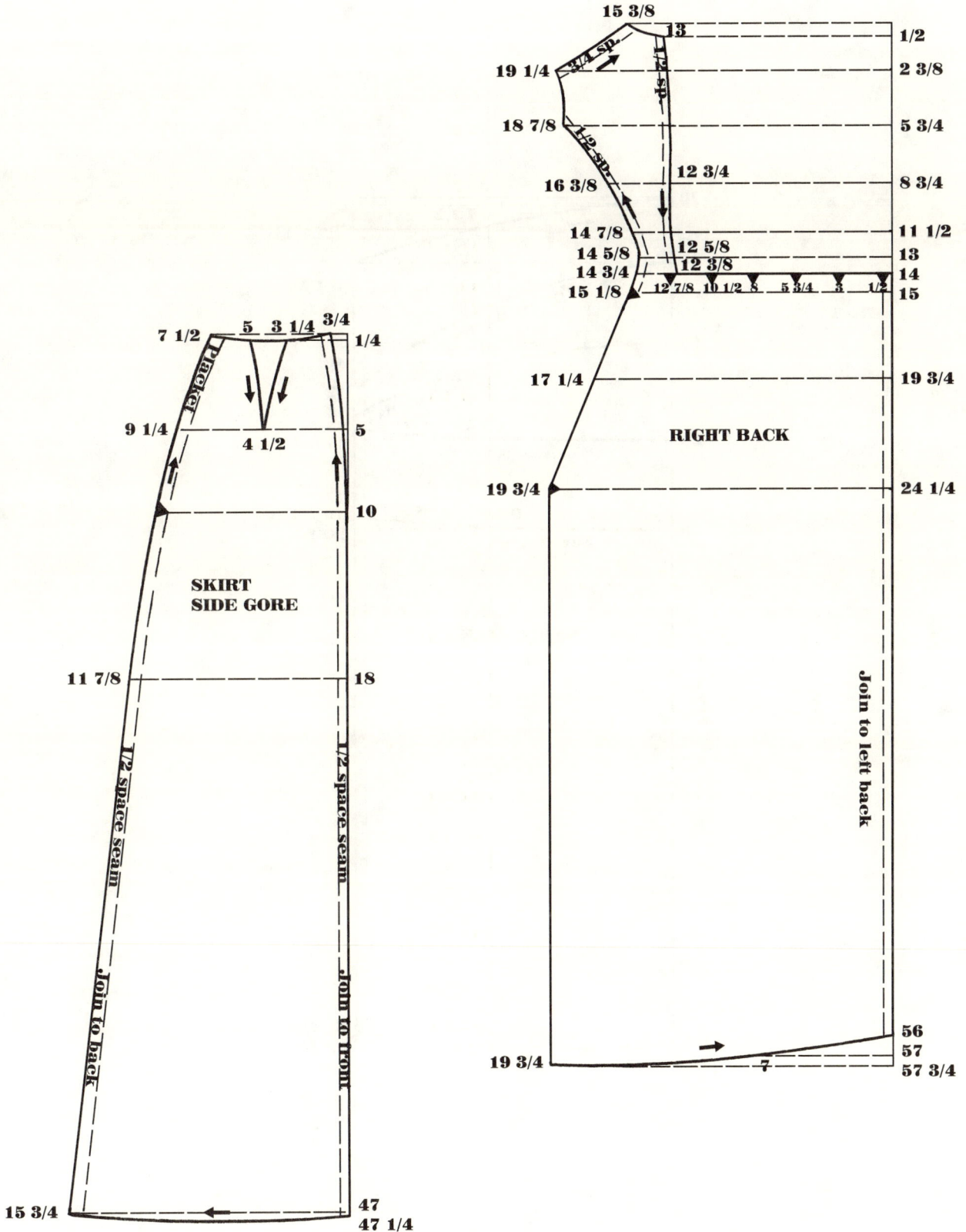

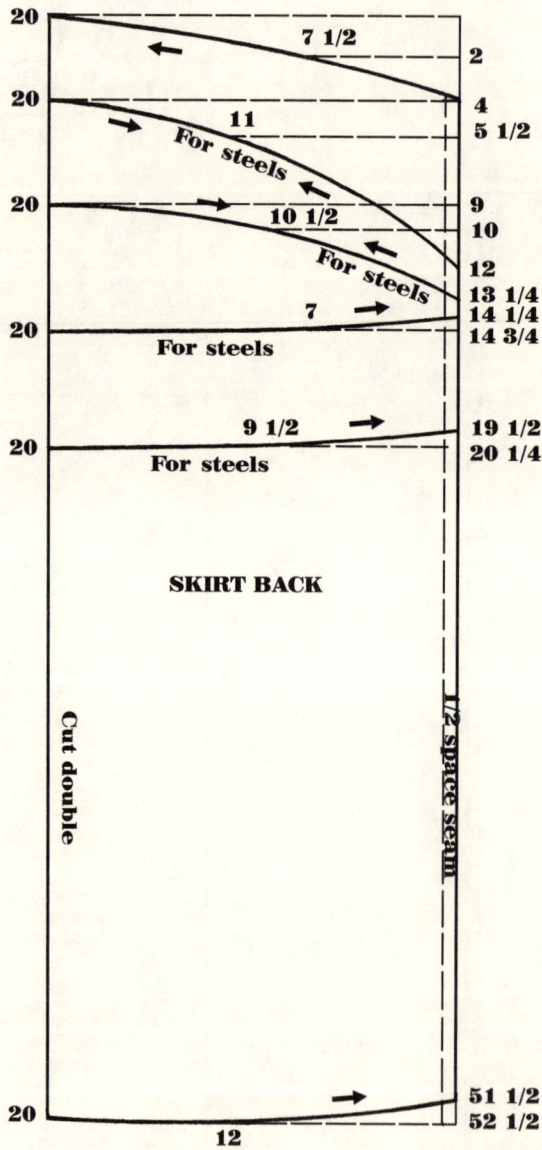

Ladies' Costume. The costume combines a skirt and a polonaise. It is shown made up in white and serpent green cashmere, and trimmed with serpent green velvet. The four-gored foundation skirt is made in the standard shape. It is hidden by a second skirt of the white cashmere, which is trimmed at the bottom with a deep velvet facing surmounted by a simple scroll of gold soutache. On each side, just back of the side-front seams in the foundation, the second skirt is laid in two forward-turning and two backward-turning plaits, which are deep and spread with a fan effect toward the bottom. The plaits are basted to tapes underneath to retain their folds. The top is gathered across the back breadth, and sewed flatly all around to the skirt some distance below the belt. The placket opening is made at the center of the back.

The polonaise bodice is adjusted by curved bust darts, side pieces, side backs, and a center back seam, the side pieces and left front being in round basque shape. The fronts close with hooks and eyes in a curve from the right shoulder to the left hip. The right front is deepened and widened to form the front drapery, while the left front is widened diagonally above the bust to extend to the right shoulder. A velvet band follows the curved edge of the right front, and along the back edge of the band is a scroll of gold braid. On the left front, above the waist-line, the band and braid trimming is duplicated. In front of it the front is faced with white material, giving the effect of a chemisette vest.

At the end of the closing, four upward-turning plaits are clustered in the front. In the right side edge five similar plaits are arranged, the plaits all falling diagonally into the drapery. This descends in a long point to the edge of the skirt on the left of the center. Contrasting with the front drapery on each side is a

narrow, pointed drapery. This hangs to the edge of the skirt, and is seamed to the side pieces and side backs some distance above their lower edges. The points are turned down over their seams and are very slightly draped by two upward-turning plaits arranged in their back edges at the seam. The points extend on the front drapery for a short distance at the top; they hang free from their seams and consequently should be prettily lined. They are held close across the hips by a strap crossing the back and basted to the side-back seams.

The bouffant back drapery is provided entirely by the center back, and hangs in a long point that shows an arrangement of soft jabot and irregular folds. On the right side, the back drapery hangs straight below a long burnous caught at the end of the side-back seam. The left side is disposed in a cluster of five deep, overlapping plaits that are basted to the top of the drapery so as to fall in folds from the top, the front folds of the plaits being caught to the top of the left pointed drapery. The top of the drapery at this side is disposed partly in a long burnous that duplicates the effect of the burnous on the right side, and the plaits are pushed under this loop so that they are only visible in folds below. At the center, the drapery is amplified by a quadruple box-plait underfolded at the end of the center back seam, the straight folds being very effective over the tournure and contrasting with the bouffant draping on the sides.

The standing collar is of velvet, its ends closing above the closing of the bodice. Along its seaming is a scroll of gold braid in harmony with a similar arrangement on other parts of the costume. The coat sleeves are finished with round cuff-facings of velvet headed by a scroll of gold braid.

Gobelin blue, suede, tan, blue-gray, and other fashionable shades are combined with white in costumes of this style. Any two colors may be similarly associated, and two or three contrasting textures may be used. The points at the sides may contrast with the rest of the polonaise. Silver, gold, copper, and other metal braids, and also worsted and silk braids, are applied in simple scrolls, in all-over embroidered designs, and in lines on the seamed skirt and polonaise. Sometimes the second skirt is ornamented at the bottom with deep embroidery. All seasonable materials are made up in this style. To make the costume for a lady of medium size, requires 17 5/8 yards of material 22 inches wide, 10 3/4 yards of material 36 inches wide, or 9 yards of material 44 inches wide. As represented, it needs 6 3/8 yards of dark and 3 1/4 yards of white cashmere 40 inches wide, with 1 3/4 yards of velvet 20 inches wide for the collar, etc., and 1/8 yard of lining material 36 inches wide for the foundation skirt.

June 1888 *Delineator*

Street Costume

The polonaise is drafted with the scale corresponding to the bust measure. There are seven pieces: Right front, left front, side piece, side back, back, and two sleeve pieces. The right front is cut diagonal. Lay the plaits according to the notches. Any style of trimming may be used.

The skirt has three pieces: Front, side gore, and back. It is drafted with the scale corresponding to the waist measure. The length is regulated with the tape measure.

Winter 1888–1889 *Voice of Fashion*

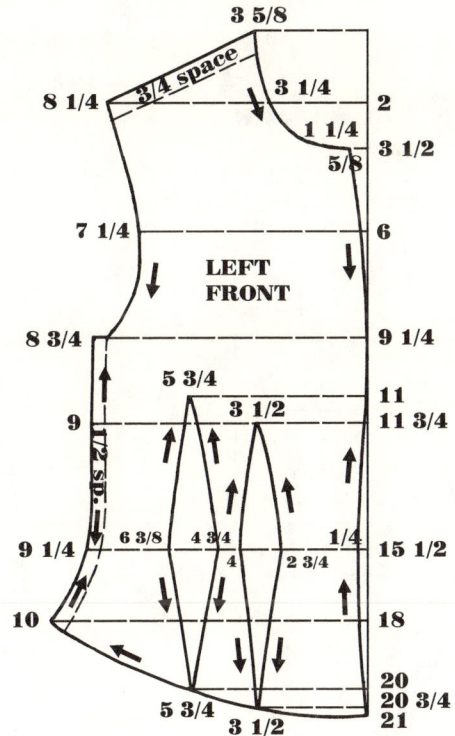

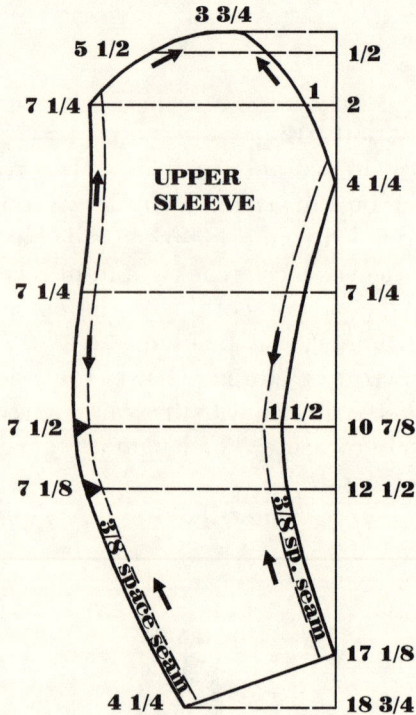

UPPER SLEEVE

3 3/4
5 1/2 — 1/2
7 1/4 — 1 — 2
4 1/4
7 1/4 — 7 1/4
7 1/2 — 1 1/2 — 10 7/8
7 1/8 — 12 1/2
3/8 space seam
3/8 s.b. seam
17 1/8
4 1/4 — 18 3/4

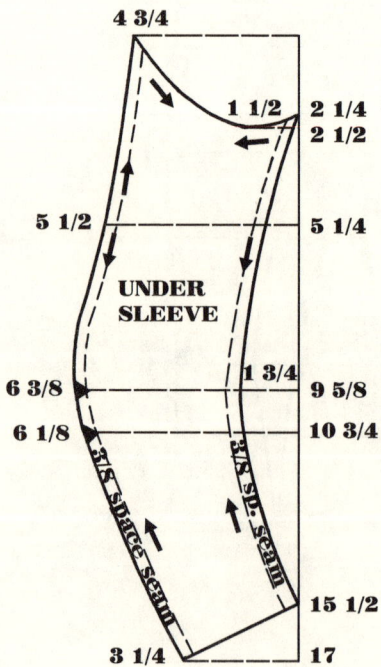

UNDER SLEEVE

4 3/4
1 1/2 — 2 1/4
2 1/2
5 1/2 — 5 1/4
6 3/8 — 1 3/4 — 9 5/8
6 1/8 — 10 3/4
3/8 space seam
3/8 s.b. seam
15 1/2
3 1/4 — 17

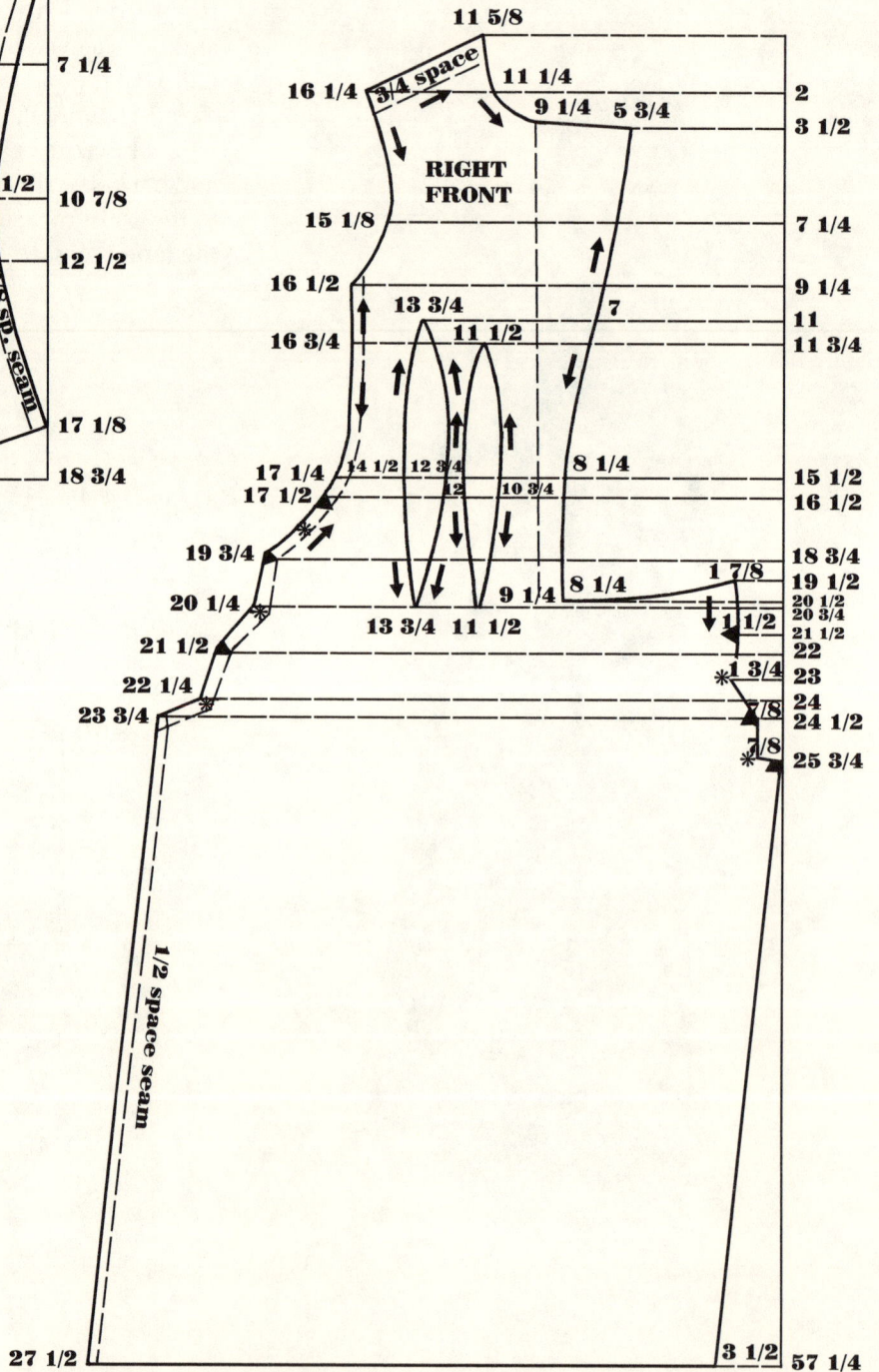

RIGHT FRONT

11 5/8
3/4 space
16 1/4 — 11 1/4
9 1/4 — 5 3/4 — 2
3 1/2
15 1/8 — 7 1/4
16 1/2 — 9 1/4
13 3/4 — 7 — 11
16 3/4 — 11 1/2 — 11 3/4
17 1/4 — 14 1/2 — 12 3/4 — 8 1/4 — 15 1/2
17 1/2 — 2 — 10 3/4 — 16 1/2
19 3/4 — 18 3/4
20 1/4 — 9 1/4 — 8 1/4 — 1 7/8 — 19 1/2
13 3/4 — 11 1/2 — 20 1/2
20 3/4
1 1/2 — 21 1/2
21 1/2 — 22
22 1/4 — 1 3/4 — 23
23 3/4 — 7/8 — 24
24 1/2
7/8 — 25 3/4
1/2 space seam
27 1/2 — 3 1/2 — 57 1/4

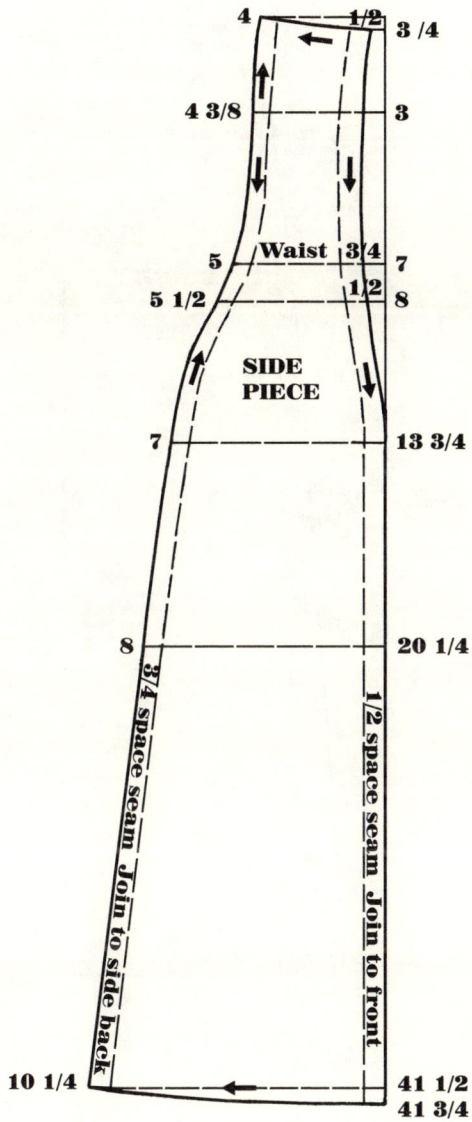

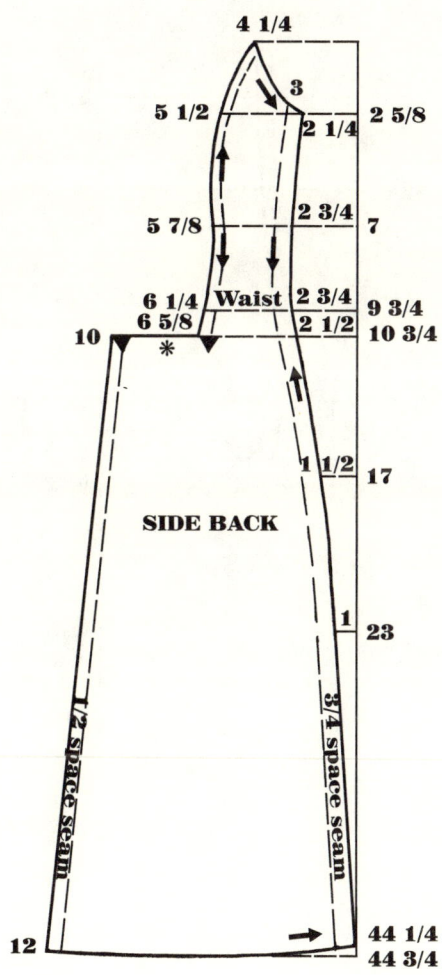

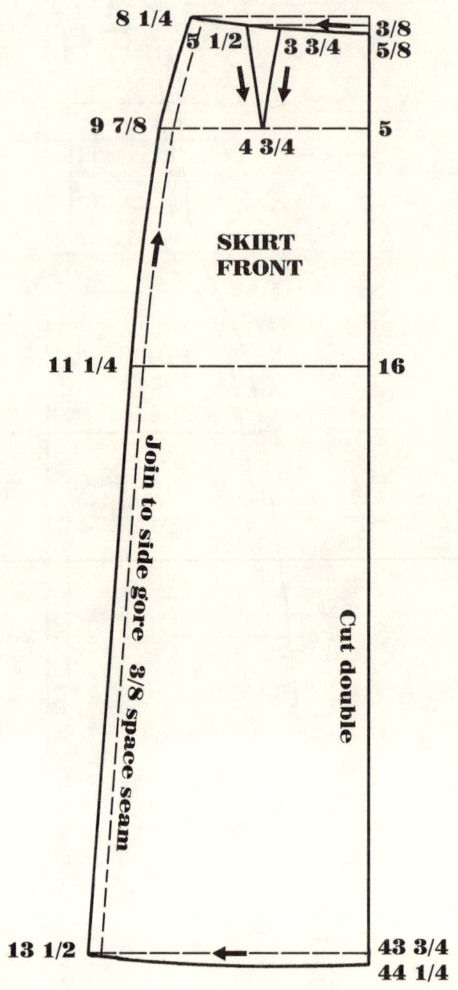

SKIRT FRONT

8 1/4
3/8
5/8
5 1/2
3 3/4
9 7/8
4 3/4
5

Join to side gore 3/8 space seam

11 1/4
16

Cut double

13 1/2
43 3/4
44 1/4

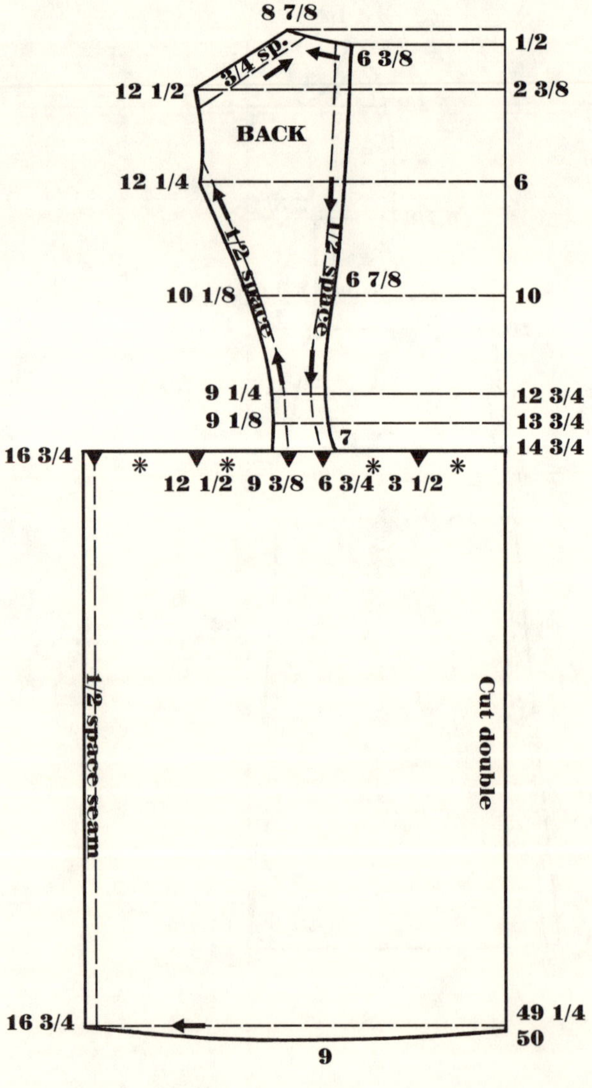

8 7/8
1/2
3/4 sp.
6 3/8
2 3/8
12 1/2

BACK

12 1/4
6

1/2 space
1/2 space
10 1/8
6 7/8
10

9 1/4
12 3/4
9 1/8
13 3/4
7
14 3/4

16 3/4 * * * * *
12 1/2 9 3/8 6 3/4 3 1/2

1/2 space seam

Cut double

16 3/4
49 1/4
50
9

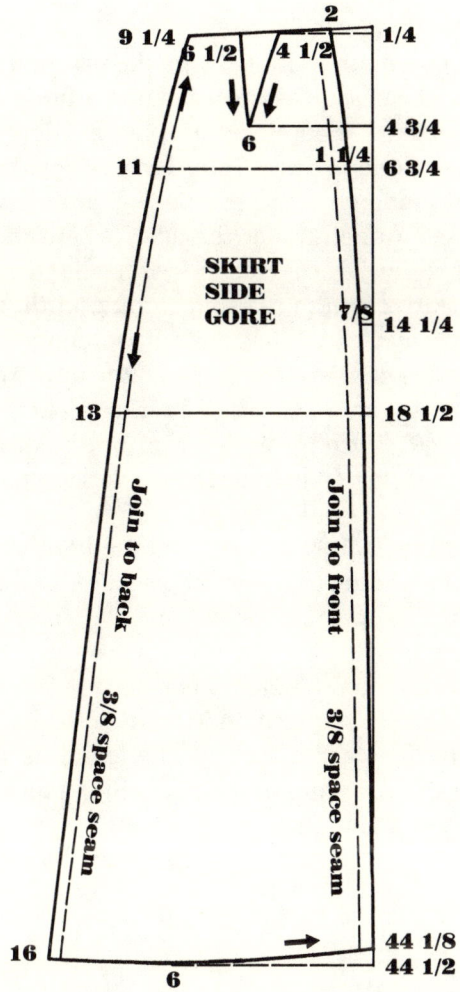

SKIRT SIDE GORE

9 1/4   6 1/2   4 1/2   2   1/4
6   4 3/4
11   1 1/4   6 3/4
7/8   14 1/4
13   18 1/2

Join to back

Join to front

3/8 space seam

3/8 space seam

16   44 1/8
6   44 1/2

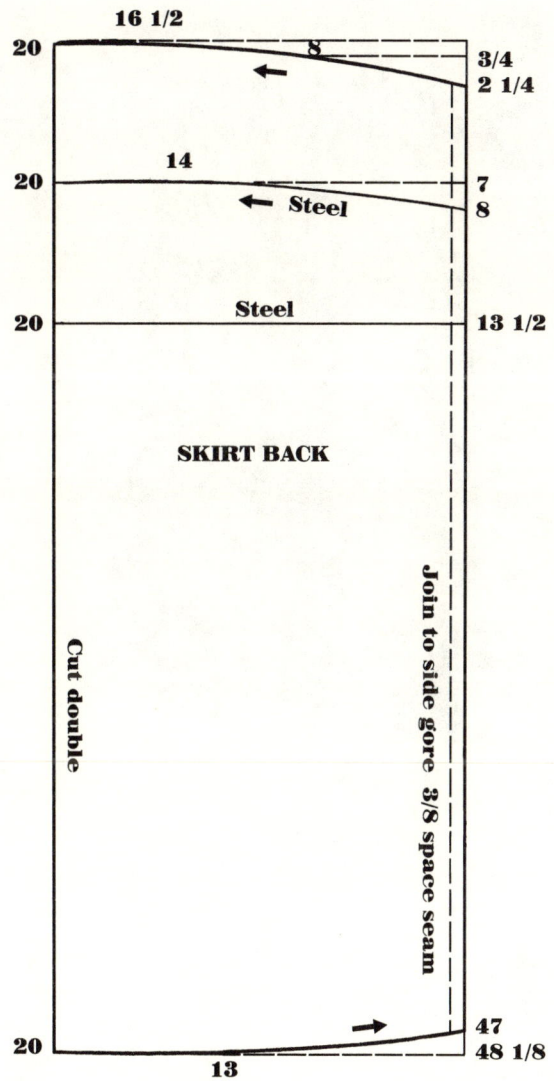

SKIRT BACK

16 1/2
20   8   3/4
2 1/4
20   14   7
Steel   8
20   Steel   13 1/2

Cut double

Join to side gore   3/8 space seam

20   47
13   48 1/8

Directoire Costume

The polonaise is drafted with the scale corresponding to the bust measure. It should be the same length as the skirt. There are ten pieces: Right and left under fronts, upper front, lapel, side back, back, front drapery, two sleeve pieces, and collar. Leave the seam open under the arms where there is no dashed line. Face each side with silk, the same as the skirt. Lay the plaits according to the notches. The center of the back can be left either open or closed from the waist-line. Cut the upper fronts on the heavy lines. Sew the under fronts in the under-arm dart. Turn away the front on the dashed line and face. The right under front overlaps the left, and fastens with hooks and eyes.

The front drapery is drafted with the scale corresponding to the waist measure. Lay the plaits according to the notches. The stars represent the under part of the plait or fold. Cascade the left side according to the notches and stars.

The skirt is drafted with the scale corresponding to the waist measure. The length is regulated with the tape measure. It has three pieces: Front, side gore, and back.

Spring 1889 *Voice of Fashion*

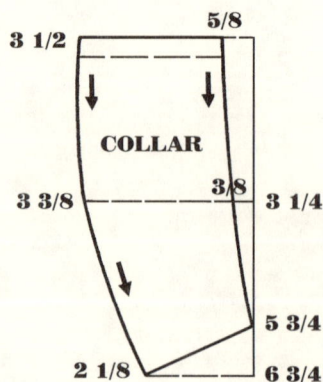

Directoire Costume

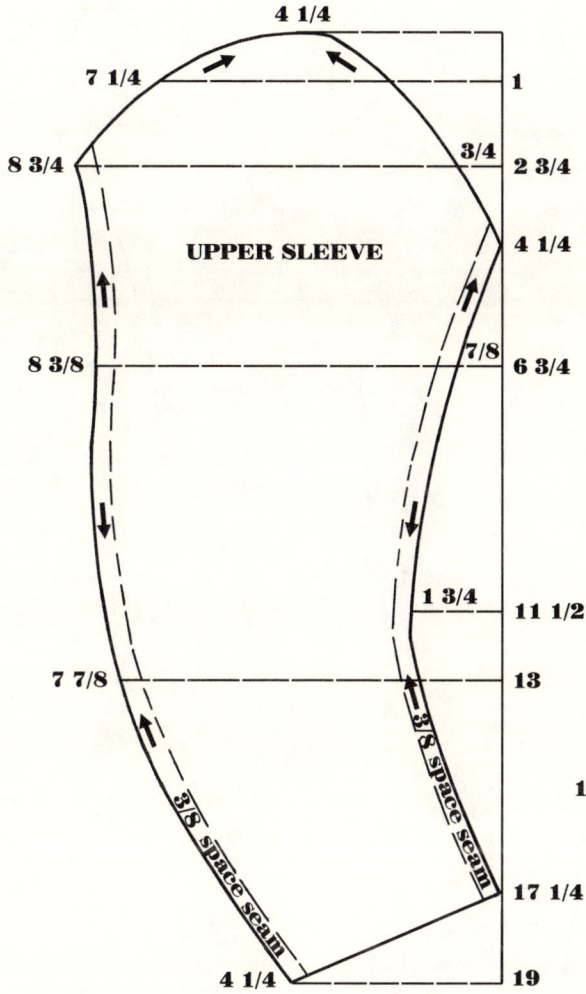

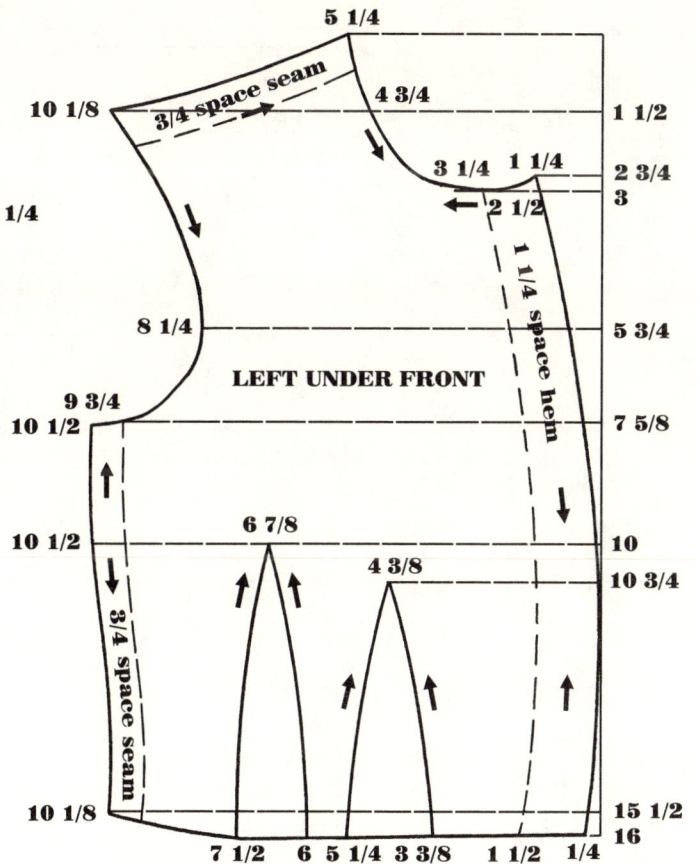

UPPER SLEEVE

- 4 1/4
- 7 1/4
- 1
- 8 3/4
- 3/4
- 2 3/4
- 4 1/4
- 8 3/8
- 7/8
- 6 3/4
- 1 3/4
- 11 1/2
- 7 7/8
- 13
- 3/8 space seam
- 3/8 space seam
- 17 1/4
- 4 1/4
- 19

LEFT UNDER FRONT

- 5 1/4
- 3/4 space seam
- 10 1/8
- 4 3/4
- 1 1/2
- 3 1/4
- 1 1/4
- 2 3/4
- 2 1/2
- 3
- 8 1/4
- 1 1/4 space hem
- 5 3/4
- 9 3/4
- 10 1/2
- 7 5/8
- 10 1/2
- 6 7/8
- 10
- 4 3/8
- 10 3/4
- 3/4 space seam
- 10 1/8
- 15 1/2
- 16
- 7 1/2
- 6
- 5 1/4
- 3 3/8
- 1 1/2
- 1/4

241

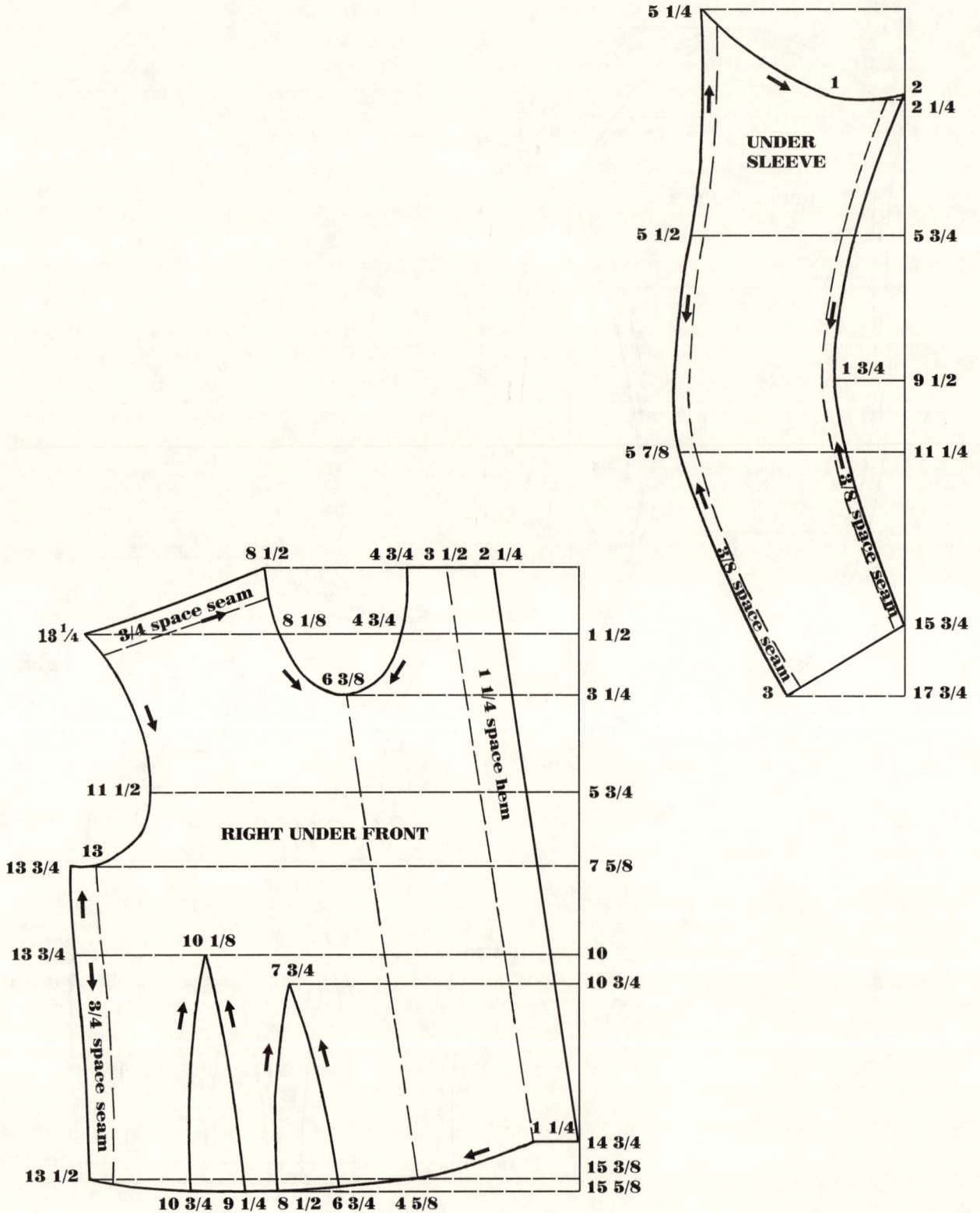

UNDER SLEEVE

5 1/4

1

2
2 1/4

5 1/2 · 5 3/4

1 3/4 · 9 1/2

5 7/8 · 11 1/4

3/8 space seam

3/8 space seam

3 · 15 3/4

17 3/4

---

8 1/2 · 4 3/4 · 3 1/2 · 2 1/4

3/4 space seam

13 1/4 · 8 1/8 · 4 3/4 · 1 1/2

6 3/8 · 3 1/4

1 1/4 space hem

11 1/2 · 5 3/4

RIGHT UNDER FRONT

13 3/4 · 7 5/8

13 ·

13 3/4 · 10 1/8 · 10

7 3/4 · 10 3/4

3/4 space seam

1 1/4 · 14 3/4

15 3/8

13 1/2 · 15 5/8

10 3/4 · 9 1/4 · 8 1/2 · 6 3/4 · 4 5/8

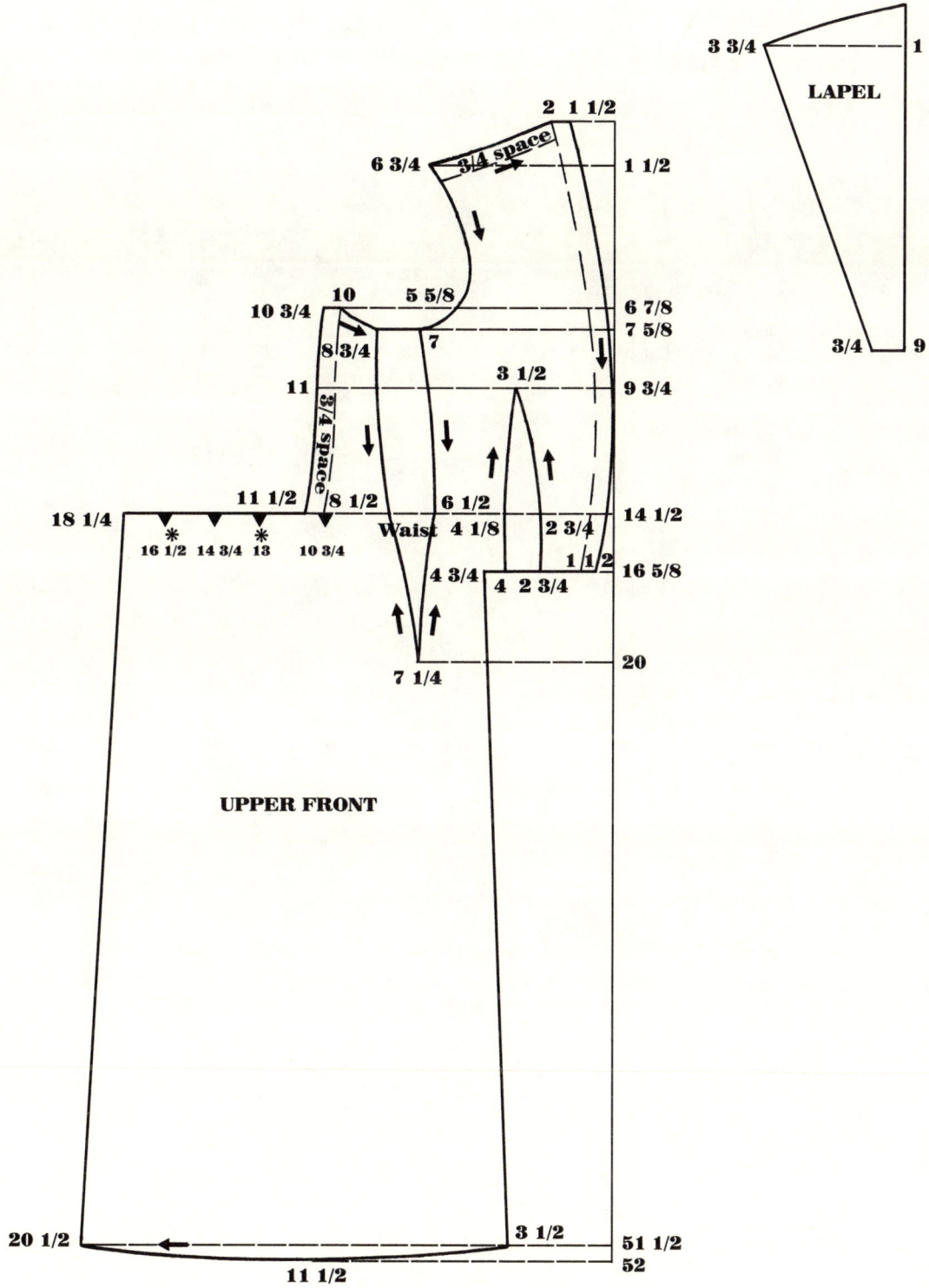

LAPEL

UPPER FRONT

Waist

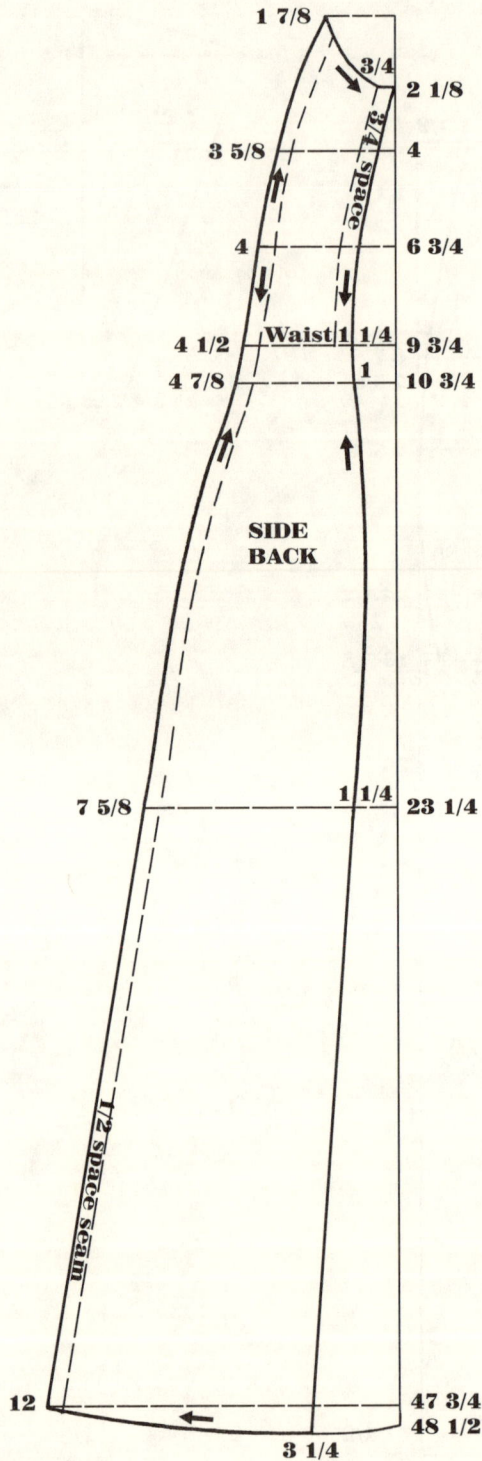

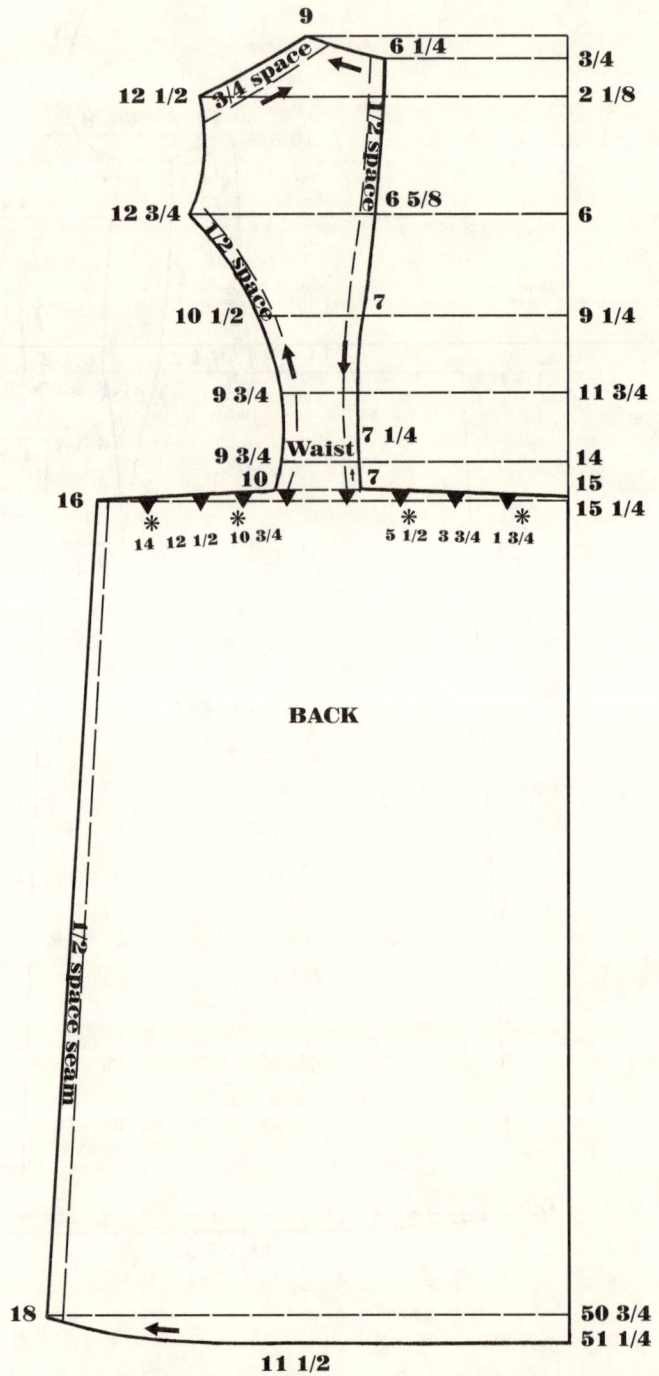

SIDE BACK

BACK

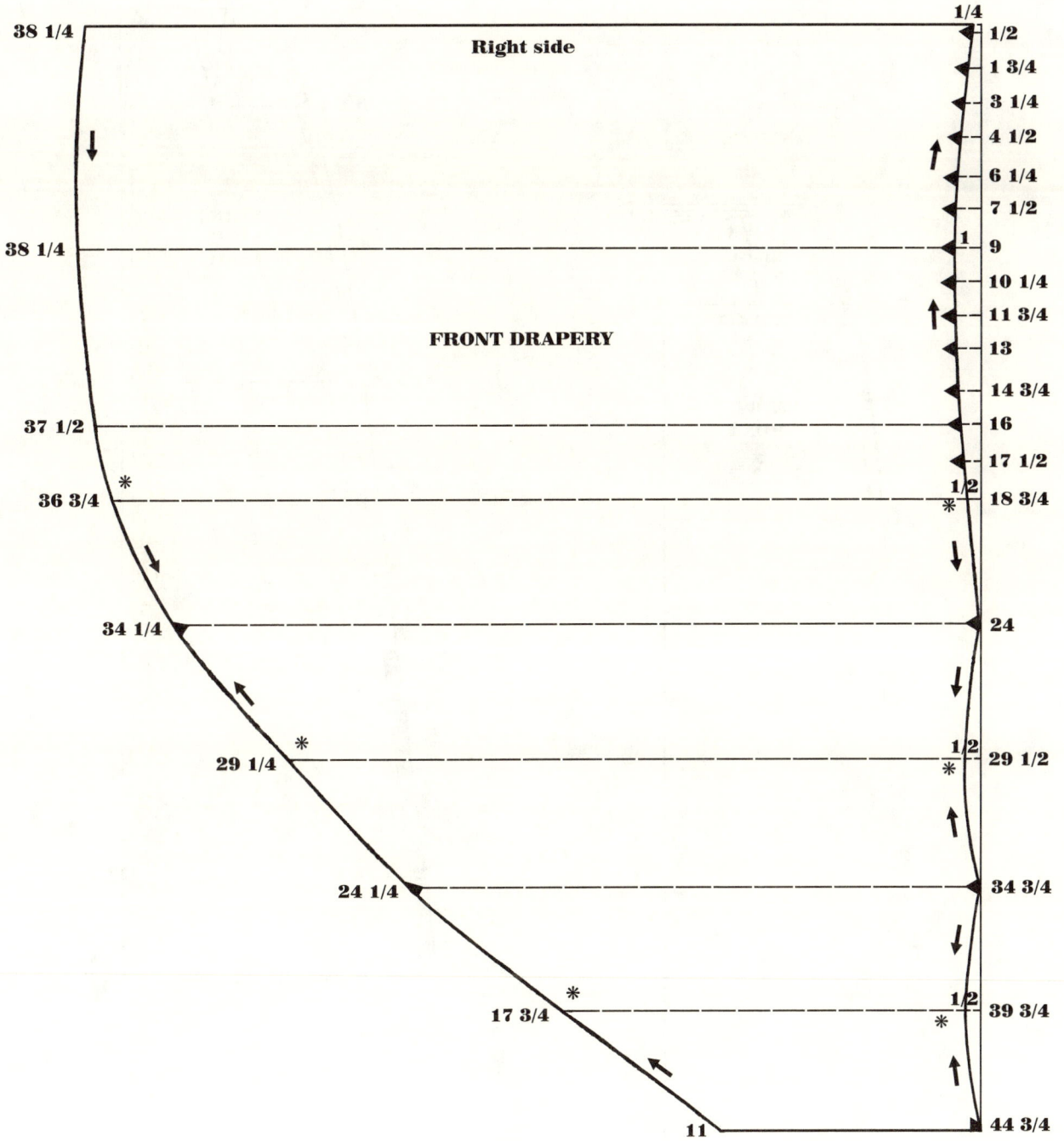

Right side

FRONT DRAPERY

38 1/4

38 1/4

37 1/2

36 3/4 ✳

34 1/4

29 1/4 ✳

24 1/4

17 3/4 ✳

11

1/4
1/2
1 3/4
3 1/4
4 1/2
6 1/4
7 1/2
1   9
10 1/4
11 3/4
13
14 3/4
16
17 1/2
1/2   18 3/4 ✳

24

1/2   29 1/2 ✳

34 3/4

1/2   39 3/4 ✳

44 3/4

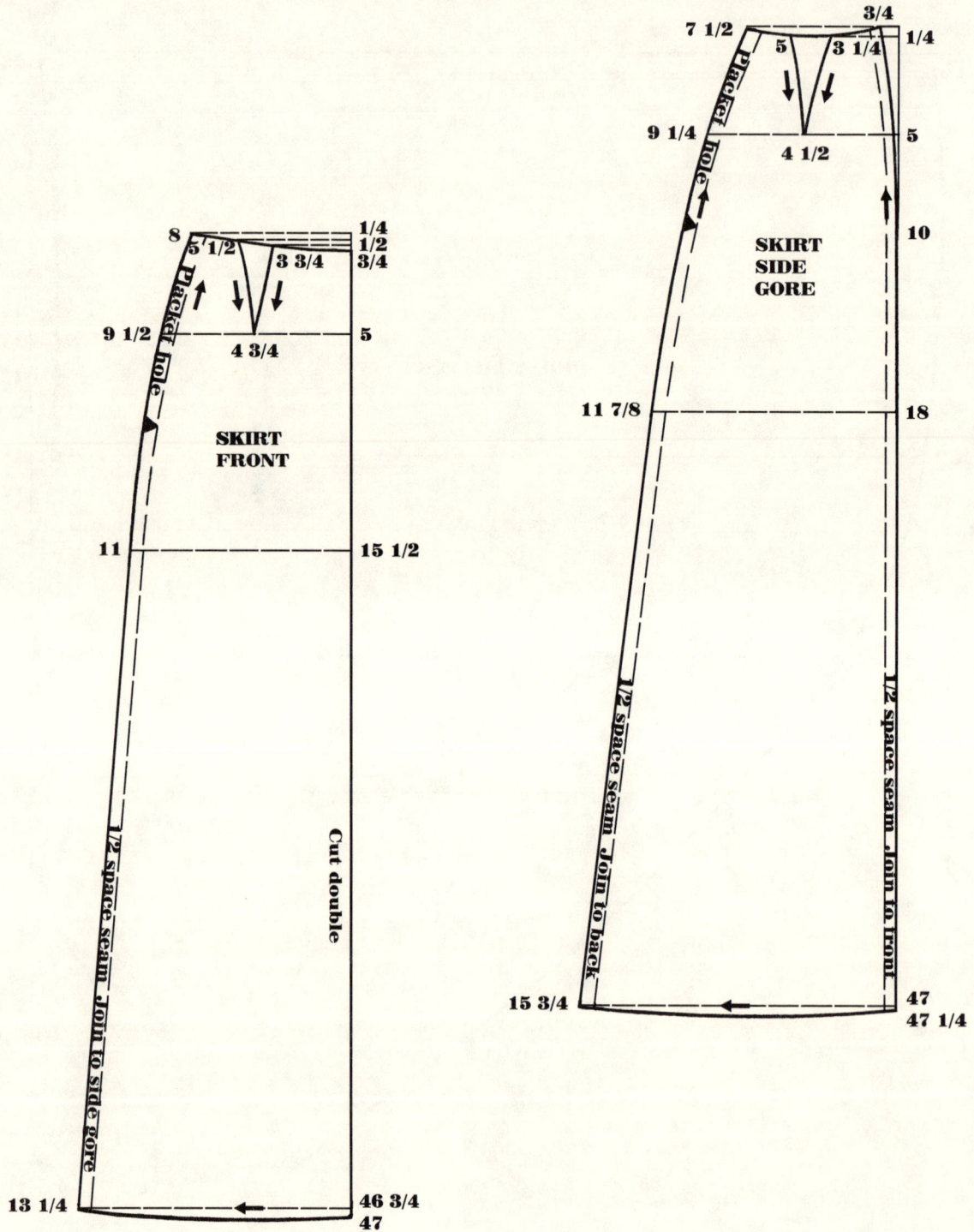

SKIRT SIDE GORE

7 1/2

3/4

5   3 1/4

1/4

Placket hole

9 1/4

4 1/2

5

10

11 7/8

18

1/2 space seam Join to back

1/2 space seam Join to front

15 3/4

47

47 1/4

8

1/4

5 1/2

1/2

3 3/4

3/4

Placket hole

9 1/2

4 3/4

5

SKIRT FRONT

11

15 1/2

Cut double

1/2 space seam Join to side gore

13 1/4

46 3/4

47

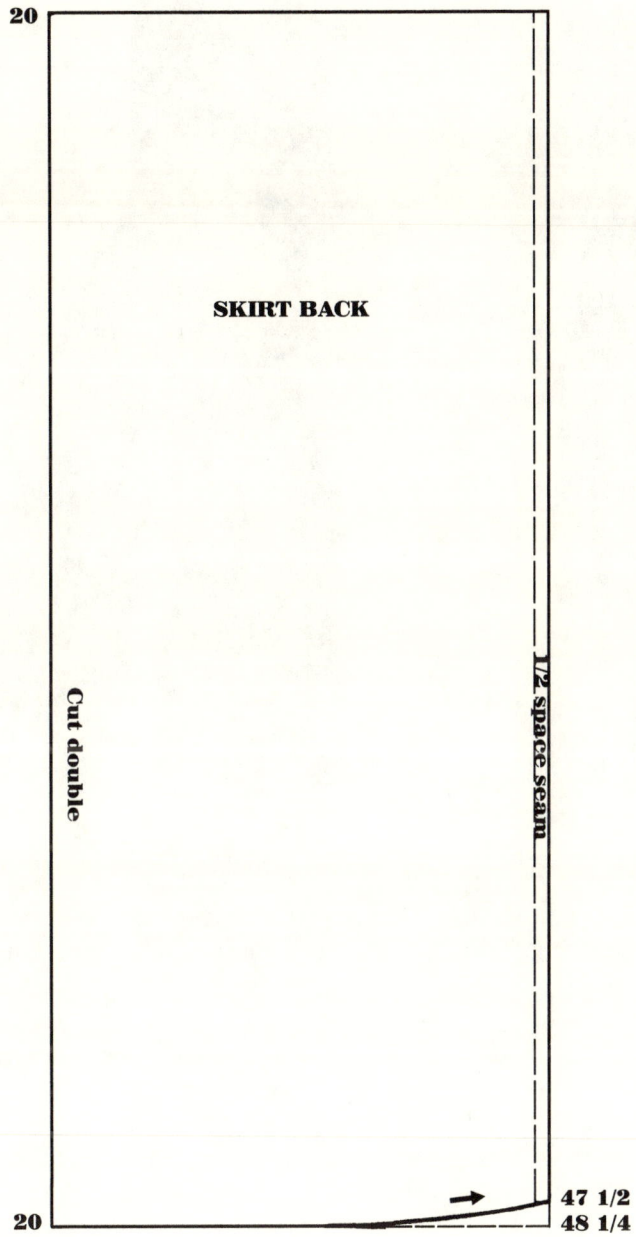

20

SKIRT BACK

Cut double

1/2 space seam

20

47 1/2
48 1/4

247

Directoire Costume. This costume is shown developed in black cashmere and black-and-white striped silk, with fancy buttons for trimming. The four-gored skirt has two steels adjusted at the back. The bouffant effect of the tournure is further increased by a pad, which may be dispensed with if not liked. The drapery that covers the gores is of the striped material. It is plaited and gathered at the top, the plaits being pressed in their folds for some distance from the belt and then falling unconfined.

The polonaise, which is of cashmere, reaches to the edge of the skirt at the sides and back. It is adjusted by double bust and under-arm darts, side backs, and a curved center back seam, the three seams at the back producing a rounded effect at the waist-line. Below the under-arm dart on each side is cut a pocket opening, which is faced with cashmere. Between the fronts is seen a vest of striped material cut bias. To the right front edge of the vest is joined a bias section, which extends well on the vest on the left side so that the stripes both meet at the seam and describe numerous Vs. This section is made close fitting by a dart on the left side. The vest and bias section are a little shorter than the fronts. The closing is made with hooks and eyes. Silk lapels are joined to the upper part of the fronts. These are pointed at the shoulders and end at the bust, where they meet a silk bias strip, which is plaited and fastened to the fronts on the outside. Three fancy buttons are placed on each front along the first dart, the highest one being placed over the

end of the strap. The fullness at the end of the center back and side-back seams is closely gathered up and fastened underneath, giving a full, plaited effect to the polonaise.

The close-fitting coat sleeves are each trimmed on the upper side of the wrist with a narrow, plaited section of silk that has its front end inserted in the seam, a button decorating its back end. The neck is finished with a standing cashmere collar, outside of which is a lower and shorter silk collar.

Any soft wool material makes up well in this way, particularly the light-weight spring cloths, cashmeres, etc. This fashion is also suitable for evening wear, for which numerous elegant materials in old rose, absinthe, reseda, etc., combine effectively with faille in the same or a contrasting shade. To make the costume for a lady of medium size, requires 15 3/4 yards of material 22 inches wide, 9 yards of material 36 inches wide, or 7 3/4 yards of material 44 inches wide. As represented, it needs 4 1/4 yards of cashmere 40 inches wide, 8 3/8 yards of silk 20 inches wide, and 3 1/8 yards of lining 36 inches wide for the four-gored skirt.

April 1889 *Delineator*

Polonaise in the Directoire Style. This polonaise is shown developed in velvet and two shades of cloth, with facings of light cloth and velvet, large buttons, and simulated button-holes of cord for trimming. Double bust and under-arm darts are used to fit the fronts, which are cut away below the waist-line from the front edge to the second dart. Three large buttons are placed along the first dart of each front over the front ends of simulated button-holes of cord, the back ends of which are arranged in a trefoil design. Above the bust, the fronts turn back in pointed lapels that are faced with velvet. Between them is revealed a double-breasted vest of light material, which is also reversed at the top and faced with the light material. It is closed with button-holes and small buttons. A row of similar buttons is arranged on the right side of the vest to carry out the double-breasted effect. Between the lapels of the vest is disclosed a chemisette, which is sewed permanently on the right side and fastened with hooks and eyes on the left.

The rest of the polonaise is adjusted by a center back seam, side seams, and side-back seams. The center back seam ends a little below the waist-line at the tops of extra widths, which are turned under for hems and underfolded in a forward-turning plait. The fullness on each side-back seam is pressed in two similar plaits. The side seams end a little below the waist-line, and the fronts fall loosely with the effect of a panel. On each hip is placed a large pocket lap that is reversed to suggest a double lap, the reversed part being faced with velvet and decorated at each corner with a large button.

The sleeves are in leg-of-mutton style and have but one seam. They are gathered full on the upper side at the top, and trimmed at each wrist with a deep, pointed cuff-facing of velvet. At the neck is a standing collar.

All kinds of seasonable dress materials are made up in this way. When a striking contrast is desired, the vest may be trimmed with Persian bands, which, with the velvet lapel facings, heighten the becoming effect. The polonaise need not be made of the skirt material; in fact it is well to have a handsome color contrast. To make the garment for a lady of medium size, requires 9 yards of material 22 inches wide, 6 3/8 yards of material 36 inches wide, or 4 3/8 yards of material 44 inches wide. Each requires 5/8 yard of light cloth 54 inches wide for the pocket laps and vest, and 1 1/4 yards of velvet 20 inches wide for the collar, etc.

June 1889 *Delineator*

Costume in the Directoire Style. Black surah, white surah, and black Chantilly lace flouncing are associated in this example. The four-gored skirt has two steels and a pad (the pad may be dispensed with). The drapery, which is of lace flouncing, overlaps the gores and is gathered at the top, from which it falls to the edge of the skirt in natural folds.

The polonaise or redingote is in the Directoire style. It is of basque depth at the front. The vest is adjusted by double bust darts. Over these are similarly fitted fronts, which are cut away to show the vest in V shape. Lapels of white surah are joined to the cutaway edges of the fronts, describing deep points at the shoulders, and reach below the bust, where the fronts are closed with button-holes and buttons. The ornamental fronts are cut off a few inches from the front edges to almost the length of the fronts, back of which they are extended to reach the lower edge of the skirt. The adjustment is completed by under-arm darts, side backs, and a curved center back seam. At the sides the polonaise hangs with a straight panel effect. At the back it falls in double box-plaits, the plaits being produced by ample underfolded fullness of the center three seams, below the waist-line. The sleeves are in coat style, and the neck is finished with a high standing collar.

Directoire Costume

Light-weight cloth, silk, satin, camel's hair, cheviot, serge, Henrietta, and cashmere make up well in this way. For the vest and fronts all kinds of fancy vestings, velvet, moiré, and novelty wools may be used. Where only one material is used, braiding in some graceful pattern will render the ornamental fronts, lapels, etc., rich looking, although it is also suitable when two or more materials are made up. When lace flouncing cannot be procured in the required width for the skirt drapery, the needful length may be obtained by applying a lace ruffle to the lower part of the gores beneath the flouncing. To make the costume for a lady of medium size, requires 13 3/4 yards of material 22 inches wide, 8 3/4 yards of material 36 inches wide, or 7 1/4 yards of material 44 inches wide. Each requires 2 yards of white surah 20 inches wide for the vest, etc., and 1 7/8 yards of lace flouncing 41 inches wide.

May 1889 *Delineator*

Redingote Costume

The polonaise is drafted with the scale corresponding to the bust measure. There are seven pieces: Front, lapel, side back, back, collar, and two sleeve pieces. Join the lapel to the front where a 1/2-space seam is marked. Connect the waist-lines. The side piece and the side back are combined to avoid an extra seam. Take up the dart, cut it open, and press it carefully. Line the lower parts of the front, side back, and back, and face them with silk or the same material as the polonaise or the skirt.

The under bodice is drafted with the scale corresponding to the bust measure. There are four pieces: Front, side piece, side back, and back.

The foundation skirt is drafted with the scale corresponding to the waist measure. The length is regulated with the tape measure. There are three pieces: Front, side gore, and back. This skirt may be made of embroidery as shown, or laid in box-plaits or side-plaits if made of a heavier material.

Summer 1889 *Voice of Fashion*

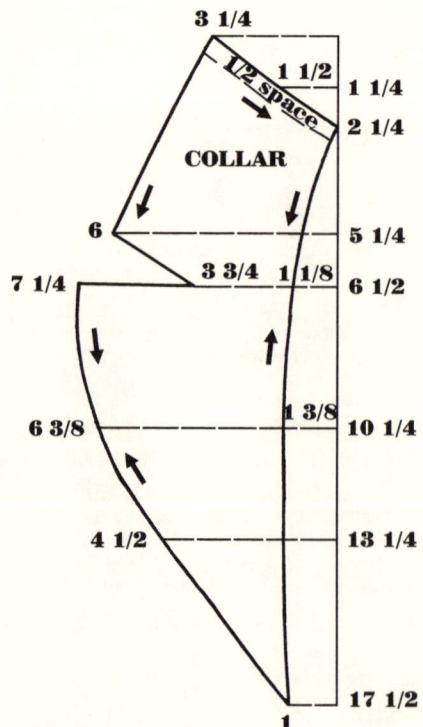

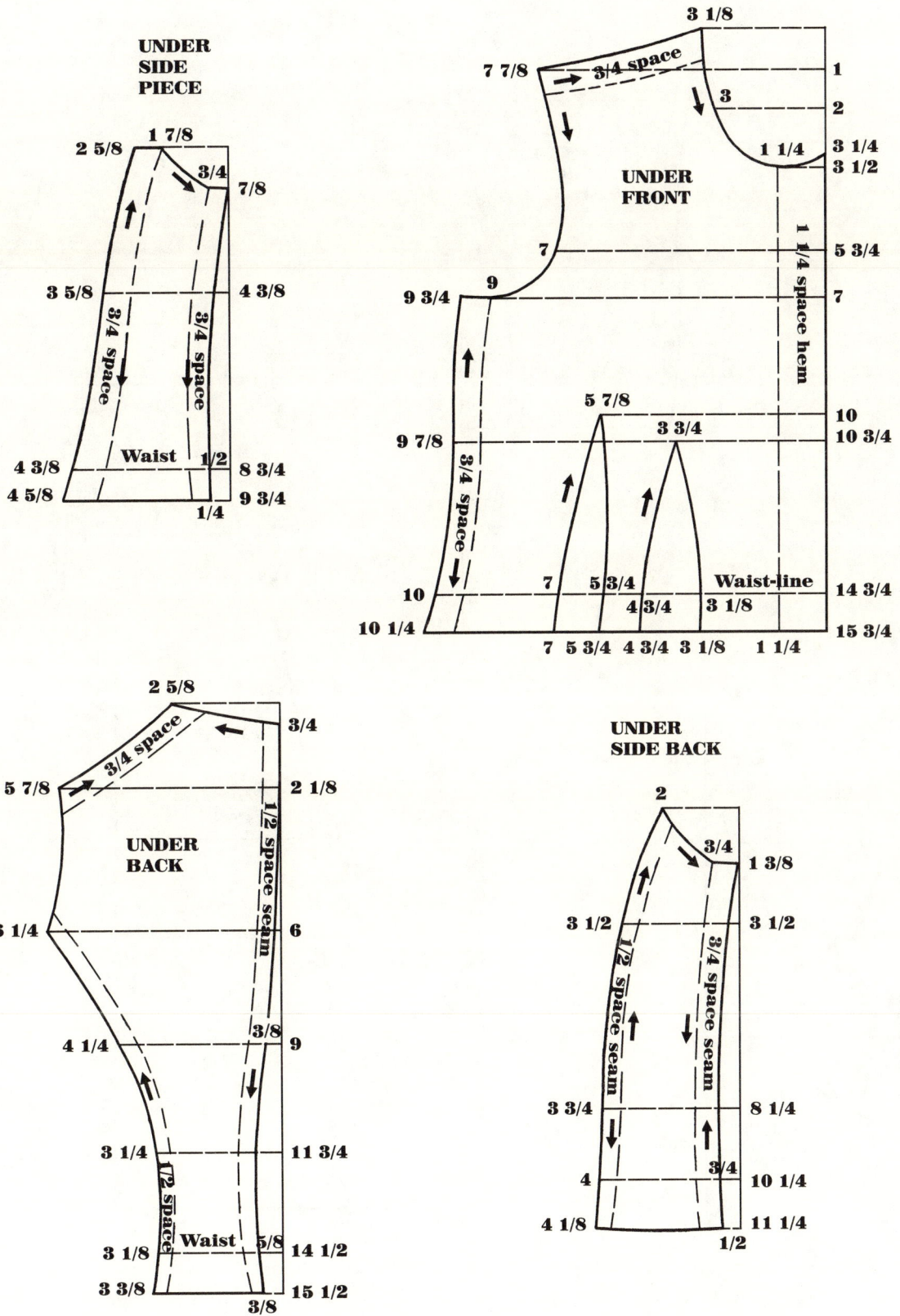

UNDER SIDE PIECE

UNDER FRONT

UNDER BACK

UNDER SIDE BACK

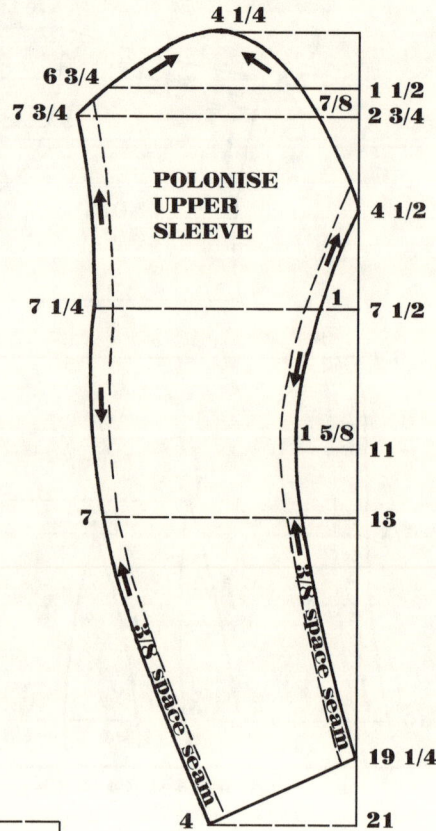

POLONISE UPPER SLEEVE

4 1/4

6 3/4

7 3/4

1 1/2

7/8

2 3/4

4 1/2

7 1/4 — 1 — 7 1/2

1 5/8

11

7 — 13

3/8 space seam

3/8 space seam

19 1/4

4 — 21

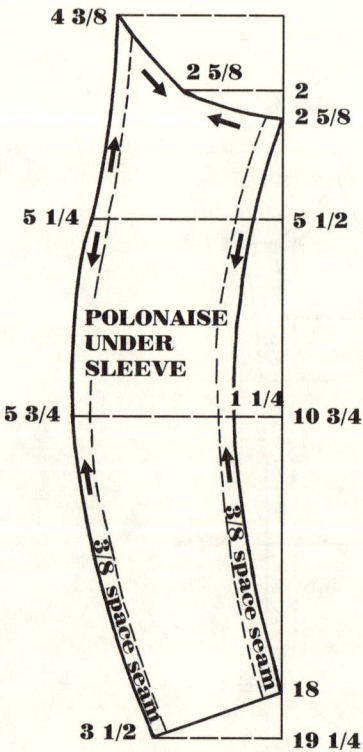

POLONAISE UNDER SLEEVE

4 3/8

2 5/8

2

2 5/8

5 1/4 — 5 1/2

5 3/4 — 1 1/4 — 10 3/4

3/8 space seam

3/8 space seam

18

3 1/2 — 19 1/4

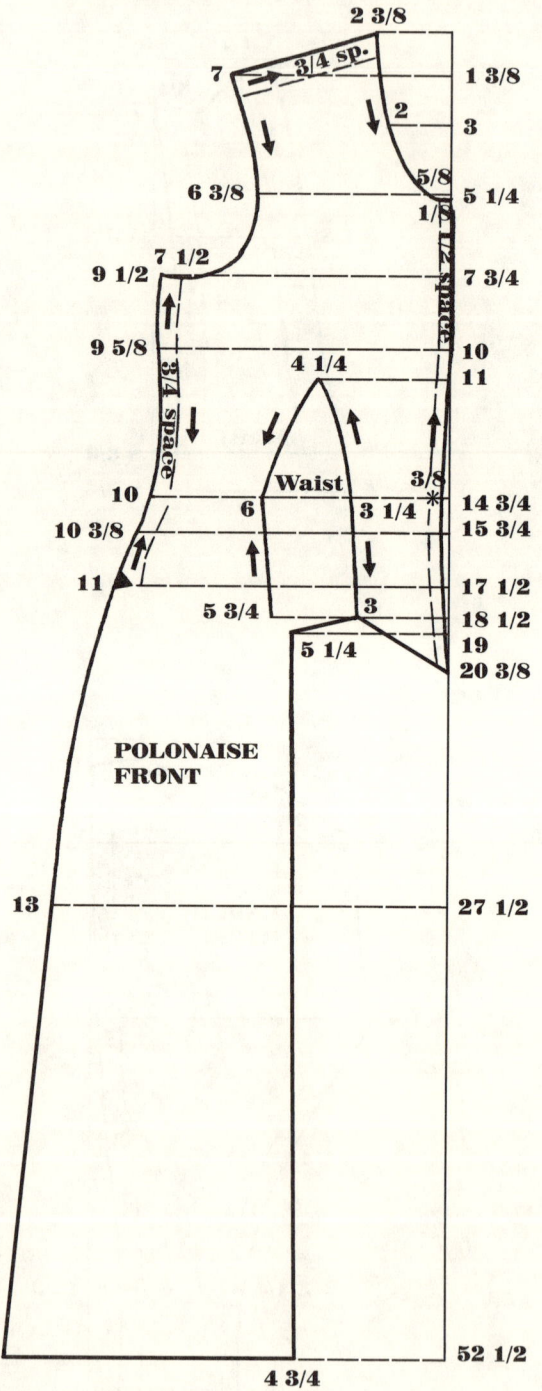

POLONAISE FRONT

2 3/8

3/4 sp.

7

1 3/8

2

3

6 3/8

5/8

5 1/4

1/8

7 1/2

3/4 space

7 3/4

9 1/2

9 5/8 — 10

4 1/4 — 11

3/4 space

Waist

10

3/8

10 3/8

6 — 3 1/4 — 14 3/4

15 3/4

11

5 3/4 — 3 — 17 1/2

18 1/2

5 1/4

19

20 3/8

13 — 27 1/2

15 3/4 — 52 1/2

4 3/4

256

Redingote Costume

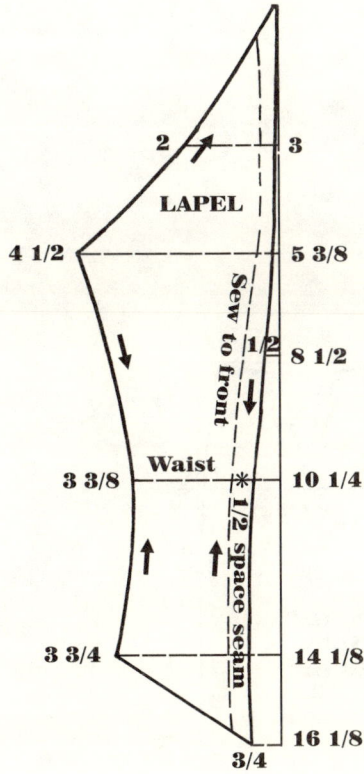

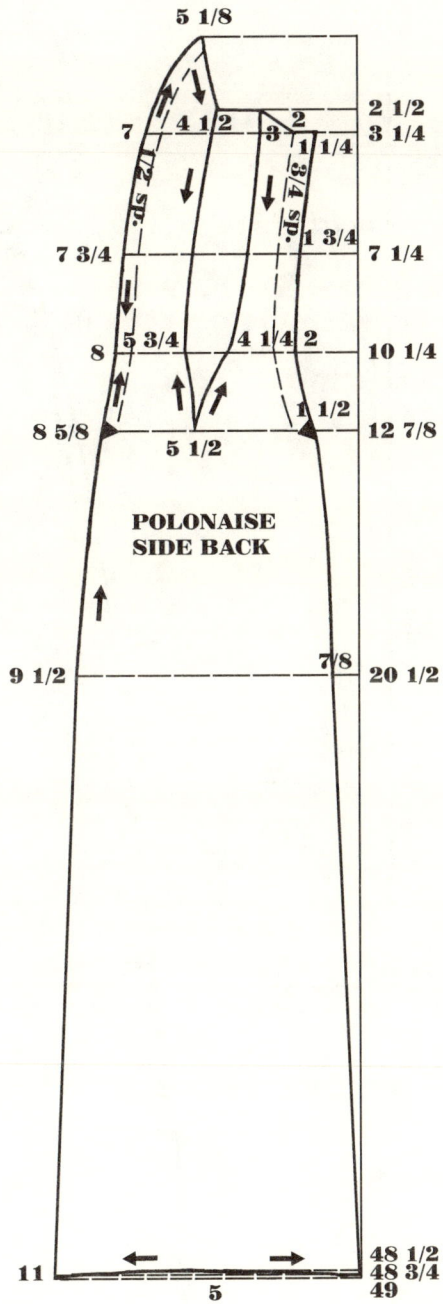

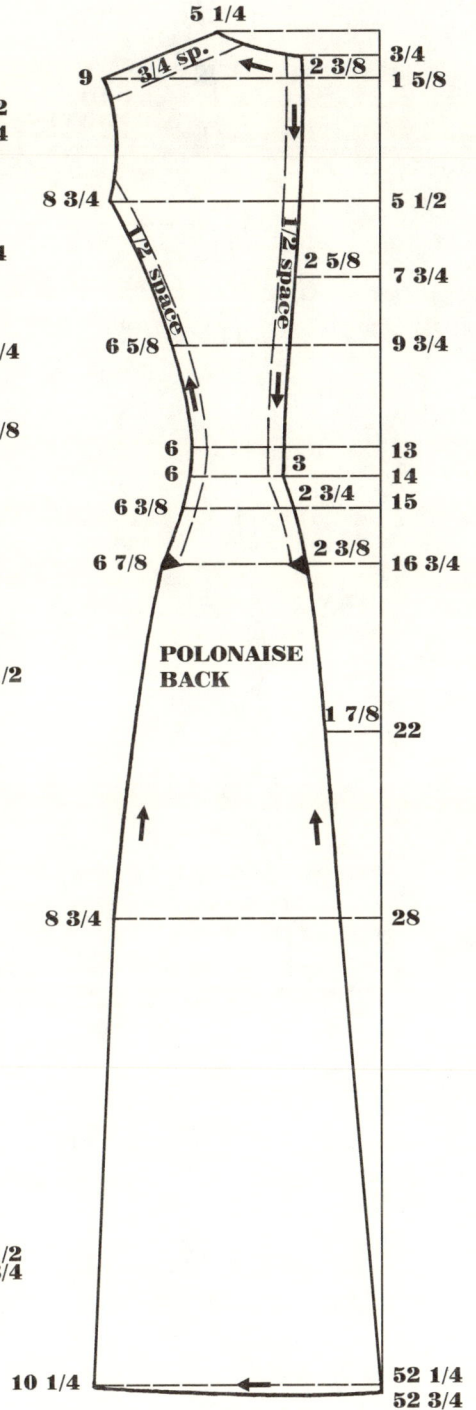

LAPEL

2 — 3
4 1/2 — 5 3/8
Sew to front
1/2
8 1/2
Waist
3 3/8 — ✱ 10 1/4
1/2 space seam
3 3/4 — 14 1/8
16 1/8
3/4

POLONAISE SIDE BACK

5 1/8
2 1/2
7 — 4 1/2 — 2 — 2 — 3 1/4
1/2 sp. — 3 — 1 1/4
3/4 sp.
7 3/4 — 1 3/4 — 7 1/4
8 — 5 3/4 — 4 1/4 — 2 — 10 1/4
8 5/8 — 1 1/2 — 12 7/8
5 1/2
9 1/2 — 7/8 — 20 1/2
11 — 48 1/2
5 — 48 3/4
49

POLONAISE BACK

5 1/4
9 — 3/4 sp. — 2 3/8 — 3/4
1 5/8
8 3/4 — 5 1/2
1/2 space — 1/2 space — 2 5/8
7 3/4
6 5/8 — 9 3/4
6 — 3 — 13
6 — 14
6 3/8 — 2 3/4 — 15
6 7/8 — 2 3/8 — 16 3/4
1 7/8 — 22
8 3/4 — 28
10 1/4 — 52 1/4
52 3/4

257

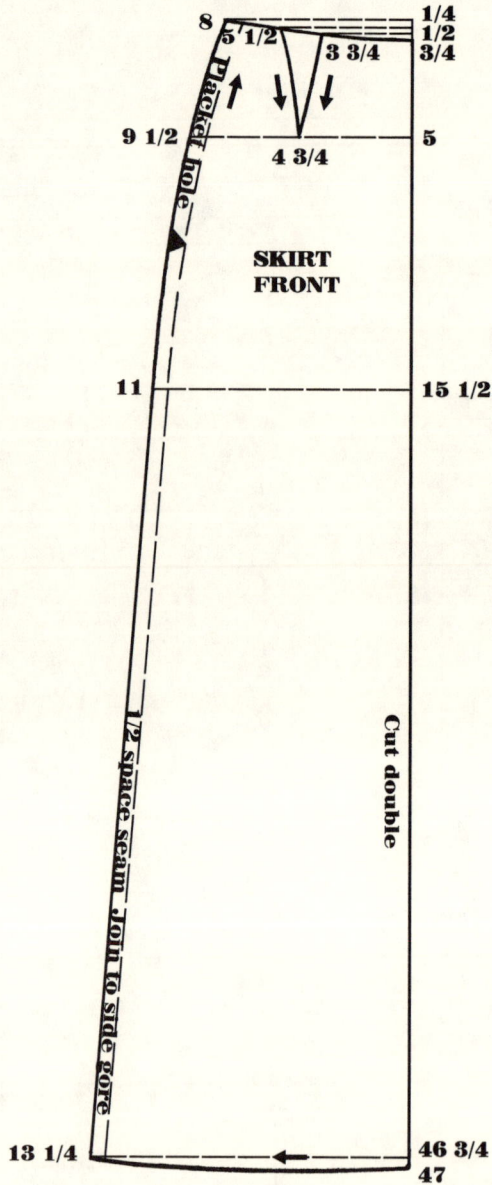

8 5 1/2   3 3/4   1/4
                     1/2
                     3/4

Placket hole

9 1/2   4 3/4   5

SKIRT FRONT

11   15 1/2

1/2 space seam Join to side gore

Cut double

13 1/4   46 3/4
                47

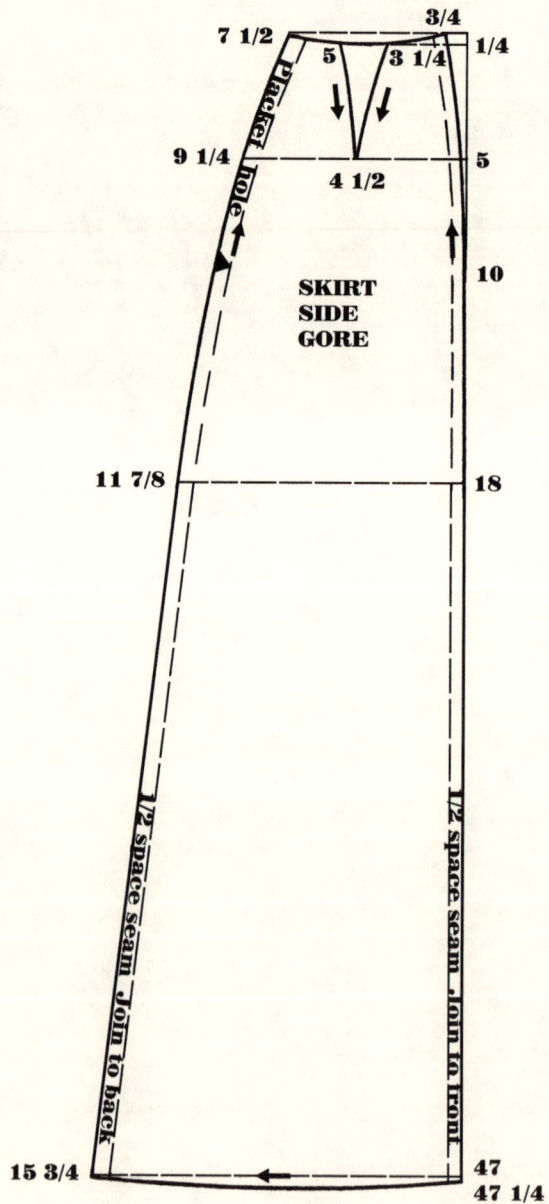

7 1/2   5   3 1/4   3/4
                       1/4

Placket hole

9 1/4   4 1/2   5

SKIRT SIDE GORE   10

11 7/8   18

1/2 space seam Join to back

1/2 space seam Join to front

15 3/4   47
                47 1/4

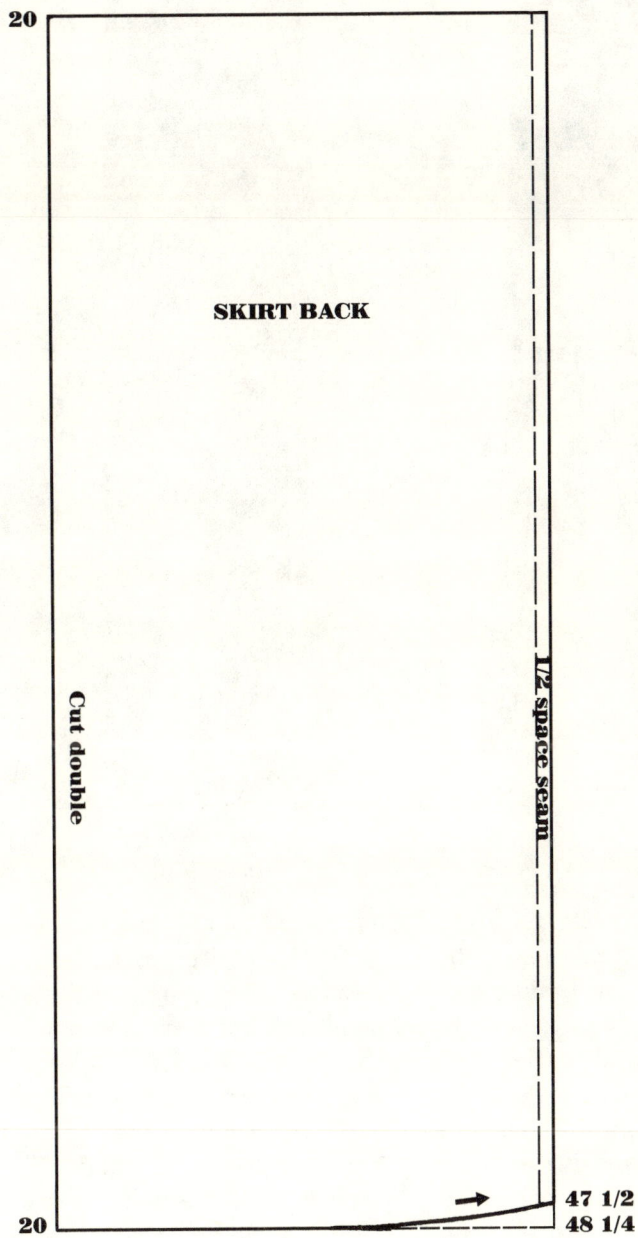

Coat Polonaise in the Directoire Style.
Dark green cloth and velvet are combined in this polonaise, with velvet, buttons, and braid passementerie for decorations. The garment is fitted by double bust and under-arm darts, side backs, and a curved center back seam. The center back and side seams are discontinued below the waist-line, extra width on the back edge of each being turned under and hemmed. The fullness on each side-back seam is pressed into a narrow coat-plait on the outside, and a button decorates its top.

The fronts are each slashed through the center from the lower edge nearly to the under-arm dart. This arrangement heightens the coat effect by forming three broad tabs. The lower edges of the tabs of the fronts are trimmed with braid passementerie. Between the first darts, the fronts are only of basque

length. They are widened above to turn back in large Directoire lapels faced with velvet, which describe deep points at the armholes. Below the lapels, the fronts are closed in double-breasted style with button-holes and buttons. Between the lapels is seen a narrow vest, which is permanently sewed to the left front and attached to the right front with hooks and eyes. A band of braid passementerie trims it along the center.

A standing collar of velvet finishes the neck. Its ends overlap a small collar part of cloth overlaid with passementerie, which completes the top of the vest. The coat sleeves have a stylish fullness gathered across the top. They are each trimmed at the wrist by a cuff-facing of velvet below a band of passementerie.

Coat Polonaise

This mode may be developed in a variety of materials and combinations, prominent among which are fancy and smooth cloths (especially light-weight cloths), heavy silks, plushes, etc. Gold or silver soutache may embroider the lapels, collar, and vest, or a chamois vest may be worn. Gimp, braid, or galloon may be used for trimming. In that case, if the coat is made of cloth, braid binding or machine-stitching may finish the edges of the collar and sleeves. An elegant garment for evening wear may be developed in absinthe faille Française lined with light pink surah. To make the polonaise for a lady of medium size, requires 7 5/8 yards of material 22 inches wide, 3 3/4 yards of material 44 inches wide, or 3 yards of material 54 inches wide. Each requires 3/4 yard of velvet 20 inches wide for the larger collar part, etc.

April 1889 *Delineator*

Ladies' Polonaise. This polonaise is really a redingote with Directoire features. It is generally worn over a skirt of contrasting material, and forms part of a carriage, visiting, or street toilette. Seal-brown suit material and tan-colored surah are associated in this example.

The fronts are made double-breasted by sections that join their front edges in curved seams, and which are also curved at the front edges. The fronts are folded back to below the bust in pronounced Directoire lapels, below which they close in double-breasted style with button-holes and large oxidized buttons, over a vest. The vest is closed down the center and is visible only for a short distance at the neck. Double bust darts are taken in the fronts and vest together. Long under-arm darts, side pieces, and a curved center back seam perfect the adjustment. The back edges of the vest are included

in the under-arm darts, and the shoulder edges pass into the shoulder seams. In front of the second bust darts the fronts are only of basque length, while back of the darts they hang smoothly to the bottom of the skirt. At the back the polonaise falls even with the fronts. Underfolded fullness below the center three seams throws the back into two broad, double box-plaits, which preserve their straight lines to the edge, straps being basted to them underneath at intervals to stay them. The high standing collar is in three parts. The front parts are of surah to match the vest, which they join, and they lap under the ends of the other part, which is of the polonaise material. The lapels are faced with surah. Deep, round cuff-facings of surah complete the coat sleeves.

Ladies' Polonaise

This mode develops admirably in cloths and suitings of all kinds, and admits of elaborate trimming. Rich brocaded materials have a special vogue, and rich braidings are in order on the lapels, vest, collar, and wrists. Handsome polonaises are usually lined throughout with changeable, striped, or plain surah, satin, or silk. To make the garment for a lady of medium size, requires 9 1/2 yards of material 22 inches wide, or 4 3/4 yards of material 44 inches wide. Each requires 1 1/2 yards of surah for the smaller collar parts, etc., and 5/8 yard of lining 36 inches wide for the vest.

March 1889 *Delineator*

Coat in the Directoire Style. Velvet, brocaded satin, and Russian lambskin are combined in this example. The fronts extend only a trifle below the waist-line, and are closely fitted by single bust darts. They are each widened by a piece that, with the front, is turned back to form a broad lapel from the shoulder to the bust, which is faced with velvet. Below this is a double-breasted closing made with button-holes and large fancy buttons, with another row of buttons placed on the overlapping side. A brocaded satin vest, which is also fitted by single bust darts, extends somewhat below the fronts. Its curved front edges are closed with button-holes and buttons, and flare with a notched effect below the closing. The back edges of the vest enter the under-arm seams. The latter, together with the side backs and a curved center back seam, complete the adjustment. The backs and side backs hang straight to the bottom of the skirt, with the effect of broad coat-tails. Below the center back seam are arranged coat laps, which lie gracefully over the tournure. At each side-back seam, in a line with the center back seam, extra widths are allowed and folded underneath in a forward-turning plait. The high standing collar is made of Russian lambskin, and so are the round cuffs on the coat sleeves.

This coat may be developed in fancy or smooth cloth, or in heavy silk, plush, etc., using one material, or combined with velvet or satin brocade or other fancy material. It may accompany a skirt made of camel's hair, cloth, Ottoman suiting, silk, or any fashionable dress material. Braid, passementerie, Astrakhan, or fur may trim both the coat and the skirt, or each may be decorated independently. Gold, silver, or worsted soutache or cord may embroider the lapels and vest, or fur may form the trimming. Chamois vests are in order, and gimp, passementerie, gallon, etc., are used for trimming. Braid binding or lines of machine-stitching may finish a coat of smooth cloth. To make the garment for a lady of medium size, requires 6 1/4 yards of material 22 inches wide, 3 1/8 yards of material 44 inches wide, or 2 1/4 yards of material 54 inches wide. Each requires 1 1/4 yards of brocaded satin 20 inches wide for the vest, 6 1/2 yards of plain satin 20 inches wide for the lining, and a piece of Russian lambskin 13 1/2 by 16 1/2 inches.

December 1888 *Delineator*

Coat with Puffed Sleeves. In this instance cloth and velvet are combined, and velvet and buttons comprise the decorations. The adjustment is performed by single bust and under-arm darts, side backs, and a curved center back seam that ends at the top of hemmed coat laps. Below the waist-line of each side-back seam, extra width is cut on the front edge of the back and the back edge of the side back. This is pressed in a forward-turning plait underneath, a button marking the top of the plait. The right front is reversed and faced with velvet. The closing is made with buttons and button-holes, from below this lapel to a trifle below the waist-line. The collar is in the high standing style. Over the coat sleeve is adjusted a long puff. Below this is applied a cloth facing, decorated with two buttons placed at the back of the arm.

Diagonal, checked, striped, and plain and fancy cloths of seasonable weight are adaptable to this mode. Braid, passementerie, velvet, etc., are suitable trimmings. A coat of golden brown smooth cloth may introduce gold-and-brown striped surah for the collar, lapel, and cuff-facings. If desired, the sleeve puffs may be made of velvet and the rest of the coat of cloth. To make the coat for a lady of medium size, requires 8 yards of material 22 inches wide, 4 1/4 yards of material 44 inches wide, or 3 1/4 yards of material 54 inches wide. Also required is 1 5/8 yards of velvet for the collar, etc.

September 1889 *Delineator*

Ladies' Jacket

Ladies' Jacket. This jacket is pictured made of navy blue cloth, decorated with gray Astrakhan and buttons. It is fitted by double bust darts, side pieces, side backs, and a curved center back seam that ends a trifle below the waist-line. The right front is widened to close in double-breasted fashion by a shapely section, which is reversed and covered with gray Astrakhan at the top and narrowed gradually toward the bottom. Both fronts are cut away below the closing. Extra width allowed at the center back and side-back seams is underfolded in a box-plait at the center back seam, and in a forward-turning plait marked by a button at the top, on each side-back seam. The coat sleeves are trimmed with bands of Astrakhan, and a standing collar overlaid with Astrakhan is at the neck.

Lady's cloth, Biarritz cloth, Bedford cord, cordelière, broadcloth, twill, diagonal, coarse serge, and a variety of fancy coatings are suitable. For dressy wear, this jacket may be made up in heavy corded silk, matelassé, velvet, etc. Fur, feather trimmings, Persian bands, cord or bead passementerie or gimp, cords and buttons, fancy braid, and velvet or silk facings are appropriate trimmings. Crocheted buttons, or those covered with velvet or silk, are selected for most materials. A lining of silk, satin, or flannel may be added. For a lady of medium size, this jacket requires 4 1/4 yards of material 22 inches wide, 2 1/8 yards of material 44 inches wide, or 1 3/4 yards of material 54 inches wide. Each requires 3/8 yard of Astrakhan 27 inches wide for the collar, etc.

December 1889 *Delineator*

Street Costume

The polonaise is drafted with the scale corresponding to the bust measure. There are seven pieces: Front, side back, bodice back, skirt back, two sleeve pieces, and collar. The skirt back is gathered and sewed to the bodice back. Lay two upward-turning plaits in the front and join it to the back, bringing the plaits up over the side, and stay it underneath.

The jacket is drafted with the scale corresponding to the bust measure. There are seven pieces: Front, vest, side piece, side back, back, and two sleeve pieces. The jacket may be made of the same material as the polonaise, or of contrasting material. Turn the front back on the dashed line running from 6 5/8 on the shoulder down to 21 1/4 on the base-line. This forms the lapel in front, and also the rolling collar at the back. Join the front and vest to the side piece and the shoulder seams of the back.

The skirt is drafted with the scale corresponding to the waist measure. The length is regulated with the tape measure. There are three pieces: Front, side gore, and back.

Summer 1889 *Voice of Fashion*

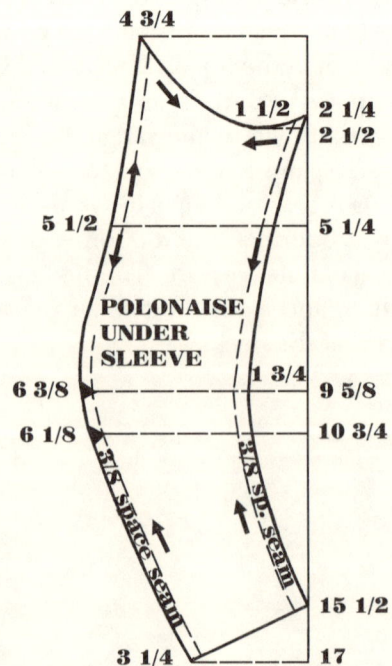

POLONAISE UNDER SLEEVE

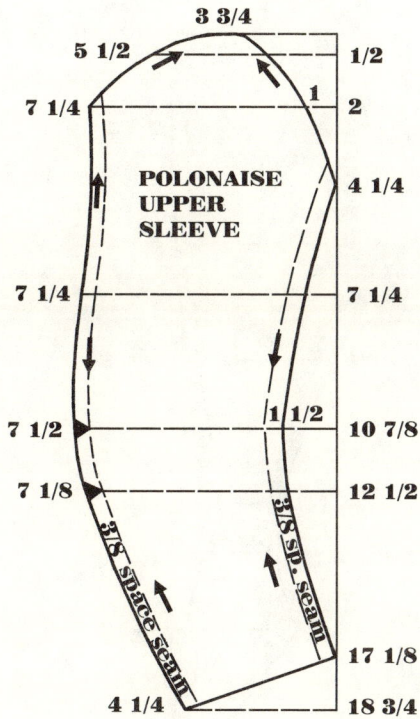

POLONAISE UPPER SLEEVE

3 3/4

5 1/2   1/2

7 1/4   1

2

4 1/4

7 1/4   7 1/4

7 1/2   1 1/2   10 7/8

7 1/8   12 1/2

3/8 space seam   3/8 sp. seam

17 1/8

4 1/4   18 3/4

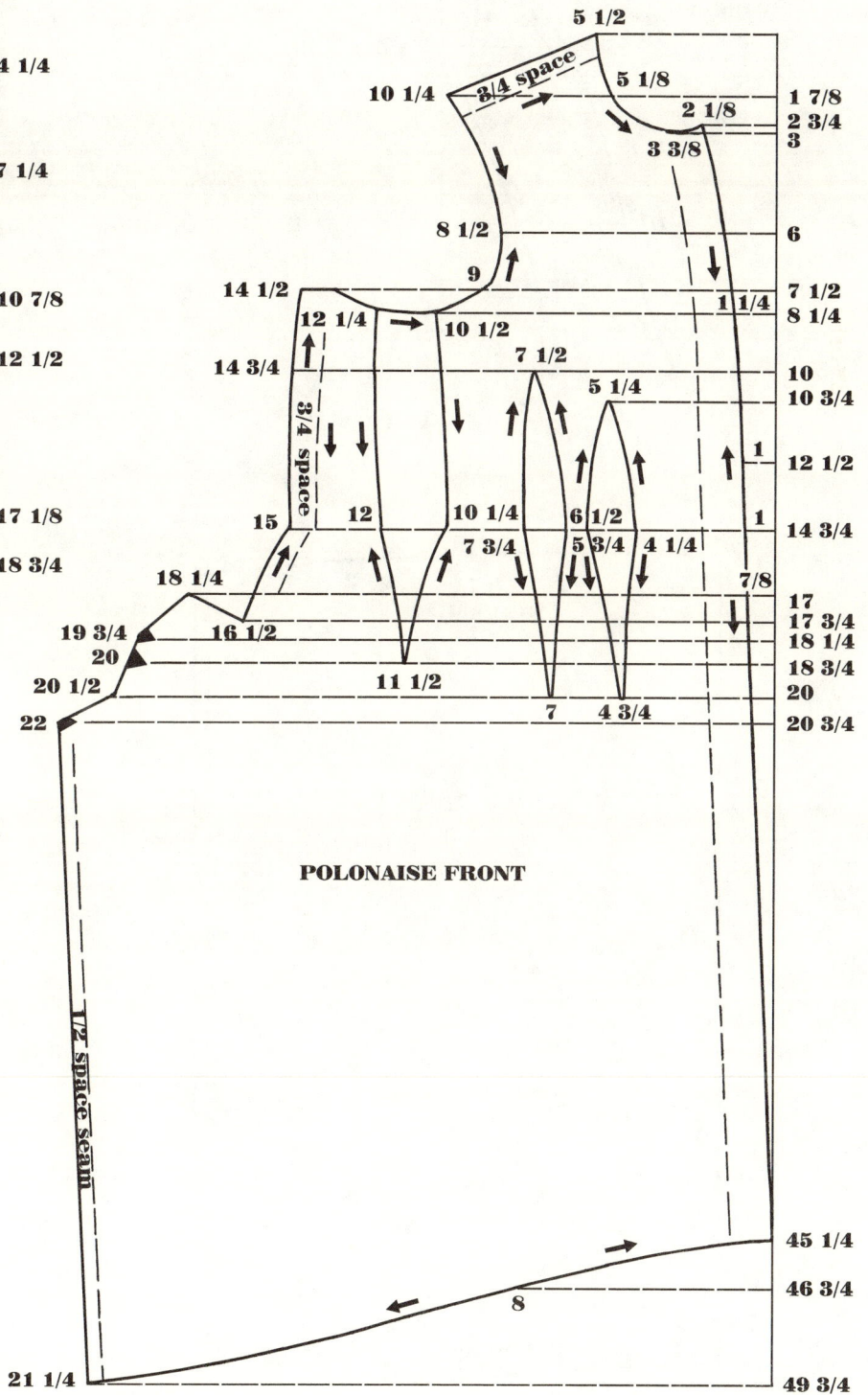

POLONAISE FRONT

5 1/2

10 1/4   3/4 space   5 1/8   1 7/8

2 1/8   2 3/4

3 3/8   3

8 1/2   6

9   7 1/2

14 1/2   1 1/4

12 1/4   10 1/2   8 1/4

14 3/4   3/4 space   7 1/2   10

5 1/4   10 3/4

12   10 1/4   6 1/2   4 1/4   1   12 1/2

15   7 3/4   5 3/4   1   14 3/4

18 1/4   7/8   17

19 3/4   16 1/2   17 3/4

20   18 1/4

20 1/2   11 1/2   18 3/4

7   4 3/4   20

22   20 3/4

1/2 space seam

45 1/4

46 3/4

8

21 1/4   49 3/4

269

POLONAISE SIDE BACK

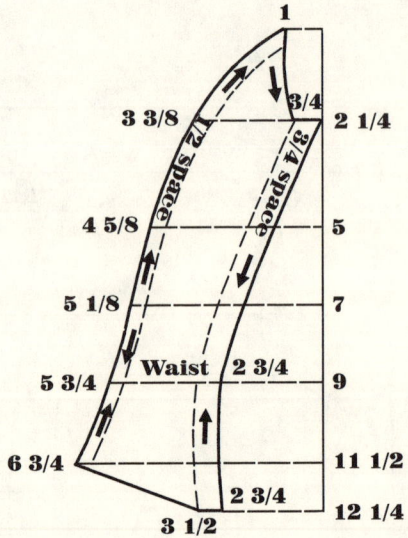

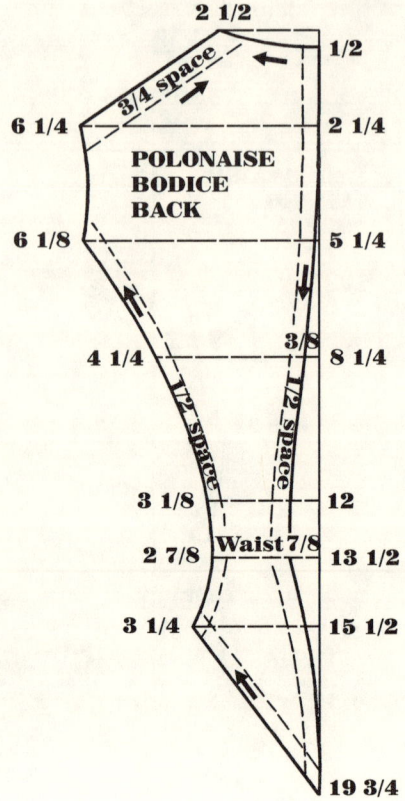

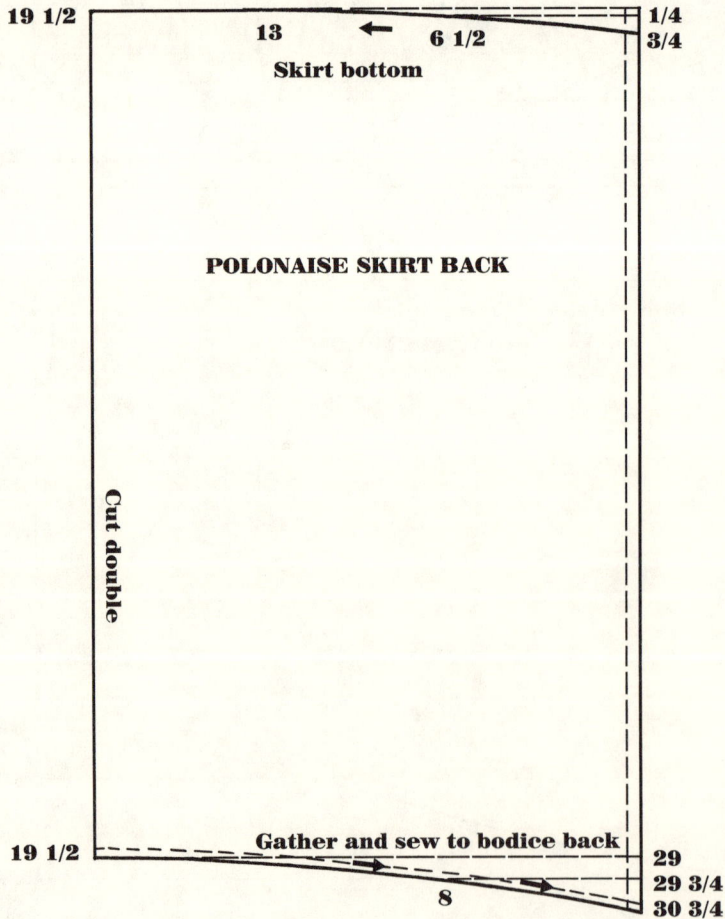

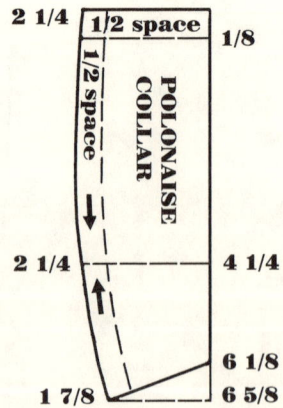

1

3 3/8   3/4   2 1/4
1/2 space   3/4 space

4 5/8   5

5 1/8   7

5 3/4   Waist   2 3/4   9

6 3/4   11 1/2

2 3/4   12 1/4

3 1/2

2 1/2   1/2

6 1/4   3/4 space   2 1/4

POLONAISE
BODICE
BACK

6 1/8   5 1/4

4 1/4   3/8   8 1/4

1/2 space   1/2 space

3 1/8   12

2 7/8   Waist 7/8   13 1/2

3 1/4   15 1/2

19 3/4

19 1/2   1/4
13   6 1/2   3/4

Skirt bottom

POLONAISE SKIRT BACK

Cut double

2 1/4   1/2 space   1/8

1/2 space   POLONAISE
COLLAR

2 1/4   4 1/4

6 1/8

1 7/8   6 5/8

19 1/2   Gather and sew to bodice back   29

29 3/4

8   30 3/4

270

JACKET FRONT

4 3/4
6 5/8
1/4 sp.
8 1/4
1 1/4
2 1/4
7
2 5/8
4 3/8
3/4 space
10 3/4
4 1/4
1 3/8
7 5/8
7 7/8
11 3/4
9 3/4
2 1/2
13 1/2
14 1/4
3/4 space seam
17 3/4
7 1/4
20
1/8
21 1/4
7
25 1/2
1/4

JACKET VEST

5 5/8
10 3/4
3/4 space
5 1/4
1 7/8
2 3/4
2 3/4
2 1/4
3
9
1 1/4 space hem
6 1/4
10 3/4
11 1/2
8
11 5/8
3/4 space
6 1/4
11 1/8
10
11 3/4
7 3/4
4 1/2
7/8
15
Waist
Cut open before basting
12 1/8
16
13 1/2
18 3/4
19 3/4
7 7/8
4 3/4
1 1/4
20

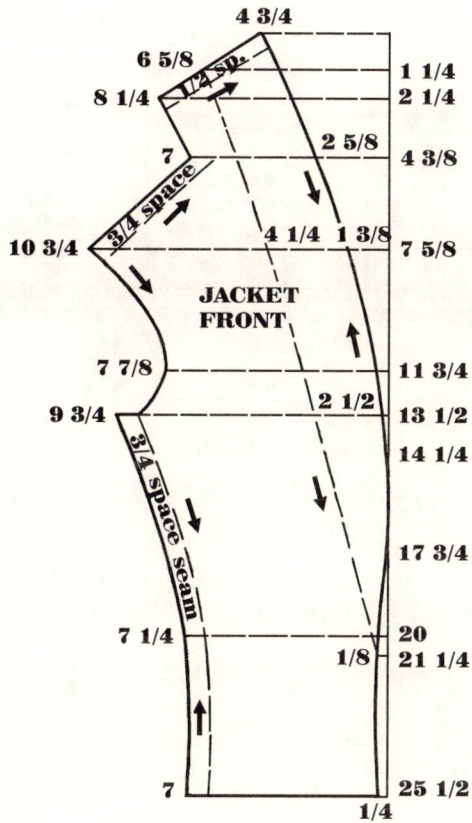

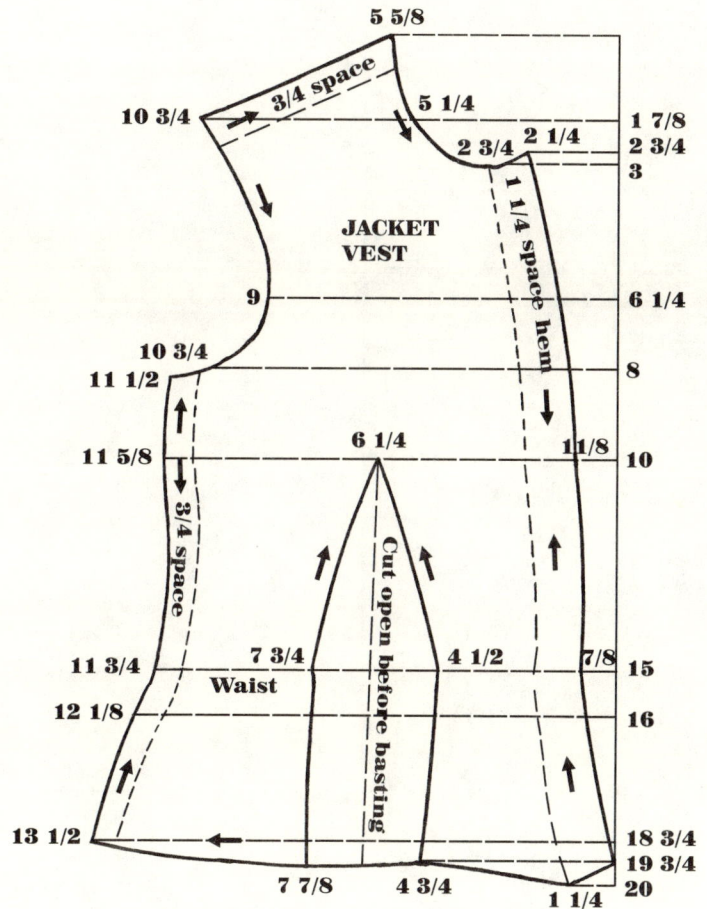

JACKET SIDE PIECE

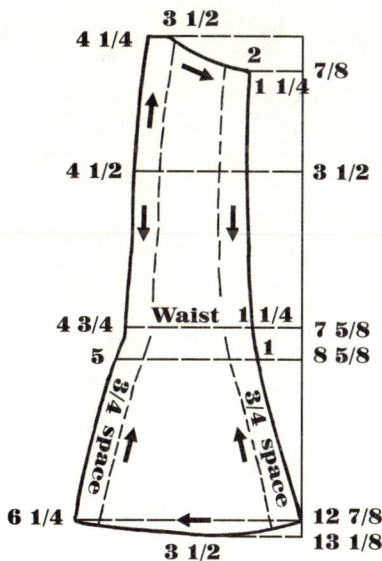

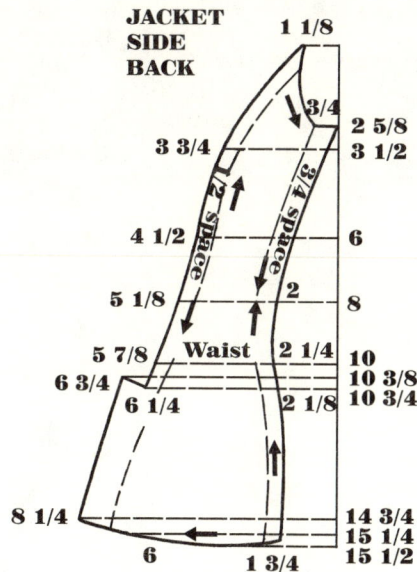

3 1/2
4 1/4
2
7/8
1 1/4
4 1/2
3 1/2
4 3/4
Waist   1 1/4
7 5/8
5
1
8 5/8
3/4 space
3/4 space
6 1/4
12 7/8
3 1/2
13 1/8

JACKET SIDE BACK

1 1/8
3/4
3 3/4
2 5/8
3 1/2
1/2 space
3/4 space
4 1/2
6
5 1/8
2
8
5 7/8
Waist
2 1/4
10
6 3/4
10 3/8
6 1/4
2 1/8
10 3/4
8 1/4
14 3/4
15 1/4
6
1 3/4
15 1/2

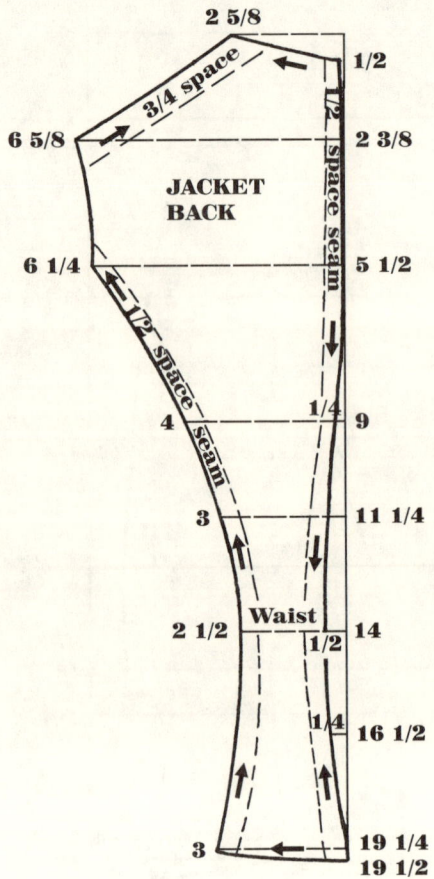

2 5/8

1/2

3/4 space

6 5/8

2 3/8

1/2 space seam

**JACKET
BACK**

6 1/4

5 1/2

1/2 space seam

4

1/4 9

3

11 1/4

2 1/2 Waist

14

1/2

1/4

16 1/2

3

19 1/4
19 1/2

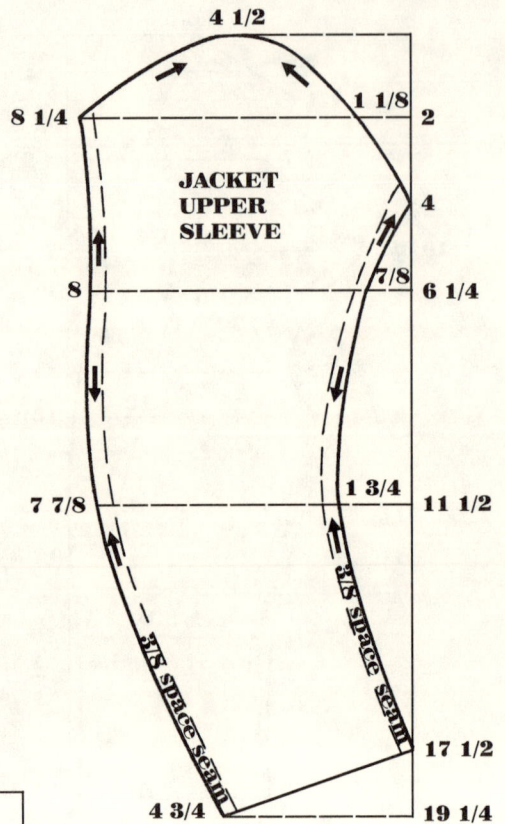

4 1/2

8 1/4

1 1/8 2

**JACKET
UPPER
SLEEVE**

4

8

7/8 6 1/4

7 7/8

1 3/4 11 1/2

3/8 space seam

17 1/2

4 3/4

19 1/4

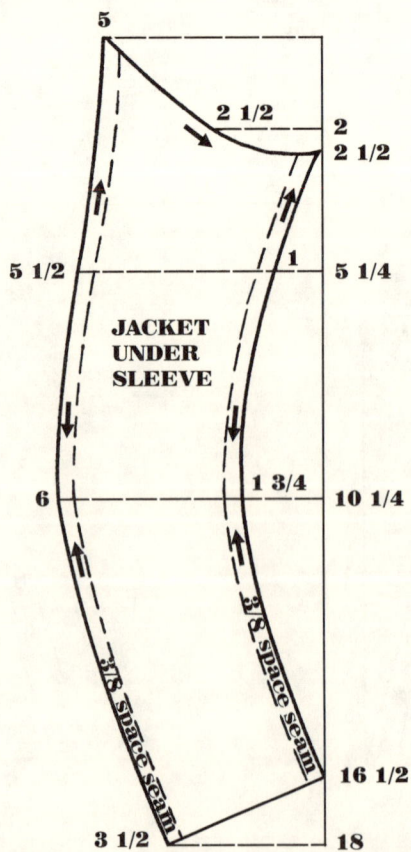

5

2 1/2

2
2 1/2

5 1/2

1

5 1/4

**JACKET
UNDER
SLEEVE**

6

1 3/4 10 1/4

3/8 space seam

16 1/2

3 1/2

18

272

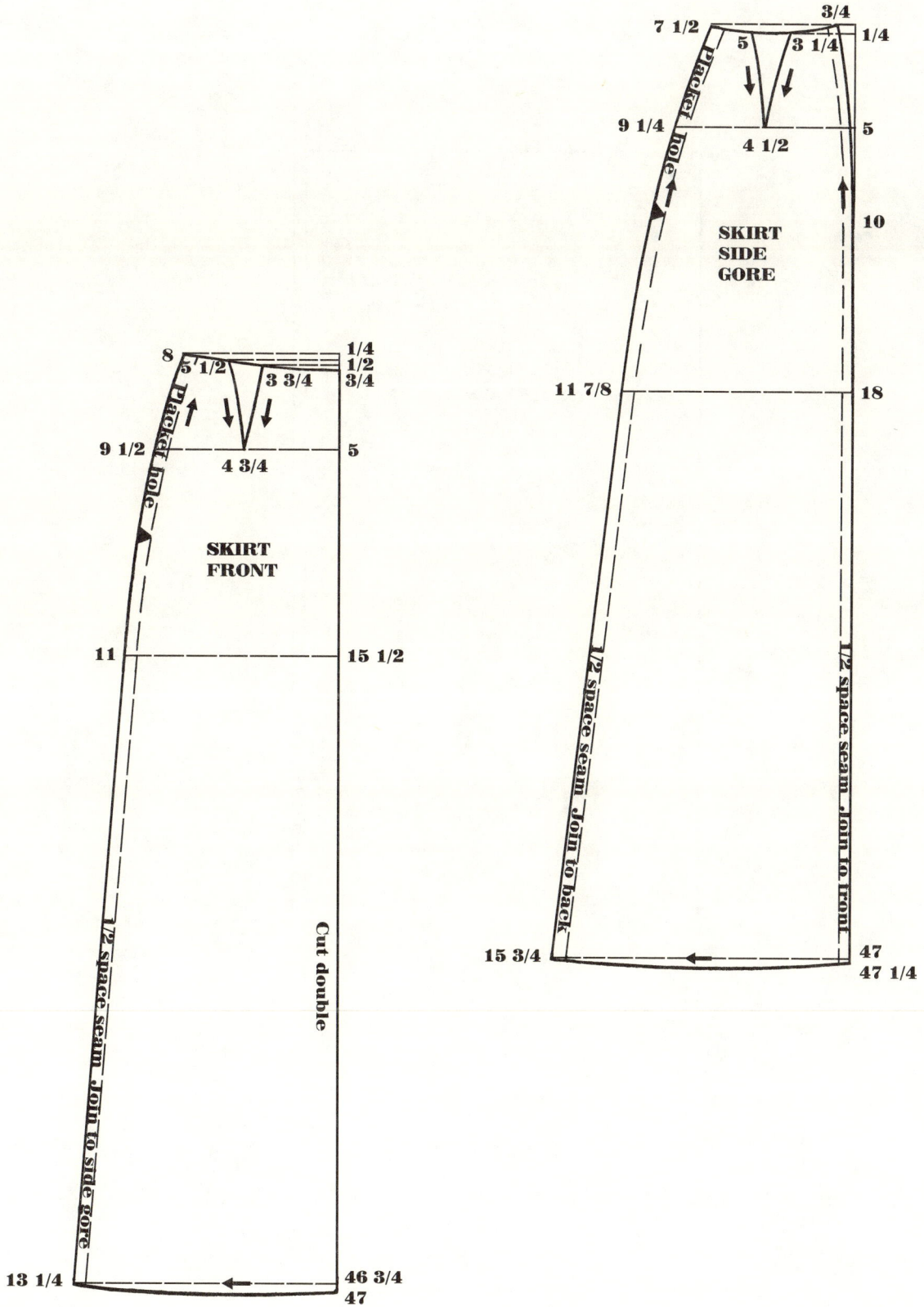

SKIRT FRONT

SKIRT SIDE GORE

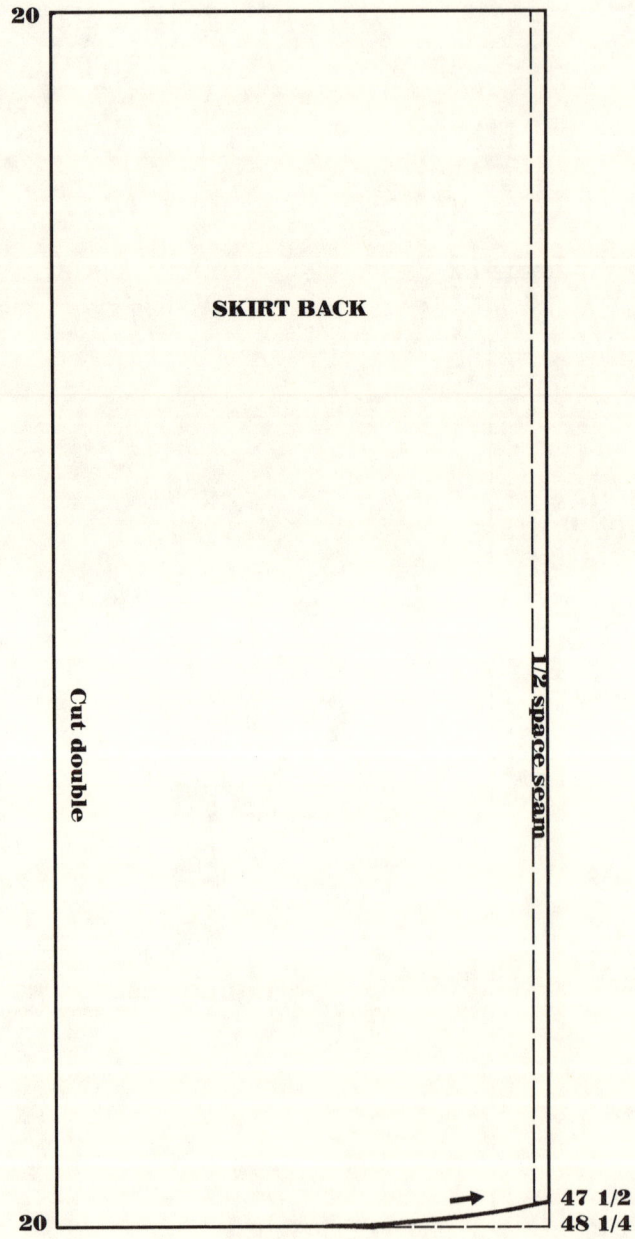

SKIRT BACK

Cut double

1/2 space seam

20

20

47 1/2
48 1/4

Ladies' Jacket. The jacket is pictured made of plain cloth and novelty figured material. The center three seams of the back are made in lapped style. The two under-arm seams are continued to the lower edge, while the center back and side-back seams end several inches from it. To the loose back edge of each back is joined a square-cornered lap, which is turned over on the outside and decorated with a row of buttons. Two lines of stitching follow the edges of the laps, and also the lower and loose edges of the garment. The end of each back seam is stayed by a triangular ornament worked with silk twist.

The fronts open from the shoulders in curves over a shorter, notched vest, which passes into the shoulder and under-arm seams. It is closely fitted by single bust darts. The curved front edges are fastened with buttons and button-holes. A line of stitching follows the outlines of the vest. To the front edges of the fronts are joined long lapels, which taper toward the bottom. The lapels are extensions of a rolling collar, which joins the back and has a center seam. A standing collar of the vest material joins the vest and also passes across the back, where it is partly concealed by the rolling collar. Its edges are outlined by a single line of stitching, while two lines are made along the edges of the lapels and rolling collar. Small laps are adjusted below the waist-line on the fronts; they may conceal pocket openings. Two lines of stitching follow the lower and side edges of the laps, and a single line is made just above their seaming to the fronts. The coat sleeves are finished with stitching. The outside seam of the sleeve is left open below the stitching, and a lap cut on the under side is lapped under the upper side and basted in place under buttons.

Smooth, corded, and twilled cloths, and cloths showing hair-lines and checks, are devoted to these jackets. Gay and unique effects may be realized in the vest, which usually accords with the standing collar. Elaborate disposals of braid and cord in fancy designs are in order, and fancy metal braids are also effective. White vests look well on jackets of all colors, and so do those of old rose, tan, cream, and other light shades. For a lady of medium size, this jacket requires 3 3/4 yards of material 22 inches wide, 1 7/8 yards of material 44 inches wide, or 1 1/2 yards of material 54 inches wide. Each requires 1 1/8 yards of figured material 22 inches wide for the vest, etc.

September 1888 *Delineator*

Ladies' Directoire

The polonaise is drafted with the scale corresponding to the bust measure. There are eight pieces: Upper front, under front, side piece, side back, back, collar, and two sleeve pieces. The side back and back are each in two pieces to be put together before drafting. Make them the same length as the skirt.

Turn back the upper front on the dashed line, and face for lapels. Join the upper and under fronts to the side piece. To make as illustrated, take a piece of surah or any soft material. Cut it on the bias, full it very slightly at the neck and waist, fasten it firmly on the right side, and close it on the left side with hooks and eyes. These extra fronts can be changed as the occasion demands, for example a cream surah for evening and darker shades for the street. One suit can be made to look like new by changing the front, girdle, and cuffs.

Lay one or more folds in the back and side back. Face them, but do not sew them up.

The skirt is drafted with the scale corresponding to the waist measure. The length is regulated with the tape measure. There are three pieces: Front, side gore, and back. The flounces are cut the width desired. Embroidered flounces are very pretty.

Summer 1889 *Voice of Fashion*

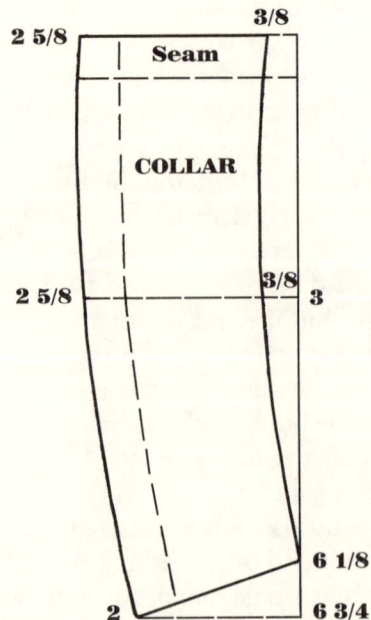

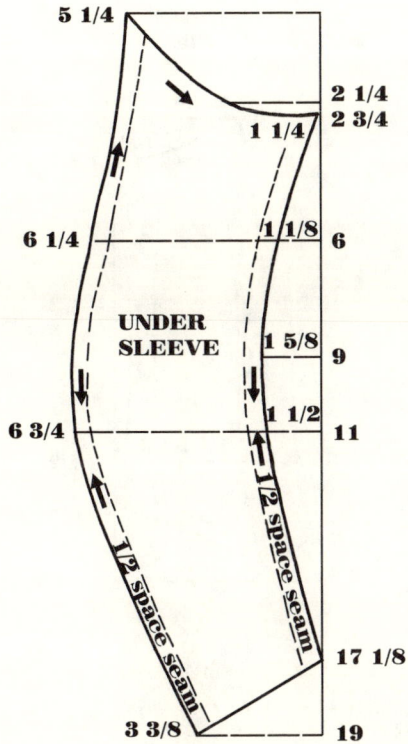

UNDER SLEEVE

5 1/4

2 1/4
2 3/4
1 1/4

6 1/4   1 1/8   6

1 5/8   9

6 3/4   1 1/2   11

1/2 space seam

1/2 space seam

17 1/8

3 3/8   19

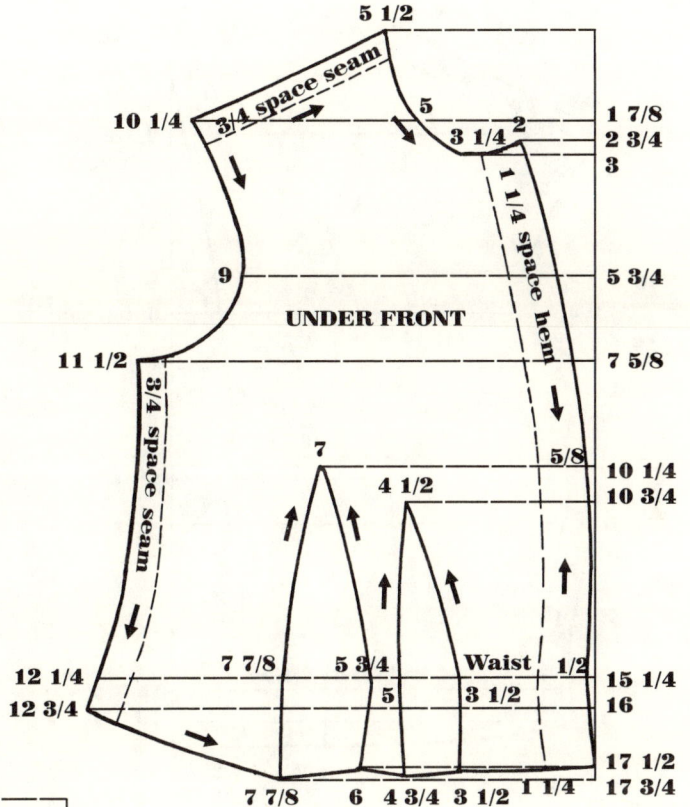

UNDER FRONT

5 1/2

3/4 space seam

10 1/4   3/4 space seam   5   1 7/8
3 1/4   2   2 3/4
3

9   5 3/4

1 1/4 space hem

11 1/2   7 5/8

3/4 space seam

7

4 1/2   5/8   10 1/4
10 3/4

7 7/8   5 3/4   Waist   1/2   15 1/4

12 1/4

12 3/4   5   3 1/2   16

17 1/2
17 3/4

7 7/8   6   4 3/4   3 1/2   1 1/4

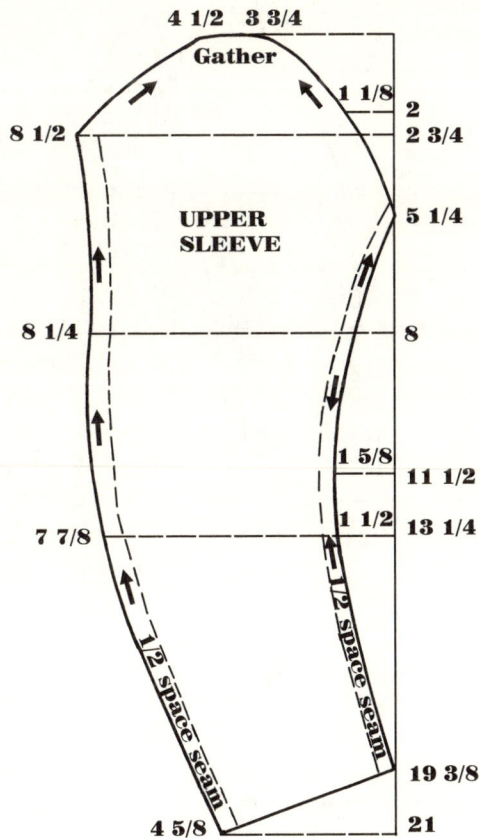

4 1/2   3 3/4

Gather

1 1/8   2
2 3/4

8 1/2

UPPER SLEEVE

5 1/4

8 1/4   8

1 5/8   11 1/2

1 1/2   13 1/4

7 7/8

1/2 space seam

1/2 space seam

19 3/8

4 5/8   21

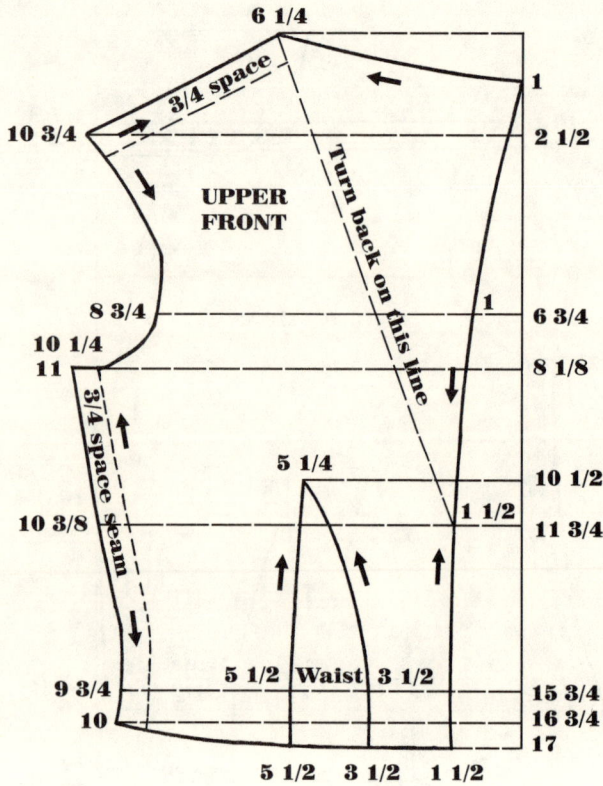

UPPER FRONT

6 1/4

3/4 space

10 3/4

1

2 1/2

Turn back on this line

8 3/4   6 3/4

10 1/4

11   8 1/8

3/4 space seam

5 1/4   10 1/2

10 3/8   1 1/2   11 3/4

9 3/4   5 1/2 **Waist** 3 1/2   15 3/4

10   16 3/4

17

5 1/2   3 1/2   1 1/2

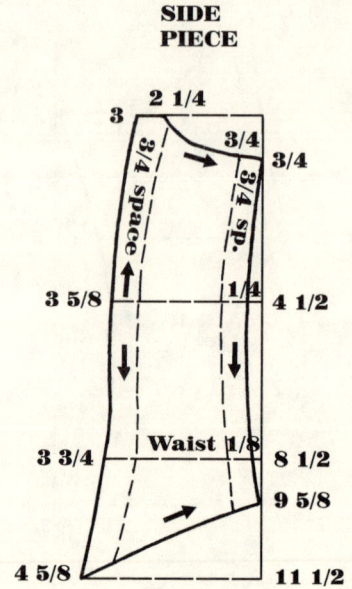

SIDE PIECE

2 1/4

3   3/4   3/4

3/4 space

3/4 sp.

3 5/8   1/4   4 1/2

3 3/4   **Waist 1/8**   8 1/2

9 5/8

4 5/8   11 1/2

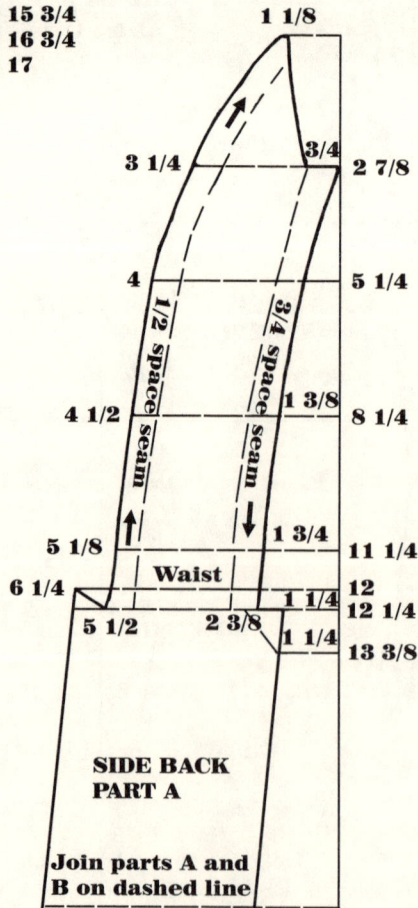

1 1/8

3 1/4   3/4   2 7/8

4   5 1/4

1/2 space seam

3/4 space seam

4 1/2   1 3/8   8 1/4

5 1/8   1 3/4   11 1/4

6 1/4   **Waist**   1 1/4   12

12 1/4

5 1/2   2 3/8   1 1/4   13 3/8

**SIDE BACK
PART A**

**Join parts A and
B on dashed line**

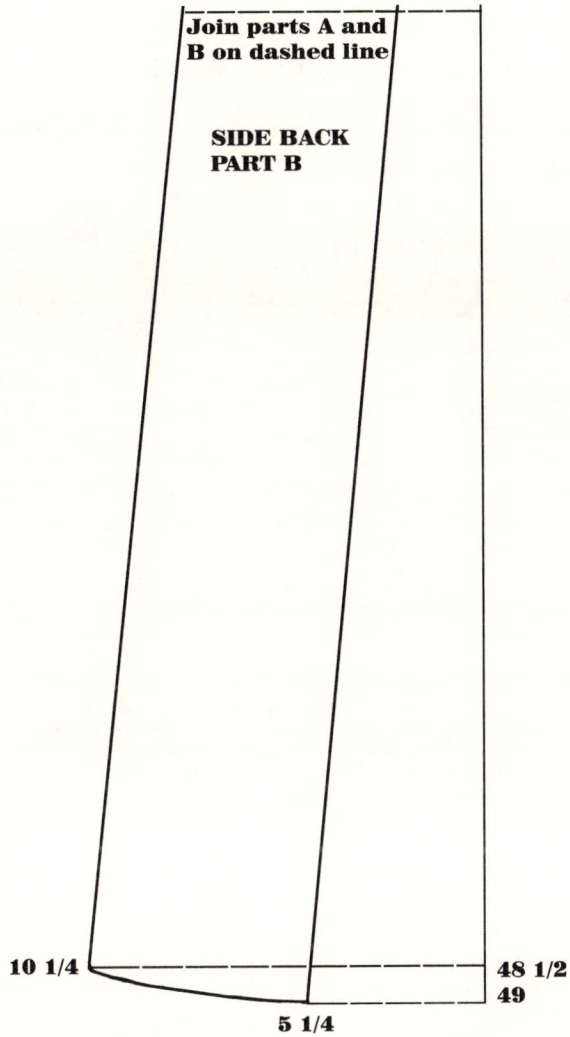

Join parts A and B on dashed line

SIDE BACK PART B

10 1/4

48 1/2
49

5 1/4

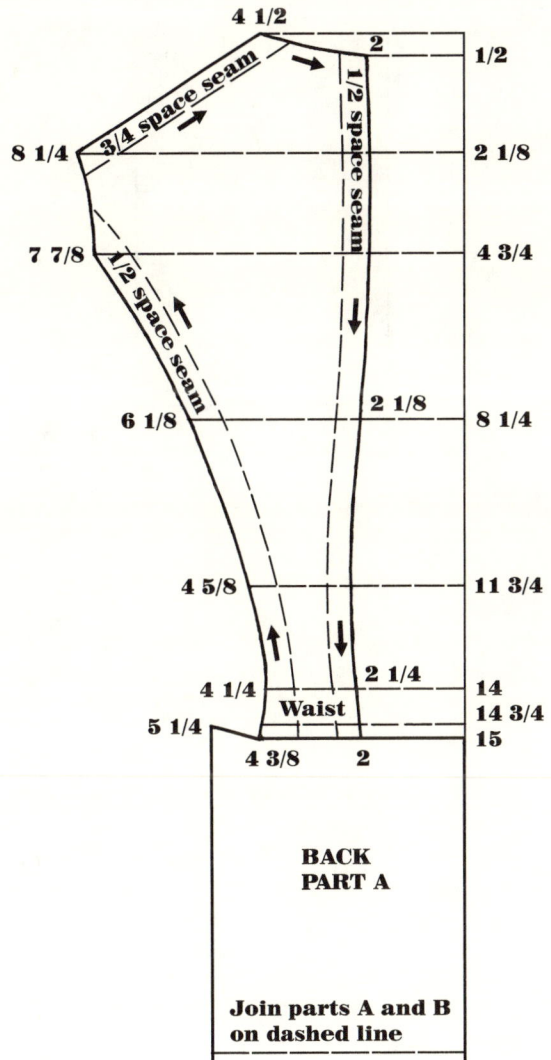

4 1/2

2

1/2

3/4 space seam

1/2 space seam

8 1/4

2 1/8

7 7/8

1/2 space seam

4 3/4

1/2 space seam

6 1/8

2 1/8

8 1/4

4 5/8

11 3/4

4 1/4

2 1/4

14

Waist

14 3/4

5 1/4

15

4 3/8

2

BACK PART A

Join parts A and B on dashed line

**Join parts A and B
on dashed line**

**BACK
PART B**

5 1/2   51 1/2

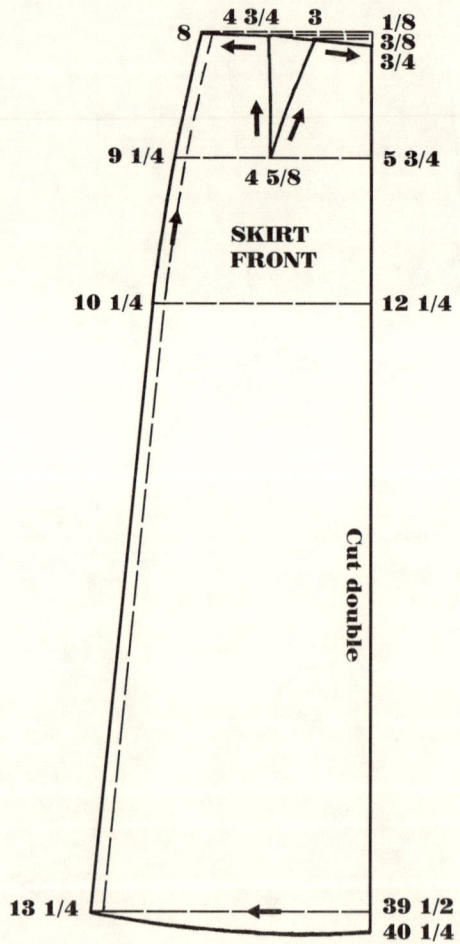

8   4 3/4   3   1/8
                     3/8
                     3/4

9 1/4   4 5/8   5 3/4

**SKIRT
FRONT**

10 1/4   12 1/4

Cut double

13 1/4   39 1/2
                        40 1/4

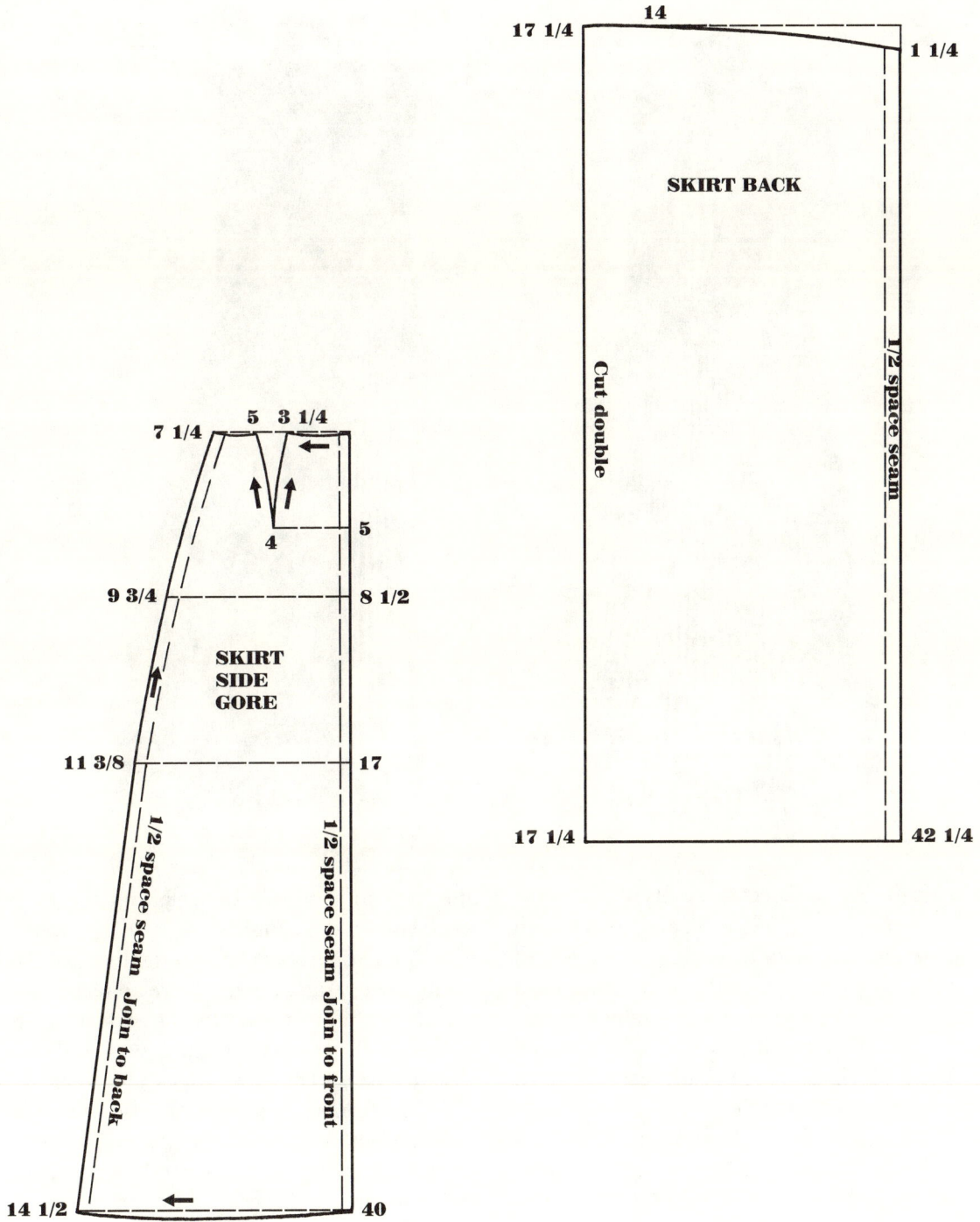

Costume in the Directoire Style. This costume is pictured developed in silk and velvet, with silk and passementerie for trimming. The effect of the four-gored skirt is brought out by wearing a long, slender bustle, although steels may be used with an equally good result. The gores are covered by a drapery, which is laid in fine kilt-plaits that turn toward the center on each side.

The polonaise is adjusted by double bust and under-arm darts, side pieces, side backs, and a curved center back seam. The latter terminates above extra width, which is underfolded in a double box-plait. Below the waist-line of the side-back seams, extra widths are allowed on the back edges of the side backs and on the front edges of the back. These widths are underfolded to form a double box-plait on each side, the arrangement forming the skirt in a double box-plait on the outside on each side of the center.

The fronts are of basque depth and are pointed at the lower edge. On them are adjusted full fronts, which are shorter than the fitted fronts. They are gathered along the neck and lower edges for some distance back of the front edges, the exposed parts of the fitted fronts being concealed by a pointed girdle overlaid with passementerie. The full fronts present a vest effect between reversed jacket fronts. The latter extend to the waist-line and are faced with silk. At the neck is a high standing collar covered with passementerie. The leg-of-mutton sleeves are gathered at their upper edges, and trimmed with passementerie.

Directoire Costume

This mode is particularly well suited to combinations. Henrietta cloth, serge, embroidered cashmere, silk-and-wool barége, Bedford cord, mohair, etc., develop stylishly; and silk, velvet, etc., may be united with any of them. Passementerie, ribbon, Persian bands, appliqué, point de Gene bands, galloon, lace, or any favored trimming may be selected. To make the costume for a lady of medium size, requires 21 1/8 yards of material 22 inches wide, or 9 7/8 yards of material 54 inches wide. As represented, it needs 18 5/8 yards of silk 20 inches wide, 8 1/4 yards of velvet 20 inches wide, and 3 3/4 yards of lining 36 inches wide for the fronts, etc.

September 1889 *Delineator*

Coat Polonaise in the Directoire Style.
Silk, velvet, and dress material are associated in this example, velvet facings and buttons providing the trimmings. The fronts are shaped by double bust darts, and are closed with buttons and button-holes. On the fronts is arranged a vest, which is shirred once at the upper edge and twice at the lower edge. It is sewed permanently to the right front, and secured invisibly to the left front with hooks and eyes. A plaited girdle is disposed over the lower part of the fronts and vest, its right end being inserted in the right under-arm seam and its left end fastened with hooks and eyes. The jacket fronts are fitted by single bust darts, and are turned back in triangular lapels. The lapels are faced with velvet and terminated at the bust, below which three buttons are ornamentally placed.

The rest of the adjustment is performed by side pieces, side backs, and a center back seam. Below the waist-line of each side-back seam, extra width is cut and underfolded to form a forward-turning plait, the top of which is marked by a button. The center back seam ends above hemmed laps. The upper sleeve part, which is gathered at the upper edge and for a short distance down each side edge, is considerably larger at the top than its coat-shaped lining. The wrist is trimmed with a round cuff-facing of velvet. A high standing collar is at the neck.

Coat Polonaise

This polonaise makes up admirably in cloth, Henrietta, etc. Any caprice may be indulged in the combination of materials, and opportunity is afforded for rich contrasts in shades and textures. The lapel facings may be of Persian embroidery or bands, if preferred to velvet. To make the garment for a lady of medium size, requires 5 7/8 yards of material 22 inches wide, 3 yards of material 44 inches wide, or 2 1/4 yards of material 54 inches wide. Also required are 1 1/4 yards of velvet 20 inches wide for the collar, etc., 2 7/8 yards of silk 20 inches wide for the vest, etc., and 3/4 yard of lining 36 inches wide for the sleeve linings.

September 1889 *Delineator*

Coat Polonaise. The polonaise is shown made of lady's cloth, contrasting silk, and Persian material, and trimmed with silk and button molds covered with Persian material. The adjustment is performed by double bust and under-arm darts, side backs, and a center back seam. The latter ends a little below the waist-line, and the side seams end somewhat lower. Below the waist-line of each side-back seam extra fullness is allowed, and underfolded in a forward-turning plait.

The right front is extended to overlap the left front, where it is closed invisibly. On the right front is arranged a vest, which is sewed flatly at the side edges. The upper edge of the vest is laid in four forward-turning plaits on each side of the center, and the lower edge is laid in three upward-turning plaits. The lower part is arranged to form a girdle. Over the fronts are adjusted outside fronts that are cut away a little below the waist-line, where they form a notch and are extended to produce a panel effect. Lapels that taper to points at the waist-line are sewed to the front edges of the outside fronts. Two buttons are ornamentally placed below each lapel, and below the notch three similar buttons are placed.

The neck is completed with a high standing collar. Each upper sleeve part is much larger at the top than its coat-shaped lining, and is laid in four downward-turning plaits on the side edges and basted at the center. At the wrist is a cuff, which is much larger than the sleeve and is extended so that the ends are basted together at the back, a button being ornamentally placed over each basting. A large pocket lap with pointed lower corners is

applied over each hip and decorated at the back edge with two buttons. The front edges of the side backs, and the side edges of the deeper part of the outside fronts, are followed with a fold of silk.

This mode is adaptable to serge, cashmere, Bedford cord, all-wool surah, foulé, Persian novelty material, Henrietta cloth, mohair, and silk-and-wool barége. Combinations make up especially well, and any of the materials mentioned may be united with velvet, silk, or a contrasting color of the same material. Surah; faille; brocaded China silk; India silk; foulard; or printed, figured, or checked silk may be combined with velvet or pretty wool material. Persian bands, passementerie, Arab trimmings,

etc., are appropriate decorations. The polonaise may be worn with a skirt of the same or contrasting material, and may be trimmed to correspond to the skirt. The skirt may consist of four straight breadths gathered to a belt. To make the polonaise for a lady of medium size, requires 6 7/8 yards of material 22 inches wide, 3 1/2 yards of material 44 inches wide, or 3 yards of material 54 inches wide. Also required are 2 3/4 yards of silk 20 inches wide for the vest, etc., 1/2 yard of Persian material 44 inches wide for the collar, etc., and 1 1/4 yards of lining 36 inches wide for the sleeve lining, etc.

October 1889 *Delineator*

Four-Gored Skirt. This skirt is illustrated made of suit material. It may be worn with a long, slender bustle, as shown by the view on the left. The view on the right shows the skirt adjusted without a bustle, in which case the back breadth is cut off straight near the top. The front and side gores are fitted by darts, the back breadth is gathered, and the top is finished with a belt. A placket opening is made at the center of the back breadth. Tapes are sewed to the side-back seams on each side to draw the fullness backward. A deep facing of canvas under a shallower facing of alpaca or soft lining material is the usual finish, and the edge is completed with braid either plain or plaited. When the skirt is to be worn with a drapery that will partially or entirely obscure it, lining material is often used for the skirt, and it is overfaced for a short distance from the bottom with the drapery material.

Cloth, cashmere, Henrietta, and other wool and silk dress materials are adaptable to this style. Passementerie, braid, appliqué, or any flat trimming may border the lower part of the skirt. For a lady of medium size, this skirt requires 4 5/8 yards of material 22 inches wide, 3 1/2 yards of material 36 inches wide, 2 7/8 yards of material 44 inches wide, or 2 3/8 yards of material 54 inches wide.

October 1889 *Delineator*

Street Costume

The polonaise is drafted with the scale corresponding to the bust measure. It consists of ten pieces: Front, back, vest lining, vest shirring, pocket lap, collar, tucked sleeve, optional cuff, and two coat sleeve pieces for an optional sleeve lining.

The back and side back are drafted together. Lay the plaits according to the notches, leaving the back open at the center. Lay the plaits at the bottom, press them carefully, but do not baste them underneath. Turn back the front on the dashed line and face the lapels. Sew the pocket lap on the curved line. It is not necessary to cut on the line extending from the first dart to 5 at the bottom of the skirt; simply turn it under.

The vest may be made plain or shirred. Cut it double. Sew the right side in the front dart and the shoulder seam, and close it on the left side with hooks and eyes.

The full sleeve is tucked on the vertical dashed lines. Draft the pattern just as it is given. Trace the lines on the material. Tuck the sleeve, and sew it to the coat sleeve on the curved dashed lines. Finish the lower part of the sleeve with a cuff. If you wish to make the tucked sleeve without the lining, use the cuff diagram given.

The over-skirt is drafted with the scale corresponding to the waist measure. The length is regulated with the tape measure. Allow for the hem. You may use either the diagram given for a tucked over-skirt, or the one for the full over-skirt shown by the engraving. A single diagram is given for each.

The foundation skirt is drafted with the scale corresponding to the waist measure. The length is regulated with the tape measure. There are three pieces: Front, side gore, and back.

Fall 1889 *Voice of Fashion*

COLLAR

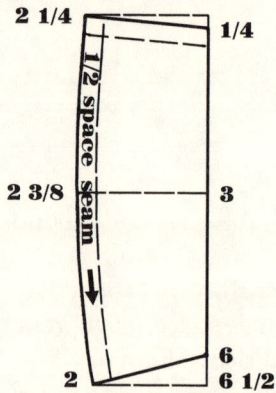

2 1/4 — 1/4

1/2 space seam

2 3/8 — 3

2 — 6
6 1/2

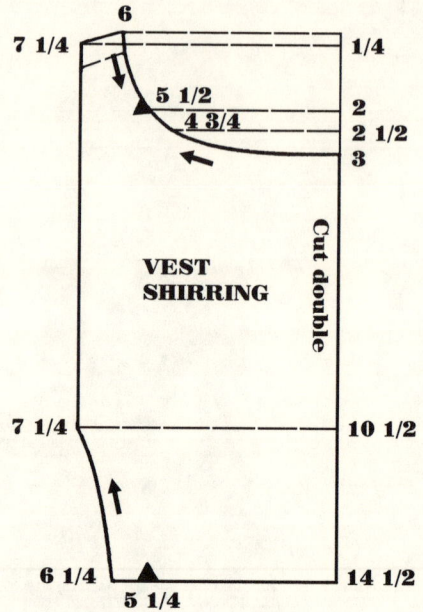

6
7 1/4 — 1/4
5 1/2 — 2
4 3/4 — 2 1/2
— 3

VEST SHIRRING

Cut double

7 1/4 — 10 1/2

6 1/4 — 14 1/2
5 1/4

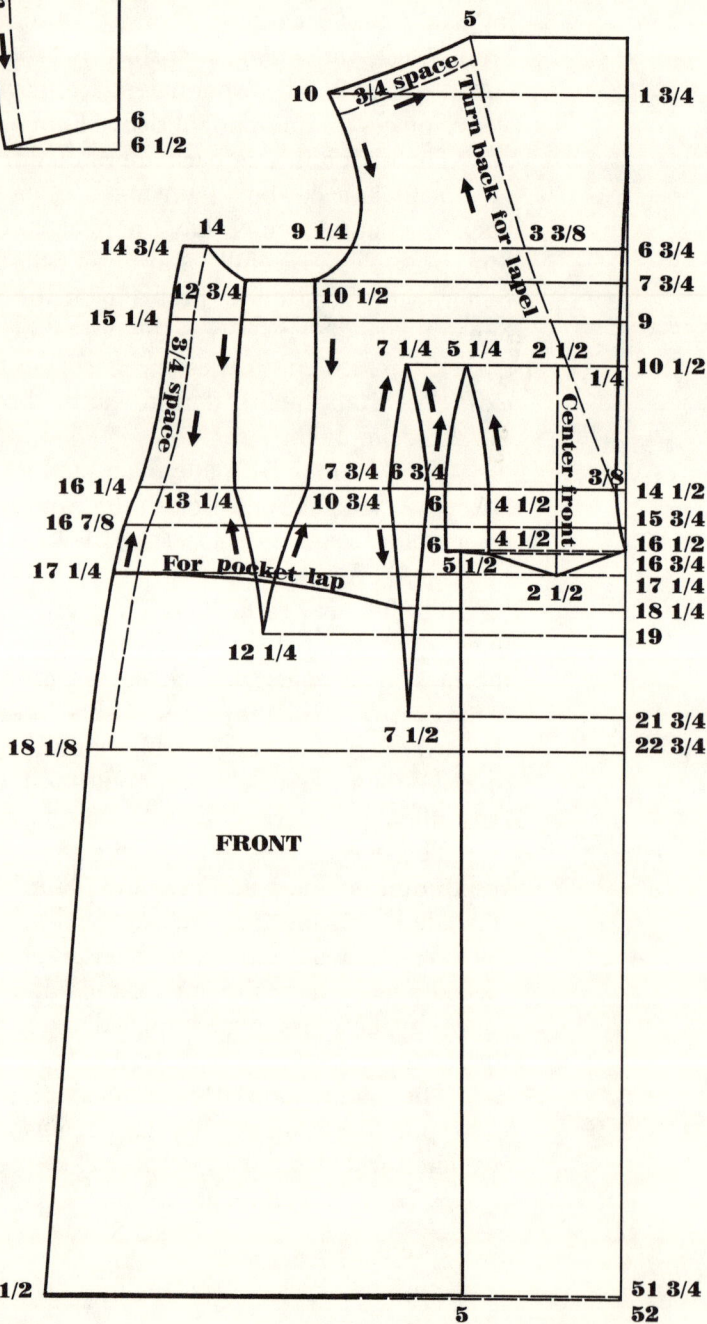

5

10 — 3/4 space — Turn back for lapel

1 3/4

3 3/8

14 — 14
14 3/4 — 9 1/4
12 3/4 — 6 3/4
10 1/2 — 7 3/4
15 1/4 — 9
3/4 space
7 1/4 5 1/4 2 1/2 — 10 1/2
1/4
Center front
3/8
16 1/4 — 7 3/4 6 3/4 — 14 1/2
13 1/4 — 10 3/4 — 6 — 4 1/2 — 15 3/4
16 7/8 — 6 — 4 1/2 — 16 1/2
17 1/4 — For pocket lap — 5 1/2 — 16 3/4
17 1/4
2 1/2 — 18 1/4
19
12 1/4

21 3/4
7 1/2 — 22 3/4
18 1/8

FRONT

20 1/2 — 51 3/4
5 — 52

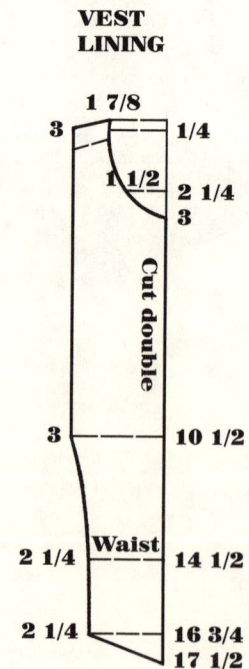

VEST LINING

1 7/8
3 — 1/4
1 1/2 — 2 1/4
— 3
Cut double

3 — 10 1/2

2 1/4 — Waist — 14 1/2

2 1/4 — 16 3/4
17 1/2

Street Costume

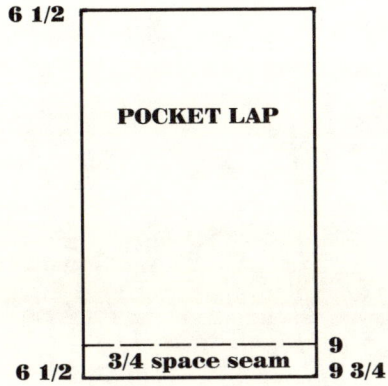

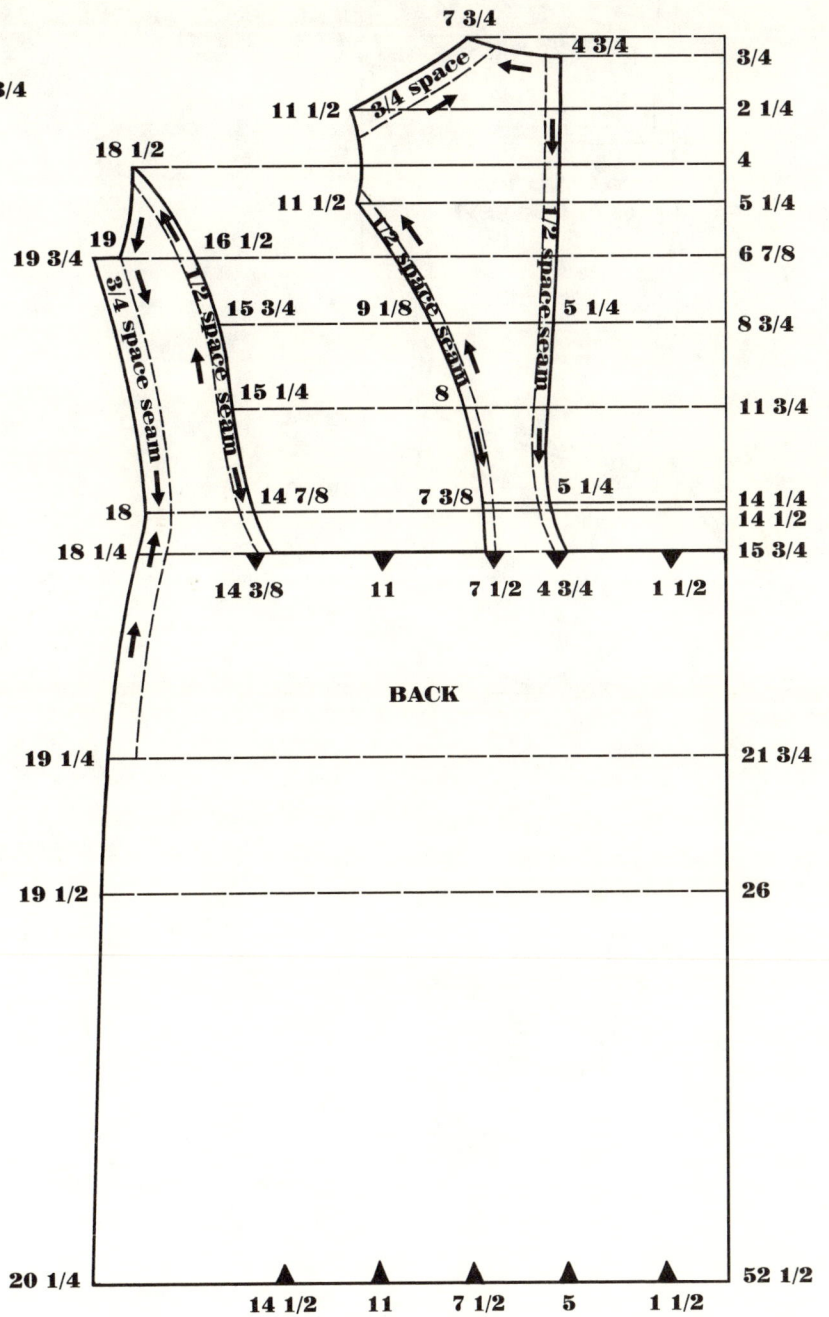

291

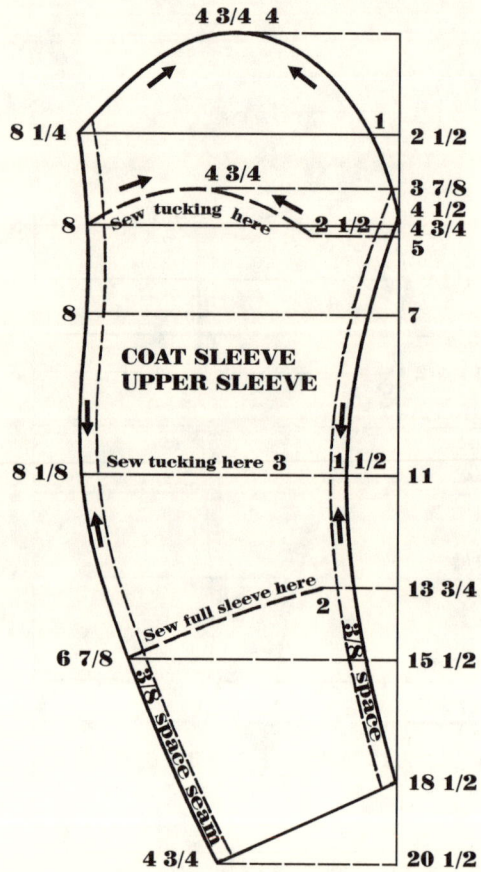

4 3/4 4

8 1/4

1

2 1/2

4 3/4

3 7/8

8

4 1/2

Sew tucking here

2 1/2

4 3/4

5

8

7

**COAT SLEEVE
UPPER SLEEVE**

8 1/8

Sew tucking here 3

1 1/2

11

Sew full sleeve here

13 3/4

6 7/8

2

15 1/2

3/8 space seam

3/8 space

18 1/2

4 3/4

20 1/2

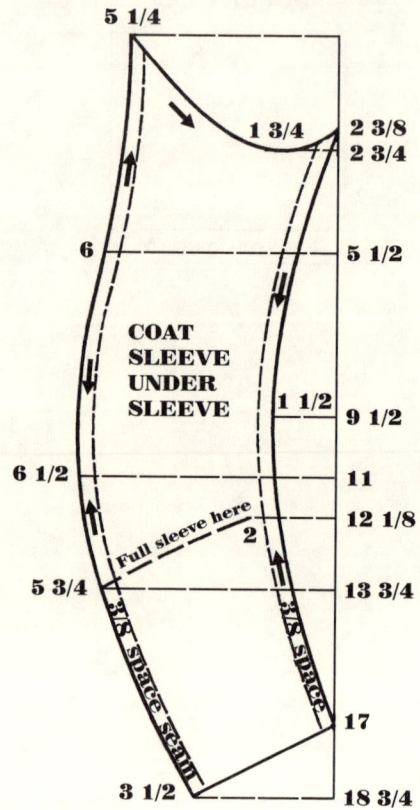

5 1/4

1 3/4

2 3/8

2 3/4

6

5 1/2

**COAT
SLEEVE
UNDER
SLEEVE**

1 1/2

9 1/2

6 1/2

11

Full sleeve here

2

12 1/8

5 3/4

13 3/4

3/8 space seam

3/8 space

17

3 1/2

18 3/4

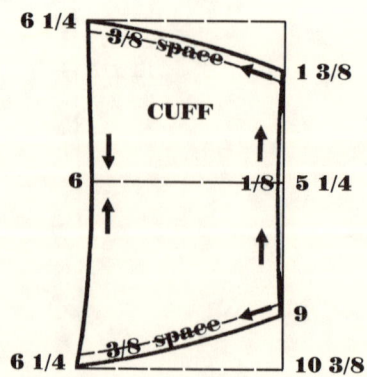

6 1/4

3/8 space

1 3/8

CUFF

6

1/8

5 1/4

6 1/4

3/8 space

9

10 3/8

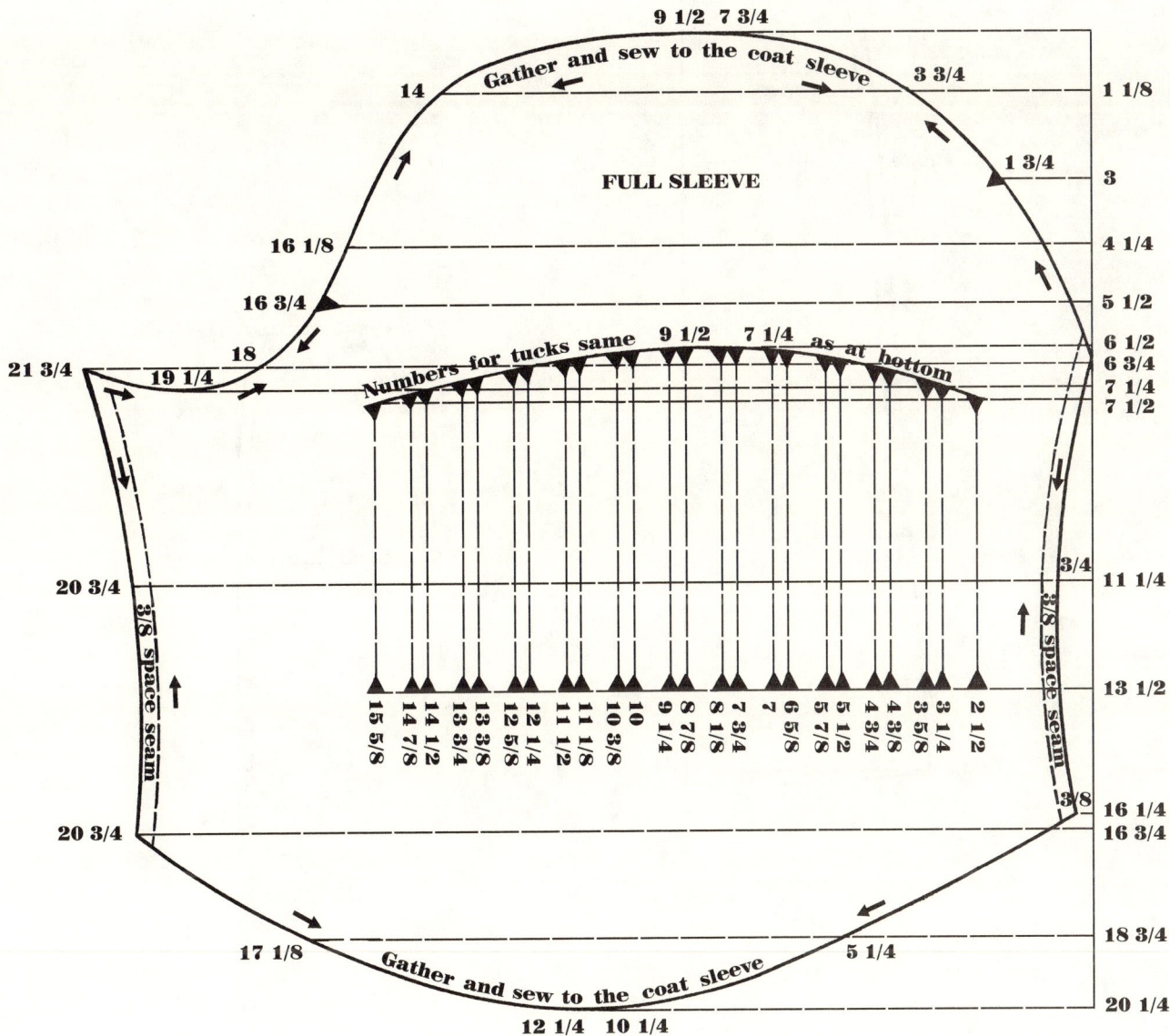

9 1/2 7 3/4

Gather and sew to the coat sleeve

14

3 3/4

1 1/8

1 3/4

3

FULL SLEEVE

16 1/8

4 1/4

16 3/4

5 1/2

6 1/2

18

6 3/4

21 3/4

Numbers for tucks same

9 1/2

7 1/4

as at bottom

7 1/4

19 1/4

7 1/2

3/8 space seam

3/4

11 1/4

20 3/4

3/8 space seam

13 1/2

15 5/8 14 7/8 14 1/2 13 3/4 13 3/8 12 5/8 12 1/4 11 1/2 11 1/8 10 3/8 10 9 1/4 8 7/8 8 1/8 7 3/4 7 6 5/8 5 7/8 5 1/2 4 3/4 4 3/8 3 5/8 3 1/4 2 1/2

16 1/4

3/8

20 3/4

16 3/4

18 3/4

17 1/8

Gather and sew to the coat sleeve

5 1/4

20 1/4

12 1/4 10 1/4

293

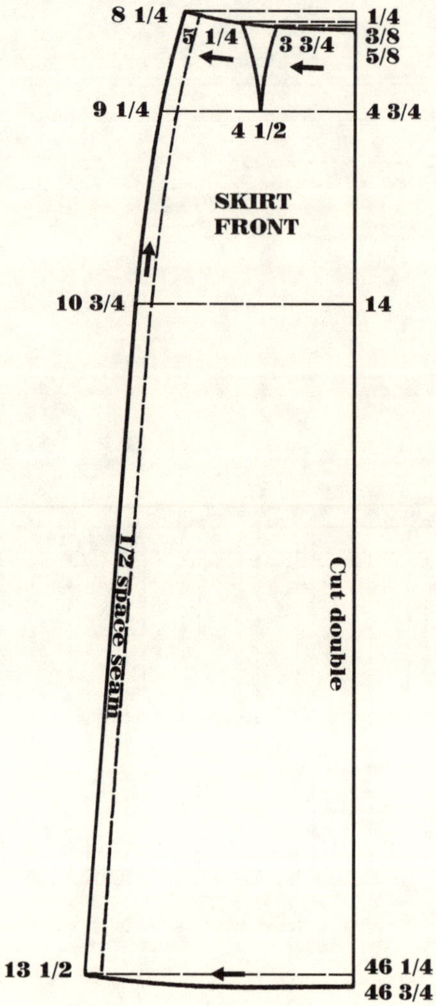

8 1/4   1/4
5 1/4   3 3/4   3/8
             5/8

9 1/4   4 3/4
4 1/2

SKIRT FRONT

10 3/4   14

1/2 space seam

Cut double

13 1/2   46 1/4
           46 3/4

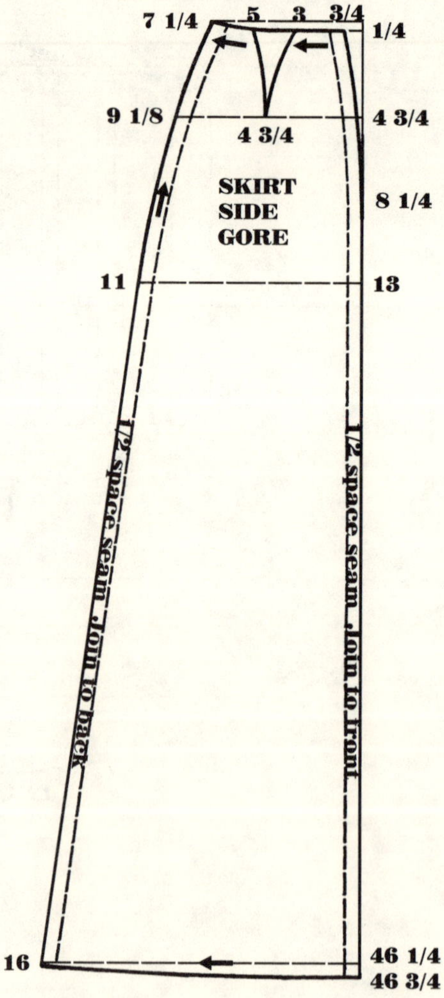

7 1/4   5   3   3/4   1/4

9 1/8   4 3/4
4 3/4

SKIRT SIDE GORE   8 1/4

11   13

1/2 space seam, join to back   1/2 space seam, join to front

16   46 1/4
         46 3/4

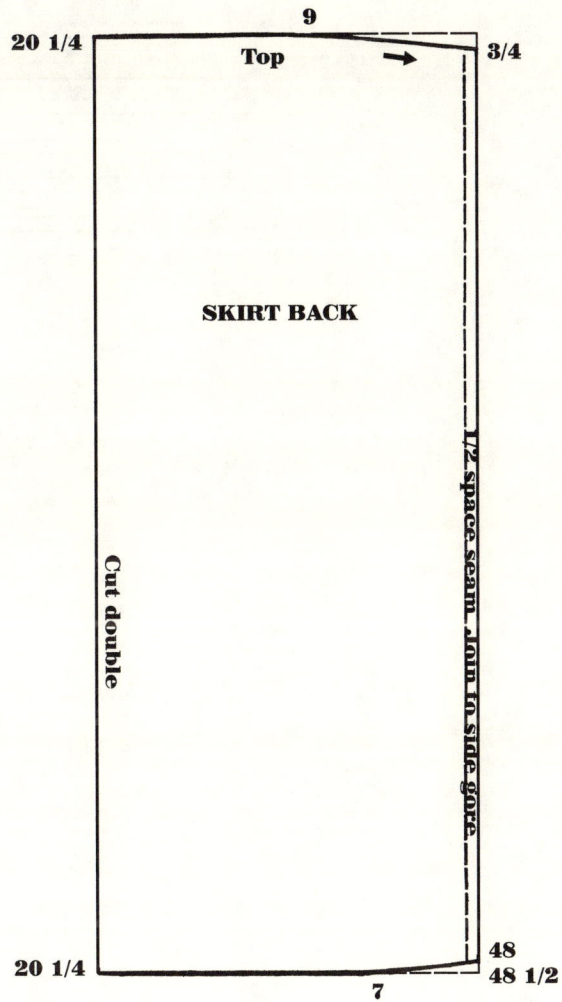

9

20 1/4   **Top** →   **3/4**

SKIRT BACK

Cut double

1/2 space seam. Join to side gore.

48
20 1/4   **48 1/2**
          7

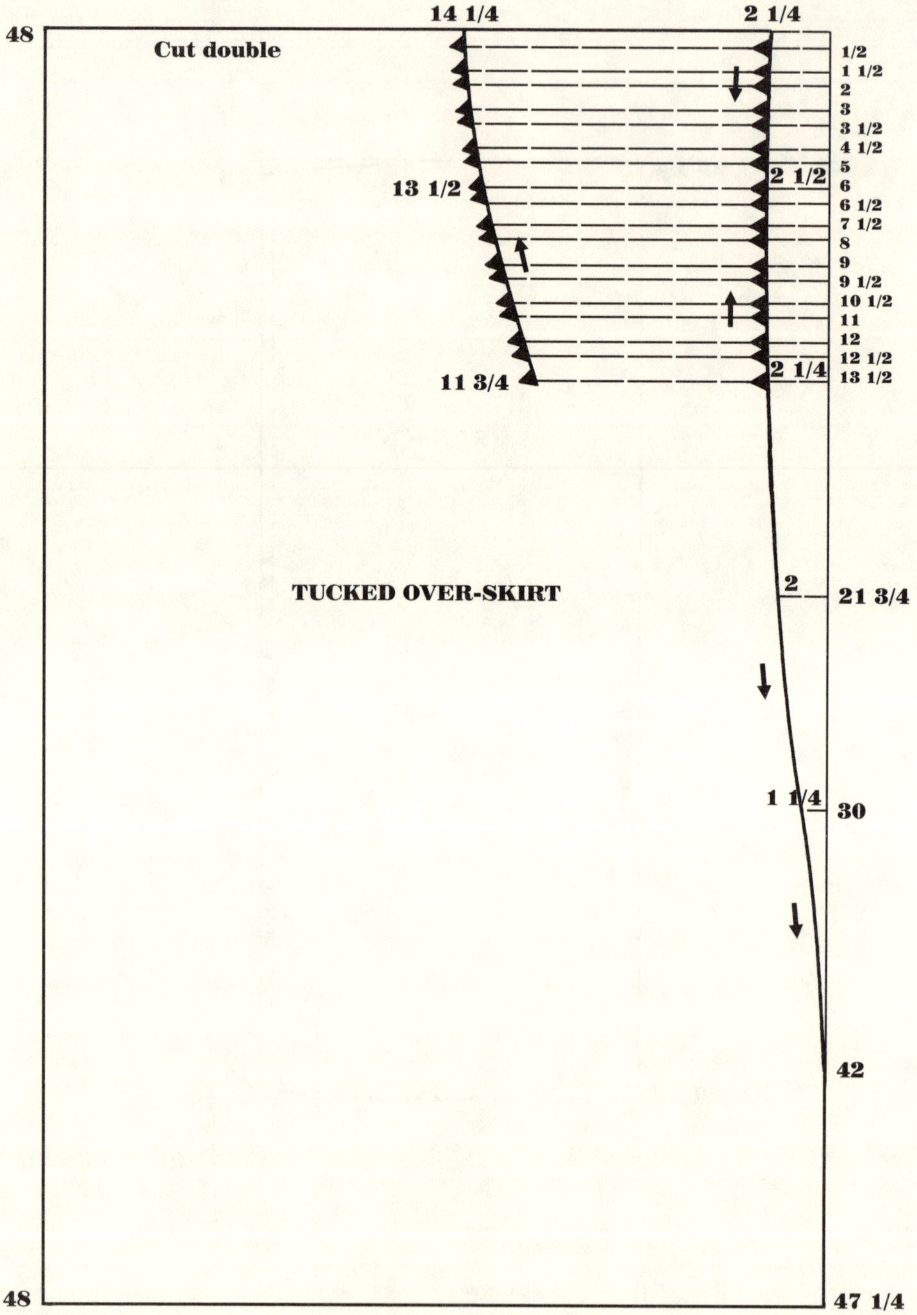

48

14 1/4   2 1/4

Cut double

1/2
1 1/2
2
3
3 1/2
4 1/2
5
2 1/2   6
6 1/2
7 1/2
8
9
9 1/2
10 1/2
11
12
12 1/2
2 1/4   13 1/2

13 1/2

11 3/4

TUCKED OVER-SKIRT

2   21 3/4

1 1/4   30

42

48   47 1/4

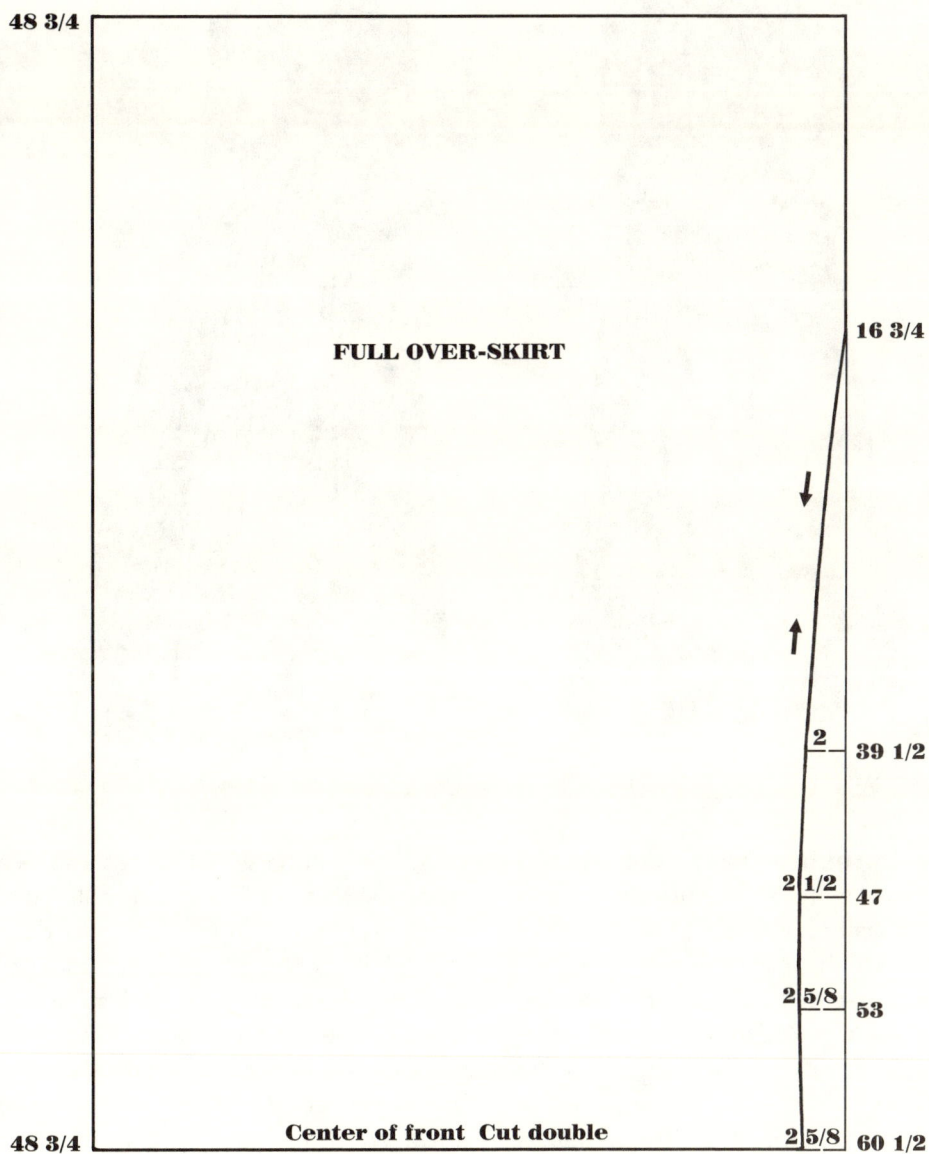

48 3/4

FULL OVER-SKIRT

16 3/4

2 — 39 1/2

2 1/2 — 47

2 5/8 — 53

48 3/4

Center of front Cut double

2 5/8 — 60 1/2

Directoire Costume. This costume is pictured made of dress material having a wide and narrow border, and silk. It is trimmed with facings of the material and with bands of the narrow border. The skirt is in the four-gored style, and the wearing of a long slender bustle will produce the desired effect, although steels may be used with equally good results. The drapery, which is all in one, hangs in long folds at the back, which result from a line of gathers at the top. In the front, nine forward-turning tucks are laid on each side of the center. They are deepest at the center, from which they graduate in yoke shape, and the fullness hangs to the edge of the skirt.

The polonaise, which resembles a Directoire coat, is shaped in front by double bust and underarm darts. Between the first bust darts the fronts are of basque length, and present a pointed lower outline. The fronts turn back in lapels, which are faced with the material and trimmed with the narrow border. Between the lapels is revealed a puff that is shirred at the upper and lower edges and arranged on a plain lining, the parts being sewed to the left front along the first dart and flatly above. The closing is effected on the right side by buttons and button-holes in a fly. Below the lapels, the fronts lap and are closed diagonally with two large buttons. The adjustment of the polonaise is completed by side seams, side-back seams, and a center back seam. The latter ends below the waist-line at the top of extra widths, which are each turned under

for a hem and pressed into a forward-turning plait underneath. The side-back seams terminate in a line with the center back seam, and the fullness is underfolded in two forward-turning plaits. The side seams also end a short distance below the waist-line, and here, as well as at the center, the coat flares to reveal the drapery. Large double pocket laps are placed on each hip, extending from the second bust dart to the side seams.

The neck is finished with a standing collar. The sleeves are arranged on coat-shaped linings. The upper parts are each gathered along the side edge near the armhole, and also across the top, and the resuling fullness is arranged in pretty folds. The wrists are completed by pointed cuff-facings below a band of the narrow border.

Heavy and light-weight cloths, and all kinds of suitings, make up well in this style. The lapels may be faced with velvet or faille, or overlaid with Persian bands. Striking contrasts may be effected by making the fancy puff of silk in some harmonizing shade. The skirt may be of different material than the polonaise, although this is unnecessary when bordered material is used. For a lady of medium size, this costume requires 15 5/8 yards of material 22 inches wide, 9 7/8 yards of material 36 inches wide, or 7 7/8 yards of material 44 inches wide. As represented, it calls for 3 1/4 yards of dress material having a wide border on one edge and a narrow border on the other, 4 1/8 yards of plain material 54 inches wide, 1/2 yard of silk 20 inches wide for the puff, and 3 3/4 yards of lining material 36 inches wide for the foundation skirt, etc.

July 1889 *Delineator*

Street Costume

Use the scale corresponding to the bust measure to draft the polonaise. It should be the same length as the skirt. It consists of ten pieces: Upper front, under front, side piece, side back, back, standing collar, rolling collar, upper sleeve, under sleeve, and cuff. The side back and back are each in two pieces to be put together before drafting.

Leave the back open from 14 1/2 down to 49 3/4, and also the side seam. Lay the extra fullness in folds or simply hem, according to fancy. Sew the rolling collar on the front and back, commencing at the center back seam and extending down to 11 1/2 on the upper front. The folded piece across the front is simply a straight piece of material laid in three or four upward-turning folds joined in the shoulder seam and brought down under the belt. Gather the under sleeve at the top to fit the upper sleeve; gather the bottom and sew it to the cuff.

The foundation skirt is drafted with the scale corresponding to the waist measure. Regulate the length with the tape measure. It has three pieces: Front, side gore, and back. The accordion-plaited over-skirt is not given, as it is simply a straight piece of material the length required, laid in very fine plaits.

Fall 1889 *Voice of Fashion*

STANDING COLLAR

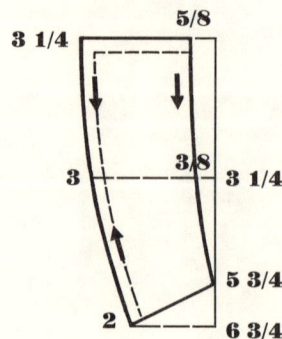

3 1/4   5/8

3   3/8   3 1/4

5 3/4

2   6 3/4

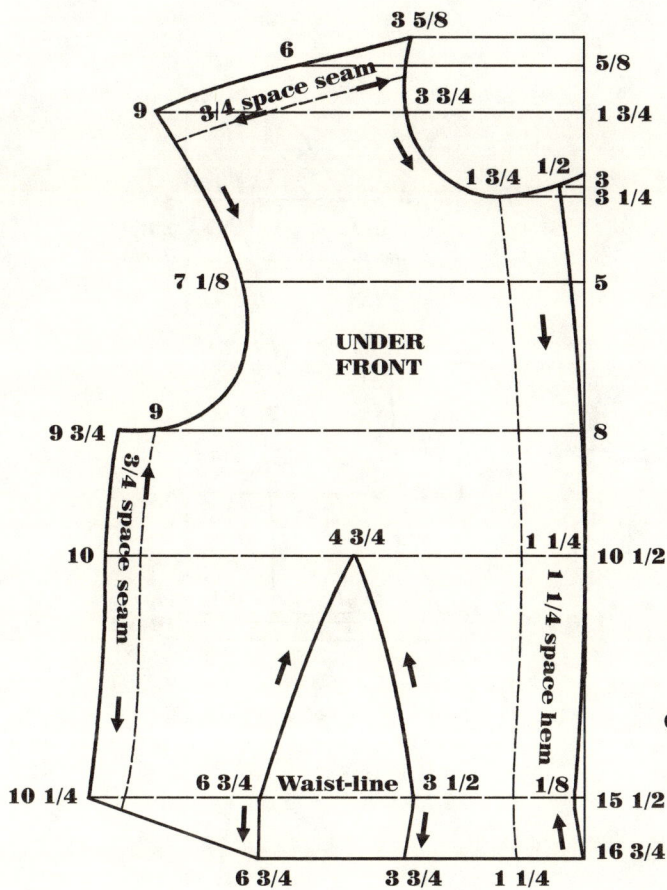

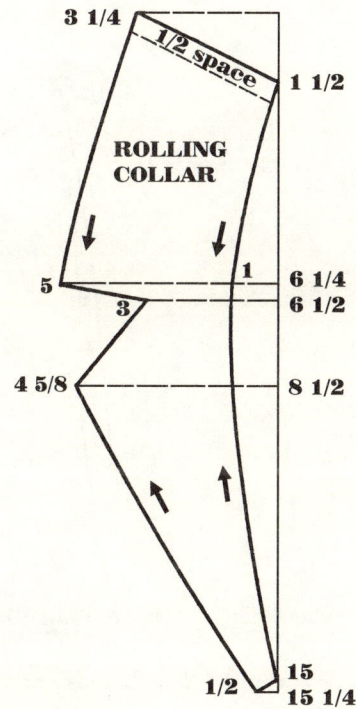

ROLLING COLLAR

UNDER FRONT

UPPER FRONT

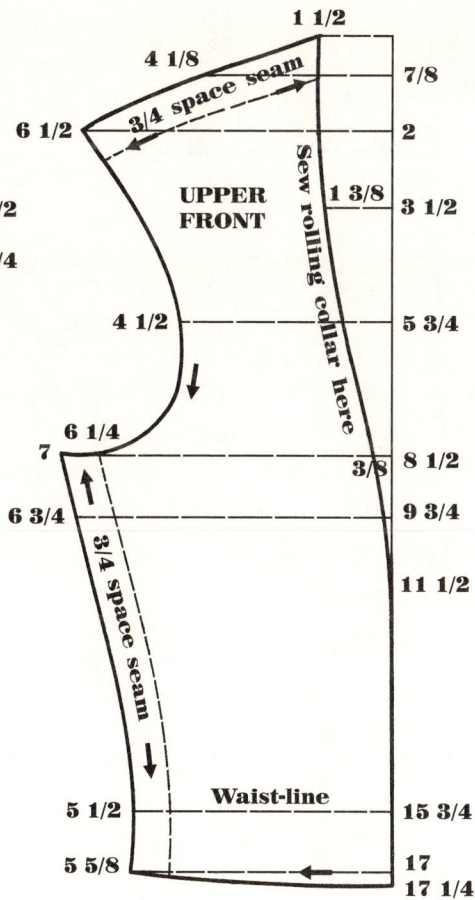

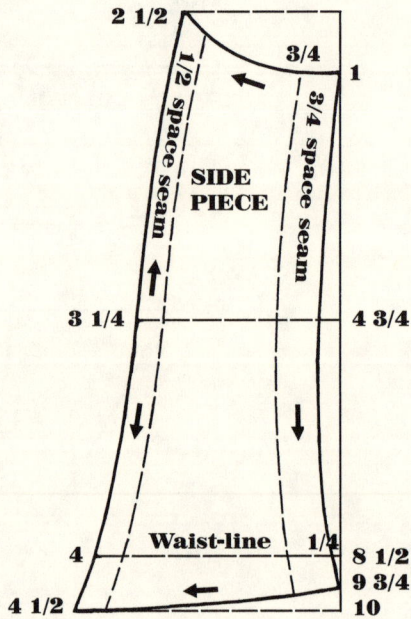

SIDE
PIECE

2 1/2

1/2 space seam

3/4

1

3/4 space seam

3 1/4

4 3/4

Waist-line

1/4

4

8 1/2

9 3/4

4 1/2

10

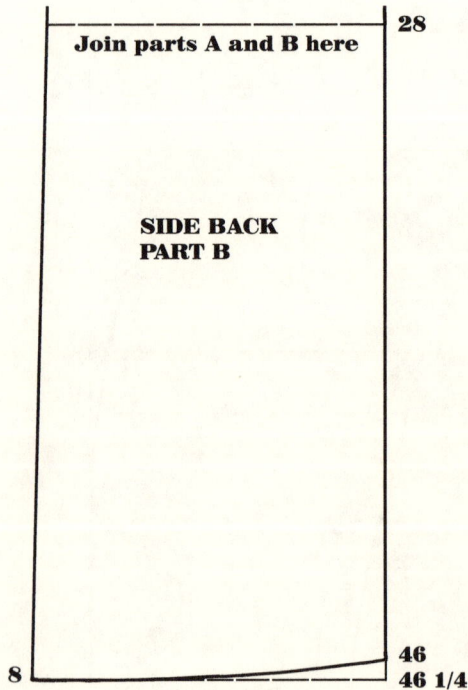

Join parts A and B here

28

SIDE BACK
PART B

8

46

46 1/4

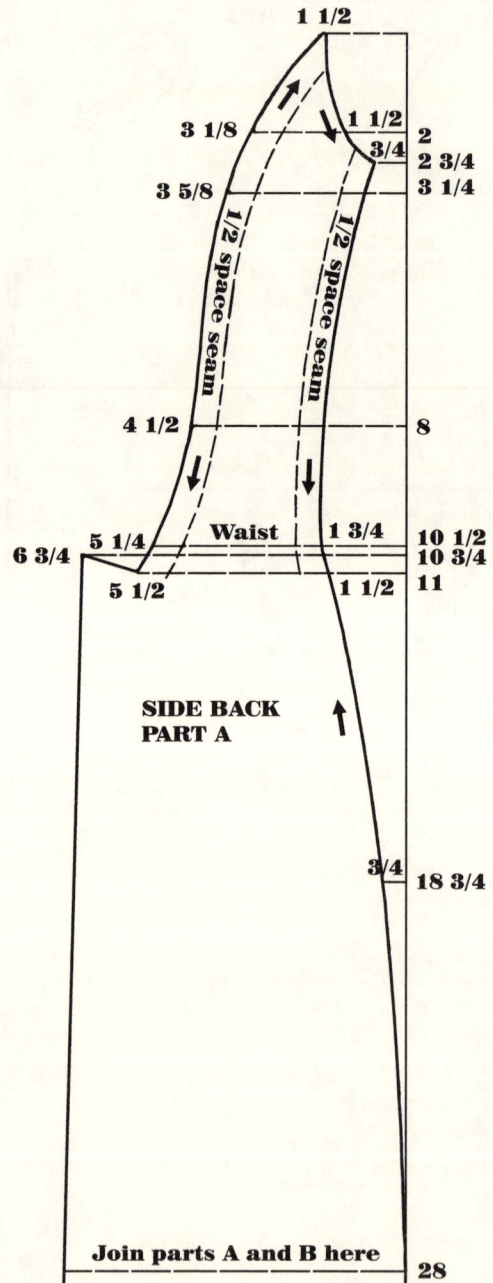

1 1/2

3 1/8

1 1/2

2

3/4

2 3/4

3 5/8

3 1/4

1/2 space seam

1/2 space seam

4 1/2

8

Waist

5 1/4

1 3/4

10 1/2

6 3/4

10 3/4

5 1/2

1 1/2

11

SIDE BACK
PART A

3/4

18 3/4

Join parts A and B here

28

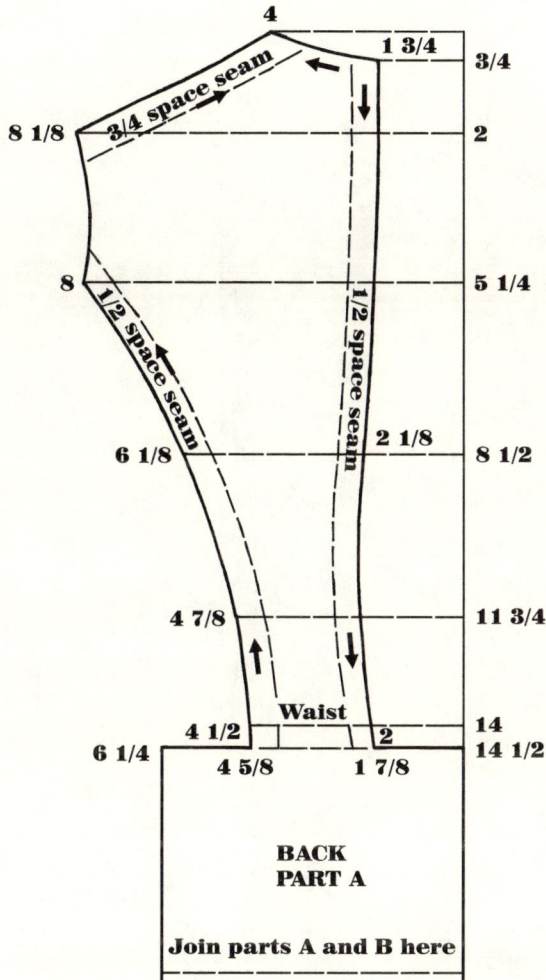

4

1 3/4   **3/4**

8 1/8   **3/4 space seam**   **2**

8   **1/2 space seam**   **1/2 space seam**   **5 1/4**

6 1/8   **2 1/8**   **8 1/2**

4 7/8   **11 3/4**

Waist   **14**

6 1/4   **4 1/2**   **2**   **14 1/2**

4 5/8   **1 7/8**

**BACK
PART A**

Join parts A and B here

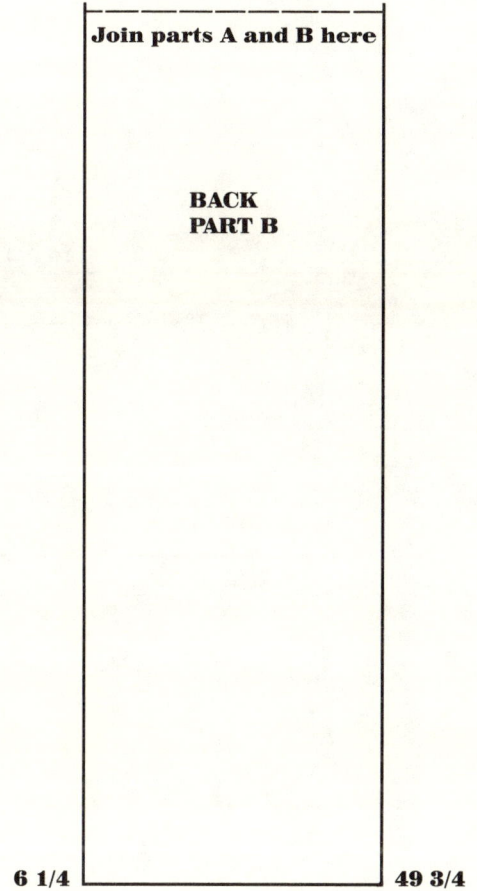

Join parts A and B here

**BACK
PART B**

6 1/4   **49 3/4**

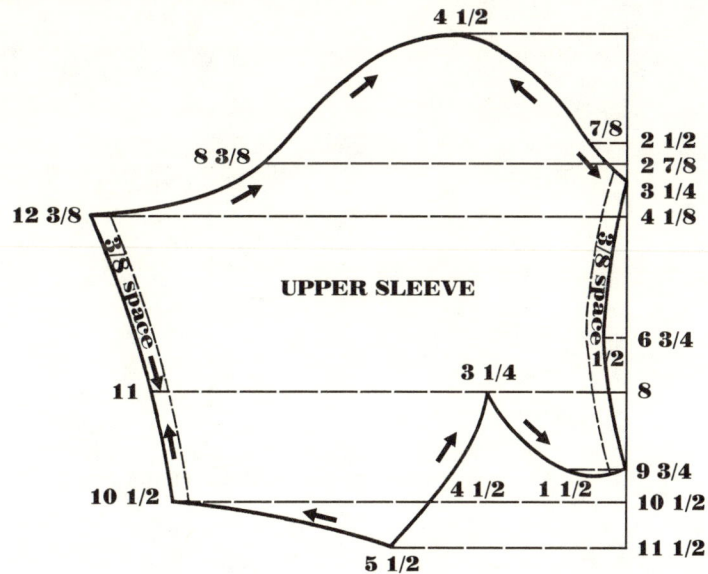

4 1/2

7/8   **2 1/2**

8 3/8   **2 7/8**

3 1/4

12 3/8   **4 1/8**

3/8 space   **3/8 space**

UPPER SLEEVE

6 3/4

1/2

11   **3 1/4**   **8**

9 3/4

10 1/2   **4 1/2**   **1 1/2**   **10 1/2**

5 1/2   **11 1/2**

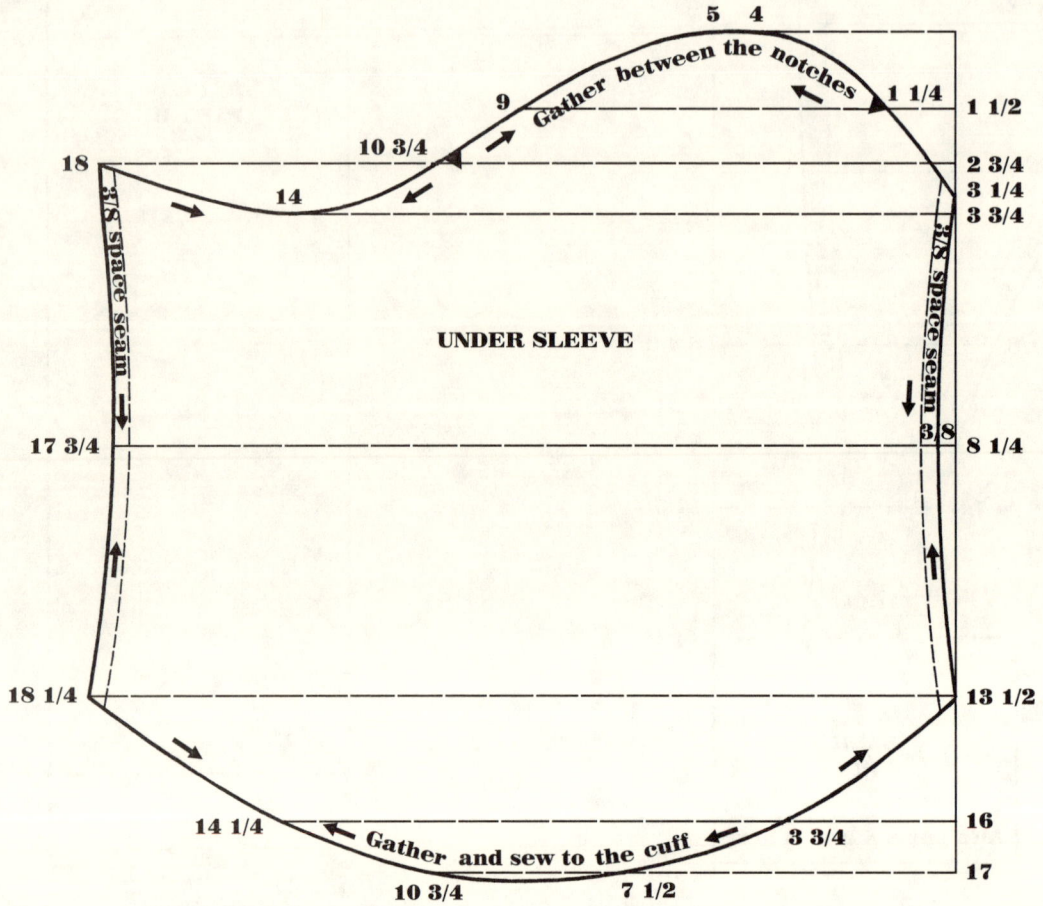

5   4

Gather between the notches   1 1/4   1 1/2

9

10 3/4   2 3/4

18   14   3 1/4   3 3/4

3/8 space seam   3/8 space seam

UNDER SLEEVE

17 3/4   3/8   8 1/4

18 1/4   13 1/2

14 1/4   Gather and sew to the cuff   3 3/4   16

10 3/4   7 1/2   17

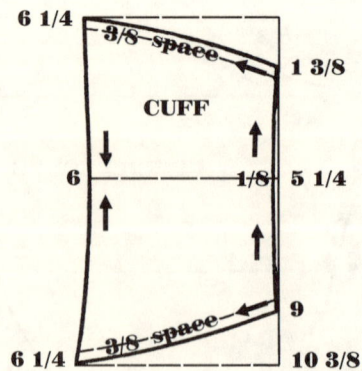

6 1/4   3/8 space   1 3/8

CUFF

6   1/8   5 1/4

6 1/4   3/8 space   9

10 3/8

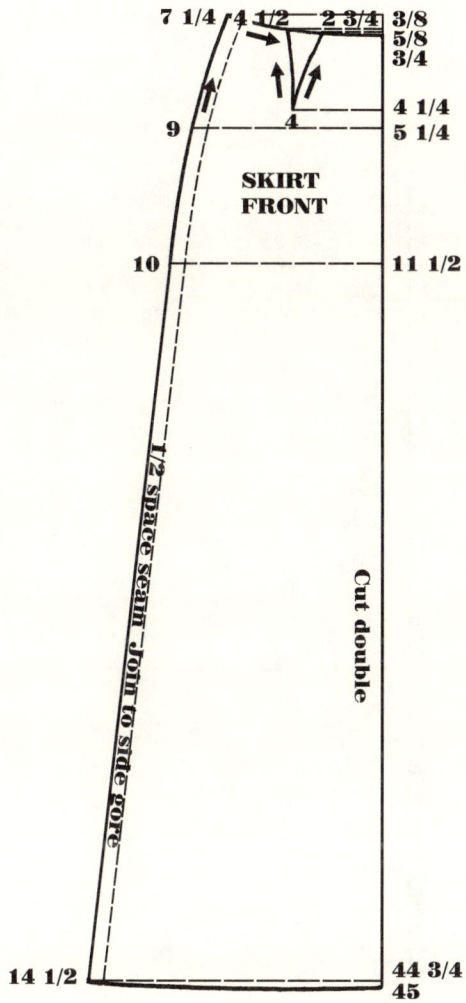

7 1/4 4 1/4 4 1/2 2 3/4 3/8
5/8
3/4

4 1/4
9 4 5 1/4

**SKIRT
FRONT**

10 11 1/2

1/2 space seam Join to side gore

Cut double

14 1/2 44 3/4
45

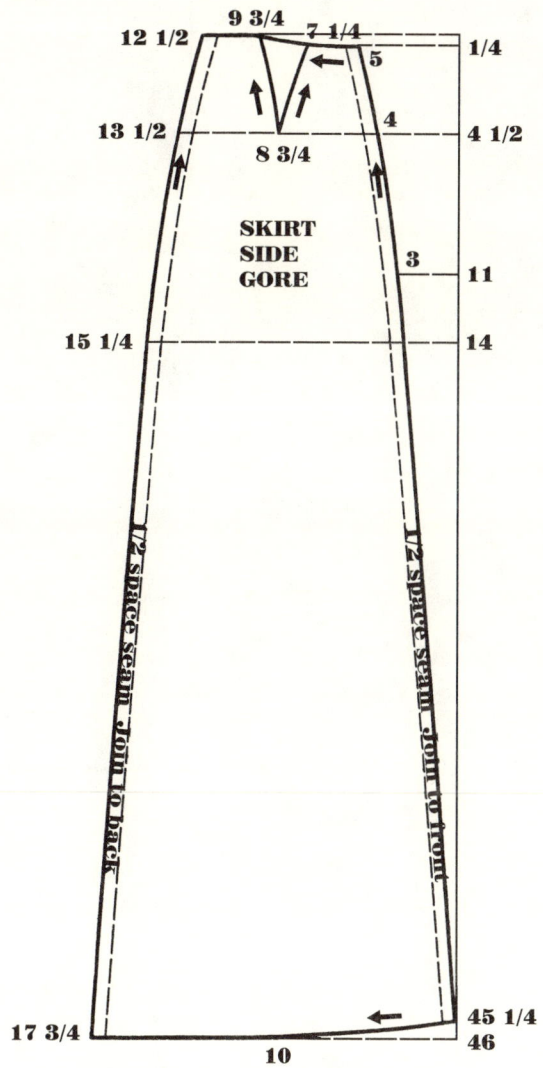

12 1/2 9 3/4 7 1/4 5 1/4

13 1/2 8 3/4 4 4 1/2

**SKIRT
SIDE
GORE** 3 11

15 1/4 14

1/2 space seam Join to back   *1/2 space seam Join to front*

17 3/4 45 1/4
10 46

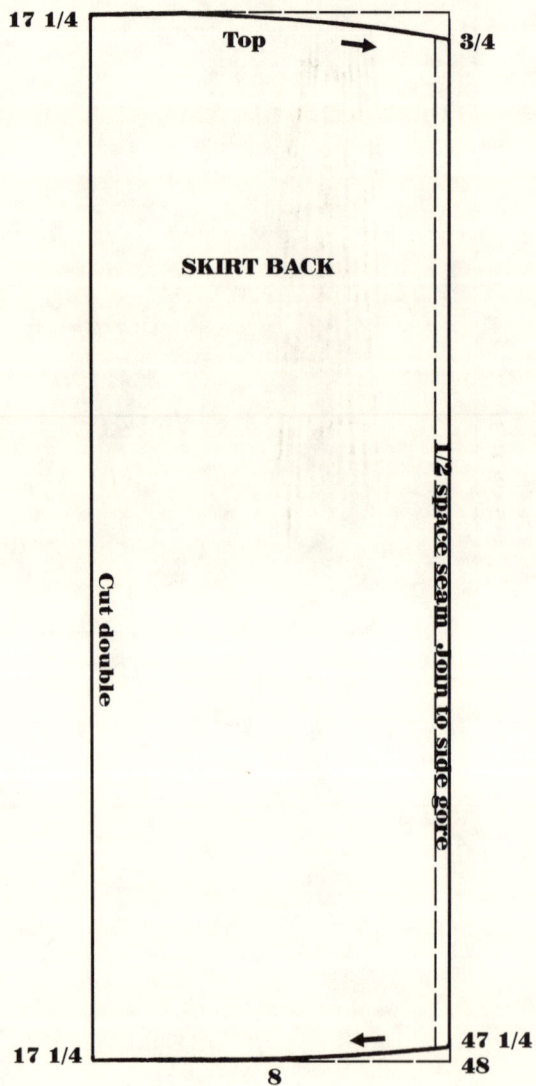

Kilt Skirt

Kilt Skirt. This skirt may be used instead of an accordion-plaited skirt, when that kind of plaiting cannot conveniently be procured. Plain dress material was selected for this example, and a perfectly plain finish was adopted. The foundation skirt, which is made of lining material, consists of three gores and a full back breadth. The gores are fitted by darts, the back breadth is gathered on each side of the placket opening, and the skirt is finished with a belt. The kilt of dress material reaches to the edge of the foundation and extends to within a short distance of the top. It is made of straight breadths joined together to obtain the requisite fullness, and is hemmed at the lower edge. It is laid in very narrow side-plaits that all turn in one direction. These are held in their folds by tapes basted to them underneath. The top of the kilt is sewed flatly onto the foundation. The lower part of the foundation, as well as the part above the kilt, is faced with the dress material.

Any style of drapery may be arranged with a kilt skirt, although none is needed if the basque or jacket is deep enough to cover the space above the plaiting. When very light materials are used, the foundation skirt may be of the material, in which case a facing is not needed. The kilt may be made up in cloths of all kinds, seasonable suitings, and faille, surah, etc. Trimming is usually dispensed with, but when the kilt is made of a wool material, braid or narrow ribbon may be used. These trimmings must be applied before the material is plaited. To make the skirt for a lady of medium size, requires 13 1/4 yards of material 22 inches wide, 7 5/8 yards of material 36 inches wide, 6 1/4 yards of material 44 inches wide, or 5 1/8 yards of material 54 inches wide. Each needs 3 1/8 yards of lining 36 inches wide for the foundation skirt.

July 1889 *Delineator*

Stout Ladies' Costume

Use the scale corresponding to the bust measure to draft the polonaise pattern, which should not be used for a figure smaller than a 36 bust. It consists of seven pieces: Front, pocket lap, side back, back, collar, and two sleeve pieces. Make the polonaise as long as the skirt.

Lay the plaits in the back according to the notches. The under-arm seams may remain open from the first line below the waist-line down to the bottom. Any style of trimming may be used to relieve the plain front. For instance, do not button it all the way up to the neck, but turn it back at the neck and face with velvet to form lapels. Fit the lining to the neck, however, and fill in with lace or soft silk.

The polonaise may be worn with either a plain skirt or a kilt skirt. The plain skirt is drafted with the scale corresponding to the waist measure. Regulate the length with the tape measure. There are three pieces: Front, side gore, and back. Any style of trimming may be used.

Winter 1889–1890 *Voice of Fashion*

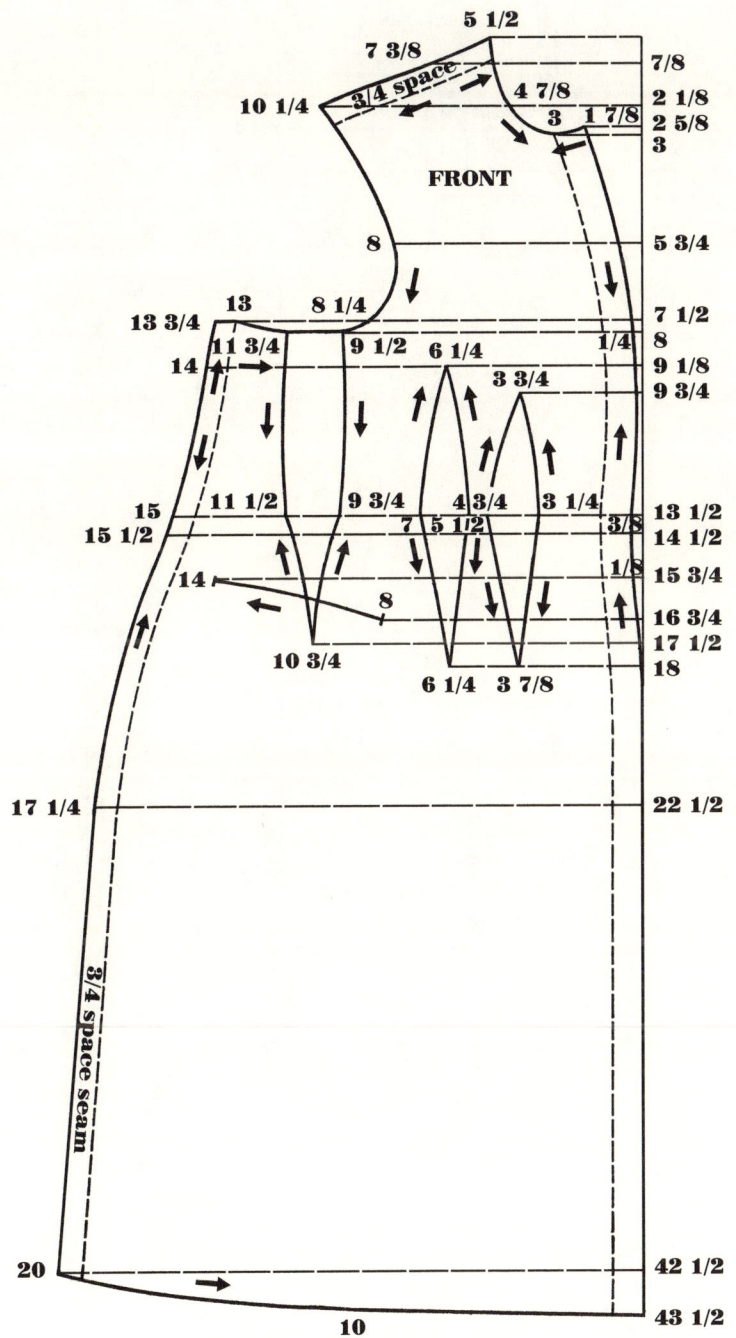

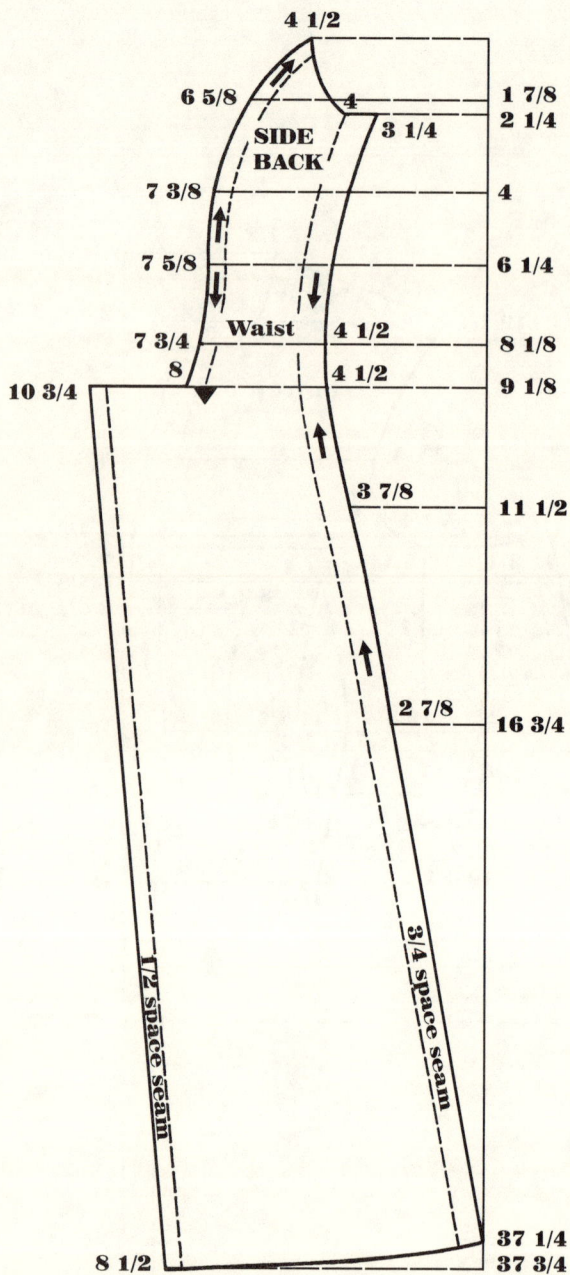

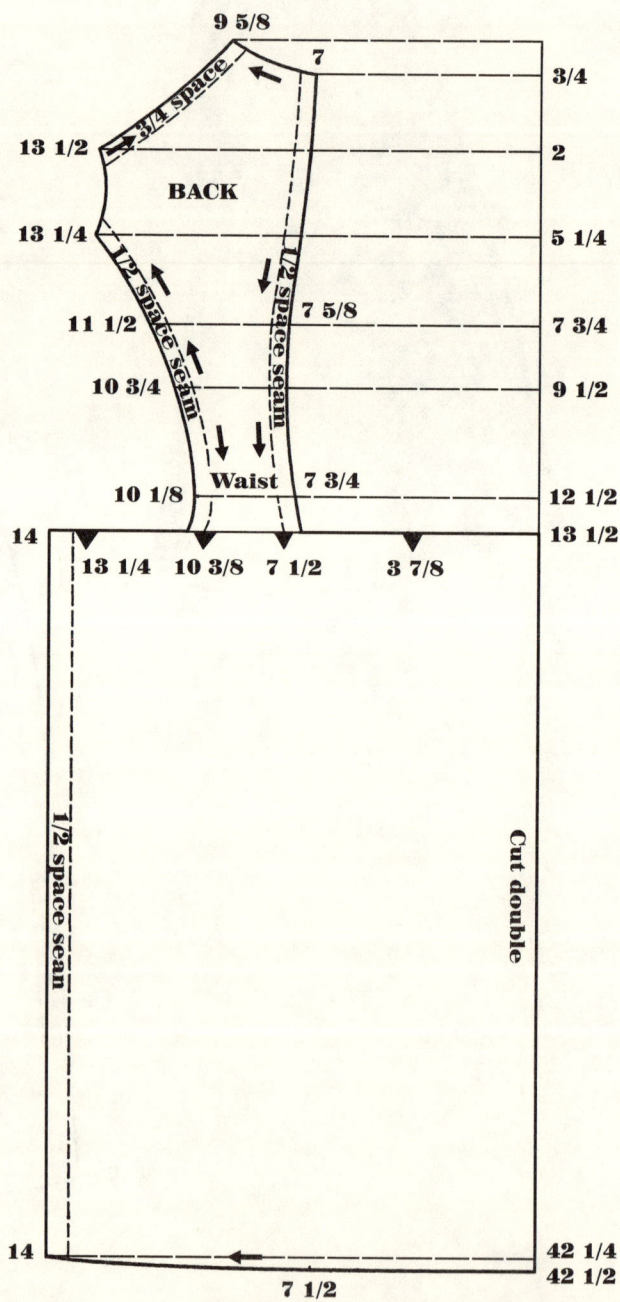

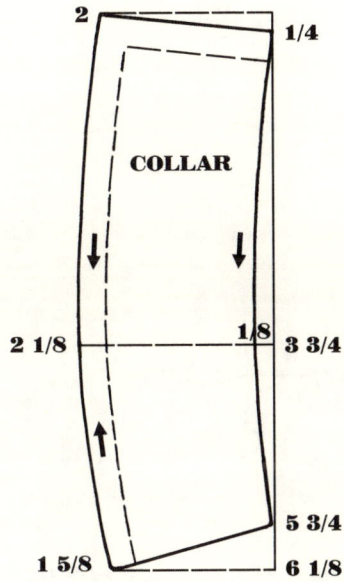

COLLAR

2

1/4

2 1/8

1/8

3 3/4

1 5/8

5 3/4

6 1/8

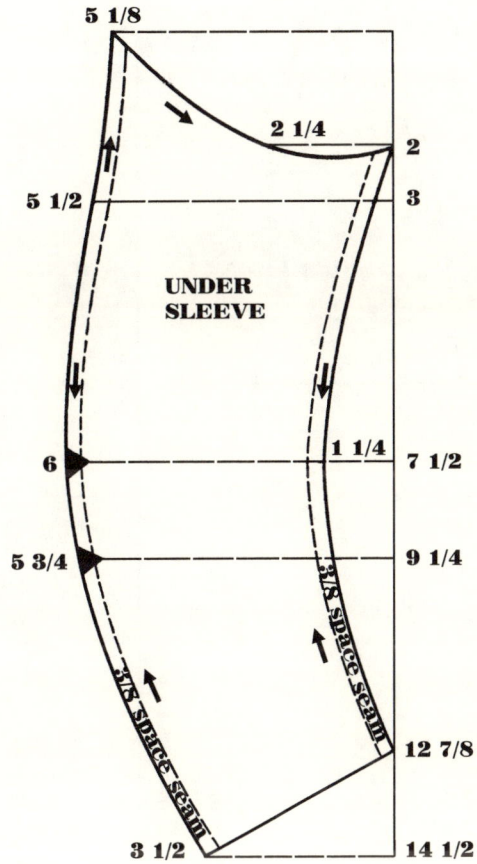

5 1/8

2 1/4

2

5 1/2

3

UNDER
SLEEVE

6

1 1/4

7 1/2

5 3/4

9 1/4

3/8 space seam

12 7/8

3 1/2

14 1/2

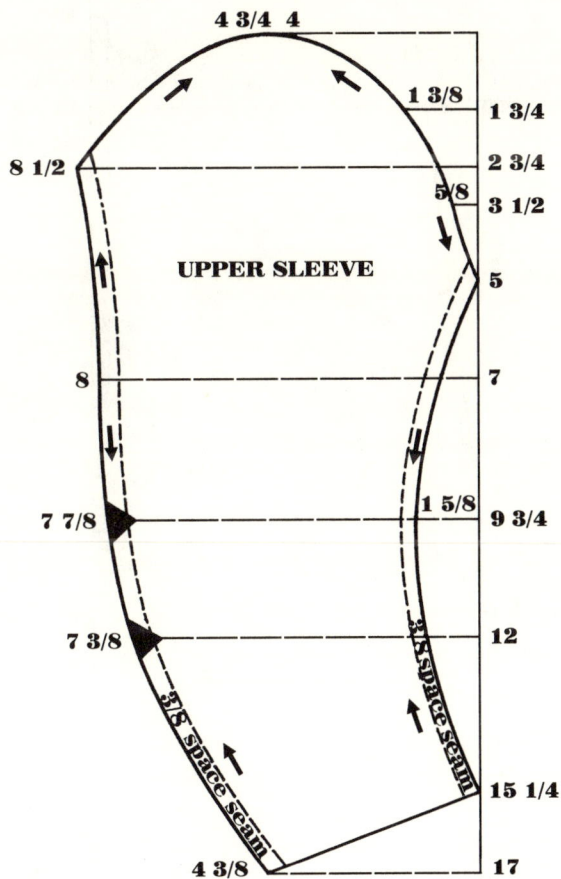

4 3/4 4

1 3/8

1 3/4

8 1/2

2 3/4

5/8

3 1/2

UPPER SLEEVE

5

8

7

7 7/8

1 5/8

9 3/4

7 3/8

12

3/8 space seam

3/8 space seam

15 1/4

4 3/8

17

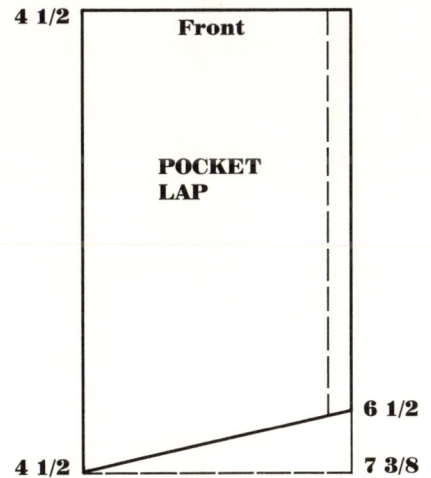

4 1/2

Front

POCKET
LAP

6 1/2

4 1/2

7 3/8

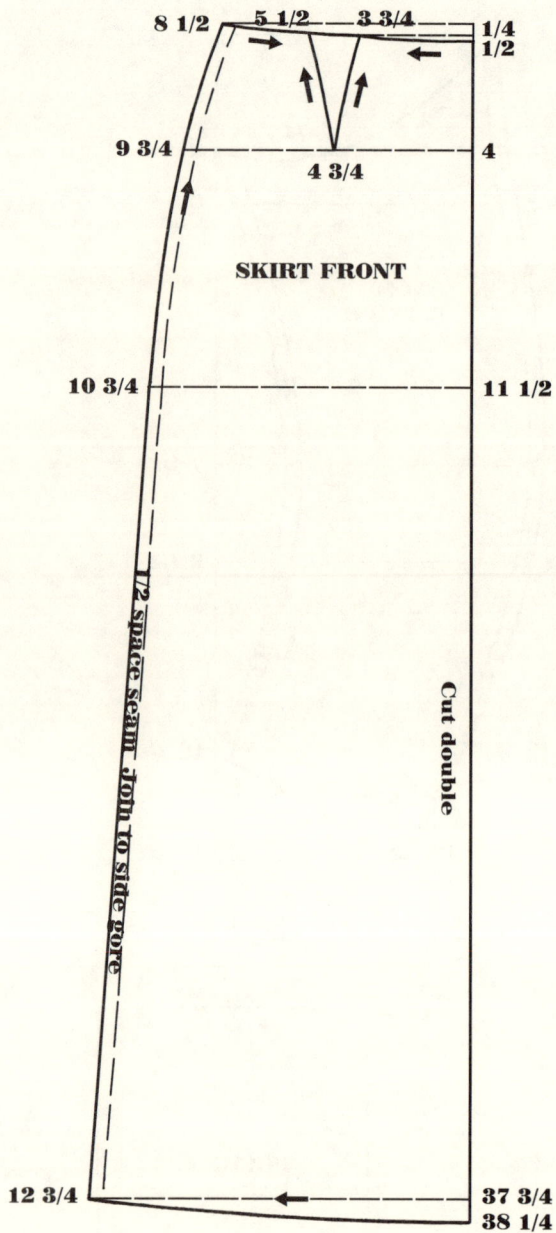

SKIRT FRONT

8 1/2 5 1/2 3 3/4 1/4
1/2

9 3/4 4 3/4 4

10 3/4 11 1/2

1/2 space seam Join to side gore

Cut double

12 3/4 37 3/4
38 1/4

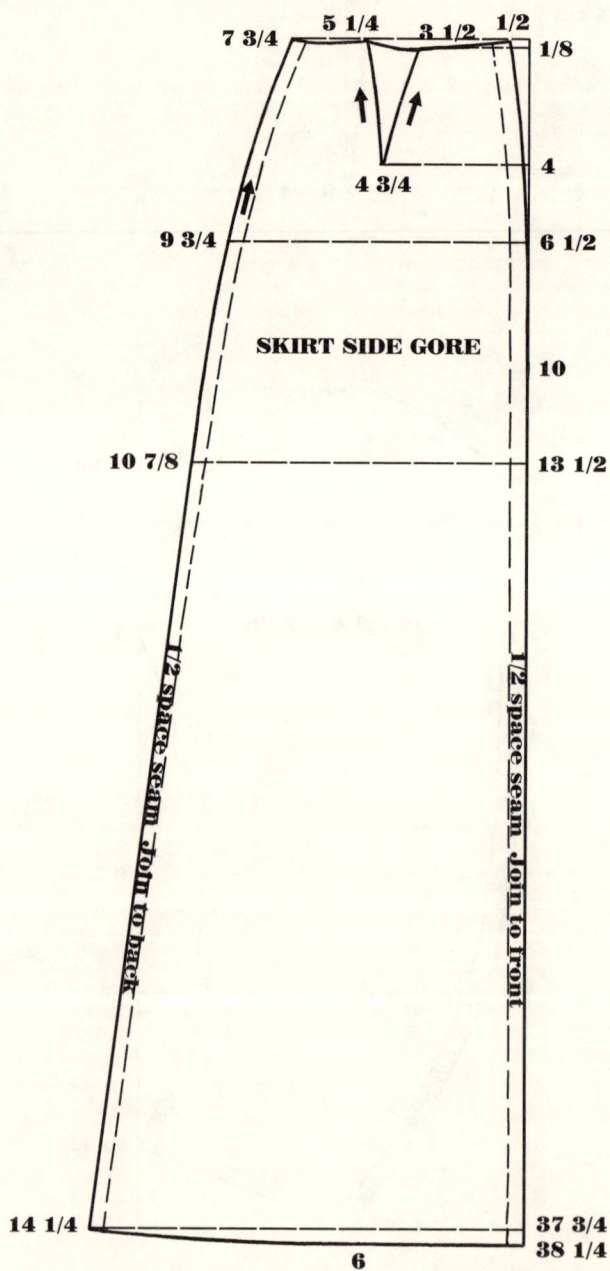

SKIRT SIDE GORE

7 3/4 5 1/4 3 1/2 1/2
1/8

4 3/4 4

9 3/4 6 1/2

10

10 7/8 13 1/2

1/2 space seam Join to back

1/2 space seam Join to front

14 1/4 37 3/4
6 38 1/4

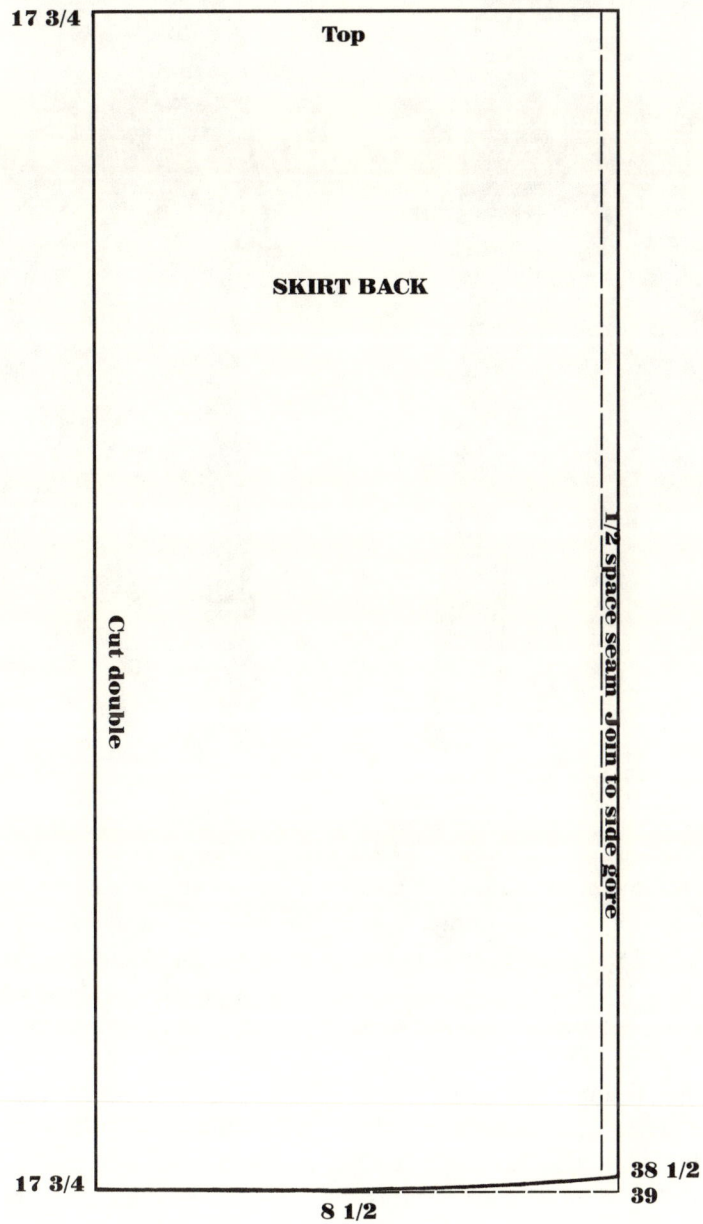

17 3/4

Top

SKIRT BACK

Cut double

1/2 space seam join to side gore

17 3/4

8 1/2

38 1/2

39

Ladies' Coat. In this example plain cloth and moiré are combined. The coat is fitted by single bust darts, side pieces, side backs, and a curved center back seam. The fullness at the three back seams is underfolded to form a double box-plait on each side of the center, on the outside. The coat fronts are closed in a slightly diagonal curve with large fancy buttons. The vest, which is exposed in the narrow V between the fronts, is fitted by single bust darts and is included in the shoulder and under-arm seams. It is closed with concealed fastenings.

To the lower edges of the shorter parts of the coat, extending as far back as the side-back seam on each side, are joined side skirts. These are gathered along the upper edges for some distance in front of the back edges, and fall gracefully over the hips. In the join of each side skirt is included a large pocket lap that describes three points at its lower edge. The back edge of each side skirt is joined to the front edge of the side back. The fullness is pressed underneath in a backward-turning plait, the back end of the pocket lap being hidden under the outer fold of this plait.

The neck is finished with a high standing collar. Below this are two collars that are in rolling style at the back. A moiré lapel is arranged on each side of the collars, and gives the effect of three collars at the front. The sleeves are in coat style, and each is finished at the wrist with a fancy moiré cuff that is pointed on its upper side.

Ladies' Coat

This mode develops effectively in light-weight cloths. The vest may be of velvet of the same or a contrasting color, or it may be of the same material as the coat, with a rich trimming of metallic braid. Passementeries applied on a harmonizing color different from the shade of the coat, often produce the effect of rich brocades and are very showy for vests, particularly those of gold or silver on a very light ground. For a lady of medium size, this coat requires 11 yards of material 22 inches wide, 5 3/4 yards of material 44 inches wide, or 5 3/8 yards of material 54 inches wide. Also required are 1 5/8 yards of moiré 20 inches wide for the pocket laps, etc.

April 1889 *Delineator*

Street Costume

Use the scale corresponding to the bust measure to draft the bodice. It consists of ten pieces: Front, vest front, V front, side piece, back and side back drafted together, rolling collar, standing collar, vest collar, and two sleeve pieces. Lay the plaits in the back according to the notches. Hem the sides and bottom, which should be just even with the foundation skirt at the back. Sew the vest in the under-arm seam and the shoulder seam.

The drapery and skirt are drafted with the scale corresponding to the waist measure. Regulate the length with the tape measure. The drapery consists of two pieces: Front drapery and side panel. Lay the plaits according to the notches. The skirt has three pieces: Front, side gore, and back.

Spring 1890 *Voice of Fashion*

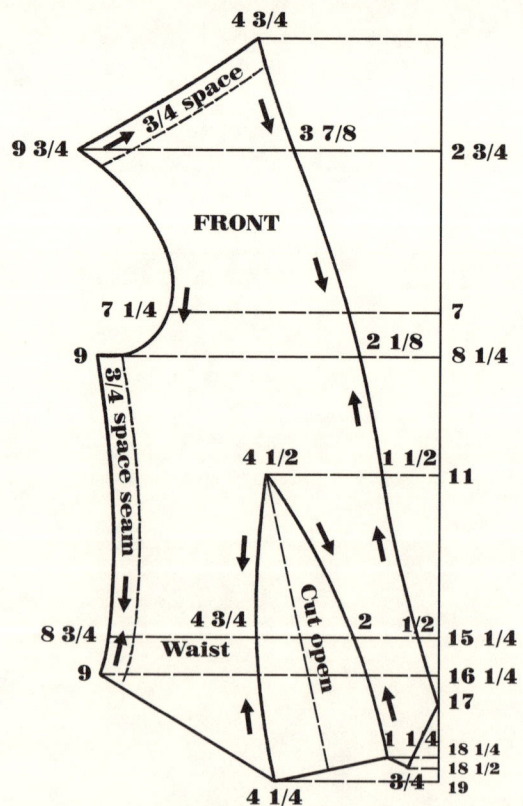

Street Costume

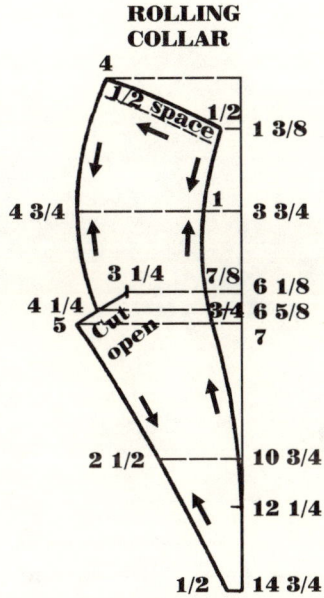

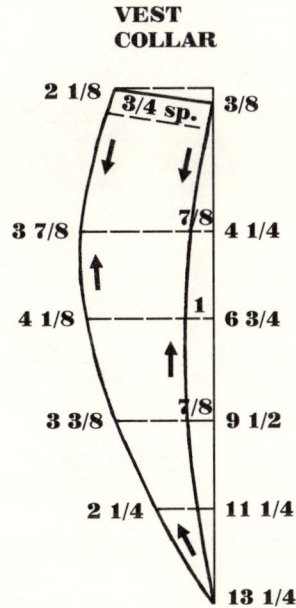

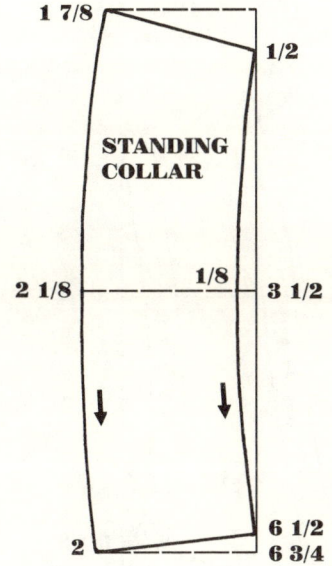

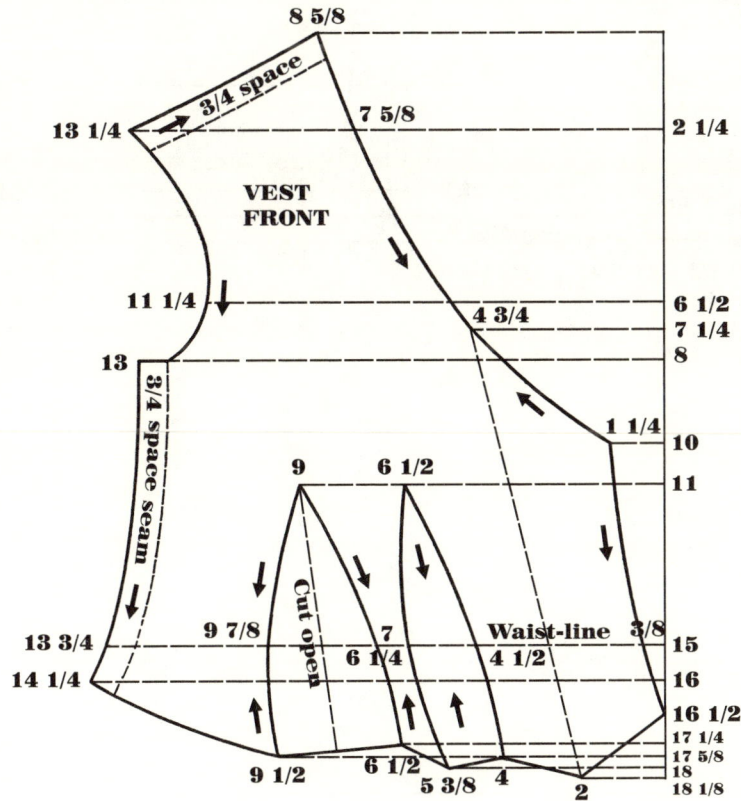

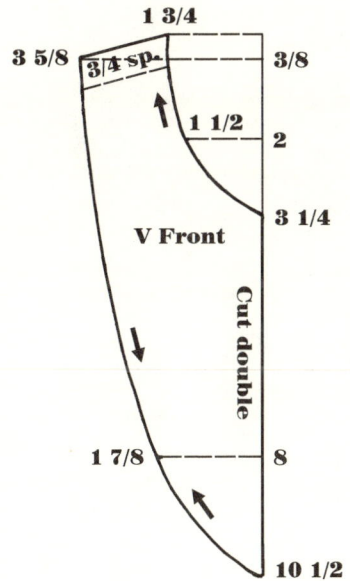

ROLLING COLLAR

4

1/2 space

1/2 — 1 3/8

4 3/4 — 1 — 3 3/4

3 1/4 — 7/8 — 6 1/8

4 1/4 — 3/4 — 6 5/8

5 — Cut open — 7

2 1/2 — 10 3/4

12 1/4

1/2 — 14 3/4

VEST COLLAR

2 1/8 — 3/4 sp. — 3/8

3 7/8 — 7/8 — 4 1/4

4 1/8 — 1 — 6 3/4

3 3/8 — 7/8 — 9 1/2

2 1/4 — 11 1/4

13 1/4

STANDING COLLAR

1 7/8 — 1/2

2 1/8 — 1/8 — 3 1/2

2 — 6 1/2 — 6 3/4

VEST FRONT

8 5/8

3/4 space

13 1/4 — 7 5/8 — 2 1/4

11 1/4 — 4 3/4 — 6 1/2 — 7 1/4 — 8

13 — 3/4 space seam — 1 1/4 — 10

9 — 6 1/2 — 11

Cut open

13 3/4 — 9 7/8 — 7 — Waist-line 3/8 — 15

14 1/4 — 6 1/4 — 4 1/2 — 16

16 1/2

17 1/4

17 5/8

18

9 1/2 — 6 1/2 — 5 3/8 — 4 — 2 — 18 1/8

V Front

1 3/4

3 5/8 — 3/4 sp. — 3/8

1 1/2 — 2

3 1/4

Cut double

1 7/8 — 8

10 1/2

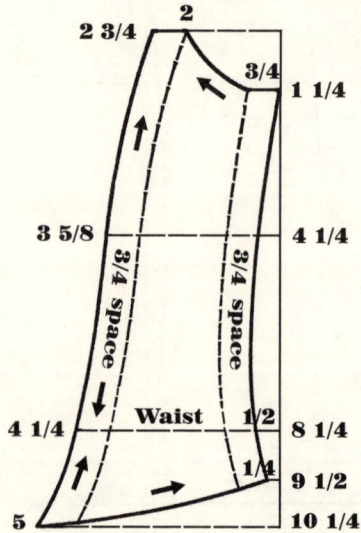

SIDE PIECE

2 3/4 2

3/4 1 1/4

3 5/8 4 1/4

3/4 space   3/4 space

4 1/4   Waist 1/2 8 1/4

1/4 9 1/2

5 10 1/4

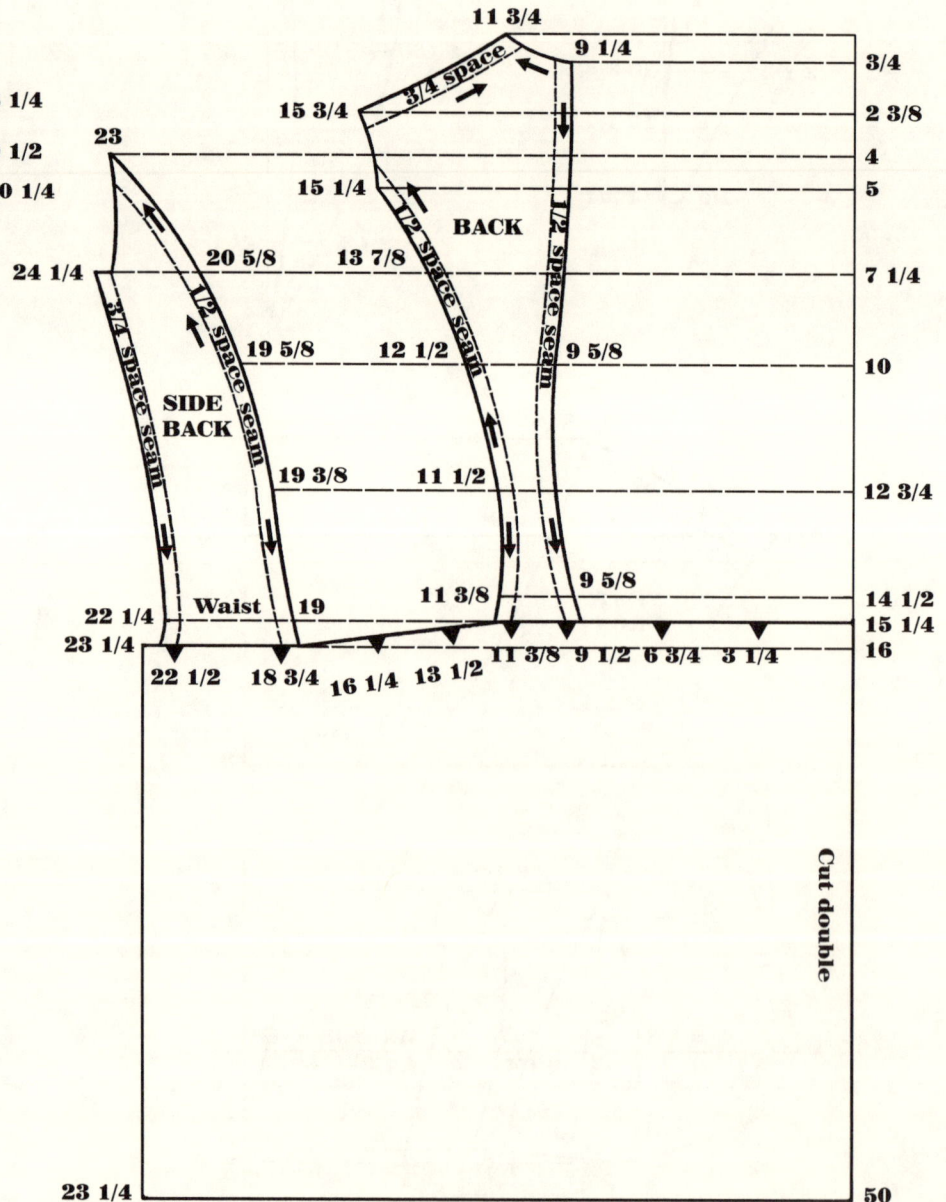

11 3/4

9 1/4   3/4

3/4 space   2 3/8

15 3/4   4

15 1/4   5

23

BACK

24 1/4   20 5/8   13 7/8   7 1/4

1/2 space seam   1/2 space seam

3/4 space seam   1/2 space seam

19 5/8   12 1/2   9 5/8   10

SIDE BACK

19 3/8   11 1/2   12 3/4

22 1/4   Waist 19   11 3/8   9 5/8   14 1/2

23 1/4   15 1/4

22 1/2   18 3/4   16 1/4   13 1/2   11 3/8 9 1/2 6 3/4 3 1/4   16

Cut double

23 1/4   50

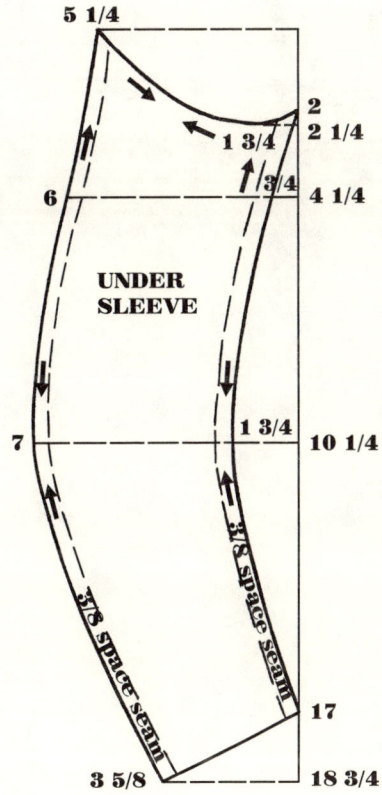

5 1/4

2
2 1/4

1 3/4

3/4

6   4 1/4

UNDER SLEEVE

7   1 3/4   10 1/4

3/8 space seam

17

3 5/8   18 3/4

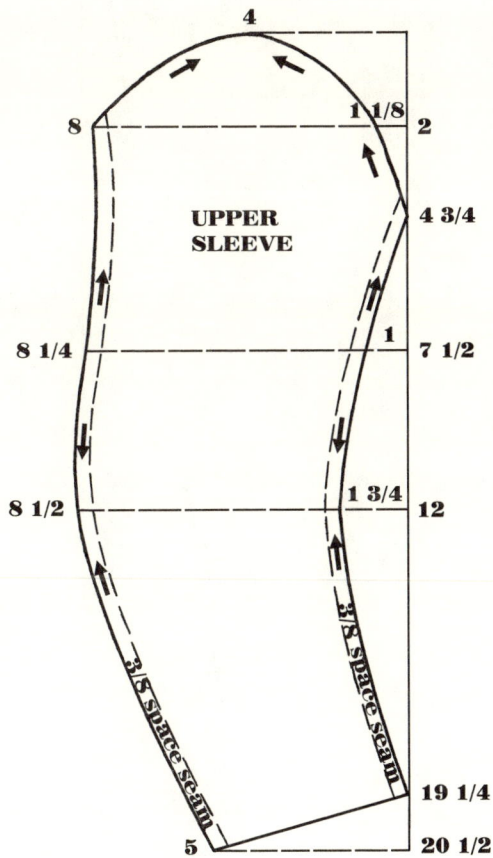

4

8   1 1/8   2

4 3/4

UPPER SLEEVE

8 1/4   1   7 1/2

8 1/2   1 3/4   12

3/8 space seam

19 1/4

5   20 1/2

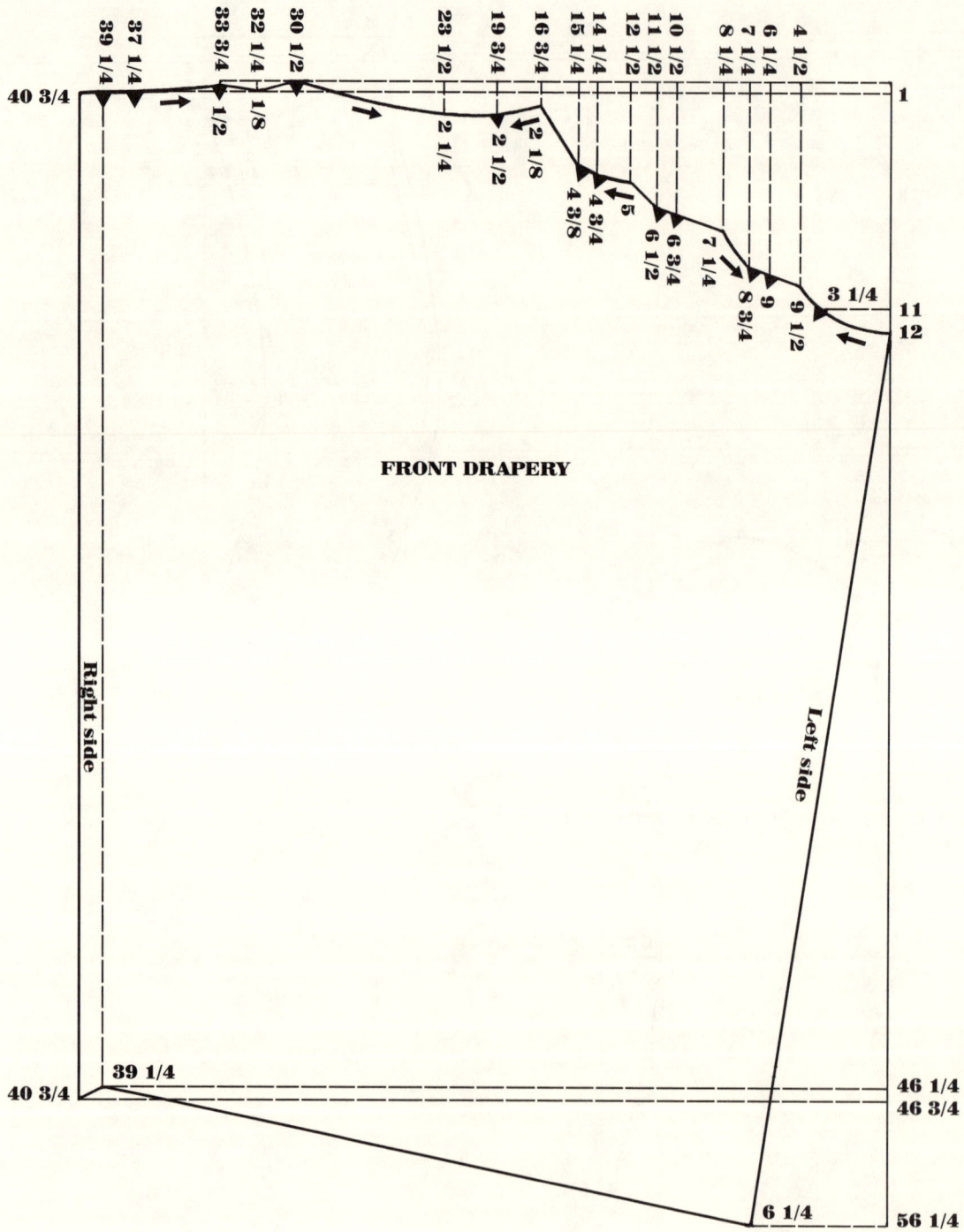

FRONT DRAPERY

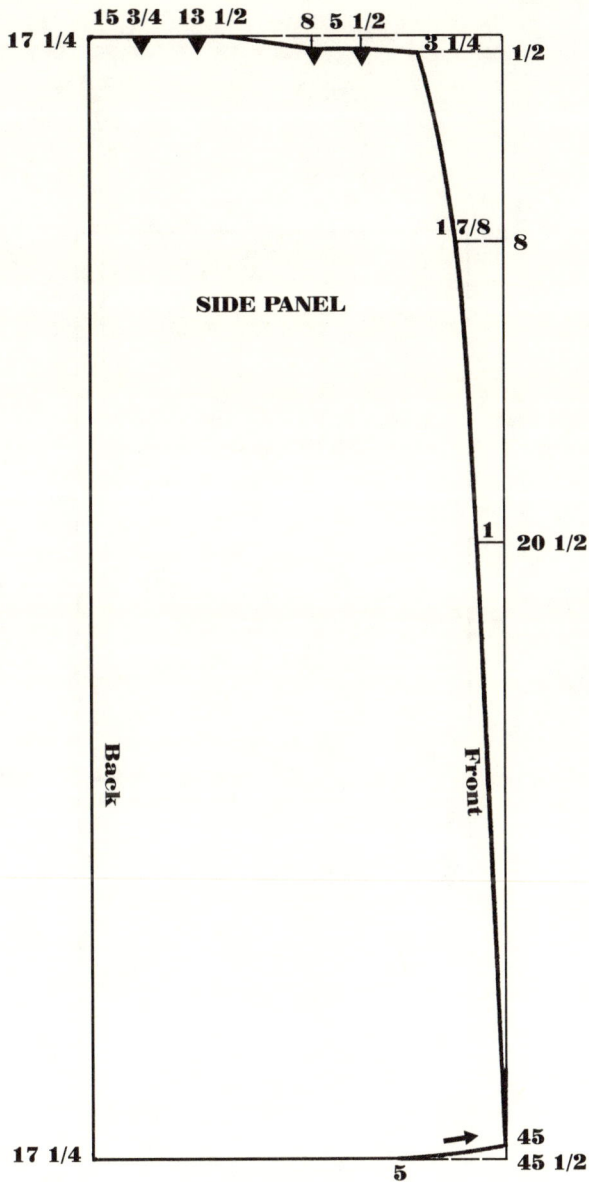

SIDE PANEL

17 1/4   15 3/4   13 1/2   8   5 1/2   3 1/4   1/2

1 7/8   8

1   20 1/2

Back   Front

17 1/4   5   45 / 45 1/2

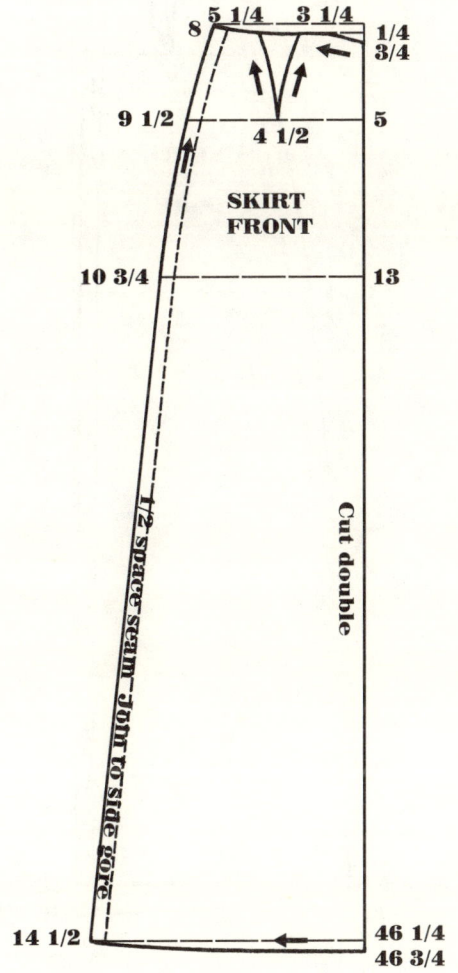

SKIRT FRONT

8   5 1/4   3 1/4   1/4 / 3/4

9 1/2   4 1/2   5

10 3/4   13

1/2 space seam join to side fore

Cut double

14 1/2   46 1/4 / 46 3/4

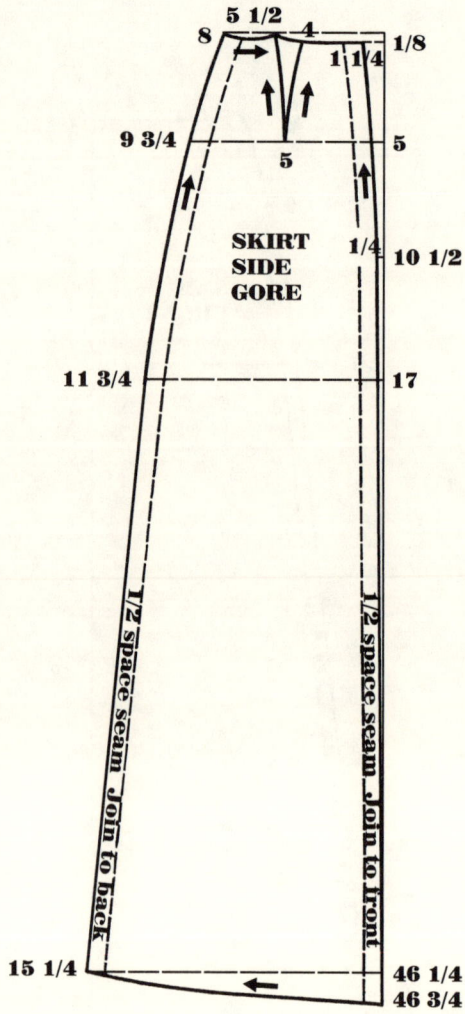

SKIRT
SIDE
GORE

5 1/2
8
4
1/8
1 1/4
5
5
9 3/4
1/4   10 1/2
11 3/4   17

1/2 space seam Join to back
1/2 space seam Join to front

15 1/4   46 1/4
46 3/4

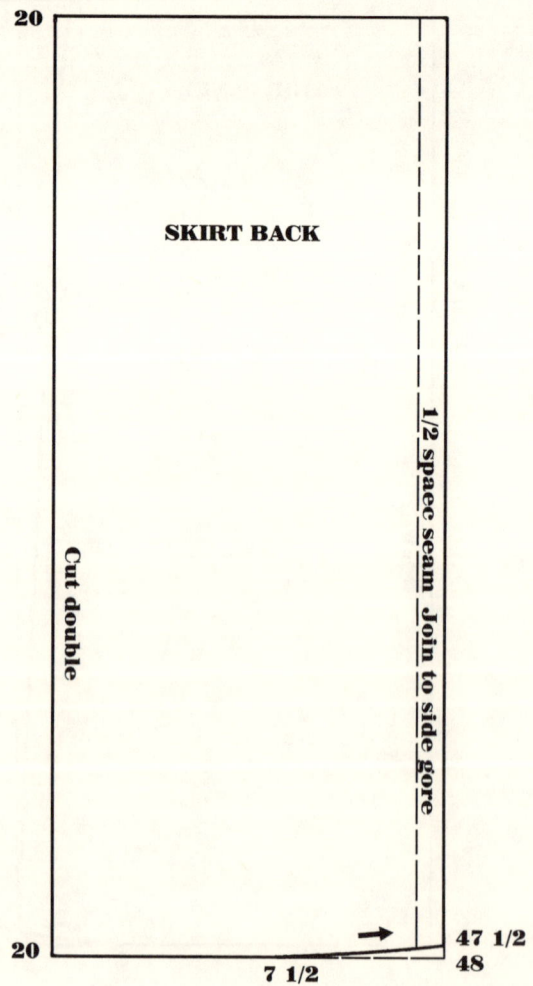

20

SKIRT BACK

Cut double

1/2 space seam Join to side gore

20   47 1/2
7 1/2   48

Ladies' Polonaise

This polonaise is drafted with the scale corresponding to the bust measure. The length is regulated with the tape measure. There are eight pieces: Right front, left front, side piece, side back, back, collar, and two sleeve pieces. The right front is cut diagonal. Lay the plaits according to the notches. Fasten the right front on the left front with hooks and eyes. Lay the plaits in the back and side back according to the notches. Make the polonaise even with the skirt at the bottom.

The skirt is drafted with the scale corresponding to the waist measure. Regulate the length with the tape measure. There are three pieces: Front, side gore, and back.

Spring 1890 *Voice of Fashion*

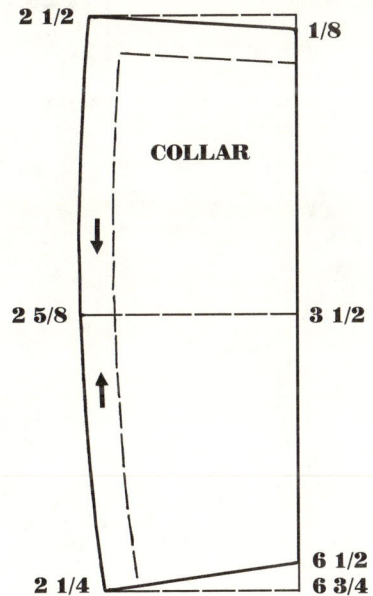

2 1/2   1/8

COLLAR

2 5/8   3 1/2

                                             6 1/2
2 1/4   6 3/4

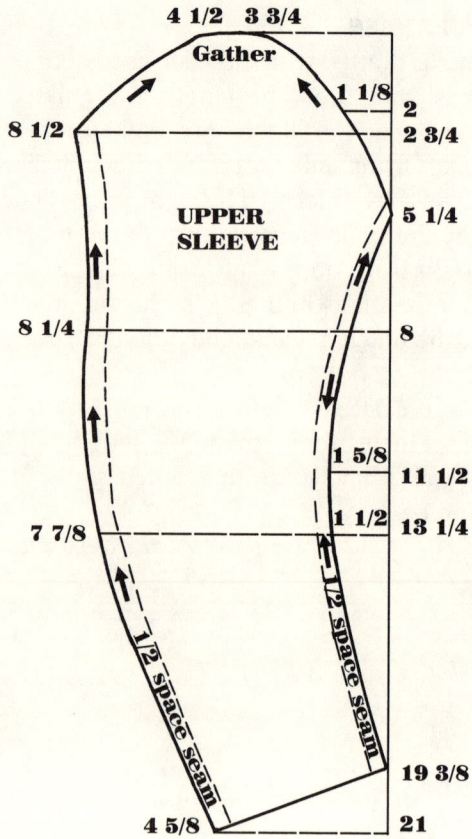

UPPER SLEEVE

4 1/2   3 3/4

Gather

1 1/8   2

8 1/2   2 3/4

5 1/4

8 1/4   8

1 5/8   11 1/2

1 1/2   13 1/4

7 7/8

1/2 space seam

1/2 space seam

19 3/8

4 5/8   21

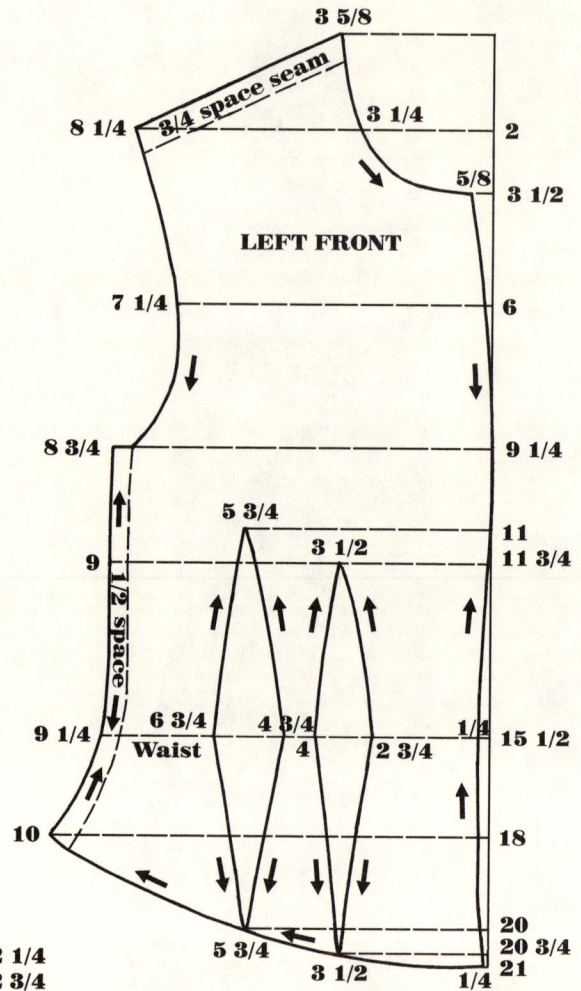

LEFT FRONT

3 5/8

3/4 space seam

8 1/4   3 1/4   2

5/8   3 1/2

7 1/4   6

8 3/4   9 1/4

1/2 space   5 3/4   11

9   3 1/2   11 3/4

9 1/4   6 3/4   4 3/4   1/4   15 1/2

Waist   4   2 3/4

10   18

20

5 3/4   20 3/4

3 1/2   1/4   21

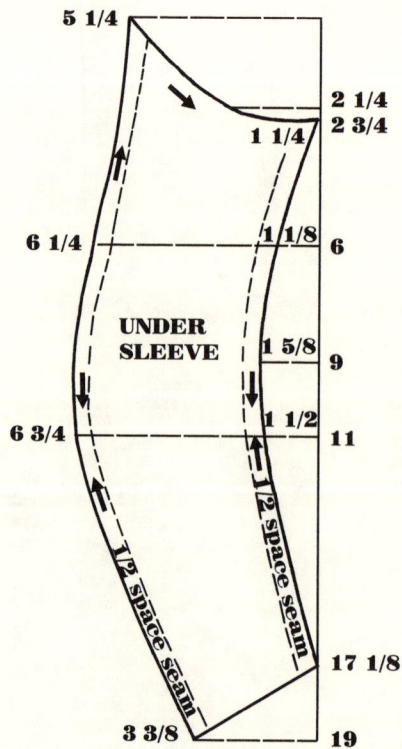

UNDER SLEEVE

5 1/4

2 1/4
1 1/4   2 3/4

6 1/4   1 1/8   6

1 5/8   9

6 3/4   1 1/2   11

1/2 space seam

1/2 space seam

17 1/8

3 3/8   19

11 5/8

16 1/4 3/4 space 11 1/4
9 1/4 5 3/4 2
3 1/2

15 1/8 7 1/4

16 1/2 9 1/4

13 3/4 11 7
16 3/4 11 1/2 11 3/4

14 1/4 12 3/4 8 1/4 15 1/2
17 1/4
17 1/2 Waist 12 10 3/4 16 1/2

19 3/4 18 3/4
1 7/8 19 1/2
20 1/4 9 1/4 8 1/4 20 1/2
13 3/4 11 1/2 1 1/2 20 3/4 21 1/2
21 1/2 22
1 3/4 23
22 1/4 24
23 3/4 /8 24 1/2
/8 25 3/4

RIGHT FRONT

1/2 space seam

27 1/2 3 1/2 57 1/4

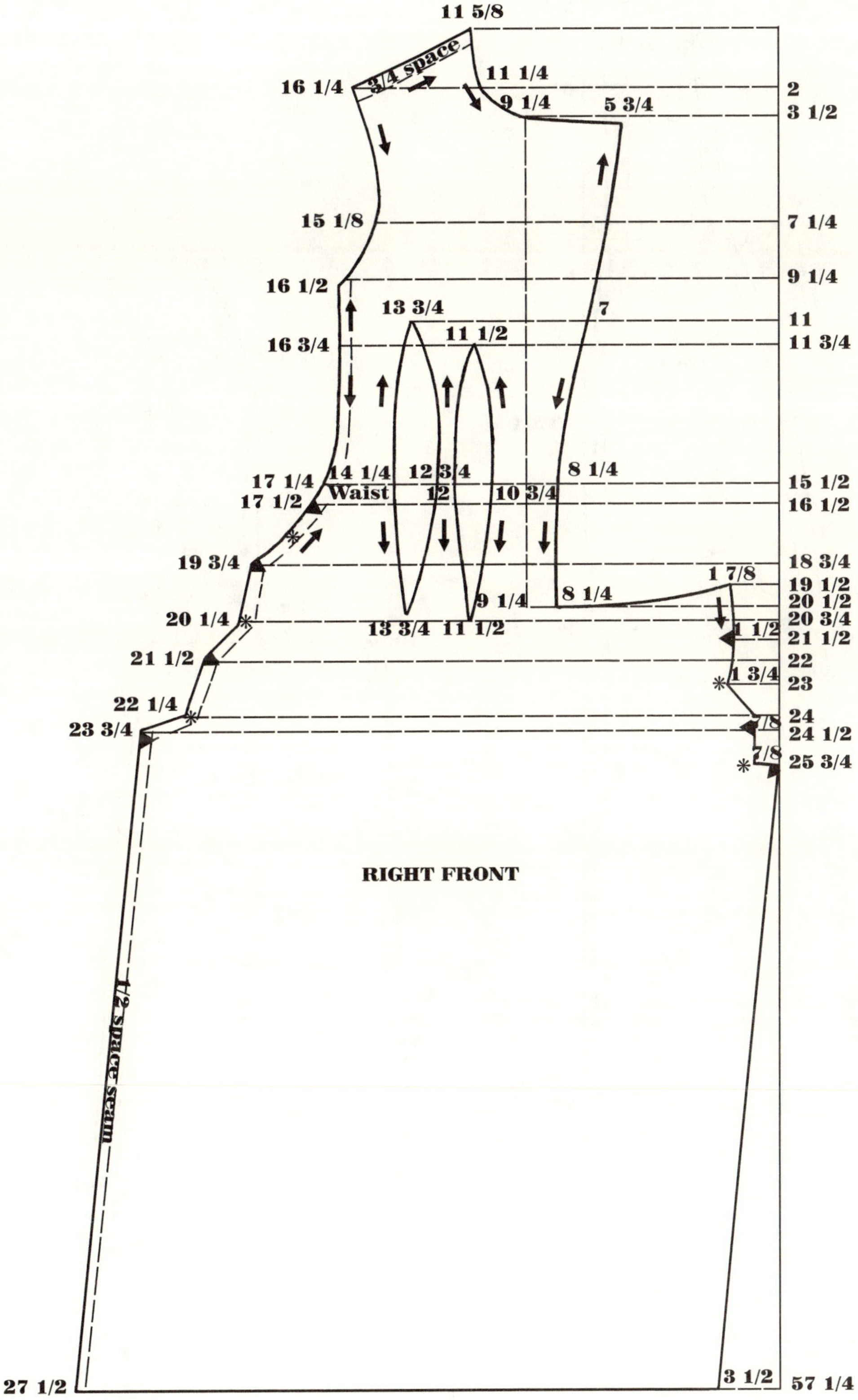

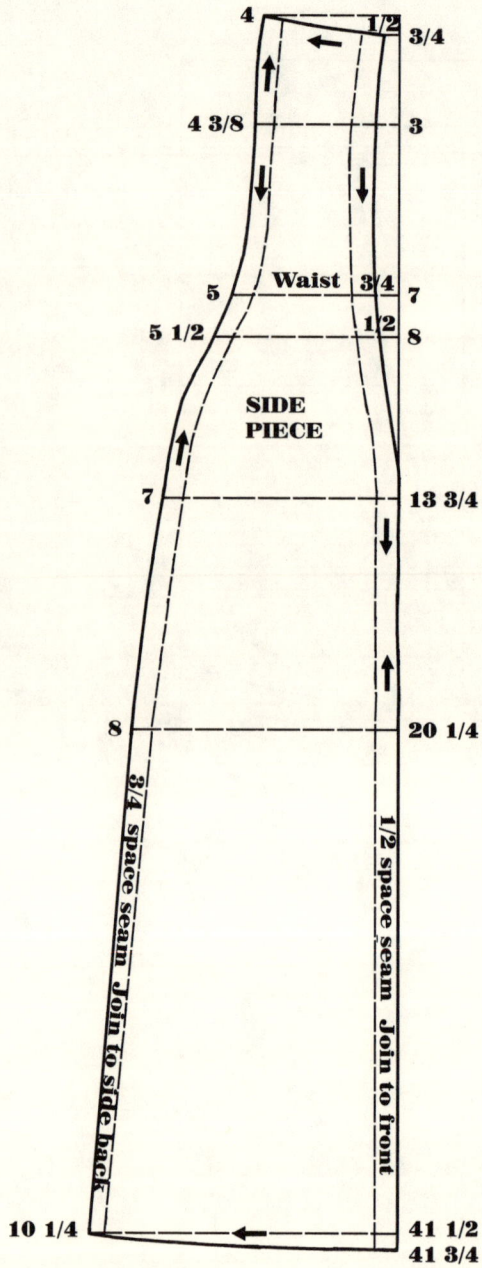

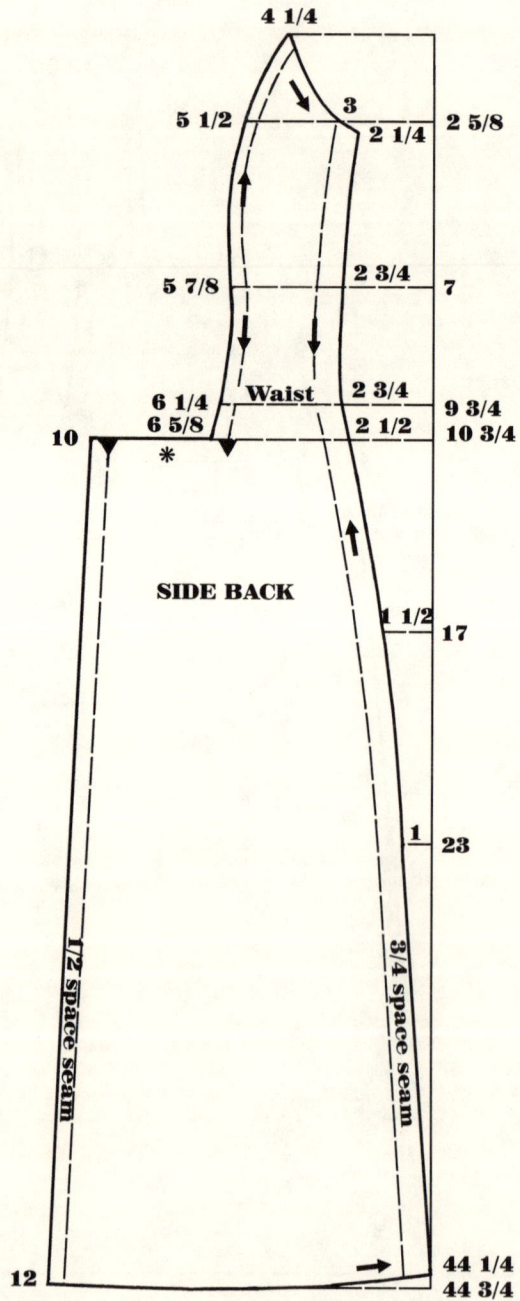

SKIRT FRONT

5 1/4   3 1/4

8

1/4
3/4

9 1/2   4 1/2   5

10 3/4   13

1/2 space seam Join to side fore

Cut double

14 1/2   46 1/4
46 3/4

8 7/8

6 3/8   1/2

12 1/2   3/4 space   2 3/8

1/2 space seam

12 1/4   6

10 1/8   6 7/8   10

9 1/4   12 3/4
9 1/8   13 3/4
7   14 3/4

16 3/4   *   *   *   *

12 1/2   9 3/8   6 3/4   3 1/2

BACK

1/2 space seam

Cut double

16 3/4   49 1/4
50

9

327

SKIRT BACK

Cut double

1/2 spaec seam Join to side gore

20

20

47 1/2
48

7 1/2

5 1/2
8   4   1/8
1 1/4

9 3/4   5   5

SKIRT SIDE GORE

1/4   10 1/2

11 3/4   17

1/2 space seam Join to back

1/2 space seam Join to front

15 1/4

46 1/4
46 3/4

Ladies' Costume. This costume is illustrated made of fancy dress material and velvet, with fancy braid and ornaments for decoration. It may be modified to be worn as an evening, dinner, or reception dress, as well as for general outdoor uses. The four-gored skirt is worn with a long, slender bustle. It is nearly concealed by the polonaise.

The polonaise is fitted by double bust darts, single under-arm darts, side backs, and a curved center back seam. The vertical seams end a trifle below the waist-line. Extra fullness allowed below the center back and side-back seams is underfolded in box-plaits, the loose front edges of the back being hemmed. The left front is cut off at basque depth in front of the first bust dart. Its longer part is slightly draped over the hip by two upward-turning plaits laid in its back edge, back of which it hangs straight to the edge of the skirt with a panel effect. The right front overlaps the left. The fullness of its drapery part is disposed in a festoon of folds at the front by three upward-turning plaits in its back edge, and a group of five upward-turning plaits in its front edge. The front and back edges flare slightly below the plaits from the edges of the adjacent parts. The skirt is revealed between the straight edges of the drapery.

The fronts are cut out in V shape above the bust, the right front crossing the left diagonally. Between the flared edges of the fronts is disclosed a chemisette overlaid with fancy braid. The chemisette is sewed permanently to the left side and fastened invisibly on the right side. The closing below the chemisette is made with buttons and button-holes in a fly. At the neck is a high

standing collar matching the chemisette. A broad, rolling collar is joined to the front edges of the fronts and rolled high at the back, where it is seamed. It tapers narrowly toward the ends, ending beneath a fancy ornament.

The coat-shaped foundation sleeves are of lining. Over them is arranged a full upper part, which is gathered at the outside and inside seams and also at the top, to produce a mousquetaire effect. The wrist is trimmed with a cuff-facing of velvet surmounted by fancy braid.

This mode invites combinations both in colors and materials. The chemisette, standing collar, and visible parts of the skirt are usually alike and in contrast with the rest of the costume. Velvet with fur trimming is handsome. Plain or brocaded silks and satins, matelassé, fine cloths, coarse serges, etc., may be used. Fancy braid, passementerie, Irish point, Genoese point, Renaissance lace, embroidery, fringe, fancy ornaments, velvet bands or Vandyke borders, etc., may supply the decorations. The chemisette may be richly decorated with gold or silver braid. To make the costume for a lady of medium size, requires 15 7/8 yards of material 22 inches wide, or 8 1/2 yards of material 44 inches wide. Each requires 1 1/4 yards of velvet 20 inches wide for the rolling collar, etc.

November 1889 *Delineator*

7. Dresses

Empire dresses are made with a belted waist and full undraped skirt of chantilly net figured in flowers or stripes, over black silk taffeta. The trimmings are black moiré ribbons around the skirt and as a wide sash, also a plastron, and perhaps a side band of net strewn with pendant beads like bugles. The bodice lining of taffeta is made like that of a basque. The foundation skirt is gored in the usual way, with a trifle more fullness at the back. It is finished at the bottom with a narrow knife-plaiting, and an inside balayeuse of one or two pinked ruffles of the silk gathered very full. The small, sloped tournure is formed by two steels (the shortest two in the usual set of three steels) placed quite low, and not tied too closely.

The net bodice is gathered on the shoulders in front and back. This fullness is sewed into the shoulder seams of the silk lining. The fronts of the net are then drawn down straight to the waistline, shirred there, and carried on down to turn under the ends of the lining. However, all the part below the waist-line is thrust out of sight under the skirt belt, which in its turn is covered by a sash. In the pointed space left open at the throat a plastron is set, made of the net placed smoothly over silk, and dotted with pendant beads. This V-shaped plastron is sewed in under the right side of the bodice, and hooks under the left side. It is finished around the neck with a high collar band of the moiré ribbon 2 inches wide. This band is folded once along the center to make it slightly narrower, and hooked on the left side, with or without a bow.

At the back, the net is gathered in the shoulder seams to make a single wide back piece. It is again gathered at the waist-line. A plain side back is on each side of this, joining to the side pieces, both side back and side piece being of the lace placed smoothly over the silk lining.

The sleeves have a close silk lining. The net is set on this lining in leg-of-mutton shape pushed up in folds—not round puffs—above the elbow. Ribbon is tied around just below the elbow and again at the wrist, with a bow on the inside seam.

The sash of moiré ribbon 5 or 6 inches wide is sewed into the left under-arm seam for nearly its full width. It is drawn across the front to the right side and around the back, encircling the whole waist. Then, crossing the front a second time, it is hooked on the right side, tied in a small bow, and descends in two ends nearly to the bottom of the skirt.

The net skirt is full and straight. It is gathered to a belt at the top (which is hidden under the sash), and is hemmed around the bottom. It is trimmed with many tucks and bands of narrow moiré ribbon, or three graduated bands of ribbon suffice. This skirt sometimes opens up on the left side (having the ribbon and tucks continued there in rows up to the waist) to show a band of beaded net set down the foundation skirt. Or the net is shirred and puffed across, or in frills crossed with moiré ribbon, or else there may be four or five lengthwise plaits, with two long bands of ribbon falling to the bottom and ending in a chou.

May 5, 1888 *Harper's Bazar*

White muslin dresses are made up in very simple fashions, or they are so elaborate with embroidery that they are suitable for very dressy occasions. For simple dresses, for either morning or afternoon, soft English nainsook without dressing is chosen, with a little embroidery or lace for the neck and sleeves. The belted bodice may be gathered on the shoulders and crossed in front in surplice fashion, leaving the neck open in V shape. The V neck is trimmed with Swiss embroidered edging, or with gathered Oriental or Valenciennes lace, which may be turned back from the front, or its scalloped edges made to meet, as best suits the wearer. The

sleeves are plain to the elbows, with a ruffle of lace or embroidery falling toward the wrists.

The skirt is five straight breadths, with shirring across the front and side breadths just below the belt. The back breadths are gathered only once and in a very small space, hanging plain to the bottom. This full round house-maid skirt is worn over handsomely tucked or embroidered petticoats under which a very small bustle is placed. A ribbon belt and rhine-stone buckle may complete this dress. Or else a wide sash of white or colored moiré ribbon is worn, with loops and ends hanging low at the back.

Still simpler white dresses are made of French nainsook, or of cross-barred muslin. The belted bodice is high at the throat and full there, also on the shoulders, and then drawn into yoke shape, back and front, by two cords run in the material. The sleeves are full, with deep cuffs or narrower wristbands of embroidery. There is a rolling collar of embroidery to match.

Very sheer mull dresses made in this way—with cords outlining the yoke—have also cords holding the full sleeves in puffs at the top, and two sets of cords holding the fullness below the belt in the front and side breadths. A rolling collar of wide lace, and deep lace cuffs, trim this sheer bodice.

Tucked bodices of nainsook have the fronts tucked in a pointed yoke shape from armhole to armhole. Or else the tucks are only just below the neck in front and back, and the shoulders are plain or gathered. Many of these tucked bodices extend below the belt a short distance, and are simply hemmed on the edges.

July 28, 1888 *Harper's Bazar*

House dresses for afternoon wear, family parties, Thanksgiving dinners, etc., are made just long enough to touch the floor, or they rest for 3 or 4 inches on the floor. Demi-trains that drag 10 inches on the floor are seen on many very elaborate dresses, while full trains are reserved for the most ceremonious occasions. The design of such dresses is a flat skirt with a long plain effect, and a full elaborate front on the bodice, which gives character to the whole. Thus the full lapped front widely belted suggests the Empire dress, while the wide plain vest with broad lapels is the feature of the Directoire costume. A round bodice and separate skirt may represent a redingote, the join in front being concealed by a sash of soft bengaline or of China crêpe, which crosses the fronts only. The back breadths of the skirt are hooked onto the bodice, giving the effect of princess breadths. Ten yards of brocade are required, with 1 1/2 yards of lady's cloth.

To make these dresses appear to be in one piece from the neck to the bottom, the round bodice is cut long enough to extend over the hips. The ends are thrust under the dress skirt. The back breadths of the skirt are hooked onto the bodice, and a very small pad is sewed to the end of the round bodice, instead of being placed inside the skirt.

The round bodice is of brocaded silk, quite plain at the back, with the fronts turned back in short lapels, and with a high collar of the brocade. A wide space on the front of the lining is covered with a vest of light faced cloth laid in folds, which may be either straight across or diagonal. It is crossed at the waist-line by a wide sash of ribbon, silk, or China crêpe. The cloth vest is in one piece, and is hooked under the lapel on the left side.

The sleeves may be plain coat sleeves full at the top. Or they may have their fullness pushed up in cross-folds around the armhole, or else in a high, soft puff, with tucks from this puff down to the elbows. The light cloth forms pointed cuffs, or short inner sleeves seen only at the wrists.

The skirt is made over a silk foundation skirt. It has three straight breadths of brocade at the back, hanging entirely plain from the waist, yet very full. A flat breadth is on each side, with its front edges loose and widely faced with silk or satin. The front is covered with light cloth put on in folds like those of the vest, or in flat lengthwise plaits. Or the center may be finished with a frill and hang as a jabot, its edges being pinked, or faced with velvet or moiré ribbon.

December 1, 1888 *Harper's Bazar*

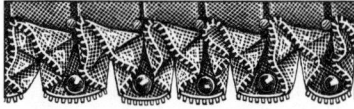

Dresses

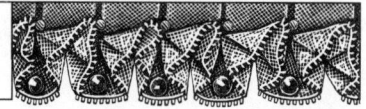

Simple dresses, with gathered bodices, full sleeves, and straight skirts, grow in favor. Anything like fussy or elaborate drapery on the skirt destroys the style of the dress. Many net or lace skirts hang perfectly straight all around. A new fancy is a foot trimming of a small lace ruffle sewed to the edge—not on it—of the net skirt. Wool skirts, and those of wash materials, are quite plain at the bottom, or have a flat border trimming.

The front of the bodice is the place for drapery or elaborate trimming if the wearer prefers it. Unless the material is thick, the bodice is usually full on the shoulders and shirred at the waist-line, or lapped diagonally and edged with a Directoire ruffle. The very long waist can be given a shorter appearance by the wide sashes and broad lapped fronts. For full figures, smooth tailor bodices are preferred. Even lace bodices can be made quite plain, and apparently lengthened by being composed of lengthwise bands of insertion alternating with ribbon stripes. Or else the lace bodice has long bretelles of ribbons passing over the shoulders and tapering to a point at the waist-line in front and back. Full sleeves, especially leg-of-mutton sleeves, with wrinkles or folds extending around the arm, are made very long, covering the wrists entirely.

The yokes so fashionable for thin wool and for cotton dresses are very shallow, not reaching quite to the armholes on the shoulders. They are round in front and back instead of being pointed. They are sometimes decorated with an embroidered collar in deep Vandyke points that nearly cover the yoke. The fullness below the yoke is attached by an erect ruffle of the material, doubled, and standing about 1 inch high above the edge of the yoke. Another fashion is to trim the neck, the edge of the yoke, and the wrists with the material drawn in a small puff with a narrow doubled ruffle on each side of it. The skirt front then has a Spanish flounce, trimmed at the top with a wider puff edged on each side with a ruffle. This is pretty for lawn, cambric, mull, and challis dresses.

Dresses of India silks, China silks, or wash silks have the back and front gores *en princesse,* all in one piece from head to foot. They are shirred at the waist-line, instead of being gored there to fit the figure. The side gores are separate from the bodice and are shirred on the hips, the join to the bodice being hidden by large gathered and square-cornered pockets. These shirred princess dresses are also made of thin wash materials, such as white mull trimmed with Valenciennes insertions, and of lawns with jardinière designs on white or light-colored grounds.

July 6, 1889 *Harper's Bazar*

House Dress

This is a plain but becoming costume for morning wear. The basque is drafted with the scale corresponding to the bust measure. It is in six pieces: Front, side piece, side back, back, and two sleeve pieces.

A quarter of the skirt is given; regulate the length and width with the tape measure. Any style of trimming may be put on the bottom. The top of the skirt may be gathered and sewed to the bodice. Or it may be turned down and shirred, leaving a portion, say 1 inch, for a heading.

Fall 1888 *Voice of Fashion*

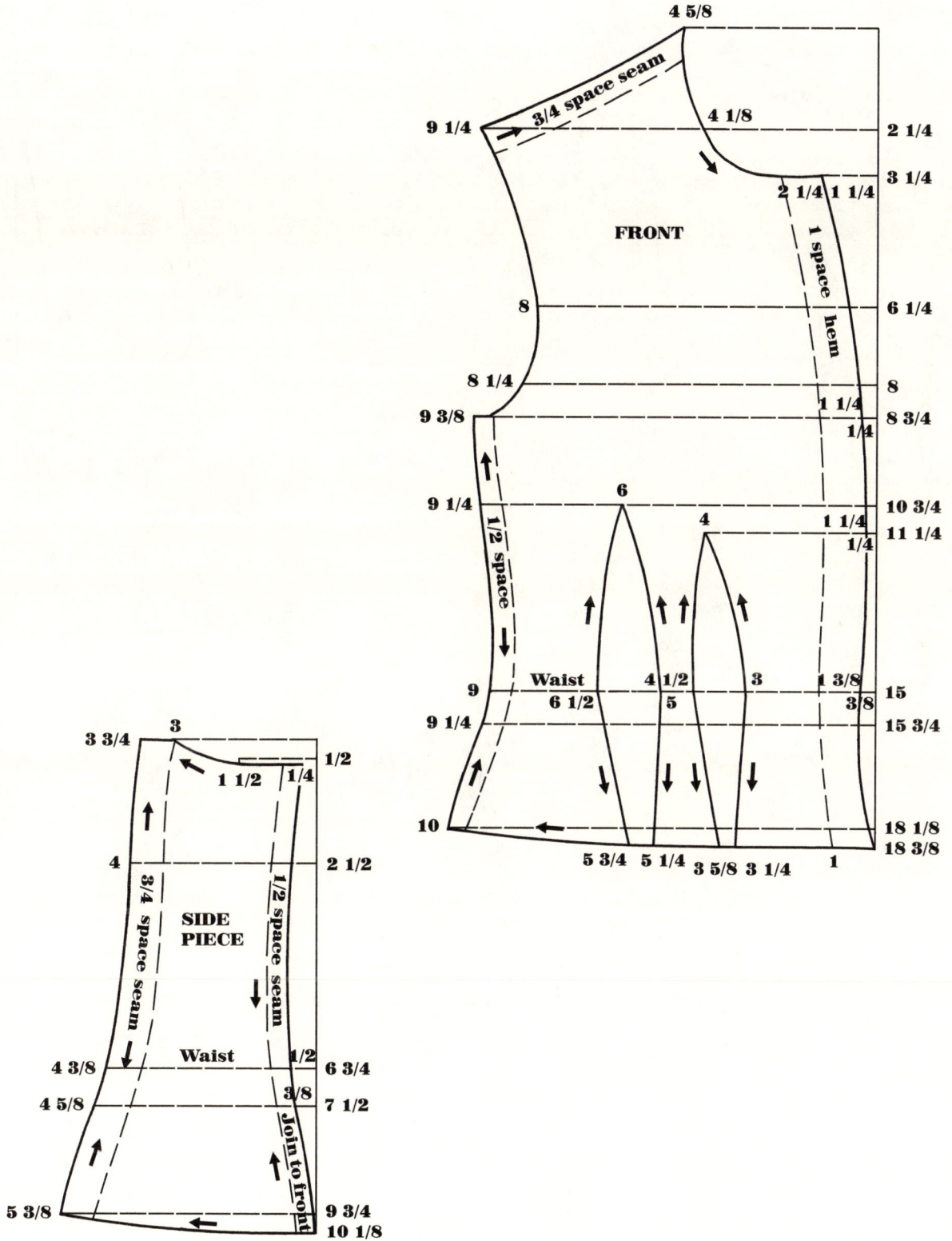

Dresses

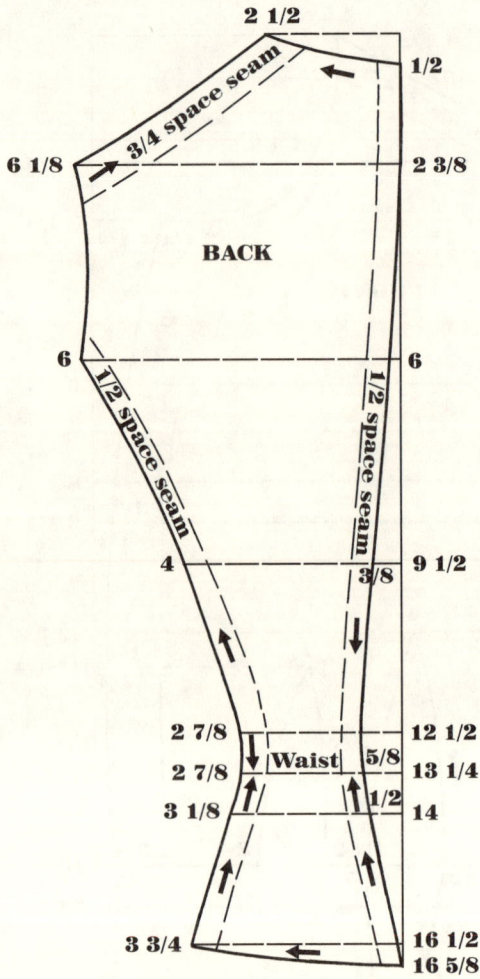

2 1/2
1/2
6 1/8
3/4 space seam
2 3/8
BACK
6
6
1/2 space seam
1/2 space seam
4
9 1/2
3/8
2 7/8
12 1/2
Waist
5/8
13 1/4
2 7/8
3 1/8
1/2
14
3 3/4
16 1/2
16 5/8

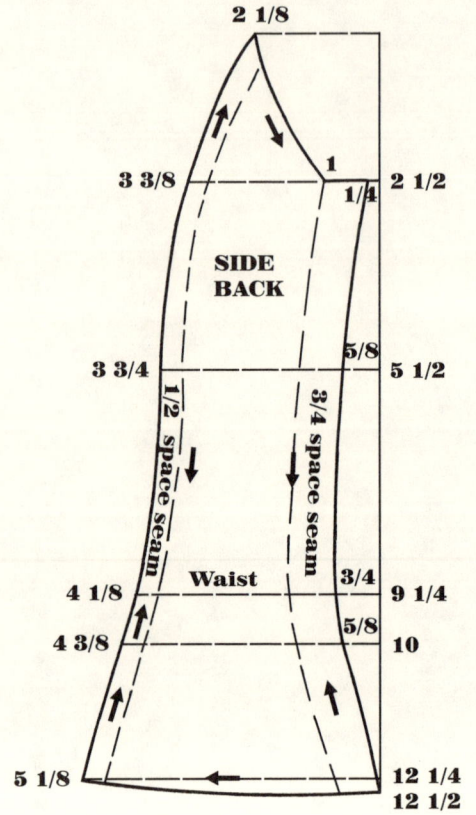

2 1/8
3 3/8
1
2 1/2
1/4
SIDE BACK
3 3/4
5/8
5 1/2
1/2 space seam
3/4 space seam
Waist
4 1/8
3/4
9 1/4
4 3/8
5/8
10
5 1/8
12 1/4
12 1/2

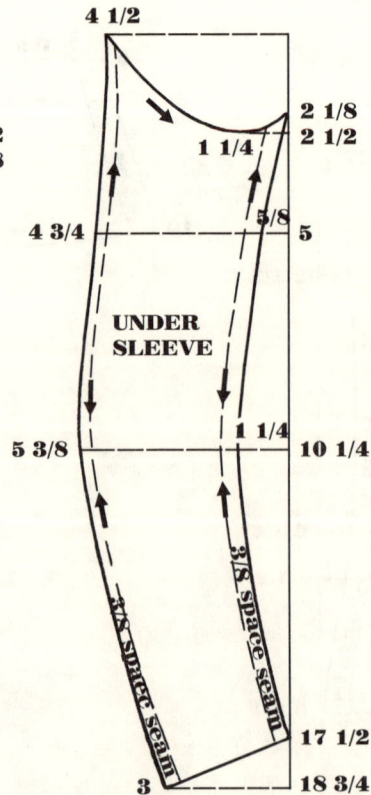

4 1/2
2 1/8
2 1/2
1 1/4
4 3/4
5/8
5
UNDER SLEEVE
5 3/8
1 1/4
10 1/4
3/8 space seam
3/8 space seam
17 1/2
3
18 3/4

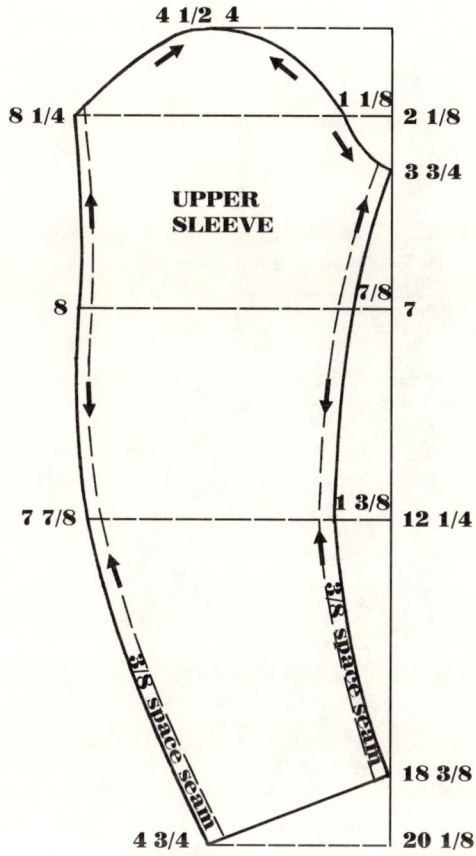

UPPER
SLEEVE

4 1/2 4

8 1/4

1 1/8   2 1/8

3 3/4

8

7/8   7

7 7/8

1 3/8   12 1/4

3/8 space seam

3/8 space seam

18 3/8

4 3/4

20 1/8

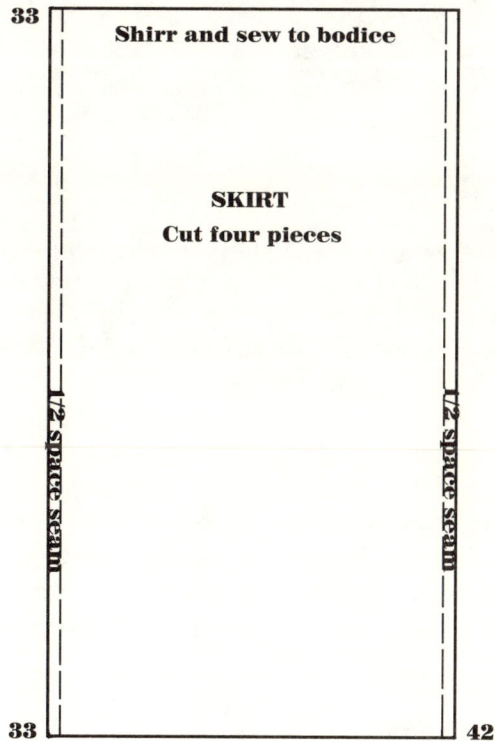

33

Shirr and sew to bodice

SKIRT
Cut four pieces

1/2 space seam

1/2 space seam

33

42

337

House Dress. This style is equally admired for wear in the house or under a long top garment. Light-weight cloth suiting was chosen for this example, with an elaborate decoration of braiding. The bodice is a short, round basque. It is closely fitted by double bust darts, side pieces, side backs, and a curved center back seam. The fronts are closed with button-holes and buttons. Down each side of the closing is a plastron decoration of soutache in a simple design that narrows toward the bottom. The braiding is continued over the shoulders and down each side of the center back seam, where it duplicates the effect on the front.

The full skirt is joined to the edge of the bodice. It is shirred to a pretty depth all around the top, but most of the fullness is arranged at the back, where it falls over a moderate bustle. The placket opening is made a short distance back of the darts on the left front. From it to the closing, the top of the skirt is left loose from the bodice and finished with a facing, hooks and eyes fastening the skirt in place. A deep decoration of braiding is visible all about the bottom of the skirt, and is deepened in inverted V shape nearly to the shirrings at the center of the front.

The upper side of the coat sleeves shows a deep decoration of braiding in pointed cuff style. The high standing collar is braided all over to correspond to the rest of the garment. This dress suggests the addition of a Directoire sash; and also of wide ribbons set into the under-arm seams and carried in wrinkles to the edge of the closing, where they are tied in a bow with long loops and ends.

Full, Round Walking Skirt

Cream, crimson, old rose, electric blue, and serpent are favored colors for house dresses. They are shown in albatross, nun's veiling, camel's hair veiling, foulé, cashmere, etc. Figured surahs and wools also make up well in this style. Braids, galloons, ribbons, passementeries, embroidered bands, coarse lace, velvet, and fancy stitching are suitable trimmings. Bordered materials are charming, the border being used at the bottom of the skirt, and in bands or in vest shape on the fronts and sleeve cuffs. For a lady of medium size, this dress requires 9 1/8 yards of material 22 inches wide, 5 1/4 yards of material 36 inches wide, or 4 3/8 yards of material 44 inches wide.

September 1888 *Delineator*

Full, Round Walking Skirt. This full, round walking skirt is made up in all kinds of soft materials and is worn with all kinds of round bodices, short basques, and fancy bodices. It is shown developed in plain dress material. The requisite width is obtained by joining together straight breadths. Care should be taken that no join comes at the center of the front or back. The lower edge is turned under for a hem. The top is gathered, or as the process is more properly called, gauged twice, about 1 inch being allowed between the two lines, and sewed to a belt. The fullness is distributed so that, while enough is left in front to produce an easy, graceful effect, the greater part of it is kept back of the hips. A placket opening is finished at the back.

Trimming is rarely added, except for a band of contrasting material, or a few bands of braid, velvet, or any simple flat decoration at the lower edge. Drapery is never added. A sash, softly wrinkled about the waist and tied at the back or the left side of the front, is not inappropriate. To make the skirt for a lady of medium size, requires 10 3/8 yards of material 22 inches wide, 6 7/8 yards of material 36 inches wide, or 4 5/8 yards of material either 48 or 54 inches wide.

December 1884 *Delineator*

339

House Dress

The basque is drafted with the scale corresponding to the bust measure. There are seven pieces: Front, side piece, rounded side back, narrow back, two sleeve pieces, and collar. Before sewing the front darts, cut them open in the center and baste on the lines given. If desired, the front may be trimmed with embroidery or braid to correspond to the drapery.

The skirt and drapery are drafted with the scale corresponding to the waist measure. The length is regulated with the tape measure. The skirt is in three pieces: Front, side gore, and back. The drapery is in two pieces: Front and back. Lay the plaits according to the notches.

Winter 1888–1889 *Voice of Fashion*

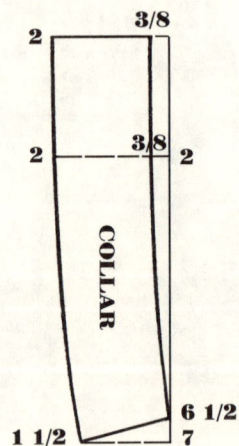

COLLAR

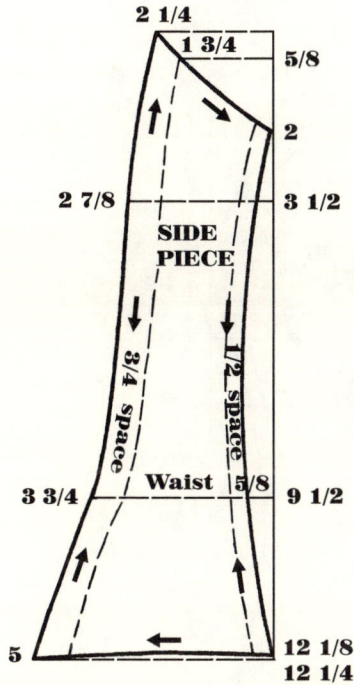

SIDE PIECE

2 1/4
1 3/4   5/8
2
2 7/8   3 1/2
3 3/4   Waist 5/8   9 1/2
3/4 space
1/2 space
5
12 1/8
12 1/4

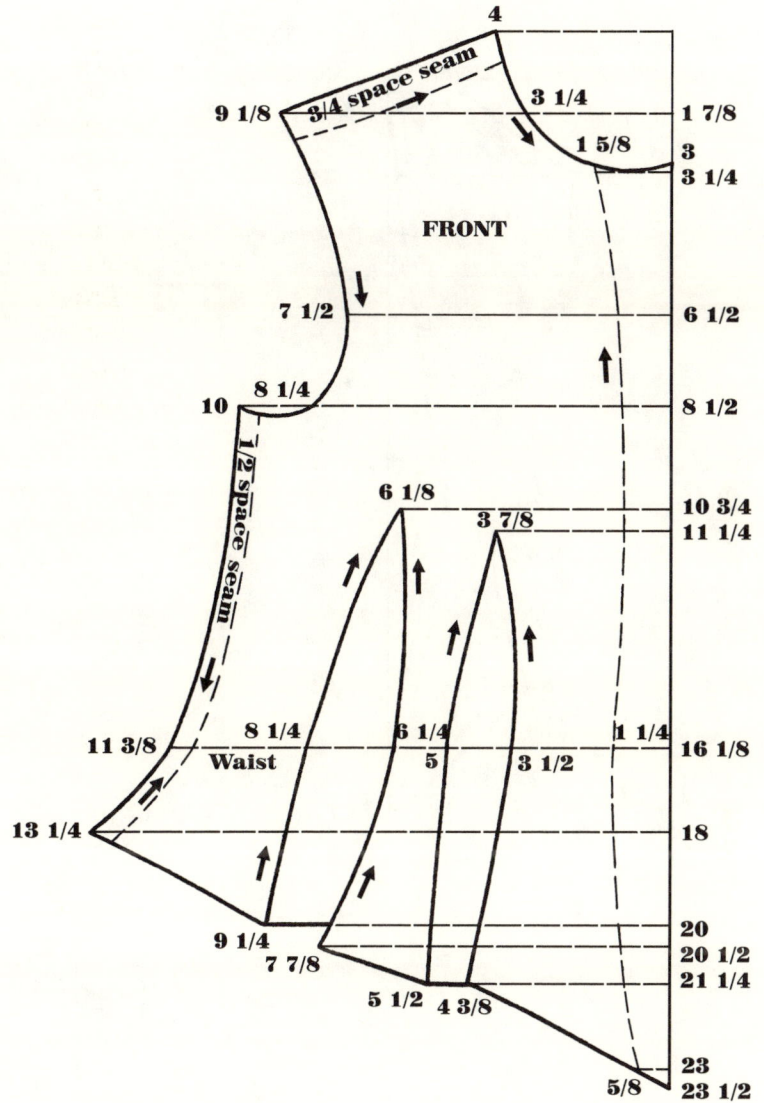

FRONT

4
9 1/8   3/4 space seam   3 1/4   1 7/8
1 5/8   3
3 1/4
7 1/2   6 1/2
8 1/4   8 1/2
10
1/2 space seam
6 1/8   3 7/8   10 3/4
11 1/4
11 3/8   8 1/4   6 1/4   1 1/4   16 1/8
Waist   5   3 1/2
13 1/4   18
9 1/4   20
7 7/8   20 1/2
21 1/4
5 1/2   4 3/8
23
5/8   23 1/2

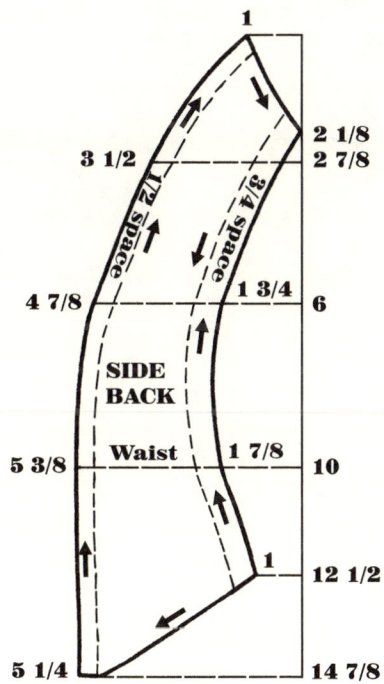

SIDE BACK

1
2 1/8
3 1/2   2 7/8
1/2 space
3/4 space
4 7/8   1 3/4   6
5 3/8   Waist   1 7/8   10
1
12 1/2
5 1/4   14 7/8

341

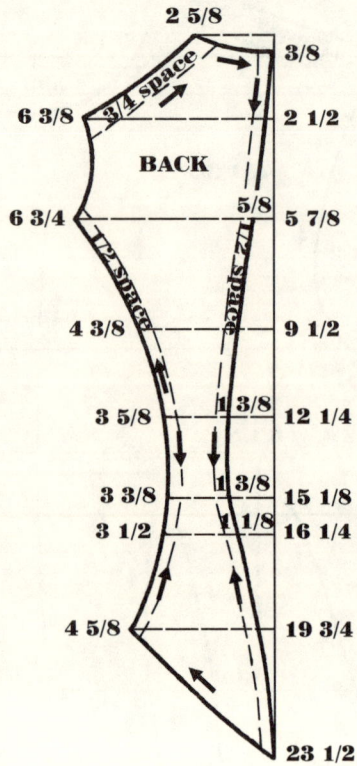

2 5/8

3/8

6 3/8

2 1/2

BACK

6 3/4   5/8   5 7/8

4 3/8   9 1/2

3 5/8   1 3/8   12 1/4

3 3/8   1 3/8   15 1/8

3 1/2   1 1/8   16 1/4

4 5/8   19 3/4

23 1/2

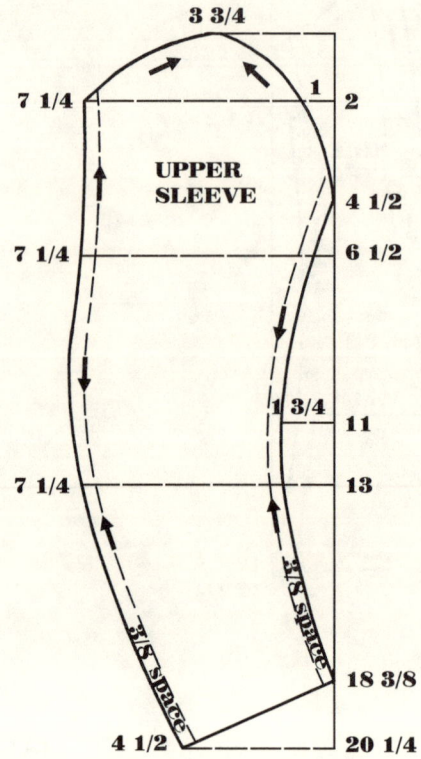

3 3/4

7 1/4   1   2

UPPER
SLEEVE

4 1/2

7 1/4   6 1/2

1 3/4   11

7 1/4   13

18 3/8

4 1/2   20 1/4

UNDER
SLEEVE

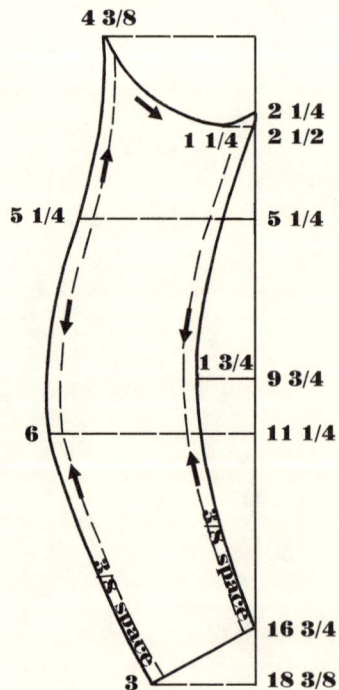

4 3/8

2 1/4

1 1/4   2 1/2

5 1/4   5 1/4

1 3/4   9 3/4

6   11 1/4

16 3/4

3   18 3/8

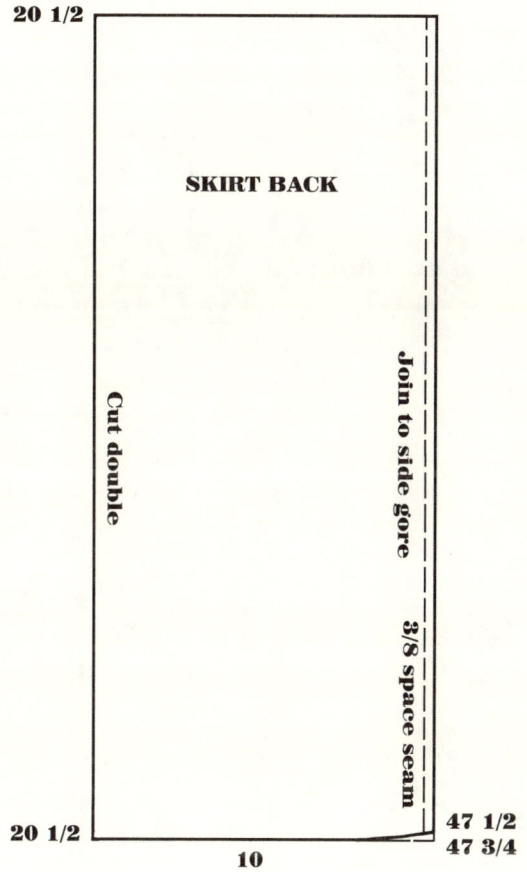

SKIRT BACK

20 1/2

Cut double

Join to side gore

3/8 space seam

20 1/2

47 1/2
47 3/4

10

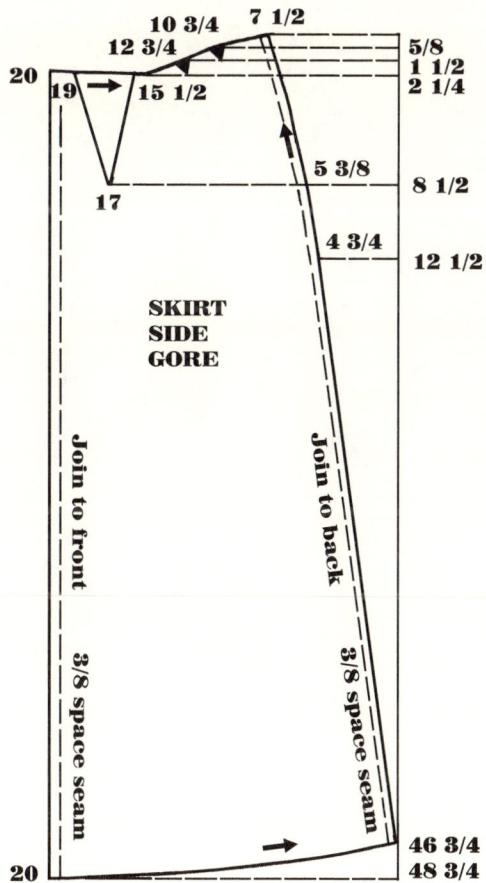

10 3/4   7 1/2
12 3/4
20   19   15 1/2

5/8
1 1/2
2 1/4

17

5 3/8   8 1/2

4 3/4   12 1/2

SKIRT
SIDE
GORE

Join to front   Join to back

3/8 space seam   3/8 space seam

20

46 3/4
48 3/4

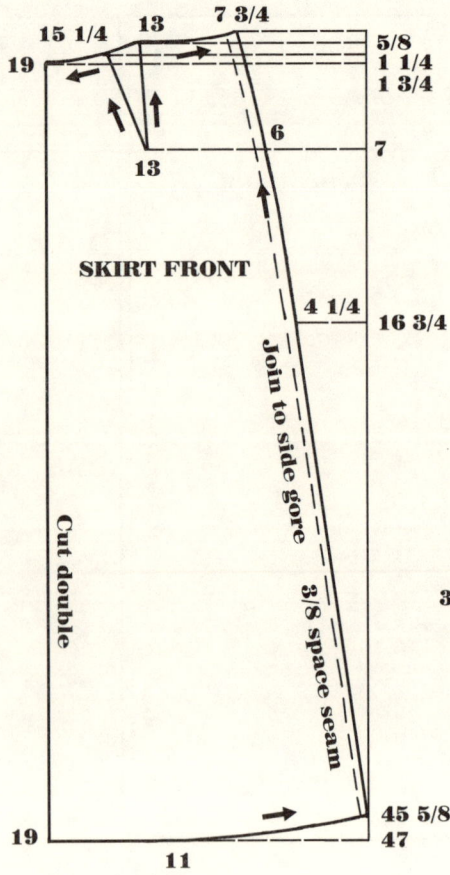

SKIRT FRONT

15 1/4   13   7 3/4

19

5/8
1 1/4
1 3/4

6   7

13

Cut double

Join to side gore

3/8 space seam

4 1/4   16 3/4

19   45 5/8
         47
11

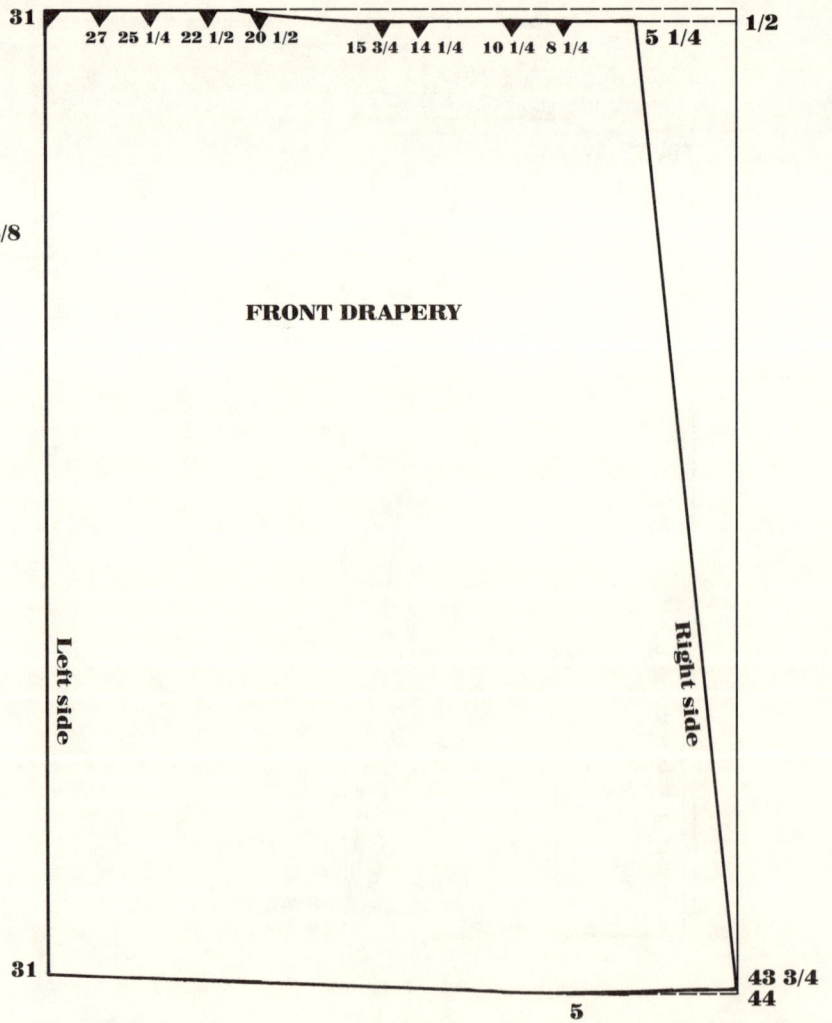

FRONT DRAPERY

31   31

27 25 1/4 22 1/2 20 1/2   15 3/4 14 1/4 10 1/4 8 1/4   5 1/4   1/2

Left side   Right side

31   43 3/4
         44
5

House Dress

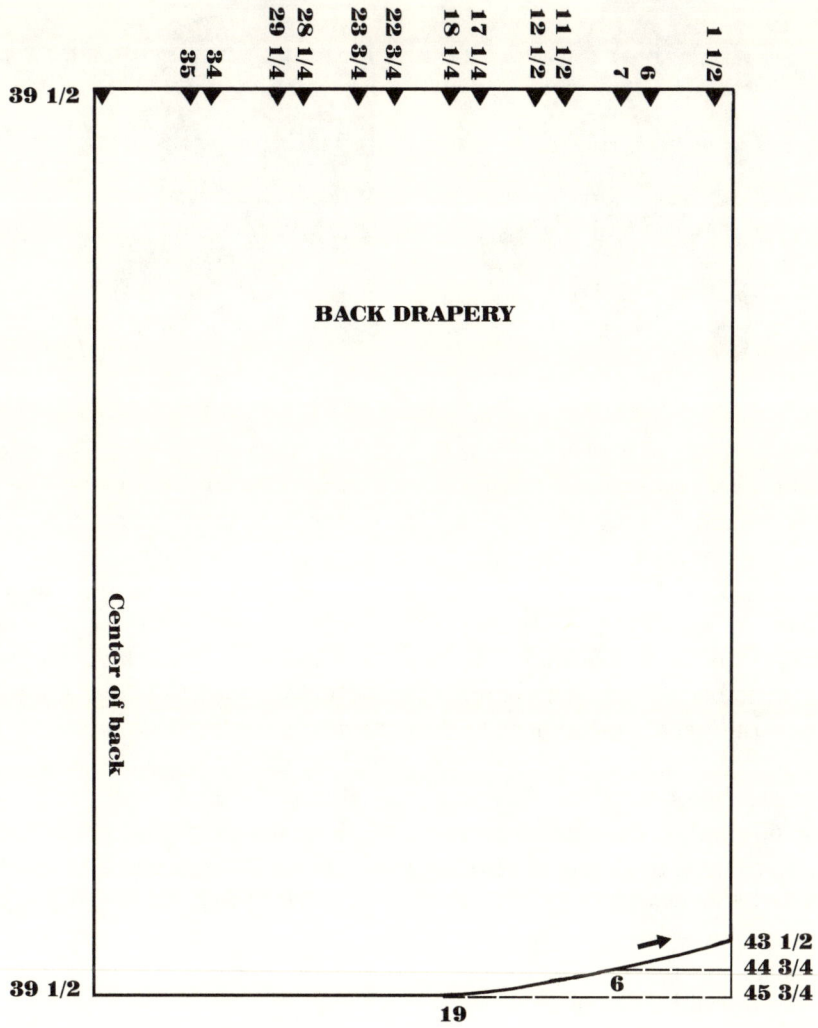

BACK DRAPERY

Center of back

39 1/2

39 1/2

1 1/2
6
7
11 1/2
12 1/2
17 1/4
18 1/4
22 3/4
23 3/4
28 1/4
29 1/4
34
35

43 1/2
44 3/4
45 3/4
6
19

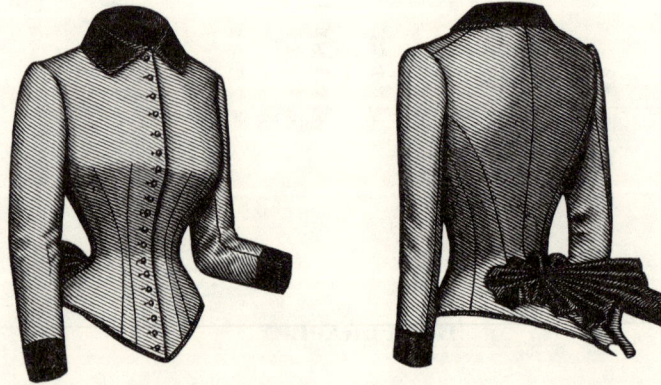

Ladies' Basque. A tasteful contrast is brought out by the selection of darker suit material for the collar, cuff-facings, and bindings, than for the rest of the garment. The fronts close with button-holes and fancy buttons, the right side being hemmed. There are two bust darts in each front. Adjoining the front are side pieces, while at the back are side backs and a curved center back seam. The latter ends a little below the waist-line, at the top of extra widths.

Each width is underfaced with the darker material, drawn into a full jabot on the outside by a shirring that begins a little below the top at the end of the seam, and is carried downward diagonally to a point at the outer edge a little less than halfway from the bottom. A basting is made through the front above the shirring to hold it in place. Extra width is also allowed on each front edge of the back in a line with those already described. It is arranged in two overlapping plaits turning backward underneath, which contribute to the bouffant effect, but have their folds concealed by the shirred part.

The lower edge of the basque curves upward over the hips, and deepens to a slight point toward the bottom of the closing. A narrow binding finishes each side, from the end of the closing as far as the side-back seam. The coat sleeves are similarly finished with narrow cuff-facings of the darker material. The high rolling collar is also of the darker material. Sometimes a vest-facing of contrasting material is applied on the front, and sometimes the contrast is limited to the facing of the jabot parts.

To make the basque for a lady of medium size, requires 3 1/2 yards of material 22 inches wide, or 1 5/8 yards of material 48 inches wide.

September 1886 *Delineator*

Pointed Bodice

Pointed Bodice. This example is made of velvet, and trimmed with fancy silk, lace, and passementerie. The front and back open in V shape for some distance over added sections. The section for the front is sewed beneath the right side and invisibly attached with hooks and eyes on the left, while below it the right side is hemmed, and closed with button-holes and buttons. The back section is sewed on both sides beneath the overlapping back edges. The overlapping edges of both the back and front are underfaced. The bodice is fitted with double bust darts, side pieces, side backs, and a curved center back seam. It is deeply pointed both back and front and curved high over the hips. Passementerie borders the edges of the openings. The added sections are overlaid with silk scantily shirred at its upper and lower edges, with only enough fullness for a graceful effect. The high standing collar is overlaid with passementerie. The ends of the collar are fastened on the left side above the closing of the front sections.

In the back view, the sleeves are of little more than elbow length. They are finished with lace ruffles surmounted by bands of passementerie. In the front view, the sleeves are cut off a little below their tops, and finished with lace ruffles. When the longer sleeves are used, they are usually in contrast with the rest of the bodice. When they are omitted, slightly shirred tulle or illusion, or any becoming arrangement of lace or crêpe, is often substituted. The richest and the simplest dress materials make up becomingly in this way. For a lady of medium size, this bodice requires 2 3/4 yards of material 22 inches wide, or 1 1/4 yards of material 48 inches wide.

September 1886 *Delineator*

347

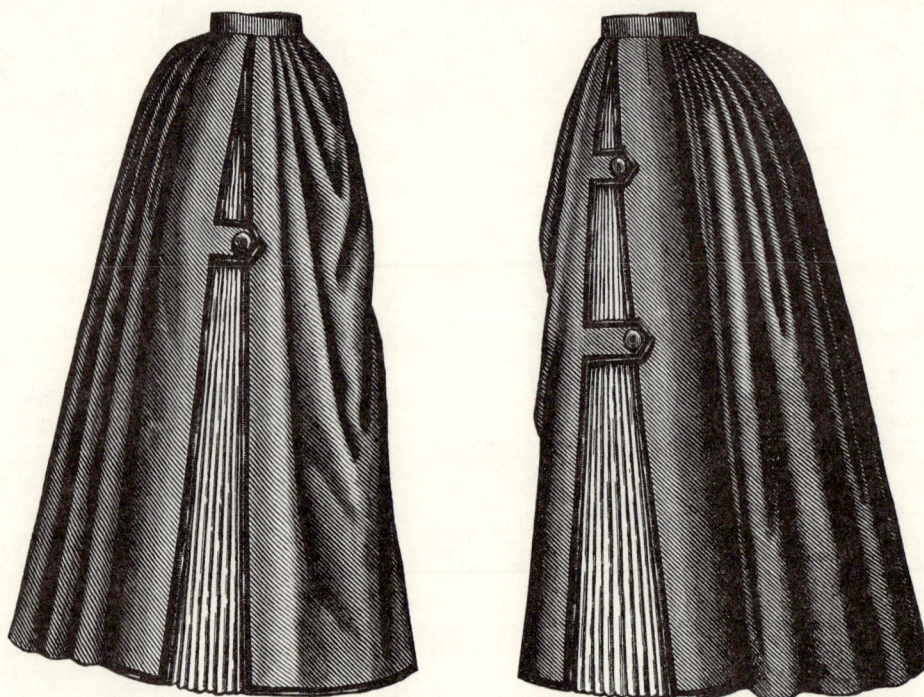

Walking Skirt. The skirt is portrayed made of dress material. It is trimmed with plaitings of the same material in a lighter shade, silk braid, and large buttons. The four-gored skirt is generally worn with a long, slender bustle, although a similar effect may be produced by steels.

On each side gore is a plain panel that is smoothly fitted over the hip by a dart, a narrow extension being allowed on the right panel. Over the front gore falls a drapery. This drapery is wrinkled by a group of forward-turning plaits laid on the right side of the center in the upper edge, and by three similar plaits on the left of the center. The front drapery is extended on the left side to form two pointed tabs, which are basted to the front edge of the left panel under large buttons. The extension on the right panel is similarly basted to the right edge of the front drapery. The loose edges of the front drapery and panels are bound with silk braid.

The back drapery is in waterfall style. Between the side edges of the front drapery and the front edge of the panel on each side, is a fan-like trimming of the material in a lighter shade.

This mode is especially adapted to cloths and other wool materials. The panels may contrast with the skirt, and a finish of machine-stitching or bands of Persian trimming may be substituted for the binding. When the skirt does not form part of a costume it may be worn with any harmonizing bodice, either plain or fancy. To make the garment for a lady of medium size, requires 12 yards of material 22 inches wide, or 6 yards of material 44 inches wide.

September 1889 *Delineator*

Empire Dress

The bodice is drafted with the scale corresponding to the bust measure. It consists of nine pieces: Upper front, upper back, under front, side back, under back, upper and under pieces for sleeve lining, outside sleeve, and collar. There is only one skirt piece. It is drafted with the scale corresponding to the waist measure. The length is regulated with the tape measure.

Gather the upper fronts between the notches, and sew them to the under front and to the back likewise. Gather the outside sleeves and sew them to the sleeve linings. Any adornment may be used to finish the sleeves at the wrist. Shirr the skirt as many times at the waist as desired. The sash is of silk, satin, or sash ribbon of the length and width desired.

Spring 1889 *Voice of Fashion*

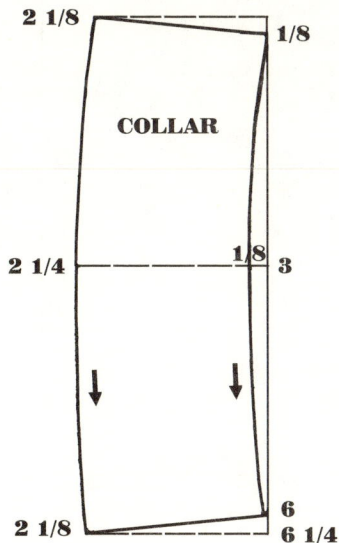

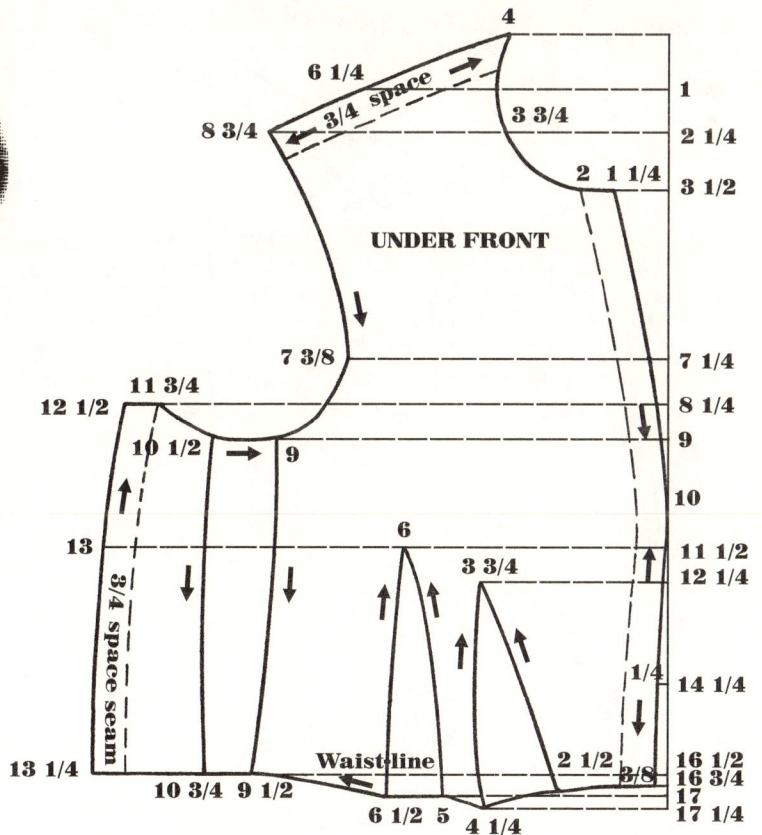

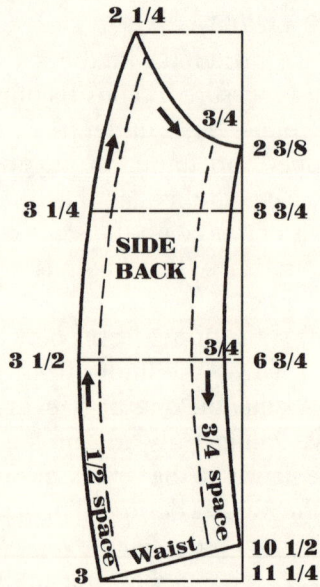

2 1/4

3/4

2 3/8

3 1/4   3 3/4

SIDE BACK

3 1/2   3/4   6 3/4

1/2 space

3/4 space

Waist   10 1/2

3   11 1/4

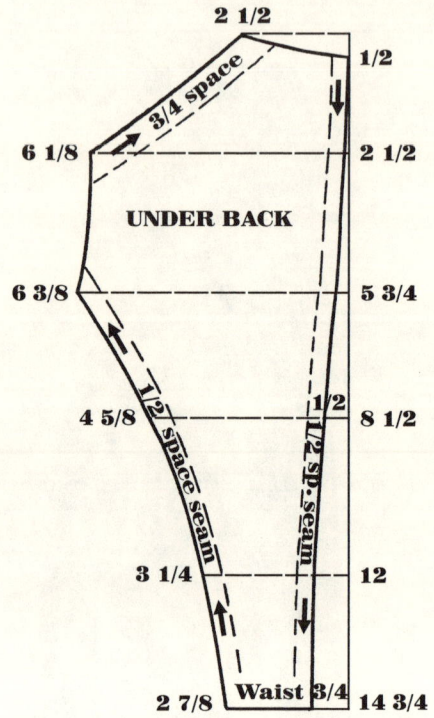

2 1/2

1/2

3/4 space

6 1/8   2 1/2

UNDER BACK

6 3/8   5 3/4

4 5/8   1/2   8 1/2

1/2 space seam

1/2 sp. seam

3 1/4   12

2 7/8   Waist 3/4   14 3/4

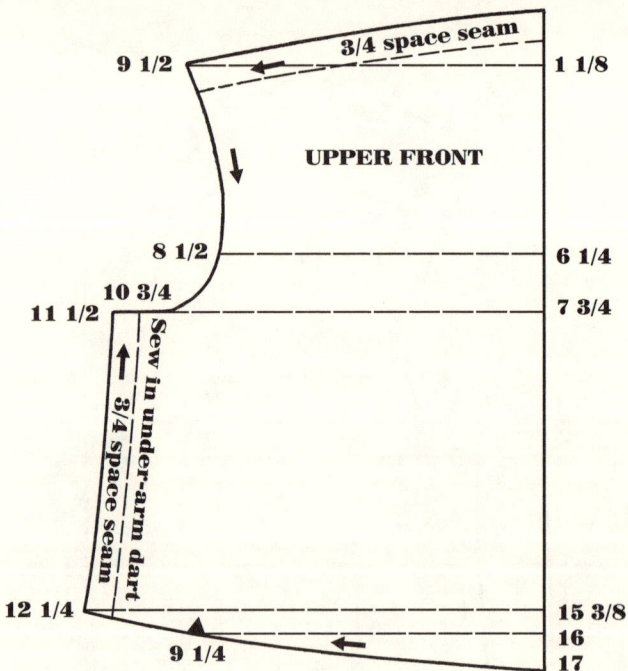

9 1/2   3/4 space seam   1 1/8

UPPER FRONT

8 1/2   6 1/4

10 3/4   7 3/4

11 1/2

Sew in under-arm dart
3/4 space seam

12 1/4   15 3/8
        16
9 1/4   17

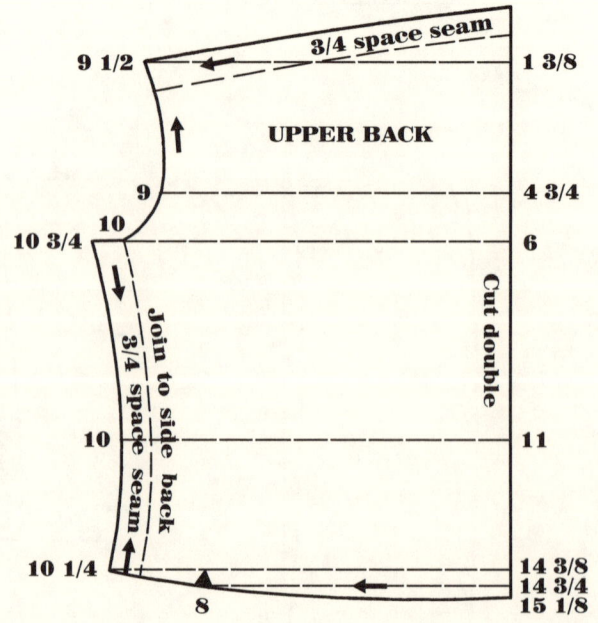

9 1/2   3/4 space seam   1 3/8

UPPER BACK

9   4 3/4

10 3/4   10   6

Join to side back
3/4 space seam

Cut double

10   11

10 1/4   14 3/8
        14 3/4
8   15 1/8

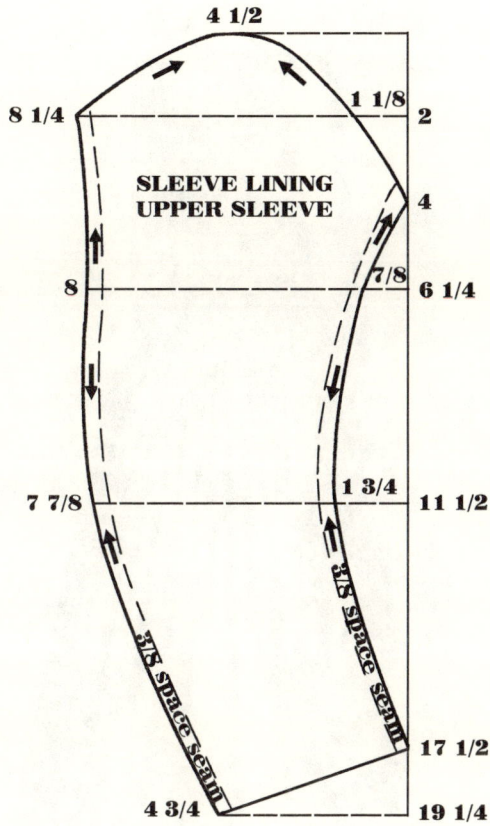

SLEEVE LINING UPPER SLEEVE

4 1/2
8 1/4
1 1/8
2
4
8
7/8
6 1/4
7 7/8
1 3/4
11 1/2
3/8 space seam
4 3/4
17 1/2
19 1/4

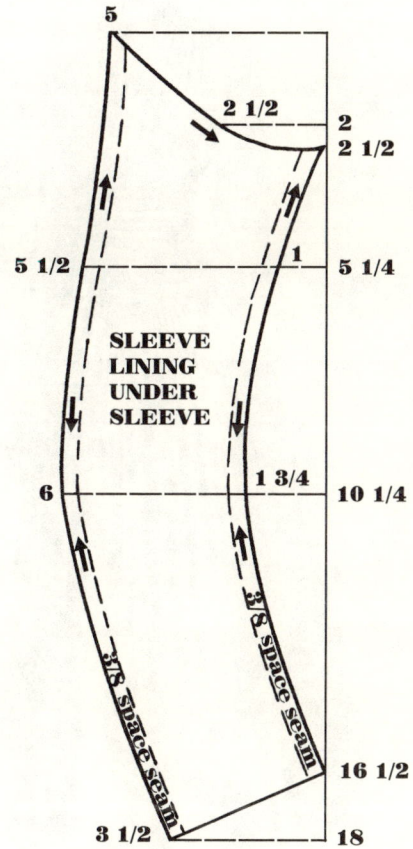

SLEEVE LINING UNDER SLEEVE

5
2 1/2
2
2 1/2
5 1/2
1
5 1/4
6
1 3/4
10 1/4
3/8 space seam
3 1/2
16 1/2
18

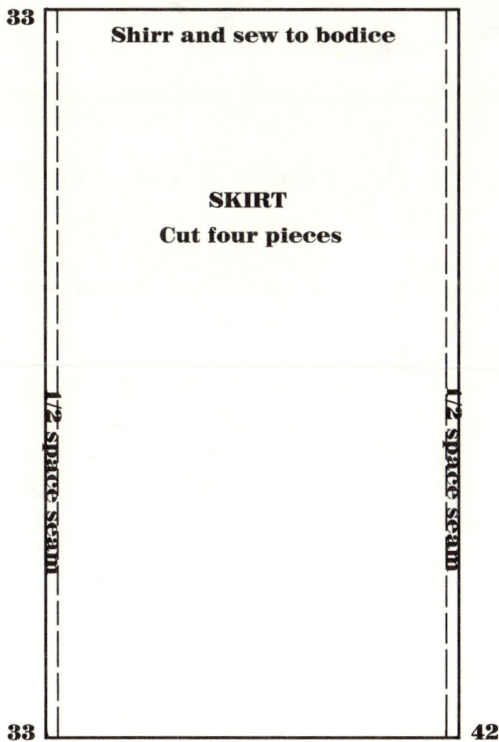

Shirr and sew to bodice

SKIRT
Cut four pieces

33
1/2 space seam
1/2 space seam
33
42

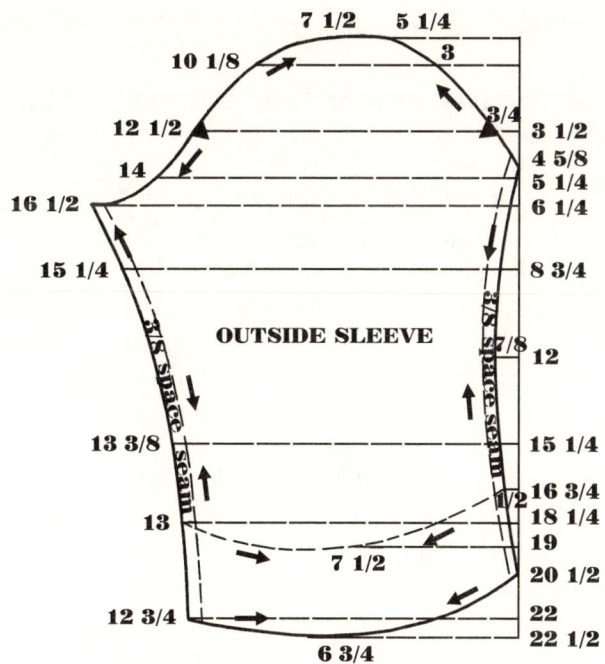

OUTSIDE SLEEVE

7 1/2
5 1/4
10 1/8
3
12 1/2
3/4
3 1/2
14
4 5/8
5 1/4
16 1/2
6 1/4
15 1/4
8 3/4
3/8 space seam
3/8 space seam
7/8
12
13 3/8
15 1/4
13
16 3/4
1/2
18 1/4
19
7 1/2
20 1/2
12 3/4
22
6 3/4
22 1/2

Dress in the First Empire Style. This dress is especially adapted to house wear, although under a long wrap it may be worn in the street. The Empire mode is brought out to good advantage by the selection of cashmere and surah, with lace for trimming. The short bodice is fitted by double bust darts, side pieces, side backs, and a curved center back seam. It is closed with hooks and eyes, back of which on each side is placed a forward-turning band of lace. On each front is arranged an ornamental front that is gathered all along the shoulder edge. Its back edge is included in the armhole and under-arm seams. The fullness is regulated with two lines of shirring made at the bottom a short distance back of the front edge, the second line being about 1 inch above the first. These ornamental fronts meet at the waist-line, from which they flare in suggestion

of the surplice style and expose the trimmed fronts between their edges.

On each side of the back is placed an ornamental back, which is arranged like the ornamental fronts. The upper edge is gathered and included in the shoulder seam, and the front edge is included in the armhole and second under-arm seam. The ornaments likewise flare from the lower edge of the bodice and show between their edges a backward-turning band of lace that trims each side of the back. The fullness of the ornaments is confined by two lines of shirring at the bottom a little back of the edge, about 1 inch apart.

Empire Dress

A belt finishes the lower edge. A lace frill falls over the high standing collar. The full sleeves have but one seam at the inside of the arm, the upper edge being gathered to within a short distance of the seam. Six lines of shirring are made at the back of the arm at the wrist, and a lace frill turns upward from the edge.

The skirt is full and round and is deeply hemmed at the bottom. At the top, five lines of shirring are made at intervals of about 1 inch. The placket opening is made a short distance back of the darts in the left front. From it to the closing, the top of the skirt is left loose from the body, the rest of the upper edge being joined to the lower edge of the bodice and belt. About the waist is draped a girdle of surah, which is laid in four upward-turning plaits and fastened at its end with hooks and eyes. Over its ends is fastened a wrinkled cross-piece, which also conceals the plaited ends of two loops and two sash ends. The loops and ends are of un-equal lengths, and the loose ends of the sash ends are fringed.

Materials that fall in pretty natural folds are preferred for this mode, as much of its grace is due to that quality. Cashmere, bordered camel's hair, mixed beige, soft-textured fancy suitings, serge, nun's veiling, flannel, etc., make up attractively in this way. Surah, moiré, and velvet are also liked. A pleasing contrast may be effected by the use of fancy surah, moiré, novelty material, figured silk, etc., for the surplice ornaments. To make the dress for a lady of medium size, requires 13 1/4 yards of material 22 inches wide, or 6 1/2 yards of material 44 inches wide. Each requires 4 3/4 yards of surah 20 inches wide for the sash ends, etc.

October 1888 *Delineator*

Evening Costume

Use the scale corresponding to the bust measure to draft the bodice. It consists of five pieces: Front, back, collar, sleeve, and cuff. Cut the back double and gather between the notches. Lay the front in two forward-turning plaits—there are three at the bottom, however. Face the bottom of the bodice. Lap the fronts across each other, and fasten at the side with hooks and eyes. Gather the sleeve at the bottom between the notches, and sew it to the cuff. Gather the sleeve at the top between the notches, and sew it into the armhole.

The one-piece skirt is drafted with the scale corresponding to the waist measure. Regulate the length with the tape measure. Gather the skirt and sew it to a belt. Or instead, shirr it four or five times. Draw the shirring thread up until the skirt fits the hips perfectly. No tournures or steels are put in these skirts at present.

The diagram is for half of the sash. It is drafted with the scale corresponding to the waist measure. The scarf may be either of the dress material, or soft silk in a matching color. Lay folds around the waist. Tie the sash in a large bow with loops and ends on the side or at the back.

Fall 1889 *Voice of Fashion*

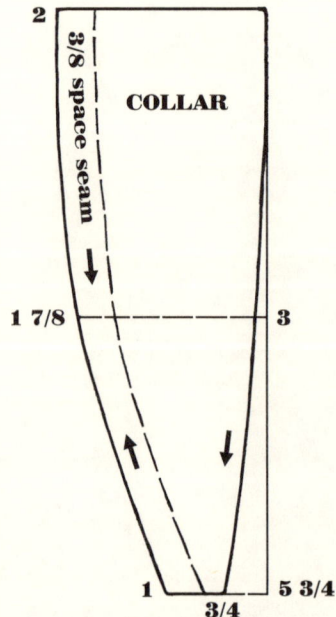

2

3/8 space seam

COLLAR

1 7/8   3

1

3/4   5 3/4

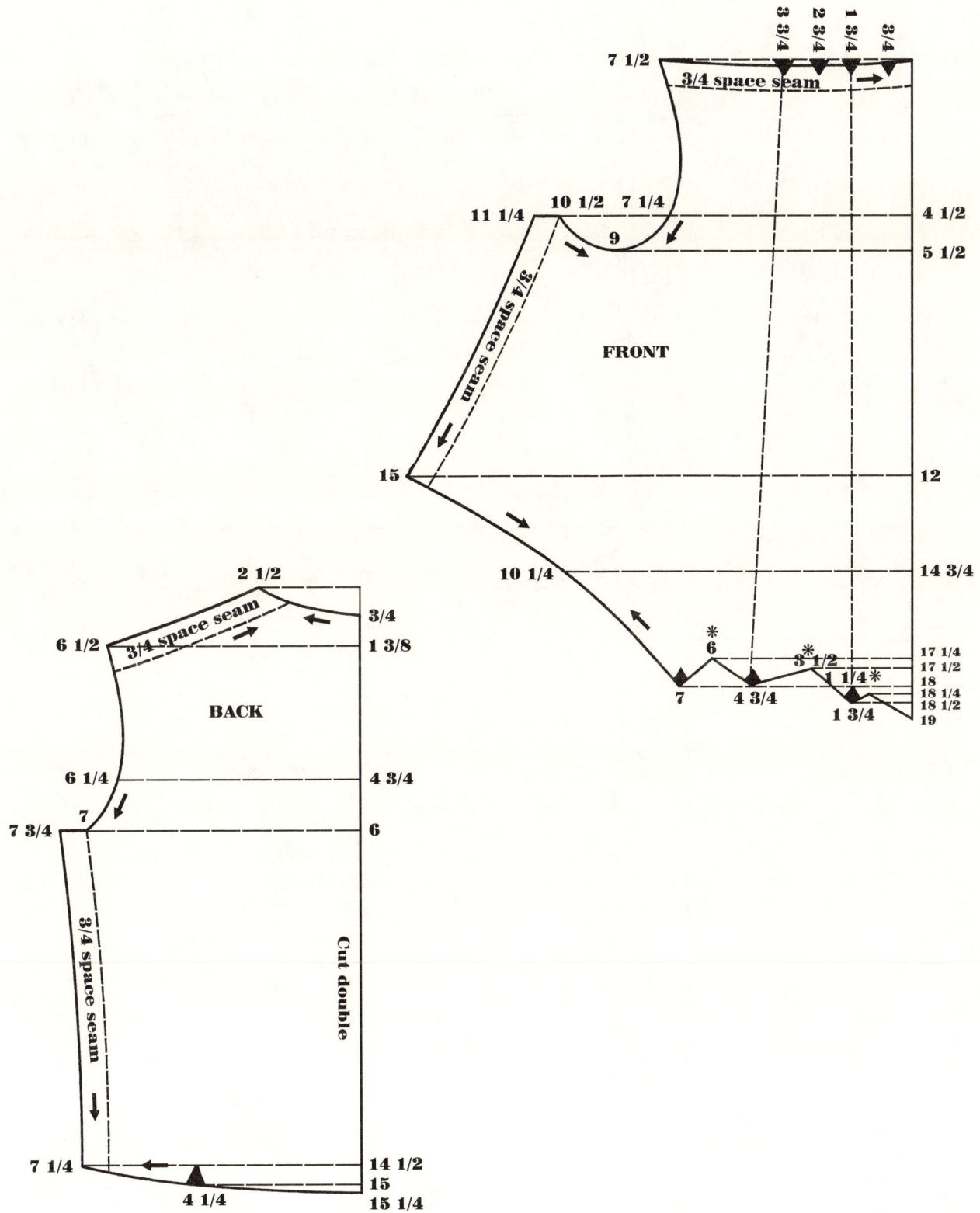

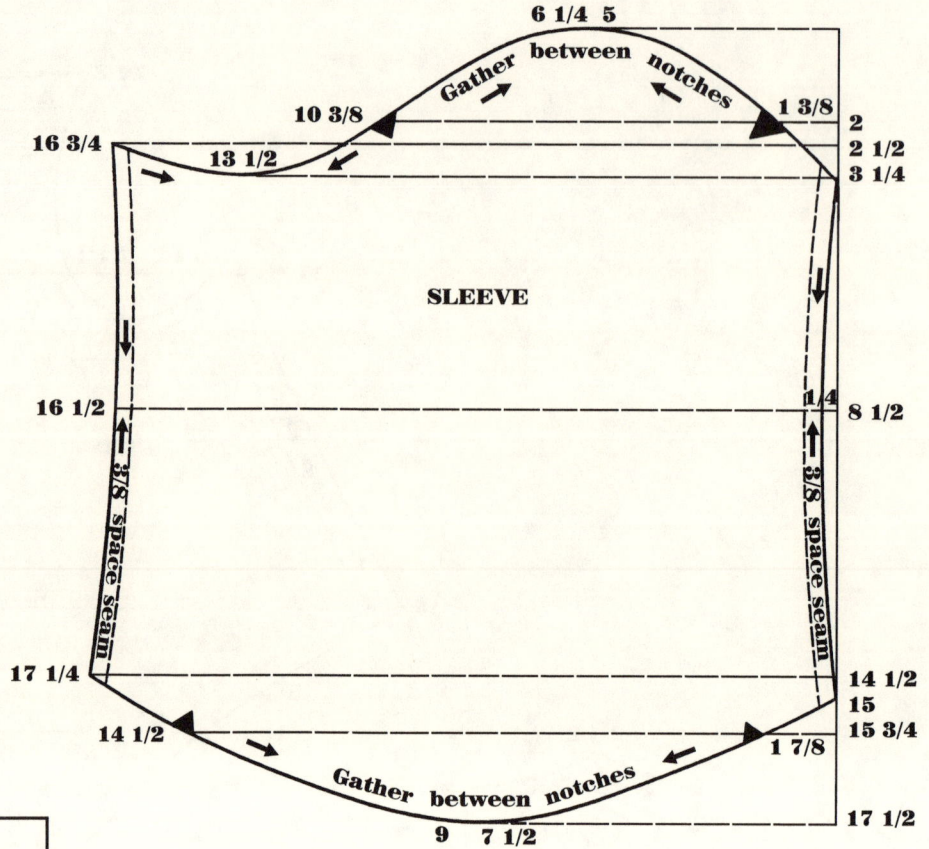

6 1/4 5

Gather between notches

10 3/8   1 3/8

16 3/4   2
13 1/2   2 1/2
                         3 1/4

SLEEVE

3/8 space seam   3/8 space seam

16 1/2   1/4 8 1/2

17 1/4   14 1/2
                         15
14 1/2   15 3/4
                    1 7/8

Gather between notches

9   7 1/2   17 1/2

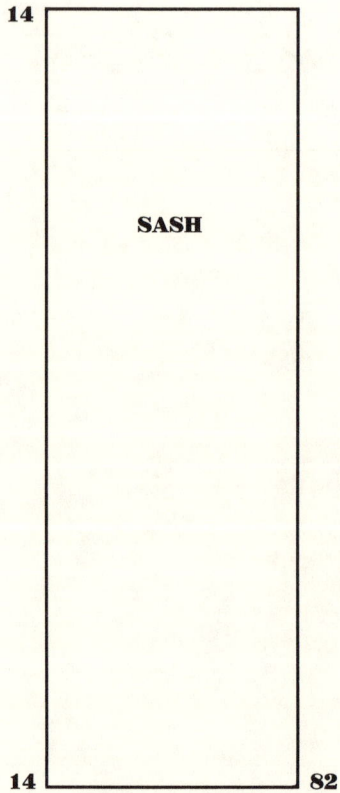

14

SASH

14   82

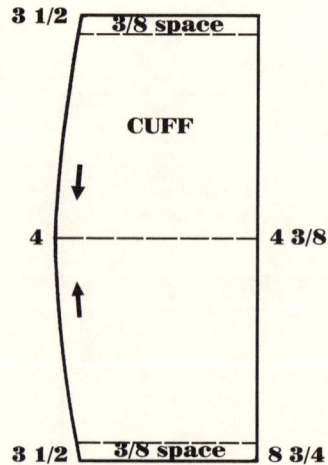

3 1/2   3/8 space

CUFF

4   4 3/8

3 1/2   3/8 space   8 3/4

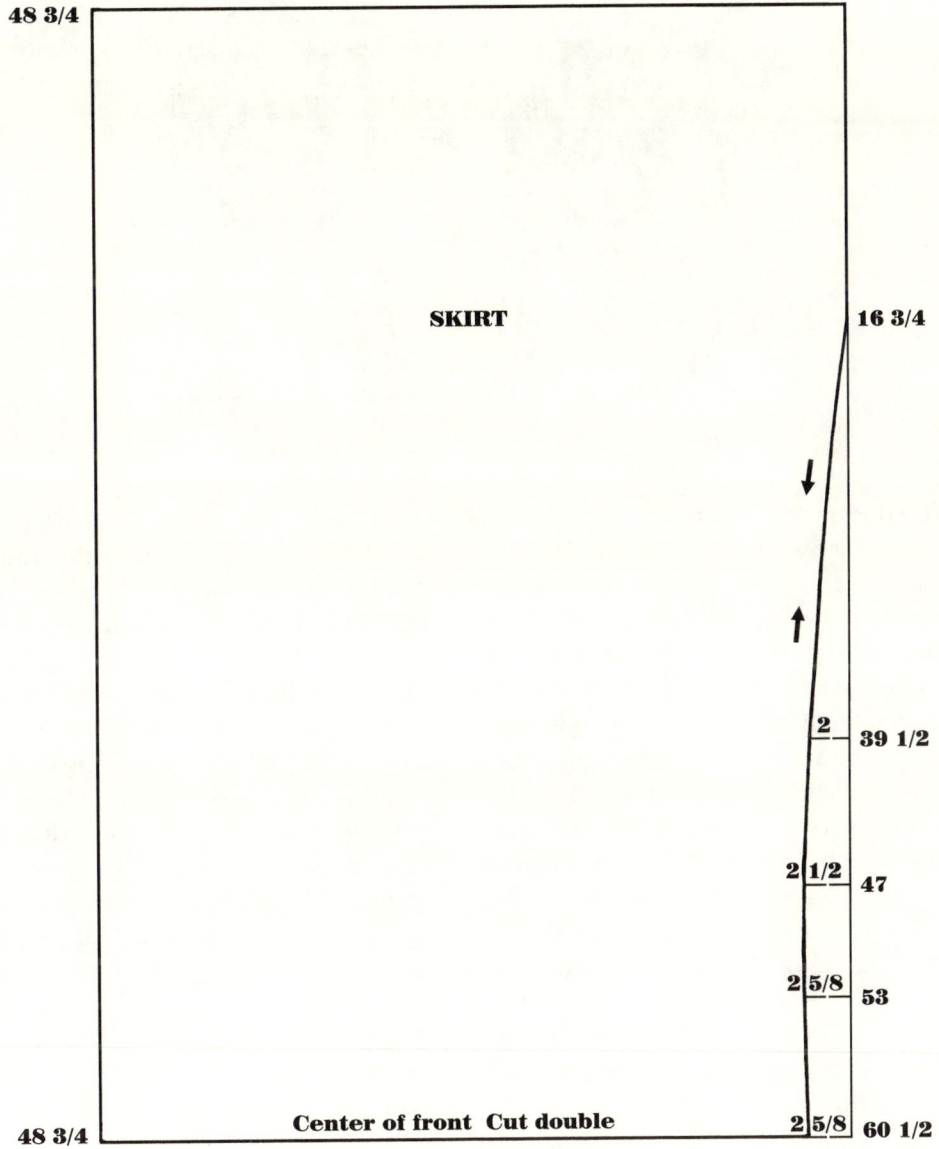

48 3/4

SKIRT

16 3/4

2 — 39 1/2

2 1/2 — 47

2 5/8 — 53

48 3/4

Center of front Cut double

2 5/8 60 1/2

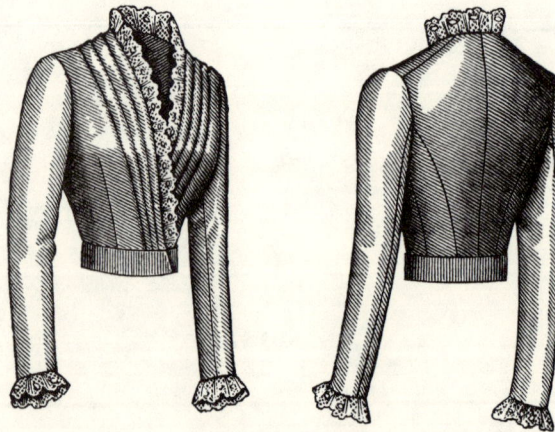

Surplice Bodice. In the engraving this bodice is shown made of dress material, with lace for trimming. Three forward-turning plaits are made in each front a little back of the front edge. These plaits extend from the shoulders to the lower edges, and are deeply lapped toward the bottom. The fronts are adjusted on fitted linings. Their front edges are turned under for hems, on which the front edges of the lining are felled. The smooth adjustment of the fronts is attained by two bust darts in each front lining, and a single bust dart made back of the plaits in each front and taken up with the corresponding dart in the lining. The right front crosses the left in surplice fashion below the bust. Above the bust the fronts flare in V shape toward the shoulders, exposing the neck. The back is adjusted by side backs and a curved center back seam, and fits with basque-like smoothness.

The waist is finished with a belt, which is sewed to the lower edge, turned up on the outside, and sewed flatly in place. Hooks and eyes close the bodice at the belt. A standing lace frill trims the neck and is continued down each front along the hem to the belt. The coat sleeves fit closely but comfortably, and each is trimmed at the wrist with a lace frill.

Cashmere, challis, nun's veiling, and light-weight wools are suited to this mode, and so are chambray, sateen, lawn, batiste, and other wash materials. Tissue and all kinds of sheer materials are especially beautiful. Lace, or embroidery applied plainly or frilled, is desirable for trimming most materials. Plain, embroidered, or lace chemisettes may be worn with this bodice, or deep frills of soft lace may be used and the edges caught together with small scarf pins. To make the bodice for a lady of medium size, requires 3 1/8 yards of material 22 inches wide, 2 1/8 yards of material 36 inches wide, or 1 3/4 yards of material 44 inches wide. The front lining requires 5/8 yard of silesia 36 inches wide.

August 1887 *Delineator*

Full Skirt

Full Skirt. The skirt is shown developed in hunter green dress material and trimmed with three bands of fancy worsted braid applied just above the wide hem that finishes its lower edge. It consists of joined straight breadths. It is gathered at its upper edge and sewed to a belt, from which it hangs in full folds. A Turkish sash of the skirt material is carried about the top of the skirt and loosely knotted low on the left side of the front. On the right side toward the back, the sash is laid in plaits and basted to the belt. The ends of the sash reach nearly to the lower end of the skirt, and are gathered up closely and tipped with worsted tassels that match the braid.

Such a skirt is pretty worn with a spencer bodice, a blouse, or a plain, round bodice. It is appropriate for house wear, and for tennis and other outdoor sports. Tennis cloth, lady's cloth, cashmere, serge, or any seasonable dress material may be used. As part of a tennis suit, this skirt is often made up in white and striped flannels and outing cloths. Many pleasing contrasts in colors between the dress material and the trimming may be effected. Skirts of dark blue, brown, green, wine, or mahogany may be trimmed with white, gold, or silver braids. With some materials, picot-edged ribbon is used for decoration. To make the skirt for a lady of medium size, requires 9 1/8 yards of material 22 inches wide, or 5 3/8 yards of material either 36 or 44 inches wide.

April 1889 *Delineator*

Empire Costume. This mode is admirable for dressy wear. It is pictured made up in dark green cashmere, velvet, and light pink serge. It is trimmed with green velvet, plaitings of pink serge, and silver braid. The four-gored skirt is of lining and worn over a long, slender bustle. The drapery, which reaches to the edge of the skirt, is gathered at its upper edge and joined to a shaped girdle that is stayed at each seam underneath. The side edges of the drapery are attached to the skirt with buttons and button-holes. The lower part of the drapery is trimmed with a double box-plaiting of serge. This is surmounted by a trimming of velvet decorated with two bands of narrow braid, the trimming describing points at its upper and lower edges.

The polonaise is shaped by double bust darts, and by under-arm, side, side-back, and center back seams. The fullness below the waist-line of the center back and side-back seams is underfolded to form a double box-plait in each. Extra width is also allowed below the waist-line of each side seam, and underfolded in a shallow backward-turning plait. The tops of all of the plaits are finished with binding. On the loose front edges of the side pieces and side backs—which are in one—extra width is allowed and turned under for a hem. The hems of the deep parts of the polonaise are attached to the drapery with hooks and eyes.

Empire Costume

The polonaise is of basque depth in front. On the front, which is closed with hooks and eyes, is arranged a velvet plastron that is sewed permanently to the right side and fastened on the left with hooks and eyes. The plastron is visible in V shape between the surplice fronts. The latter are gathered along their shoulder caps nearly to the armholes, and laid in four forward-turning plaits at the lower edge. The surplice fronts cross at the bust, a hook and eye fastening each lower front corner in place. The girdle is trimmed at its long edges with three bands of narrow braid. The right end of the girdle is sewed to the right under-arm seam. The left end is caught in place with hooks and eyes, the girdle holding the surplice fronts in place.

The coat sleeves are cut away below each seam to form points on the upper and under side. On them are arranged full, plaited puffs that extend below the elbow, the lower edge of each puff being gathered and sewed in place. The sleeves are trimmed at each wrist with a narrow side-plaiting of pink serge, above which is a pointed trimming of velvet corresponding to the trimming on the drapery. The standing collar is trimmed with braid.

Effective contrasts may be produced by a judicious selection of materials, for example the union of cashmere, Henrietta, camel's hair, camelette, serge, etc., with velvet or silk in a harmonizing shade. To make the costume for a lady of medium size, requires 14 yards of material 22 inches wide, or 7 3/8 yards of material 44 inches wide. As represented, it needs 4 3/4 yards of cashmere 40 inches wide, 3 7/8 yards of serge 40 inches wide, and 1 5/8 yards of velvet 20 inches wide. Also required are 2 1/8 yards extra of serge 40 inches wide for plaiting, and 3 3/4 yards of lining 36 inches wide for the foundation skirt, etc.

September 1889 *Delineator*

Street Costume

Use the scale corresponding to the bust measure to draft the bodice. It consists of eight pieces: Under front, upper front, side piece, side back, back, collar, girdle, and leg-of-mutton sleeve. Shirr the upper front two or three times between the curved lines, and sew each line to the under front. Also gather the bottom and sew it to the under front. Take up the darts. Close the front with hooks and eyes. Lay the plaits for the girdle according to the notches. Sew it into the under-arm seam. Then bring it halfway up to the arm, bring it across the front, and fasten it on the side with hooks and eyes. Finish the end with a bow or ornament.

The draperies are drafted with the scale corresponding to the waist measure. Regulate the length with the tape measure. There are three pieces: Front drapery, plaiting for the left side of the front, and back drapery. Lay the plaits in the front and side draperies according to the notches. The side drapery consists of one double box-plait. Press it carefully, but do not baste it at the bottom. Gather the back at the top and sew it to the belt.

The skirt is drafted with the scale corresponding to the waist measure. Regulate the length with the tape measure. There are three pieces: Front, side gore, and back.

Spring 1890 *Voice of Fashion*

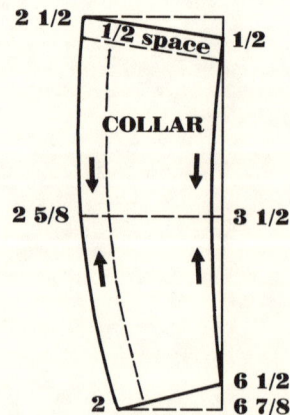

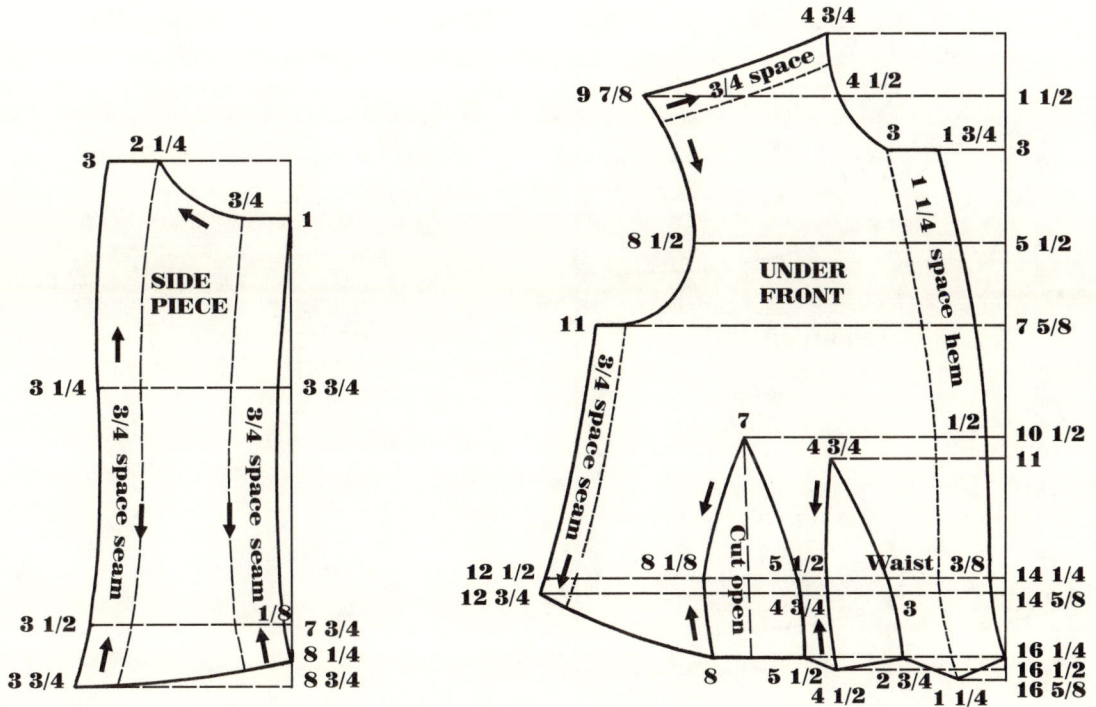

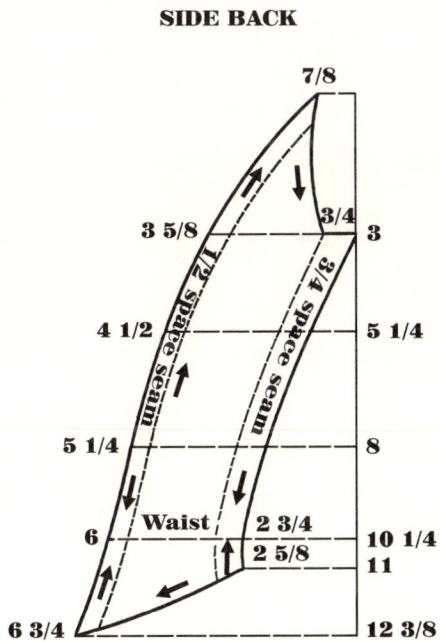

SIDE BACK

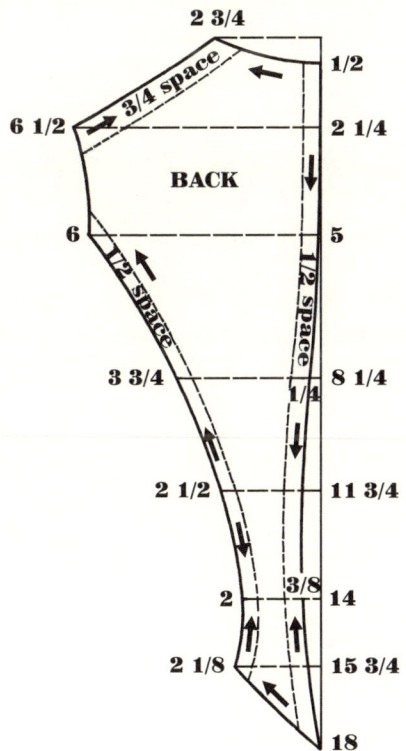

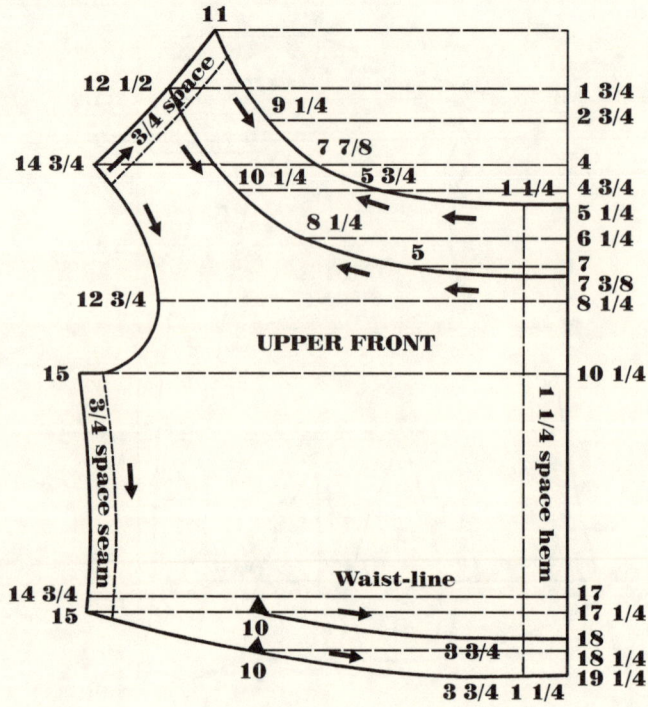

UPPER FRONT

11

12 1/2

3/4 space

14 3/4

9 1/4

7 7/8

10 1/4   5 3/4

8 1/4

5

12 3/4

1 3/4
2 3/4
4
4 3/4
5 1/4
6 1/4
7
7 3/8
8 1/4

1 1/4

15

3/4 space seam

Waist-line

1 1/4 space hem

10 1/4

14 3/4
15

10

3 3/4

10

17
17 1/4
18
18 1/4
19 1/4

3 3/4 1 1/4

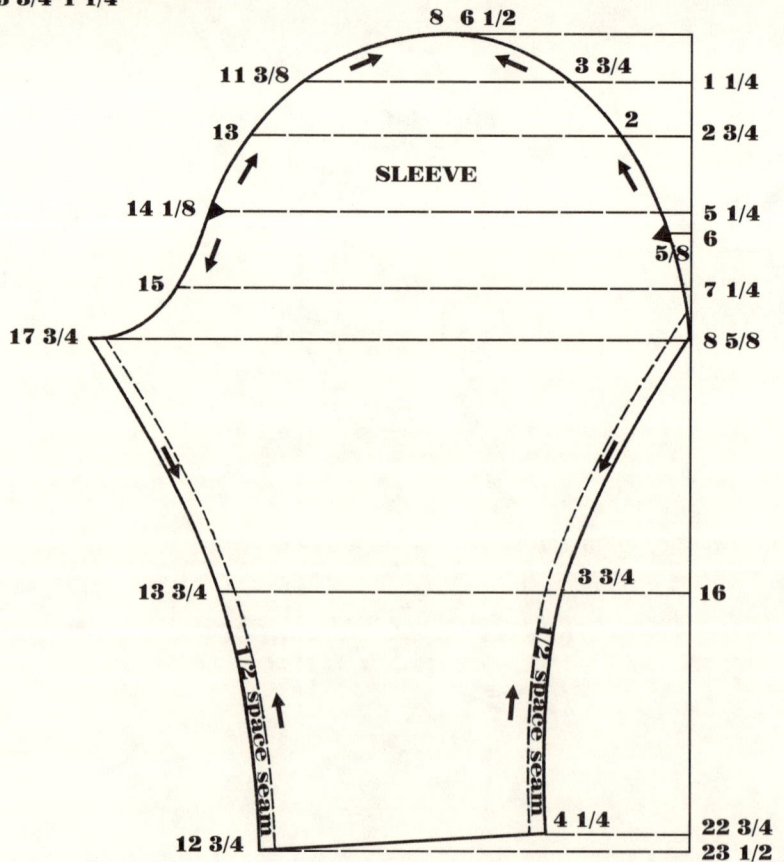

SLEEVE

8   6 1/2

11 3/8   3 3/4

13   2

14 1/8

15

17 3/4

5/8

1 1/4
2 3/4
5 1/4
6
7 1/4
8 5/8

13 3/4   3 3/4   16

1/2 space seam   1/2 space seam

12 3/4   4 1/4

22 3/4
23 1/2

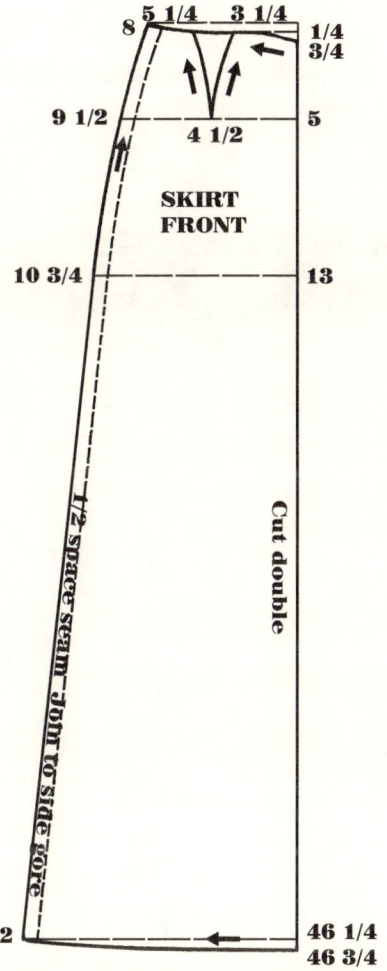

SKIRT
FRONT

5 1/4   3 1/4
8   1/4
                     3/4
9 1/2   5
        4 1/2

10 3/4   13

1/2 space seam — joint to side for ?

Cut double

14 1/2   46 1/4
                   46 3/4

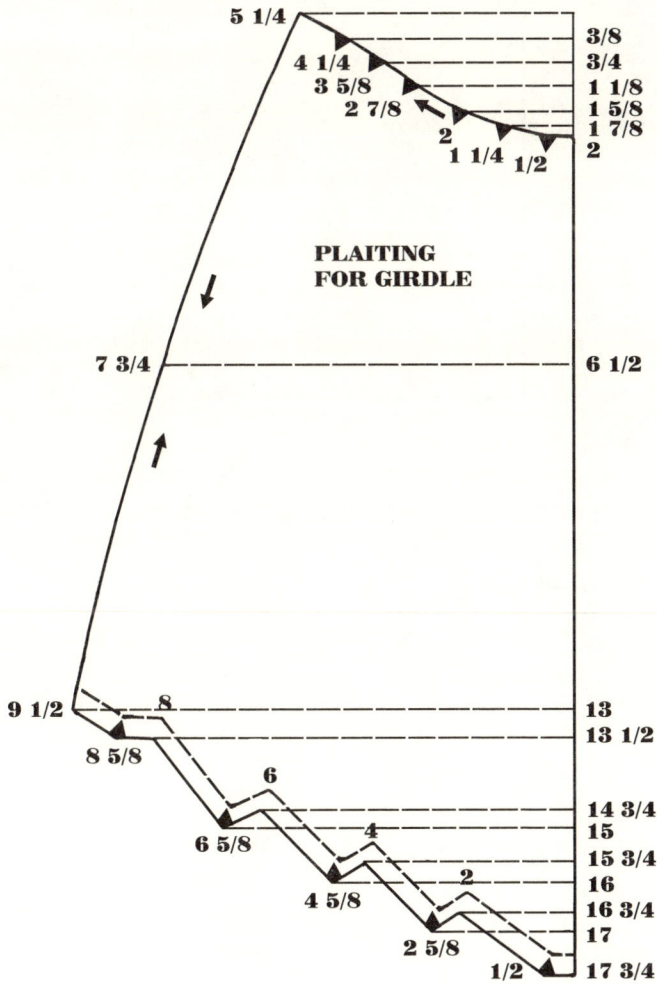

5 1/4
                    3/8
4 1/4   3/4
3 5/8   1 1/8
  2 7/8   1 5/8
      2   1 7/8
  1 1/4   1/2   2

PLAITING
FOR GIRDLE

7 3/4   6 1/2

9 1/2   8   13
                    13 1/2
8 5/8
         6
                    14 3/4
6 5/8   15
         4   15 3/4
                    16
4 5/8   2   16 3/4
                    17
  2 5/8   17 3/4
        1/2

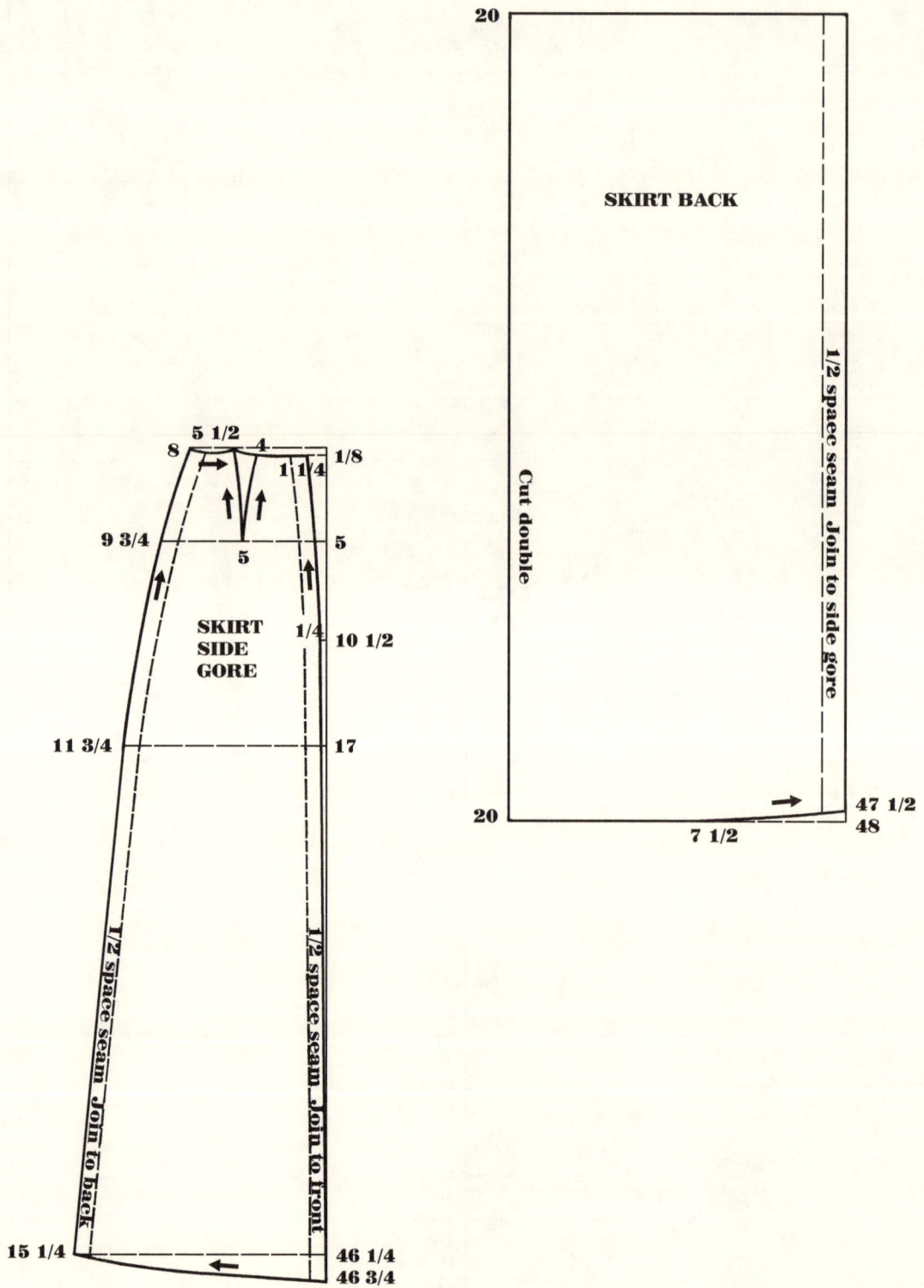

SKIRT BACK

Cut double

1/2 space seam   Join to side gore

20

20

7 1/2

47 1/2

48

5 1/2

8

4

1/8

1 1/4

9 3/4

5

5

**SKIRT
SIDE
GORE**

1/4

10 1/2

11 3/4

17

1/2 space seam   Join to back

1/2 space seam   Join to front

15 1/4

46 1/4

46 3/4

Street Costume

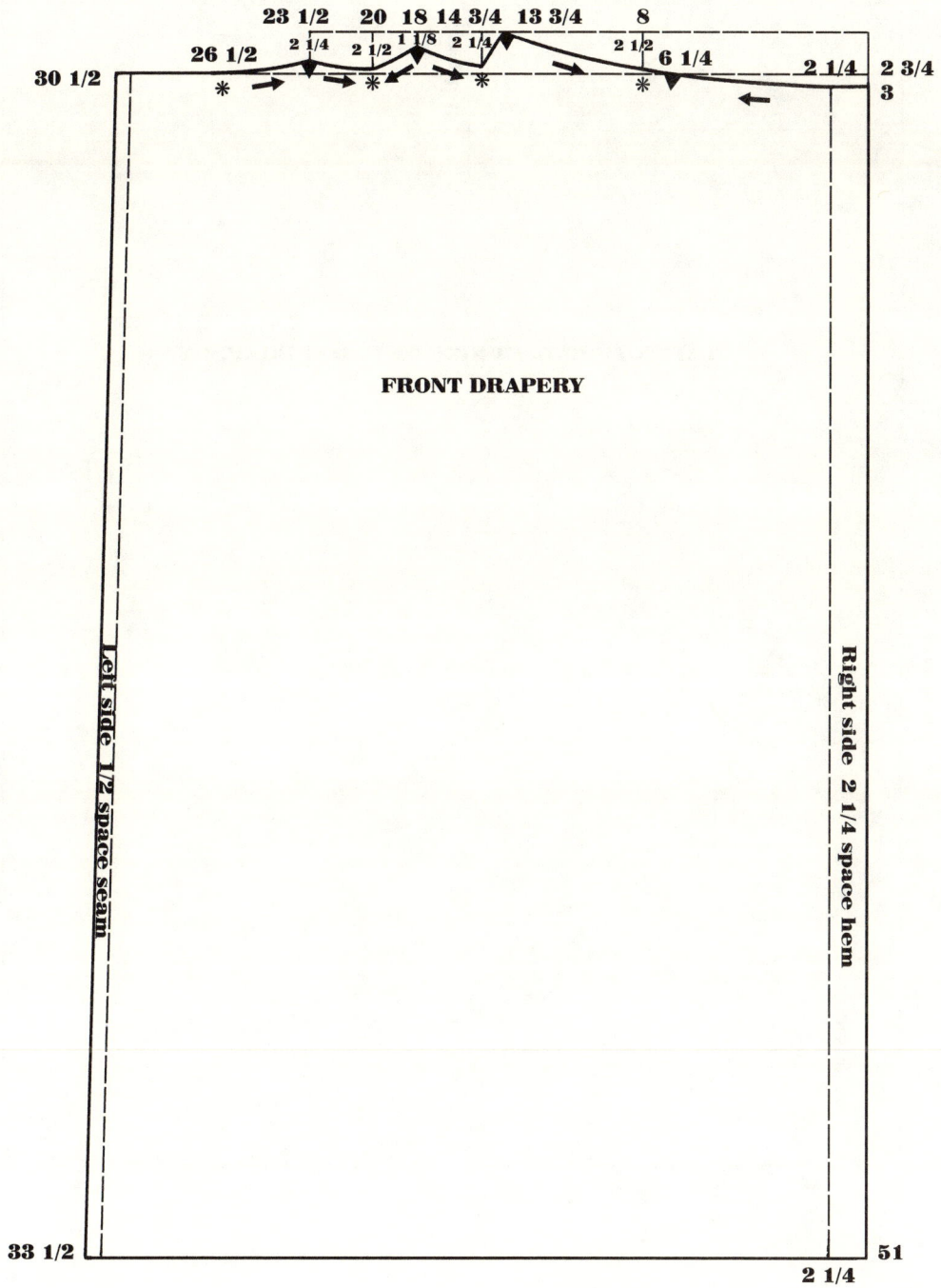

FRONT DRAPERY

Left side 1/2 space seam

Right side 2 1/4 space hem

367

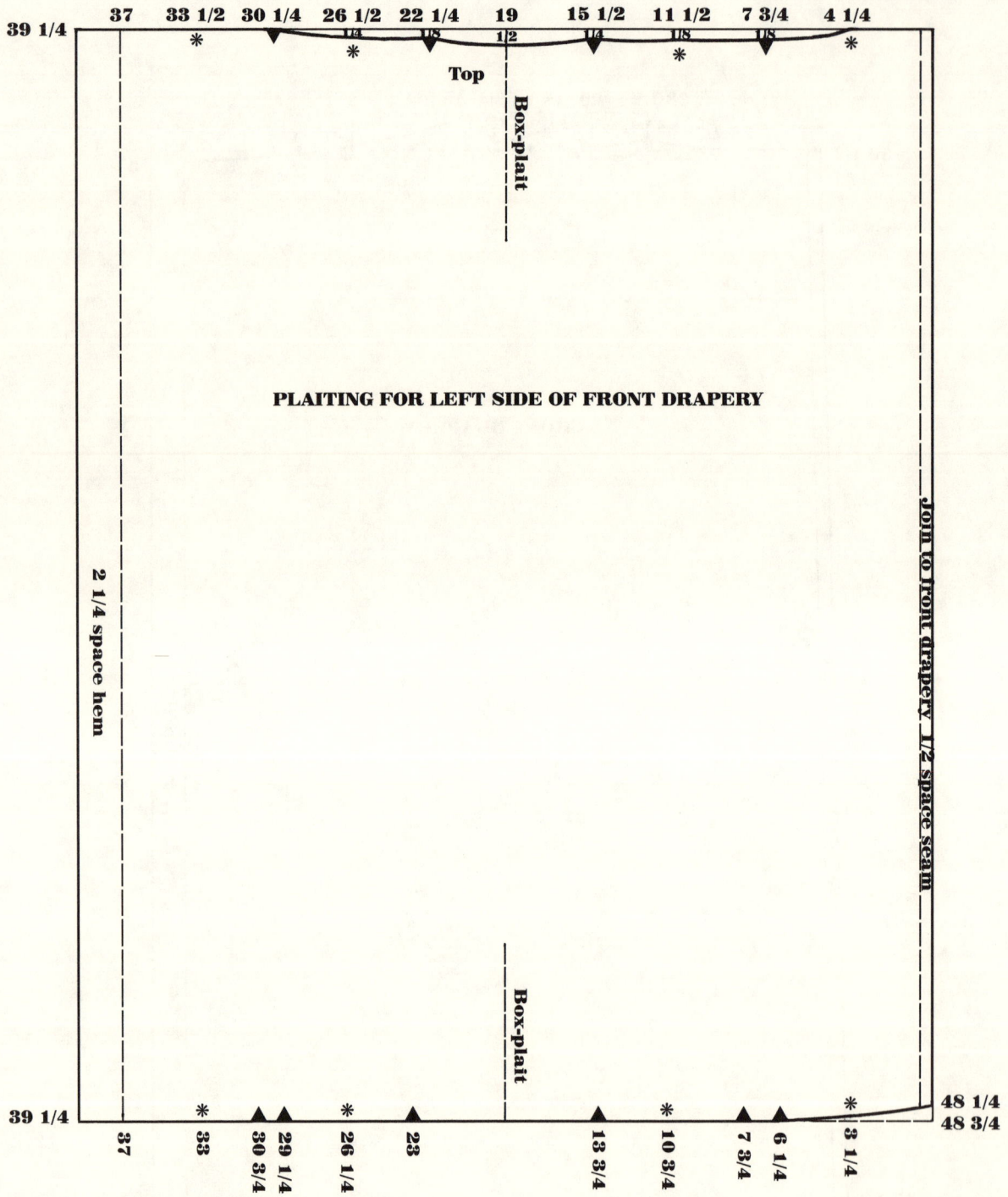

PLAITING FOR LEFT SIDE OF FRONT DRAPERY

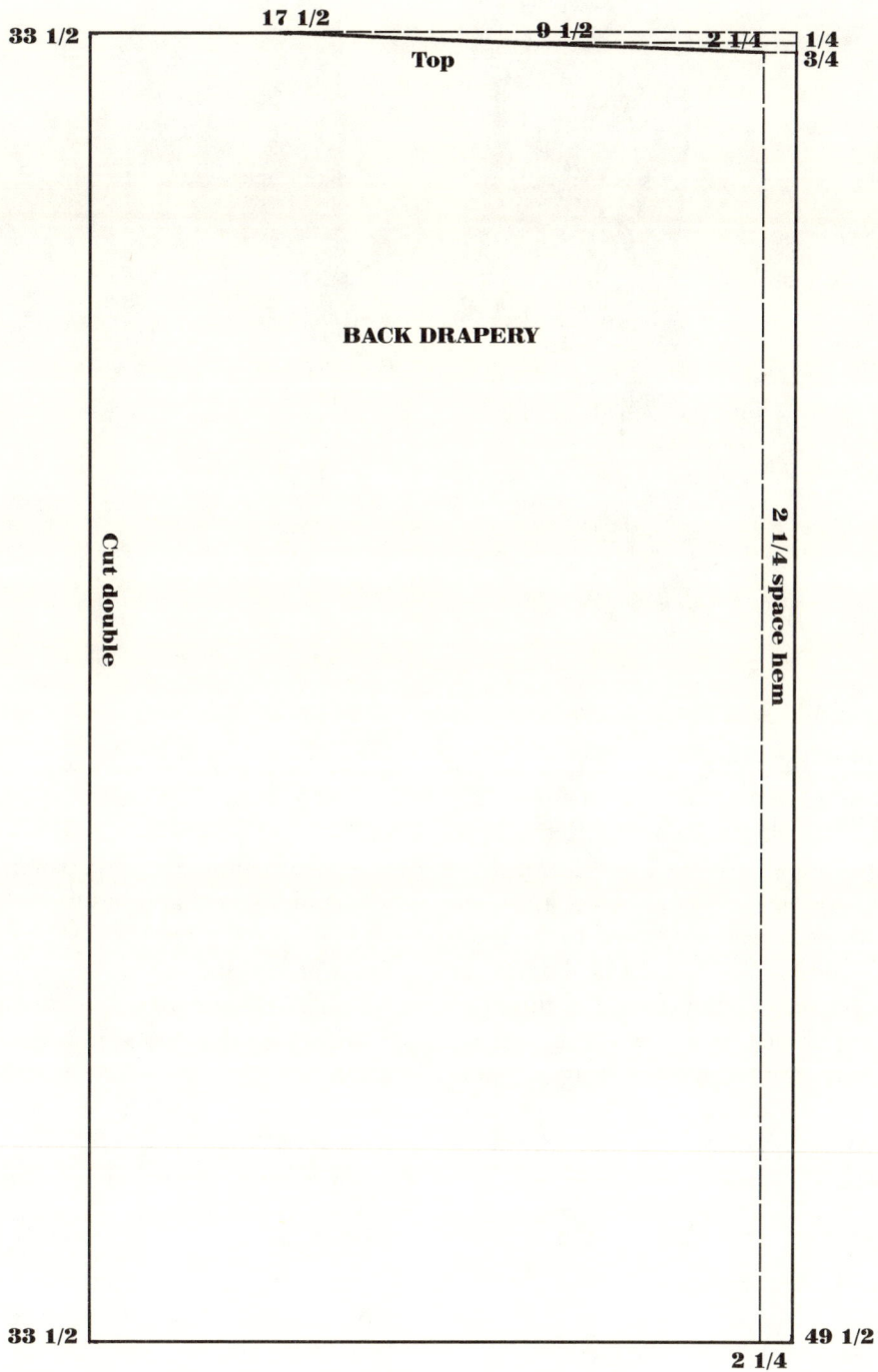

33 1/2   17 1/2   9 1/2   2 1/4   1/4

Top   3/4

BACK DRAPERY

Cut double

2 1/4 space hem

33 1/2   49 1/2

2 1/4

Old English Basque. This example is made of old rose cashmere and olive-dotted silk, and trimmed with olive ribbons. The lining fronts are closely fitted by double bust darts, and closed down the center with hooks and eyes. Over these are arranged full fronts, which are sewed to the lining fronts along the darts. The fullness of the fronts is drawn in on each side of the closing at the lower edge. At the top of each front, two tuck shirrings are made with the effect of a full ruching, outlining the yoke. The yoke is arranged on the upper parts of the lining fronts and displays a similar arrangement at the neck.

The adjustment is competed by side pieces, side backs, and a curved center back seam. The basque is short over the hips and pointed at the center of the back. Its lower edge in front is outlined by a plaited ribbon arranged in a point below the closing. A ribbon bow hangs in long loops and ends on the right side. At the neck, a fold of silk is gathered to form a narrow frill. The full upper part of each sleeve is plaited at the top and arranged over a coat-shaped lining. The fullness is basted to the upper part of the lining, to rise in a puff above the shoulder. At the wrist of each sleeve is applied a puff. This puff is narrowed toward the inside of the arm and has tuck shirrings at the top and bottom to correspond to the yoke. Gathers are made at the elbow.

This basque may form part of a house toilette, or it may be developed in bright- or dark-colored materials to wear with a number of skirts. For evening wear, soft silks and wools are combined in *fleur de pêche*, turquoise, serpent, pearl gray, or any preferred shades. The yoke and the puffs at the wrists are often of white peau de soie, surah, China silk, or some similar material; and the rest of the basque is of albatross, veiling, or camel's hair in a delicate shade. To make the basque for a lady of medium size, requires 3 yards of material 22 inches wide, or 1 1/2 yards of material 44 inches wide. Each requires 7/8 yard of silk 20 inches wide for the yoke, etc.

December 1889 *Delineator*

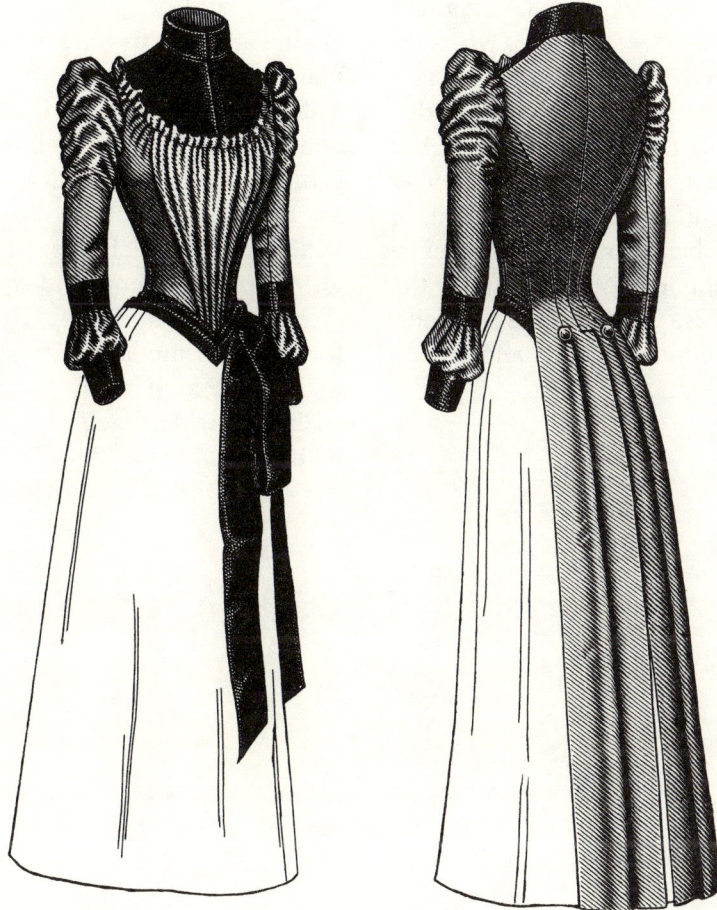

Old English Polonaise. This polonaise is equally appropriate for street and house wear. Plain chaudron suit material and velvet of a darker shade are united in this example, with buttons, velvet, and velvet ribbon of the same shade for decoration. The fronts are of basque depth, and closely fitted by double bust darts. They are closed with hooks and eyes at the center and are pointed below the closing. Over these fronts are arranged outside fronts. The latter are fitted by single bust darts, in front of which the fullness is brought to the center. The outside fronts are turned down at the upper edge, below which a single shirring forms a frill that outlines the upper part of the fronts with the effect of a round yoke. The fullness at the lower edge is drawn to the center of the front by shirrings on each side of the closing. The exposed parts of the fronts are faced with velvet. A standing collar of velvet is about the neck.

The adjustment is completed by short side pieces, side backs, and a curved center back seam. The latter terminates above coat laps and forms the back in long coat-tails. Extra fullness allowed at the side-back seams is underfolded in coat-plaits, each of which is marked by a button at the top.

The full outer part of each sleeve is applied over a coat-shaped lining. Its fullness is wrinkled in mousquetaire fashion by gathers along the edges above the elbow. The sleeves reach only a short distance below the elbow. To the lower edge of each is joined a deep wrist section, which is ornamented at the top by a drooping puff and below by a band of velvet ribbon, a similar band encircling the sleeve above the puff. Velvet ribbon is folded to outline the lower edge of the polonaise in front of the coat-tails, and is arranged to hang in long loops and ends a trifle to the left of the closing.

This polonaise may be made up in lady's cloth, camel's hair, serge, brocaded wools, Scotch plaids, Lorne stripes, and other plain and fancy suitings and silks. Combinations of dress materials and silk also develop well in this way. Silk ribbon is often used for the collar facings and other trimmings when the polonaise is worn with a silk skirt. When one material is used throughout, passementerie, appliqué, embroidery, fancy galloon, etc., are favored trimmings. To make the polonaise for a lady of medium size, requires 5 5/8 yards of material 22 inches wide, or 2 3/4 yards of material 44 inches wide. Each requires 5/8 yard of velvet 20 inches wide for the collar, etc.

December 1889 *Delineator*

Evening Costume

Use the scale corresponding to the bust measure to draft the bodice. It consists of five pieces: Front, side piece, side back, back, and sleeve. Close the front with hooks and eyes, or lace it with a silk cord. Any style of trimming may be used at the neck and the bottom of the sleeve. Make the sash of soft silk that harmonizes with the dress. Join it in the under-arm seam on the right side, bring it across the front, and fasten it on the left side with hooks and eyes.

The skirt is drafted with the scale corresponding to the waist measure. Regulate the length with the tape measure. It is in one piece. Bring nearly all of the fullness to the back.

Spring 1890 *Voice of Fashion*

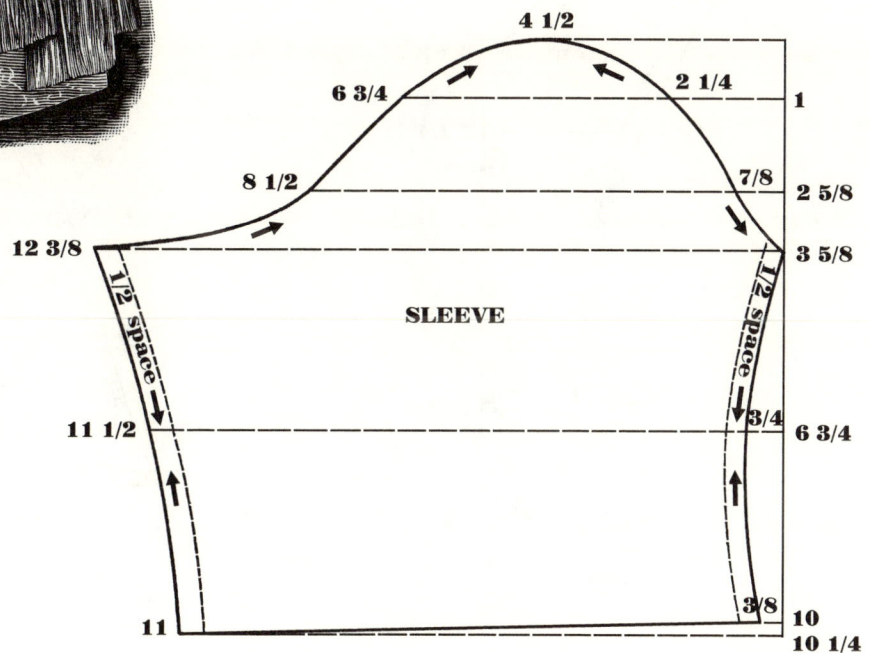

SLEEVE

4 1/2 · 6 3/4 · 2 1/4 · 1 · 8 1/2 · 7/8 · 2 5/8 · 12 3/8 · 3 5/8 · 1/2 space · 1/2 space · 11 1/2 · 3/4 · 6 3/4 · 11 · 3/8 · 10 · 10 1/4

SIDE PIECE

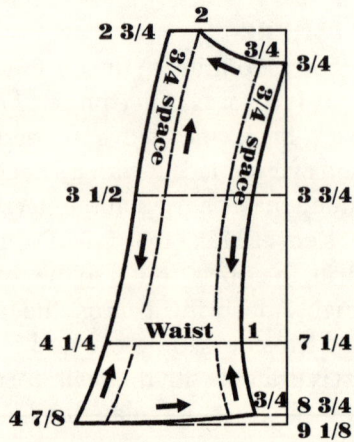

FRONT

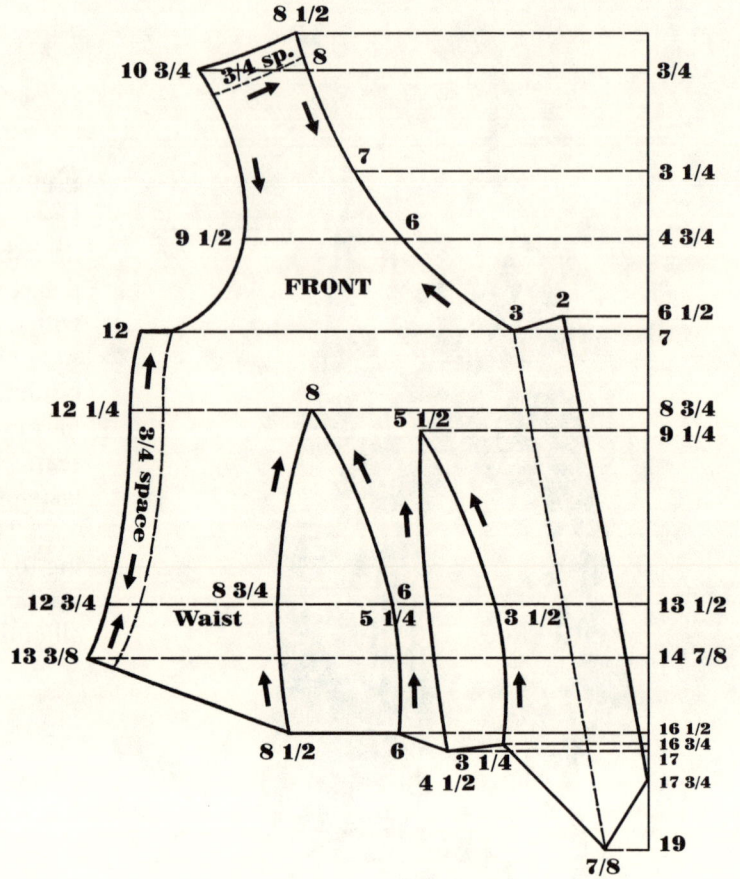

BACK

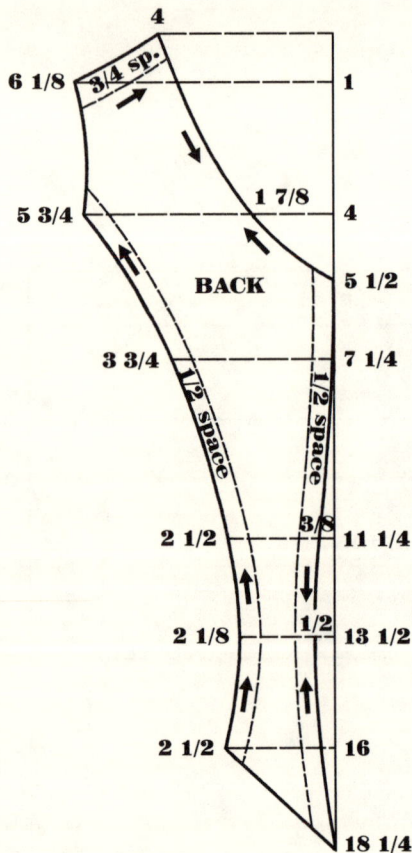

SIDE BACK

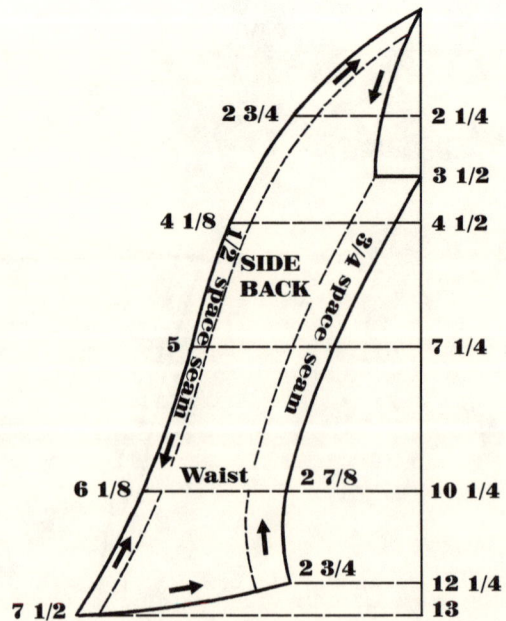

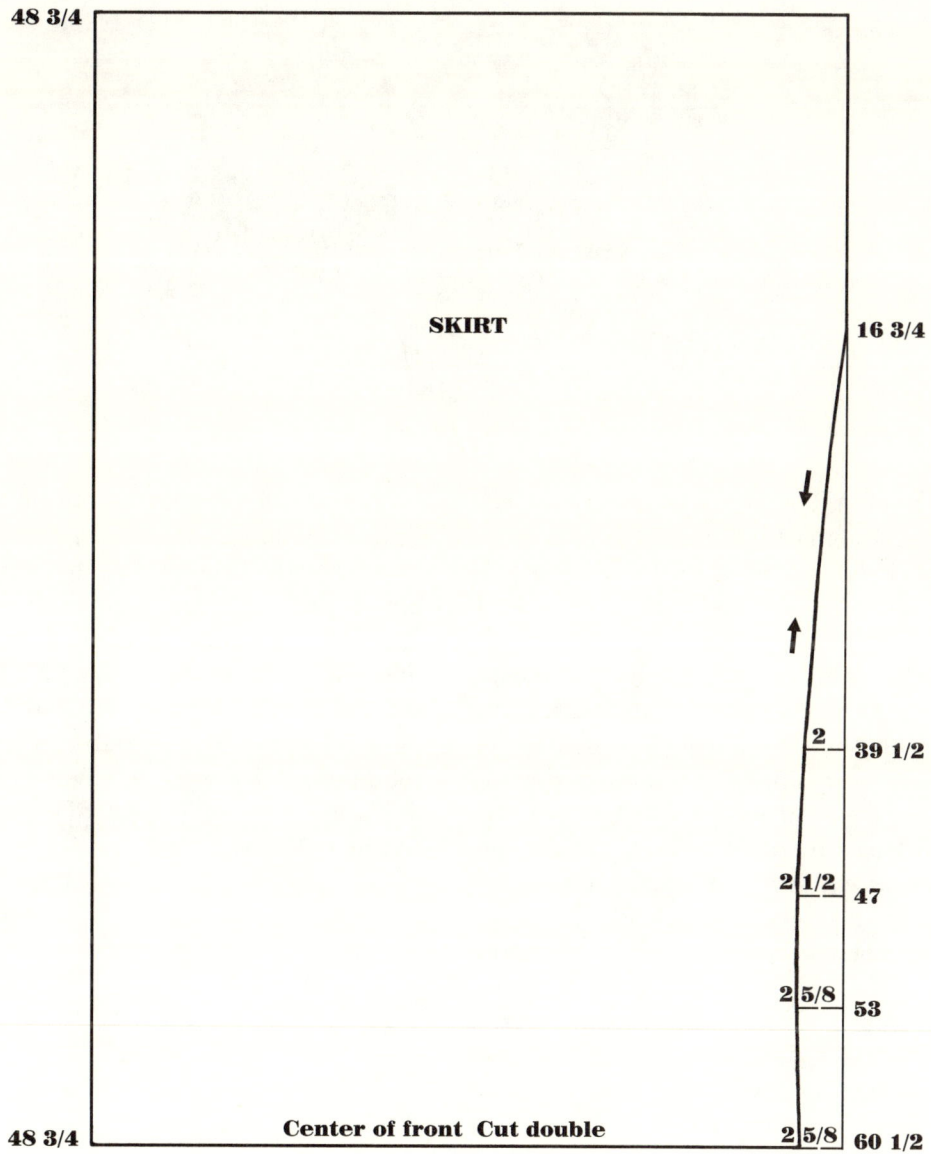

48 3/4

SKIRT

16 3/4

2 — 39 1/2

2 1/2 — 47

2 5/8 — 53

48 3/4

Center of front Cut double

2 5/8 — 60 1/2

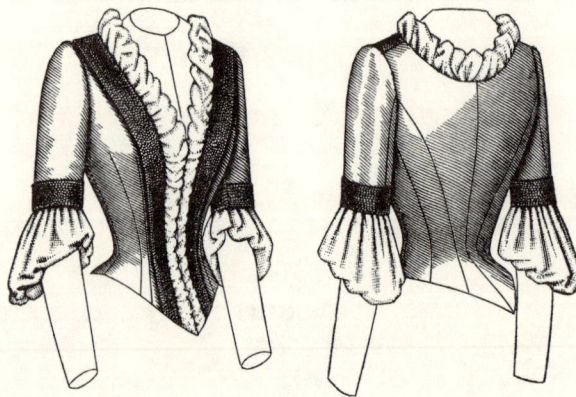

Court Bodice. This style is especially adapted for evening wear. It may form part of a costume, or be worn with a contrasting skirt. In this example lilac silk and old rose velvet and tulle are associated, velvet supplying the trimming.

The bodice is fitted by double bust darts, side pieces, side backs, and a curved center back seam. It is closed with hooks and eyes, an underlap being sewed to the left side. The bottom is pointed at the center of the front and back and arches over the hips. The backs are cut in a low, round outline, while the fronts are shaped in a V to the bust. A puff outlines the front edges and extends about the neck edge at the back; it is arranged over smooth linings that are seamed at the shoulders. A lapel is turned back from each front edge, its upper end being basted in place along the shoulder seam and its lower end along the lower edge of the front. To the lower edge of the short coat sleeve is sewed an ornament, which is widened toward the back of the arm and surmounted by a velvet band.

Any soft silk may be developed in this way, India, China, and faille being preferred. The silk may be in a solid color or figured, and may be combined with velvet and tulle, mull, crêpe de Chine, etc. The neck may be filled in with lace, crêpe, tulle, etc. To make the bodice for a lady of medium size, requires 2 1/2 yards of material 22 inches wide, or 1 1/4 yards of material 44 inches wide. Also required are 7/8 yard of velvet 20 inches wide for the lapels, etc., and 1 yard of tulle 72 inches wide for the puff, etc.

October 1889 *Delineator*

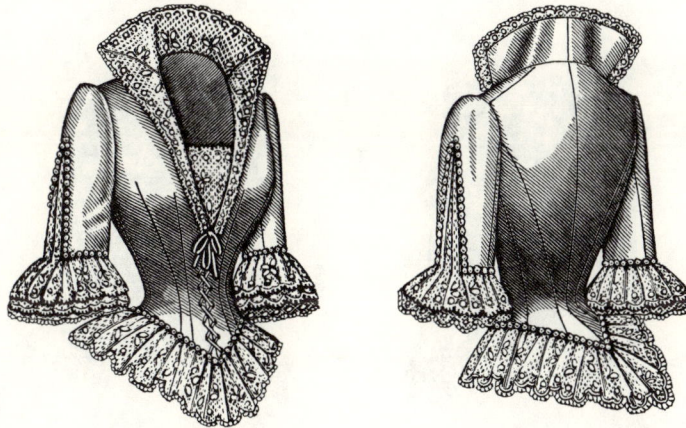

Evening Bodice with Medici Collar. This bodice is shown developed in pink silk, with lace edging, lace net, and narrow beaded trimming. It is adjusted by double bust darts, side pieces, side backs, and a center back seam. It is pointed both back and front, with a high curve on each side. The edge is trimmed with a frill of deep lace headed by a band of beaded trimming. The coat sleeves come just above the elbow. Each is slashed through the center of the upper part. The opening is filled in with a plaited section of lace net, the edges of the slash being ornamented with a band of beaded trimming. The bottom edges of the sleeve are finished with a double frill of lace edging and a bead arrangement corresponding to that on the edge of the basque. The fronts are cut low with a V effect. They have a small, lace-covered ornament of similar outline inserted at the bust. The ornament is permanently attached to the right front and fastened to the left with hooks and eyes. The Medici collar at the neck is covered with lace and interlined with crinoline, which makes it stand up well. The collar rolls high at the back, describes points above the shoulders, and narrows gradually toward the bust. Below the bust, the closing of the bodice is effected with narrow ribbon laced through eyelets. The ribbon is arranged in a bow at the top of the closing.

This mode is equally suitable for all colors and materials used for evening costumes. It develops nicely in black lace. It also makes up prettily in white, with trimmings of gold and white lace and pearl bead trimming. This bodice may form part of a costume, or it may be designed to be worn with almost any skirt, particularly one of black lace, with which any fancy bodice is appropriate. To make the garment for a lady of medium size, requires 2 3/4 yards of material 22 inches wide, 1 5/8 yards of material 36 inches wide, or 1 3/8 yards of material 44 inches wide.

May 1889 *Delineator*

Evening Bodice with Pompadour Neck.
This bodice is pictured made of silk. The neck is in V shape at the back and a low Pompadour shape in the front. The sides of the Pompadour opening are considerably slanted, and V shaped at the lower edge. The front edges are curved and underfaced. Instead of being buttoned, they are laced with silk cord. Double bust darts, side pieces, side backs, and a curved center back seam perform the adjustment. The lower edge is pointed at the front and back and curved high over the hips. The sleeves extend to a little below the elbows, the lower outline showing a gradual shortening toward the back of the arm. Beaded lace net is draped in a soft twist about their lower edges above a lisse frill, and a bow of picot-edged ribbon is fastened at the inside of the arm. Lace net and ruching border the neck edges. Ribbon bows are fastened at the tops of the shoulder seams and at the corners of the front opening.

Bodices of this style are often made of velvet or satin to wear with skirts of tulle, lace net, or silk. When intended for this purpose they are usually black, or a darker or lighter shade than the skirt. For instance, a bodice to wear with dark brown skirts may be golden brown; one to wear with pale heliotrope may be the darkest shade of the flower; and one to wear with a skirt of white tulle or lace may be white. The sleeves may be of lace net, or they may be omitted altogether. The neck decoration may be varied in any becoming manner. To make the bodice for a lady of medium size, requires 2 1/2 yards of material 22 inches wide, or 1 1/4 yards of material 44 inches wide.

February 1887 *Delineator*

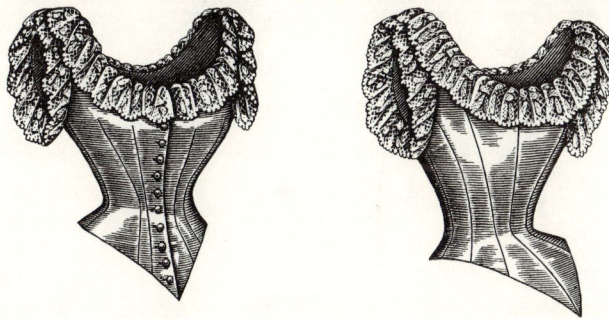

Pointed Evening Basque. This basque is shown developed in satin, with lace for trimming. The fronts close with button-holes and buttons, the right side being hemmed. The adjustment is performed by double bust darts, side pieces, side backs, and a curved center back seam. The back seams are sprung out below the waist-line to give the proper fullness for any style of drapery. The outline is raised high over the hips and deepened into a decided point at the center of the front and back, the lower edge being plainly finished. This basque may be made with the low, round neck pictured, or a square Pompadour shape.

With either shape, a lace frill is the usual finish. Lace frills also finish the armholes. Sometimes the lower edge of the basque is single, double, or even triple piped, or it may be bordered with a silk cord. If the wearer is slender, passementerie, lace, down, or feather bands may be added about the lower edge and about the neck. To make the basque for a lady of medium size, requires 2 yards of material 22 inches wide, or 3/4 yard of material 48 inches wide.

November 1885 *Delineator*

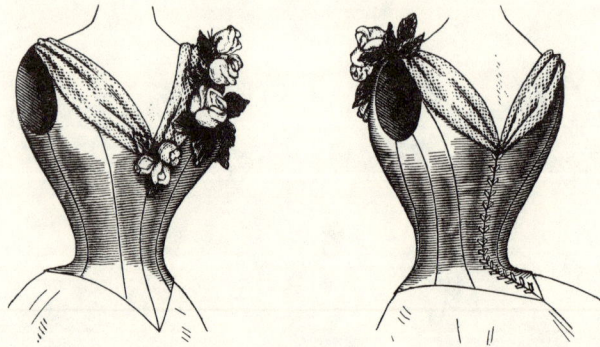

Evening Bodice. This décolleté bodice is shown developed in white satin, with white tulle and roses and buds for trimmings. The bottom is deeply pointed at the center front and back, and arched high at the sides, where the basque is quite short. The bodice is fitted by a curved seam at the center of the front, side fronts, side pieces, side backs, and curved back edges. The latter are boned and laced together with white silk cord, an underlap being sewed to one back. The neck is cut in V shape both back and front, but is much lower in front. It is draped with tulle, which is caught up closely on the shoulders at the closing edges at the center of the front, forming soft puffs or festoons between the bastings. The tulle forms a cloudy nest for a spray of roses, buds, and foliage, which extends well down from the right shoulder. A trio of small buds surrounded by their leaves is fastened where the drapery is caught at the center of the front. The armholes and lower edges are plainly finished.

Soft wools, silks, and velvets are equally desirable materials, and all colors are appropriate. Bodices of black or colored velvet are worn with lace skirts. Black velvet or satin bodices, with gold or silver tinsel net, or with a small figured net having the pattern outlined with tinsel thread, are elegant. The neck and armholes may be draped with beaded, embroidered, or tinsel net. Guimpes of tulle laid in soft folds, or of tinsel and embroidered or tufted net, are fashionable. Puffed sleeves of the same material reach nearly or quite to the wrists. Lace frills draped up on the shoulders and falling low under the arms are liked by many ladies. Sometimes only a cording or heading edges the neck and armholes, and the remaining edges are similarly finished. For a lady of medium size, this bodice requires 1 3/4 yards of material 22 inches wide, or 7/8 yard of material 44 inches wide.

February 1888 *Delineator*

8. Sports Outfits

The bodice of a riding habit may have a step collar, notched and open at the throat (precisely like that of a man's morning coat), for wearing with a white chemisette and necktie. What are perhaps the most acceptable bodices button closely up to the throat and are canvased throughout. The front edges curve outward, are double stitched, and are further rounded out or fashioned by the tailor's iron. When made in tailor fashion, the cloth of the bodice is fitted to the wearer and is bound in all the lengthwise seams. The satin or flannel lining is then made up separately, and all its seams are concealed, as they are set inside. A good plan is to add a corset belt in front, sewed in the under-arm seams at the waist-line. This is pointed like a girdle at the top and bottom in front, has several whalebones, and is laced closely. The close coat sleeves have two buttons and button-holes at the wrist. The high collar is stiffly interlined. Two buttons define the waist-line at the back.

The habit skirt is cut about 80 inches broad at its greatest width. The top should fit without a wrinkle when the rider is in the saddle. The skirt drops within 2 inches of the floor when she stands. It is shaped by curves and cross-cuts to fit over the right knee, and to allow room for the pommel. Inside the under half of the front is a loop in which the right boot of the rider is thrust just to the toe. On the back of the skirt is another loop, which is fastened under the heel of the left boot. These loops keep the skirt smooth and hold it in place.

The long trousers are seated with chamois. They are attached to a wide satin belt shaped out over the hips, which laces at the back to give greater latitude. Short breeches have a similar belt. They are made long enough to button just below the knee. Each leg buttons differently, that worn on the right leg buttoning inside, and that on the left leg outside, so as not to come between the limbs and the saddle.

1892 Home Dressmaking

Gay striped coats for tennis players, and for country wear generally, are made of thick twilled serge, either white, pale blue, or rose, with irregular stripes of brown, red, and green. These coats are quite short, with adjusted back pieces and a loose front. The front fastens at the top with one or two large pearl buttons, then slopes away gradually. Several small pockets with laps are added, and the edges are double stitched. The collar turns over deeply, or there is a rolling notched collar.

March 24, 1888 Harper's Bazar

Lawn Tennis Costume

The bodice is drafted with the scale corresponding to the bust measure. It is in eight pieces: Front yoke, back yoke, shirred front, shirred back, sailor collar, standing collar, and two sleeve pieces. The belt is not given, as it is simply a straight piece of material of the length and width desired. Gather the top of the shirring and sew it to the yoke. Also gather it between the notches on the waist-line, and fasten it to the belt. The sailor collar may be separate, or fastened to the bodice at the back of the neck.

The skirt and skirt yoke are drafted with the scale corresponding to the waist measure. Regulate the length with the tape measure. The yoke is cut double in front. The skirt consists of ten box-plaits. But two are here given; the remaining eight are made in the same manner. Press carefully and stay two or three times underneath with tape, and sew the plaited part to the yoke.

The skirt drapery is drafted with the scale corresponding to the waist measure. It is in one piece; the front and back are drafted together. It is simply a straight piece of material laid in five upward-turning plaits on the sides, and fastened firmly to the skirt. The front is laid in three backward-turning plaits to give the required fullness in front. The back is hemmed and left open. There are two large loops at the back.

Summer 1888 *Voice of Fashion*

STANDING COLLAR

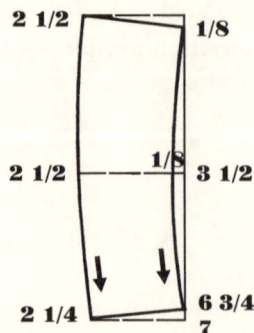

2 1/2		1/8
2 1/2	1/8	3 1/2
2 1/4		6 3/4
		7

Lawn Tennis Costume

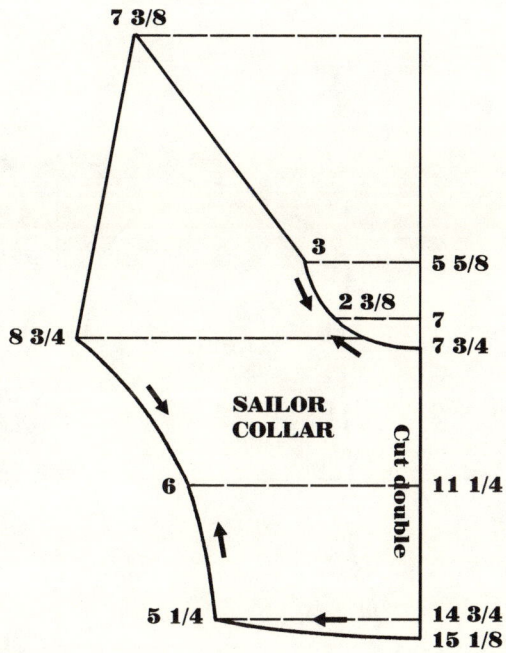

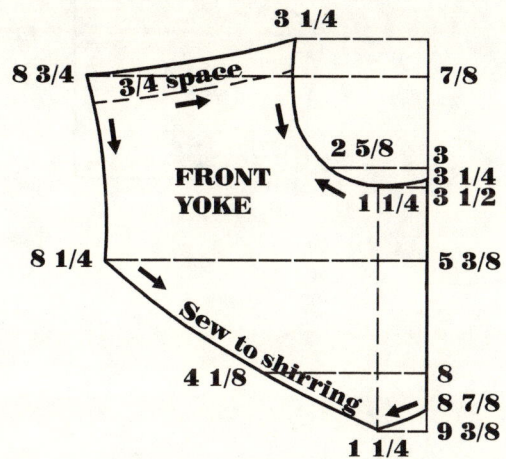

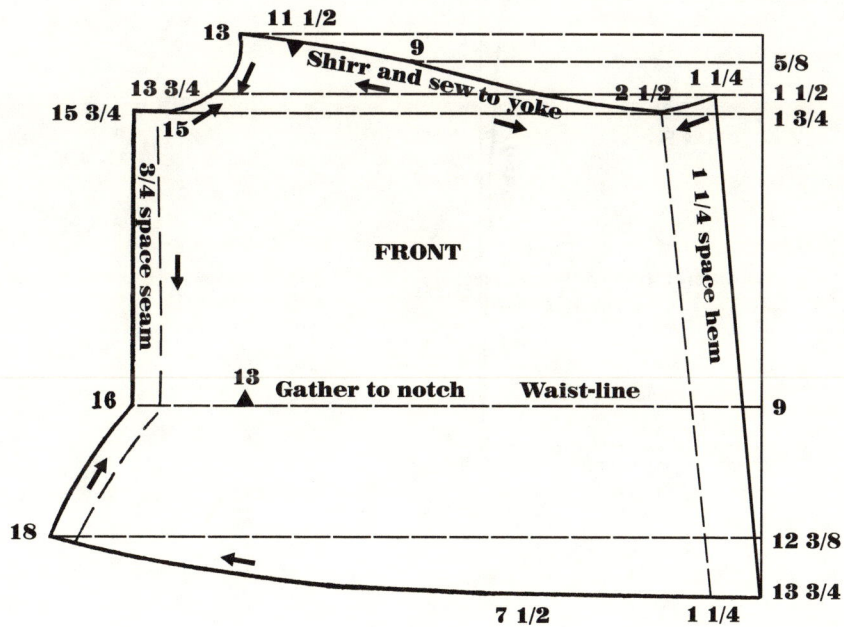

SAILOR COLLAR

7 3/8

3

5 5/8

2 3/8

7

7 3/4

8 3/4

6

11 1/4

Cut double

5 1/4

14 3/4

15 1/8

FRONT YOKE

3 1/4

8 3/4

3/4 space

7/8

2 5/8

3

3 1/4

1 1/4

3 1/2

8 1/4

5 3/8

Sew to shirring

8

4 1/8

8 7/8

1 1/4

9 3/8

FRONT

13

11 1/2

9

Shirr and sew to yoke

5/8

2 1/2

1 1/4

1 1/2

13 3/4

1 3/4

15 3/4

15

3/4 space seam

1 1/4 space hem

16

13

Gather to notch

Waist-line

9

18

12 3/8

13 3/4

7 1/2

1 1/4

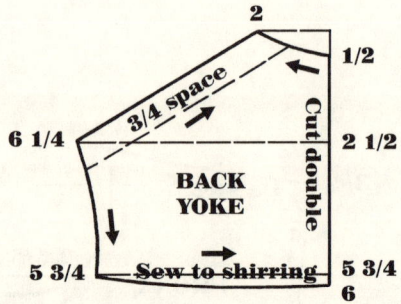

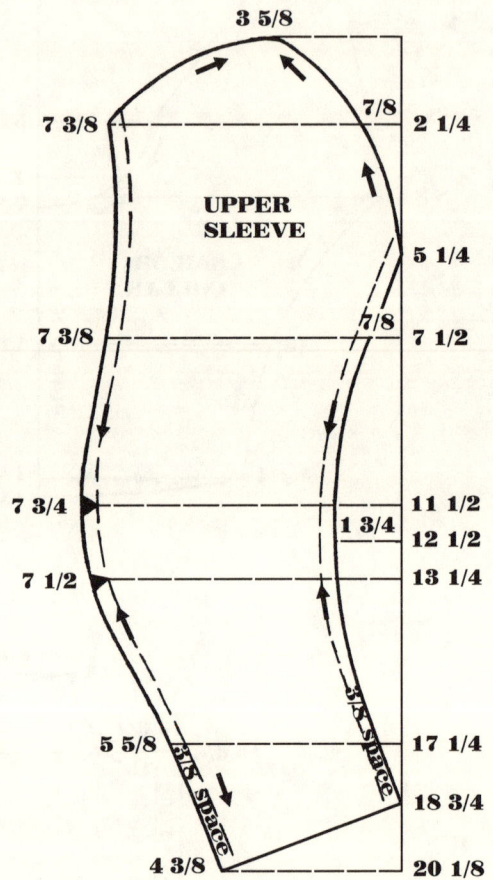

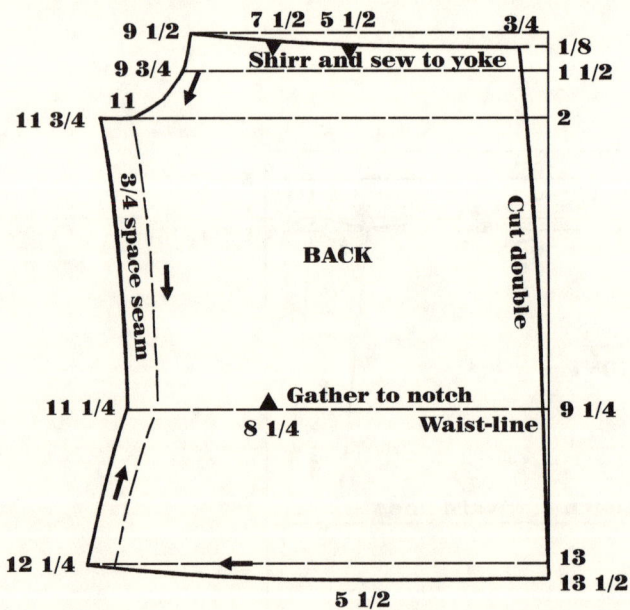

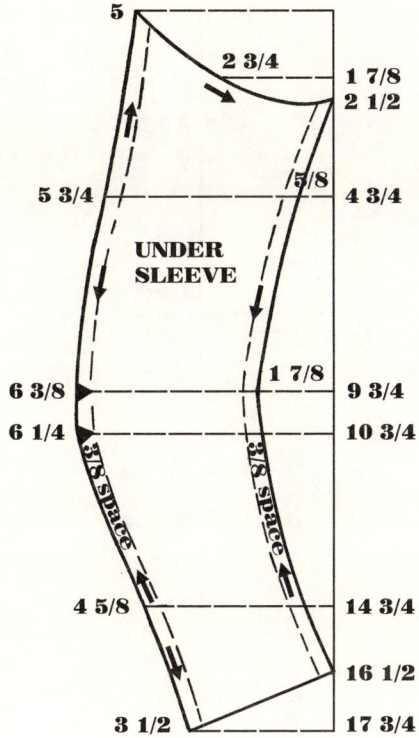

UNDER SLEEVE

5

2 3/4

1 7/8
2 1/2

5 3/4   5/8   4 3/4

6 3/8   1 7/8   9 3/4
6 1/4   10 3/4

3/8 space   3/8 space

4 5/8   14 3/4

16 1/2
3 1/2   17 3/4

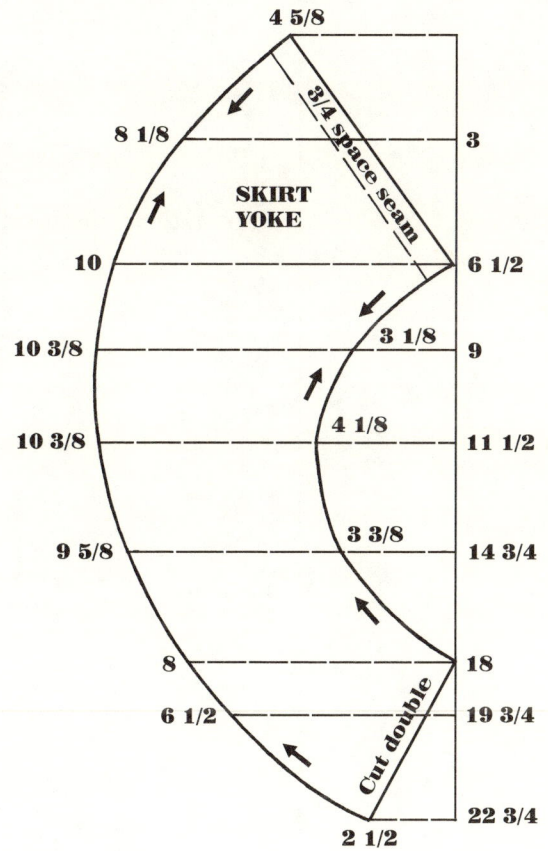

SKIRT YOKE

4 5/8

8 1/8   3/4 space seam   3

10   6 1/2

10 3/8   3 1/8   9

10 3/8   4 1/8   11 1/2

9 5/8   3 3/8   14 3/4

8   18

6 1/2   Cut double   19 3/4

22 3/4
2 1/2

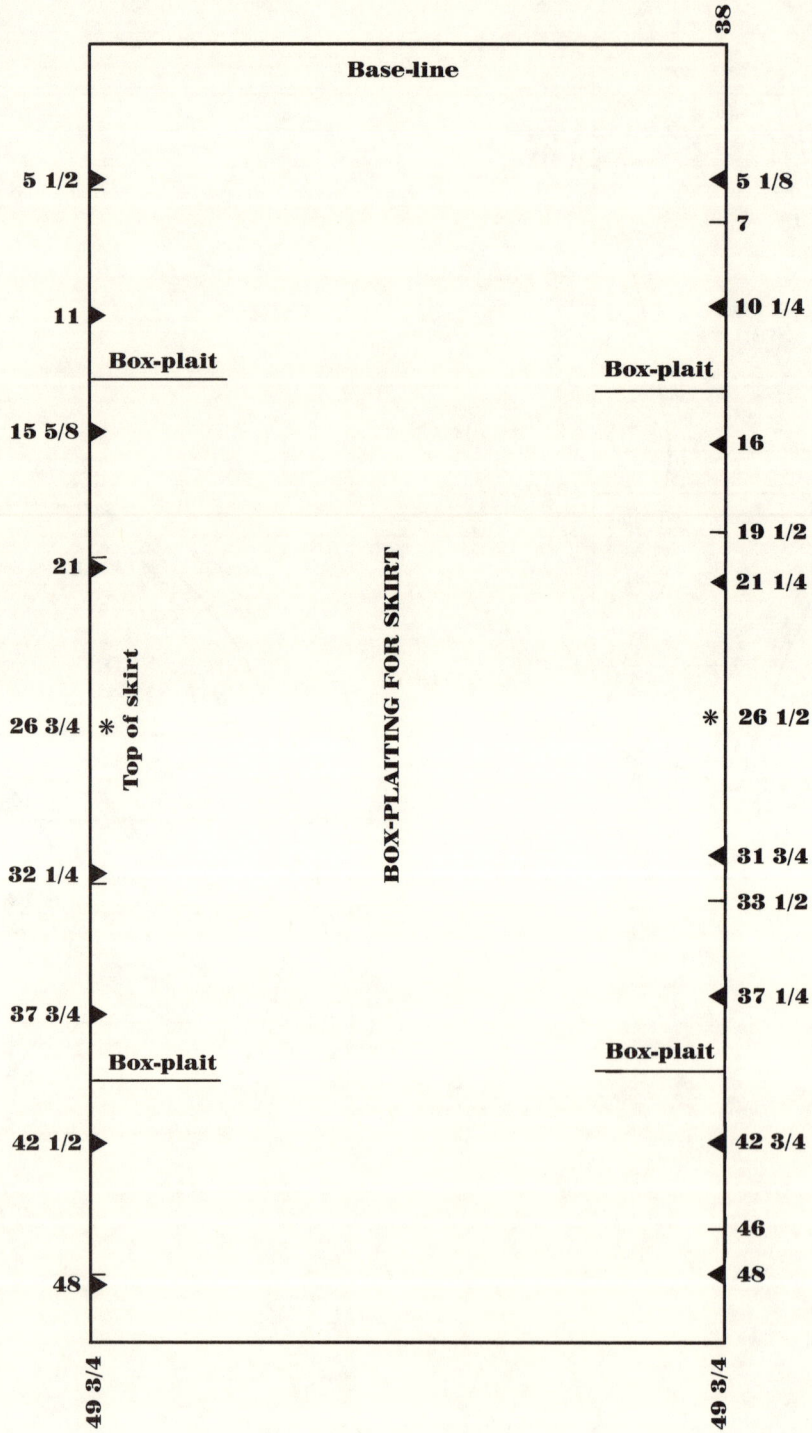

Base-line

38

5 1/2   5 1/8

7

11   10 1/4

Box-plait   Box-plait

15 5/8   16

19 1/2

21   21 1/4

Top of skirt

26 3/4 ✱   ✱ 26 1/2

BOX-PLAITING FOR SKIRT

31 3/4

32 1/4   33 1/2

37 3/4   37 1/4

Box-plait   Box-plait

42 1/2   42 3/4

46

48   48

49 3/4   49 3/4

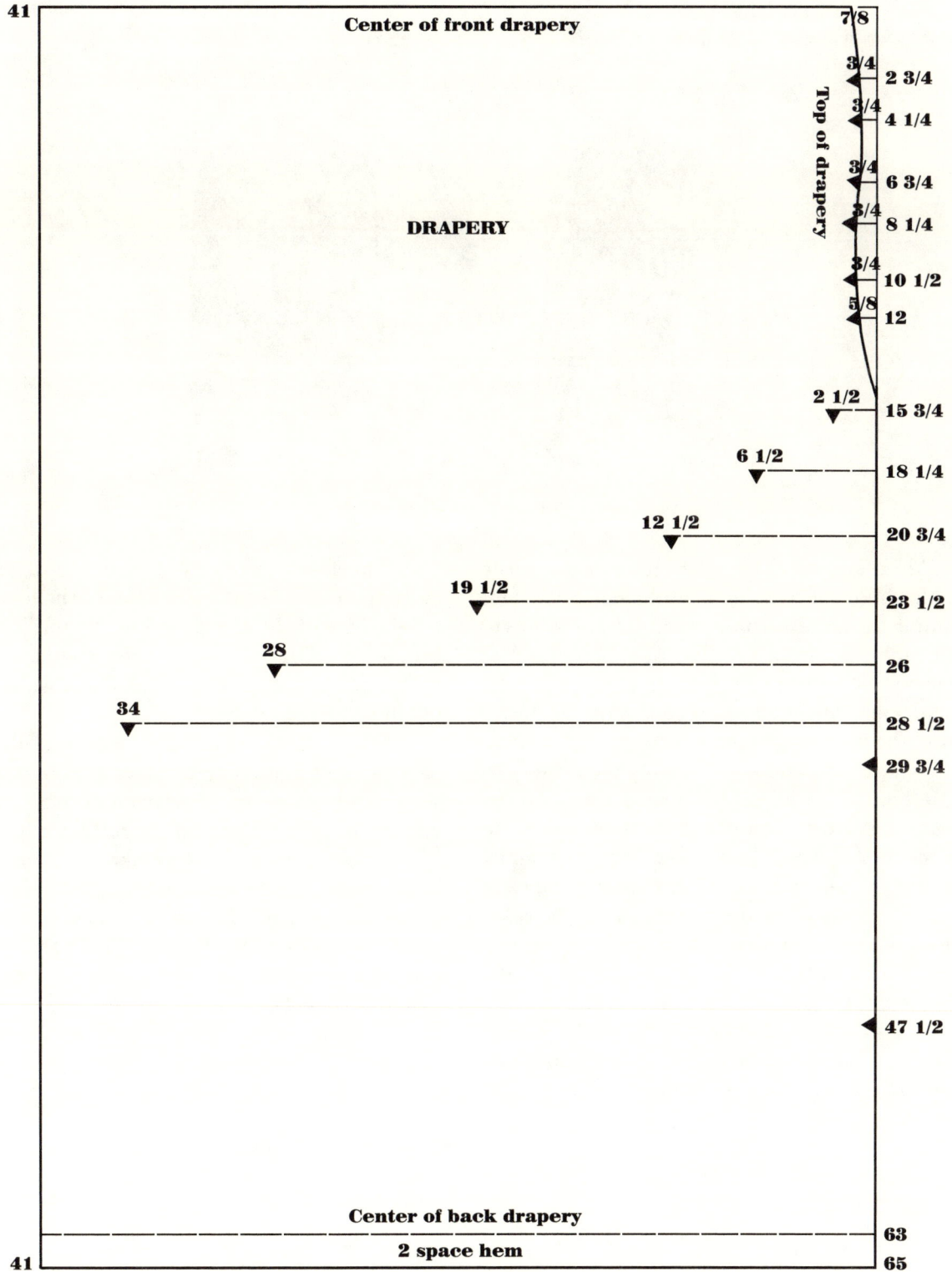

41 Center of front drapery 7/8

DRAPERY

Top of drapery

3/4 ◄ 2 3/4
3/4 ◄ 4 1/4
3/4 ◄ 6 3/4
3/4 ◄ 8 1/4
3/4 ◄ 10 1/2
5/8 ◄ 12

2 1/2 ▼ 15 3/4

6 1/2 ▼ 18 1/4

12 1/2 ▼ 20 3/4

19 1/2 ▼ 23 1/2

28 ▼ 26

34 ▼ 28 1/2

◄ 29 3/4

◄ 47 1/2

Center of back drapery 63
2 space hem

41 65

Yoke Blouse. The yoke blouse is a favorite style for both wash materials and fancy ones. This example is made of plain cambric and all-over embroidered cambric. The yoke is pointed at the center of the front and back. It is seamed at the shoulders. Its lower edge is piped before the lower part of the blouse is joined to it.

The three sections comprising the lower part of the blouse are joined by curved seams on the sides. They are sloped out above these seams to perfect the shape of the armholes. They are scantily gathered at their tops to within a short distance of the armholes, to adapt them to the size of the yoke. The blouse is closed with buttons and button-holes, the right side of both the yoke and the lower part being hemmed.

A belt with leather straps draws the blouse in at the waist-line. The blouse extends to about basque depth below it, the lower edge being plainly finished.

The front of the yoke is made of all-over embroidery. The coat-shaped sleeves have pointed cuff-facings of the same, and narrow frills of embroidered edging turning toward the hands. The rolling collar is of all-over embroidery, with a finish of embroidered edging.

Prints, lawn, percale, piqué, and all kinds of white and figured cottons, as well as linen and seasonable wools, make up well in this way. The entire yoke, the collar, and the cuff-facings may be of contrasting material. To make the blouse for a lady of medium size, requires 3 1/2 yards of material 22 inches wide, or 1 7/8 yards of material 44 inches wide. As represented, it needs 2 1/8 yards of cambric 36 inches wide, and 7/8 yard of embroidered material 20 inches wide.

March 1887 *Delineator*

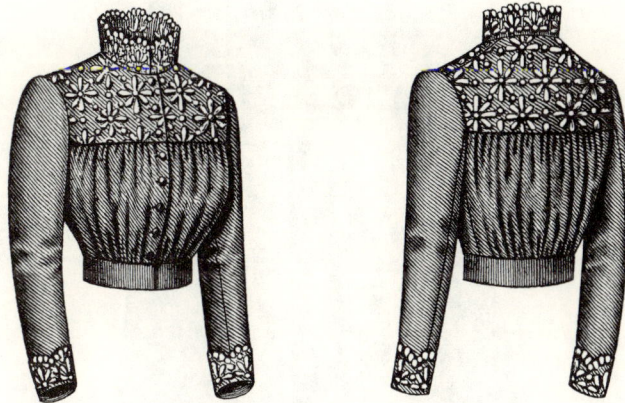

Yoke Bodice. This example shows the yoke made of all-over embroidered webbing. The lower part of the bodice is made of plain wash material. So are the coat sleeves, which have embroidered edging turned back in cuff fashion from their wrists.

The yoke is of becoming length, curves well up over the tops of the arms, and has seams on the shoulders. The full part has seams at the sides. Its top is drawn to the proper dimensions by gathers that end a little to the front and back of the arm-holes. After the gathers are made, the lower part is seamed to the corresponding edges of the yoke. The lower edge is reduced to the proper size by two lines of gathers in the back and two in each side of the front, a space of about 2 inches being allowed between the lines. The gathers end some distance from the side seams. A belt is stitched on the out-side, with its top over the upper gathers; its lower edge is turned under and hemmed on the under side. Button-holes and buttons close the fronts, the right side of both the yoke and the full part being turned under for a hem. The high standing collar is of embroidered edging.

Bodices of this style are especially adapted to embroidered materials, open-work materials of all kinds, and plain wash materials. However, they may be made of any kind of wool or silk dress material not devoted especially to wear on ceremonious oc-casions. To make the bodice for a lady of medium size, requires 2 3/4 yards of material 22 inches wide, or 1 3/8 yards of material 48 inches wide. In the combination pictured, it needs 1 3/8 yards of mate-rial 36 inches wide, and 5/8 yard of embroidered webbing 20 inches wide.

July 1886 *Delineator*

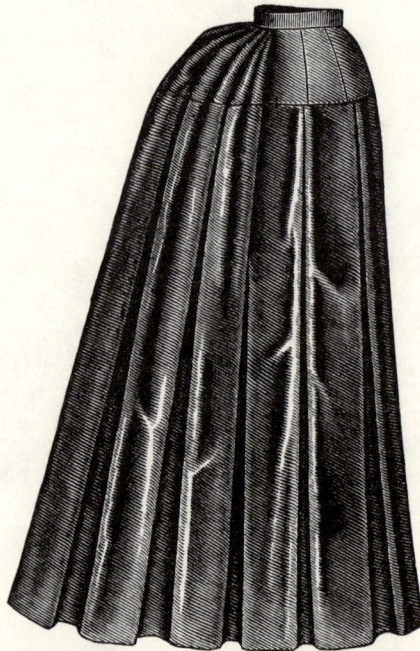

Box-Plaited Skirt. The foundation or skirt proper comprises three gores for the back and sides, and a full breadth for the back. The gores are fitted smoothly by darts, while the breadth is gathered on each side of the placket opening. A bustle may be allowed for by adding extra length at the top. The bouffant effect is enhanced by steels run through casings that are set on the breadth and tied into curves by tapes sewed at their ends. The top is finished with a belt.

Straight breadths are joined together to form the plaited part. The lower edge is turned under for a hem. Two tapes sewed to the box-plaits underneath retain them in their folds. When the plaited part is arranged on the foundation, the lower edges fall evenly, and the top is sewed flatly not far below the top of the foundation.

Plain dress material was chosen for the skirt pictured, and the finish is quite plain. Flat decorations, however, may be applied if desired. Instead of being hemmed, the plaiting is sometimes faced to the depth of 4 or 5 inches with contrasting material before the plaits are laid. Wide braid is sometimes arranged in the same manner. All kinds of dress materials make this skirt up handsomely, and any style of bodice may be worn with it. A broad sash may be draped about the figure to conceal the skirt above the plaiting, and its ends are bowed at the back. Any style of drapery may be added; but with a basque long enough to cover the skirt above the plaiting, drapery is unnecessary. To make this skirt for a lady of medium size, requires 15 1/2 yards of material 22 inches wide, 8 3/4 yards of material 44 inches wide, or 6 5/8 yards of material 54 inches wide.

February 1887 *Delineator*

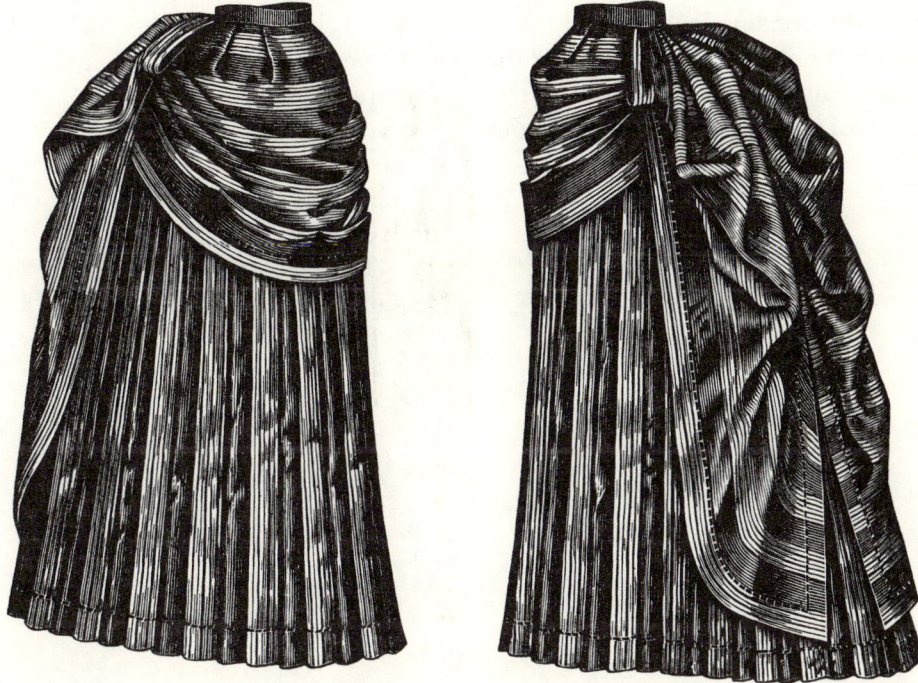

Tennis or Walking Skirt. Striped tennis suiting was used for this skirt. The upper part is in yoke shape and fits smoothly about the figure. Its ends are hemmed, and it is closed at the back with button-holes and flat buttons, or with hooks and eyes. To the yoke is sewed a kilt composed of straight breadths joined together, turned under for a hem at the lower edge, and laid in plaits all turning one way. The plaits are held in place by tapes sewed to their underfolds. A placket opening is made beneath the plait at the center of the back. Before the kilt is sewed to the yoke it is gathered, most of the fullness being kept at the back. As the kilt has no foundation skirt, it is light-weight and is easily freed from dust and wrinkles.

The front drapery is in tablier style and is cross-wrinkled by means of four upward-turning plaits in each side. The folds of the lower plaits are basted to form pockets for tennis balls. The top of the drapery is conformed to the yoke by shallow plaits, the side edges being sewed on the skirt.

Two full breadths are united in the back drapery; they are seamed together and their front edges turned under for hems. When they are adjusted on the skirt, they are sewed through the underfolds of these hems smoothly over the side edges of the tablier, from the lower edge of the latter as far as the fold of the topmost plait, where a single, loose loop is folded in each edge of the back drapery. Above the looping, they are sewed in the same manner as far as the top. In the seam joining the two breadths, five upward-turning plaits are folded, one on the other, even with the top, and are basted to the top of the yoke on the right end. In the seam lower down are basted two similar plaits, which are basted at the lower edge of the yoke on the same side. In the top, turning toward the hem of the front edge, a single plait is folded in each side. Back of this plait, nearly all of the length remaining at the

top of the right side is sewed in a burnous loop. On the left side the corresponding length is left loose, save for a basting that holds it to the left end of the yoke to facilitate putting on the skirt. However, this falls amid the folds of the drapery like the burnous when the garment is on the figure.

The top of the tablier, and the top of the part of the back drapery neither included in the burnous nor needed for the corresponding loose length at the opposite side, are turned in for a finish. They are sewed in place near the top of the yoke, which is itself finished with a narrow bias underfacing. Machine-stitched hems finish the lower edges of both drapery sections.

To make the skirt for a lady of medium size, requires 18 1/2 yards of material 22 inches wide, or 9 1/4 yards of material 44 inches wide.

June 1887 *Delineator*

Lawn Tennis Costume

Lawn Tennis Costume

This costume is shown made up in plain white and bourette-striped tennis cloth, with a cashmere sash trimmed with pompon fringe. The blouse bodice is drafted with the scale corresponding to the bust measure. It consists of six pieces: Back, front, pocket, collar, sleeve, and cuff. The front is tucked as marked on the diagram. The buttons are sewed underneath, and the button-holes are made on the under side. The lacing in front may be omitted if preferred. The bottom of the bodice is hemmed and elastic inserted in the hem, as marked on the diagrams. If preferred, it may be gathered and sewed to the belt.

The skirt is drafted with the scale corresponding to the waist measure. The length is regulated with the tape measure. There are four pieces: Belt, half of the yoke, half of the sash, and half of the kilt skirt. The sash may be cut double if preferred. Tie it around the waist and make a large knot and ends on the side. The ends of the sash may be gathered and finished with a tassel.

1889 *National Garment Cutter Book of Diagrams*

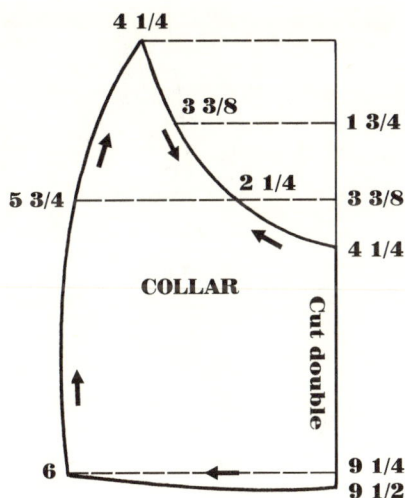

4 1/4

3 3/8   1 3/4

5 3/4   2 1/4   3 3/8

4 1/4

COLLAR   Cut double

6   9 1/4
9 1/2

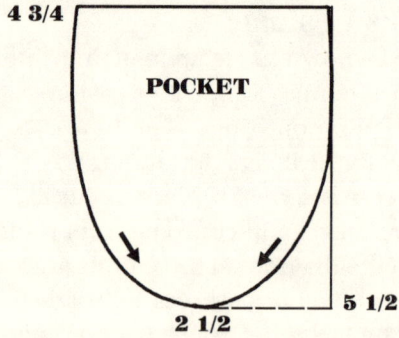

POCKET

4 3/4

2 1/2   5 1/2

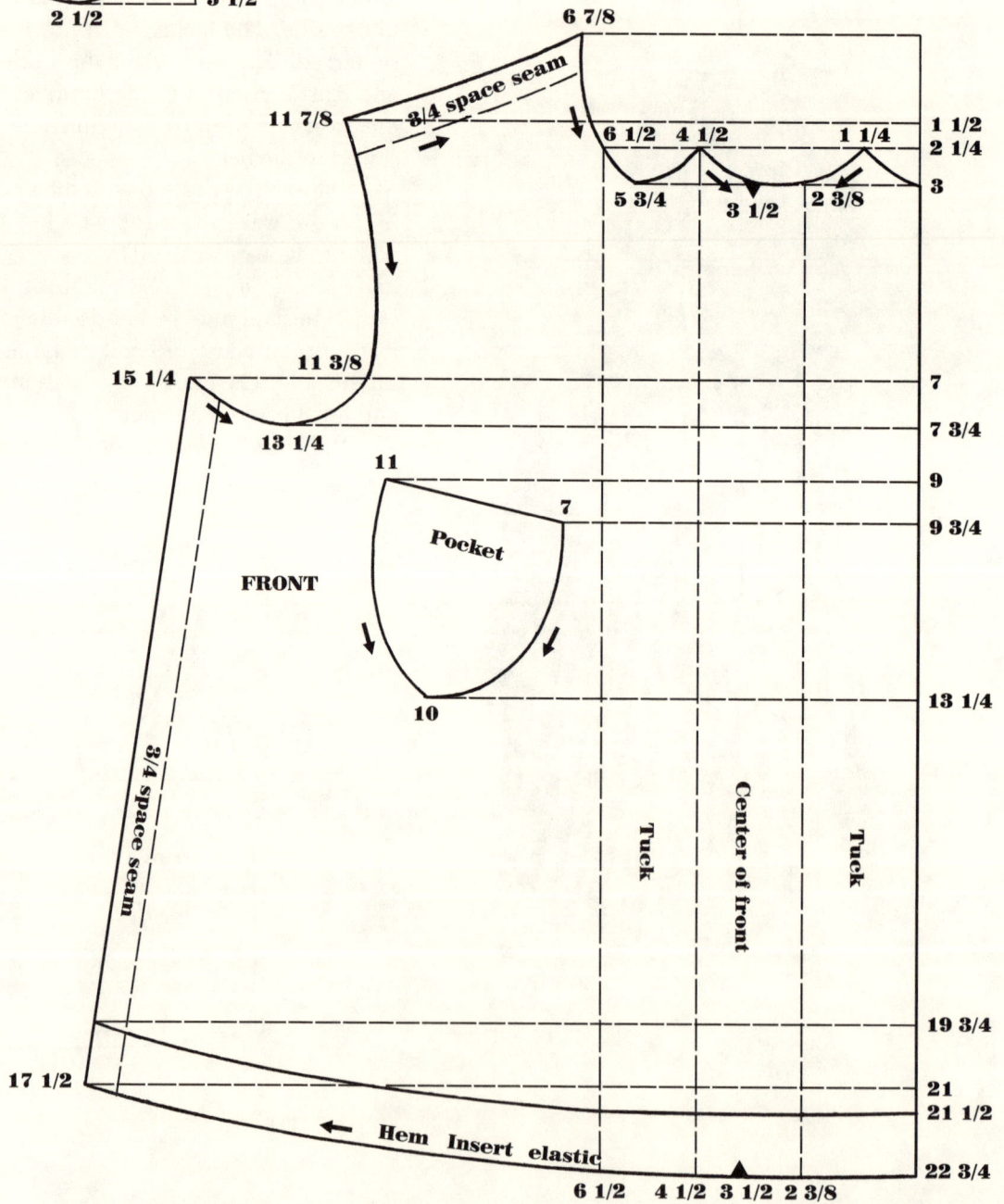

6 7/8

3|4 space seam

11 7/8

1 1/2
6 1/2   4 1/2   1 1/4   2 1/4
5 3/4   3 1/2   2 3/8   3

11 3/8

15 1/4   7

13 1/4   7 3/4

11   9

FRONT   Pocket   7   9 3/4

10   13 1/4

3/4 space seam   Tuck   Center of front   Tuck

19 3/4

17 1/2   21
                                         21 1/2

← Hem Insert elastic   22 3/4

6 1/2   4 1/2 3 1/2 2 3/8

Lawn Tennis Costume

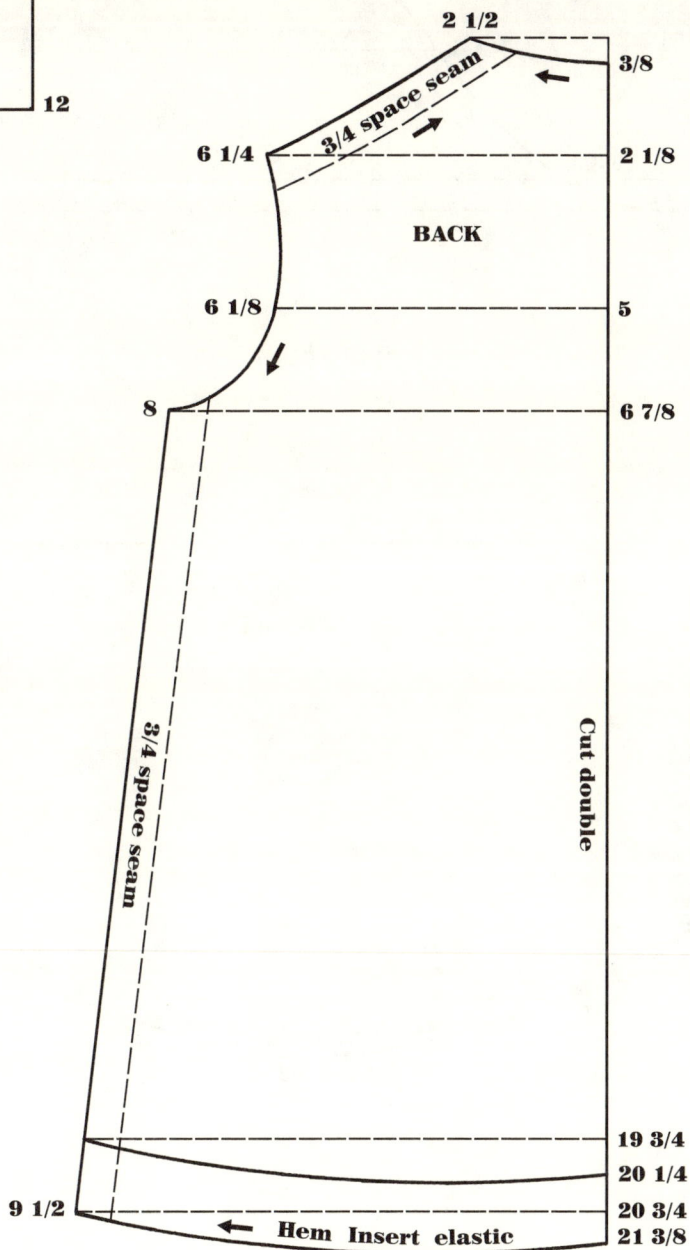

BELT

3

3   12

2 1/2

3/8

3/4 space seam

6 1/4   2 1/8

BACK

6 1/8   5

8   6 7/8

3/4 space seam

Cut double

19 3/4

20 1/4

9 1/2   20 3/4

Hem Insert elastic   21 3/8

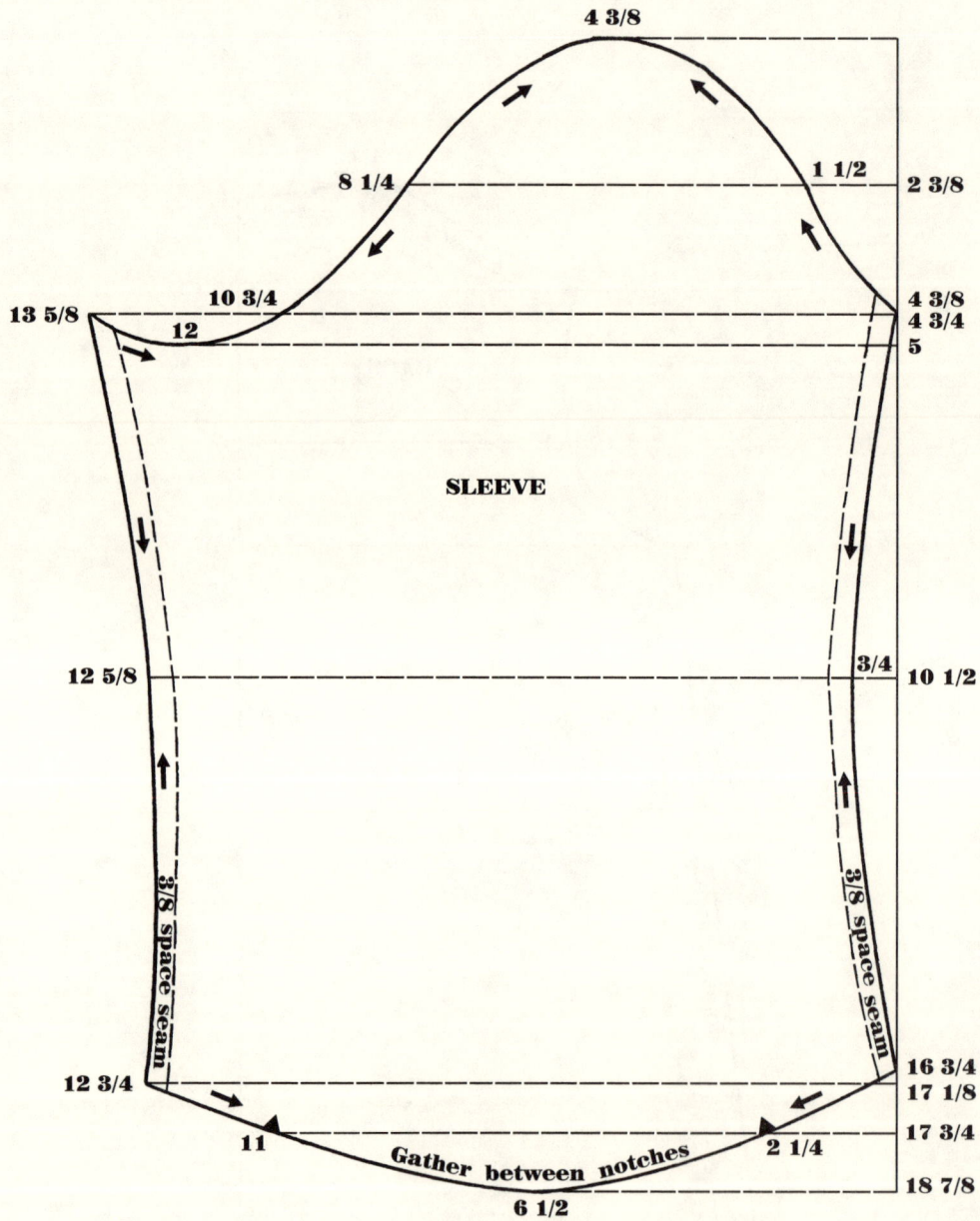

SLEEVE

Gather between notches

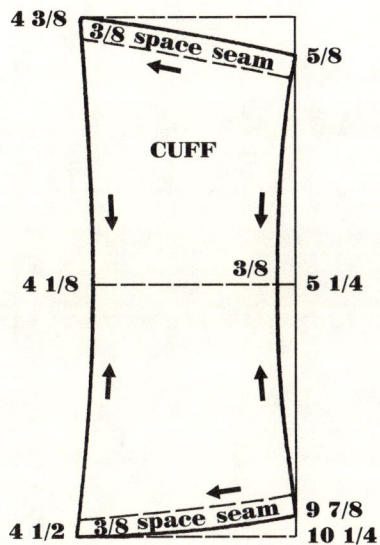

CUFF

4 3/8

3/8 space seam

5/8

4 1/8   3/8   5 1/4

4 1/2   3/8 space seam   9 7/8   10 1/4

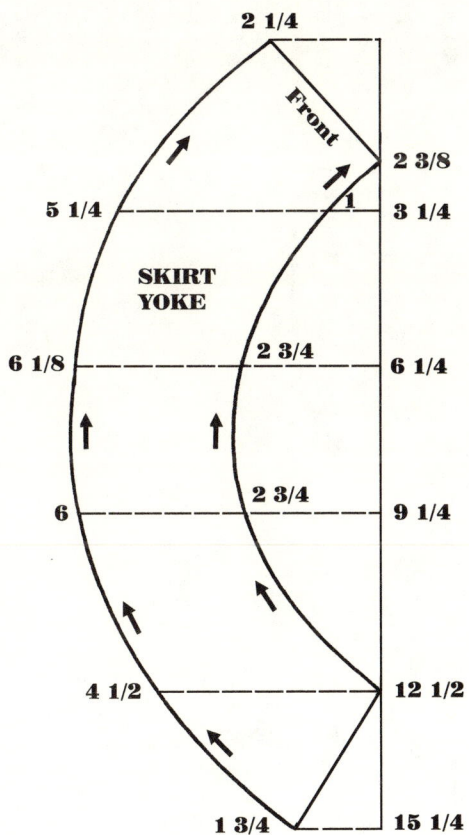

SKIRT YOKE

Front

2 1/4

2 3/8

5 1/4   1   3 1/4

6 1/8   2 3/4   6 1/4

6   2 3/4   9 1/4

4 1/2   12 1/2

1 3/4   15 1/4

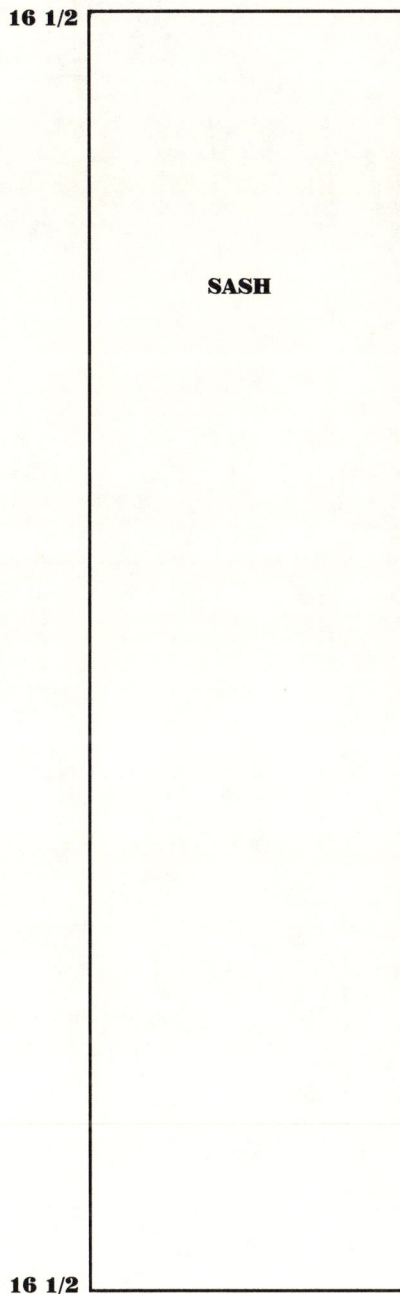

SASH

16 1/2

16 1/2   60

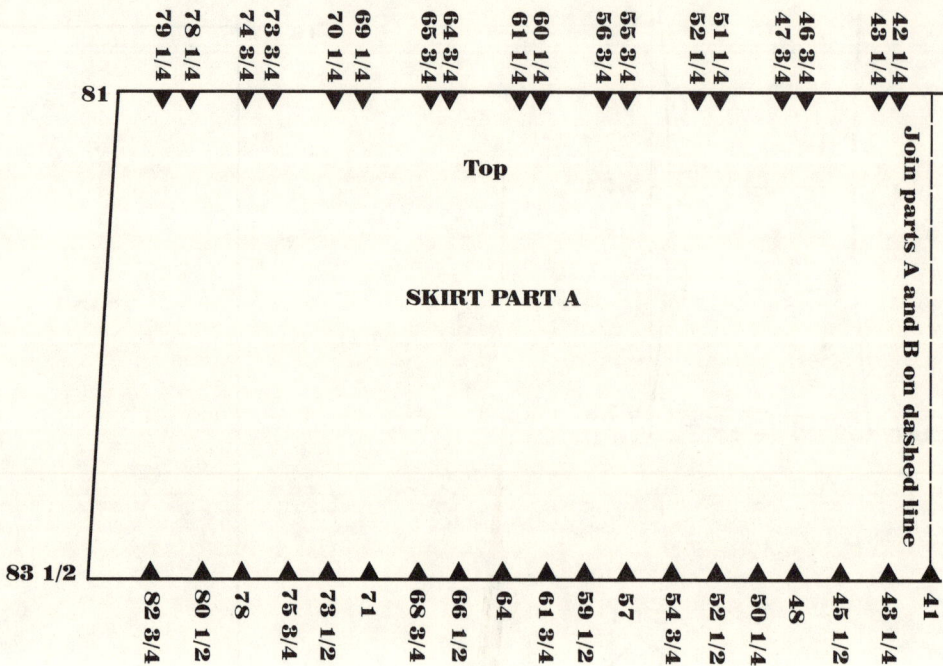

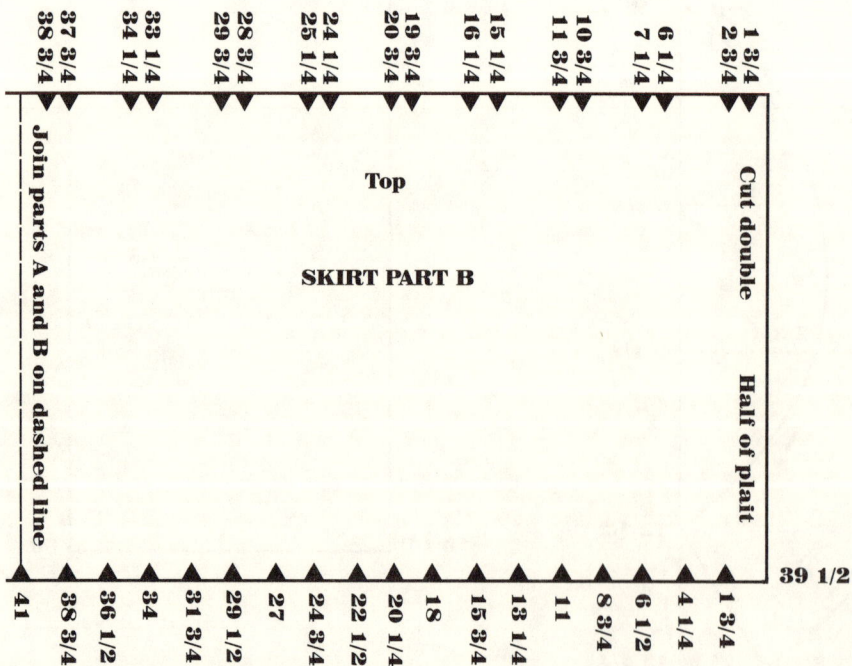

Lawn Tennis Costume

Lawn Tennis Costume. This costume is shown developed in striped tennis cloth and plain suiting. The skirt is of the striped material, and comprises a kilt and a yoke. The yoke is shallow and smoothly fitted. The left end is hemmed and lapped over the right at the back, the lower edges being basted. The kilt is formed of straight breadths joined together, with a hemmed lower edge. The skirt is laid in medium-wide side-plaits all turning one way and stayed by tapes basted to them underneath. The top is sewed to the yoke, and the placket opening is finished beneath the plait at the end of the yoke. A belt finishes the top.

About the upper part is draped a sash, formed of a straight strip of the plain material hemmed at its longest edges, gathered in Turkish fashion at the ends, and tipped with tassels. When the sash is adjusted, it is knotted on the left side of the back. It is basted securely through the knot and at intervals through the top to the yoke seam, the latter bastings being concealed by the folds of the sash.

The bodice is an easy-fitting blouse, which has a forward-turning tuck stitched in each side of the front. Both sides are hemmed. The left side is extended sufficiently beyond the center of the front to permit of making the closing beneath the hem of the right side, with button-holes and flat buttons matching the material. As these are invisible, the blouse is apparently closed by a cord laced through eyelets made in the upper part of the blouse. The cord is knotted at the top and tipped with tassels. On the left side of the front is a rounded breast pocket, which is turned in at the top and hemmed. Seams on the shoulders and the sides shape the blouse, which is quite loose. The lower edge is turned under for a casing, into which an elastic tape is run, the ends

being fastened just back of the closing edges. When the blouse is adjusted on the wearer, the extra length falls over and conceals the skirt yoke.

The sleeves are wider than the coat shape. Each is composed of a single section, which has its inner edges joined by a seam, and which is sewed with an easy fullness into the armhole. The lower edge is scantily gathered across the outside of the arm and is sewed to a deep wristband of the striped material, which is wide enough to slip easily over the hand. A broad sailor collar of the striped material is sewed to the neck, and turned down over its own seam.

For a lady of medium size, this costume requires 15 1/8 yards of material 22 inches wide, or 7 3/8 yards of material 44 inches wide. As pictured, it requires 6 1/2 yards of plain material and 8 5/8 yards of striped material 22 inches wide. Sometimes a jersey bodice matching the brightest or darkest shade in the skirt is worn instead of the blouse for mountain trips, seaside excursions, etc.

May 1887 *Delineator*

Riding Habit

The basque is drafted with the scale corresponding to the bust measure. It consists of eight pieces: Front, side piece, side back, back, skirt that finishes the bottom of the basque, collar, and two sleeve pieces. Sew the basque up, then sew the basque skirt onto the bottom, as illustrated. Lay two side-plaits in the back, according to the notches.

The skirt is drafted with the scale corresponding to the waist measure. The length is regulated with the tape measure. There are two pieces: Front and back. Join the corresponding seams. Take up the darts in the front, and gather the extra fullness at the back. Sew the skirt to a belt. The skirt may be caught up with a hook and eye, or simply held up while the wearer is off the horse.

Spring 1889 *Voice of Fashion*

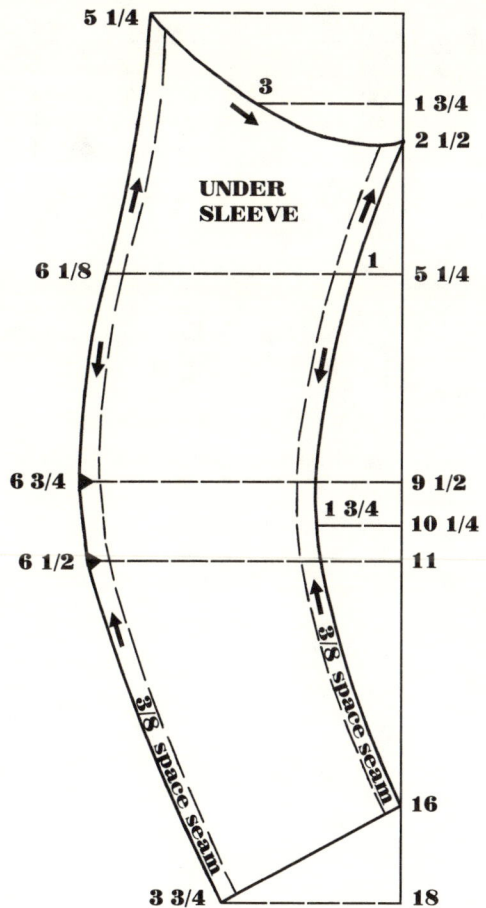

COLLAR

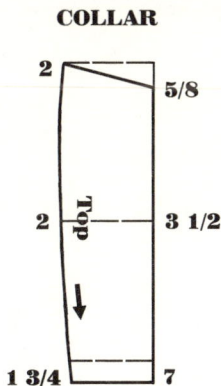

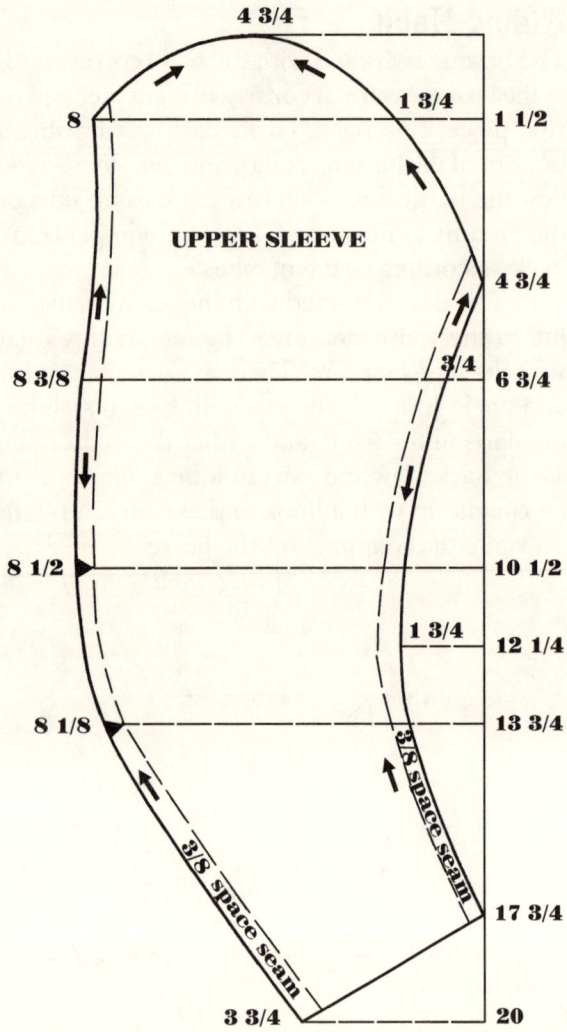

UPPER SLEEVE

4 3/4

8

1 3/4 — 1 1/2

4 3/4

8 3/8 — 3/4 — 6 3/4

8 1/2 — 10 1/2

1 3/4 — 12 1/4

8 1/8 — 13 3/4

3/8 space seam

17 3/4

3 3/4 — 20

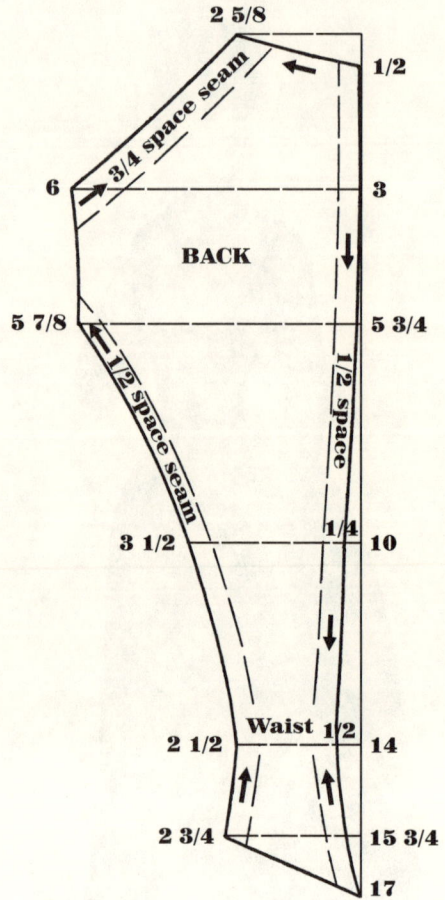

BACK

2 5/8

1/2

3/4 space seam

6 — 3

5 7/8 — 5 3/4

1/2 Space seam

1/2 space

3 1/2 — 1/4 — 10

Waist 1/2

2 1/2 — 14

2 3/4 — 15 3/4

17

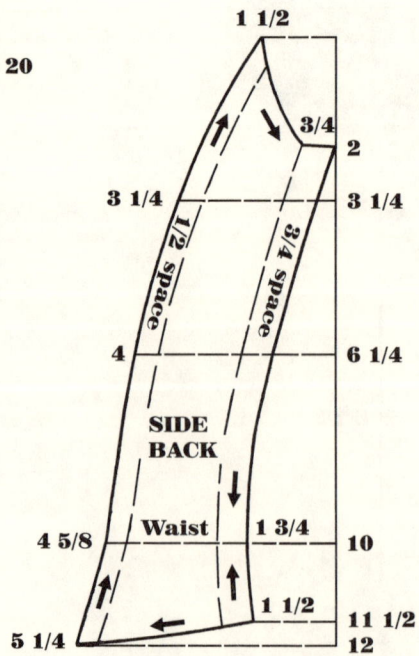

SIDE BACK

1 1/2

3/4 — 2

3 1/4 — 3 1/4

1/2 space

3/4 space

4 — 6 1/4

Waist

4 5/8 — 1 3/4 — 10

1 1/2

5 1/4 — 11 1/2 — 12

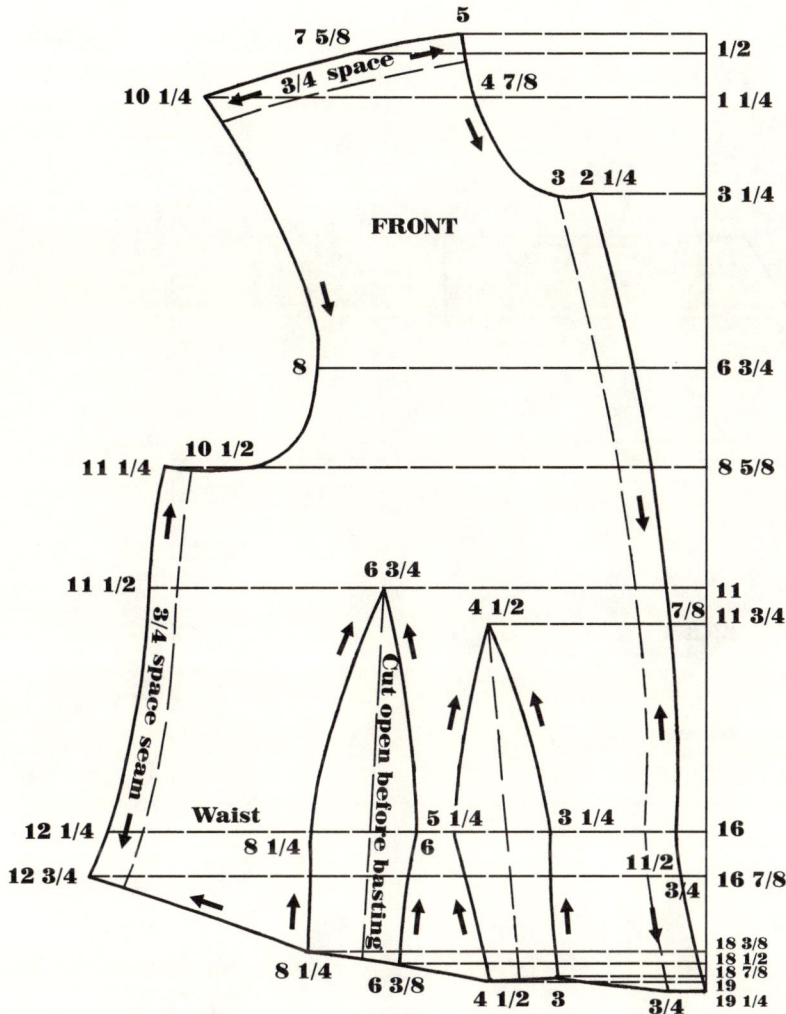

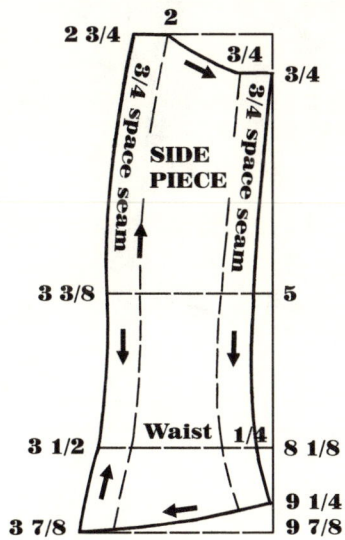

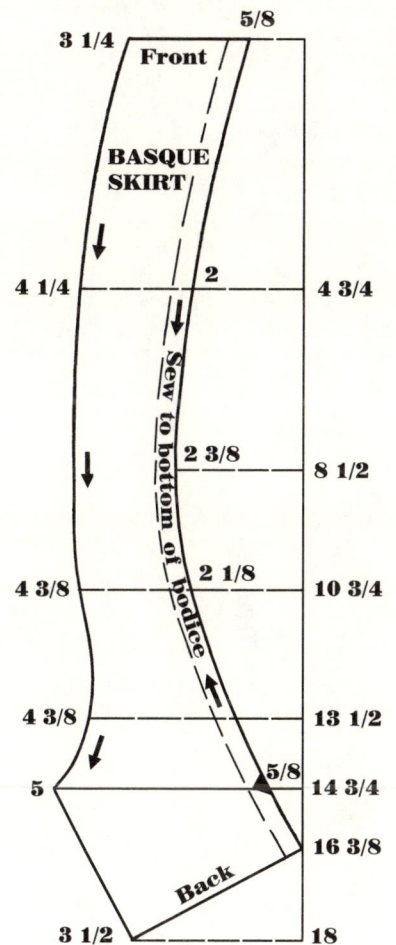

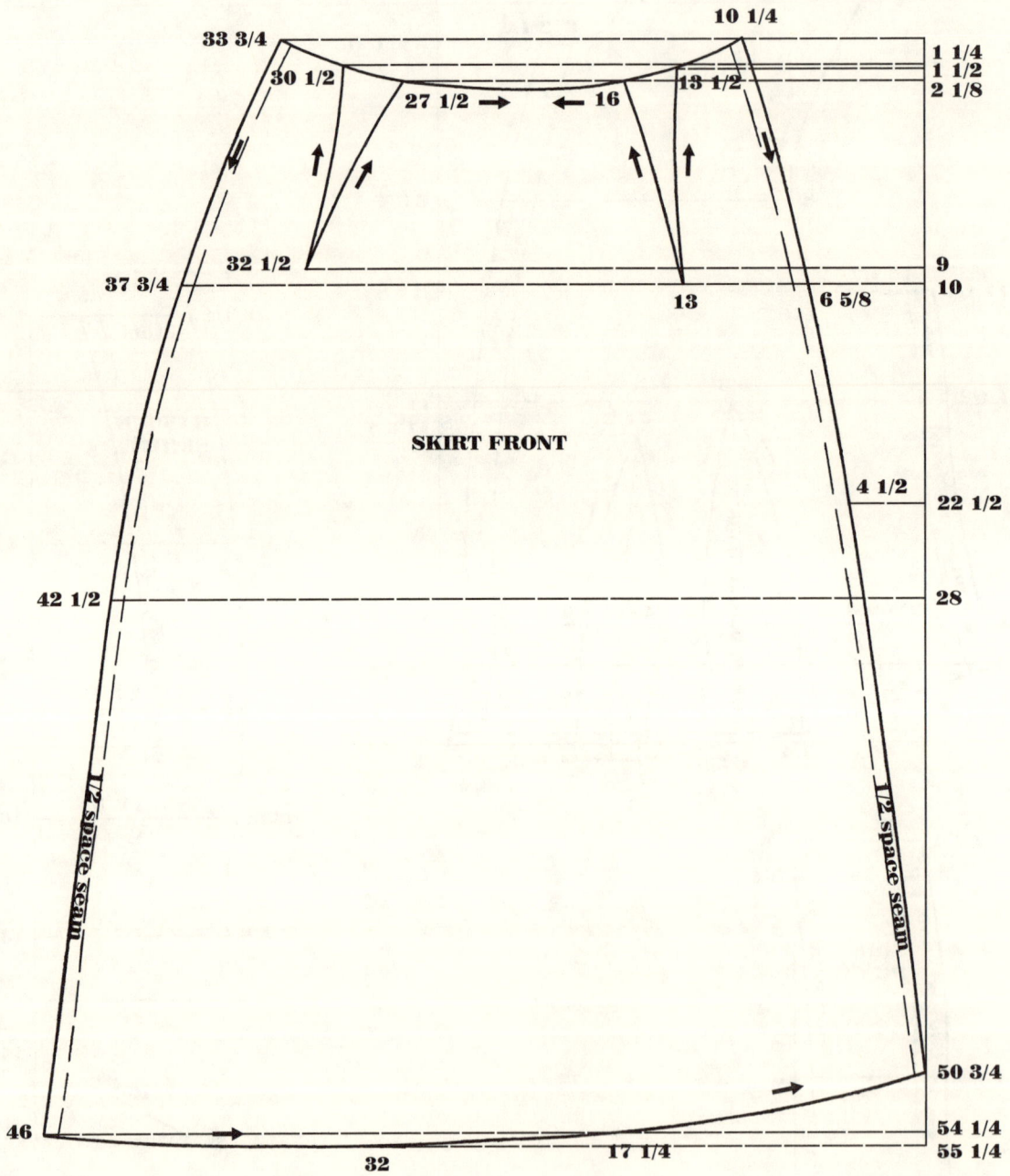

SKIRT FRONT

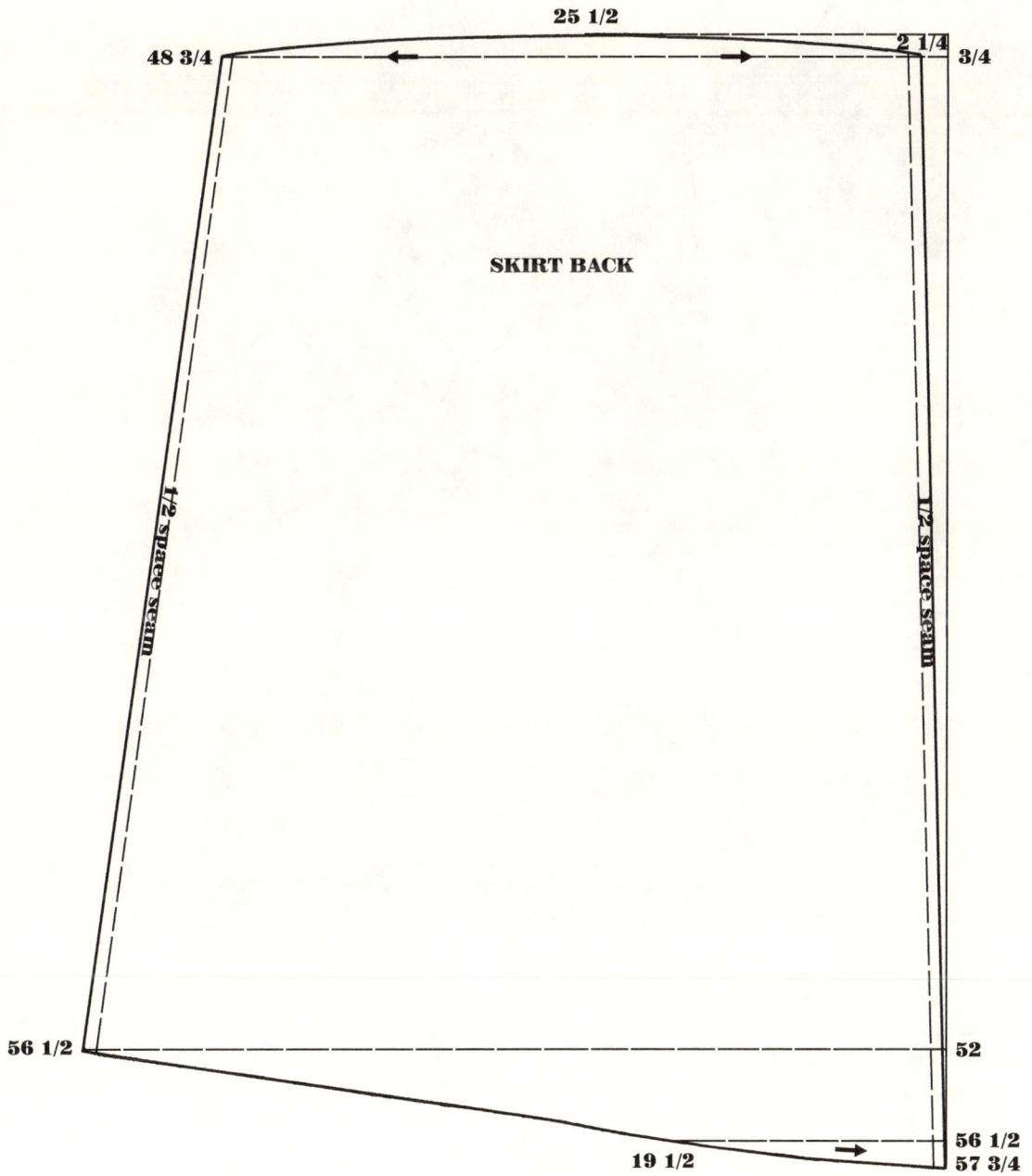

SKIRT BACK

25 1/2

48 3/4

2 1/4   3/4

1/2 space seam

1/2 space seam

56 1/2

52

19 1/2

56 1/2
57 3/4

Riding Habit. Finely woven, smooth-finished cloth was chosen for this habit. The finishings include buttons, machine-stitching, and braid binding. The trousers are smoothly fitted at the top by darts, and by seams at the center of the back and front. They also have seams at the inside and outside of the legs. The outside leg seams end a short distance from the top, and above them extensions are cut on the fronts and pass under the backs. The free edges and the tops are bound with braid, and the side openings are closed with button-holes and buttons. To strengthen the top, narrow, fitted underfacings are applied before the binding is added, and that on the front is carried the length of the extensions on the sides. The bottoms of the legs are hemmed. The right leg is longer than the left, to permit of its comfortable adjustment when this limb is bent over the saddle. Straps fastened beneath the side seams and passed under the boots hold the trousers securely in position. If these straps are of

elastic, they can be sewed in place. If they are of the habit material or of leather, they can have button-holes worked in their ends and slipped over buttons sewed underneath to the leg seams of the trousers.

The skirt is designed to be comfortable and graceful whether the wearer is mounted or walking. It has two sections, which are united by seams on the sides. Three darts of graduated lengths are taken in the top. There is only a single lengthwise dart in the front, and this is near the right side seam and is quite long. There are several crosswise darts in the saddle side, two in the front and two in the back, beginning on the right side seam and extending respectively a short distance back and front of this seam. In the back is a longer, diagonal dart. This dart extends from a little back of the crosswise darts, to within a short distance of the end of the lengthwise dart nearest the right side edge of the back. These darts give a smooth, easy adjustment, permitting the skirt to follow the outlines of the figure without introducing fullness. The skirt is enough longer at this side than on the left to allow for the amount taken up on the saddle side; consequently the lower outline is uniform when the garment is on the wearer. The lower edge is finished with a hem. The length is a matter of personal taste, although it is more convenient if the skirt is not so long as to be cumbersome when the wearer dismounts.

The left side seam terminates at placket length from the top. Above it extra width for an underlap is allowed on the back breadth, a fly with button-holes being sewed beneath the front edge. Flat buttons are sewed on the underlap. In front of these buttons, it forms the facing for a pocket composed of two sections seamed together at their rounded edges. After the back edge of the under part of the pocket is sewed beneath the underlap, the corresponding edge of the upper side is sewed over the latter for some distance from the top and bottom. However, the opening is left wide enough to permit of the hand being easily slipped in. The placket opening is closed, and the pocket concealed by the button-holes and buttons mentioned, and two hooks and eyes are added at the top.

The top of the skirt is provided with a fitted, yoke-like facing. The upper edges of both skirt and facing are bound together with silk braid. The binding is carried along the top of the pocket, and enough extra length is allowed at the end to tie to a short piece fastened considerably in front of the placket opening. A piece of stout elastic is fastened beneath the front gore, and its free end is fastened in a loop into which the left foot is slipped to hold the skirt in place. A tiny loop of braid is fastened at the back end of the lower crosswise dart in the right side of the back. When the wearer is not in the saddle, this loop is passed over a button sewed near the top of the center lengthwise dart in the back, the extra length of the skirt at this side being thus lifted to walking length.

The basque is fitted by double bust darts, side pieces, side backs, and a curved center back seam. Below the waist-line, narrow extensions are cut on the back edges of the side backs. After these seams are closed, the extensions are pressed in shallow plaits on the backs. The back and side backs fall below the remainder in a narrow postilion. The sides curve upward over the hips. The fronts have curved edges and form short, double points below the closing. The closing is made with button-holes and small buttons, the right side being underfaced.

A high standing collar finishes the neck. Its edges, as well as the lower edges of the basque, are finished with machine-stitching. The sleeves are shaped to fit the arms smoothly and permit of their easy movement. The outside seam of each is discontinued some distance from the wrist, and below it extra width is cut on the under side to form an underlap. Buttons are placed on the underlap, and button-holes are made in the overlapping edge. By these means the sleeve is closely adjusted to the wrist without making it difficult to slip on. A line of machine-stitching finishes the lower and overlapping edges. Below the waist-line of the back seams, are sewed straps of the lining in which button-holes are made. These are slipped over buttons sewed near the tops of the darts in the skirt, to prevent marring of the adjustment when the wearer leans forward.

The basque and sleeves are both well wadded and padded. The wadding is placed between the outside and the lining, and attached to the lining with long stitches. Such a garment should be close but easy, and the padding and wadding permit of this and do away with wrinkles.

Smooth-faced cloth, tricot, serge, and plain cheviot are among the most satisfactory materials for habits, dark colors and a plain finish being the best form. The basque may have its edges bound instead of stitched. Sometimes the trousers are made of chamois above the knees. To make the habit for a lady of medium size, requires 5 3/8 yards of material 54 inches wide, with 1/2 yard of silesia 36 inches wide for the yoke, facing, and pocket.

August 1887 *Delineator*

Ladies' Basque

Ladies' Basque. The style of this basque adapts it to the association of two contrasting materials. In this instance fancy dress material is united with velveteen. The fronts are closed with button-holes and buttons, the right side being hemmed and the left underfaced. Below the closing, the lower edge is slightly pointed. There are two bust darts in each side, and side pieces of even length are joined to them. The back is considerably longer, and is fitted by side-back seams and a curved center back seam. All three end a little below the waist-line.

Extra width is allowed below each of these seams. The width at the end of the center back seam is arranged to form a double box-plait underneath, while that on each side-back seam is underfolded in a forward-turning plait. Beneath the upper fold of each side-plait is sewed a velveteen revers ornament, which turns backward. The difference in length between the back and the rest of the basque is partially decreased by the addition of a shallow, ornamental skirt part, which is sewed to the side piece and adjoining side of the front as far as the dart nearest the closing. The skirt part is sewed at its back edge to the corresponding edge of the back and is deepened slightly toward its front end. Owing to the addition of these ornaments the center front assumes a vest effect, which may be enhanced by the application of a facing of the contrasting material.

The coat sleeves are fitted closely about the lower part of the arms, enough fullness being allowed across the top to give a curved effect. A plain, round cuff-facing of velveteen finishes each wrist. The high standing collar is also of velveteen.

To make the basque for a lady of medium size, requires 3 3/4 yards of one material and 5/8 yard of contrasting material 22 inches wide, or 1 7/8 yards of one material and 3/8 yard of contrasting material 48 inches wide.

April 1885 *Delineator*

9. Jackets and Outer Wear

With modifications, a well-fitting basque pattern will answer for a jacket. The seams must be cut 1/2 inch wider than for a dress, and the armholes cut 1/2 inch lower. This extra allowance is required because of the thickness of the materials used and because the jacket is to be worn over a bodice. Two darts are put in a basque, but usually one in a jacket, whether it is cut close, half-fitting, or loose. It is best to fit the jacket in inexpensive muslin, and then use the muslin as a pattern. Always allow for generous seams when cutting out the material.

When the seams of a jacket or cloak are to be bound with satin, silk, or farmer's satin cut in bias strips, and the garment is not lined, the binding is sometimes put on before the seam is stitched. The binding is cut wide enough to extend a trifle beyond the seam basting. It is applied by the usual binding process on each side, and then the seam is stitched through the binding as well as the material. Seams finished in this way are not pressed until the binding has been added and sewed in. A line of stitching may be made along the rolled edge of the binding, on the upper side of the seam edge.

A safer way is to baste the binding on after the seams are stitched and pressed. Use the rolled method just described, turning the binding under on the wrong side, so that one line of machine-stitching will hold both it and the roll of the basted edge in place.

Pocket openings are cut in the material, and the pockets are cut and made to lie flat. They are always put in before the lining is attached and do not appear in it at all. The pocket welt or opening must always be stayed with a strip of canvas or silesia sewed in the fold of the welt.

The lining of a jacket or cloak is merely put on as a neat finish. Two distinct garments are made, one of the material and the other a silk or satin lining. The only points of connection are along the lines of the edges. If there are sleeves, the material and lining are only joined at the wrists and shoulders.

For cloaks an interlining is frequently used. Canvas placed over the chest and across the shoulders makes the cloak set well. Flannel is sometimes introduced in the same way for extra warmth. These interlinings are sewed together with the material, but the silk lining always remains separate. The seams of each portion must be laid open, notched, and pressed flat before they are laid together.

1892 *Home Dressmaking*

A jacket that may be worn with half a dozen different dresses is a useful garment in a spring or summer outfit. A copper or a suède-colored cloth jacket is worn not only with a dress of the same color, but with a blue, green, or brown dress, or one of black lace. Coats of bluish gray or drab cloth are worn with gray, brown, or black dresses.

Suède, iridescent, and bronze beads are made up in entire mantles and shoulder capes. Handmade net mantles heavily jetted are very stylish. Others have the netted meshes made entirely of fine beads, with a closer design of vine passementerie made of larger beads wrought amid these meshes for a trimming. V-shaped vines and epaulettes of leaves, balls, and berries are in fine diamond-meshed jetted capes, with a rain fringe of beads falling over the shoulder. Pointed patterns of beading are now making a pointed cape in front and back from the neck to the waist-line, or just below it. The arms are covered with close dropping pieces of a different pattern, or with fringes and drops of beads. Shoulder capes of beads come in various sizes, some scarcely reaching the tips of the shoulders, while others are pointed to the waist-line. Still others drop nearly to the elbows, and are even all around.

The pointed capes are also made of black faille Française richly wrought with jets, reaching to the waist at the back and front, and tied there with a waist ribbon. The arms are covered with jetted net of an elaborate design. Rows upon rows of jet or suède-colored bead fringe cover other small silk wraps.

March 3, 1888 *Harper's Bazar*

Some cloth cloaks have appliqué cloth designs of another shade all over them, or put on in stripes, or as a border, or forming wing-like sides. These cloth figures are cut out in very open designs that show the material beneath them. They are outlined with braid set up on one edge. Cloaks made of velvet or plush are trimmed likewise, in arabesques.

October 6, 1888 *Harper's Bazar*

The favorite style is a jacket that is half wrap, half jacket, rather longer than the usual tailor jacket, and with long, ornamented fronts opening over a short vest of plain material. Fine qualities of faced cloth, in creamy fawns, steel grays, bright dragon green, coffee, chocolate, dark marine blues, and greens are used for these jackets. The usual trimming is braiding in self-color, contrasting shades of color, black, gilt, or silver. Persian-patterned silks are used for the facing and vest of some jackets.

Redingotes or coats to match or complete the costume in Directoire style are hardly to be classed as wraps, although they take the place of the latter and are often made to be worn with various skirts.

Dressier additions to the costume, called wraps by courtesy, include jet-beaded capes or collarettes, the Empire scarf, and the wide, three-cornered mull fichu for morning wear. The Empire scarf is simply a single width of lace or material 3 yards long, or long enough to encircle the neck with both ends reaching the bottom of the skirt. It may be of surah that is embroidered or lace trimmed at the ends, India silk, crêpe, or crêpe de Chine. Most popular is black Chantilly lace or lace net fastened at the waist with a ribbon tied with long, drooping ends.

April 1889 *Demorest's Monthly Magazine*

Some of the fur-trimmed winter wraps are transformed for spring merely by replacing the fur with a handsome trimming of gilt cord passementerie and embroidery.

May 1889 *Demorest's Monthly Magazine*

Certain costumes have short capes in the Directoire style, much resembling the once popular coachman's cape. From three to five overlapping layers of the material are mounted on a cape reaching nearly or quite to the waist. When made to match the costume, these capes are sometimes finished with broad lapels faced with contrasting material. Separate capes are made of light-colored, rough-finished cloths, in russet, suède, argus gray, and the whitish gray shade known as *parchemin*.

October 1889 *Demorest's Monthly Magazine*

Street Jacket with Hood

This jacket is drafted with the scale corresponding to the bust measure. It is in nine pieces: Front, side piece, side back, back, collar, two sleeve pieces, cuff, and hood. The jacket may be made of material to match the suit, or of contrasting material, according to the fancy of the wearer.

1889 *National Garment Cutter Book of Diagrams*

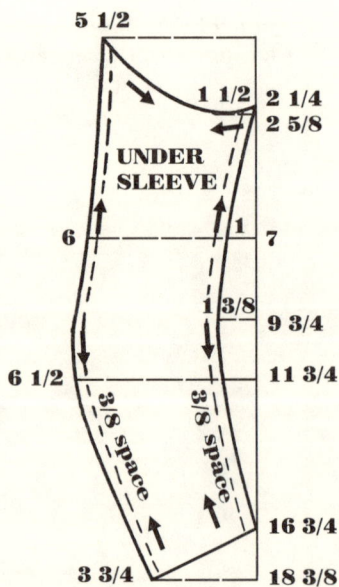

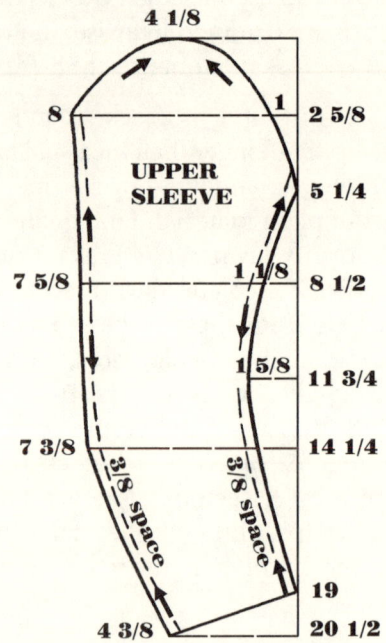

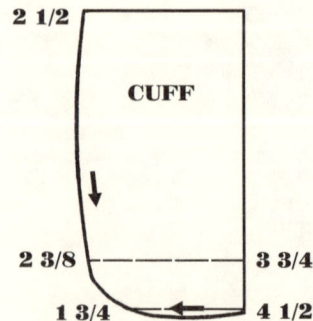

UPPER SLEEVE

4 1/8

8
1
2 5/8

5 1/4

7 5/8
1 1/8
8 1/2

1 5/8
11 3/4

7 3/8
14 1/4

3/8 space   3/8 space

19

4 3/8
20 1/2

UNDER SLEEVE

5 1/2

1 1/2   2 1/4
2 5/8

6
1
7

1 3/8
9 3/4

6 1/2
11 3/4

3/8 space   3/8 space

16 3/4

3 3/4
18 3/8

CUFF

2 1/2

2 3/8
3 3/4

1 3/4
4 1/2

Street Jacket with Hood

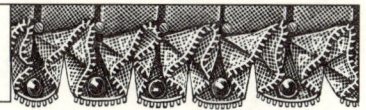

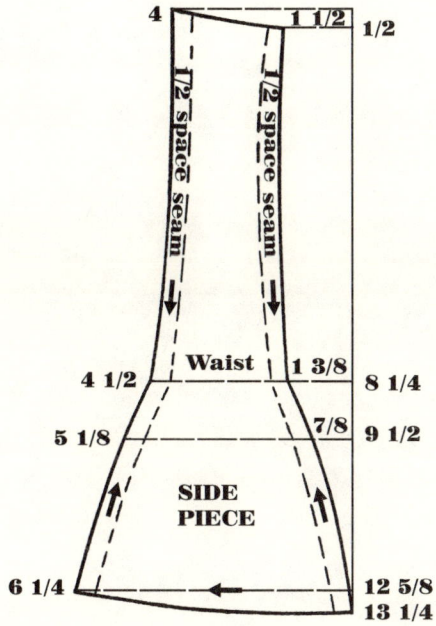

SIDE PIECE

4   1 1/2   1/2

1/2 space seam   1/2 space seam

4 1/2   Waist   1 3/8   8 1/4

5 1/8   7/8   9 1/2

6 1/4   12 5/8   13 1/4

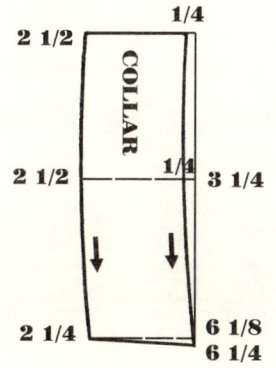

COLLAR

1/4
2 1/2
2 1/2   1/4   3 1/4
2 1/4   6 1/8   6 1/4

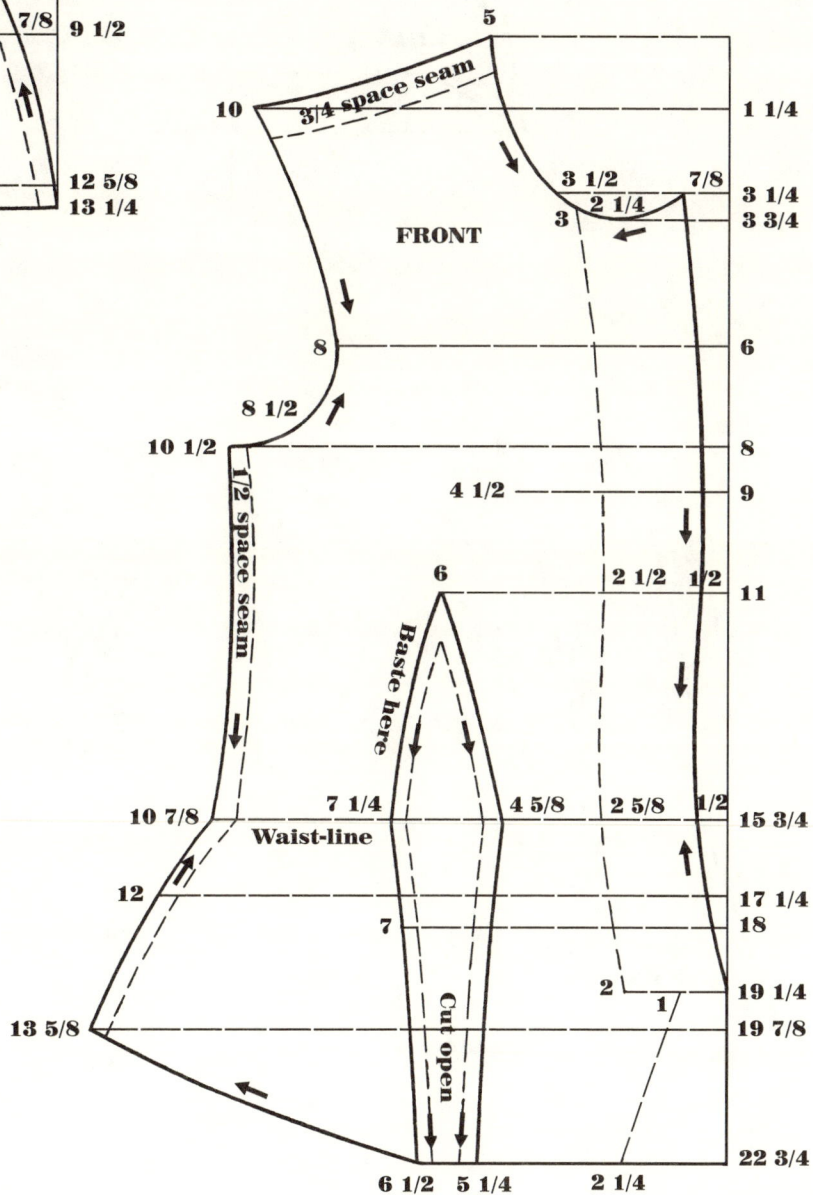

FRONT

5

3/4 space seam

10   1 1/4

3 1/2   7/8   3 1/4
2 1/4   3 3/4
3

8   6

8 1/2
10 1/2   8

4 1/2   9

1/2 space seam

6   2 1/2   1/2   11

Baste here

10 7/8   7 1/4   4 5/8   2 5/8   1/2   15 3/4
Waist-line

12   17 1/4
7   18

2   19 1/4
1

13 5/8   19 7/8

Cut open

6 1/2   5 1/4   2 1/4   22 3/4

413

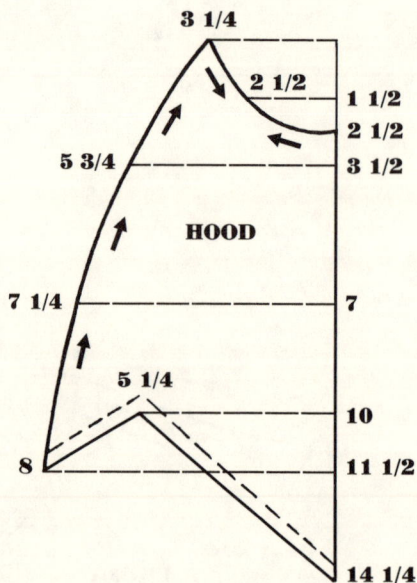

HOOD

3 1/4
2 1/2
1 1/2
2 1/2
5 3/4
3 1/2
7 1/4
7
5 1/4
10
11 1/2
8
14 1/4

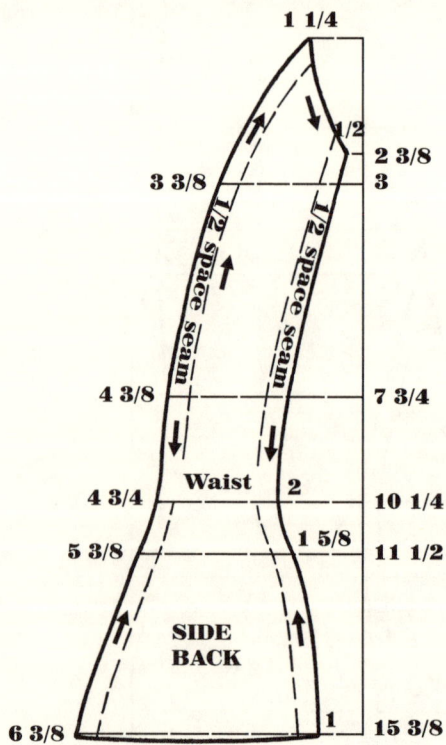

1 1/4
1/2
2 3/8
3 3/8
3
1/2 space seam
1/2 space seam
4 3/8
7 3/4
Waist
2
4 3/4
10 1/4
5 3/8
1 5/8
11 1/2
SIDE
BACK
6 3/8
1
15 3/8

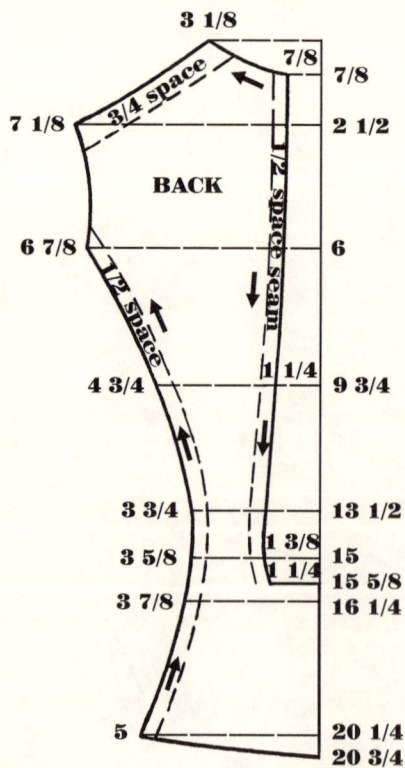

3 1/8
7/8
7/8
7 1/8
3/4 space
2 1/2
BACK
1/2 space seam
6 7/8
6
1/2 space
4 3/4
1/4
9 3/4
3 3/4
13 1/2
3 5/8
1 3/8
15
1 1/4
15 5/8
3 7/8
16 1/4
5
20 1/4
20 3/4

Jacket with Hood

Jacket with Hood. Fancy striped coating was selected for this jacket. It is shaped by single bust darts, side pieces, side backs, and a curved center back seam. The center back seam ends at the top of narrow extensions arranged in regular coat-lap fashion, with the left over the right. The lower edges are cut in curves toward the ends of the back under-arm seams. The closing edges are hollowed to assist in the adjustment. The closing is made from the neck to below the waist-line, with button-holes and medium-sized tailor buttons. Below the closing, the edges are cut away with sufficient flare to prevent the jacket from crushing light draperies.

On each side of the front rests a pocket lap having its front corners rounded off. These laps, as well as the overlapping front, the opposite side of the front below the closing, the overlap at the back, and the bottom of the jacket, are bound with braid.

A pocket is inserted in a straight opening high up in the left front, and the edges of the opening are bound with braid. Each coat-shaped sleeve is ornamented with a band of braid stitched at cuff depth from the wrist, two buttons being placed inside the braid in front of the outside seam. In the same seam with the standing collar is sewed a hood, which falls in a point and has its outer edges reversed quite broadly. The hood is lined with silk, and the collar is finished with braid.

Jackets of light-weight, smoothly finished cloths in beige and mastic, and in soft gray and fawn, are among summer wardrobes prepared for time spent in varying altitudes. Many jackets matching the costumes with which they are to be worn are also made up in this fashion, always with a simple finish. To make the garment for a lady of medium size, requires 3 7/8 yards of material 22 inches wide, 1 3/4 yards of material 44 inches wide, or 1 1/2 yards of material 54 inches wide. Each requires 1/2 yard of silk 20 inches wide to line the hood.

May 1887 *Delineator*

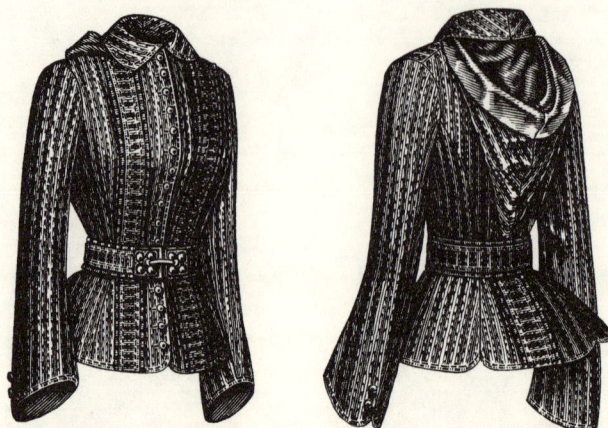

Norfolk Jacket. This jacket may be worn either instead of or outside of a dress bodice. It is shown made of striped fancy cloth. The fronts, which are curved to assist in the adjustment, are closed with button-holes and bone buttons, the right side being underfaced. In each side is a single bust dart. At the back are side-back seams and a curved center back seam. The edges below the side-back seams are rounded off to give the jacket an easy adjustment over any style of drapery.

On the center of the back is what appears to be a double box-plait, although it uses much less material than for such a plait. It is really formed of a straight strip, which is folded under for a finish at its lengthwise edges, and then a narrow plait turning toward each edge is also folded. A line of stitching made through each plait and folded edge holds it in place on the jacket and renders permanent the double box-plait effect. A similar ornament is arranged on each side of the front, considerably back of the closing, its top entering into the shoulder seam.

The sleeves widen with a flowing or drapery effect toward the wrists, and at their tops fit closely in coat style. The outside seam of each terminates a little above the lower edge, and the corners below it are rounded off. Two buttons are placed on the upper side of each sleeve, in front of the outside seam. Single lines of stitching finish the bottom of the sleeves, the overlapping front, and the bottom of the jacket. A belt of the material is worn about the waist. This is made to harmonize with the plait

ornaments by having its long edges turned under, and narrow plaits turning toward each edge folded in it, stitching holding the plaits and reversed edges in place. A metal clasp closes the belt in front, and bastings made beneath the plaits attach the belt conveniently to the back.

About the neck is a high rolling collar. Its ends are rounded, and its edges are finished with double lines of stitching. Beneath the collar is adjusted a hood in capuchin style, which rolls over about the edges, and reaches almost to the waist. It is formed of a single section of material seamed along its lower end, and is lined with surah of a darker shade. It is finished at its neck edge with a narrow binding, which may be basted or hooked beneath the collar.

This jacket may be made of all kinds of plain and fancy suitings, light coatings, and flannels. Aside from the linings for the hood and the lower parts of the sleeves, and fancy belt clasps, it should have little if any decoration. However, binding, braid, or stitching about the edges is always appropriate. Plush; velvet; and plaid, plain, or striped silk or surah may be used for the linings. Mode, beige, brown in all its variations, dark blue shot with red, red shot with blue, and black shot with yellow are more favored for lining than the very high tints. For a lady of medium size, this jacket requires 4 3/4 yards of material 22 inches wide, 2 3/8 yards of material 44 inches wide, or 1 7/8 yards of material 54 inches wide. In each instance 5/8 yard of surah 20 inches wide is needed to line the hood and sleeves.

March 1887 *Delineator*

Short Wrap

Short Wrap

This wrap is drafted with the scale corresponding to the bust measure. It consists of four pieces: Front, back, collar, and sleeve. Use material suitable for early fall or spring wear. In putting this garment together, connect the corresponding notches and stars. Lay the back in two plaits. If the waist-line has been lengthened or shortened, lengthen or shorten the sleeve just the same. Gather the bottom of the front, and finish with bows of ribbon, or fancy balls.

1889 *National Garment Cutter Book of Diagrams*

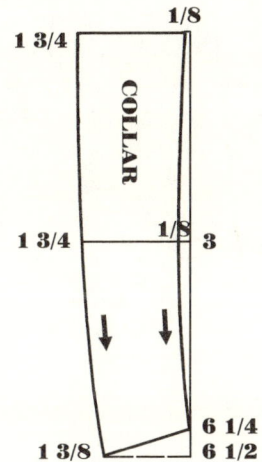

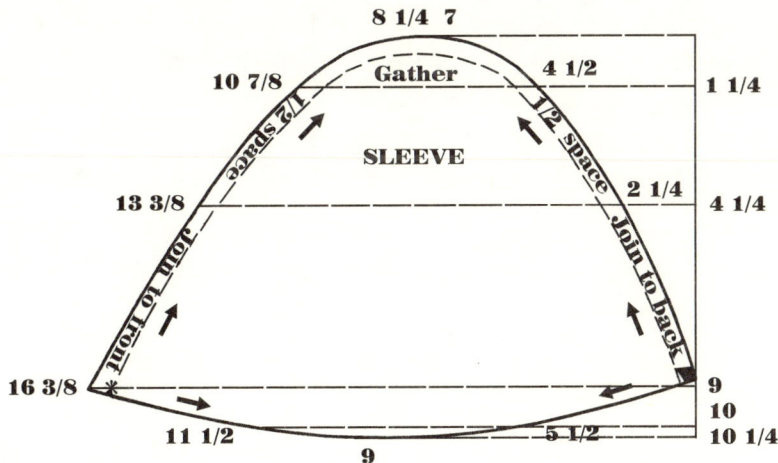

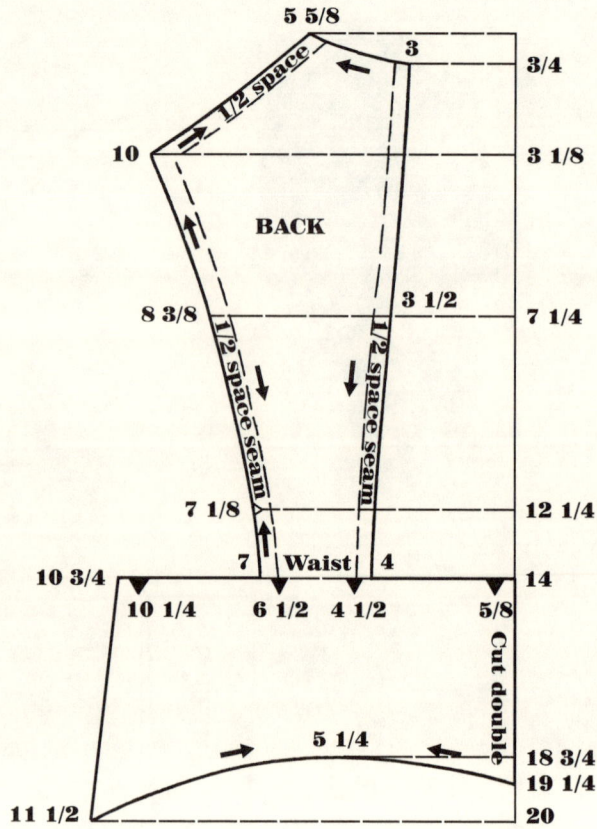

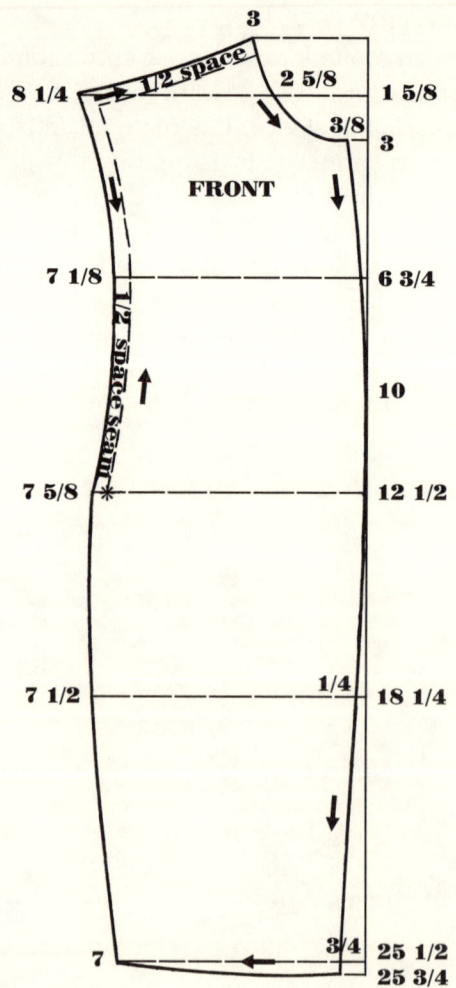

BACK

5 5/8

3

3/4

1/2 space

10

3 1/8

8 3/8

3 1/2

7 1/4

1/2 space seam

1/2 space seam

7 1/8

12 1/4

7 Waist 4

10 3/4

14

10 1/4 6 1/2 4 1/2 5/8

Cut double

5 1/4

18 3/4
19 1/4

11 1/2

20

FRONT

3

8 1/4

1/2 space

2 5/8

1 5/8

3/8

3

7 1/8

6 3/4

1/2 space seam

10

7 5/8

12 1/2

7 1/2

1/4

18 1/4

7

3/4

25 1/2
25 3/4

418

Ladies' Wrap

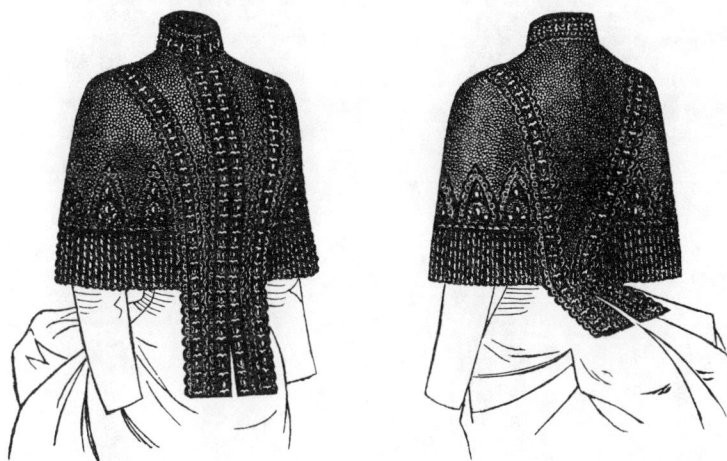

Ladies' Wrap. Velvet was selected for this wrap, and jet passementerie and fringe form the trimmings. Between the fronts and back are inserted side or sleeve sections that fall over the arms nearly to the elbows. The back is rendered smooth fitting by a curved center seam. This seam is discontinued a trifle below the waist-line, the parts below falling in two tabs. The front edges of the fronts are curved to assist in the adjustment, and are closed with hooks and eyes to a little below the waist-line. Below the closing, they fall in half-long narrow tabs. Back of the closing, on each side, is a band of passementerie. Across each shoulder seam is a similar band, which passes down the front and back along the side sections and extends to the lower edge of the tabs both back and front. The lower edge of each side section is trimmed with fringe, above which is sewed four passementerie ornaments. Passementerie also overlies the high collar.

Sicilienne, faille Imperiale, radzimir, or jetted lace over a silk or satin foundation make up well, in any preferred color. Lace, silk, or jet passementeries; down; or feather trimming provide the trimmings. For less dressy wear, cloth or some pretty wool material may be used, with braid for decoration. To make the wrap for a lady of medium size, requires 1 5/8 yards of material 22 inches wide, 7/8 yard of material 44 inches wide, or 3/4 yard of material 54 inches wide.

March 1888 *Delineator*

419

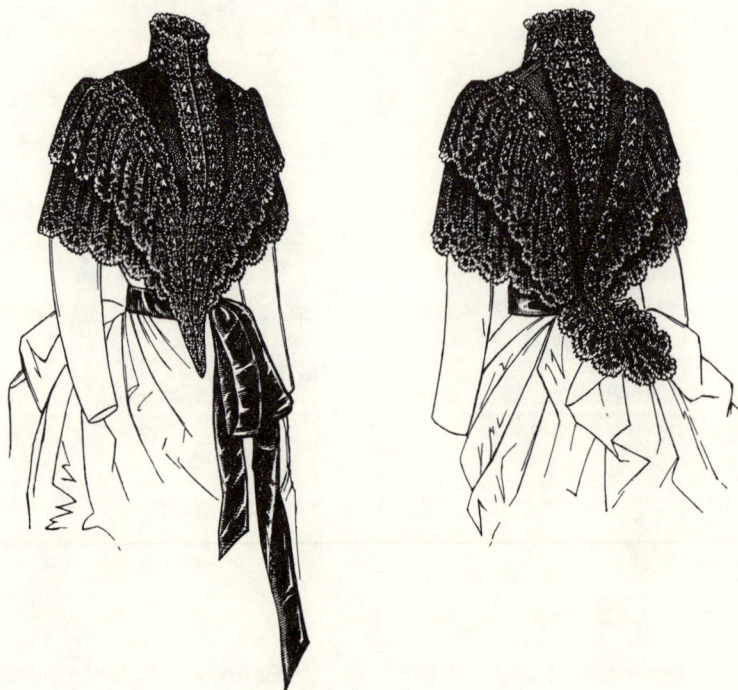

Ladies' Wrap. This wrap is shown made of black velvet richly trimmed with lace, ribbon, and jet bands. The fronts and back taper to decided points and fall to a short distance below the waist-line. They are joined by shoulder seams and fit with perfect smoothness. The sides join the fronts and back in curved seams to the waist-line, and are curved on the lower edge. They are covered with frills of wide lace, the lower frill extending slightly below the edge. Their seams are each followed by a jet band, which is continued to the points of the back and fronts. A similar band trims the front edges of the fronts, which are closed with hooks and eyes. A handsome jet V ornament lies on the back nearly to the waist-line. The standing collar is covered with a jet band, and a narrow lace frill stands above its edge. A wide lace frill follows the point of the back. Under the back is basted a wide ribbon, which is carried about the waist and tied in long loops and ends on the left side of the front. The wrap is lined throughout with silk.

This wrap is often made entirely of lace, and a single lace flounce may form the sides. In material and decoration the sides may differ entirely from the rest of the wrap. Ottoman, sicilienne, bengaline, faille Française, brocades, and other silks in all colors are also suitable, as are beaded and figured nets, velvet, plush, etc. Lace, ribbon, passementerie, feather trimming, etc., will make a stylish trimming, and a lining of silk, satin or surah in a fancy color is often preferred. Cashmere, Henrietta cloth, serge, camel's hair, drap d'été, and many seasonable dress materials also make up well, with trimmings of braid, galloon, passementerie, Persian bands, all-over braiding, etc., which may be arranged to please the fancy. Black wraps are stylish with all kinds of costumes. To make the garment for a lady of medium size, requires 2 yards of material 22 inches wide, 7/8 yard of material 44 inches wide, or 3/4 yard of material 54 inches wide. Each requires 2 1/2 yards of silk 20 inches wide for the lining.

March 1889 *Delineator*

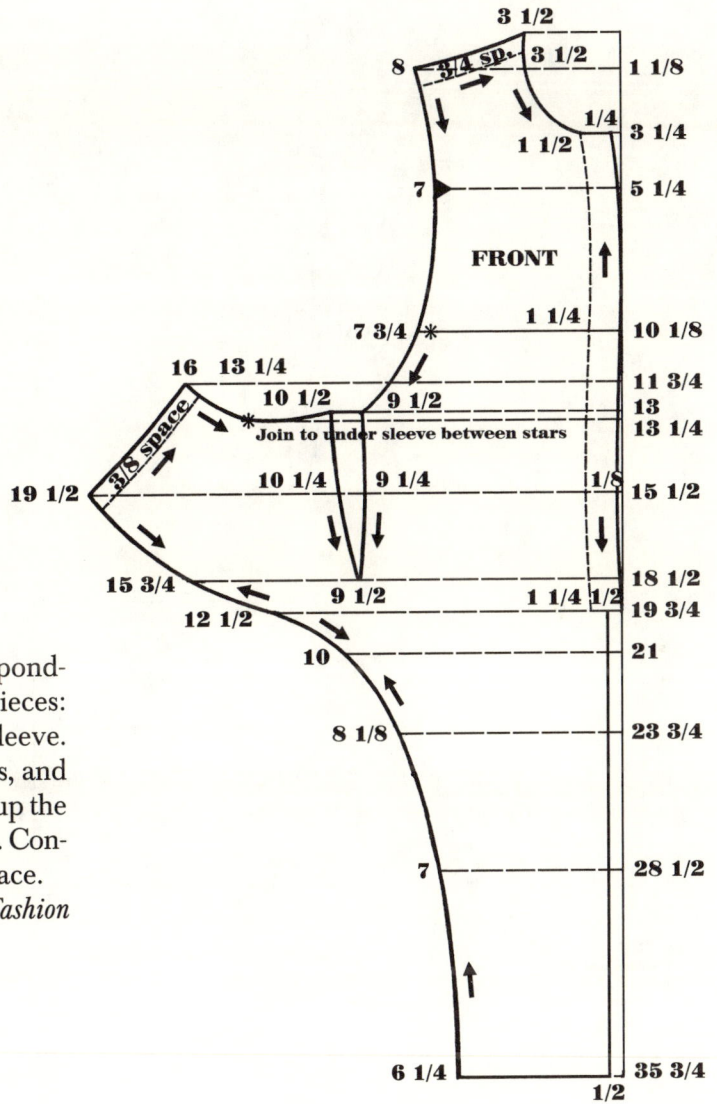

Ladies' Wrap

This garment is drafted with the scale corresponding to the bust measure. It consists of five pieces: Front, back, collar, upper sleeve, and under sleeve. Be careful to mark all of the notches and stars, and notice the instructions on the diagrams. Take up the dart under the arm before sewing in the sleeve. Connect the stars. Trim the wrap with fringe or lace.

Summer 1890 *Voice of Fashion*

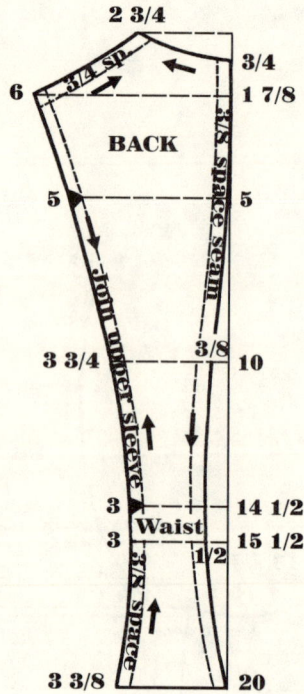

BACK

2 3/4
3/4 sp.
6
3/4
1 7/8
5 — 5
3 3/4 — 3/8 — 10
3 — 14 1/2
3 — Waist — 15 1/2
1/2
3 3/8 — 20

Join under sleeve

3/8 space seam

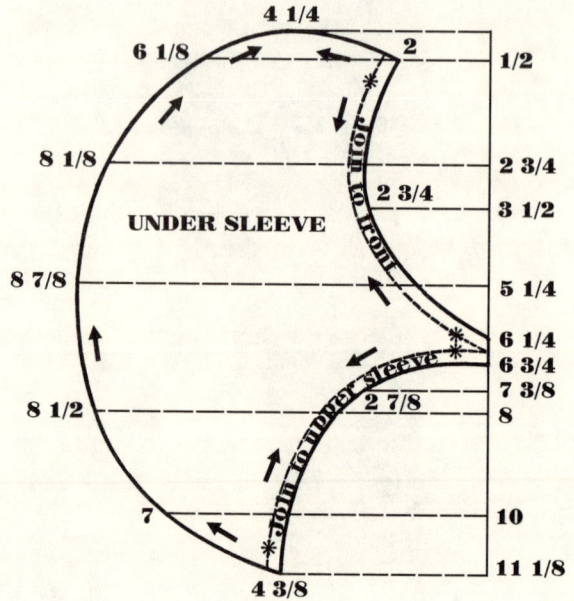

UNDER SLEEVE

4 1/4
6 1/8 — 2 — 1/2
8 1/8 — 2 3/4
2 3/4 — 3 1/2
8 7/8 — 5 1/4
6 1/4
6 3/4
8 1/2 — 2 7/8 — 7 3/8
8
7 — 10
4 3/8 — 11 1/8

Join to front

Join to upper sleeve

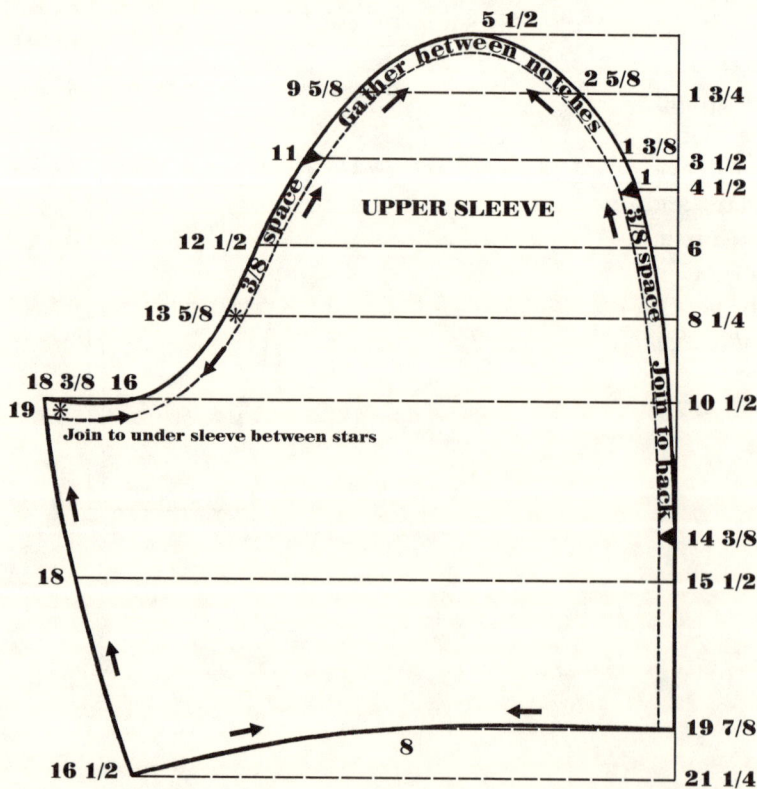

UPPER SLEEVE

5 1/2
Gather between notches
9 5/8 — 2 5/8 — 1 3/4
11 — 1 3/8 — 3 1/2
1 — 4 1/2
12 1/2 — 6
13 5/8 — 8 1/4
18 3/8 16 — 10 1/2
19
Join to under sleeve between stars
14 3/8
18 — 15 1/2
19 7/8
16 1/2 — 8 — 21 1/4

3/8 space

3/8 space

Join to back

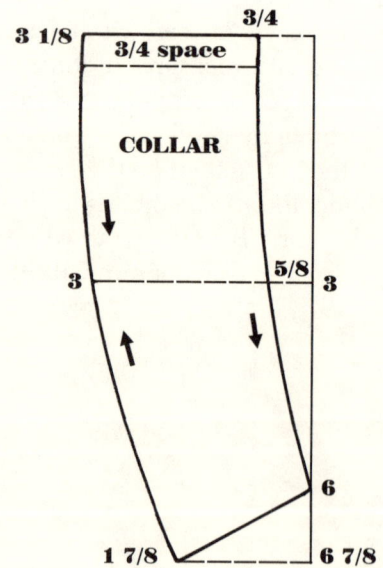

COLLAR

3 1/8 — 3/4 space — 3/4
3 — 5/8 — 3
1 7/8 — 6
6 7/8

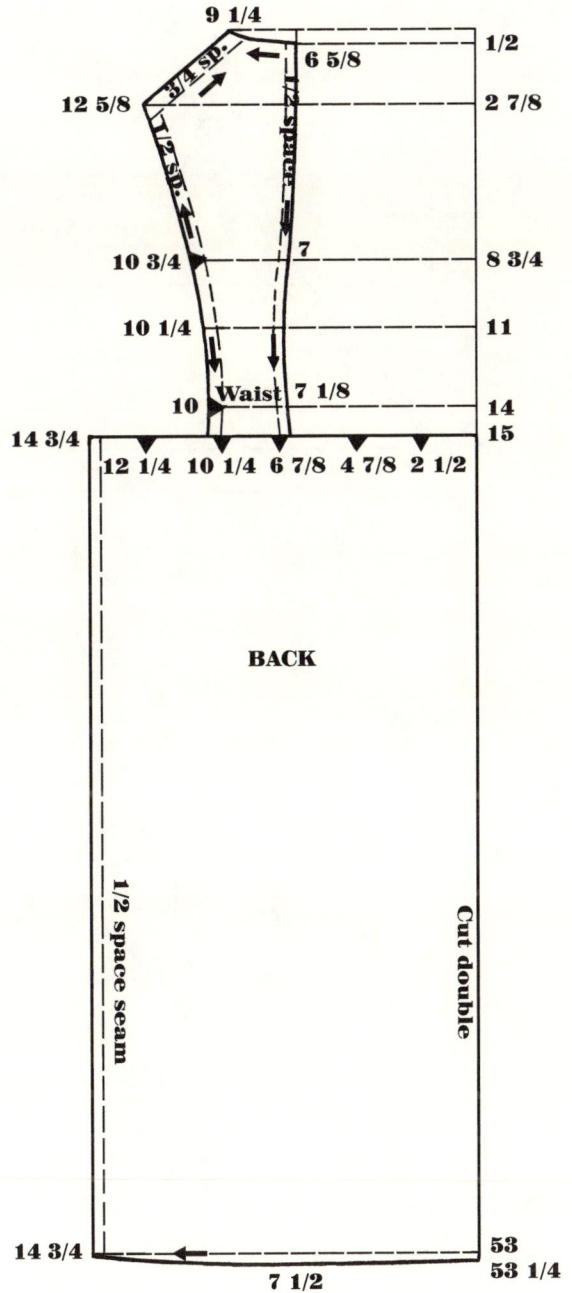

Long Wrap

Draft this garment with the scale corresponding to the bust measure. Regulate the length with the tape measure. There are six pieces: Front, side piece, back, two sleeve pieces, and collar. Connect the waist-lines and the corresponding notches. The fur trimming gives a comfortable appearance but may be omitted, and a fur boa worn around the neck instead.

Winter 1888–1889 *Voice of Fashion*

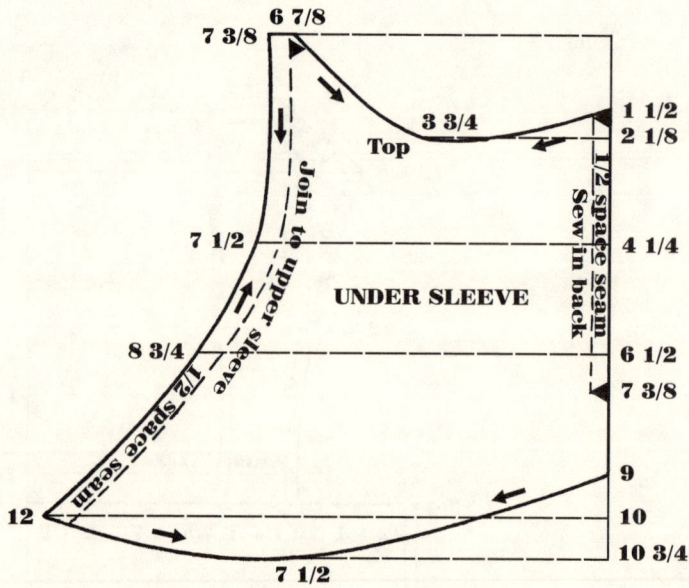

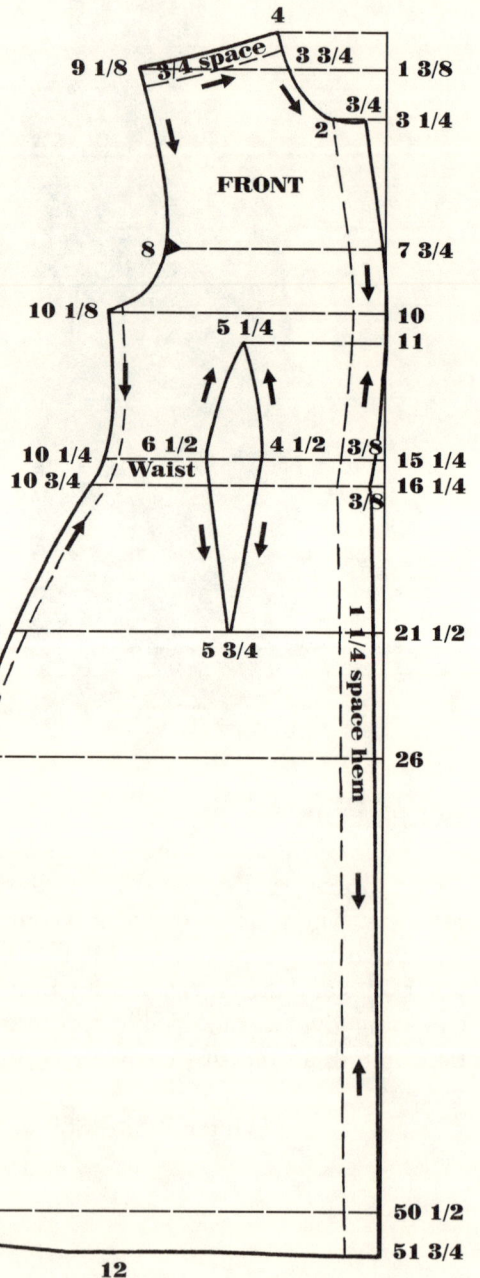

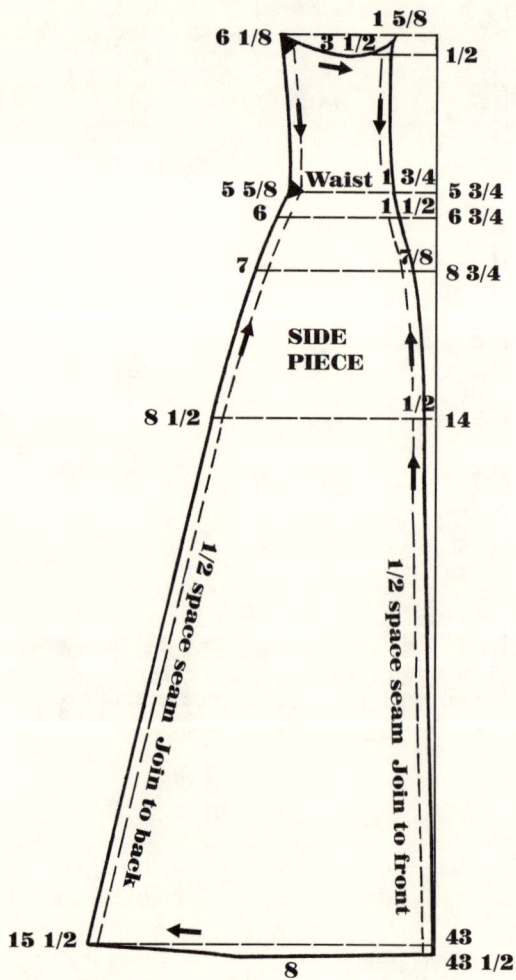

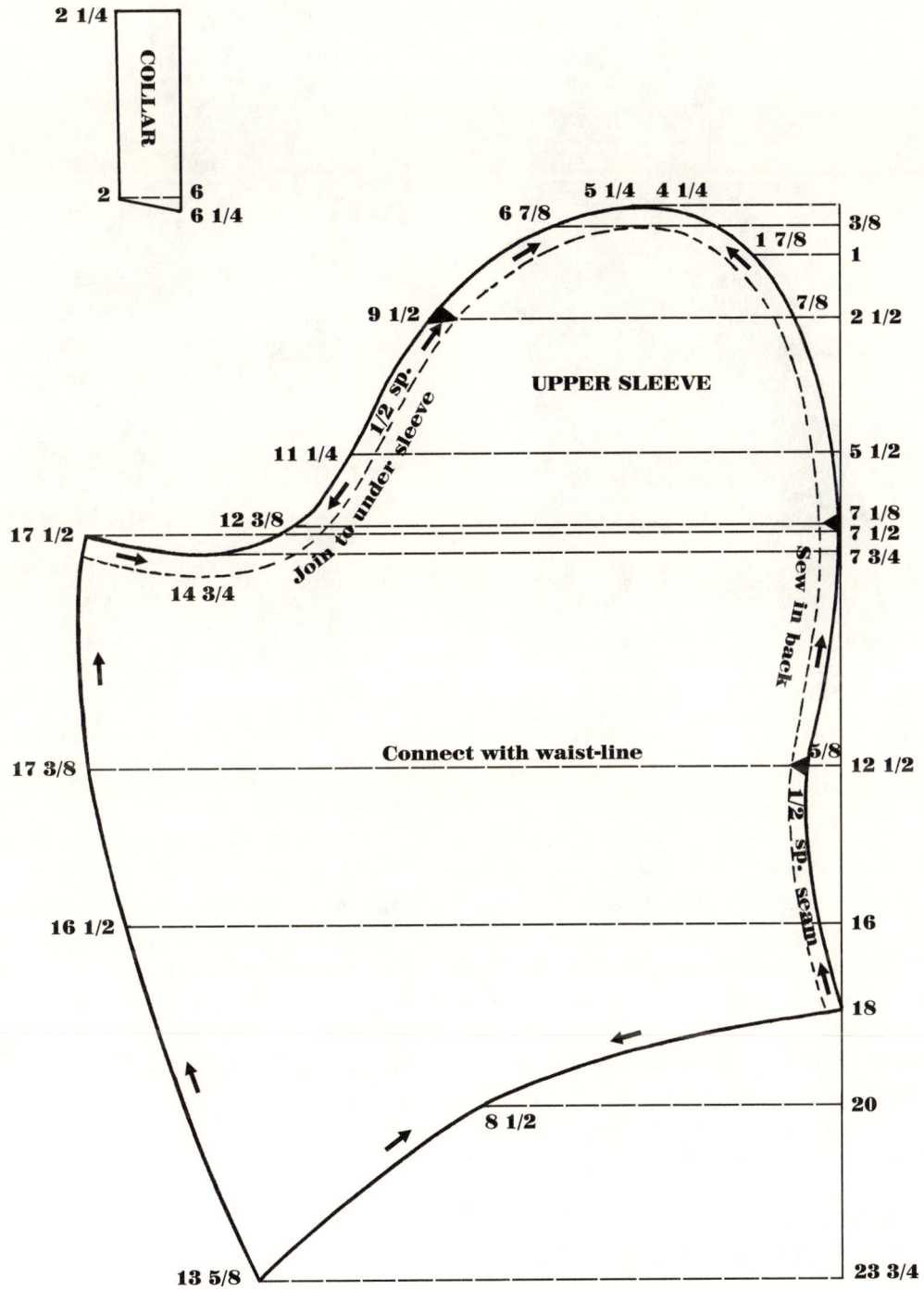

COLLAR

2 1/4

2

6
6 1/4

5 1/4 4 1/4

6 7/8

3/8
1 7/8   1
7/8
9 1/2   2 1/2

1/2 sp.

11 1/4

Join to under sleeve

12 3/8

17 1/2

14 3/4

UPPER SLEEVE

5 1/2

7 1/8
7 1/2
7 3/4

Sew in back

Connect with waist-line

17 3/8

5/8   12 1/2

16 1/2

1/2 sp. seam.

16

18

20

8 1/2

13 5/8

23 3/4

425

Long Wrap. The style of this wrap is adapted to traveling and general wear. Cloth of seasonable texture was chosen for this example, and braid forms the trimming. The fronts are closed all the way down with button-holes and buttons, the edges being curved and the right side underfaced. There are two darts in each side. One curves below the bust, while the other begins at the armhole and extends some distance below the waist-line. The back has a curved center seam that ends a little below the waist-line. At the end of this seam, and at corresponding points on the front edges of the back, extra widths are allowed. These are underfolded to form two triple box-plaits, which are held in their folds by tapes basted to them underneath. The tapes do not, however, prevent the plaits from springing out gracefully toward the bottom of the wrap.

Each sleeve is composed of two sections, one of which curves over the top of the arm, while the other forms the under part. The two are joined in a curved seam along the inside of the arm. The under part is sewed as far as it extends with the upper section into the side-back seam of the garment below the armhole. The upper part is, however, much deeper than the under and falls considerably below it in wing shape.

A band of braid borders the lower edges of the sleeve. Another band crosses each shoulder and passes down the back to the top of the corresponding plait, where it is terminated in a loop and short, pointed end. In front of the shoulder seam, this band of braid passes along the closing to a point some distance below the waist-line, where it is terminated in a longer pointed end and three loops. A high standing collar completes the neck.

Plain and checked cloths, coatings, and fancy cloakings, as well as the handsomest of ottomans and siciliennes, are made up in this way. Passementerie or drop ornaments often take the place of braid on rich materials. A nice lining is always a commendable addition. To make the wrap for a lady of medium size, requires 10 yards of material 22 inches wide, 5 1/8 yards of material 44 inches wide, or 4 1/4 yards of material 54 inches wide.

November 1886 *Delineator*

Ladies' Wrap. In this instance this wrap is very elaborately developed, the back and front being of plain velvet and the sleeves of Spanish lace net over crimson surah. The back is quite short, and its center seam ends below the waist-line at the top of an underfolded triple box-plait. The sleeves are gathered to stand high at the shoulders and fall in deep points quite low on the hips. They are trimmed with three deep ruffles of Spanish lace, the upper ruffle being headed by a ruche of narrower lace. On the back is an elaborate passementerie ornament. This covers the back across the neck and almost between the shoulders, and tapers toward the waist-line. Below the waist-line, it falls in two large tassel-like ornaments that descend quite a distance below the edge. A similar but smaller ornament is fastened beneath the folds of the plait. The front has full jabots of lace at the closing, and a standing plaited frill of lace is arranged outside a standing collar.

Wraps of this style are very often developed in combinations of two materials. Lace or beaded net over colored surah or silk is much liked for the sleeves, in conjunction with velvet-brocaded silk; ottoman; frisé brocades in silks, wools, and velvets; and rich materials of all kinds in black and colors. Of course, one material may be used throughout. Fringe of the chenille or passementerie variety, feather bands, or plaitings of silk, surah, lace, or embroidery may be used as trimmings. The back seldom has an edge trimming, but the sleeves and front may be as fancifully decorated as desired.

April 1885 *Delineator*

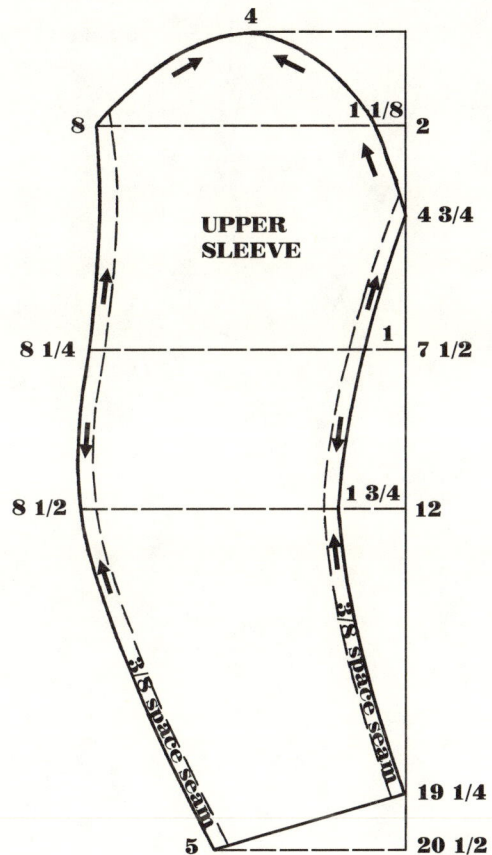

Long Wrap

This wrap is drafted with the scale corresponding to the bust measure. The length is regulated with the tape measure. It is in seven pieces: Front, side back, back, collar, upper sleeve, under sleeve, and ornamental sleeve.

Gather the extra fullness in the side back and sew it to the back. Line the ornamental sleeve with silk. Lay the plaits according to the notches. Finish with fancy balls, tassels, or ribbon bows. Sew the ornamental sleeve in with the plain sleeve.

Fall 1888 *Voice of Fashion*

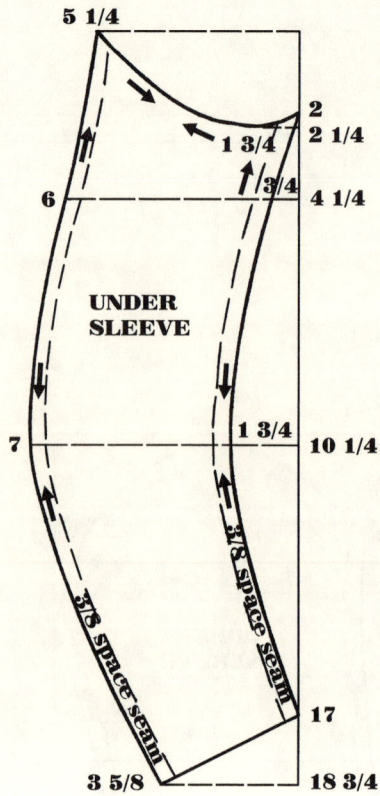

UNDER
SLEEVE

5 1/4

2
2 1/4
1 3/4

3/4
4 1/4

6

7   1 3/4   10 1/4

3/8 space seam
3/8 space seam

17

3 5/8   18 3/4

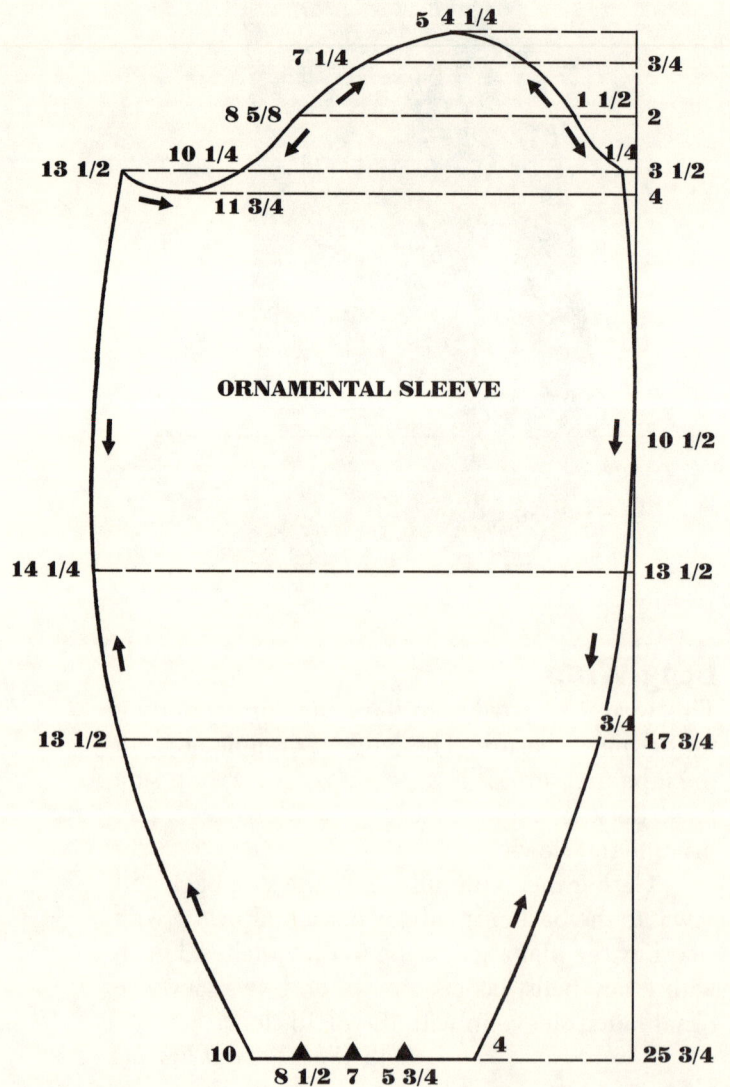

ORNAMENTAL SLEEVE

5 4 1/4

7 1/4   3/4

8 5/8   1 1/2
2

10 1/4   1/4
3 1/2

13 1/2   4
11 3/4

10 1/2

14 1/4   13 1/2

13 1/2   3/4
17 3/4

10   4   25 3/4
8 1/2 7 5 3/4

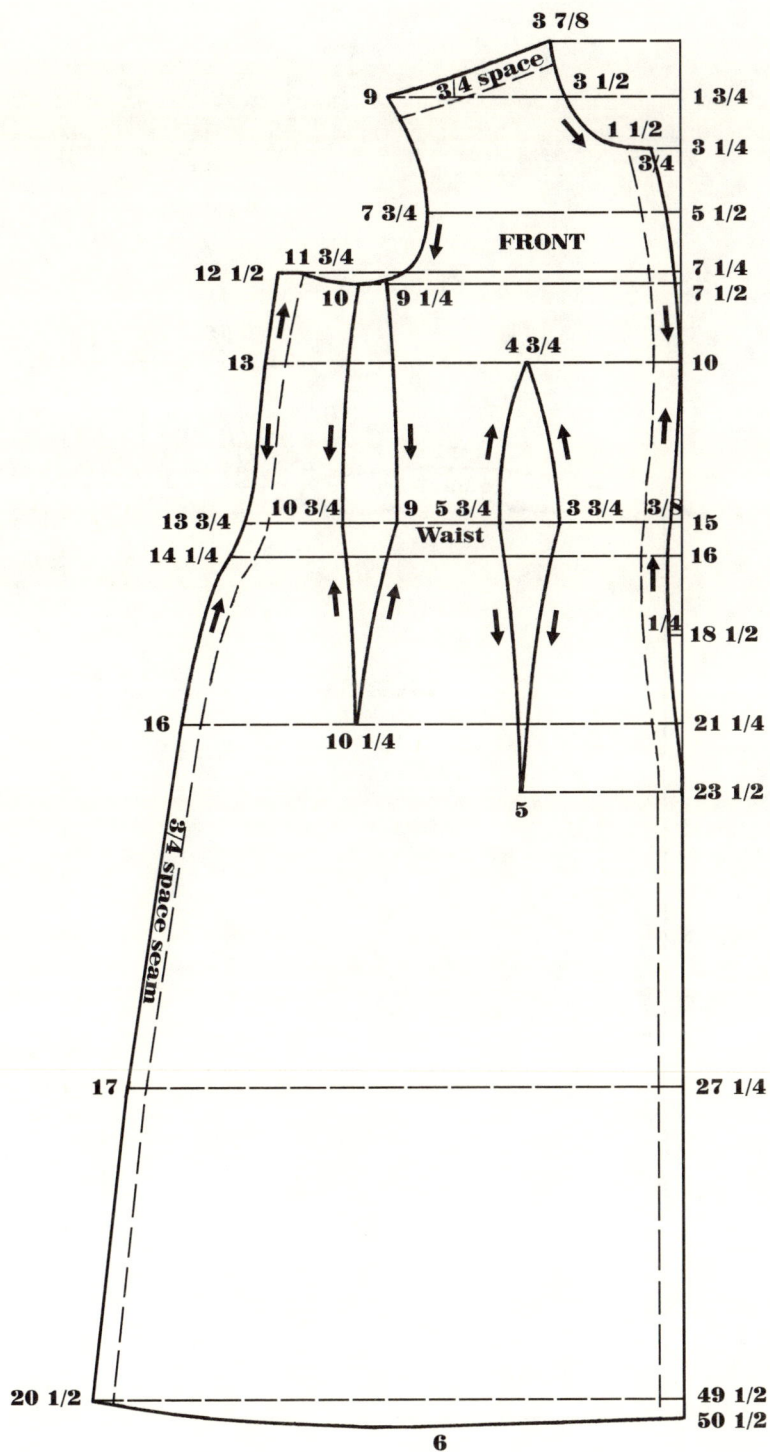

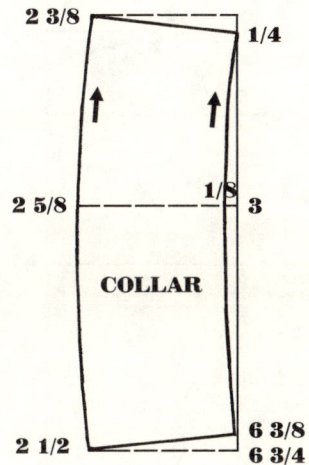

COLLAR

2 3/8 — 1/4

2 5/8 — 1/8 — 3

2 1/2 — 6 3/8 / 6 3/4

3 7/8

3/4 space — 3 1/2

9 — 1 3/4

1 1/2

3 1/4

3/4

7 3/4 — 5 1/2

FRONT

7 1/4

12 1/2 — 11 3/4 — 7 1/2

10 — 9 1/4

13 — 4 3/4 — 10

13 3/4 — 10 3/4 — 9 — 5 3/4 — 3 3/4 — 3/8 — 15

Waist

14 1/4 — 16

1/4

18 1/2

16 — 10 1/4 — 21 1/4

5 — 23 1/2

3/4 space seam

17 — 27 1/4

20 1/2 — 49 1/2 / 50 1/2

6

431

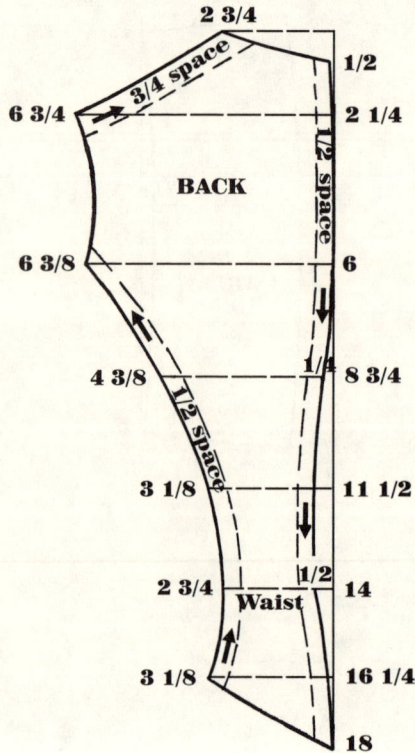

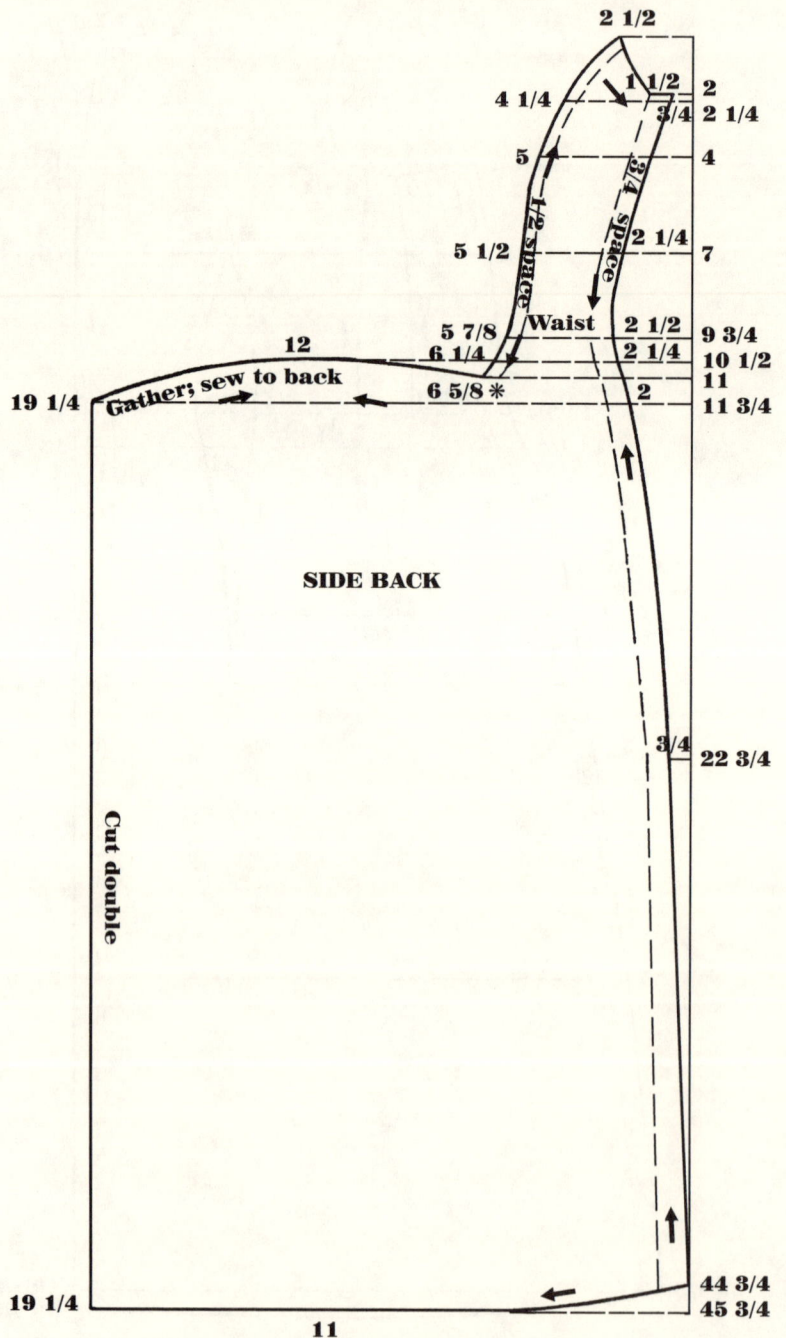

Ladies' Coat

Ladies' Coat. The material illustrated is cloth of firm weight, and the facings are of heavy white silk. The construction of this coat renders it alike suitable for moderate and cold weather, the fronts being made to roll back in lapels when open and lap well when closed. The closing is made only at the neck, a button and an elastic loop being used. The collar stands high, and rolls back with the lapels to the shoulders when the fronts are open. The lapels are faced with white silk cut bias, the facing being extended up on the collar so that the lapels appear as if there were no collar join when the fronts are rolled back. An interlining of buckram, such as tailors use in collars, etc., is placed under the facing to make the lapels stiff enough to stand out instead of lying flat. Although the fronts are loose fitting, they are conformed to the figure by long under-arm darts.

The back is rendered close fitting by side backs and a curved center back seam. The side backs fall even with the fronts at the bottom. The back extends only a little below the waist-line, where it is deepened considerably by a full skirt that is shirred three times across its top. The skirt is sewed onto the back at the lowest shirring and is rolled over a small pad. The coat sleeves are plainly finished at their wrists.

These coats are in fashionable demand for visiting, etc., and are made up in all kinds of stylish cloths and coatings. Smooth and ribbed effects are liked. For the facings moiré, corded, or brocaded silk is preferred and most colors are generally favored, especially white and light shades of green. The material should be firm enough to hold the facings out well, and the facing on the lapels is generally cut bias. Fur, Astrakhan, or a line of narrow metallic braid may define the edges and simulate deep cuffs. These coats are generally prettily lined. To make the garment for a lady of medium size, requires 8 3/8 yards of material 22 inches wide, 4 3/4 yards of material 44 inches wide, or 3 3/8 yards of material 54 inches wide. Also required are 1 5/8 yards of silk 20 inches wide for facings.

February 1889 *Delineator*

Coat with Organ-Pipe Plaits. Cloth of a seasonable quality was chosen for this coat, and machine-stitching, buttons, and a passementerie ornament constitute its finishings. The length suggests the newmarket style. The fronts are curved, and are closed with button-holes and braid buttons matching the coat material. In each side are a bust dart and an under-arm dart. Back of the bust dart, below the hip, is a curved pocket opening, its edges being machine-stitched and its ends stayed by triangles outlined with silk twist. Side backs and a curved center back seam fit the back to the figure.

A little below the waist-line, the backs are cut off straight across, and the side backs are extended at their back edges to supply the fullness necessary for the plaits. These are six in number and are arranged as follows. The upper edge is turned in quite deeply for a finish, and this edge is caught together by six loops with short spaces between them. The edges of the loops are pushed to the inside and creased in bias folds. Between the plaits, the top is slip-stitched to the backs. This arrangement produces what are known as organ-pipe plaits, and is very practical for arranging heavy material that is not easily gathered or plaited in the usual way. The plaits are stayed in their folds by elastic straps or tapes basted to them underneath. A passementerie ornament with tasseled ends covers the attached edge of the skirt. A line of machine-stitching holds in place the underfacing about the lower edge.

435

The sleeves are in coat shape. Double lines of stitching close to the wrist, and three buttons at the outside seam, ornament each sleeve. A high rolling collar, with double lines of stitching about the edges, completes the neck.

When material that is not heavy enough to preserve the round folds of the plaits is chosen, the back skirt is lined with material of appropriate weight to produce the effect pictured. This style may be made up in all kinds of seasonable cloths and coatings, and in pongee, surah, mohair, etc. A fancy clasp or ribbon ties may be fastened at the neck. To make the coat for a lady of medium size, requires 7 1/4 yards of material 22 inches wide, 3 3/8 yards of material 48 inches wide, or 3 1/4 yards of material 54 inches wide.

February 1885 *Delineator*

Coat with Bell Sleeves. The coat pictured is made of light-weight cloth, with a plain finish. It is adjusted by single bust and under-arm darts, side backs, and a curved center back seam. The back extends only a little below the waist-line, and is pointed at the end of the center back seam. The back skirt is provided by a full breadth that is gathered across the top and joined to the lower edge of the back, its side edges being seamed to the skirt edges of the side backs. The fullness is held back by elastic straps, which are sewed at intervals underneath to the side-back seams. The front edges of the fronts are curved to aid in the adjustment, and the right side is hemmed. Button-holes and fancy buttons are employed for the closing. The closing extends a considerable distance below the waist-line, the edges below falling apart to disclose the costume worn underneath. The collar is of fashionable height and fits closely about the neck. The sleeves have the two seams characteristic of the coat style, but widen in bell shape toward the wrist.

Cloths and suitings in small or broken plaids, as well as in stripes, checks, and plain colors, are popular for such coats. The collar may be of velvet in any becoming shade. A long ribbon bow at the neck is an effective adjunct. Braid, passementerie, or galloon are used for trimming. Pongee, mohair, camel's hair, and linen are suitable for traveling, and lines of machine-stitching may serve as their finish. To make the coat for a lady of medium size, requires 8 3/4 yards of material 22 inches wide, 4 1/4 yards of material 44 inches wide, or 3 1/2 yards of material 54 inches wide.

May 1888 *Delineator*

Coat with Angel Sleeves. Plaid coating was used for this coat. The angel sleeves open at the arm-holes in front over the coat sleeves and are curved at the open edges. The tips are narrowed by two plaits that turn from each edge and are then folded double and decorated with a pendant ornament. The sleeves are lined with silk of a harmonious color. A line of stitching follows the free edges of the angel sleeves. The coat sleeves are plainly finished.

The adjustment is effected by single bust and under-arm darts, side backs, and a center back seam. The back describes a pigeon-tail point at the end of the center seam. The full skirt is provided by the side backs, which are all in one below the back; ample fullness being allowed between the side-back seams to permit of a full gathering at the edge joined to the bottom of the back. The effect is graceful over the tournure, and the fullness keeps the draperies from crushing. Buttons and button-holes close the fronts

down the center to within some distance of the lower edge. The latter is finished with a line of stitching. The standing officer's collar is high and close fitting, and a line of stitching is made close to its edges.

Repped, corded, twilled, and plain cloths are admired for dressy coats, and are sometimes very elaborately embroidered. For serviceable garments changeable, checked, striped, mixed, and plaid coatings and cloths are stylish. The finish on them is generally plain, or a simple decoration of braid or passementerie. The angel sleeves should always be lined with silk, satin, etc., as in this way a bright effect may easily be given a sober-hued cloth. For a lady of medium size, this coat requires 8 1/2 yards of material 22 inches wide, 4 1/4 yards of material 44 inches wide, or 3 3/4 yards of material 54 inches wide. Each requires 1 5/8 yards of silk 20 inches wide to line the angel sleeves.

September 1888 *Delineator*

438

Ladies' Pelisse. The garment pictured is made of navy blue cloth. The fronts close nearly to the bottom with button-holes and buttons, the front edges being curved. The pelisse is closely adjusted by single bust and under-arm darts, side backs, and a curved center back seam. An emphatic coat-like appearance is given to the back by arranging coat-plaits below the waist-line of the side-back seams, and hemmed coat laps below the end of the center back seam. A button marks the top of each coat-plait. A line of stitching confines the hems of the coat laps, and is continued about the bottom of the pelisse. The standing collar is high and close fitting, and its edges are followed by a line of machine-stitching.

The coat sleeves are finished with two lines of stitching several inches from the wrist edges. They are encased in wide fancy sleeves, which are lined with silk and are open at the front of the arm in the Japanese style. The fancy sleeves are widest at the bottom, where they fall with a square effect considerably below the coat sleeves. Their edges are finished with a line of machine-stitching.

For traveling, promenading, and general wear, this pelisse is practical, comfortable, and stylish. It may be developed in all kinds of cloths and coatings; corded, changeable, striped, checked, and mixed effects are fashionable. The fancy sleeves may be lined with gay or sober colors, and they may be handsomely braided. Braidings on the back, down both sides of the closing, and on the collar and wrists produce an elaborate effect. Fur is a handsome trimming. To make the pelisse for a lady of medium size, requires 8 7/8 yards of material 22 inches wide, 4 1/2 yards of material 44 inches wide, or 3 7/8 yards of material 54 inches wide. Each requires 1 5/8 yards of silk 20 inches wide to line the ornamental sleeves.

January 1889 *Delineator*

Ladies' Cloak. The cloak is illustrated developed in cloth. It is adjusted by single bust and under-arm darts, side backs, and a curved center back seam that ends at the top of an underfolded box-plait. Below the waist-line of the side-back seams, fullness is allowed and is gathered up closely and basted in place. A belt-tie is sewed underneath at the waist-line to the center back and side-back seams to draw the back in closely to the figure. At the neck is a high standing collar with an invisible closing.

Over each coat sleeve falls a wing sleeve that resembles the angel style. At the inside of the arm is a short seam, below which the edges fall free to the edge of the garment. The high effect visible above the shoulders is produced by a plaiting of crinoline placed under the gathered top of the wing sleeve.

Bedford cord; striped, checked, and brocaded wools; plain armure, brocaded silk, and sicilienne are stylish for these cloaks, as are all kinds of winter cloakings. Passementerie, braid, or velvet may be chosen for trimming, and the wing sleeve is often lined with silk. To make the cloak for a lady of medium size, requires 12 1/2 yards of material 22 inches wide, 6 1/4 yards of material 44 inches wide, or 5 1/8 yards of material 54 inches wide.

November 1889 *Delineator*

Ulster and Garrick Cape

The ulster is drafted with the scale corresponding to the bust measure. The length is regulated with the tape measure. The ulster consists of six pieces: Front, side back, back, collar, and two sleeve pieces. Lay the plaits in the back according to the notches.

The garrick cape is drafted with the scale corresponding to the bust measure. It consists of five pieces: Four overlapping capes and the collar. The cape is often made to match the ulster, but it may be made of almost any material. Two alternating shades are frequently seen, but there should be a similarity, say two shades of brown or two of gray. Sew the center capes onto the under cape on the curved dashed lines, then take up the shoulder darts. The cape may be finished on the edges with machine-stitching or feather-stitching, or left perfectly plain.

Fall 1889 *Voice of Fashion*

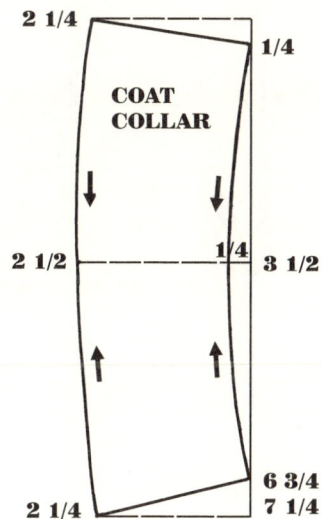

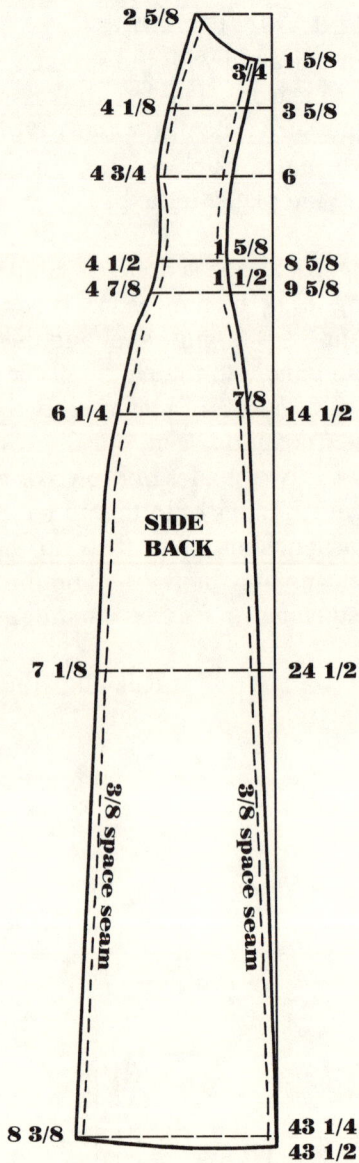

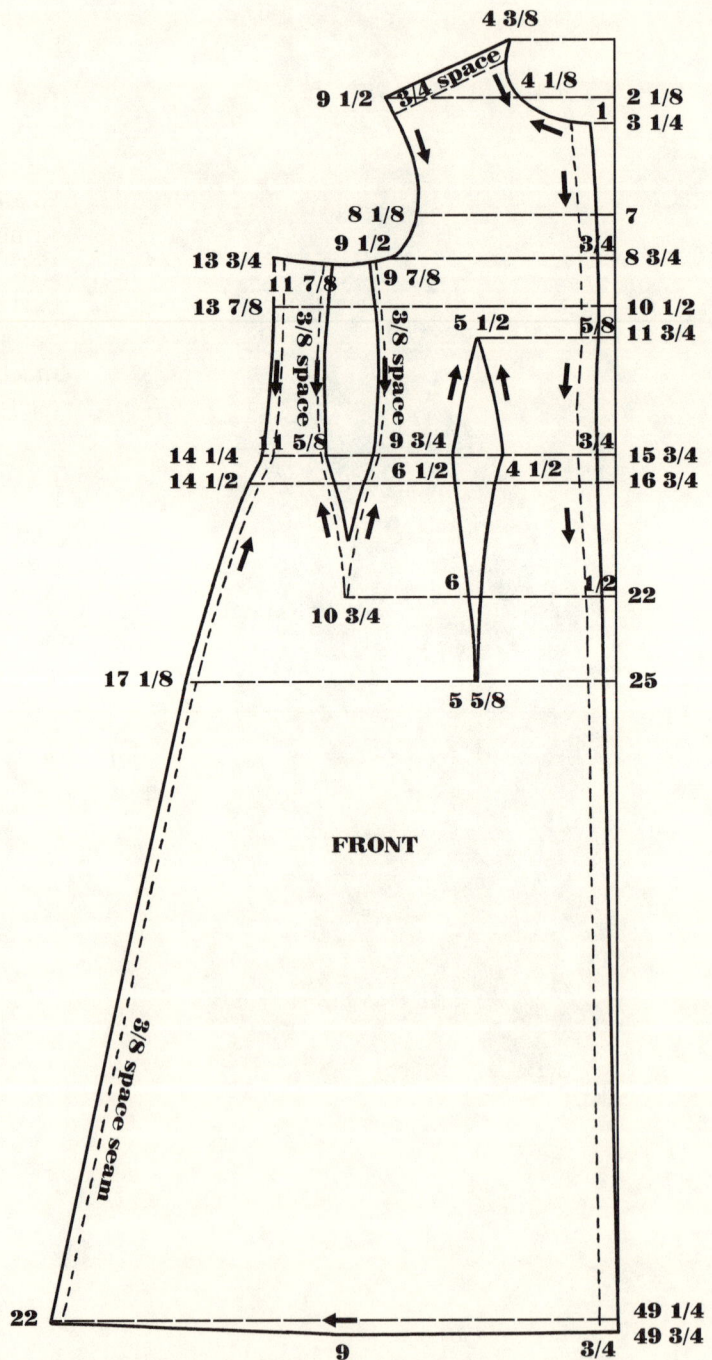

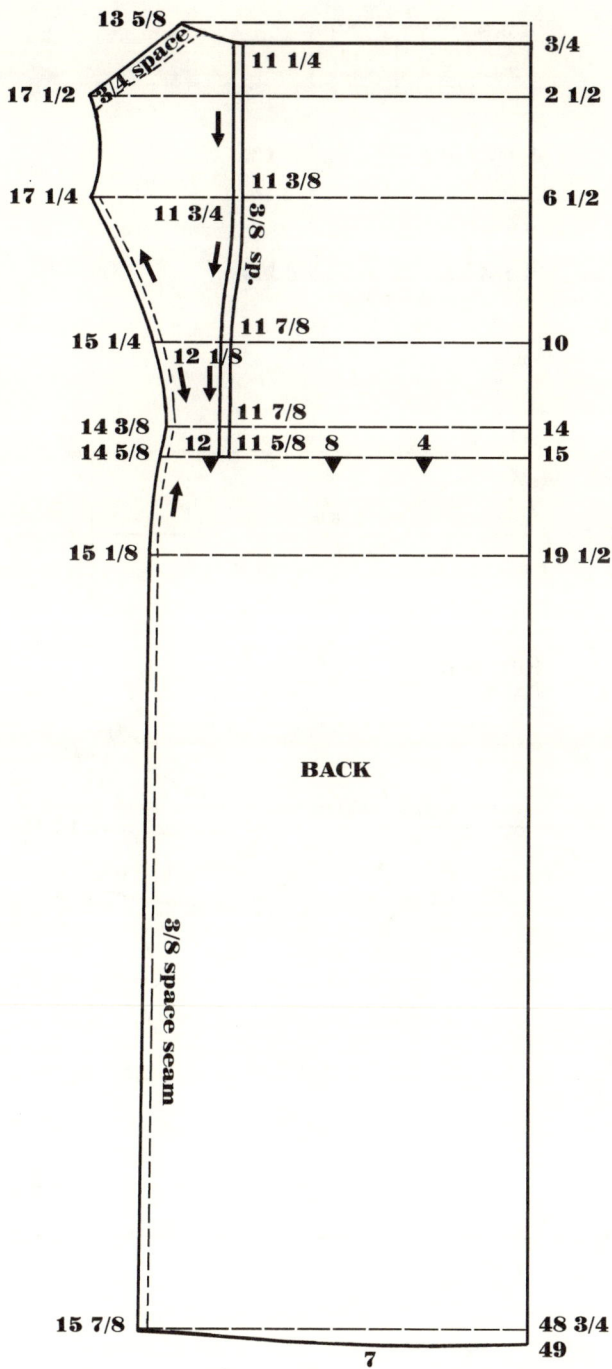

13 5/8

17 1/2   3/4 space

11 1/4   3/4

2 1/2

17 1/4

11 3/8   6 1/2

11 3/4   3/8 sp.

15 1/4   11 7/8   10

12 1/8

14 3/8   11 7/8   14

14 5/8   12   11 5/8   8   4   15

15 1/8   19 1/2

BACK

3/8 space seam

15 7/8   48 3/4
49
7

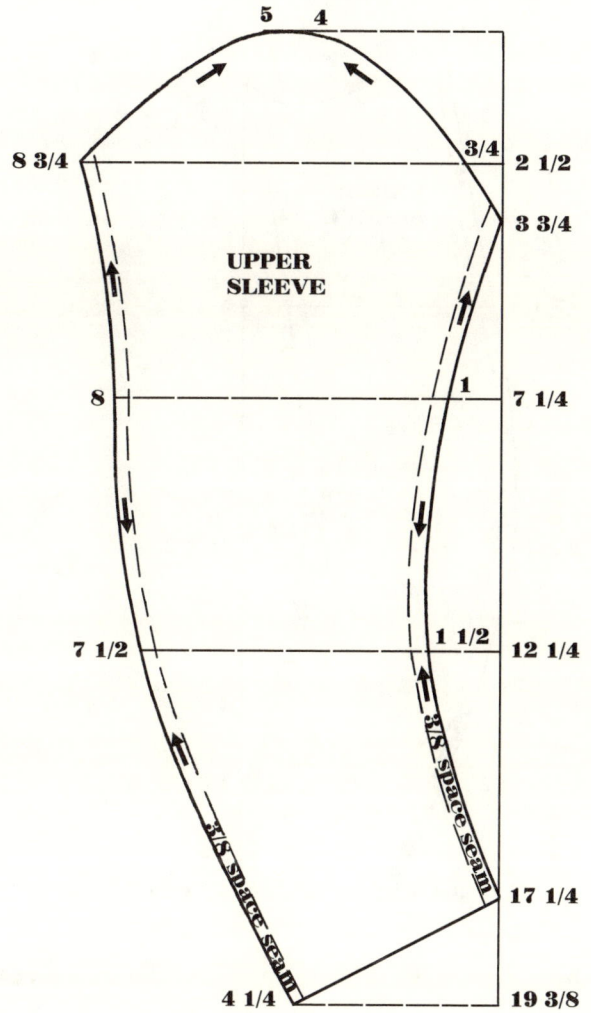

5   4

8 3/4   3/4   2 1/2

3 3/4

UPPER SLEEVE

8   1   7 1/4

7 1/2   1 1/2   12 1/4

3/8 space seam

17 1/4

4 1/4   19 3/8

443

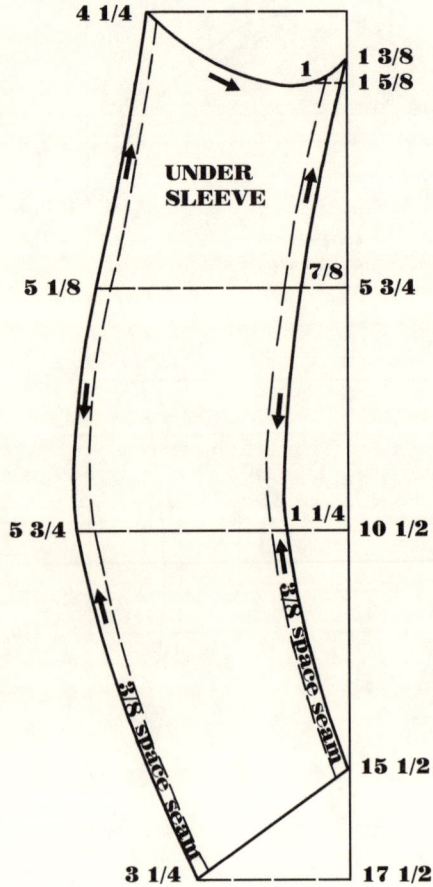

UNDER SLEEVE

4 1/4
1 3/8
1
1 5/8
5 1/8
7/8
5 3/4
5 3/4
1 1/4
10 1/2
3/8 space seam
3/8 space seam
15 1/2
3 1/4
17 1/2

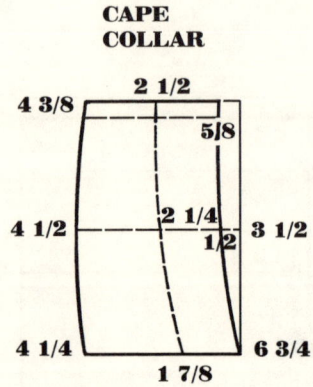

CAPE COLLAR

4 3/8
2 1/2
5/8
4 1/2
2 1/4
1/2
3 1/2
4 1/4
6 3/4
1 7/8

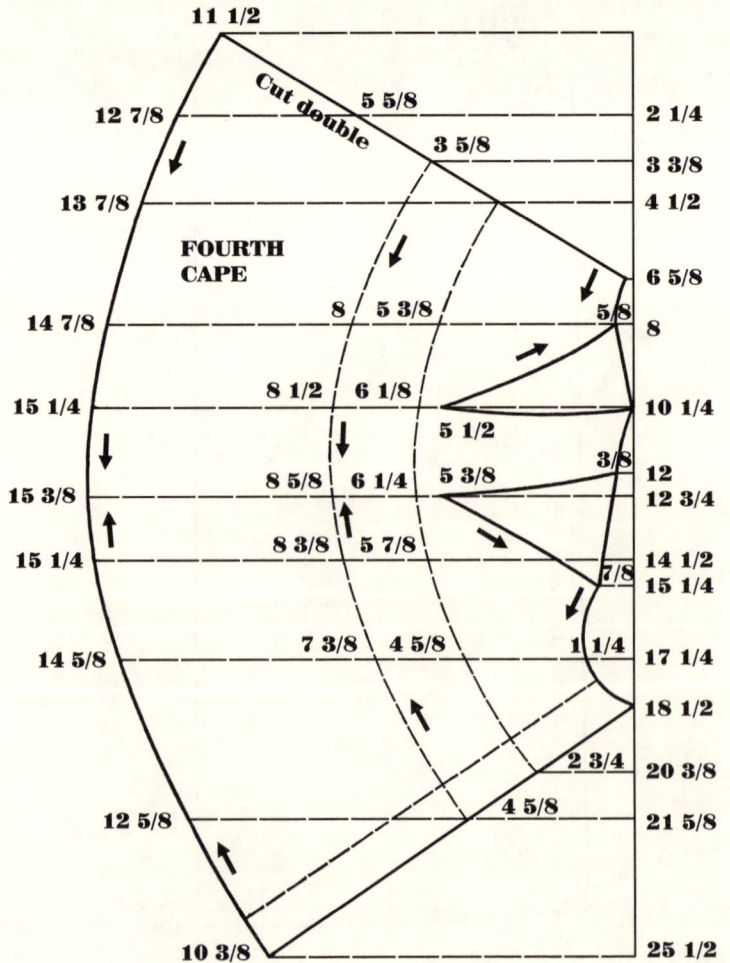

FOURTH CAPE

Cut double

11 1/2
12 7/8
5 5/8
2 1/4
3 5/8
3 3/8
13 7/8
4 1/2
6 5/8
14 7/8
8
5 3/4
5/8
8
8 1/2
6 1/8
10 1/4
15 1/4
5 1/2
3/8
12
15 3/8
8 5/8
6 1/4
5 3/4
12 3/4
15 1/4
8 3/4
5 7/8
14 1/2
7/8
15 1/4
14 5/8
7 3/8
4 5/8
1 1/4
17 1/4
18 1/2
2 3/4
20 3/8
12 5/8
4 5/8
21 5/8
10 3/8
25 1/2

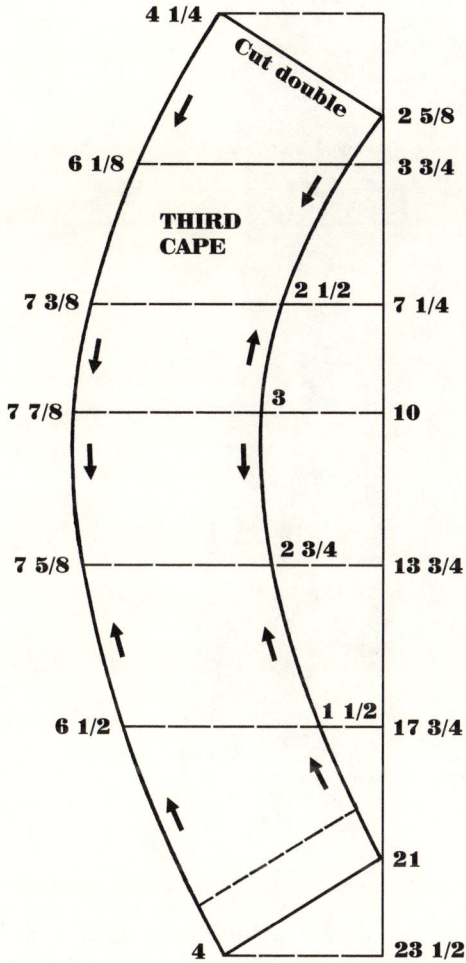

THIRD CAPE

4 1/4
Cut double
2 5/8
6 1/8 — 3 3/4
7 3/8 — 2 1/2 — 7 1/4
7 7/8 — 3 — 10
7 5/8 — 2 3/4 — 13 3/4
6 1/2 — 1 1/2 — 17 3/4
21
4 — 23 1/2

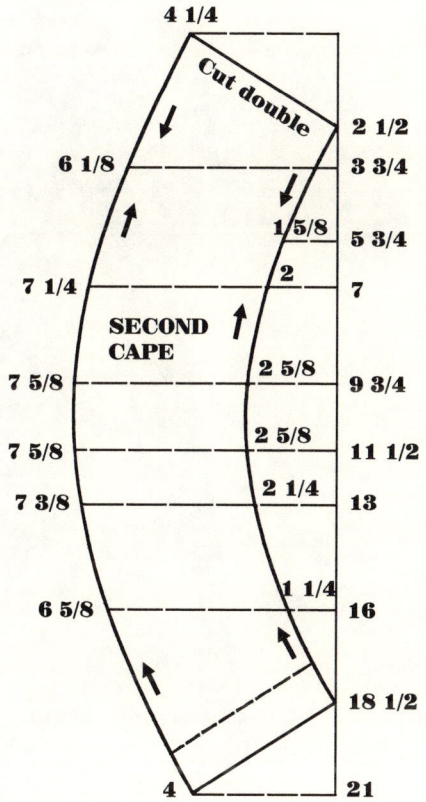

SECOND CAPE

4 1/4
Cut double
2 1/2
6 1/8 — 3 3/4
1 5/8 — 5 3/4
7 1/4 — 2 — 7
7 5/8 — 2 5/8 — 9 3/4
7 5/8 — 2 5/8 — 11 1/2
7 3/8 — 2 1/4 — 13
6 5/8 — 1 1/4 — 16
18 1/2
4 — 21

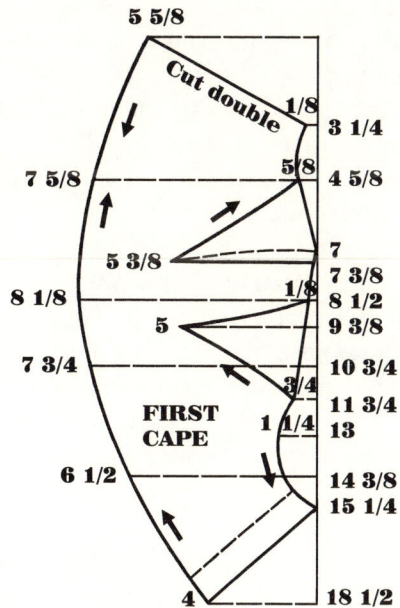

FIRST CAPE

5 5/8
Cut double
1/8
3 1/4
7 5/8 — 5/8 — 4 5/8
5 3/8 — 7
7 3/4 — 7 3/8
8 1/8 — 1/8 — 8 1/2
5 — 9 3/8
7 3/4 — 10 3/4
3/4 — 11 3/4
1 1/4 — 13
6 1/2 — 14 3/8
15 1/4
4 — 18 1/2

Coat with Triple Cape. This coat is shown made of cloth and trimmed with silk braid. It is fitted by long under-arm darts, side backs, and a curved center back seam that is discontinued at the top of extra widths. The extra width on the left back is turned back on the outside to form a revers. The extra width on the right back is lapped under the left back and caught in place at intervals with hooks and eyes. A button is placed at the top of the revers, and a similar button is placed on the top of the right back. The side-back seams have fullness allowed in a line with that of the center back seam, which is underfolded in a forward-turning plait.

The fronts are turned back to a little below the waist-line in triangular lapels, and are closed invisibly to the bust. Below this, they lap diagonally to some distance below the waist-line. They are closed with two buttons and button-holes below the lapels, from which to the lower edge the lap is straight and wide. The lapels are faced with the material, and their edges and the overlapping front edge are bound with braid. If desired the right front, instead of being reversed, may be lapped over the left.

At the neck is a high standing collar, to the upper edge of which is sewed a rolling collar. In the seam of the standing collar to the coat is included a triple cape, each section of which is fitted smoothly by two darts on each shoulder. The

pointed upper corner of each lapel is secured to the upper cape with a button and button-hole. The coat sleeves are finished at the wrists with deep, rolling cuffs that are wider than the sleeves. The edges of the cuffs, capes, and collar, and the upper and side edges of the revers on the back, are bound with braid matching that on the fronts.

This mode is adaptable to all kinds of cloakings, such as lady's cloth; diagonal, beaver, twilled, or brocaded cloth; tricot, corkscrew, or rough-surfaced cloth, etc. The cape sections may be made of Astrakhan or corduroy. The trimming may consist of braid, cord, or drop trimming, or the loose edges may simply be followed by machine-stitching. Velvet may be used for the cuffs, collar, and lapels. To make the coat for a lady of medium size, requires 11 1/8 yards of material 22 inches wide, 5 1/2 yards of material 44 inches wide, or 4 1/2 yards of material 54 inches wide.

November 1889 *Delineator*

Coat Polonaise with Removable Capes.
The polonaise is shown made of cloth, decorated with Astrakhan, and lined with silk. It is fitted by double bust and under-arm darts, side backs, and a curved center back seam that ends at the top of hemmed coat laps. The side seams end in a line with the center back seam, and the fronts fall with the effect of panels. Below the waist-line of each side-back seam, extra width is underfolded in a forward-turning plait underneath. The fronts, which lap in double-breasted style, are short between the darts, and their front edges are reversed and faced with Astrakhan. The closing is effected with hooks and eyes.

At the neck is a rolling collar. About the shoulders is worn a cape consisting of three graduated sections. Each is fitted by two darts on each shoulder. The loose edges of the sections are followed by a line of machine-stitching. The coat sleeves are finished at the wrists by a double cuff, which is left open at the back and has pointed upper back corners. The deeper part of the cuff is followed along its free edges by a line of machine-stitching. On each hip is applied a double pocket lap with a square front and pointed lower back corners, the deeper part of the lap being finished by a line of machine-stitching. The skirt parts of the polonaise are lined with silk.

Lady's cloth; cashmere; camel's hair; serge; Pera material; Bedford cord; diagonal, tricot, brocaded, corded, or repped cloth; matelassé velvet; faille, etc., are the materials most frequently chosen. Velvet or plush may be combined with cloth, and Astrakhan, fur, etc., unite well with heavier materials. The capes may be made of velvet or plush, and the polonaise of cloth or a lighter-textured material. A lining of contrasting silk adds greatly to the effect. For a lady of medium size, this coat polonaise requires 9 yards of material 22 inches wide, 4 3/4 yards of material 44 inches wide, or 4 yards of material 54 inches wide. Also required are 7/8 yard of Astrakhan 27 inches wide for the collar, etc., and 3 1/2 yards of lining silk 27 inches wide.

October 1889 *Delineator*

Directoire Cape. This cape may form part of a toilette, or it may be made up to accompany a number of different costumes. It is shown made of golden brown and tan cloth, with an edge finish of machine-stitching. The cape consists of five sections. On the largest, which is fitted by two darts on each shoulder, are arranged four sections that are graduated in length, the second section from the top being also fitted by two darts on each shoulder. The lowest two of these four sections are sewed flatly to the largest section, while the other two extend to the neck. The ends of all of the sections are hemmed. A rolling collar is at the neck. Its edges, and all of the loose edges of the cape sections, are followed by a line of machine-stitching. The closing is made at the neck with a hook and eye.

This mode is adaptable to all kinds of materials, for example light-weight cloth, faille, Ottoman, and armure. Combinations have a particularly good effect. Mode, green, and light gray are the most popular shades. A lining of the preferred shade may be added. The trimming may consist of braid, drop trimming, gimp, fringe, etc.; or the edges may be followed with cord, piping, machine-stitching, etc. To make the cape for a lady of medium size, requires 3 5/8 yards of material 22 inches wide, or 1 7/8 yards of material either 44 or 54 inches wide.

September 1889 *Delineator*

10. Trimmings

Some of the large decorative buttons are works of art. They are meant to be placed at the back or on the coat fronts of Empire coats. On some buttons, bits of enamel are arranged in kaleidoscope fashion. On others are depicted groups of shepherdesses and their swains, while on still others are miniature likenesses of dead and departed beauties. Flashing buttons of finely cut steel are used on both long and short coats. Small buttons, either crocheted or covered with velvet or the dress material, are chosen for use, because a garment may really be secured with them.

June 1889 Delineator

Fringes are available in a wide variety of patterns and textures. Fancy knotted or meshed fringes and Milan droppings are much admired for bordering panels, and for trimming sash ends and broad Directoire pocket laps. They are frequently carried across the lower edges of short draperies. An elegant decoration consists of a tablier or side gore combining a network of twisted cord and knotted sewing-silk fringe. A deep beading of black gimp known as bullion, edged with bead-and-silk fringe, is extended diagonally from one shoulder of a bodice to the waist-line, where a pointed girdle is attached.

Trimmings of kid in Grecian patterns are especially appropriate as border decorations for classic or full, straight draperies. They form effective frames for vests of plain leather or kid.

August 1889 Delineator

Velvet is the ruling garniture. It may or may not differ in color from the material on which it is placed, and it may be used either sparingly or lavishly. Both full and plain sleeves are made of velvet. Velvet may be used for a long fold in a plain skirt; when it is heavy grosgrain or figured moiré velvet, it is outlined with silk passementerie. The girdle, collar, and pocket laps may be of velvet, as may a deep Russian or shawl collar. Velvet is much used for plastrons, and for the lapels that often form the only decoration on a plain basque. Vests of brocaded velvet are rather a novelty. Fine pipings of velvet are favored as the edge finish for jackets. The draperies of cloth dresses are outlined with broader pipings, 1 inch wide. When velvet is the trimming, velvet buttons may be used.

Passementeries and heavy cord fringes are receiving special attention. The cord fringe, however, is impossible on any but very heavy dresses. The passementeries made entirely of silk are often as fine as lace, and are shown in all of the popular colors. Most of the designs can be cut in motifs, so that none of the trimming is wasted; but motifs can also be purchased separately.

Black lace that seems like a first cousin to yak lace is used on serpent, blue, golden brown, black, or any other color that harmonizes with it. It is shown both as an insertion and an edge finish. Several bands of insertion set in the material, with an edging to match, form a favored decoration. The lace is sewed on the material that is to be decorated. The material is then cut from under it, the edge being rolled and hemmed with long invisible stitches. Usually there are three bands of insertion and then the full frill of lace. At least 1/8 yard of the material should show between each two bands of lace. On long coats with capes this heavy lace is considered very smart, and it is very effective on smooth cloth or heavy suiting.

Feather trimming is noted on short velvet wraps for evening wear. Most frequently this is black, while the velvet is serpent, garnet, army, or golden brown. The wrap is lined with silk of the same shade as the velvet.

October 1889 Delineator

Ensembles

Ensembles

Chantilly and marquise laces are used for entire dresses. They are made over black satin surah, or over changeable surah in shades of moss green with rose, pink with gray, or red with blue. Very wide flouncing, deep enough for a skirt, is draped long and full above a narrow flounce (5 inches wide) at the bottom, which is laid over a puff or a pinked flounce of changeable silk. The lace skirt is plaited very full at the top, with especially full plaits in the center of the back, and has Arab folds dropping over at the top. On the left side it is carried up to the hips, the scallops meeting. Flounces of narrower lace cross the open space on the left side, or are draped as jabots, on which falls a bridle of black satin ribbon from the belt to the bottom, tied in three places in clusters of long loops.

The wide lace covers the changeable silk for the basque. It is gathered on the shoulders, and plaited to a point in front. Knife-plaited lace 3 inches wide edges the V-shaped opening. Two other frills of

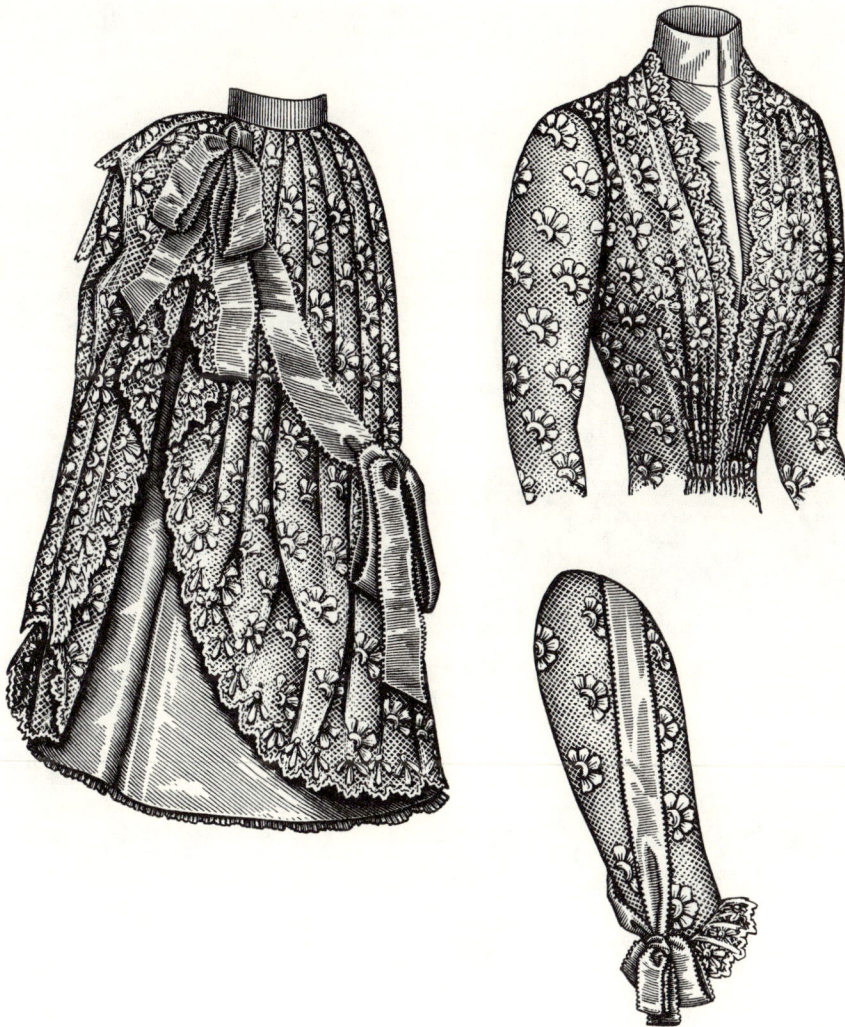

Figure 1. Lace trimming for bodice, sleeve, and skirt

451

plaited lace fill in this space, while a single plaiting is upright around a high collar of the changeable silk. Four frills of plaited lace are set on the back of the basque, and two frills trim the wrists of the coat sleeves.

Such dresses require 8 or 9 yards of lace over 40 inches wide. The Chantilly lace most used is an imitation of real thread lace known as French lace. The marquise lace has large Spanish designs on the small irregular meshes of Chantilly lace. Nets of various kinds, striped, dotted, and cross-barred, and in large square meshes, are used for black lace dresses.

March 24, 1888 *Harper's Bazar*

Silk embroidery on cloth is a fashionable trimming for tailor dresses. A length of 3 or 4 yards is used for each dress, as a border or lengthwise in front, or for side stripes, lapels, and collar. The designs are leaves and arabesques. They are in shades of one color, or in the India cashmere colors, with some tinsel threads added to the silks.

October 20, 1888 *Harper's Bazar*

White, black, or tinted lace may be arranged as shown by Figure 1 over silk, satin, moiré, etc., of the same or a contrasting color. The lace represented is white over white surah. The basque has surplice fronts of lace flouncing that open over a surah vest, which is revealed in chemisette shape.

Figure 2. Decoration for bodice, sleeve, and skirt

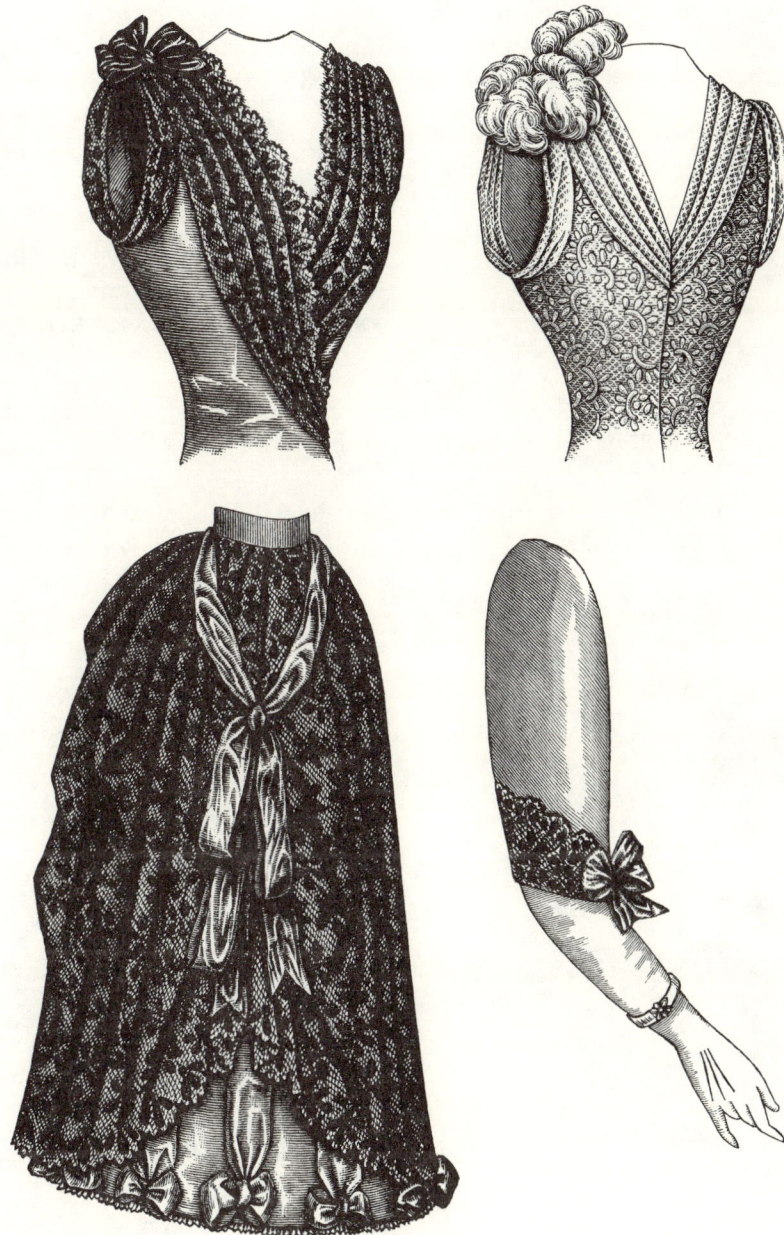

Figure 3. Decorations for evening costume

The surplice fullness is gathered at the shoulders and shirred at the waist-line.

The sleeve is made of lace net. It is cut off to elbow length and edged with a lace frill. It may be lined or not, as desired. It is decorated with a ribbon strap passing from the top near the front of the arm, to the bottom of the sleeve near the outside seam, where it is tied in a full bow.

The skirt has a protective knife-plaiting of surah that is revealed slightly below the edge. The decoration consists of feather-edged ribbon. This is tied in a bow and basted near the belt on the right

453

hip, from which it is carried to the left knee and there tied in a similar bow.

May 1888 Delineator

This mode is particularly adapted to yachting, tennis, etc., and Figure 2 pictures it in plain and striped flannel. The decorative anchors may be embroidered in metallic threads or in braids, or may be of metal or appliquéd, as preferred.

The fronts of the basque open all the way down over a Breton vest. The vest is decorated down the center with cord laced evenly over small buttons. The sailor collar extends in tapering lapels down the front edges to the bust. Below its ends a small anchor decorates each front. A knot of ribbon is fastened at the neck, although the cord may be tied there, if desired. A round cuff-facing of plain material finishes the coat sleeve. If desired, an anchor may be embroidered on it.

The drapery is bordered at the bottom to the depth of at least 9 inches with plain flannel. The long strap that lies on a bunch of plaits below the right hip is of plain flannel decorated in the point with an anchor. On the left side the drapery hangs straight below a loose loop, revealing the skirt in panel fashion and affording a fine opportunity for a display of braid in any preferred arrangement.

July 1888 Delineator

White, black, or tinted lace may be arranged as in Figure 3 on silk, satin, moiré, etc., of the same or a contrasting color. Two views of the basque are given, with different trimmings. The front view shows black lace over cream surah, while the back

Figure 4. Trimmings for walking costume

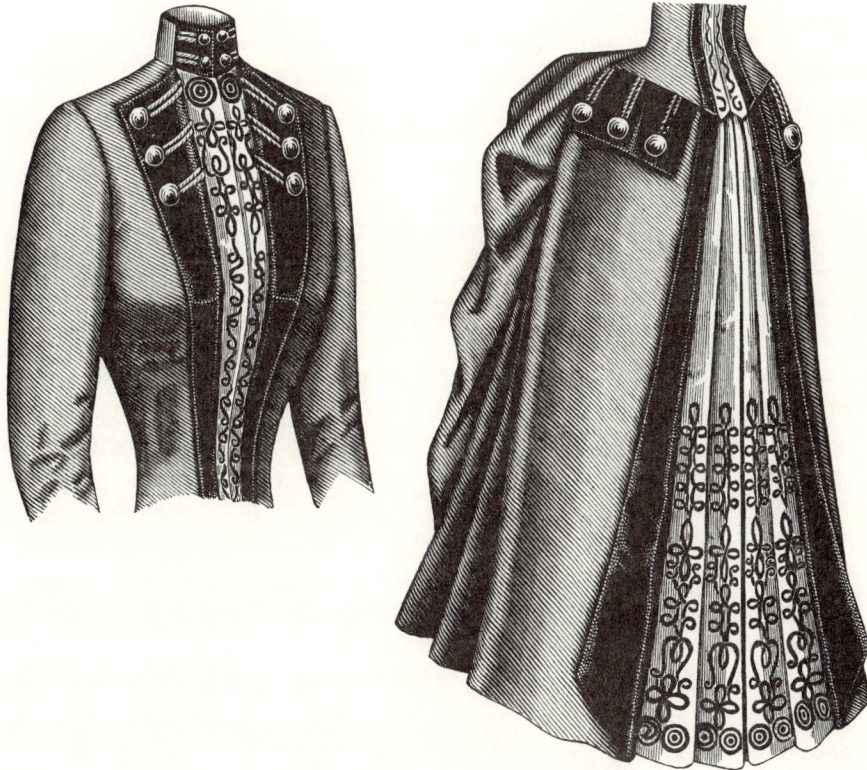

Figure 5. Decoration for polonaise and skirt

view shows cream net over satin. The front view shows broad surplices that cross each other. The neck is cut in V shape, and the scalloped edge of the lace turns toward the front. A soft twist of net outlines each armhole, and a little bow of moiré ribbon rests on the right shoulder.

The back view shows a V neck, which is followed by a drapery of point d'esprit. The armholes are also draped with net, and a bunch of ostrich tips waves over the left shoulder.

The sleeve, if used, is cut off to elbow length. Lace edging turns back on it, the full depth of the lace being visible at the outside of the arm, and from this narrowing toward the inside seam, where a tiny bow rests.

A protective plaiting of surah peeps from under the edge of the skirt. At intervals on the right side are set strips of soft ribbon, which are each held beneath their gathered lower ends by a tiny

bow of similar ribbon. The flounce is draped so as to reveal the strips. Moiré ribbon falls in loops and ends on the right side.

November 1888 *Delineator*

Hunter green velvet, dove gray cashmere, and Oriental lace net are combined in the walking costume shown by Figure 4. On the basque, a plaited net chemisette is revealed in V shape from the neck to the bust. Velvet vest sections overlap each other below this. Picot-edged ribbon is arranged as illustrated. A row of crocheted buttons ornaments each edge of the jacket front above the bust. The high military collar is of velvet. The inside seam of the coat sleeve ends a little above the wrist, which is reversed to form a graduated cuff that displays a round under cuff. The reversed part is faced with velvet, and the under cuff is overhung by a frill of Valenciennes lace. A bow of fancy-edged ribbon is placed above the flared ends of the reversed part.

Hunter green velvet is used for the four-gored foundation skirt. The right and left side draperies expose the front and right side gores between them. Starting from the right side-back seam are three straps of picot-edged grosgrain ribbon, the uppermost strap being the shortest and the lowest the longest. A bow conceals the front end of each strap. When a union of materials is not liked, the exposed parts of the gores may be braided.

November 1888 Delineator

The materials are twilled suiting, white corded silk, and velvet. The upper part of the polonaise is shown on the left of Figure 5. Back of the closing on each side is a velvet Directoire lapel that narrows toward the bottom. Between the lapels, the front is faced with silk and braided with metal soutache in a delicate tracery pattern. Near the back edge of each lapel at the top are three metal buttons, from beneath which extend obliquely loops of metal cord that pass under the front edges. The collar part crossing the vest is of velvet, and is trimmed with two smaller buttons and short loops of cord.

The skirt and the lower part of the polonaise are shown on the right. The plaited panel is of white silk. On the upper fold of each plait, an application of soutache is observable. The skirt sections of the polonaise are joined to the short bodice parts. In their seams are included the tops of velvet pocket laps, which are decorated with cord loops and buttons. A velvet revers turns from the front edge of each skirt section.

November 1888 Delineator

Figured India silk was chosen for this costume, and surah, velvet, lace, and moiré ribbon supply the trimmings. The front view, at the top left of Figure 6, shows the neck cut out and the sleeves shortened. The fronts are trimmed with bands of moiré ribbon tapering to points at the waist-line, where they meet. A section of lace, gathered up closely at the shoulder and front edge, is applied to each front, the scalloped edge of the lace coming at the neck edge. The sleeves are deepest at the inside seam. They are trimmed with a lace frill and two bands of ribbon, the ribbons meeting at the back of the arm, where they are formed into a butterfly bow.

The back view is shown at the bottom left. The parts cut low in V shape are covered by a plaited section of surah. The edges of the V are gathered up closely at the center back seam and on each shoulder. The neck is finished with a high velvet collar. Braided or embroidered material may replaced the plaited surah.

The lower part of the skirt drapery is trimmed with bands of moiré ribbon corresponding to the ribbon on the front of the basque.

December 1888 Delineator

Figure 7 shows this costume developed as an evening dress in pale green silk, with trimmings of white lace, plain net, and passementerie. The skirt is in the standard four-gored shape. Two steels adjusted across the back breadth support the fullness of the train and produce a slightly bouffant effect. A pad may be worn, if desired.

On the back is arranged a full train that sweeps out in either oval or square outline, as preferred. The sides of the train are basted to the back breadth. The front and side gores are covered from the belt to the edge with a lace flounce. On each side of the center of the front is a narrow panel that hangs free from the belt, where it is gathered. These panels are lined with silk and interlined with crinoline. They are trimmed down each side edge and across the bottom with a band of passementerie. Flaring sharply from these panels are much narrower panels, which pass into the side-back seams and are similarly lined and interlined. They are trimmed at their front and lower edges with a band of passementerie.

The bodice is a close-fitting basque, which is deeply pointed at the center of the front and back and curved high across the sides. It is fitted by double bust darts, side pieces, side backs, and a curved center back seam. The fronts open from the point toward the shoulders over a vest, which is sewed in place underneath on one side and secured with hooks and eyes on the other. The vest is trimmed with a shirred puff of plain net, which passes under a band of passementerie heading a full arrangement of lace net. The standing collar shown by the back view is omitted when the low neck shown by the front view is desired. When the collar is used, it is covered with passementerie. When the low neck is used, a jabot of

Figure 6. Decoration for bodice and skirt

lace outlines it from the shoulders to the bust, and a band of passementerie crosses the neck at the back and passes down the front edges of the fronts. Similar passementerie trims the front of the armholes. The coat sleeve is shortened somewhat. On it is arranged a full puff that is shirred just above the elbow under a band of passementerie, to resemble a double puff. Lace is arranged to turn up from the wrist, and passementerie hides the lower edge of the puff.

Striped velvets and silks, plain velvets and plushes, rich brocades, etc., are used for the train, which may differ entirely from the rest of the costume. The train should be handsomely lined, and an interlining is usually added to hold the material out well. The skirt gores may be made of fancy material and plainly finished; or they may be made of plain velvet or silk and embroidered all over with braid, cord, or beads. Appliqué trimmings in cloth or velvet are elegant, and they may be outlined with metallic braid, cord, or thread, or with beads. The drapery panels and vest also invite elaborate applications of these trimmings. All materials devoted to dressy wear make up handsomely in this style. A bride's dress may be made up in white satin and white tulle, with point lace, pearl bead passementerie, and pearl bead ornaments for trimmings.

February 1889 *Delineator*

Figure 7. Evening or bridal dress

Figure 8. Decoration for basque, sleeve, and skirt

The materials combined in the example shown by Figure 8 are cashmere, velvet, and silk. The skirt shows the panel made of silk and decorated with rope shirrings in V shape. The back drapery is deeply bordered at the bottom with a velvet band. Above the band is a scroll design of metallic cord, the band and cord being continued across the front drapery.

The basque shows a pointed vest, on which are rope shirrings in V shape. The front edges of the fronts are trimmed with a velvet band, back of which is a scroll design of metallic cord. The high standing collar is of velvet and is plainly finished, although it may have gold cord scrolled along its edges.

The sleeve decoration consists of an oval puff of silk with three rope shirrings applied at the back of the wrist. The material is cut away to accommodate the puff, and the edges are blind-stitched in place. A pointed revers-facing of velvet trims the sleeve in front of the puff. It is followed at its upper and front edges by a scroll of metallic cord.

February 1889 *Delineator*

This Directoire evening costume is pictured by Figure 9 made of figured bengaline and pea green surah. The skirt has four gores, which are covered to the edge with a full drapery that is gathered at the top and hangs in natural folds from the belt. Two steels are adjusted across the back breadth to support the train. A pad may be worn or not, as preferred.

Figure 9. Directoire evening costume

Figure 10. Trimmings for Directoire costume

The train is a continuation of the polonaise, and it lies in square outline for some distance on the floor. If a demi-train or walking length is preferred, the train may be cut off. The plaits in the train take the form of two quadruple box-plaits, which result from underfolded plaits below the waist-line of the center three seams. The side pieces and side backs extend to the bottom of the skirt, and fall free from the train below the knees. They are in one piece in the skirt on each side, and their seam ends at the top of a broad, underfolded box-plait that is basted underneath to retain its folds to the edge. The plaits in the train are pressed to flare gracefully, and are stayed by tapes basted across them underneath. The sides of the train are caught to the skirt with hooks and eyes just above where the gores hang free.

The fronts fold back in large Directoire lapels and extend only a little below the waist-line. They are narrow, and reveal the vest widely all the way down the center of the front, and more than halfway down the shoulders. The lapels are faced with surah and ornamented at the point with a large button. The fronts are decorated with similar buttons below the lapels. The vest is fanciful in effect and may be low or high in the neck. It is fitted by double bust darts. Its upper part is a chemisette or deep Pompadour yoke. On each side of this is arranged a surplice ornament of surah, which is gathered at the neck and lower edges.

With the high neck, as shown by the side view, is worn a high Directoire collar. The collar rolls over deeply in front, is square at the rolled corners, and is stiffened so as to stand and roll properly. An incroyable lace cravat is usually worn with the Directoire collar. When the low neck, as illustrated by the front view, is desired, the collar and yoke are omitted and the back is cut out slightly. A lace ruffle passes from underneath the surplices and hangs well over on the vest. A broad Directoire girdle crosses the vest in soft folds, its right end being gathered and inserted in the right under-arm seam, while the opposite end is bound and caught with hooks and eyes.

The coat sleeves are of but little more than elbow length. They are finished with surah Directoire cuffs, which are each trimmed at the back of the wrist with two small buttons. When the costume is made low in the neck, the sleeves are omitted, and the armholes are trimmed with lace frills.

This costume may be developed in all kinds of rich brocaded materials, and also in moiré, plush, velvet, peau de soie, bengaline, crêpe, figured and plain nets, etc. India muslin; embroidered or plain gauze; tulle; dotted, figured, or plain net, etc., are used for the vest, girdle, and front drapery. The effect is that of a filmy dress worn with a trained Directoire coat of velvet, brocade, or other material.

March 1889 *Delineator*

The materials combined in this Directoire costume are surah, velvet, and lace net (see Figure 10). The bodice is in the Empire style. Its fronts are faced in V shape to the bust with velvet, and are closed with button-holes and tiny velvet buttons. The surplice fronts are of lace net. The Directoire lapels are of velvet overlaid with Etruscan galloon. The neck is finished with a high standing collar of velvet, and the girdle is also of velvet. The sleeve decoration

Figure 11. Trimmings for bodice, sleeve, and skirt

Figure 12. Decoration for coat

consists of a triangular facing of velvet overlaid with galloon, and a length of lace edging that is draped up narrowly at the inside of the arm.

The skirt has the panels made of velvet and the front gore overhung by lace flouncing. The panels are decorated with Etruscan galloon in a geometrical pattern about 1/4 yard deep, the lower edge of the galloon extending to about 1 inch from the bottom.

March 1889 *Delineator*

Venetian red cashmere and Sappho pink crêpe de Chine are united in the costume shown by Figure 11. The right front of the basque laps diagonally on the left below the bust. Above the bust the left front is folded back in a lapel, below which are placed three large ornamental buttons. This arrangement produces a broad V opening, which is filled in by a finely plaited chemisette of crêpe de Chine. Two passementerie ornaments of silver cord decorate the right front. The high military collar is overlaid with a band of silver cord passementerie. The plain coat sleeve is trimmed on the upper side of the wrist with a triangular passementerie ornament.

Crêpe de Chine is used for the full panel that covers the left side gore of the skirt. It has three pairs of double shirrings crossing its upper part, and a

line of shirring at its upper edge. Below the shirrings, the fullness is pressed into plaits. The front drapery is bordered with silver cord passementerie.

March 1889 Delineator

This coat is made of tan surah and invisible green cloth, and decorated with fine silk soutache braid of a jet black. The bodice is illustrated on the left of Figure 12, with a wing sleeve adjusted over a coat-shaped sleeve. The neck of the vest is of surah and completed with a high standing collar of the same. Two flat collars, one of cloth and one of surah, finish the fronts, the cloth collar showing a scroll pattern done in soutache. Lapels of cloth, also braided, rest on the front ends of the upper flat collar. The coat sleeves each have a braid-trimmed cuff. The wing sleeve is gathered across the top of the arm, where it is raised to present a high effect. It is lined with old gold surah, and the outer part is entirely braided.

The side skirts of the coat, with pointed pocket laps resting on them, are shown on the right. A braiding pattern is outlined on the laps, and a larger design is followed along the front edges of the skirt and partway around the lower edge.

April 1889 Delineator

The Empire costume in Figure 13 combines pale green India silk, white lace flouncing, and dark green velvet. The skirt gores are faced with velvet for several inches from the bottom, and over them falls a white lace flounce. The front drapery and the long sash ties are of silk. The sash ties hang from the belt on one side of the front, and have their closely gathered lower ends tipped with fluffy silk tassels.

The front of the bodice is covered with lace in front of full silk surplices that pass under the broad, fitted velvet girdle. A narrow silver buckle, reaching

Figure 13. Decoration for Empire costume

Figure 14. Decoration for Empire dress

Figure 15. Decoration for bodice, sleeve, and skirt

the entire depth of the girdle, apparently closes the girdle on the left side of the front. The scalloped edge of the lace on the right front loops over the closing, which is invisibly made. On the top of the coat sleeves, which are of velvet, are deep puffs of silk. Below the puffs, a band of lace is arranged to turn forward from the outside seam all the way to the wrist edge, which may be finished with lace frills. Lace also overlies the standing collar.

May 1889 *Delineator*

This decoration for an Empire dress is suitable for afternoon and evening wear. (See Figure 14.) It combines India silk and black, white, or colored lace flouncing. The skirt has a full front drapery that extends to below the knees between the front edges of the back drapery. The bottom of the front drapery passes under a Spanish flounce that falls gracefully to the bottom. The flounce is headed by a frill of lace edging.

The front of the bodice is shown at the top left of the engraving, and the back is shown on the right. The full yoke is of silk. The low surplice fronts are of lace flouncing arranged so that the scallops come at the free edges. The low V neck at the back is outlined with a falling frill of lace edging.

The broad Empire sash is of silk with deeply fringed ends. It is draped in soft folds about the waist, and tied in loops and ends of different lengths on the left side of the back. The decoration of the sleeve corresponds to the bodice and skirt. The soft puff of silk is headed by a wrinkled band of ribbon, which also conceals the bottom of an upward-turning band of lace and is tied in a bow at the front of the wrist. If desired, the sleeve or the puff may be of lace.

May 1889 *Delineator*

The materials represented by Figure 15 are tan Henrietta cloth, golden brown velvet, and tan surah. The decorations are tan and brown silk passementerie ornaments and buttons. On each front of the polonaise is cut a lapel, which is faced with velvet and overspread with passementerie. Below each lapel are ornamentally placed two groups of three buttons each. Between the fronts are displayed a full, puffed vest and a shaped ornamental section, the latter being decorated with passementerie. The high standing collar is faced the width of the vest with surah, the remainder being cut from velvet and decorated with a tan passementerie ornament. The coat sleeve is finished at the wrist with a pointed cuff-facing of velvet overlaid with tan passementerie.

Over the skirt gores falls a drapery, the wrinkled surface of which is the result of plaits laid in each side. A brown passementerie ornament decorates the lower part of the drapery. The drapery is framed by box-plaited panels of velvet, the ornaments being placed at the bottom of each panel.

September 1889 *Delineator*

The evening costume in Figure 16 is made of dark green and cream fancy-striped velvet, plain dark green velvet, cream faille, and dotted tulle. It is decorated with tulle and bands of seed pearl passementerie. The four-gored skirt falls over a slender bustle in a long, oval train at the back. A demi-train may be used, instead of the full-length train illustrated. The front gore, which is framed by tulle puffings, is trimmed with three bands of passementerie arranged to flare toward the bottom.

The bodice is pointed at the back and front, the sides curving high. At the back the neck is cut round. In front a V shape is observable, the neck and front edges being followed by a tulle puff that is mounted on linings. Lapels are sewed to the fronts and overspread with passementerie. The short coat

Figure 16. Evening costume

sleeve is lengthened by an ornament that gradually narrows toward the inside of the arm. A band of passementerie is placed just above it, a second band being disposed diagonally across the upper side of the sleeve.

This mode favors brocades, which combine handsomely with heavy silks or velvets. Gold and silver braid, passementerie, and appliqué are fashionable trimmings. Dotted tulles, lace nets, and drapery nets unite well with surah or China silk.

October 1889 *Delineator*

Bodices and Jackets

Basques are more simply shaped at the back than formerly, while the front is most elaborately trimmed. One of the simplest fashions is that of putting a silk sash 8 inches wide (when doubled) across the ends of the front of the basque, and letting it fall nearly to the bottom of the skirt. Above this are a vest and lapels. The back is rounded or pointed, with the skirt sewed above its edges.

Dressy basques have short Eton jacket fronts cut off squarely at the waist-line. The front edges are turned back in lapels that begin in a point at the waist, and gradually widen to 3 or 4 inches at the top, turning over there almost enough to touch the armhole seams. The vest inside may be of contrasting material, or cross-striped silk or velvet, lying perfectly flat; or it may be double breasted and smooth. Or else it may be very full, and crossed from the top, leaving a V-shaped space to be filled by a plastron or chemisette and standing collar. The back may be plainly curved below the waist-line, with the back breadths of the skirt hooked upon it. Or it may be cut in points on the side, which hang with tasseled ends or are merely bordered with gimp. Or else the center fronts end in two soft leaf points longer than the pointed ends of the side pieces.

October 27, 1888 *Harper's Bazar*

The deep lapels on Directoire coats and basques are elaborately beaded with tinsel or jet, although facings of silk, moiré, velvet, and satin are also in vogue.

May 1889 *Delineator*

The bodice in Figure 1 may be made up in silk, satin, velvet, plush, or moiré. It closes at the back with lacing cord. Its neck is cut in V shape both back and front. On the center of the front, a V decoration is formed with crosswise folds of narrow lace edging, which turn upward. The V is outlined on each side by a full surplice drapery of lace net. The drapery is plaited to a point at the lower end, caught in a rosette puff on the shoulder, and continued across the neck of the back, where it is plaited to a point at the closing. Three soft, fluffy tips rise from the left shoulder. A lace frill completes each armhole. Tulle, gauze, or crêpe may be used instead of lace, and flowers may be substituted for the tips.

February 1888 *Delineator*

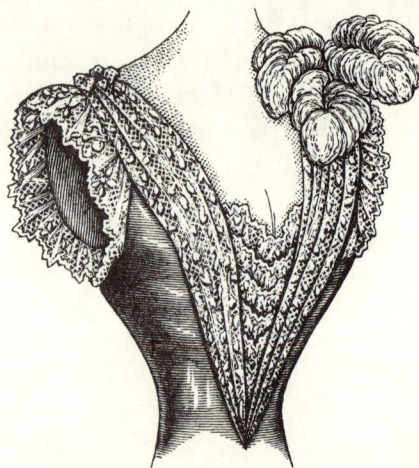

Figure 1. Evening bodice

Velvet-figured wool, plain velvet, plain silk, and crêpe are combined in this basque. (See Figure 2.) The fronts meet at the neck, and separate below in curves over a fancy vest, which has a plaited upper part of crêpe and a pointed bodice piece of silk. The vest is mounted on a plain lining and is attached in Breton fashion. A row of buttons decorates each front along the sides of the bodice piece. Above the buttons the fronts are faced in lapel fashion with velvet, the facing being widest at the neck. The standing collar is shown in crêpe, but may be of velvet if preferred.

On the illustration of the basque, a plaited crêpe puff is set into the top of the sleeve. On each side of the puff is a revers-facing of velvet, the facings outlining a point. If desired, the sleeve may be completed as shown by the separate sleeve on the left, where the puff and revers-facings are omitted in favor of a plain pointed facing. The inside seam of the sleeve is left open for some distance from the edge. The wrist is folded up on the outside in a rolling cuff that is faced with velvet, a full frill of soft lace falling toward the hand. A ruff may be added instead of the lace.

February 1888 *Delineator*

On the bodice in Figure 3, large lapels are applied on the fronts and finished with the front edges, which are invisibly fastened with hooks and eyes. The lapel on the left front is of velvet, and appears to be fastened in place along its top and back edge with button-holes and large buttons. The lapel on the right front is of white billiard cloth, and is embroidered in a scroll pattern with gold soutache. With the billiard cloth and velvet in dark green, terra-cotta, brown, mahogany, or blue, the contrast with the white and gold is notably stylish. The standing collar is of velvet.

On the sleeve, a deep, round cuff of white billiard cloth completes the wrist. The cuff is braided in harmony with the lapel on the right front. Turning upward from its top is a shallow cuff of velvet, which is lined with thin crinoline and has its ends slanted off at the inside seam.

February 1888 *Delineator*

The blouse in Figure 4 may be made up in crêpe, cashmere, India and China silks, batiste, organdy, etc. Silk or cotton thread may be used for the smocking, according to the material. Beads are effective on wools and silks. The smocking on the blouse extends to the depth of a round yoke, and beads are fastened in at the bastings. It is underlaid with a smooth yoke of lining, and a crinoline interlining cut like the lining is added to give the needful firmness. The high standing collar is covered with a smocked section of the material. The sleeve has a full upper part that droops over a deep, smocked cuff. Both puff and cuff are adjusted on a coat-shaped lining.

The illustrations of the method of smocking in Figure 5 are to be read in two columns, first down the left and then down the right. The first thing to do is space evenly, and this is shown by the first

Figure 2. Decoration for bodice and sleeve

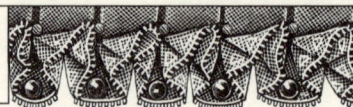

Figure 3. Braid decoration for bodice and sleeve

figure. The section to be smocked may be creased, or marked off in lines with thread or chalk, in the direction the smocking is to run. Then on each side, dots are made to indicate where the material is to be caught together. This method will do for all but sheer and delicate-hued materials, when marked paper will have to be used as in tucking. The dots indicated by the arrows are to be caught together, and those connected by the dashed lines are to be similarly caught.

Begin at the topmost space. Catch together the dots indicated by the arrows, beginning on the right. Insert the needle as shown by the second figure, and make the fastening secure; usually two or three over-and-over stitches suffice. Then pass the needle underneath and out through the next arrow dot below, as indicated by the third figure. Continue to the end of the line.

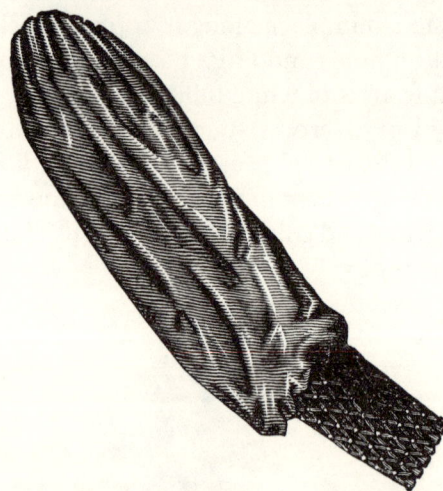

Figure 4. Smocked blouse and sleeve

Now begin at the second space. Catch together the dots connected by the dashed lines, passing the needle underneath and out through the lined dot just below as shown by the fourth figure. Then pass the needle through as shown by the fifth figure and make the stitches secure as above. Each succeeding row is done in the same way. The sixth figure shows the smocking perfected, and also how it may be run to a point when desired.

June 1888 *Delineator*

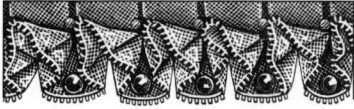

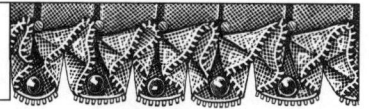

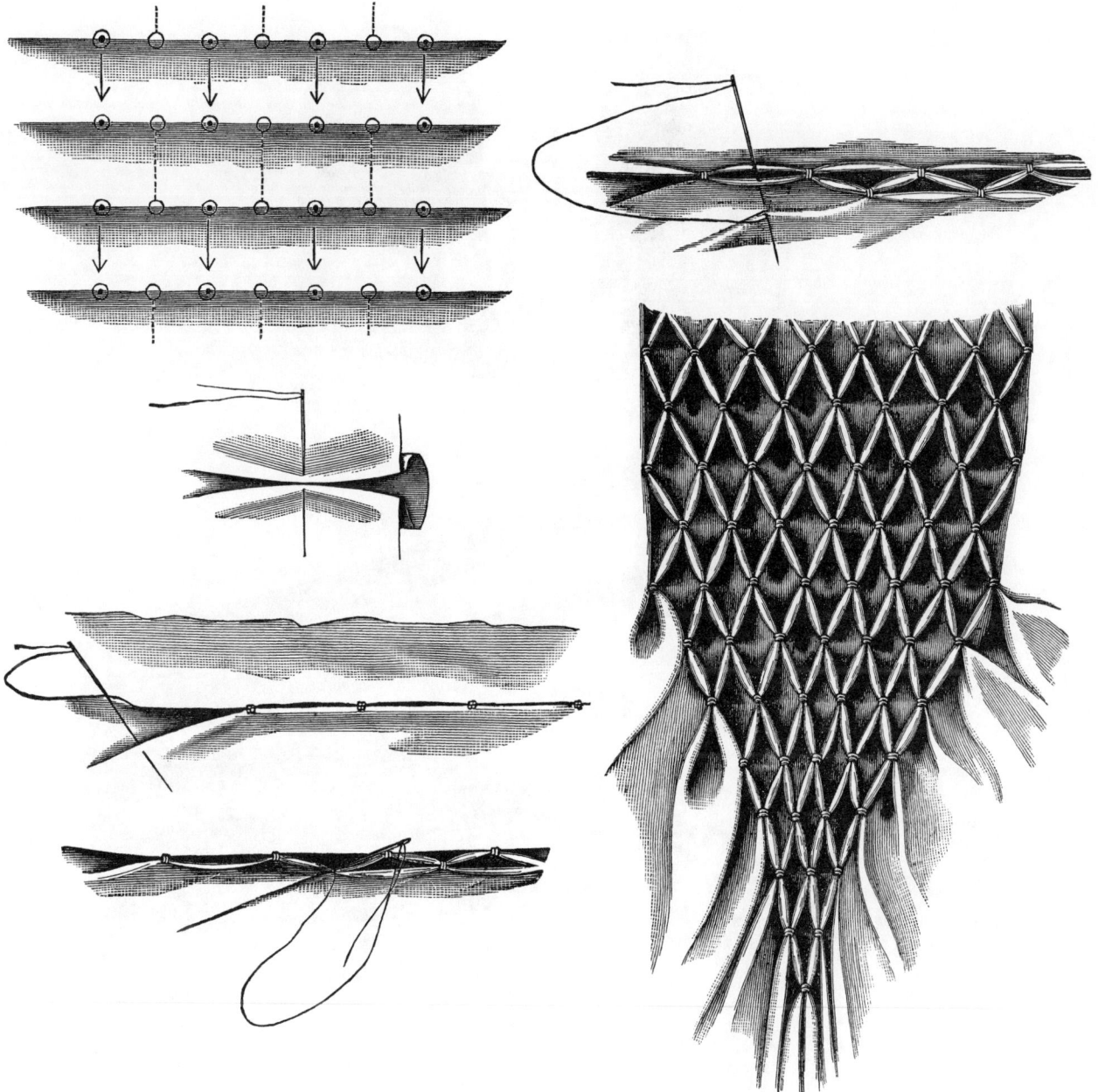

Figure 5. The method of smocking

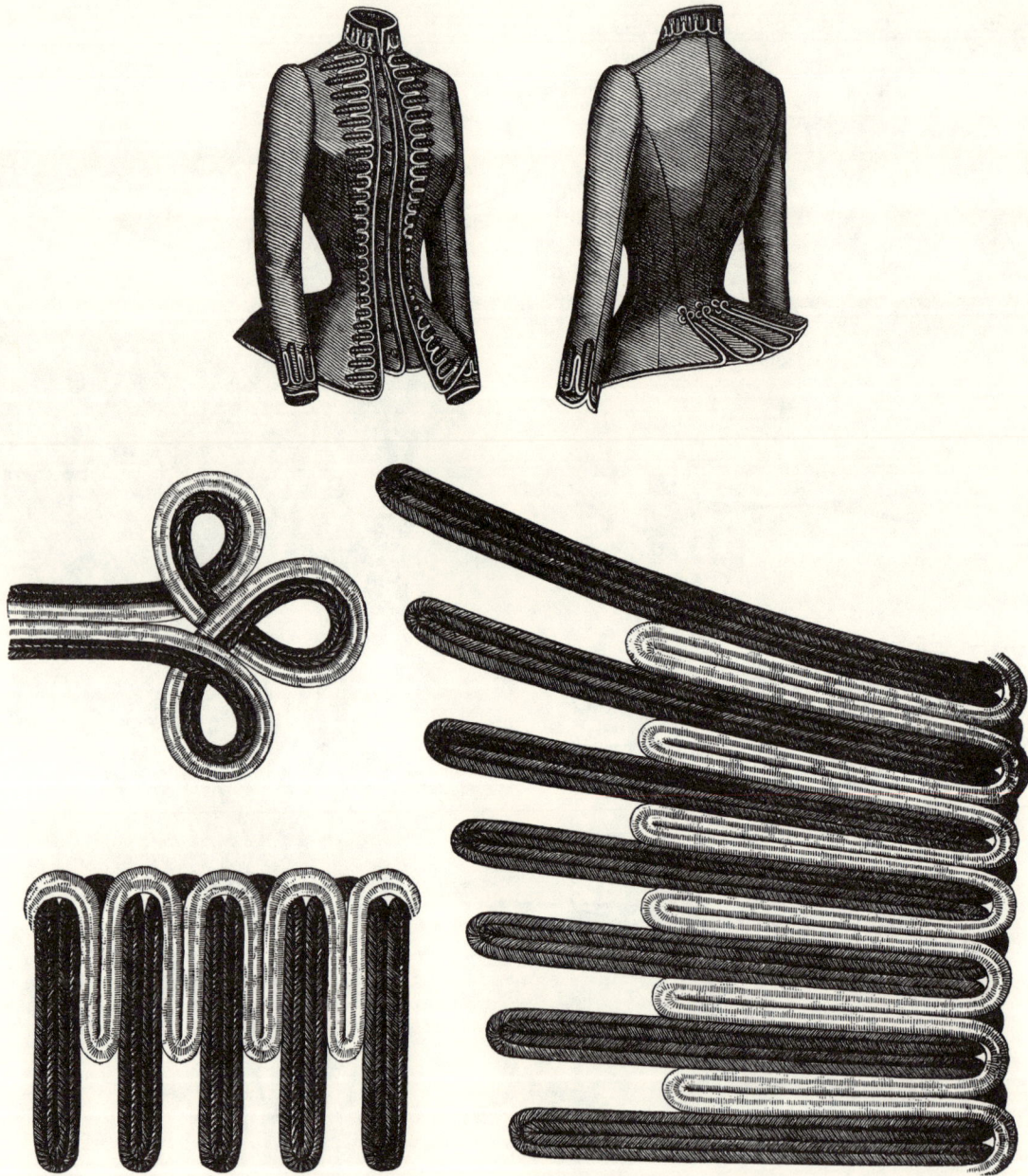

Figure 6. Braided jacket and the method of braiding

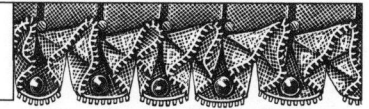

Tan lady's cloth was used for the jacket in Figure 6, with metallic gold soutache and brown worsted soutache for trimming. The jacket also looks handsome in hunter green cloth, with silver and black soutache. It is shown completed at the top of the engraving. The worsted soutache may be of the same color as the jacket, and the metal soutache may be copper.

The fronts flare from the neck over a vest, which is somewhat shorter and closed down the center with button-holes and tailor buttons. The lower front corners of the front and vest are sharply rounded. The front edges of both the front and vest are curved to assist in the adjustment. The jacket is additionally fitted by single bust darts, side pieces, side backs, and a curved center back seam, which like the side-back seams ends below the waist-line. The back falls in two narrow, oval tabs on an added skirt. This skirt is sewed flatly in place at the top, and also at its front edges underneath to the side backs, the lower back corners of which are rounded off. The vest is joined to the fronts along the bust darts, and the added skirt at the back renders the depth of the garment uniform.

Two bands of braid—one of each kind—follow the front edges of the fronts and vest. They are continued along the lower and loose edges of the garment, and coiled in a trefoil over the ends of the center three seams of the back, as shown by the figure at the center left. For the trefoils, the two braids are joined together by stitches carefully taken up underneath, and then coiled and firmly sewed on the garment. The fronts are elaborated with two braids arranged in a narrow loop design, the brown braid describing the longer loops, and the design broadening gradually above and below the waist-line. This is shown in detail at the bottom right. The worsted braid is first arranged in loops and sewed on very firmly; then the metal braid is arranged in the spaces and is crossed over as shown. The standing collar has a similar decoration of braid, as shown at the bottom left. The decoration is repeated on the coat sleeves, where it is deepened gradually on the upper side toward the back of the wrist. The outside seam of the sleeve is left open for a short distance at the bottom, and the corners are rounded off. Two bands of braid follow the loose edges of the sleeve.

The vest may be made of embroidered, flowered, figured, striped, or other fancy material. Dark and light colors are fashionable for this jacket, and white is largely used for carriage and evening wear. The jacket may be lined with surah, glacé or striped silk, satin, etc.

October 1888 *Delineator*

The design in Figure 7 is effective on wraps, vests, etc. It can be traced onto paper, which can be cut out for the pattern. It is so arranged that it can

Figure 7. Design for appliqué and for outline embroidery

be repeated continuously by placing the left end of the design on the right end of the part traced, so that the lower lines meet. The design may be simply outlined with cord or braid. Or it may be cut out in cloth, velvet, etc., and applied with fancy stitching, braid, or cord.

January 1889 Delineator

Silk and velvet are the materials pictured in Figure 8. The flared collar, which is in the Directoire style, may be adjusted on any plain dress bodice. It stands higher than the bodice collar at the back and has broad, square ends, which roll with a flare on each side of the Molière Pompadour. A passementerie ornament rests on each end of the bodice collar. A larger ornament arranged with Directoire girdle effect trims the waist on each side of the closing.

The sleeve is made of velvet. The inside seam ends a little above the wrist, which is reversed to form a graduated cuff that displays a round under cuff of white silk. The reversed part is faced with white silk, and a passementerie ornament overlies it. Sometimes the under cuff is overhung by a lace frill.

March 1889 Delineator

The materials shown by Figure 9 are plain silk, striped silk, and lace net. The Directoire lapels, which roll back from the fronts, are faced with striped silk. Three large buttons are placed below them on each front. On the vest are arranged surplices of plain silk and a chemisette of lace net. Across the lower part of the surplices is drawn a Directoire girdle of net, which is laid in three upward-turning plaits. The sleeve has a bias cuff-facing at the wrist, from the top of which extends an upward-turning band of lace edging.

March 1889 Delineator

The decoration in Figure 10 is suitable for an Empire dress. Plain white net, lace net, and black velvet are united, with lace edging and ribbon for trimming. The sleeve has a long, full puff arranged above the elbow. A fold of ribbon conceals the lower edge of the puff. A bow is arranged at the back of the arm, and another at the wrist above a lace frill. The bodice has a deeply pointed, gathered yoke. This is finished with an upward-turning band of lace and a drooping frill of wide lace edging. A ribbon bow is placed on the left side just below the collar.

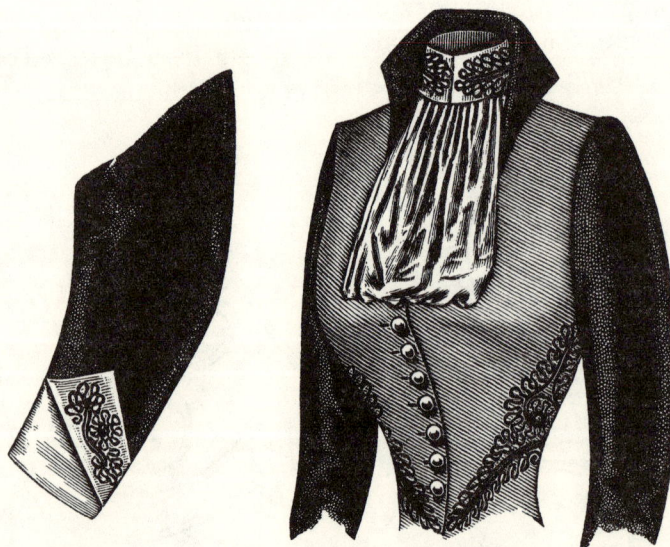

Figure 8. Directoire decoration for bodice and sleeve

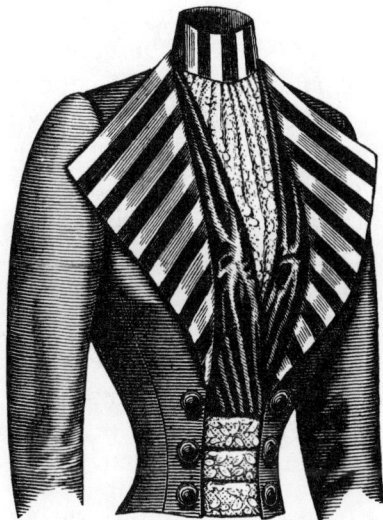

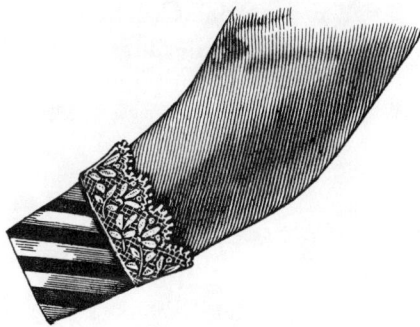

Figure 9. Decoration for Directoire bodice and sleeve

A shaped girdle of black velvet, which is passed through a slide, encircles the waist.

The evening bodice in Figure 11 is made of old rose faille. The fronts are cut low in heart shape. An ornament decorated with upward-turning lace frills is inserted at the bust. A band of seed pearl passementerie decorates each front in the outline of a rounded jacket. On the short sleeves, which are slashed on the upper side, are applied two bands of seed pearl passementerie. The collar is also decorated with the passementerie.

The collar may be cut from velvet, and the bodice from silk of the same or a different shade or color. Lace may be frilled along the edges of the slash in the sleeve and fall over the arm from its lower edge.

November 1889 *Delineator*

The bodice on the left of Figure 12 is made up for dinner and evening wear with the draped sleeve puff alone, which gives the appearance of a short, shaped sleeve. A deep lace frill falls from the edge of the puff, and a similar frill surrounds the neck.

If the sleeve on the right is worn, the draped puff is of velvet and the sleeve is of the dress material. A wrinkled band of velvet heads a deep lace frill at the wrist, the lace falling well over the hand.

December 1889 *Delineator*

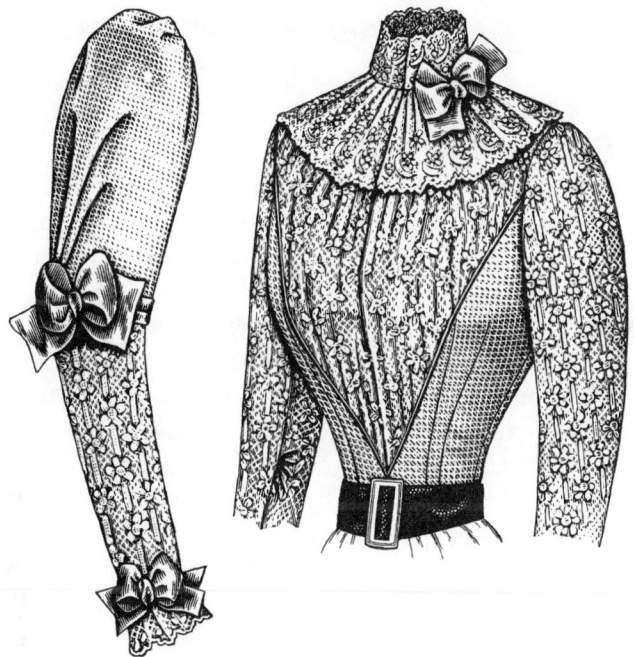

Figure 10. Decoration for Empire bodice and sleeve

475

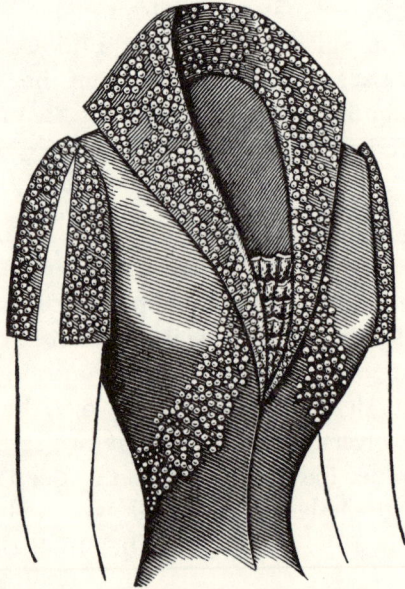

Figure 11. Evening bodice

For home or evening toilettes, the fancy sleeve is most artistic. Plaitings or tucks diminish the fullness slightly, and the remainder of the shaping is performed by deep cuffs. Many sleeves are firmly held in place by sewing the plaitings, but quite as often the folds are machine made, and caught by the cuff. Many persons insist that the folds should really be tucks, and this is best for very thin materials and those that do not crease easily. When the dress shows two colors, the upper part of the sleeves may be of the light shade and the cuffs of the dark, with velvet Vandykes of the same shade outlined upon them with narrow silver or gold braid.

March 1889 *Delineator*

Tiny round pearl buttons, or bone buttons matching the dress color, are used when the sleeve is made of cotton material. Crocheted or gold buttons are used on other materials.

June 1889 *Delineator*

Sleeves

Some coat sleeves drop down from the top in a cross-fold separate from the lining, and are sewed very full in a point at the top of the armhole. Cloth sleeves are full from the armhole to halfway below the elbow, where they are gathered over an inner sleeve of cloth of contrasting color. The inner sleeve fits more closely, but not tightly; when finished with its turned-back cloth cuff, it is large enough for the hand to pass through. Sometimes the cloth is shirred in a point at the armhole, and a band of galloon forms a cap or jockey around the armhole. A similar band conceals the seam that joins the full part to the deep cuff. Velvet or plush sleeves are also full, with a deep cuff covered with passementerie. In some coat sleeves, fullness is added by lengthening and widening the upper end, and folding it carelessly around the armhole in thick irregular folds. Some deep cuffs flare outward like gauntlets, and extend in two or three points above the end of the full sleeves.

October 27, 1888 *Harper's Bazar*

Figure 12. Decoration for bodice and sleeve

Sleeves

The sleeve in Figure 1 looks picturesque on tea gowns, matinées, and all styles of indoor costumes. White China silk and apple green velvet are united in this example. The coat-shaped foundation is faced in deep cuff style with velvet. Above this facing, a soft silk puff extends above the elbow to meet a deep, smocked band, which is surmounted by a short, full puff. A ribbon conceals the join of the long puff and band, and is tied in a bow at the back of the arm.

August 1888 *Delineator*

The tucks may be sewed in place with lines of fancy stitching of a contrasting color. The cuff-facings may be of the material, or of velvet embroidered with soutache in a pretty design or arranged in parallel lines. If the sleeve is of cotton material, the cuff-facings may be of all-over embroidery, and the lining may be cut away under them.

March 1889 *Delineator*

Figure 2. Ornamental sleeve

Figure 1. Smocked sleeve for indoor costumes

The sleeve in Figure 2 is shown made of dress material and trimmed with velvet. It is arranged on a coat-shaped lining. It is gathered across the upper side of the top, and also at the bottom, where it is sewed in place under the top of a deep cuff-facing of velvet. In the fullness are made eleven backward-turning tucks that start some distance above the elbow and end some distance below it. Above and below the tucks, the fullness forms soft puffs. The side edges pass into the inside seam of the lining.

This sleeve in Figure 3 is shown developed in plain suit material. It is made over a coat-shaped lining and has but one seam. Below the elbow, it fits smoothly over the lining. At the top, it is gathered across the upper side to rise with a puff effect above the shoulder, bastings being made below the gathers to produce the rounded curves illustrated. For tea gowns or very fancy house dresses, the foundation is usually of light-colored silk when the outside is of lace.

December 1889 *Delineator*

Figure 3. Sleeve for a bodice or polonaise

Skirts and Draperies

Plaited flounces are in vogue as panels for the front of dress skirts, with plain side gores next to them. There are also series of flounces—three, five, or seven—up the left side of the skirt, with long drapery covering it elsewhere.

January 21, 1888 Harper's Bazar

Extremely narrow ribbons are especially favored. On accordion or other plaited skirts they are arranged like rows of tucks about the edge and then plaited in with the material. Wider velvet ribbon is used in the same way; sometimes only one band nearly 1/4 yard wide is placed about the edge of the skirt. Ribbons may also be formed into ornamental fringes. The narrowest width is chosen, and the fringe is made up very full on a foundation composed of a band of the very narrowest galloon. As a finish for the edges of dress panels it is very handsome, and a little of it produces a good effect.

March 1889 Delineator

White cloth street skirts are bordered with a Grecian design in soutache braid. When the skirt is for house or carriage wear, the braid is outlined with beads or tiny spangles. Occasionally a color appears on the white ground, but oftener the braid

is gold, silver, or white. When white braid is used, crystal beads or silver spangles are combined with it. They do not outline the pattern precisely, but are placed here and there so that they are effective without making the trimming look crowded. Silver braid with silver spangles is much liked. The spangles must be firmly secured, but without being made to look stiff.

July 1889 Delineator

Black fox, bear, natural beaver, Astrakhan, blue fox, sable, mink, and all of the brown furs are popular trimmings. They are applied in long strips and bands. Fur borders are a favorite decoration for skirt edges. They are often made more elaborate by placing them just above a band of passementerie that contrasts strongly with the fur, either by reason of the fineness of the braid or the glitter of jet or gold beads. These beads are never very large, but are so numerous that they are very effective.

November 1889 Delineator

Coarse coffee-colored lace imitating point de Venise is noted as a skirt trimming on dresses intended for evening or reception wear, and its effect is strongly reminiscent of the dresses in old-time portraits. This lace is also used for making deep cuffs on tea gowns, and looks well on dark velvet, especially green, brown, or black.

December 1889 Delineator

Plain dress material and faille Française are shown combined in Figure 1. The skirt is in the standard round walking shape, with two steels across its back breadth. As it is almost concealed by the draperies, it is usually made of lining.

On the right side of the skirt gores is a full drapery, which extends from the belt to the edge and laps well on the left side gore. On each side of the drapery, three deep tuck shirrings are made close together and present a soft ruche effect, the fullness falling like a flounce below and between them. This drapery is also gathered at its top and is arranged to resemble long puffs above the tuck shirrings. On the right side, the drapery enters the side-back seam of the skirt. On the left it is sewed in place under a broad, flat panel that is hemmed at its front edge and plaited at its upper and back edges.

A long tablier drapery hangs to the edges of the skirt on the left side of the front. This drapery is shaped to be quite short where it crosses the right hip. Groups of deep plaits laid in the top fall into it, producing irregular folds.

The back drapery is alike on both sides and falls nearly to the edge at the center. It hangs in two burnouses at the top and is made slightly bouffant by a downward-turning plait in each side edge. A small pad may be worn if desired.

The shirred drapery should always be of soft material. Bands of braid, ribbon, or Persian bands may be arranged across the bottom of the front drapery. Soft-finished cottons, such as foulards, sateens, etc., are particularly friendly to the mode. Point embroideries or coarse laces may be added to them. A velvet bodice is often worn with this skirt.

April 1889 *Delineator*

The train in Figure 2 may be attached and detached as required. It may be made either round or square. Velvet, plush, corded and moiré silks, brocaded and striped materials, etc., are stylish. The color may contrast with that of the dress, but care must be taken to preserve a harmonious effect. Flowered or striped moirés in light and dark colors make elegant trains to wear with contrasts of airy or thick materials. Sometimes a contrasting breadth is introduced at the center of the train. Pompadour and Louis Quinze brocades make superb trains to wear with dresses of corded silk, and sometimes one breadth of the dress material is arranged between breadths of the brocade. The train should be lined with material that harmonizes with it. The added weight given by an interlining of padding will ensure its graceful hanging. The edges may be finished plainly or with cord, and a balayeuse plaiting is needful.

May 1888 *Delineator*

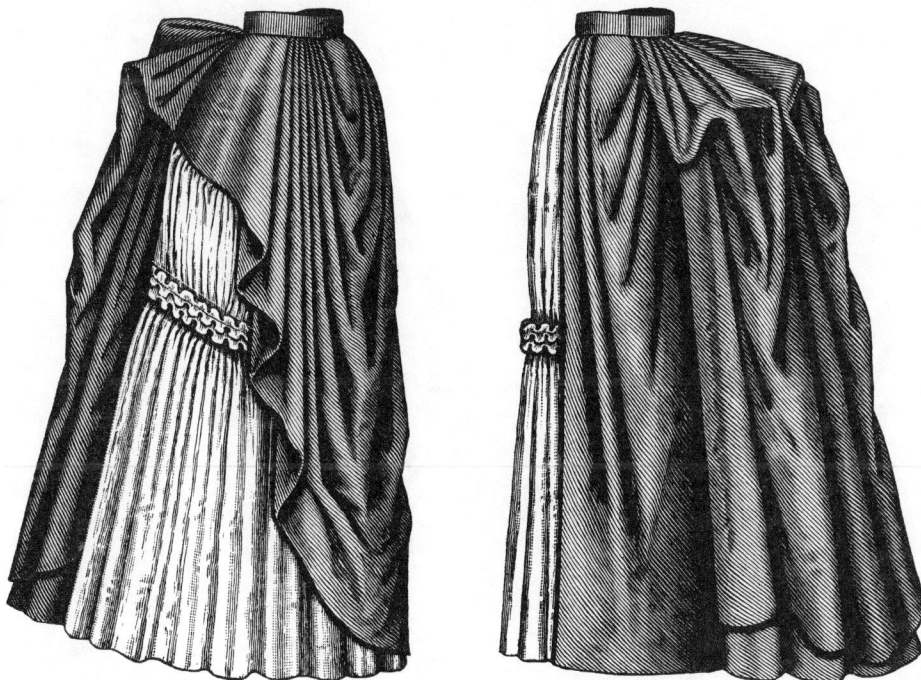

Figure 1. Drapery for walking skirt

Figure 2. Adjustable train

The over-skirt in Figure 3 is well adapted for wear over plaited skirts of all kinds, whether box, side, or accordion. It also looks well over full or plainly trimmed skirts. The front drapery is in a short apron style. It is smoothly fitted at the top by two backward-turning plaits on each side of the center, while the sides are lifted by three upward-turning plaits that wrinkle the surface prettily. A narrow hem facing finishes the lower edge, being held in place by a line of machine-stitching.

The back drapery is in butterfly style. It is in two sections and is finished with machine-stitched hems. The top is laid in five deep, forward-turning plaits. In the back edge near the bottom are folded four downward-turning plaits, which are brought up to the top beneath the other plaits to form a long loop and jabot folds. The side edges of the front drapery are sewed to the back drapery on each side along the hem of the latter. A belt finishes the top.

All kinds of seasonable dress materials are suitable for this style. Braid, passementerie, or bands of narrow ribbon may be applied. If the skirt and bodice of the costume are of silk, the over-skirt may be of wool. Over a plainly finished skirt of golden brown and cream striped wool may be worn an over-skirt of camelette matching the brown stripe in the skirt.

June 1889 *Delineator*

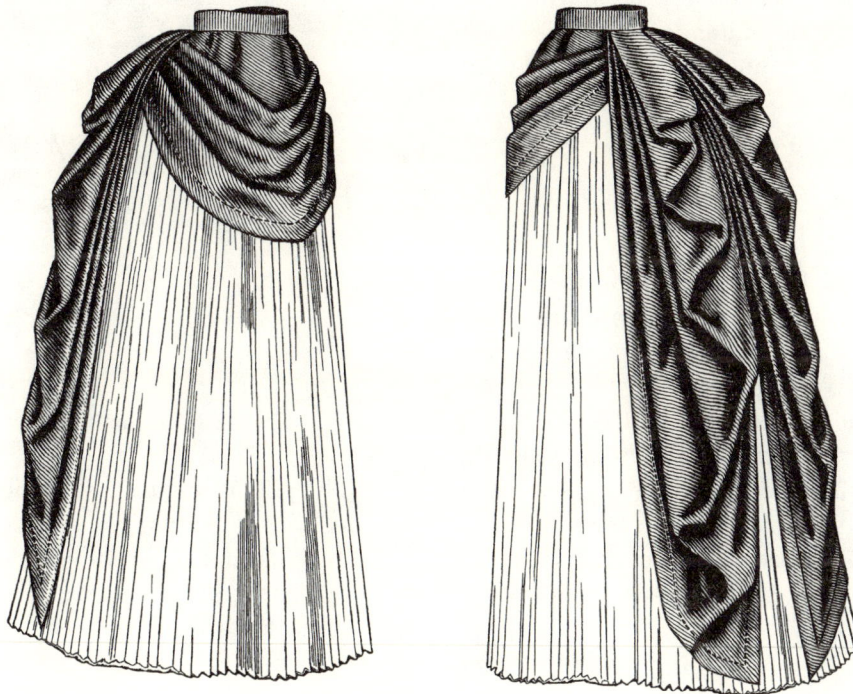

Figure 3. Butterfly over-skirt

11. Accessories

Any bodice that is quite untrimmed may, by the deft application of a gilet, a collar, or a plastron, be made to look as if it were originally so arranged; and the decoration can be changed at any time. Jet, ribbon, passementerie, and laces of thread, gold, or silver are all used. Gilets made of ribbon or braid are liked, while for elaborate dresses those formed of jabots of lace are especially in vogue. The latter are especially suited to jacket basques. A full jabot of the yellowest lace that can be found is a necessary adjunct to an Empire coat, and frills about the wrists are proper when the coat is not a simple one intended only for street wear. Folds of lisse are much more popular than plaited ruchings.

March 1889 *Delineator*

Collars, Jabots, Fichus, Chemisettes, Etc.

Boas of lace, flowers, feathers, or ribbon are thrown around the neck when wearing low full-dress bodices at the opera or at evening parties generally. Lace boas may be either black or white, and are made of 3-inch lace gathered around and around. They are seen occasionally with morning toilettes, but are more suitable with carriage dresses when mantles are omitted. Long lace scarves are also worn, passing closely around the neck and falling to the bottom in front. Natural gray ostrich feather boas are worn at seaside resorts.

July 21, 1888 *Harper's Bazar*

The collar in Figure 1 is shaped over a net foundation and is closed at the back. It is of golden brown moiré ribbon. Its top is outlined with small amber beads, while a full fringe of the same kind of beads falls on the collar about 1 inch deep all around. The jabot consists of a fan of Valenciennes lace mounted on a strip of net and drawn in the lines illustrated. Ends of golden brown ribbon are notched and placed in two groups, one on the outside of the fan, and the other underneath so that it seems to peep out. Black and white with jet beads, scarlet and black with jet beads, gray and blue with steel beads, or all white with pearl beads, are good combinations.

February 1888 *Delineator*

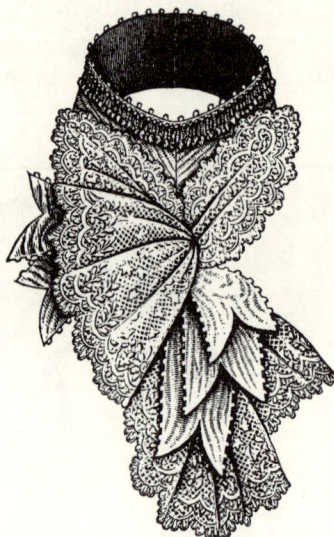

Figure 1. Ribbon and lace jabot

The gilet in Figure 2 is made of two kinds of ribbon—pale rose grosgrain and deep absinthe velvet. The collar fits the neck in military fashion, the reversed corners showing the rose-colored inside in contrast with the green velvet of the outside. At the neck is a bow of velvet ribbon. The gilet is composed of folds of rose ribbon arranged on a net foundation of the proper shape. It extends considerably below the waist-line, where it is drawn in very closely and then allowed to flare. A velvet strap is drawn across the gilet at the waist-line. Beneath it fall two loops; while from under the lower edge comes a fringe of velvet loops and ends. This gilet may be made in pale blue and green, rose and blue, olive and rose, or yellow and black.

March 1888 *Delineator*

Figure 2. Ribbon gilet

Figure 3. Roman scarf

The chemisette in Figure 4 is mounted on a firm foundation of white net, which is as carefully cut and fitted as the lining of a dress. The lace is one of the fancy varieties with a point d'esprit background. It is put on very full and gathered in lines that are hidden under golden brown velvet straps. A lace ruffle finishes the neck, and a broad band of velvet matching the straps gives the chemisette the appearance of a dog-collar. Plain point d'esprit, Spanish net, plain net, or tulle may be used for the chemisette, and the velvet may be of any color.

May 1888 *Delineator*

For the scarf in Figure 3, the Roman combination of colors is shown on a pale rose background. At each end is a deep rose-colored knotted fringe. The scarf is drawn closely about the neck, and the loops and ends are arranged as illustrated. If a collar is worn, it should be one that rolls over slightly and shows the folds of the scarf coming from under it.

March 1888 *Delineator*

Figure 4. Lace chemisette

The gilet in Figure 5 is suitable for brightening an evening dress. The high collar is made of ciel blue Ottoman silk and is overlaid with a band of Fedora lace edging. Just in front is an arrangement of wider Fedora lace, which suggests a pouf and is formed of a long strip turned so that the picoted edges meet. On each side is a lapel of Ottoman silk, and below it is a soft, spreading fan of lace. Underlying the latter is a second fan that terminates in a jabot. The lapels are outlined with lace in a width that corresponds to the lace on the collar.

June 1888 *Delineator*

Figure 6. Lace gilet

The gilet in Figure 6 is very pretty worn with a Directoire jacket or bodice that has flared fronts. It is made of lace flouncing plaited very finely and mounted on a net foundation. The lace is caught at the waist and neck, and flares between and below the bastings. On one side is sewed a lace edge that is held down at the top by a knot of light yellow ribbons, and extends beyond the knot to form a full jabot on the other side. At the waist-line are many loops and ends of yellow ribbon.

July 1888 *Delineator*

Figure 5. Silk and lace gilet

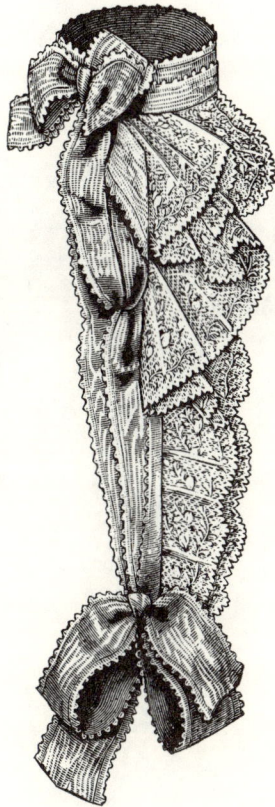

Figure 7. Lace and ribbon gilet

Rose moiré ribbon and Valenciennes lace are combined in the gilet shown by Figure 7. The collar is formed of a strip of ribbon folded over so that the edge shows, and has a bow on one side. From under this, on a net foundation, are two strips of ribbon that extend to the waist-line, one being knotted halfway of the distance. Both are knotted at the waist-line in a long-looped bow and ends. The lace also starts from under the collar in two frills, which extend to the waist-line and form a double jabot to below the bust.

July 1888 *Delineator*

The fichu in Figure 8 is especially suited to a summer dress, and is prettiest when the dress is turned in at the neck. It is pictured made of brocaded crêpe de Chine, the pattern showing oblong figures. All of the edges are outlined with a plaited double frill of Breton lace, the lower frill coming well below the upper one. The fichu may be fastened to the bodice with tiny pearl beads or a brooch.

August 1888 *Delineator*

Figure 8. Crêpe de Chine and lace fichu

Figure 9. Beaded plastron

The plastron in Figure 9 is made of steel lace and beads, and is very smoothly fitted, the closing being at the back. The high military collar is of lace in harmony with the plastron, its metallic texture causing it to retain its position well. Such plastrons are seen in gold, silver, jet, or plain passementerie. One is all the trimming that is needed on a bodice. It may be either fastened permanently to one garment, or made detachable and worn with several.

October 1888 *Delineator*

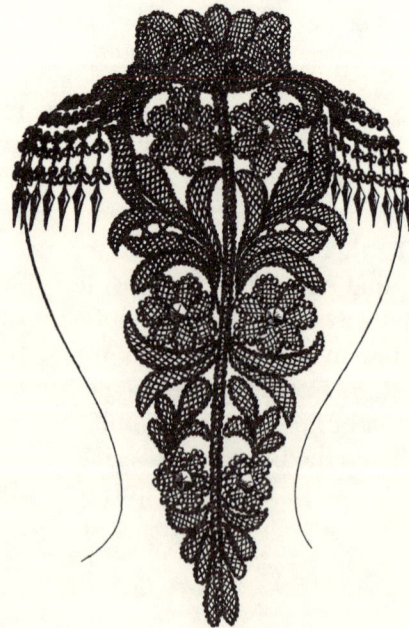

Figure 10. Jet gilet

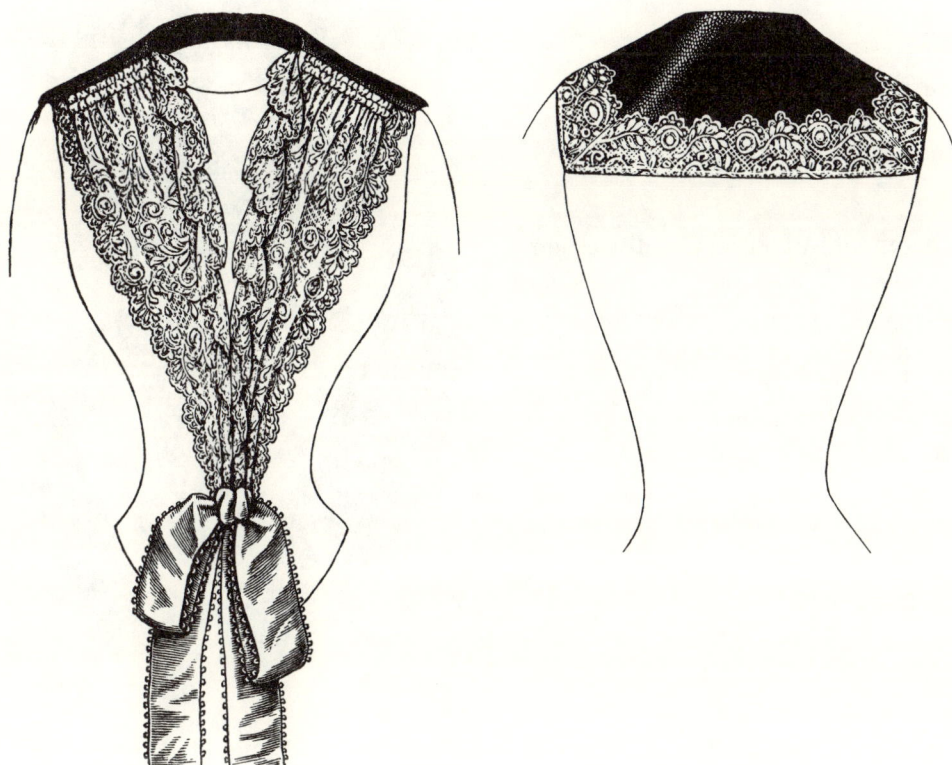

Figure 11. Sailor collar with fichu front

Figure 10 shows a very rich decoration for a bodice or close-fitting wrap. The design is a floral one wrought in fine silk passementerie and large cut jet beads. The high collar seems formed of the leaves, and the gilet is of the leaves and flowers. The epaulettes are swaying fringes finished with long oval jet beads.

October 1888 *Delineator*

The front view is shown on the left of Figure 11, and the back view on the right. The velvet sailor collar is of Russian green outlined in appliqué with white Valenciennes lace. At the shoulder a Valenciennes scarf is shirred on, and this is drawn down over the bodice to the waist-line, where it is fastened under a green ribbon bow. On the inner side a V shape is achieved, and the lace edging is arranged in cascades. The side edges may be folded under and carefully pressed without being sewed, for a particularly neat finish. This collar may be made in black velvet trimmed with gold lace and a black Spanish lace scarf.

December 1888 *Delineator*

The arrangement in Figure 12 will freshen a worn bodice or decorate a simple one. A white or black lace scarf is slightly shirred on the shoulders, and then drawn in V shape in the center. The lace is folded over so that the edges come on the inside. It is then knotted on the bodice and apparently caught by a pale green moiré ribbon in long loops and ends.

December 1888 *Delineator*

Figure 13. Jet trimmings

Figure 13 illustrates a set of finely cut jet so shaped that it may be easily arranged in position. It may be used for decoration on a costume of claret, green, brown, blue, or black. Sets of this kind are also available in steel, gold, iridescent, and silver beads, as well as in passementerie with or without beads. The passementerie may be obtained in all colors.

January 1889 *Delineator*

Figure 12. Lace scarf

Figure 14. Lace and mull fichu

The fichu in Figure 15 is made of point d'esprit lace. The outer plaiting is very deep. The next is a little narrower, corresponding in width to the one that stands à la Medici about the neck. By this arrangement a V shape is produced. Where the fichu is crossed near the waist, are placed loops and ends of moiré ribbon that fall to a considerable depth.

January 1889 *Delineator*

Rose mull forms the fichu in Figure 14. The mull is laid in fine folds in the back and about the shoulders, and flares in a soft puff just in front. The fichu is edged with Valenciennes lace put on sufficiently full to permit of being caught down in cascade fashion. In front it reaches to the waist. Picot-edged moiré ribbon in a deep rose color is knotted just in front and seems to hold the fichu in place.

January 1889 *Delineator*

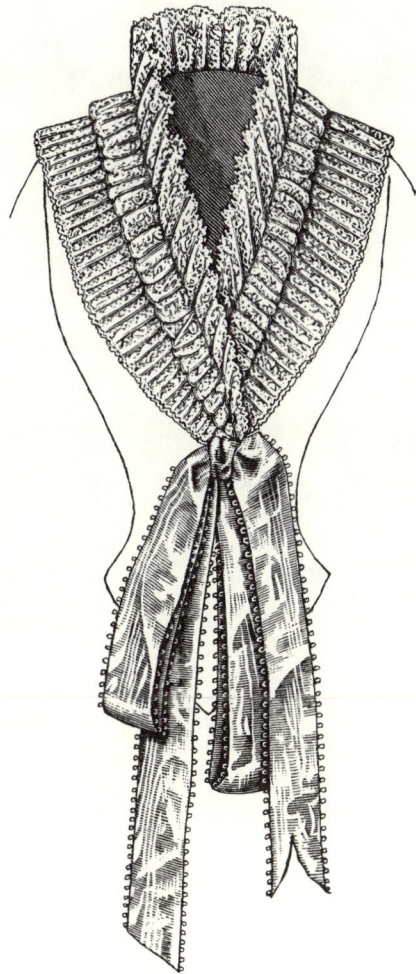

Figure 15. Lace fichu

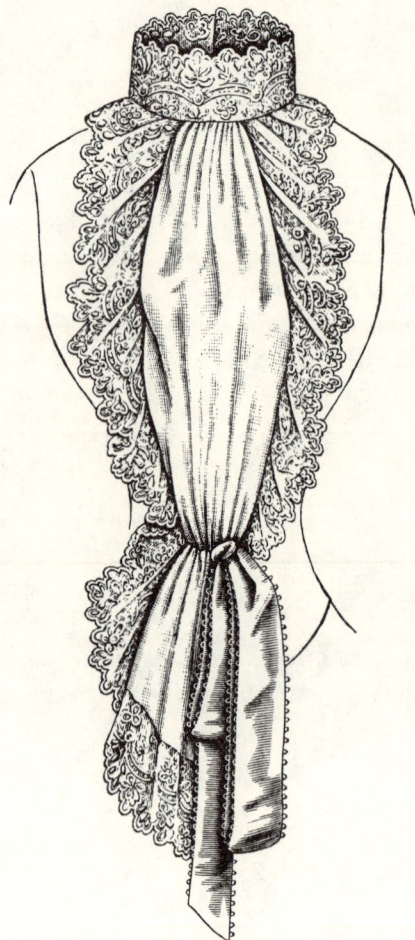

Figure 16. Mull and lace gilet

The gilet in Figure 16 is of pale blue mull. The high collar is formed of rather heavy lace that looks like Venetian point. The gilet is outlined with similar lace and is fastened to the collar. It falls in a soft pouf to the waist-line, where it is gathered and fastened to a band of strong net, and an arrangement of pale blue ribbon placed on top. The mull falls naturally below the gathering. Rose, yellow, or white mull may be used in place of blue.

February 1889 *Delineator*

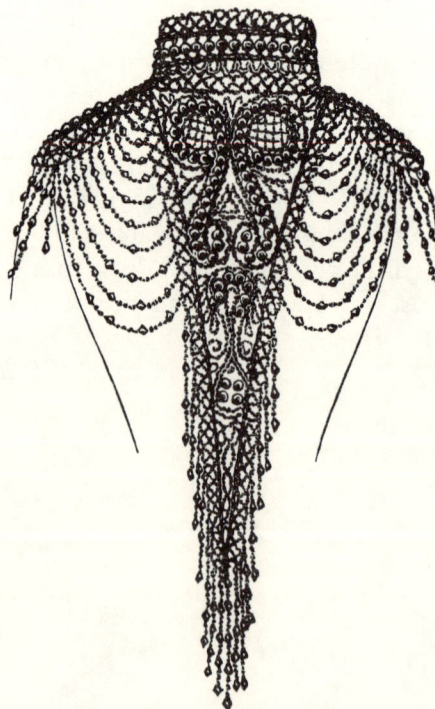

Figure 17. Jet decoration for bodice

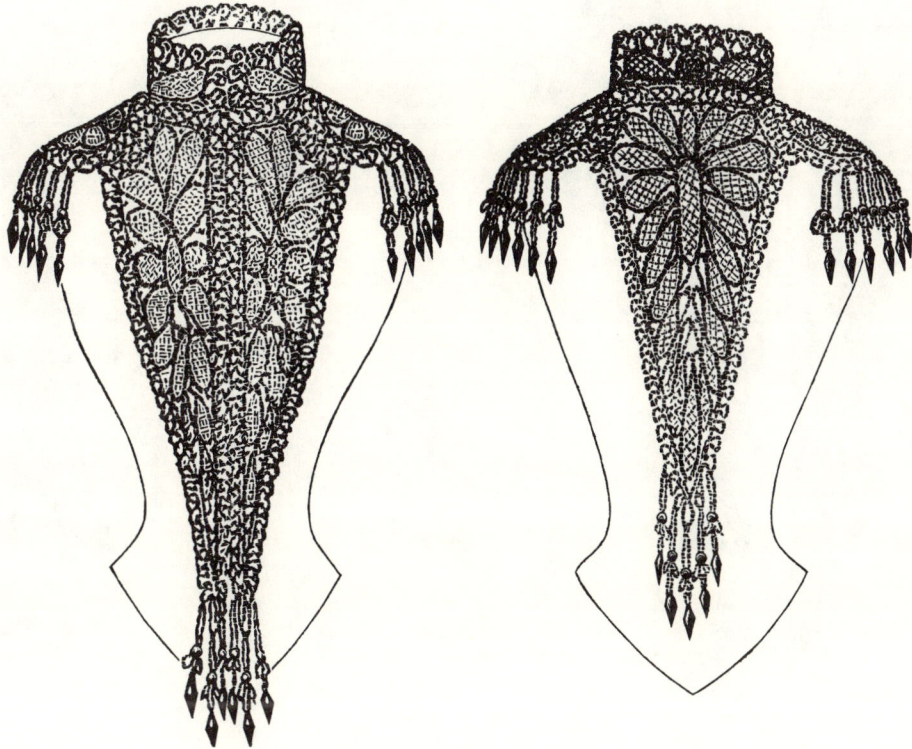

Figure 18. Jet trimming

This jet decoration really forms the collar, plastron, epaulettes, and a V-shaped ornament for the back. The front view is shown at the top of Figure 17, and the back view at the bottom. This decoration is effective with black, green, or garnet dresses.

February 1889 *Delineator*

This trimming comprises a gilet, a shoulder decoration, a collar, and an ornament for the back of the bodice. The front view is shown on the left of Figure 18, and the back view on the right. The beads follow a floral pattern, and on the shoulders, finely cut jet beads swing in the manner of fringe. This trimming is especially appropriate on green or blue velvet or silk.

March 1889 *Delineator*

This moiré ribbon with a picot edge will prove a becoming change to those who like embroidered and beaded ribbons. (See Figure 20.) On the part that encircles the neck, is set a very full ruching that stands out when the ends are tied.

June 1889 *Delineator*

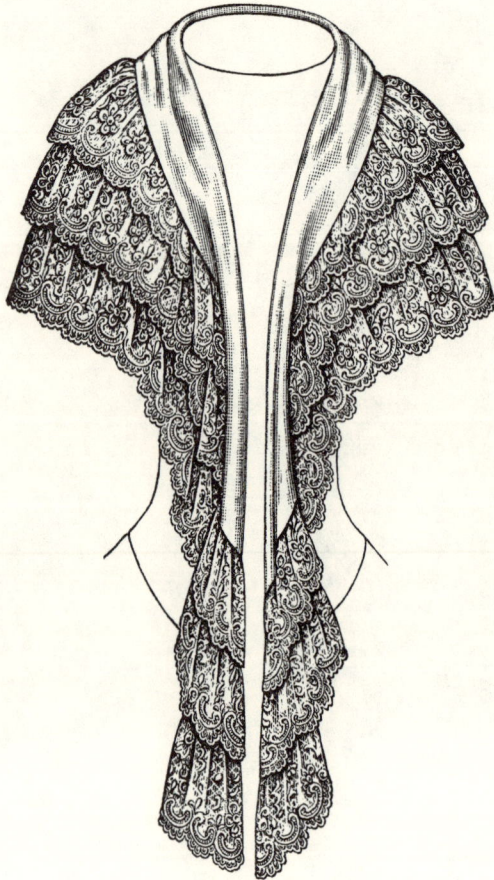

Figure 19. Mull and lace kerchief

Figure 20. Neck ribbon

This kerchief is of pale yellow mull. It is trimmed with three full frills of Valenciennes lace much yellowed by time–presumably. Arranged as illustrated by Figure 19, the effect is that of a jabot down the front. However, the long ends of the kerchief may be carelessly knotted rather high on the bodice and then let fall. Rose, pale green, blue, or mauve mull may be used for the center of this fichu.

March 1889 *Delineator*

The decoration in Figure 21 is of old pink surah. The high collar is formed of folds of surah drawn down on one side. The broad strip of surah forming the gilet and sash is plaited to the collar. From there it falls in loose Molière style to the waist, where it is drawn around to one side and caught with a knot, the end falling far down on the skirt. Any becoming shade may be used, and the silk looks especially well on muslin dresses.

June 1889 *Delineator*

Figure 22. China silk gilet

The gilet in Figure 22 is developed in white China silk. It is folded in plaits on each side of the center, where a forward-turning band of fine lace is arranged on each side, both the plaits and the trimming narrowing toward the waist-line and then flaring to the pointed lower edge. The edges are machine-stitched, but fancy stitching worked with white silk may be substituted. The collar is composed of folds of the silk separated by an upward-turning band of lace.

July 1889 *Delineator*

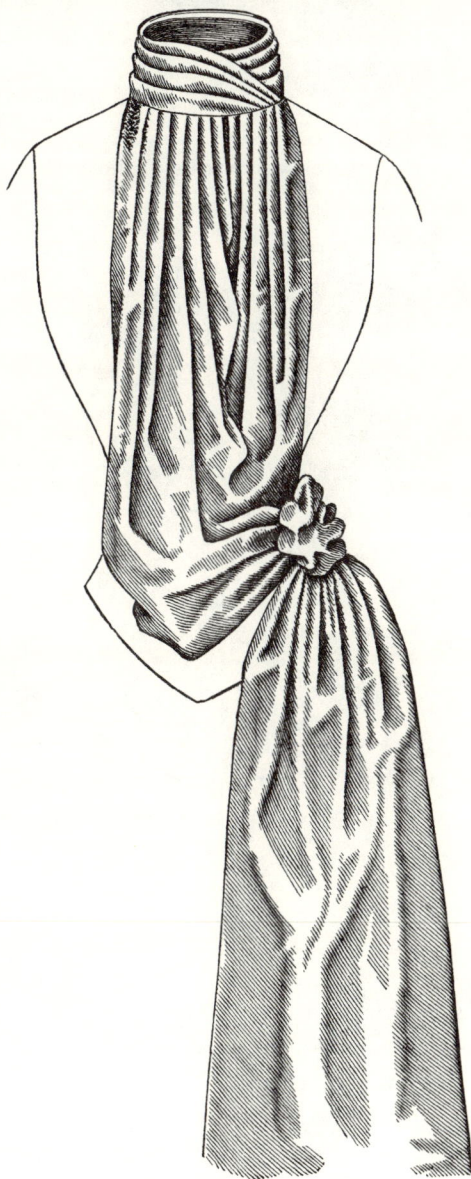

Figure 21. Combination collar, gilet, and sash

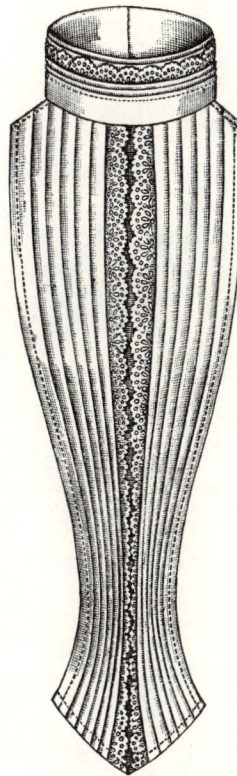

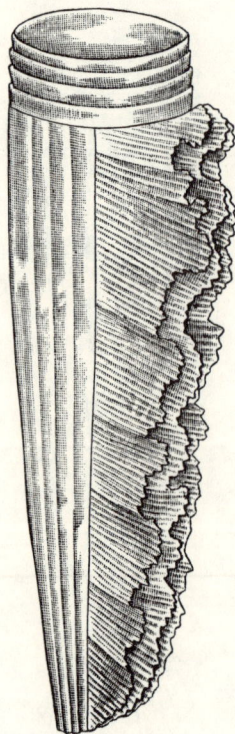

Figure 23. Crêpe lisse gilet

The crêpe lisse gilet in Figure 23 may be worn with any style of plain bodice. It is formed by plaits that extend the full depth and lap toward the bottom, and by three deep, overlapping plaited frills on the side, which are graduated narrower toward the bottom. The collar stands quite high and shows several soft folds of the material. Surah may be introduced for the plaited frills, and the edges may be fringed.

July 1889 *Delineator*

Figure 24. Black lisse jabot

Figure 25. Lace jabot

This jabot decreases in width toward the lower end, which comes at the bust. (See Figure 24.) The plainest of mourning costumes will be rendered dressy by this accessory, although its use is not limited to mourning.

August 1889 *Delineator*

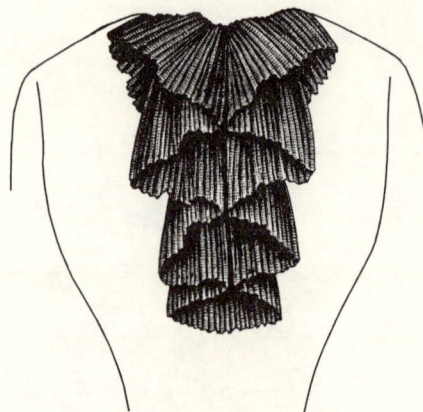

Venetian point lace was used for the jabot in Figure 25. The lace is arranged on a straight foundation of net, in a full cascade that narrows as it nears the lower end. Loops and a knot of lawn are deftly introduced. The jabot may be made of mousseline de soie edged with fine, narrow Valenciennes. Point d'esprit nets and laces are also favored.

September 1889 *Delineator*

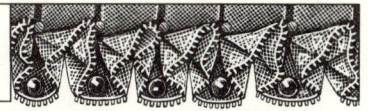

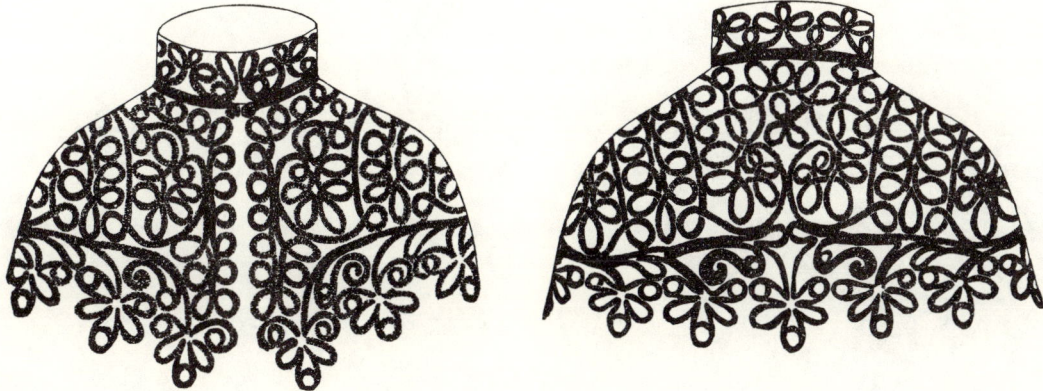

Figure 26. Shoulder cape

This cape is suitable for trimming plain wool or silk bodices, or coats or cloaks. It is made of black silk braid. The front view is shown on the left of Figure 26, and the back view on the right.

October 1889 *Delineator*

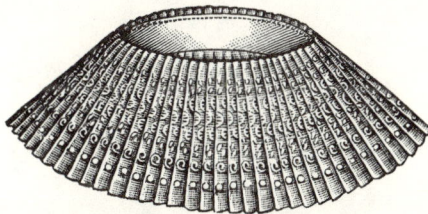

Figure 27. Directoire collar

The collar in Figure 27 lends itself well to plain bodices. It is made of deep lace net plaited to a broad linen band, which is adjusted beneath the dress collar.

October 1889 *Delineator*

The collar in Figure 28 is made of embroidered Swiss muslin. It is edged with Valenciennes lace, plaited, and then arranged as a rolling collar. From each side come the ties; they are of soft white surah finished at the edge with Valenciennes lace. The ties may be knotted in sailor fashion, or carelessly looped so that one bow is shorter than the other.

November 1889 *Delineator*

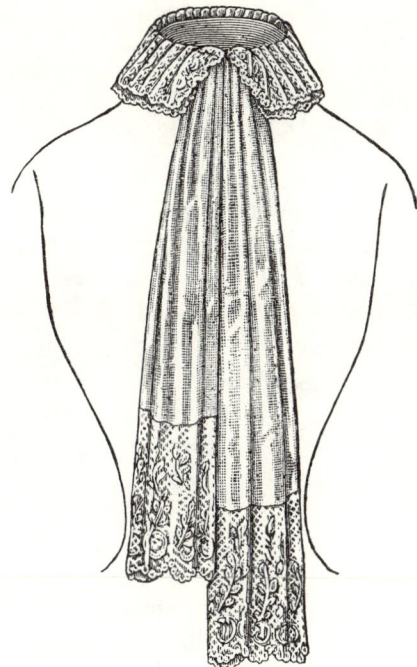

Figure 28. Fancy collar and tie

Figure 29. Fancy collar and cuff

Figure 30. Mousseline de soie and lace scarf-fichu

The accessories in Figure 29 are made of Irish point embroidery. The tabs of the collar fall deeply on the shoulders and on the bust, while those of the cuff extend almost to the elbow. The standing collar may be omitted, and beads or velvet ribbon worn about the neck.

December 1889 Delineator

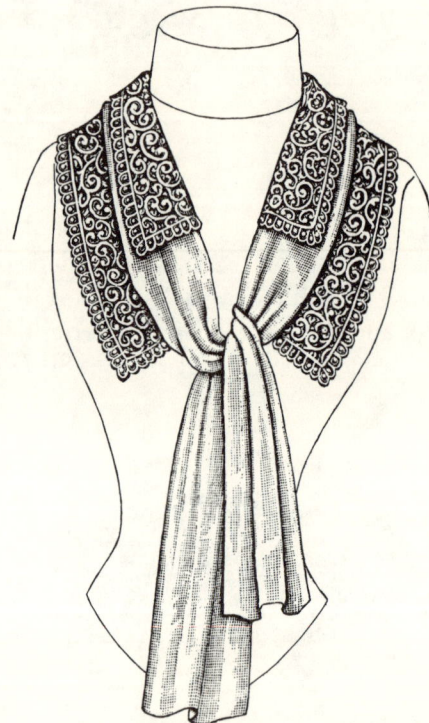

Mousseline de soie is used for the scarf or fichu part of the accessory in Figure 30. This scarf opens over the bust, where it is softly knotted, the ends falling almost to the edge of the bodice. Over the scarf falls a square-cornered collar of heavy lace. A similarly shaped, but longer collar extends to the bust from beneath the scarf. This decoration may be made of lace net, China crêpe, or surah, with fine lace. The scarf material may be colored.

December 1889 Delineator

The collar in Figure 31 is fashioned from point de Gene lace. It flares from the neck, displaying sharply pointed lower corners. From the upper edge rises a frill of lace edging. To the front edges of the collar are gathered fichu ends of crêpe de Chine, the lower ends of which are edged with deep lace. The side edges of the collar and fichu are followed with softly frilled lace, which is gradually narrowed to a little above the waist-line. The fichu may be confined at the waist-line by a belt, or it may be knotted at the bust.

December 1889 Delineator

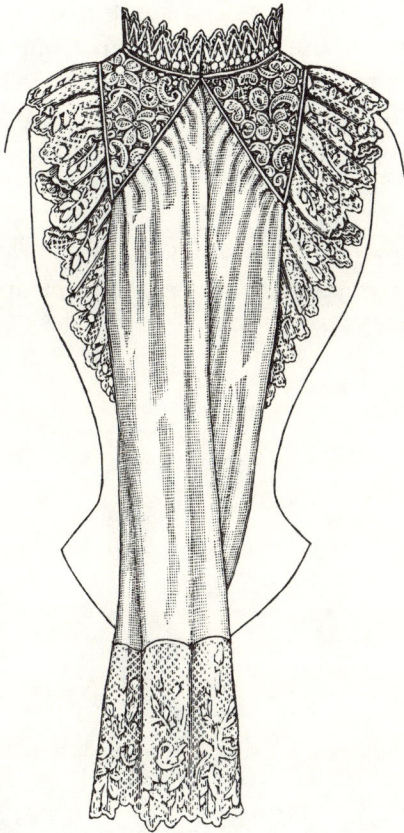

Figure 31. Lace collar with crêpe de Chine ties

Hats and Bonnets

There are shops where the most desirable shapes or frames can be purchased ready made. If the exact shape wanted is not obtainable, something very near to it generally is, and it is an easy matter to alter it. The shape can be bent, fastened up or down on one side or the other, and generally changed as taste or fancy dictates. If the brim is too wide, rip off the wire cord that furnishes the edge and trim off the buckram or stiff net of which the shape is made. Using long overcast-stitches, fasten the wire on again to the new and shorter edge. If the brim is too narrow, take some stiff crinoline or buckram and lay it on the present brim, allowing it to extend to the desired size. Finish this new edge with an extra wire. If the crown is too small, slash it at the back or side where greater room is required. A wire sewed all around the crown and over the opening

will hold it in place. All enlarging or reducing must be completed before you cover the frame with the outside material.

The first step in doing so is to cut a pattern for each part. There should be a pattern for the top of the crown, another for the sides, another for the upper side of the brim, and yet another for the under side of the brim. These patterns should be cut by laying smooth, not overly stiff paper on each part and creasing it until it fits the frame exactly. The crown top is easily cut, but the brims demand more patience. For them take a straight piece of paper as wide as the widest part of the brim. Gradually lay it around the brim until it fits, by laying plaits to make it do so. Pin each plait in place. Trim off the edges to correspond with the edges of the brim. Lay the plaited paper on a large square of smooth paper and, allowing for seams on each edge, cut out another pattern without plaits in it. Lay this on the brim to make sure no mistake has been made. Then cut out the under brim pattern and the sides of the crown in the same manner.

When the patterns are prepared, lay them all on the velvet, silk, or cloth to be used for the hat. Make the coverings of the brims and crown bias in front, even if they slope until quite straight at the back.

When the pieces have been cut, lay the crown on the frame smoothly. Fasten it in place with pins stuck through just once, then stitch it fast permanently with long back-stitches. Cotton works better here than silk thread. Then lay the two brim covers together with their right sides next to each other, and seam their outer edges together. All seams and overlapping edges should be pared off as narrow as possible. Slip these covers over the brim, which will require bending it a little, but it will easily bend back into the proper shape.

An alternative to covering the brim flat is to make a fulled brim. Take a bias piece of the material almost twice as long as the brim is around. Gather it on each edge. Take a roll of soft tissue paper as large as your finger, and baste it down on the edge of the brim, to give extra softness to the edge. Then draw the gathered material over the brim.

Let the inside edges of the brim covers extend up on the crown, and notch these edges until they set into the frame properly. Next is the cover for the sides of the crown. It must cover the raw edges of both the crown and the upper brim cover. Baste a turn-over on each side of this side cover. Draw it tightly around the crown, and fasten the ends together. Clip the bastings here and there and draw them all out.

The last touch is the crown lining. This is a double piece of gauze sewed by long stitches at the edge of the crown, then drawn up tightly at the center.

1892 Home Dressmaking

The hat in Figure 1 is of brown velvet. Its crown is soft and full. The brim is bent considerably on one side, smoothly covered, and outlined with small gold horse-shoes. On the left side, two golden brown plumes are drawn over the crown, and from their midst stand fluffy aigrettes. A large gold pin with a fancifully cut head is stuck through the crown so that it shows well from the front.

February 1888 Delineator

The hat in Figure 2 is of dark green felt. It has a square crown, and a rolling brim that is much higher on one side than on the other. A green velvet band outlines the brim and the top of the crown. On the side, absolutely on the crown, are long, full loops of fancy ribbon showing two shades of green, and from among them protrude heron feathers of the lightest green shade. When the loops are knotted, a strap is brought down over the brim, apparently to hold it in place.

February 1888 Delineator

Figure 2. Felt hat

The hat in Figure 3 is of fine mode straw. The crown is laid in double plaits at regular intervals, while the brim is gracefully curved. A silk cord encircles the crown. The trimming is massed in front. It consists of high, pointed loops of moss green velvet, against which are three full mode tips that fall over the crown, as well as in front. Dark blue, olive, russet, or any shade of brown may be substituted for the green velvet.

March 1888 Delineator

Figure 1. Velvet hat

Figure 3. Straw hat

The hat in Figure 4 is of cream straw. The brim is faced with deep red velvet, and where it curves most is placed a cluster of pale pink roses with their foliage. At the back are loops of red ribbon and a fan of cream silk pinked at its edges. Against these rests a bunch of roses and some wild flowers, the stems being tied together as if the wearer had gathered the blossoms and placed them on her hat.

March 1888 *Delineator*

The hat in Figure 5 is of gray straw, the broad brim being underfaced with dark blue velvet. Covering the back in Mercury fashion are two large blue wings, which rest against the crown and just meet in front. At the back are many high loops of blue-and-gray striped ribbon. From under these loops come ties that are brought forward and looped under the chin.

March 1888 *Delineator*

Figure 4. Straw hat

Figure 5. Straw hat

Figure 6. Straw hat

A view of the left side of the hat is shown on the left side of Figure 6, and a view of the right side on the right. The straw is of a serpent shade. The hat has a square crown with a fold just in front. The brim is flat and spoon shaped in front. It rolls slightly on one side, and very high on the other, where it lies close to the crown and is then cut to form a point, leaving no brim at the back. The brim is outlined with a narrow band of velvet the same shade. About the crown is a broad band of velvet overlaid with silver lace. At the back, extending forward on the crown, are loops of serpent moiré ribbon edged with satin in a darker shade, and a great bunch of serpent pompons and aigrettes. The clasp that confines the band is of steel and gold.

May 1888 *Delineator*

The toque in Figure 7 has an oval outline. It is pictured made of gray silk laid on a soft frame, and the fullness is gathered over cords on the top. At the edge the effect is quite plain, but just in front the silk is drawn up very high to form a double fan. The only decoration is a fine steel buckle placed on one side. Two silver quills may be substituted for the buckle. The toque may be made of cloth, suiting, or cloth of gold.

May 1888 *Delineator*

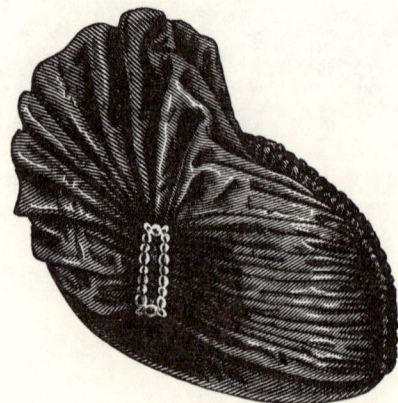

Figure 7. Silk toque

This hat, with its rather low crown and its high, curved, and almost pointed brim, is of fine black straw. (See Figure 8.) A wide band of black ribbon with a silver edge starts from the back, encircles the crown, and is arranged in strap fashion over the brim. Another band starts high up on the side and extends to the point in front, where its end is hidden under a clasp of finely cut jet. The trimming is all at the back. Black ribbon loops stand far up on the crown. Resting against them is a long, full fan of black Spanish lace that extends the entire depth of the crown. A black semi-plume, long and fluffy, falls far down over the edge from amidst the ribbon and lace.

May 1888 *Delineator*

The view on the left of Figure 9 shows this shape made of sienna brown satin straw without any trimming. It is worn well forward. The view on the right illustrates it in café-colored chip, trimmed with ombré ostrich tips and écru grosgrain ribbon showing a velvet edge. The ribbon is passed about the bottom of the crown, knotted directly at the center of the front, and arranged at the back in long loops that extend forward on the crown. Three ostrich tips are poised on the left side.

June 1888 *Delineator*

Figure 8. Straw hat

Figure 9. Straw hat shown untrimmed and trimmed

The brim of the close-fitting toque in Figure 10 is overlaid with a puffing of stone-colored velvet. The crown is hidden by a section of smocked, French gray surah. A soft twist of surah ribbon passes about the bottom of the crown. Upright loops of the ribbon are placed in front, in marked contrast with the shell pink marabou pompon that is placed *à la militaire* around them.

June 1888 *Delineator*

Figure 10. Toque

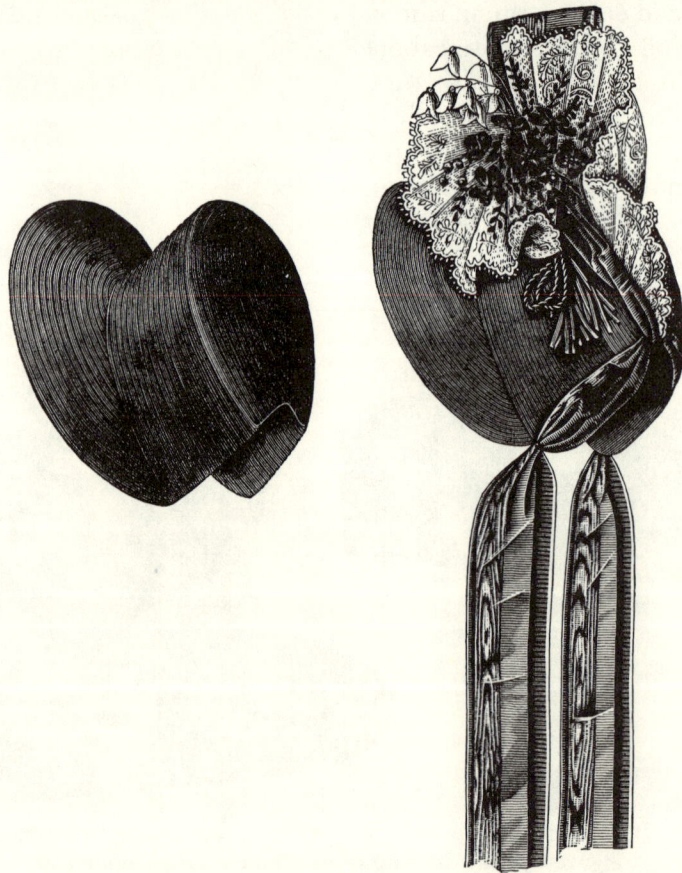

Figure 11. Straw bonnet shown untrimmed and trimmed

Figure 12. Straw hat shown untrimmed and trimmed

An untrimmed view of this bonnet is given on the left of Figure 11, and a trimmed one on the right. The former shows tabac brown Dunstable straw. The latter portrays silver-gray chip, with trimmings of point d'Alencon lace, absinthe ribbon, and green and yellow flowers. The ribbon is arranged in loops that rest against a rosette-like disposal of lace, and is then carried down on each side of a jabot that rests on the crown. Below this it is folded to outline the back of the brim, and then depends in a long tie on each side. The flowers are placed on the left side.

June 1888 *Delineator*

The untrimmed view on the left of Figure 12 shows this hat made of fine split straw in bronze-green. The trimmed view on the right shows a fine split-straw crown of heliotrope color and a brim of fancy straw uniting heliotrope and gilt. Outlining the brim at the inner edge is a tiny bias fold of heliotrope velvet. About the base of the crown is a soft twist of similar velvet. Fancy ribbon showing heliotrope and absinthe is arranged in loops on the left side, and a bunch of wild thistles and other wild flowers is placed in their midst.

June 1888 *Delineator*

The figure at the top of Figure 13 illustrates a shade hat of fancy straw, the broad brim being outlined with olive velvet. A cluster of light olive ribbon loops is on one side. On the other side is a fan of lace. A cluster of enormous daisies with long stems tied with grasses is placed on the side, extending far to the front.

The figure in the center shows a perfectly flat hat of deep yellow fancy straw. It is made to fit the head by a band of buckram covered with green ribbon, which also keeps it in place. The hat extends far forward, the trimming being placed on top well to the back. It consists of loops of soft green grosgrain ribbon with a satin edge. The loops fall to the back, and from under them come clusters of yellow blossoms and their foliage. The ties also come from the back and should be looped rather loosely.

The hat at the bottom is a large Leghorn. The crown is quite high, and the brim is broad and turned up only at the back. A band of brown velvet in three folds encircles the crown, tiny gilt crescents fastening the two upper folds. At the back, falling forward on the crown, are two golden brown tips.

Figure 13. Three shade hats

Straps of cream ribbon with a brown border hold the brim up and form loops in front. On one side are two folds of cream lace, and another shows at the back against the ribbon.

August 1888 *Delineator*

The straw hat in Figure 14 is a pale shade of green. The crown is of fine straw, while the rolling brim is a fancy braid. The trimming consists of white grosgrain ribbon and two gold quills spangled with silver. The ribbon is carried up from each side to form a double set of loops just in front. The quills are placed in the knot so that the ribbon loops form a background for them. Gray and white, white and pale yellow, and pale rose on a white hat, are smart contrasts.

August 1888 *Delineator*

One of the box-turban shapes is shown by Figure 15. The brim narrows to the back and resembles the coronet shape, permitting of wearing the hat a little off the face. The hat is of mode felt, and the edge is bound with braid. The ribbon trimming is deep green with a fancy gold border. It is passed about the crown and is turned on each side. Near the front and slightly to one side it is arranged in very high loops, wired to retain their position. Two smaller loops fall carelessly over the brim. Gold quills may be placed among the loops.

September 1888 *Delineator*

Figure 14. Straw hat

Figure 15. Felt turban

Figure 17. Leghorn hat

The crown of the bonnet in Figure 16 is of golden brown crêpe shirred on wires. The brim is smoothly covered with crêpe. The edge of the brim and the bottom of the crown are outlined with gold braid. A fan of cream lace, then one of black lace, and then a large cluster of yellow roses with their foliage form the decoration, which is placed on the front of the crown. At the back is noticeable a pointed outline, which is described by folded brown ribbons that flare at the edge and are firmly tied under the chin.

September 1888 *Delineator*

The broad brim of the fine Leghorn hat in Figure 17 is bent near the crown in such a way that it seems to flare up in poke fashion in front. The trimming is a rich, red ribbon bordered with quaint outlines in gold. The loops are brought forward from the back of the crown and are arranged stiffly but quaintly. From under the loops two ribbon straps come out on the sides and appear to hold in the brim. Any preferred color of ribbon is allowable, but a fancy variety is usually chosen.

September 1888 *Delineator*

Figure 16. Crêpe-covered bonnet

The bonnet in Figure 19 is suitable for driving, visiting, or evening wear. The shape is a pointed capote, with a twist of olive velvet arranged in front just under the brim. White silk embroidery dotted here and there with pearl beads outlines its shape, and is drawn up in front to form a high fan. Starting from the back and coming forward high up on each side, are broad loops of olive grosgrain, and against them are wings covered with pearl beads. A band of olive velvet outlines the back and forms the bridle.

October 1888 *Delineator*

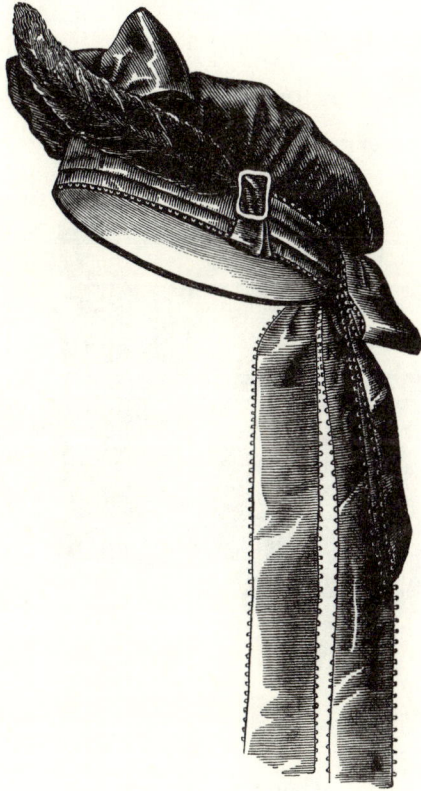

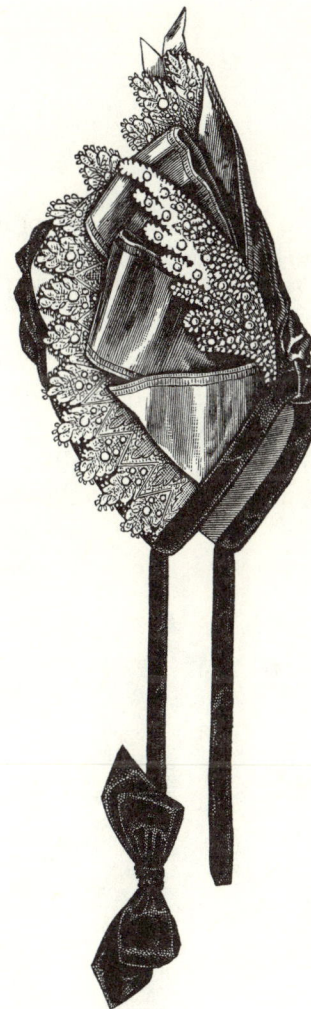

Figure 18. Tam o' shanter cap

The flat, drawn-out crown of this tam o'shanter cap is of dark blue cloth. The narrow band brim, which fits the head, is of dark blue ribbon with a fancy edge, folded as illustrated by Figure 18. At the back the ribbon falls in long loops and ends. On one side of the cap is placed a gray quill, which points to the front and is apparently held in place by a ribbon knot and a silvered buckle. Such caps are usually made of the suit material, but black velvet is always appropriate.

September 1888 *Delineator*

Figure 19. Embroidery and velvet bonnet

Figure 21. Velvet hat

The hat in Figure 20 is made of light brown straw. It fits the head easily and firmly, and is worn far enough back to show the bangs. A double band of dark green velvet is about the brim, which is drawn in a full high puff in front. Above this are loops of green moiré ribbon. Standing up quite high, yet massed against the ribbon, are greenish white blossoms and moss rosebuds that tower far above them.

October 1888 *Delineator*

This picturesque hat has a smoothly covered brim of warm brown velvet, and a crown puffed in Henri Quatre fashion. (See Figure 21.) The trimming is massed on the crown. It consists of pale yellow ostrich tips, metal quills, and bows of pale yellow ribbon placed slightly on one side. From among the tips falls one long plume, which comes quite over the brim and touches the knot of hair. This style is smart in yellow and black, black and red, or blue and pale green.

October 1888 *Delineator*

Figure 20. Round straw hat

Figure 22. Felt poke hat

The poke shape is shown in dark blue felt, and its broad brim is overlaid with silver embroidery. (See Figure 22.) The crown is quite hidden under the decorations. In front are massed blue velvet loops, and against them is a dark blue bird. From the back towers a mass of cream feathers, and amid them may be distinguished metal quills that harmonize with the embroidery on the brim. Blue velvet strings may be added.

October 1888 *Delineator*

The toque in Figure 23 is well adapted for street wear. It is an oval shape and shows a stylish combination of velvet and felt. The brim is smoothly covered at the back, but in front it is arranged in folds that are smoothly placed, yet do not look stiff. The crown is formed of a circular piece of tan felt a shade lighter than the velvet. The edge is elaborately pinked. In the center it is braided with fine gold braid and chenille. The square is drawn well to the front as illustrated. It is held in fluted style by bastings. It is finished by a gold clasp on one side, and loops of tan ribbon and wings a shade lighter on the other.

November 1888 *Delineator*

Figure 23. Velvet and felt toque

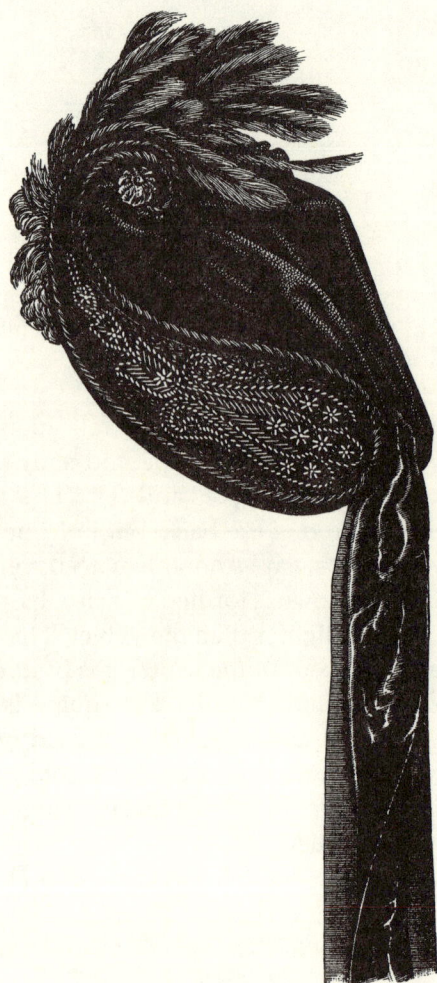

Figure 24. Velvet bonnet

Figure 25. Felt bonnet

The crown of the bonnet in Figure 24 is a soft, full pouf of rich absinthe velvet. On each side, laid flatly against it, are palm leaves wrought in gold threads and chenille cords in cashmere effect; the narrow part is brought to the front. In front, where the bonnet flares, are backward-turning clusters of absinthe feathers that come far up on the crown. Ties of absinthe velvet ribbon are knotted at the back. When the bonnet is put on, they should be brought carefully forward and loosely knotted under the chin.

November 1888 *Delineator*

The bonnet in Figure 25 is made of gray felt braided with silver soutache. Milliner's folds of deep green velvet finish the back, and velvet is also used on the sides and in front. On the sides it is pinked and laid on flatly, but in front a full pouf is placed. The decorations consist of ribbon loops and ends, which rest against the crown and show a steel ornament in their midst. The ribbon is striped with alternate lines of dark green and silver-gray. The bridle has long, narrow velvet straps, which are simply fastened over each other.

November 1888 *Delineator*

Figure 27. Velvet hat

Figure 26. Velvet hat for elaborate costume

The picturesque hat in Figure 26 is only suitable for a very elaborate costume. It has a medium crown, and a broad brim slightly curved on one side and rolled up very much on the other. Over the crown, toward the rolled-up side, fall white ostrich tips. Starting from near the back is a full boa of Valenciennes lace that falls at the back, is brought forward carelessly, drawn around the neck, and the end allowed to hang loosely. This hat may be made in all black.

November 1888 *Delineator*

The square, rather sloping crown of the hat in Figure 27 is smoothly covered with black velvet. The brim, which reaches well forward at the front, is also of velvet, overlaid with a netting of silver cord. The brim turns up at the back, and the contrast is shown against the crown. A cluster of milliner's folds is arranged about the crown. On one side stand high loops of moiré ribbon, and black and silver-gray feathers. Two long plumes showing the same colors start from under the loops and extend over the side of the hat toward the back, where they fall some distance over the brim.

December 1888 *Delineator*

Warm brown velvet was used for covering the bonnet in Figure 28. Over the brim the velvet is drawn in full, soft folds. Rich mode ribbon with a gold border is drawn about the crown and massed in small and large bows in front, the fluffy decoration just underneath resulting from the close placing of many little mode feathers. Strings of mode ribbon are fastened at the back and flare on each side. They are then brought forward and knotted either under the chin or on one side. This bonnet looks well made in Russian green and gold.

December 1888 *Delineator*

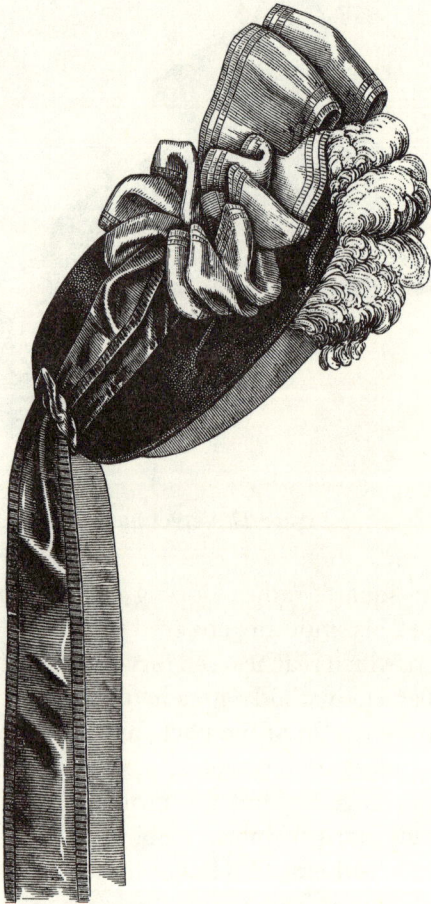

Figure 28. Velvet bonnet

Figure 29. Felt hat with veil

The hat in Figure 29 is of gray felt, which is sufficiently fine that no binding is necessary. It has ribbon bows placed on top and coming toward the front, the ribbon showing a stripe of deep pink satin and gray grosgrain. About the crown, and reaching under the loops, is a monture of pale pink blossoms that almost wreathes the hat.

The Empire veil is of dotted net, the upper frill being of two bands of French lace and the lower frill of one. It is fastened at the back, and then the narrow ribbons are drawn to make it fit under the chin. The net hangs in bag fashion and the lace frill frames the face. Large dotted net is liked for these veils, although a few are of plain Brussels net.

February 1889 *Delineator*

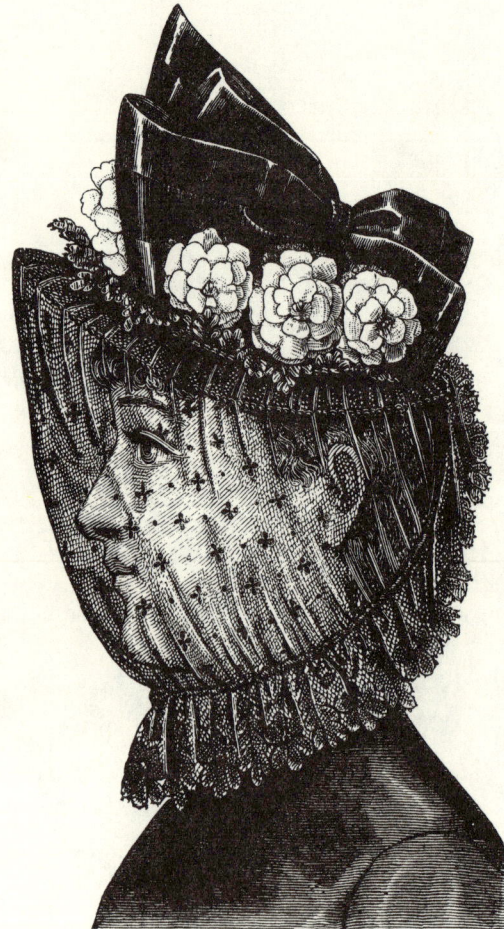

The hat in Figure 30 is of fancy straw of a natural yellow shade. It has a broad brim that flares toward the front and a very low crown. Under the crown, fitting close to the head, is a band covered with gold passementerie. On this, just in front, is a cluster of small pink roses that rest on the hair, although they are slightly shadowed by the brim. The edge of the brim is outlined with passementerie. About the crown is a band of rose ribbon heavily embroidered in gold. Three tall, stiff loops of similar ribbon arranged just in front form the only other trimming.

March 1889 *Delineator*

The hat in Figure 32 is intended for wear at garden parties and summer fêtes of all kinds. Over a shape of stiffened net, deep Oriental lace is laid in such a way that the hat seems made of it. The brim is bent to suit the face. The crown is hidden under loops of grosgrain ribbon, and from under and about these are deep green ornaments that in size and shape suggest pine cones.

April 1889 *Delineator*

Figure 30. Straw hat

The bonnet in Figure 31 is of black Neapolitan fancy straw. The crown is low and square. The brim is very narrow on the sides but flares high in front. About the crown is a wreath of green leaves and berries. Just in front are loops of black velvet ribbon and some black velvet drapery. Back of them are pale green aigrettes, a butterfly, and some fine green beads that dance airily.

March 1889 *Delineator*

Figure 32. Lace hat

The crown of the hat in Figure 33 is smoothly covered with golden brown velvet. The brim of fancy braid is of a genuine straw color. On the inner side the brim is of Leghorn, and in front, where it turns up, the edge is finished with a narrow fold of brown velvet. About the crown, against the velvet, is a band of ribbon that shows gold, and many shades of brown and yellow, combined in Persian fashion. On one side the fan-like arrangement of ribbon comes well up on the crown, the ribbon being straw color, with a border of brown velvet. Against these fans are three short, full tips of the straw shade. These are so poised that two turn toward the back and one toward the front, all three seeming like balls of down.

April 1889 *Delineator*

Figure 31. Straw bonnet

513

The toque in Figure 35 is worn off the face just like a bonnet, and the hair should be arranged low to complete the effect. The toque has a brim of fancy straw, which is bent so as to present a poke outline in front. The crown is of light olive cloth embroidered with silk a shade darker. The cloth is laid smoothly over the frame and looped just in front. The facing is of deep olive velvet. It is smoothly applied on each side, but is arranged in front in a high mass that fills in the brim and provides a face trimming. On the crown are bunches of leaves in different shades of green. Loops of olive satin ribbon conceal their fastening.

May 1889 *Delineator*

Figure 33. Velvet and straw hat

The hat in Figure 34 is of black figured net over a Gainsborough shape. The brim is not raised in the usual way, but curved up on one side, permitting three large pink roses to be placed just under it. Against the crown on this side, are high drapings of net and of black ribbon. One long plume, starting from under them, falls over the brim and seems to caress the flowers. Yellow or white roses may be substituted for the pink ones; or if an all-black hat is desired, a fanciful bow of ribbon may take the place of the flowers.

April 1889 *Delineator*

Figure 35. Cloth and straw toque

The bonnet in Figure 36 is of black Neapolitan braid, with a broad border of gold passementerie. The crown is hidden under a handsome lace scarf so placed that it has the appearance of a draped crown, and has on it bunches of purple grapes and green grape leaves. The ends of the scarf fall over at the back and form the ties. The bonnet is worn so that the hair shows plainly, and the ties are looped under the chin or on one side.

May 1889 *Delineator*

Figure 34. Net Gainsborough hat

The crown of the bonnet in Figure 37 is formed of cloth of gold laid in soft but not thick plaits. The brim is outlined by two folds of dark mauve velvet, just back of which is a broad band of gold embroidery laid flatly against the bonnet. The trimming is arranged just in front and on top. It consists of a fanciful knot of cloth of gold, from out of which springs a short, full ostrich tip of a deep yellow color. At the side of this is a pompon of the same shade, with a gold aigrette standing in its midst. Across the back is a folded mauve velvet ribbon that flares on each side to form the ties, which are bowed under the chin in a formal way.

June 1889 *Delineator*

Figure 36. Straw bonnet

Figure 37. Cloth of gold and velvet bonnet

Figure 38. Leghorn hat

The hat in Figure 38 is of Leghorn, with its brim finished so that a binding is unnecessary. The brim droops a little at the back and front. Beneath it on one side are placed three large, deep pink roses that rest against the hair. The crown is hidden by two long, cream plumes. One starts from the side and enwreathes the crown, while the other comes from under the first and falls down on one side far over the brim. Yellow feathers may be substituted for the cream ones.

May 1889 *Delineator*

The toque in Figure 39 is of golden brown faille, and over it is adjusted fancy gold net. A puffing of golden brown faille and dark brown velvet forms the edge, the puffing flaring in poke fashion in front. Back of this is arranged a large fan of golden brown faille covered with gold net.

July 1889 *Delineator*

Figure 39. Faille toque

20 1/2

12 3/8   **4 1/4**

Cut double

Turn back on this line for facing

20 1/4

1/2 space seam   **1/2 space seam**

4 3/8   **5**

20 5/8

3 7/8   **10 1/8**
11

12 3/4   **12 3/8**

FRONT

5   **1 3/4**

12 1/4   **16 3/4**

7 1/8   **5 1/2**

BACK

Gather Sew to front

10   **20**
6   **21**

8   **11 1/4**
12

1/2 space seam

9 1/4   **21 3/4**
22 1/4

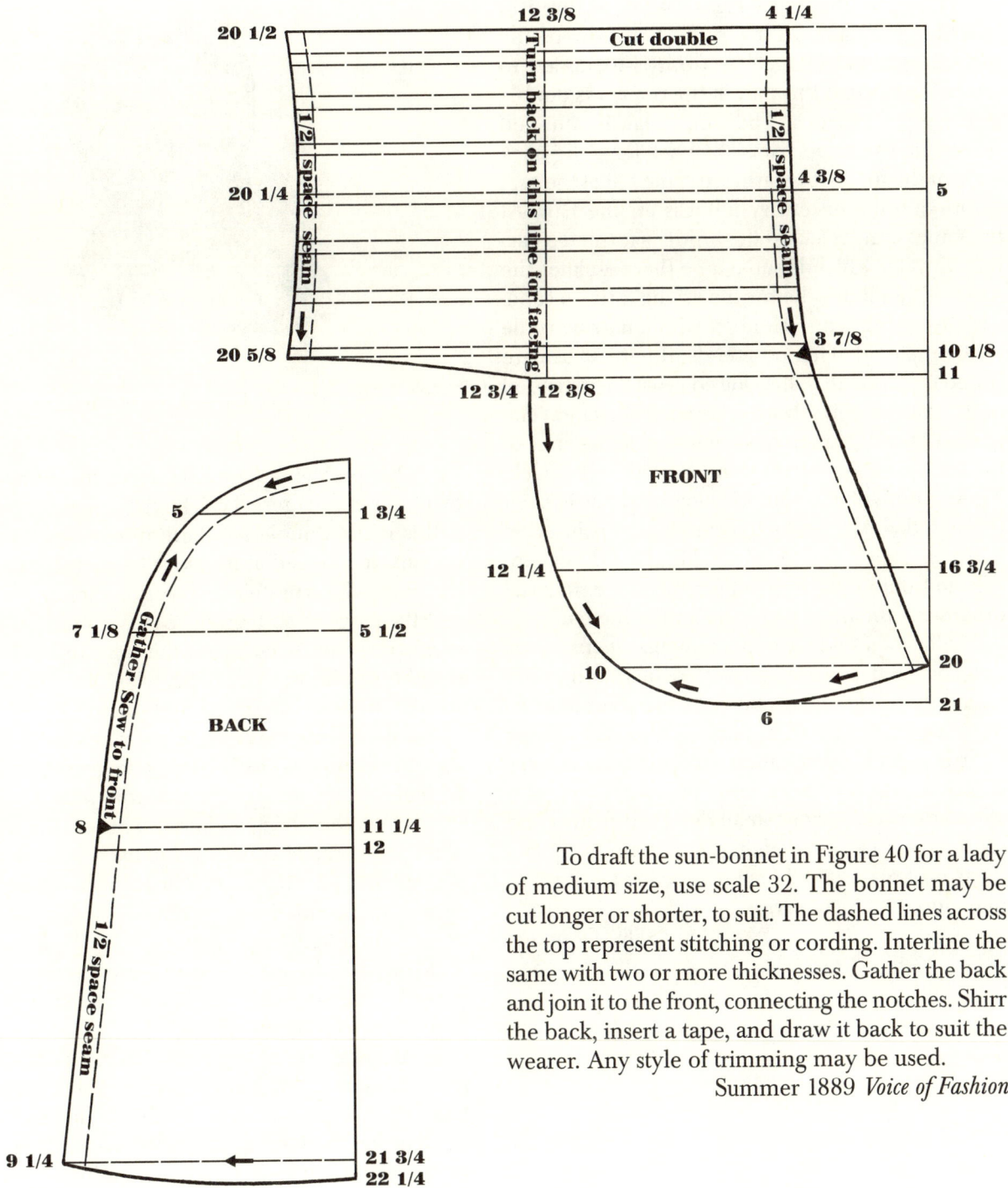

To draft the sun-bonnet in Figure 40 for a lady of medium size, use scale 32. The bonnet may be cut longer or shorter, to suit. The dashed lines across the top represent stitching or cording. Interline the same with two or more thicknesses. Gather the back and join it to the front, connecting the notches. Shirr the back, insert a tape, and draw it back to suit the wearer. Any style of trimming may be used.

Summer 1889 *Voice of Fashion*

Figure 40. Sun-bonnet

The sun-bonnet in Figure 41 is pictured in checked gingham, with a ruffle and bow of the material for trimming. The front is extended to fold under so that this part of the bonnet is double at the top and sides. The front edge is rounded below the extended part. The back joins the back edge of the front. It is gathered quite full at the top, to provide the necessary fullness for the hair. At the nape of the neck on the inside is formed a casing, through which is run a tape that regulates the width. The fullness below the casing forms a cape. The loose edges are trimmed with a narrow ruffle of the material. The loose ends of narrow ties are sewed underneath to the side edges of the extended parts, the ties being bowed beneath the chin. The plaited ends of similar ties are sewed to the ends of the casing on the outside, and bowed at the back. Three groups of machine-stitching are made in front through the extended parts, and a cord is inserted between each two lines of stitching to aid in keeping the front in place. A small bow of the material ornaments the front along the join to the back.

Checked and striped ginghams, seersuckers, embroidered cottons, piqués, prints, and other materials in use for sun-bonnets may be made up by this pattern. Braid in lines or a tracery design affords a pretty decoration for the front. A very dainty bonnet may be made of pale pink lawn with all-over embroidery in small detached figures and trimmed with a pretty edging. This bonnet requires 2 yards of material 22 inches wide, or 1 5/8 yards of material 36 inches wide.

May 1889 *Delineator*

Figure 41. Corded sun-bonnet

Pale pink gingham was chosen for the protective bonnet in Figure 42. The front is in one piece and is made double to where it forms part of the curtain. It is sewed at intervals to form broad casings, into which pasteboard sections are inserted to give the required stiffness. The crown joins the front and is deepened to complete the cape. Its front edge is gathered almost to a casing, which is formed of a strip of the material sewed underneath at the nape of the neck. Into this casing are run tapes, which shirr the bonnet up to fit easily and give the cape a flounced effect. Ties of the material pass from the seams over the casing and tie in a bow at the center of the back, the attached end of each being laid in two upward-turning plaits. The front corners of the curtain are rounded off, and the edges of the bonnet are trimmed with a hemmed ruffle of the material. Ties sewed underneath at the lowest pasteboard are bowed under the chin, their attached ends being each narrowed by two plaits.

All kinds of cotton materials are adapted to these bonnets, and they may be plain, striped, figured, checked, or embroidered. When the bonnet requires laundering, the pasteboards should be removed. A bonnet of pale blue chambray trimmed with chambray or Hamburg edging is dainty and serviceable. To make this bonnet requires 2 yards of material 36 inches wide, with 1/4 yard extra for the ruffle.

July 1888 *Delineator*

The turban-shaped hat in Figure 44 is of medium gray straw. The brim slopes toward the back and forms a coronet above the hair. It is smoothly faced with dark gray velvet, a narrow rim of the straw being left exposed at the top. The trimmings consist of clustered bows of ribbon in white and two shades of gray. These are so arranged at the front and on one side of the hat, that the butterfly loops come just above the brim and the longer ones stand upright about the crown.

October 1889 *Delineator*

Figure 42. Sun-bonnet with pasteboard

The cap in Figure 43 is made of a square of fine lawn that is drawn easily over a very light, stiff foundation so as to cover it completely. The entire edge is outlined with a fine plaiting of lisse. The plaiting is drawn up in front and on one side in rosette fashion. In the center of each rosette is a full bunch of dark red velvet ribbon intricately wound in and out. Knots of narrow satin ribbon, or a tiny bunch of violets or forget-me-knots, may be substituted for the velvet ribbon.

September 1889 *Delineator*

Figure 44. Straw hat

Figure 43. Lawn and lisse cap

A covering of gray-and-white checked cloth is drawn over the close-fitting bonnet shape. (See Figure 45.) The bonnet is finished at the edge of the front and sides with a fold of cardinal velvet. A narrower fold of the same outlines the lower edge of the back and is continued to form a bridle. A fan-shaped ornament consisting of a plaited fold of the velvet is extended from the front edge. Back of this two broad, plaited loops of velvet are crossed and caught together at the center with a fancy buckle, from which they spread toward the back.

October 1889 *Delineator*

Figure 46. Beaded bonnet

Figure 45. Cloth bonnet

The covering for the bonnet in Figure 46 is lady's cloth of a steel blue shade, elaborately embroidered with beads. At the front is placed a bunch of cream ostrich tips. A bridle of ribbon matching the cloth is folded narrowly across the lower edge and tied under the chin.

Felt, velvet, or silk may be used instead of cloth, and braid embroidery or rosettes of baby ribbon may be used for trimming. Wings or fancy feathers may take the place of the tips.

December 1889 *Delineator*

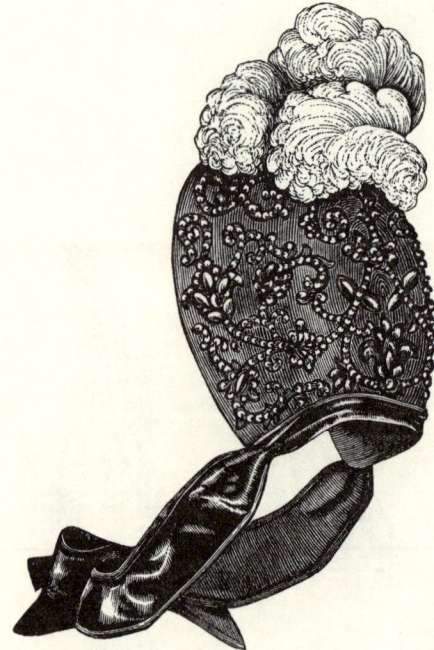

The black velvet hat in Figure 47 is designed for dressy wear. The crown is low, and the broad brim, which is edged with thick silver cord, rolls high on the left side. A section of velvet, the soft folds of which are basted on the right side of the back, extends over the crown. It is twisted at the center and then formed into a deep, full loop that falls lightly on the crown at the center of the front. A black ostrich tip peeps from under the loop. Two similar tips fall over the brim on the left side. A large plume is brought forward from the twist at the center of the crown, drooping gracefully over the brim. A long, fancy silver pin is thrust in on the left side of the hat.

December 1889 *Delineator*

Figure 47. Velvet hat

Other Accessories

Silk moirés, changeable surahs, plaid and striped silks, and brocades with designs of stripes and coin patterns, are the materials of spring and summer parasols. Their trimmings are ribbon loops forming fringes, and ruffles of lace—black, beige, and white—with many covers of lace, and drapings of lace or net, leaving the center of the parasol in relief in pointed star shapes.

The large and elaborate handles are of light natural woods heated until pliable, then twisted into large rings, knots, or hooks. Or they are richly carved in relief, or else countersunk, showing two shades of the wood. Or they are polished like lacquer, with a ball at the end, or a hand holding a carved mask. Others are of dull black wood like teak with applied flowers of ivory, or an ivory Japanese figure holding a tiny parasol of carved wood. Still other handles are of horn intricately twisted, or smoothly polished and inlaid with gold or bits of color in Japanese fashion.

March 24, 1888 *Harper's Bazar*

Ribbon muffs to match costumes are made up with alternate rows of ribbon and fur going around the muff, and long-looped ribbon bows on top. For example, sage green and gilt ribbon may alternate with natural beaver bands. Other muffs have wide ribbon ends hanging below them, while black net is shirred over the muff itself, and drops over the hands on the sides.

November 3, 1888 *Harper's Bazar*

Ostrich feather muffs are carried with the ostrich feather boas that are worn with dressy toilettes. They are of unique shape, with square corners, and are quite flat when not filled out by the hands.

November 17, 1888 *Harper's Bazar*

It seems as if velvet ribbons cannot be too wide for the sashes now so popular. A pretty arrangement for a dress when the sash is on the bodice, is to fasten one end of the ribbon to the belt on one side, then let it fall till it reaches the edge of the skirt, where it is turned and the end fastened far at the back under the sash. This will look very scanty unless wide ribbon is used and plenty of length allowed for the turn, which must not be abrupt.

April 1889 *Delineator*

521

Girdle clasps of cut steel, jet, silver, and occasionally gold are popular, particularly the long, narrow shapes. These fastenings are not really clasps, but buckles.

October 1889 *Delineator*

The ribbon shown by Figure 1 is moiré, but any preferred variety may be chosen. The girdle consists of wide ribbon narrowed by plaits in the ends, which close at the center of the back with hooks and eyes. In front the ribbon is drawn out to give a pointed effect at the top and bottom, and is retained in place by a wired tape basted to it underneath. Three loops of different lengths, and two longer ends, fall low down on the skirt from beneath the girdle on each side.

September 1888 *Delineator*

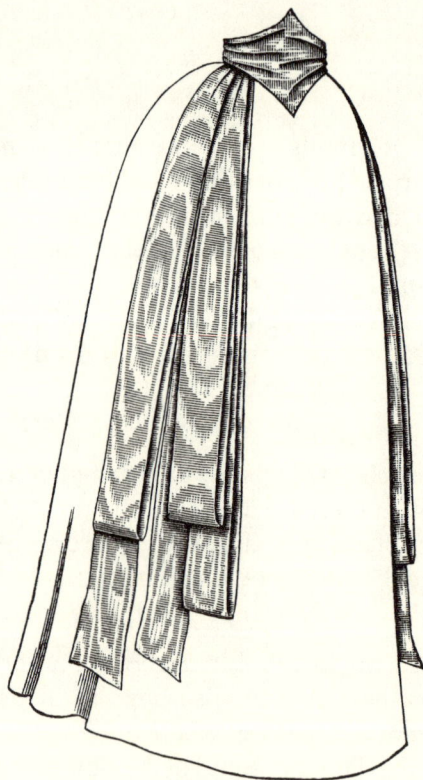

The style of girdle in Figure 2 is particularly adapted to a round bodice. A broad ribbon laid in many folds covers it, and the closing is invisibly made. A whalebone fastened securely at the center of the front and back holds it in place. From underneath the points at the front, fall loops and ends of ribbon narrower than the ribbon that covers the girdle proper. Moiré, grosgrain, or satin ribbon may be used.

November 1888 *Delineator*

Figure 2. Ribbon girdle

Figure 1. Directoire ribbon girdle

For the girdle in Figure 3, one end of the ribbon is inserted in the under-arm seam on each side of the bodice just above the waist-line. The ribbons are carried forward and knotted a little to one side of the center to fall in two long loops and two longer ends, which are deeply fringed.

November 1888 *Delineator*

Other Accessories

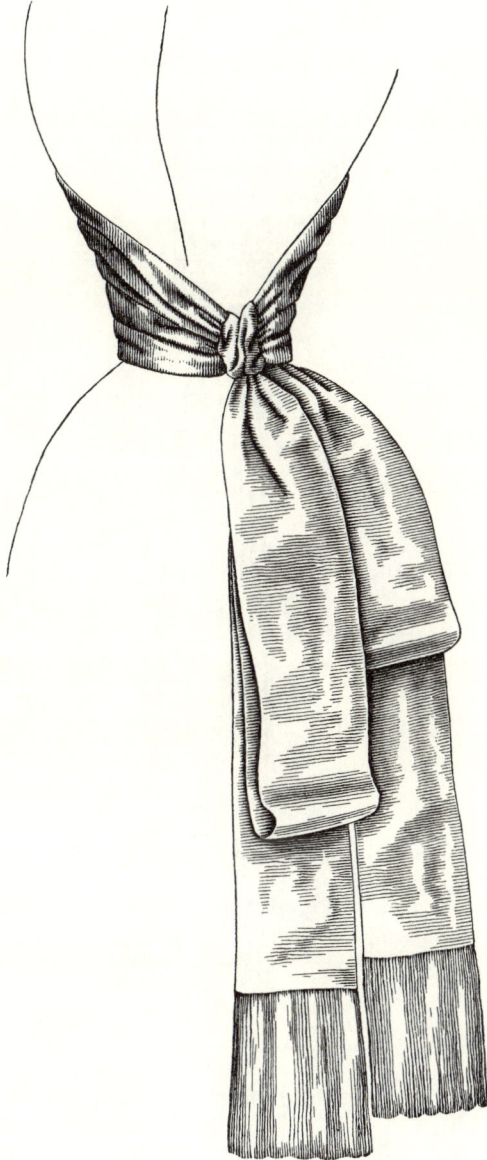

The popularity of the blouse, Spencer bodice, and skirtless bodice has created a demand for novelties in girdles and belts. The figure on the left of Figure 4 shows a belt of red Russian leather with medallion-shaped sections arranged to overlap neatly on a plain foundation. The belt is closed with a large frosted buckle, with a riveted nickel link fastened on one side. Such belts are shown in cream, black, and brown. The buckles are of various kinds. Some are set with precious stones. Others display oxidized, burnished, and hammered surfaces, while one shows the initials of the wearer.

The belt in the center is of sandalwood brown leather. It is slashed at regular intervals along the upper and lower edge to admit a 1-inch-wide strap of seal brown. Oval buckles secure the straps in place. A link of nickel is hung as shown, from which may be suspended the watch or *ammonière* of the lady.

The belt on the right is made of russet leather. It comprises four 1-inch-wide sections, which are stayed at intervals by diamond-shaped pieces of leather the depth of the belt. Its ends are fastened with a long nickel buckle. A pendant link of nickel is riveted on the left side for the attachment of the chatelaine, etc.

February 1889 *Delineator*

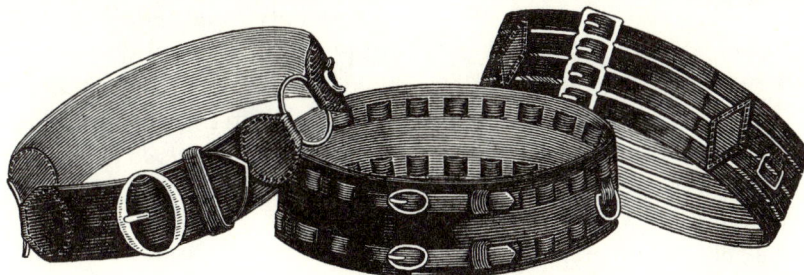

Figure 3. Ribbon girdle

Figure 4. Three belts

The ends of the black surah sash in Figure 5 are trimmed with fancy black silk fringe. The sash is draped about the waist and arranged in loops and ends at the back.

October 1889 *Delineator*

Figure 5. Black surah Fauntleroy sash

The ends of the white surah sash in Figure 6 are trimmed with white silk fringe having a fancy heading. The sash encircles the waist and is then brought to the front, its ends falling on the skirt on the left side of the center from a loose knot.

October 1889 *Delineator*

Figure 6. White surah Fauntleroy sash

The apron on the upper left of Figure 7 has a scalloped edge, and is embroidered with braid, the design being deepest at the lower corners. The ties are deeply hemmed. The cambric apron on the upper right is deeply hemmed, a wide tuck being laid above the hem. A band of wide lace insertion is added above the tuck, and another tuck is made just above the lace.

Figure 7. Six fancy aprons

In the second row, the India muslin apron on the left is edged with a band of wide Swiss embroidery. Above the hem are made five tucks, the center one being the deepest. The center apron is made of cambric and has two deep tucks above a wide hem. The apron on the right is made of lace-striped nainsook, with no additional trimming.

The lowest apron is made from printed cambric designed for the purpose, with no other decoration. Aprons whose edge finish consists simply of a hem may be trimmed with lace or narrow embroidered edging.

December 1889 *Delineator*

A. Apportioning Scales and Scroll

The National Garment Cutter system includes 45 scales, 44 of which are provided here. If you require a larger size, use the scale that corresponds to half that size and mark off twice as many units for each measure. For example, if you need a 46 scale, use scale 23; and where the diagram says to mark off 10 units, mark off 20. If you are drafting garments for dolls and need a smaller scale than is provided, use the scale that corresponds to twice the desired size and mark off half as many units. Before drafting, it is best to photocopy the pattern, determine the new measures with a pocket calculator, and write them on the pattern.

Only 10 units have been provided for each scale, as on the originals (plus a little extra length to facilitate pasting). These scales are too short to draw some pattern lines, and the page size did not allow them to be lengthened. In fact, most scales had to be divided in half. (And scale 45 was too long to fit on a page even when divided in half.) However, a scale long enough to draw any line can be created by photocopying.

First figure out which scale(s) you need to enlarge the desired pattern (see Chapter 1). Then find the longest line to be drawn with each scale. The number of units the line requires is indicated on the end farthest from the base-line. You need to lengthen the scale to at least that many units.

The scales read top to bottom for vertical lines and right to left for horizontal ones, due to the placement of the pattern base-lines. If a scale was not divided into halves, copy it as many times as required. Cut out the copies. Lay the first segment of the scale vertically on the table with the identifying tab at the top. On the second segment, fold under (or cut off) the tab at the heavy line under the label. Align this line with the line indicating the "10" unit on the first segment, covering the "1" of the "10." Tape or paste in place. Use a pen to rewrite the covered "1," or change it to "2" to indicate 20 units. Paste any additional segments in the same way.

If the scale was divided, make one copy of each half. Paste the 6–10 segment to the 1–5 segment. Copy and paste this 10-unit scale as described above.

The scales may then be pasted to cardboard or inexpensive yardsticks, cut out (if cardboard), and used for drafting. Or they may be used for measurement only, and lines drawn with a yardstick.

The National Garment Cutter scroll had to be divided into three sections to accommodate the book pages. The sections are laid out vertically in the order of assembly. Photocopy the relevant pages, and carefully cut out each section. Fold under the tab of the top section at the dashed line marked "A." Align this with line "A" on the center section, and tape or paste the sections together. Likewise attach the bottom of the center section to the bottom section, at the dashed line marked "B." Then paste the entire scroll onto light-weight cardboard, let it dry, and carefully cut out the scroll. You may find an X-Acto knife helpful.

Note: In 1998, Lavolta Press published *The Voice of Fashion: 79 Turn-of-the-Century Patterns with Instructions and Fashion Plates.* That book contains patterns from 1900 through 1906 issues of *The Voice of Fashion.* They are designed to be drafted with William H. Goldsberry's Diamond Cutting System. At the time no National Garment Cutter scales were available for examination, but the introduction theorized that the National Garment Cutter and the Diamond Cutting System were one and the same. The patent descriptions agree, the method of use is identical, and a few patterns were repeated in publications for both systems with no change in their measures.

When some National Garment Cutter scales became available, it became apparent that the two systems are slightly different. The National Garment Cutter and the Diamond Cutting System each have a base scale, where 1 unit equals 1 inch. All of the other scales are calculated from that base. In 1895, the firm, at that time Goldsberry & Doran, changed their scales so that the unit corresponding to 1 inch was assigned to the 30 scale instead of the 29, which required small changes to all of the other scales. They also redesigned the visual appearance of the scales, began to use the new units for the patterns in *The Voice of Fashion,* and announced that their patterns now required the Diamond Cutting System.

All of this may have convinced prospective customers that the system had somehow been technically improved or updated. Existing National Garment Cutter customers who continued to use their old scales, would have discovered that the patterns in their new issues of *The Voice of Fashion* did not fit as well. This may have persuaded customers to upgrade to the Diamond Cutting System.

Frances Grimble

18 in.
46 cm

1
2
3
4
5
6
7
8
9
10

19 in.
48 cm

1
2
3
4
5
6
7
8
9
10

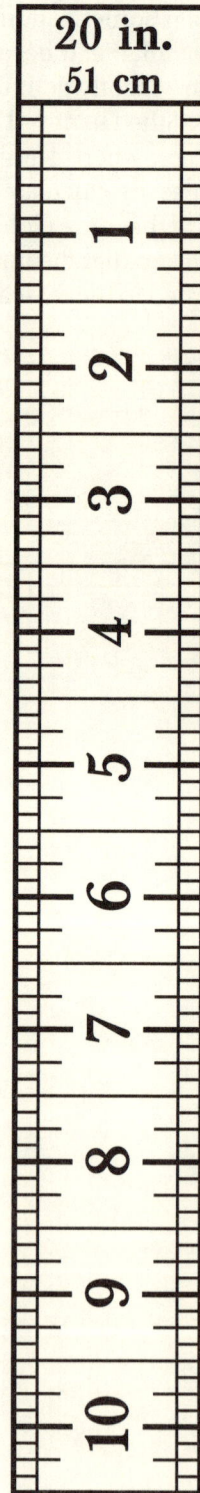

20 in.
51 cm

1
2
3
4
5
6
7
8
9
10

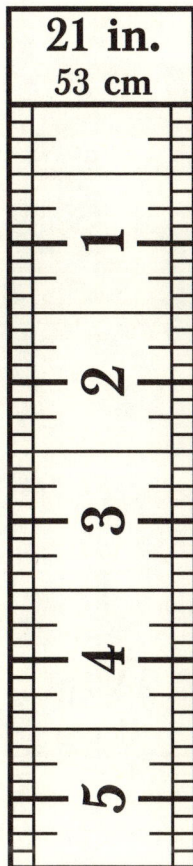

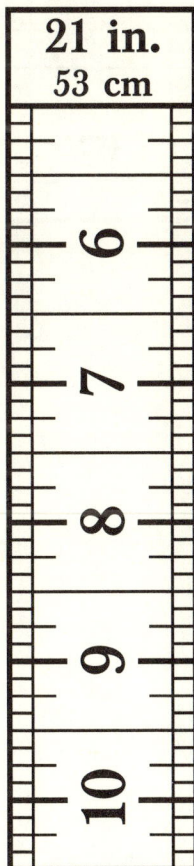

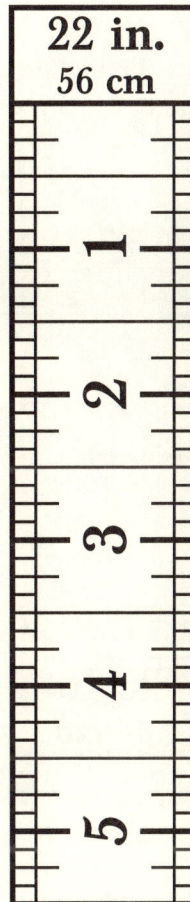

23 in.
58 cm

1 2 3 4 5

24 in.
61 cm

1 2 3 4 5

23 in.
58 cm

6 7 8 9 10

24 in.
61 cm

6 7 8 9 10

25 in.
63 cm

1 2 3 4 5

25 in.
63 cm

6 7 8 9 10

26 in.
66 cm

1 2 3 4 5

26 in.
66 cm

6 7 8 9 10

Apportioning Scales

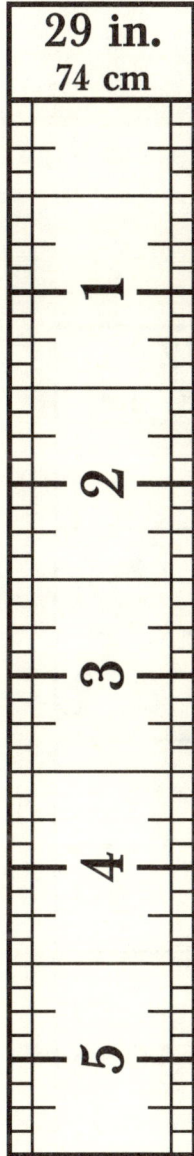

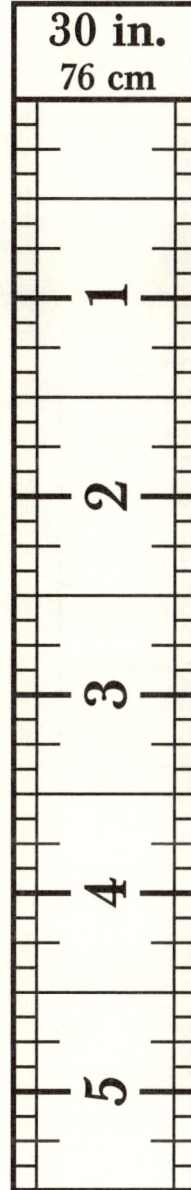

29 in.
74 cm

1 2 3 4 5

29 in.
74 cm

6 7 8 9 10

30 in.
76 cm

1 2 3 4 5

30 in.
76 cm

6 7 8 9 10

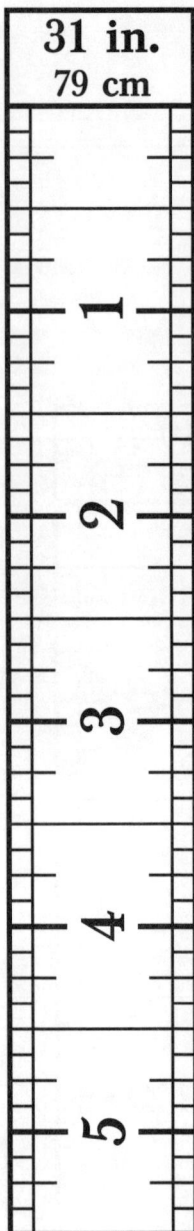

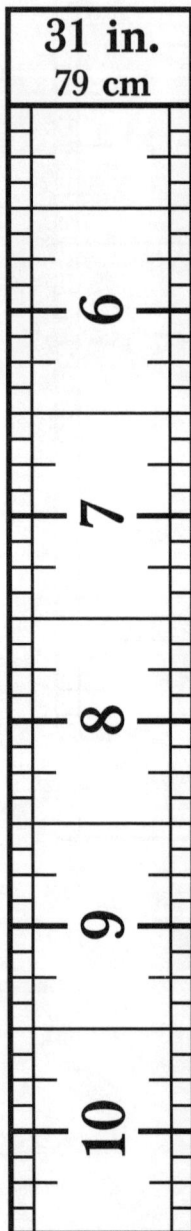

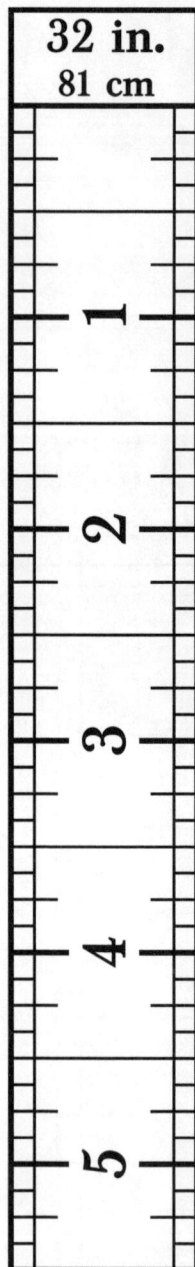

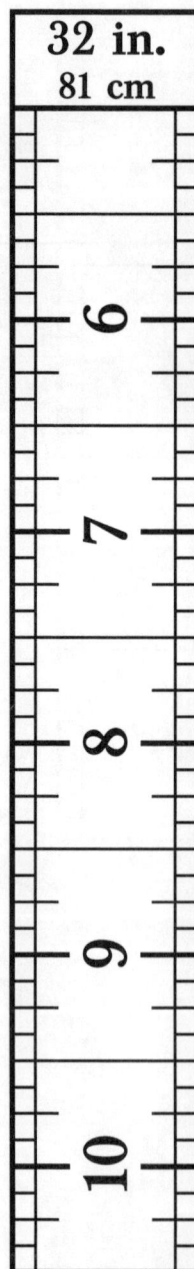

534

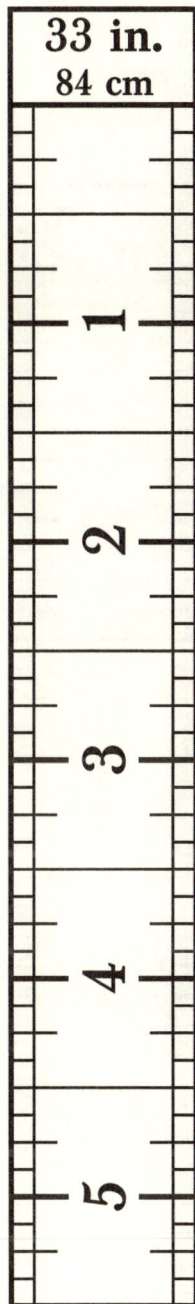

33 in.
84 cm

1
2
3
4
5

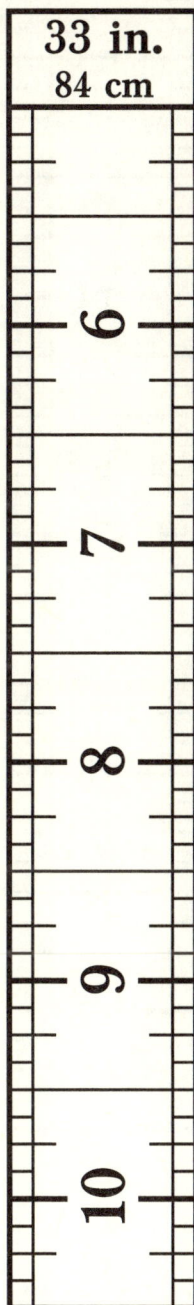

33 in.
84 cm

6
7
8
9
10

34 in.
86 cm

1
2
3
4
5

34 in.
86 cm

6
7
8
9
10

535

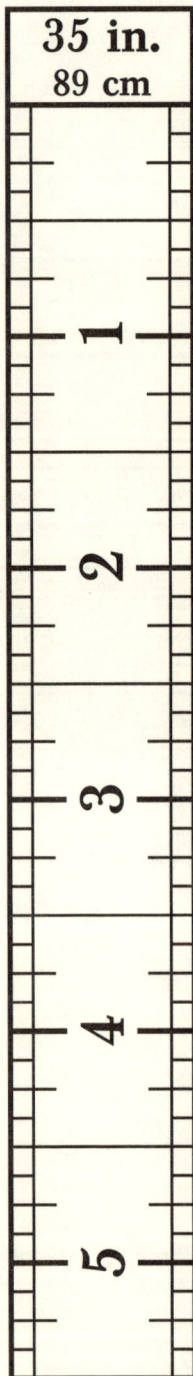

35 in.
89 cm

1
2
3
4
5

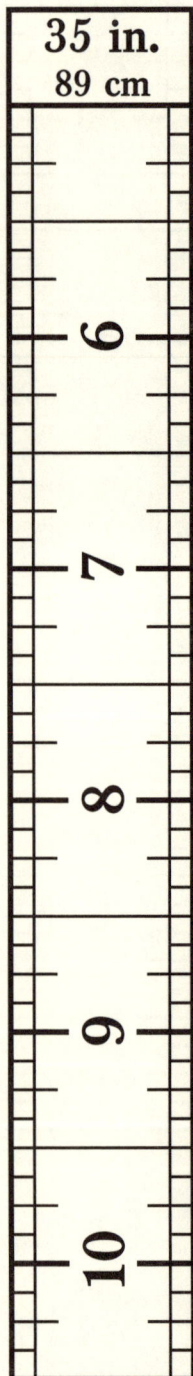

35 in.
89 cm

6
7
8
9
10

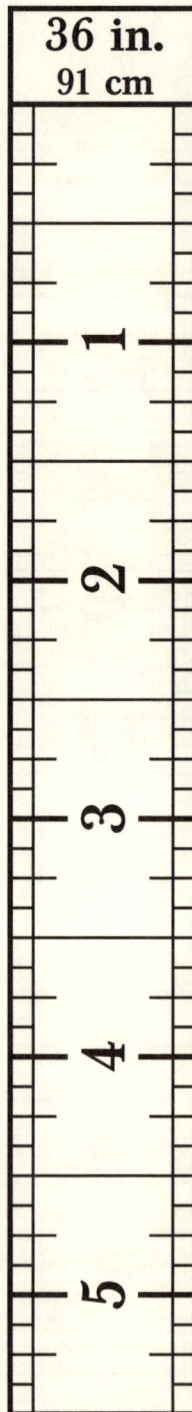

36 in.
91 cm

1
2
3
4
5

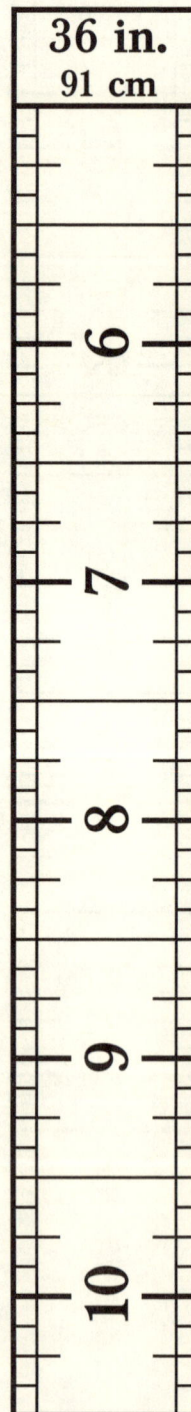

36 in.
91 cm

6
7
8
9
10

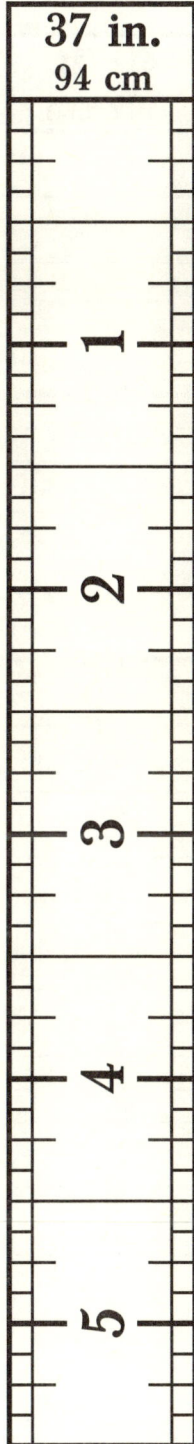

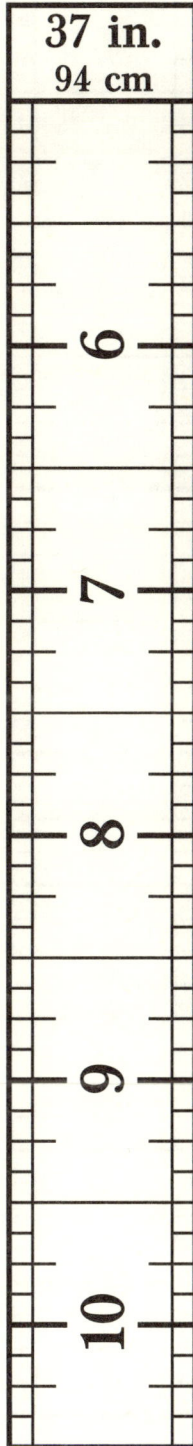

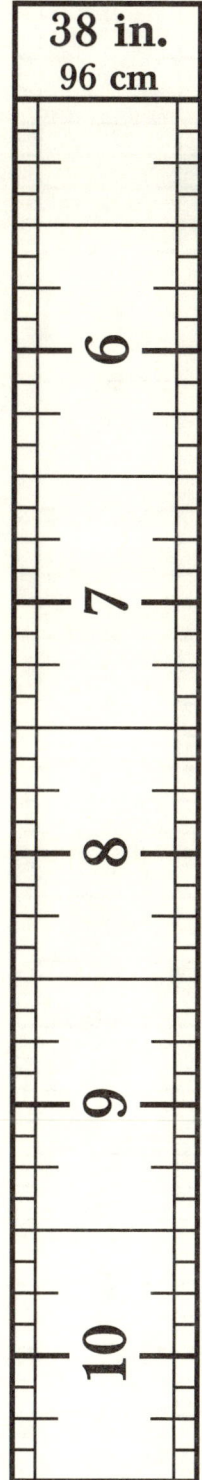

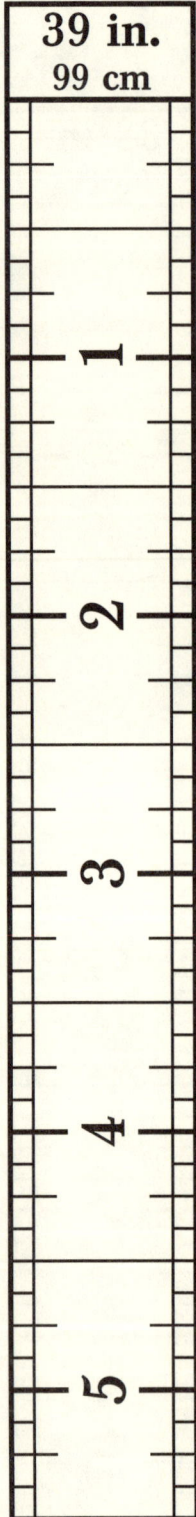

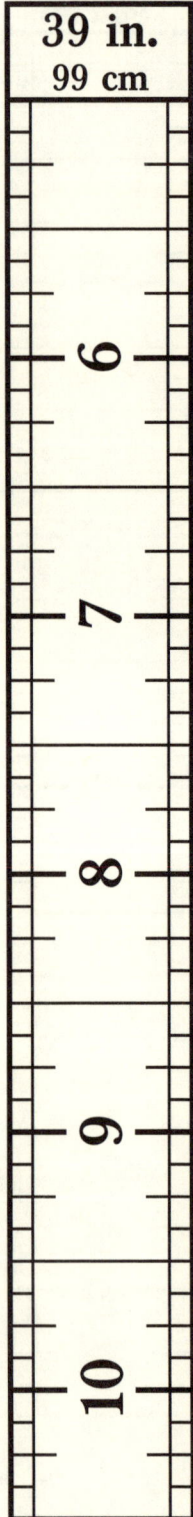

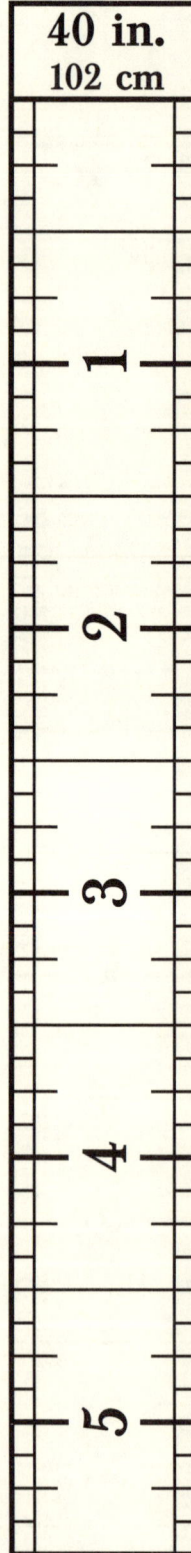

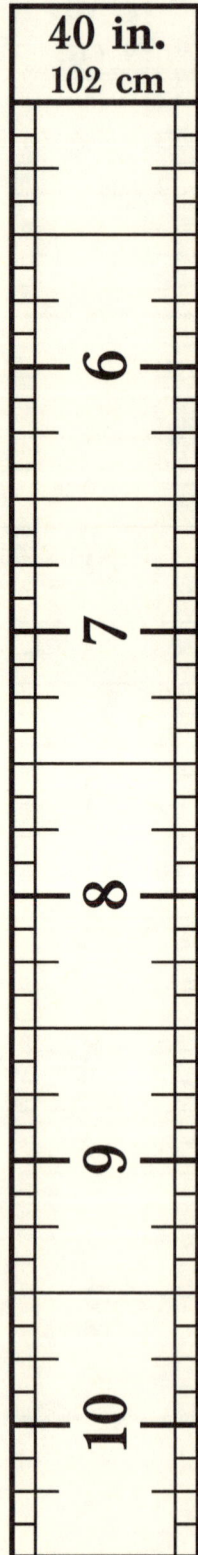

39 in.
99 cm

1
2
3
4
5

39 in.
99 cm

6
7
8
9
10

40 in.
102 cm

1
2
3
4
5

40 in.
102 cm

6
7
8
9
10

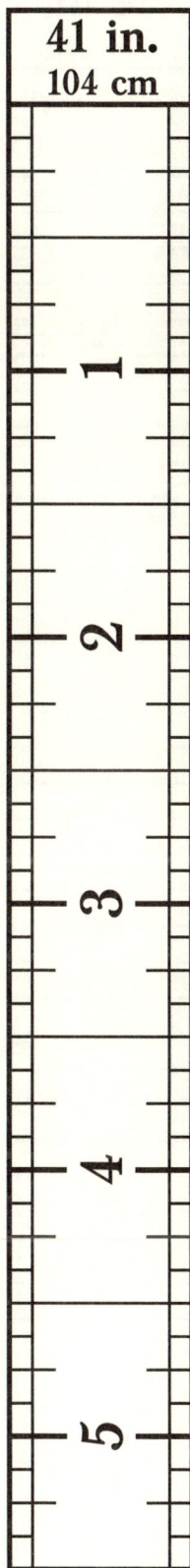

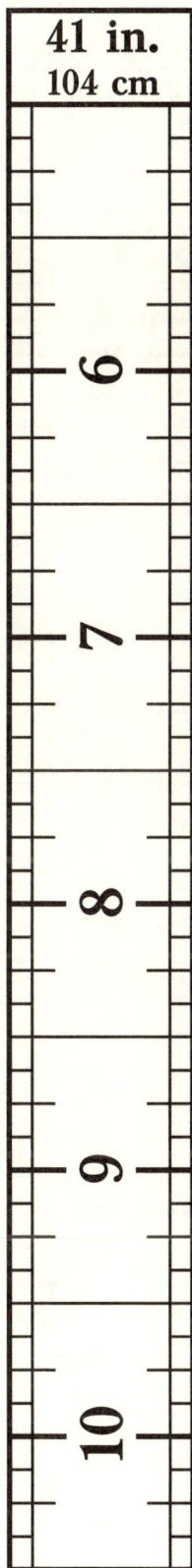

41 in. 104 cm	41 in. 104 cm	42 in. 107 cm	42 in. 107 cm
1	6	1	6
2	7	2	7
3	8	3	8
4	9	4	9
5	10	5	10

43 in.
112 cm

43 in.
112 cm

43 in.
112 cm

44 in.
114 cm

44 in.
114 cm

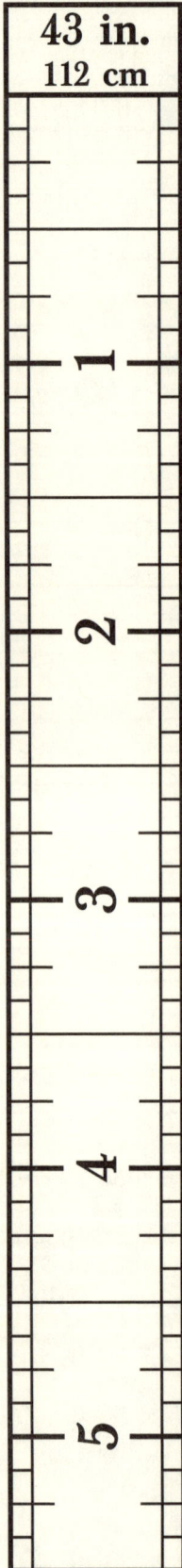
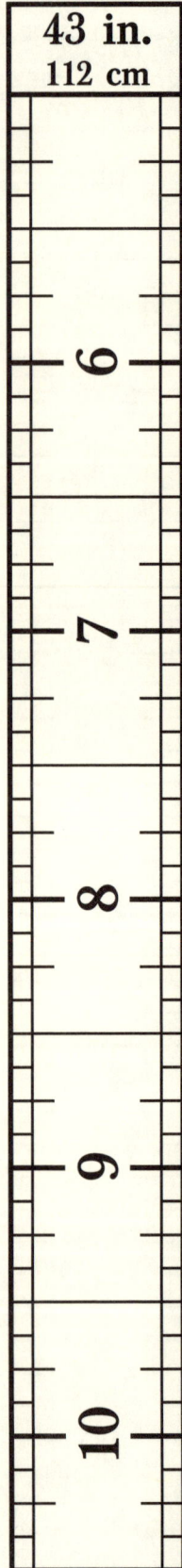
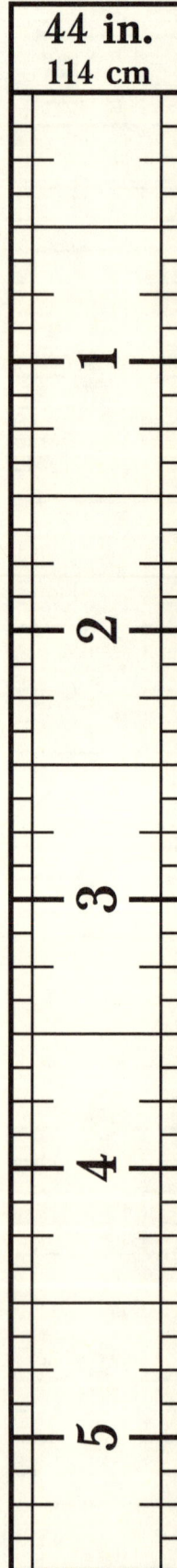
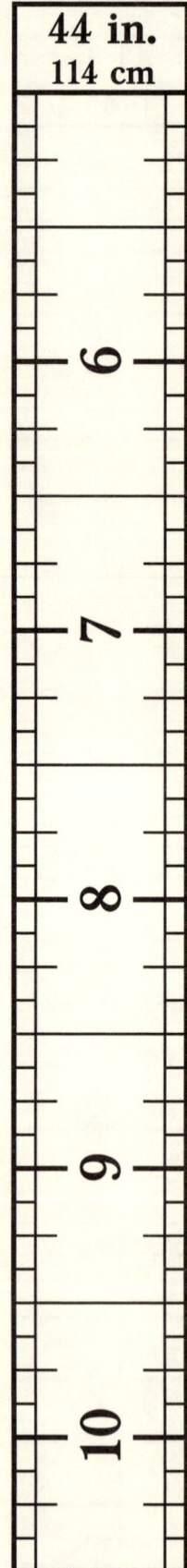

Scroll

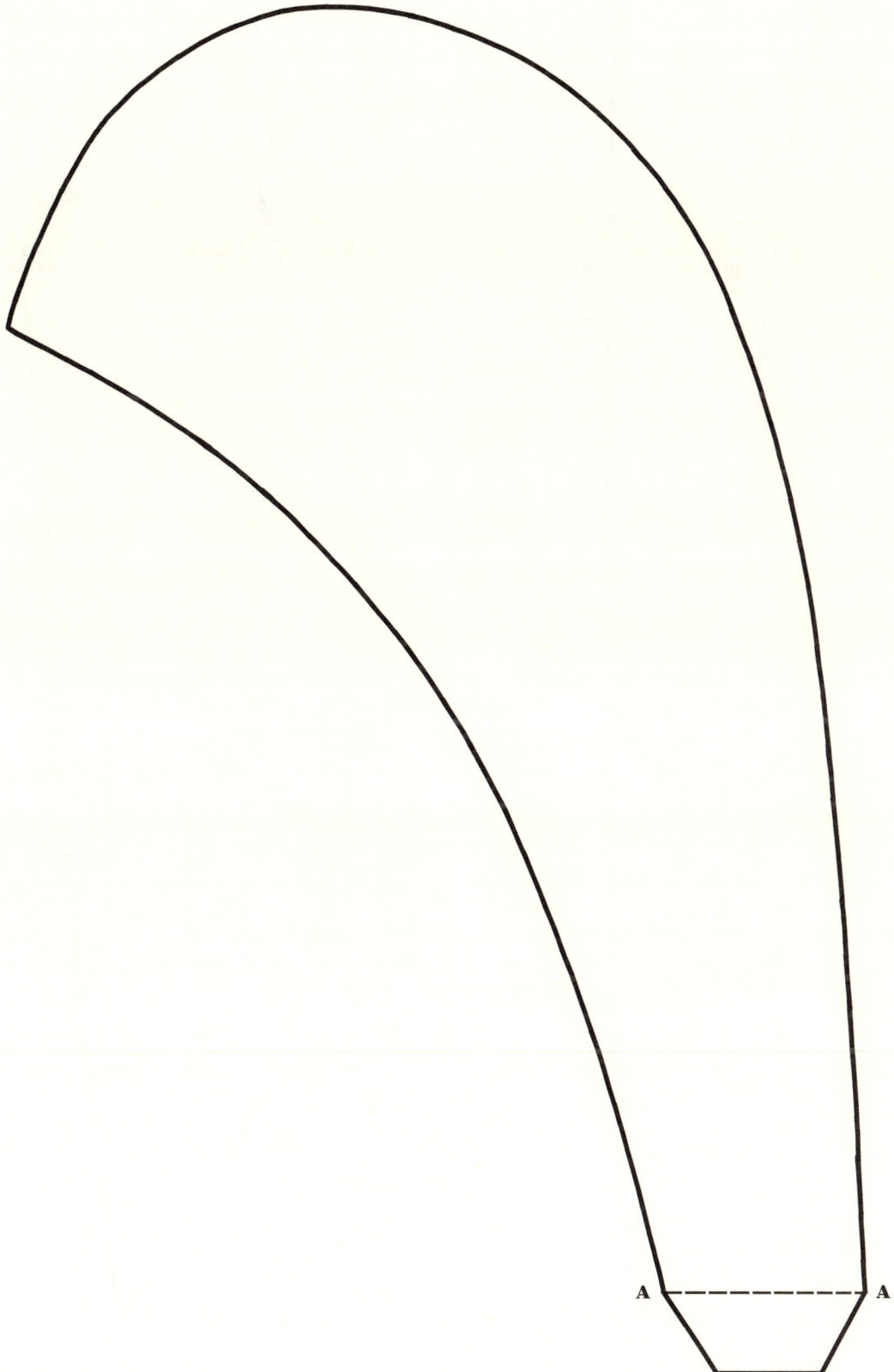

A - - - - - - - - A

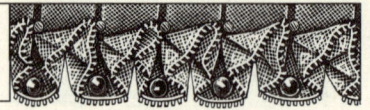
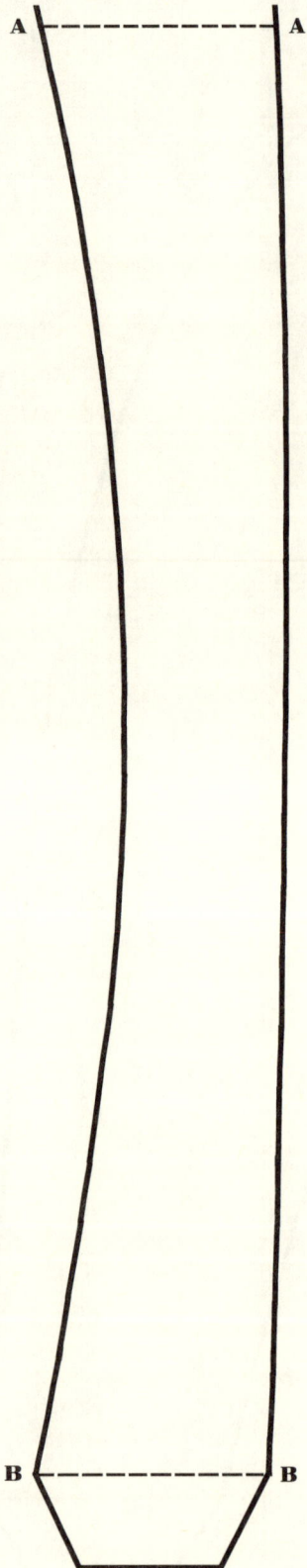

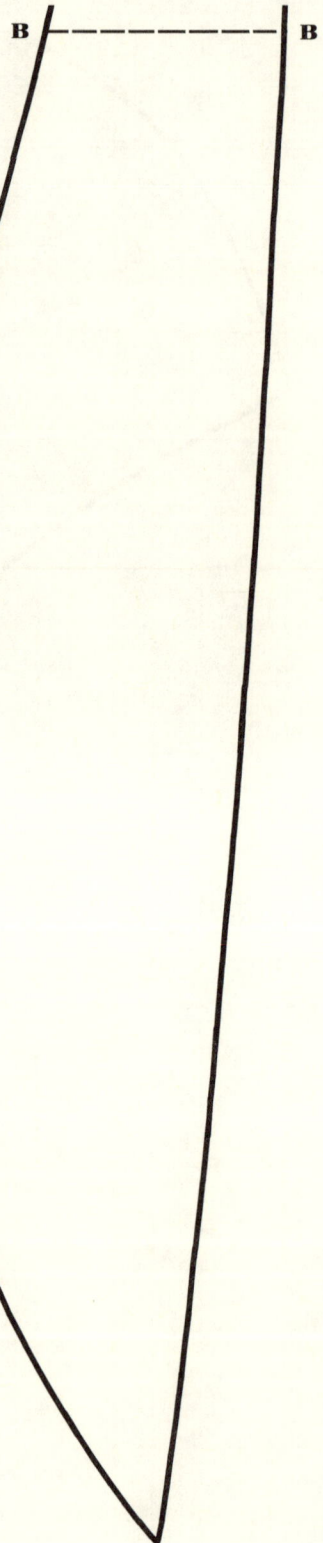

B. Metric Conversion Table

Although apportioning scale units are independent of the English and metric systems, many sewing instructions in this book use the English system, which is still common in the United States.

This table is provided for the convenience of readers who reside in other countries. Numbers running to several decimal places and (most) fractions under 1/16 inch have been rounded for easy use.

English Measurement	Metric Equivalent	Metric Measurement	English Equivalent
1/8 in.	3.2 mm	1 mm	1/32 in.
1/4 in.	6.4 mm	2 mm	1/16 in.
3/8 in.	9.5 mm	3 mm	1/8 in.
1/2 in.	1.3 cm	4 mm	5/32 in.
5/8 in.	1.6 cm	5 mm	7/32 in.
3/4 in.	1.9 cm	6 mm	1/4 in.
7/8 in.	2.2 cm	7 mm	9/32 in.
1 in.	2.5 cm	8 mm	5/16 in.
1 1/4 in.	3.2 cm	9 mm	11/32 in.
1 1/2 in.	3.8 cm	10 mm (1 cm)	13/32 in.
1 3/4 in.	4.4 cm	2 cm	3/4 in.
2 in.	5.1 cm	3 cm	1 3/16 in.
2 1/4 in.	5.7 cm	4 cm	1 9/16 in.
2 1/2 in.	6.4 cm	5 cm	2 in.
2 3/4 in.	7.0 cm	6 cm	2 3/8 in.
3 in.	7.6 cm	7 cm	2 3/4 in.
3 1/4 in.	8.3 cm	8 cm	3 1/8 in.
3 1/2 in.	8.9 cm	9 cm	3 1/2 in.
3 3/4 in.	9.5 cm	10 cm	3 15/16 in.
4 in.	10.2 cm	15 cm	5 7/8 in.
4 1/2 in.	11.4 cm	20 cm	7 7/8 in.
5 in.	12.7 cm	25 cm	9 13/16 in.
5 1/2 in.	14.0 cm	30 cm	11 13/16 in.

Metric Conversion Table

English Measurement	Metric Equivalent	Metric Measurement	English Equivalent
6 in.	15.2 cm	35 cm	13 3/4 in.
6 1/2 in.	16.5 cm	40 cm	15 3/4 in.
7 in.	17.8 cm	45 cm	17 11/16 in.
7 1/2 in.	19.1 cm	50 cm	19 11/16 in.
8 in.	20.3 cm	55 cm	21 5/8 in.
8 1/2 in.	21.6 cm	60 cm	23 5/8 in.
9 in. (1/4 yd.)	22.9 cm	65 cm	25 9/16 in.
9 1/2 in.	24.1 cm	70 cm	27 9/16 in.
10 in.	25.4 cm	75 cm	29 1/2 in.
10 1/2 in.	26.7 cm	80 cm	31 1/2 in.
11 in.	27.9 cm	85 cm	33 7/16 in.
11 1/2 in.	29.2 cm	90 cm	35 7/16 in.
12 in. (1 ft.)	30.5 cm	95 cm	37 3/8 in.
1/2 yd. (18 in.)	45.7 cm	100 cm (1 m)	39 3/8 in.
3/4 yd. (27 in.)	68.6 cm	1.25 m	1 yd. 13 3/16 in.
1 yd. (36 in.)	91.4 cm	1.50 m	1 yd. 23 1/16 in.
1 1/4 yd.	1.14 m	1.75 m	1 yd. 32 7/8 in.
1 1/2 yd.	1.37 m	2.00 m	2 yd. 6 3/4 in.
1 3/4 yd.	1.60 m	2.50 m	2 yd. 26 7/16 in.
2 yd.	1.83 m	3.00 m	3 yd. 10 1/8 in.
2 1/2 yd.	2.29 m	3.50 m	3 yd. 29 13/16 in.
3 yd.	2.74 m	4.00 m	4 yd. 13 1/2 in.
3 1/2 yd.	3.20 m	4.50 m	4 yd. 33 3/16 in.
4 yd.	3.66 m	5.00 m	5 yd. 16 7/8 in.
4 1/2 yd.	4.11 m	5.50 m	6 yd. 9/16 in.
5 yd.	4.57 m	6.00 m	6 yd. 20 1/4 in.
5 1/2 yd.	5.03 m	6.50 m	7 yd. 3 7/8 in.
6 yd.	5.49 m	7.00 m	7 yd. 23 9/16 in.
6 1/2 yd.	5.94 m	7.50 m	8 yd. 7 1/4 in.
7 yd.	6.40 m	8.00 m	8 yd. 26 15/16 in.
7 1/2 yd.	6.86 m	8.50 m	9 yd. 10 5/8 in.
8 yd.	7.32 m	9.00 m	9 yd. 30 5/16 in.

C. Glossary

Definitions of fashion and textile terms change over time. The information used to write these was drawn from late 19th-century sources wherever possible.

Absinthe: A light green with a bluish cast.

Accordion-plaiting: One plait laid on another by machinery, steamed and dried so as to retain this position.

Aigrette: An upright tuft of feathers, or an ornament of similar shape, used to decorate a head-dress, hat, or bonnet.

Albatross cloth: A soft, untwilled, wool dress material.

Alençon lace: A needle lace with a thick cordonnet, or outer edge, around each design, which renders the lace firm, durable, and heavy.

All-over: Embroidered or lace material in which the design or pattern extends over the entire surface.

Alpaca: Made from the wool of the llama, mixed with silk or cotton, producing a thin and durable material. What are mostly sold as alpacas now are really a fine make of Orleans cloth, which is a mixture of wool and cotton, dyed in all colors.

Ammonière: Probably a container for smelling salts.

Angel sleeve: A long sleeve flowing from the shoulder, with an open wrist.

Apple green: A light green with some yellow.

Appliqué: Lace, embroidery, or material that is sewed onto another material. The appliqué may be a piece, or a design of leaves, figures, etc.

Arabesque: A scroll effect or design, which may be made with cords, stitching, or applied pieces outlined.

Arab trimming: Possibly Arabian embroidery, or a machine-woven imitation. Arabian embroidery has elaborate geometrical designs in bright colors. It sometimes includes gold and silver thread.

Armure: A silk material, which may be plain, striped, ribbed, or with a small design. Sometimes armure is made of wool and silk.

Arrow-head: One of several kinds of triangular patterns worked in rather coarse silk or twist, to ornament and reinforce the tops of plaits, etc.

Astrakhan braid: Astrakhan braid has a rough surface somewhat similar to Astrakhan. It is made in all of the leading colors and in various widths.

Astrakhan cloth: A silk or worsted material with a long and closely curled pile.

Astrakhan fur: The pelts from young lambs reared in Astrakhan, dyed black.

Balayeuse: The frilling of material or lace that lines the extreme edge of a dress skirt to keep the train clean.

Barège: A kind of gauze, composed of silk and wool, or of wool only. Cheap kinds are made with a cotton warp.

Basket weave: A style of weaving that produces a pattern resembling the plaited work of a basket.

Basque: The end of a jacket or bodice falling below the waist, or a close-fitting bodice that extends below the waist.

Batiste: A fine linen or cotton muslin made in various colors. It is used for dresses, dress linings, and trimmings.

Batting: Raw cotton or wool prepared in thick, but lightly matted, lapped sheets.

Bayadère stripes: Stripes that run from selvage to selvage, giving a round appearance.

Beading: A woven or lace edging with openings through which to run a ribbon.

Bedford cord: A particular style of weave consisting of heavy ribs running lengthwise of the material.

Bell sleeve: A full sleeve that flares at the lower edge.

Belt: The waistband for a bodice, skirt, or overskirt, or else a separate belt worn outside the garment.

Bengaline: A corded silk of India make, slight in texture, and manufactured in all colors. Or else a French material made of silk and wool, similar to poplin, but with more silk in its composition and a much larger cord.

Biarritz cloth: An all-wool dress material, with a flat rep or cord.

Billiard cloth: A thick, stout material, made of fine merino spun on the wool principle and felted in the finishing.

Bison cloth: A substantial wool material.

Blouse: A loose-fitting dress bodice.

Border: Any trimming put on an edge or above it, and used as a finish to a garment.

Button stand: An allowance or addition to the left front of a garment, for sewing on buttons.

Bouclé: A wool material whose surface is raised in little tufts at regular intervals or in patterns; a rough material.

Bourette: A material on which rough threads or knots appear as straight or broken stripes.

Brandenburg: A military ornament of braid and loops with which a jacket or bodice is fastened, or appears to be fastened.

Breadth: The full width of the material, or else the straight piece forming the back of a skirt.

Bretelles: Ornamental shoulder straps.

Breton lace: An embroidered net. It may be worked in colored silks or floss, and the foundation made of colored net. Or it may be fabricated of Brussels net and cream lace thread.

Brilliantine: A dress material composed of mohair or goat's wool. Brilliantines are silky looking, durable, light, and to be had in all colors.

Broadcloth: The stoutest and best kind of wool cloth. It has a slightly napped face and a twilled back.

Brocade: A material, woven of any fiber, with a pattern of raised figures.

Broché: Any style of weaving ornamented with threads that form a pattern on the surface in imitation of stitching.

Brussels net: A linen or silk net sold by the yard for evening dresses and other articles of wear.

Buckram: A coarse linen or cotton material, stiffened with glue. It is used as an interlining and for making bonnet shapes. It is made in both white and black.

Bullion fringe: A heavy, twisted cord fringe, having intermixed fine gold or silver threads.

Butterfly bow: A bow with the loop and end on each side spread apart like butterfly wings.

Byron collar: A turn-down collar, the fronts of which are not creased, but broadly and softly rolled.

Calico: A cotton material, which varies from coarse material to the finest muslin, and from the richest printed chintz to plain white.

Cambric: A beautiful and delicate linen material. There is also a cheap cotton cambric manufactured for dress linings.

Camel's hair cloth: This material is thick, warm, light, and has a fine gloss. It is unshaved, and the long hairs are of a paler color than the close substance of the cloth. Camel's hair is often mixed with wool or cotton.

Canton flannel: A cotton material napped heavily on one side, used chiefly for under-garments.

Canvas: A plain-woven cotton or linen, used for tailoring.

Canvas cloth: A plain, open-weave wool material, or else a plain-woven cotton made of hard-spun thread.

Capote: A small, close-fitting bonnet.

Capuchin: A small hood, which may be attached to or separate from a cape, jacket, etc.

Cardinal: A deep rich red, somewhat less vivid than scarlet.

Carriage wear: Garments suitable for public display when driving about in a carriage.

Cascade: A fall of lace; usually used for a lace that is made to flow, with zig-zag bends, like a river.

Cashmere: A soft, twilled material, made of the wool of the Thibet goat, mixed with

sheep's wool. Other varieties are made entirely of sheep's wool, or of Angora rabbit fur.

Cashmere colors: A mixture of the colors used in cashmere shawls.

Challis: An extremely light-weight dress material of cotton and wool, woven without twill; soft and free from dressing.

Chambray: A plain-woven gingham, of one color and without any pattern. It is made of extra-fine cotton thread and stiffly sized with starch.

Chamois leather: The skin of the Alpine goat of that name.

Changeable, or shot: A material may be made to change in color according to the different positions in which it is viewed. This is effected by using a weft of a different color than the warp.

Chantilly lace: A delicate bobbin lace made in both silk and cotton, and in both black and cream.

Chemisette: An article used for covering the neck, made of some light material such as lace or cambric, usually worn under a low-cut bodice.

Chenille: A kind of cord used for embroidery and decorative purposes. The name means "caterpillar" in French, and denotes the hairy appearance of the material. Chenille is made of silk, of silk and wool, and of wool only.

Cheviot cloth: A rough cloth, twilled, and coarser than homespun.

China silks: A term applied to the plain silks woven in China, on a primitive hand loom. The warp and weft are identical in size and color, producing a natural luster. Some of the threads being heavier than others, a somewhat irregular surface is produced.

Choker collar: A close, straight, standing collar.

Chou: A large, soft, cabbage-shaped rosette, made of ribbon, material, or lace.

Chuddah: A light camel's hair material.

Claret: A dark, purplish red.

Cloakings: Heavy materials used for making cloaks.

Cloth: A wool material of several descriptions. Also a generic term applied equally to linen and cotton.

Cloth of gold: A material woven entirely or partly of gold-colored threads.

Coatings: Materials used to make coats.

Coat sleeve: A two-piece sleeve that comprises an under-arm and an upper piece. Used for dresses and other garments as well as coats.

Coquille: Material arranged in a shell-like design.

Corded silk: A silk with a rib or cord forming the predominating characteristic of the material.

Corduroy: A heavy, durable, cotton material. It is woven with a twill foundation and a pile surface, and is corded or ribbed on the surface. There is a very superior kind made especially for ladies' jackets and for the trimmings of warm cloth dresses, which has a very broad rib and a high pile, and is soft and pliable.

Corkscrew cloth: A warp-faced material, woven in fancied resemblance to a corkscrew. The best grades have a French thread worsted warp, while the weft may be of cotton or wool.

Crêpe: A thin, semi-transparent material made of silk or cotton, finely crinkled or crisped, either irregularly or in long parallel ridges. It is made in black, white, and colors. Mourning or "hard" crêpes are woven of hand-spun silk thread in its natural condition.

Cresson: A medium yellowish green.

Crinoline: A stiff material woven of horsehair and linen, or of cotton. It is used as a cheap material for stiffening ladies' dresses, linings, and the like, after the manner of buckram.

Crocheted button: A button mold covered with fine tight crochet.

Crow's foot: A three-pointed silk embroidery stitch, often put at the tops of plaits and the like for ornament and reinforcement.

Cuff-facing: An outside facing at the wrist of a sleeve, in contrasting material, that imitates a simple or fancy cuff.

Darned net: A lace with designs worked on a net ground with a needle handled as if in darning. It may be worked with fine lace thread, with

colored purse silks, or with floss and filoselles, upon white, colored, or black net.

Delaine: A plain-woven, muslin-like dress material, made of wool, cotton, or mixed materials.

Demi-train: A short train.

Diagonal material: A worsted twilled so that the diagonal ridges are somewhat prominent and noticeable.

Directoire styles: Imitations of the styles of the French Directory, from 1795 to 1799.

Dog-collar: A wide necklace worn about the throat.

Dolman: A style of ladies' wrap, in various lengths, and characterized by a hanging piece over the arm instead of a sleeve.

Dotted: A material ornamented with small dots.

Dove gray: A pinkish gray.

Down: The fine, soft covering of fowls under the feathers. The eider duck yields most of the down of commerce.

Drab: A dull brownish gray.

Drap d'été: A fine worsted material for summer wear.

Drawn-work: A kind of ornamental work done by cutting out, pulling out, or drawing to one side some threads of the material, while leaving others, or by drawing all into a new form, to produce fancy patterns.

Drilling: A stout twilled material of either cotton or linen, used for bodice linings, pockets, etc. Found in all colors.

Écru: Having the color of unbleached silk or linen, hence by extension any similar shade. Much lace is sold of this color, a hue that may be more accurately described as café au lait.

Egyptian lace: A knotted lace, often beaded.

Eider-down flannel: A thick, soft material with a knitted foundation and a surface of heavy wool, which is brushed to a thick, heavy nap. Available in many colors, and in fancy squares and stripes.

Epaulette: A shoulder ornament or trimming.

Étamine: A coarse wool or cotton bunting or canvas, with fluffy threads, and more or less transparent. It is used as a dress material,

and is usually intended to be worn over a contrasting color.

Eton jacket: A short jacket with lapels.

Faille: A soft, ribbed dress silk distinguished by a prominent grain or cord extending from selvage to selvage. It has a slight gloss.

Faille Française: A silk faille made in France. It is similar to grosgrain, but softer and brighter.

Farmer's satin: A glossy material in satin weave, with a cotton warp and a wool weft. Used for linings.

Fawn: A rather light yellowish brown.

Feather-edged ribbon: Having an ornamental edging composed of picots or tufts.

Fedora lace: An imitation Mechlin lace. Mechlin is a light bobbin lace with a pattern of flowers, buds, etc., outlined by a fine but very distinct thread or cord.

Festoon outline: An outline with open loops or curves.

Fichu: A small covering of silk, muslin, lace, or tulle, for the neck or shoulders.

Figured material: A material ornamented with woven, printed, or another kind of patterns or designs.

Finger: A measure of length, comprising 4 1/2 inches, and much used by needlewomen.

Fisher's net: A coarse, open-mesh material.

Flannel: A loose-woven wool, cotton-and-wool, or silk-and-wool material. The nap may be raised on one or both sides. It may be white, colored, striped, or checked.

Flannelette: A soft, loose-woven cotton material, with a short nap raised on both sides, which gives the appearance of flannel. It may be white, self-colored, or woven in stripes or checks.

Fleur de pêche: A delicate violet-gray.

Floss silk: A soft, fluffy, untwisted embroidery silk.

Fly: A strip of material sewed under the edge of a dress or coat, at the button side of the opening, extending sufficiently far beyond it to underline the buttonholes at their extreme ends. The fly thus conceals the clothing under the dress or coat.

Foot trimming: A short plaited or gathered ruffle sewed at the bottom of a skirt, to hold it out and to ornament it.

Foulard: A soft, thin, washable dress silk, woven without twill. It is usually printed in colors on black or white grounds. An imitation is also made of cotton, with a medium-soft finish, printed with mingled patterns.

Foulé: A general term applied to twilled materials with a rough face, the material being given considerable shrinking to increase the roughness.

Fraise: A ruff or frill.

French cambric: A very fine, silky, linen or cotton cambric.

French fell seam: What is now called a French seam.

French gray: A light greenish gray.

French lace: A rich and expensive lace. The foundation is of plain cotton illusion. The design, which is often very elaborate, is formed by chain-stitching in coarse cotton thread.

Frisé velvet: A velvet with a looped pile.

Frog: An ornament made of braid in a fancy pattern, which has a loop that fastens on the opposite button or olive. A pair of these ornaments is always used for each fastening.

Gainsborough hat: A large, plumed hat.

Galloon: Originally worsted lace, especially a close-woven lace like ribbon or tape for binding. In modern use a trimming similar to the above, of wool, silk, cotton, tinsel, or a combination of any of these.

Garnet: A subdued, yet warm shade of dark red.

Gauging: A series of close parallel lines of running stitches, which are all drawn up to make the material between them set full by gatherings.

Gauze: A very thin, transparent material made of silk, silk and cotton, silk and linen, or linen. It is either plain, or brocaded in patterns with silk.

Genoese point lace: A rather heavy guipure lace, usually made by the yard.

Gilet: A vest front for a bodice, often a removable accessory.

Gimp: An open-work trimming. It is made of silk, worsted, or cotton twist, having a cord or a wire running through it. The strands are plaited or twisted to form a pattern.

Gingham: A checked or striped material made of cotton or linen, the threads dyed in the yarn.

Girdle: A sash, cord, or belt worn around the waist.

Glacé: A shiny surface applied to silk materials and ribbons.

Gobelin blue: A subdued grayish blue.

Greek plait: A box-plait with about 2 inches of the outside cut away at the hem, and the under sides of the fold sloped to the point where they touch.

Grenadine: A dress material woven in small square meshes or open-work of coarse threads, very transparent. It is manufactured of cotton, silk, wool, and their intermixtures. It is made both plain and figured.

Grosgrain: A firm, close-woven, finely corded or grained dress silk, finished with but a slight luster.

Guimpe: A chemisette worn with a low or square-necked dress.

Guipure lace: This name is applied to all laces having large patterns and coarse, open grounds not filled with delicate work.

Gum Arabic: A water-soluble gum used for glue and to finish textiles.

Hair-line stripes: A color and weave effect in which fine lines, one or two threads wide, occur lengthwise or crosswise in the material.

Half-low neck: A neck-line below the throat, but higher than a full décolletage.

Hamburg: A cotton embroidery worked on cambric, used as an edging or trimming.

Heliotrope: A dull purple-brown.

Hem-stitching: An ornamental edging in linen and cotton materials, produced by drawing out a few threads parallel to the hem, and catching together in smaller groups those running the other way.

Henrietta cloth: A material woven entirely of wool, or with a silk warp and a worsted weft. It has

a twilled face and a plain back, and is like cashmere dress material in all other respects, except for being more lustrous.

Henri Quartre: Imitations of styles worn during the reign of Henry IV of France, from 1589 to 1610.

Hercules braid: A thick, corded, worsted braid, available in widths from 1/2 inch to 4 inches.

Herring-bone stitch: A kind of cross-stitch worked backwards, from left to right. It is often used to secure the raw edges of seams made in flannel.

Hollow: To cut in a concave shape.

Horsehair cloth: A loose, open material, woven with a herring-bone twill. The warp is composed of unbleached cotton, and the weft of horsehair. It is used for stiffening garments.

House-maid skirt: A full, round skirt made of straight breadths of material.

Hunter green: A dark yellowish green.

Illusion: A thin and very transparent silk tulle.

India lawn: A clear, white lawn, woven of very fine cotton threads.

India silks: India silks are classified as cultivated and wild. Among the cultivated are imported corah, mysore, nagpore, and rumchunder; and from the wild, tussah. The kincobs are satins decorated with designs in gold flowers and are employed for ladies' skirts. The mushroos have a silk surface and a cotton back, and are decorated with loom-embroidered flowers.

Insertion: Strips of lace, or embroidered muslin or cambric, with straight edges.

Invisible green: A dark bluish green.

Invisible stripes: Possibly stripes in two similar shades of one color.

Irish lawn: Pure linen lawn.

Irish linen: Irish linen is superior to that manufactured elsewhere in the evenness of the threads, the softness of the texture, and the gloss of the surface.

Irish point embroidery: A cutwork embroidery.

Japan silks: There are three kinds of dress silks, which vary in weight, and all of which may be had in a variety of light and dark colors.

These are the double warp grosgrain; the damassé Japanese, which has a rather small floral design closely covering the ground; and the plain silks.

Jardinière: Of many colors, resembling a flower garden.

Jersey: A close-fitting upper garment made of elastic wool or silk material.

Jet beads: Lustrous black glass beads.

Jetted lace: Black machine lace beaded with jet beads.

Kilt-plaiting: Flat single plaits placed closely side by side, so that the double edge of the plait on the upper side lies half over the preceding plait on the inside.

Lace net: A machine-made mesh.

Ladder-stitch: A cross-bar stitch in embroidery.

Lady's cloth: A class of fine, wide flannels slightly napped, used for ladies' light wraps and dresses.

Lapboard: A board held in the lap as a substitute for a table.

Lawn: A thin, open cambric, slightly sized with pure starch.

Leghorn straw: The straw of a kind of wheat grown in Tuscany, which is plaited and used for hats and bonnets.

Lincoln green: A medium olive green.

Lisse: A sheer, delicate, gauzy material, made of either silk or cotton. It is used for ladies' neckwear and ruchings. When crimped it is called crêpe lisse.

Lustring: A glossy silk material, neither figured nor corded.

Maltese lace: A heavy guipure bobbin lace, with simple geometrical patterns.

Marabou feathers: These are procured from a species of stork. They may be had white, gray, or dyed. They are employed as plumes for head-dresses and bonnets, and as trimmings for dresses, fans, and muffs.

Marguerite: Daisy.

Marquise lace: A black lace with the patterns bordered by a cord.

Marseilles: A stiff, corded cotton material.

Mastic: A light olive brown.

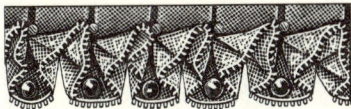

Matelassé: A silk or wool material with a raised figured or flowered design, having a quilted appearance. Those of silk are made in white and in colors, and are much used for opera cloaks.

Medici lace: A simple, rather heavy bobbin lace, similar to torchon, but with one scalloped edge.

Melton: A stout, smooth cloth used for ladies' coats. The nap is sheared close to the surface and is finished without pressing or glossing.

Merino: A thin wool twilled material.

Military collar: A narrow standing collar.

Milliner's fold: A strip of velvet, silk, or the like, folded near both edges, and then again so as to bring one of the original folds above the other.

Mode: A light brown.

Mohair: A material with a cotton or silk warp and a mohair weft. It is strong and defies dust, which makes it especially suitable for traveling. It is often printed with attractive floral designs.

Mohair braid: A black or colored braid, available in various widths.

Moiré: A wavy undulating effect produced on the surface of materials by wetting, crumpling, and great pressure.

Molière: Imitations of the styles of the time of Molière, from 1622 to 1673.

Mordoré: A mixture of crimson with a little brown.

Moss green: A medium yellow green.

Mother Hubbard: A wrapper or night-gown with a long, full skirt falling from a yoke.

Mucilage: An aqueous solution of gum or of substances allied to it, used as an adhesive.

Mull: An extremely soft, thin, and transparent muslin.

Muslin: A thin, plain-woven cotton material, bleached or unbleached. The fancy kinds include Arni muslin, an extremely fine muslin; book muslin, a thin, starchy muslin used for lining cheap dresses; corded muslin, with a thick cord; coteline muslin, a hair-line cord muslin printed in all patterns and colors; Decca muslin, a fine thin variety; figured muslin, with machine-woven figures imitating tamboured muslin; and tamboured muslin.

Nainsook: A fine, soft, bleached muslin, woven in small damasked checks and stripes, and used as a summer dress material.

Neapolitan straw: Horsehair.

Net: An open material of cotton, linen, hemp, silk, or another material, tied and woven with a mesh of any size. Cotton net is employed for stiff linings and foundations.

Nile green: A yellowish green.

Nun's veiling: A wide, untwilled wool dress material, very soft, fine, and thin. It is dyed black, white, and in colors.

Oatmeal cloth: A cotton, linen, or wool material having a corrugated face. Oatmeal cloths are thick, soft, and pliant, and may be had in all colors.

Oiled silk: Silk made waterproof by saturation in oil. It is semi-transparent. It is much used in dressmaking to prevent perspiration from passing through, at the under-arms of garments and as bonnet linings.

Old pink: A pinkish light brown.

Ombré: Shaded with various colors or different shades of the same color.

Open-work: A term used in embroidery, lace-making, crochet, and fancy work of every other kind. It means that the work is made with interstices between several portions of close work, or of cut and open material.

Organdy: A fine, white cotton material, woven plain, cross-barred, striped, and printed with figures.

Organ-pipe plaiting: Large, rounded plaits.

Oriental embroidery: All of the various kinds of embroidery produced in the East. Characterized by bold designs and costly materials.

Oriental lace: Machine embroidery on machine net with coarse, soft thread.

Ostrich tip: The tip of an ostrich feather.

Ottoman silk: A fine, soft, undressed silk dress material, woven in large cords, extending from selvage to selvage.

Panel: A piece of different material or color placed vertically on a dress skirt as an ornament, usually in front or on the side.

Pannier drapery: An over-skirt draped or looped at the sides.

Passementerie: Heavy embroidery or lace edgings and trimmings, especially those made of gimp and braid, or covered with beads, colored silk, metals, etc.

Pea green: A light yellowish green.

Pearl button: A button made of mother-of-pearl.

Peasant bodice: A low-necked bodice worn with a chemisette, and which laces or appears to lace in front.

Peau de soie: A silk dress material woven like grosgrain, but with very fine, close ribs.

Pekin: A trimming material, made in alternate stripes of satin and velvet, which vary in width from 1/2 to 2 inches.

Percale: A very closely and firmly woven cotton material. It is printed in fancy patterns on white and colored grounds.

Picot: A small loop used as an ornamental edging on ribbons and laces.

Pinking: A mode of decorating material by means of a sharp stamping instrument called a pinking iron. The edge of the material is cut in points, scallops, or other designs.

Piping: A bias fold, or corded bias fold, put on the edge of a band or garment as a finish.

Piqué: A washable cotton material, woven with a small pattern in relief, usually a lozenge, cord, or rib. It is usually rather stiff and thick. It may be white, or printed with small delicate patterns.

Pistache: A yellowish green.

Placket: The opening left in a skirt to allow the garment to be put on and off the person.

Plastron: A trimming for a dress front, of a different material.

Plomb: Lead gray.

Plush: A shaggy, hairy silk or cotton material. It is sometimes made of camel's or goat's hair. The pile is softer and longer than that of velvet, and resembles fur.

Point de Gene: A machine imitation of Genoese needle lace.

Point de Paris: A simple, narrow bobbin lace or machine imitation. Those made on the Levers machine have simple designs of flower heads or animals outlined with thick cordonnets.

Point d'esprit lace: Net or tulle with embroidered or woven dots.

Polonaise: An over-dress, worn either straight or looped up.

Pompadour lace: Lace in Pompadour colors; that is, a mixture of pink and blue, and sometimes other pastels.

Pompadour neck: A low, more or less square neckline.

Pompon: A fluffy ball of silk or wool, used for trimming.

Pongee: A thin, soft, washable silk material, woven from the natural, undyed raw silk.

Poplin: A kind of rep made of silk and wool or worsted, having a fine cord on the surface. It is produced brocaded, moiré, and plain.

Postilion: An extension of the back pieces of a basque or jacket, or extra tabs set on at the back.

Princess: A long, close-fitting dress with no waist seam.

Radzimir: A rich dress silk, in the weaving of which a weft thread is dropped at regular intervals, usually 1/16 to 1/4 inch apart. This produces a crosswise sunken line on both sides of the material. Between the sunken lines the weave is fine and close.

Redingote: A coat-dress worn over a skirt.

Renaissance lace: A heavy tape lace, also known as Battenberg. A popular kind of fancy work.

Rep: A material with thick crosswise cords, of silk, silk and wool, or wool only.

Reseda: A grayish to dark grayish green.

Revers: A part of the garment reversed, or turned back, such as a cuff, or a corner of a basque. May show a lining of a contrasting color or material.

Revers-facing: An applied facing, in contrasting material, that imitates a revers.

Glossary

Rhadames: A twilled material of all silk or part cotton, of strong texture and with a bright satin finish.

Roman stripes: Vivid horizontal stripes in different widths.

Rope shirring: A tuck is made in the material, a cord is threaded through it, and the material is drawn to position with the cord.

Rosary beads: Wooden beads, either carved and varnished of a natural color, or black and unvarnished. They are also to be had to match all shades in the material.

Rosette: A collection of bows of narrow ribbon, arranged to form a circle, and attached to a circular foundation of stiff, coarse muslin or buckram.

Round bodice: A bodice that is of even length all around, and usually ends at the waist or a little below it. It may be either full or close-fitting.

Royal armure: The weave of this silk material imitates medieval fish-scale armor, the surface edge always forming a small diamond or other angled figure. It is heavier than ordinary dress silk.

Royale: A plain-colored, ribbed dress silk, in which the ribs are not regular, but run into each other.

Ruching: A plaiting or shirring of net, lace, ribbon, or other light material into bands, which are worn in the necks and wrists of garments and used for trimmings.

Running: A line of running stitches, or of machine stitches.

Russet: A reddish brown.

Russian embroidery: Embroidery in simple and formal patterns, especially on wash materials.

Russian green: A rich dark green.

Sailor collar: A collar that is deep and square at the back, and has square ends in front.

Salmon: A pinkish yellow.

Sandalwood: A light yellowish brown.

Sappho pink: A light purplish red.

Sateen: A twilled cotton material of satin make, glossy, thick, and strong. It is employed for corsets, dresses, and boots. It may be procured in black and white, various colors, and figured in many color combinations.

Satin: A silk twill, very glossy on the face, and dull on the back. Some satins are figured and brocaded.

Satin merveilleux: A twilled satin material, of an exceedingly soft and pliable character, and having but little gloss.

Scarf: A band or strip of material.

Scrim: A soft and loose-woven cotton material, often of a fancy, lacey weave.

Seal plush: A heavy material with a pile of tussah silk, made in imitation of sealskin fur. It is dyed brown or golden color. It is designed for mantles, jackets, hats, and trimmings.

Seed pearl passementerie: Passementerie beaded with small mother-of-pearl or imitation pearl beads.

Seersucker: A washable cotton material, woven in stripes, usually blue and white or brown and white.

Serge: A loose-woven, very durable twilled material. It may be had in either silk or wool. Wool serge may be rough on one or both sides of the material, or smooth on both sides. Serge is dyed in every color, besides being sold in white and black.

Serpent: A pale bluish green.

Shell ruching: A trimming gathered and fulled in a shell-like design.

Shirring: Two or more lines of gathers having a space between.

Sicilienne: A fine poplin, made of silk and wool, and especially used for mantles.

Side-plaiting: Single plaits with the crease not pressed all the way down.

Silesia: A fine-twilled cotton, highly dressed and calendered, used for linings. It is piece dyed in all conceivable solid colors, and sometimes printed, although usually the patterns are woven.

Silk muslin: A thin and gauzy silk, either plain, printed in small patterns in color, or ornamented with raised woven figures.

Skirt braids: These are made of alpaca and mohair. They are cut into lengths of sufficient quantity for a dress, and tied up for sale in knots.

Skirtings: Materials used for skirts.

Slide: A tongueless buckle or ring used as a fastener.

Smocking: Accordion-plaiting caught together alternately in rows, making an elastic material.

Soutache braid: A very narrow silk braid, available in several widths, and having an open-work center. It is produced in many colors, and employed for embroidery and the braiding of dresses, mantles, etc.

Spanish flounce: A deep flounce that is graduated in depth.

Spanish guipure lace: A heavy lace with thick silk designs and cordonnets.

Spanish lace: Any lace made in Spain, or in imitation of a lace made in Spain. Includes a kind of darned net.

Split straw: Plaits of wheat or rye straws that were split before plaiting.

Sprig: An ornament or pattern in the form of a sprig, spray, or leaf.

Sprung out: Widened or flared.

Steel: A dark bluish gray.

Steels: Thin strips of steel or whalebone used to support a skirt or bone a corset.

Stud: A removable button, which is passed through eyelet holes.

Suède: A brownish tan color.

Suitings: Materials used for suits, or complete costumes.

Surah: A soft, fine-twilled silk or silk-and-wool mixture, employed for dresses.

Surplice effect: A bodice that overlaps diagonally in front.

Swiss embroidery: A kind of needle-work in white cotton on fine white linen or muslin. Often made by machine.

Swiss girdle: A belt or belt effect that is pointed at the top and bottom in front, and sometimes also the back.

Swiss muslin: A thin, transparent material, woven rather open, with simple patterns of dots, stripes, or sprigs.

Tabac: Tobacco brown.

Tablier: Part of a dress resembling an apron.

Taffeta: A thin, glossy silk, of a wavy luster. It is to be had in all colors, some plain, others striped, checked, or flowered.

Tamise: A fine, plain-woven wool dress material, the warp and weft of which are of the same size and woven in equal proportions.

Tam o'shanter: A cap with a headband and a large, flat crown.

Tape: A narrow, stout strip of woven cotton or linen, used for innumerable purposes.

Tarlatan: A thin, gauze-like cotton material, much stiffened, so open as to be transparent, and often of a rather coarse quality.

Tassel fringe: A fringe composed of separate bundles of threads or cords tied to a braiding or gimp.

Tennis flannel: A soft, loose-woven cotton flannelette, finished with a slight nap.

Tennis stripes: A light, twilled wool dress material with narrow colored stripes.

Terra-cotta: Reddish orange.

Thibet cloth: A material made of wool with a very slight nap and a rough, unfinished appearance. Or else one made of goat's hair, with a shaggy appearance.

Thread lace: Made of linen as distinguished from cotton and silk.

Tinsel: An ornamental material or cord overlaid with glittering metallic sparkles or threads.

Tissue: Any light, gauzy material, such as is used for veils.

Toilette: A dress or costume.

Toque: A small bonnet with a round, close-fitting crown and no brim.

Torchon lace: A simple bobbin lace with geometrical patterns. Much of it is made by machinery. It is especially suitable for trimming undergarments.

Tournure: The bustle, or the fullness at the back created by the combination of the bustle, the pad and steels in the skirt, and the drapery.

Tricot: A knitted weave, often found in flannel and other wool materials.

Tucking: A fine, white cotton material of lawn, muslin, or cambric, with rows of tucks stitched across, either close together over the entire surface, or in clusters.

Tuck shirring: The tucks are basted, then gathered through both layers of material.

Tulle: A fine silk net, used for bonnets, veils, and dress trimmings. It may be had in black and white, and every color. Sometimes it is ornamented with dots.

Turkey red: A brilliant red.

Turkish cloth: Terry cloth.

Tussah: A raw silk without any cord or woven pattern, although some are stamped or printed. It is very suitable for summer costumes, and will bear washing.

Tweed: A twilled wool material. It is soft, flexible, and durable.

Twill: A weave of any fiber, where the weft threads pass over two and under one, or over three or more warp threads. Many different patterns or surfaces may be produced by changing the order of passing the weft.

Valenciennes lace: A narrow, cotton or linen lace, often machine made.

Vandykes: A series of pointed shapes cut out as a decorative border or trimming.

Velvet: A close-woven silk that has a very thick, short pile or nap on the right side. Inferior kinds are made with a cotton back.

Velveteen: Cotton velvet.

Venetian red: A dark, dull red.

Vest: A simulated vest, applied under the edges of the main part of the bodice. The latter are cut too narrow to meet, so as to expose the vest. The vest may be permanently attached, or be a changeable accessory.

Vest-facing: Contrasting material applied to the outside of a bodice to imitate a vest front.

Vestings: Materials used to make vests.

Victoria lawn: A semi-transparent muslin, to be had in black and white. It is used for skirt linings, for petticoats worn under clear muslin dresses, and for frills.

Wadding: Carded cotton wool. It is available bleached, unbleached, slate colored, and black, cut into sheets of various sizes. It is placed between the outer material and the lining of any garment.

Wash materials: All washable dress materials.

Waterfall drapery: A back drapery that hangs straight down, instead of being puffed or looped.

Watteau plait: An arrangement of the back of a woman's dress in which broad plaits or folds, or more commonly a separate piece imitating them, hang from the neck to the bottom of the skirt without interruption.

Webbing: Heavy, stout tape of various widths, and materials used for purposes where strength is desired.

Worsted: The yarn prepared from the best long-staple wools, well combed and hard twisted. Any of many materials woven from such yarns.

Yak lace: A coarse bobbin lace, made of wool, that imitates Maltese lace. Yak lace may be successfully imitated in crochet.

Zephyr gingham: An extremely soft and pliable kind, woven of fine threads, frequently in small checks or plaids.

Zephyr prints: These are delicate materials, resembling cotton batiste, designed for summer wear, and produced in pale but fast colors.

Zouave: A short open jacket with a rounded front, or a trimming in the outline of a Zouave jacket.

D. References

The bibliography lists (mostly antique) sources for the original patterns, fashion plates, and text. The "further reading" section lists modern and reprinted sources that will help you use the patterns in this book. These include books containing photographs of 1880s garments, books on altering pattern styles, and books on Victorian needle-work.

Selected Bibliography

Butterick Publishing Co. *The Delineator,* Vols. 25–26. London and New York: Butterick Publishing Co., 1885.

Butterick Publishing Co. *The Delineator,* Vols. 27–28. London and New York: Butterick Publishing Co., 1886.

Butterick Publishing Co. *The Delineator,* Vols. 29–30. London and New York: Butterick Publishing Co., 1887.

Butterick Publishing Co. *The Delineator,* Vols. 31–32. London and New York: Butterick Publishing Co., 1888.

Butterick Publishing Co. *The Delineator,* Vols. 33–34. London and New York: Butterick Publishing Co., 1889.

Charles J. Peterson. *Peterson's Magazine,* Vols. 95–96. Philadelphia: Charles J. Peterson, 1889.

Goldsberry, Doran & Nelson. *The National Garment Cutter Book of Diagrams.* Chicago: Goldsberry, Doran & Nelson, 1889.

Goldsberry, Doran & Nelson. *The Voice of Fashion.* Chicago: Goldsberry, Doran & Nelson, Summer 1888.

Goldsberry, Doran & Nelson. *The Voice of Fashion.* Chicago: Goldsberry, Doran & Nelson, Fall 1888.

Goldsberry, Doran & Nelson. *The Voice of Fashion.* Chicago: Goldsberry, Doran & Nelson, Winter 1888–1889.

Goldsberry, Doran & Nelson. *The Voice of Fashion.* Chicago: Goldsberry, Doran & Nelson, Spring 1889.

Goldsberry, Doran & Nelson. *The Voice of Fashion.* Chicago: Goldsberry, Doran & Nelson, Summer 1889.

Goldsberry, Doran & Nelson. *The Voice of Fashion.* Chicago: Goldsberry, Doran & Nelson, Fall 1889.

Goldsberry, Doran & Nelson. *The Voice of Fashion.* Chicago: Goldsberry, Doran & Nelson, Winter 1889–1890.

Goldsberry, Doran & Nelson. *The Voice of Fashion.* Chicago: Goldsberry, Doran & Nelson, Spring 1890.

Grimble, Frances. *The Voice of Fashion: 79 Turn-of-the-Century Patterns with Instructions and Fashion Plates.* San Francisco: Lavolta Press, 1998.

Harper & Bros. *Harper's Bazar,* Vol. 21. New York: Harper & Bros., 1888.

Harper & Bros. *Harper's Bazar,* Vol. 22. New York: Harper & Bros., 1889.

Myers, Annie E. *Home Dressmaking: A Complete Guide to Household Sewing.* Chicago: Charles H. Sergel & Co., 1892.

W. Jennings Demorest. *Demorest's Monthly Magazine and Mirror of Fashions,* Vol. 24. New York: W. Jennings Demorest, 1888.

W. Jennings Demorest. *Demorest's Monthly Magazine and Mirror of Fashions,* Vol. 25. New York: W. Jennings Demorest, 1889.

References

Further Reading

Armstrong, Helen Joseph. *Patternmaking for Fashion Design.* New York: HarperCollins Publishers, 1995.

Caulfeild, S. F. A. and Blanche C. Saward. *Encyclopedia of Victorian Needlework.* New York: Dover Publications, 1972.

de Dillmont, Thérèse. *The Complete Encyclopedia of Needlework.* Philadelphia: Running Press, 2002.

Johnston, Lucy. *Nineteenth-Century Fashion in Detail.* London: V & A Publications, 2005.

Kidwell, Claudia. *Cutting a Fashionable Fit: Dressmaker's Drafting Systems in the United States.* Washington: Smithsonian Institution Press, 1979.

Kopp, Ernestine, Vittorina Rolfo, and Beatrice Zelin. *Designing Apparel Through the Flat Pattern.* New York: Fairchild Publications, 1971.

Kopp, Ernestine, Vittorina Rolfo, and Beatrice Zelin. *New Fashion Areas for Designing Apparel Through the Flat Pattern.* New York: Fairchild Publications, 1972.

Kyoto Costume Institute. *Fashion: A History from the 18th to the 20th Century.* Köln: Taschen, 2002.

Musée de la Mode et du Costume–Palais Galliera. *Femmes fin de siécle 1885–1895.* Paris: Paris-Musées, 1990.

Olian, JoAnne, ed. *Full-Color Victorian Fashions 1870–1893.* Mineola: Dover Publications, 1999.

Severa, Joan L. *Dressed for the Photographer: Ordinary Americans and Fashion, 1840–1900.* Kent: Kent State University Press, 1995.

Index

This index provides a different method of locating patterns, illustrations, and descriptions than the table of contents. Because the patterns for the main parts of ensembles—bodices, polonaises, draperies, and skirts—can be exchanged to achieve the desired style, they are indexed separately, in addition to the complete ensembles. If exactly the same pattern (such as one for a foundation skirt) is given with several different ensembles, only the first instance of it is indexed separately. Smaller sections, such as sleeves, are also interchangeable but are not indexed separately. Because some ensembles and accessories have the same name, different references apply to different ones, even if the page number is the same.

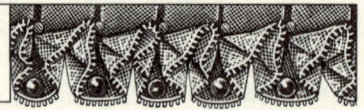

Books by Lavolta Press

After a Fashion: How to Reproduce, Restore, and Wear Vintage Styles, by Frances Grimble. Covers medieval through Art Deco styles for women and men. Guides readers through each stage of a reproduction project and advises them on all aspects of collecting vintage clothes. 356 pages, 147 illustrations.

The Lady's Stratagem: A Repository of 1820s Directions for the Toilet, Mantua-Making, Stay-Making, Millinery & Etiquette, by Frances Grimble. Contains six French manuals with instructions for dressmaking, corset making, millinery, needlework, hygiene, and etiquette, now available in English for the first time, plus considerable supplementary information from English and American sources. 755 pages, 134 illustrations.

Reconstruction Era Fashions: 350 Sewing, Needlework, and Millinery Patterns 1867–1868, by Frances Grimble. Women's fashion plates, patterns, and instructions from the first 14 months of *Harper's Bazar.* Includes articles on needlework techniques and fashion trends. 529 pages, 609 illustrations.

Fashions of the Gilded Age, Volume 1: Undergarments, Bodices, Skirts, Overskirts, Polonaises, and Day Dresses 1877–1882, by Frances Grimble. Women's sewing patterns from a German manual made available in English for the first time, plus fashion plates, sewing patterns, and needlework patterns from *Harper's Bazar* and other sources. Includes apportioning scales for a German drafting system. 469 pages, 160 patterns, 200 illustrations.

Fashions of the Gilded Age, Volume 2: Evening, Bridal, Sports, Outerwear, Accessories, and Dressmaking 1877–1882, by Frances Grimble. Women's sewing patterns from a German manual made available in English for the first time, plus fashion plates, sewing patterns, and needlework patterns from *Harper's Bazar* and other sources. Includes apportioning scales from a German drafting system and an 87-page dressmaking manual. 541 pages, 184 patterns, 598 illustrations.

Bustle Fashions 1885–1887: 41 Patterns with Fashion Plates and Suggestions for Adaptation, by Frances Grimble. A complete wardrobe of women's sewing patterns, with illustrations and detailed descriptions for variations that can be produced by flat pattern alteration. The patterns were selected from *The Voice of Fashion* magazine and National Garment Cutter pattern books. Includes apportioning scales for the National Garment Cutter system, a manual on 1885–1889 dressmaking, and instructions for trimmings and accessories. 446 pages, 438 illustrations.

Directoire Revival Fashions 1888–1889: 57 Patterns with Fashion Plates and Suggestions for Adaptation, by Frances Grimble. A complete wardrobe of women's sewing patterns, with illustrations and detailed descriptions for variations that can be produced by flat pattern alteration. The patterns were selected from *The Voice of Fashion* magazine and National Garment Cutter pattern books. Includes apportioning scales for the National Garment Cutter system, and instructions for trimmings and accessories. 563 pages, 286 illustrations.

The Voice of Fashion: 79 Turn-of-the-Century Patterns with Instructions and Fashion Plates, by Frances Grimble. Women's sewing patterns for all occasions from 1900 through 1906, selected from *The Voice of Fashion* magazine. Includes apportioning scales for the Diamond Cutting System. 463 pages, 95 illustrations.

The Edwardian Modiste: 85 Authentic Patterns with Instructions, Fashion Plates, and Period Sewing Techniques, by Frances Grimble. Women's sewing patterns for all occasions from 1905 through 1909. The patterns were selected from the *American Garment Cutter Instruction and Diagram Book* and *The American Modiste.* Includes chapters of a 1907 dressmaking manual and apportioning scales for the American System of Cutting. 430 pages, 112 illustrations.

Our books can be purchased in brick-and-mortar and online bookstores, or ordered directly from Lavolta Press. See www.lavoltapress.com for more information.